Estrildid finches of the world

Estrildid finches of the world

Derek Goodwin

COLOUR PLATES BY MARTIN WOODCOCK

British Museum (Natural History)
Comstock Publishing Associates, a division of
Cornell University Press
Ithaca, New York

First published 1982 by Cornell University Press

International Standard Book Number 0-8014-1433-4
Library of Congress Catalog Card Number 81-70708

Filmset and printed in England by
BAS Printers Limited, Over Wallop, Hampshire

Contents

Introduction

The estrildid finches range in size from a little smaller than a House Sparrow, *Passer domesticus*, to markedly more tiny than a Goldcrest or Kinglet. They vary in shape, some being rather stumpy-looking, with large bills and short tails, but the majority are pleasing and some elegant in shape. Some are rather dull, a few vividly coloured and most have pleasing, often bright, colour patterns. They occur naturally only in the old world, in Africa and east through Arabia and India to southern China, south-eastern Asia, Australasia and many of the Pacific islands. Most are birds of tropical or subtropical regions but one species is found as far south as Tasmania and several occur in essentially temperate climatic zones on high mountains. Estrildids include, among others, the firetails and grassfinches of Australia; the waxbills, firefinches and twinspots of Africa; the munias or mannikins, the avadavats and the parrot-finches. Many of them have long been popular cage and aviary birds in Britain, Europe, North America and Japan and so are well known to many people who have never seen them in a wild state. Three of them, the Bengalese Finch, the Zebra Finch and the Java Sparrow, have been domesticated.

At this stage and at risk of seeming to justify the French saying: 'Qui s'excuse, s'accuse', I feel I must try to justify my use of the rather unpleasant sounding term 'estrildid finches' (shortened to estrildids in the text) for these delightful birds. The name finch has been so long and widely used for many estrildids that it would be pedantic, and probably futile, to argue against its use. To an Australian, for example, all his native finches are estrildids. The terms 'waxbills' and 'grassfinches' are sometimes used as English names for the whole family but can cause misunderstanding as they are more often and more widely used to specify some of the smaller African species and some of the members of the Australian genus *Poephila* respectively. Either 'waxbills' or 'grassfinches' is, however, much to be preferred to the now unfortunately more widely used 'weaver-finches' which is misleading as it suggests that the estrildids are a link between the weavers and the true finches and/or that they weave when building their nests, neither of which is true.

The word 'finch' was originally applied to the Chaffinch, *Fringilla coelebs*, and derived from one of its calls. It was later used as group name for the many small birds which have relatively stout or conical bills and usually de-husk the seeds on which they largely feed. In fact their bills are by no means homogeneous (Ziswiler). Detailed studies of their structure, behaviour and biology have shown that these small seed-eating birds fall into several groups of which the true finches – Fringillidae – and the buntings and their allies – Emberizidae – probably evolved independently both from each other and from the estrildids – Estrildidae – and the weavers and sparrows – Ploceidae.

The estrildids and the sparrows and weavers may also have evolved independently from presumably more generalised and (probably) insectivorous forms or they may have shared a common ancestor subsequent to the latter's having developed seed-husking adaptations. Ziswiler has shown that the bills of estrildids and those of some weavers show apparently homologous similarities in structure. Sibley's comparative studies of egg-white proteins also suggest close relationship between the weavers and the estrildids. Two rather anomalous species, the Speckled-fronted Weaver, *Sporopipes frontalis*, and the Scaly Weaver, *S. squamifrons*, show some behaviour characters in common with estrildids and others in common with sparrows (Kunkel). They are usually put with the latter in the subfamily Passerinae, within the family Ploceidae but may represent a connecting link between sparrows and estrildids.

The whydahs and indigo-birds – *Vidua* spp – are parasitic on some species of estrildids. Their nestlings show a very close resemblance in mouth markings and juvenile plumages to those of their respective hosts. When adult the males of most viduines mimic the calls of their host species as well as uttering their own innate (and weaver-like) calls. This has led some ornithologists to assume close relationship between them and even to place the viduines in the family Estrildidae. However, as has been pointed out by Delacour, Mayr, Nicolai and others, all the resemblances that the viduines show to estrildids are connected with their nest parasitism and each viduine species resembles in detail one particular estrildid – its host. There is, I think, little doubt that the viduines are now rightly included in the Ploceidae.

The estrildids are characterised by the following behaviour patterns, some of which sharply differentiate them from finches, buntings and weavers: a strong pair bond and apparent deep attachment between the members of a pair; building an unwoven, covered nest with a side entrance that is often extended in the form of a porch or a tube; both sexes take part in incubating the eggs and brooding the young; the young beg for food with the neck held low and twisted to one side and the open mouth directed upwards; the male does not feed the female at any time; the male always gathers much, or all, of the nesting material and helps to build, or entirely builds, the nest; mandibulation, a rapid opening and shutting of the mandibles, is used in many agonistic contexts; the song has no territorial or hostile significance; the female solicits copulation with quivering tail but without any obvious wing movements. Not every species of estrildid shows all the above-listed behaviour patterns but most of them (whose behaviour is known) do so and all show the majority of them. All estrildids, so far as known, lay unmarked white eggs (which may appear pinkish when fresh and oddly dark or even bluish when about to hatch, presumably owing to the contents partly showing thorugh the shell or affecting the reflection of light). Their nestlings have conspicuous gape flanges or tubercles and usually have striking patterns of spots and/or lines on the insides of their mouths. In some species the palate pattern is retained in adult life and may function in mandibulation displays. Clumping and allo-preening between male and female of a pair, and sometimes between flock members also, are habitual and frequent in many but not all species.

Estrildids are found in many types of country from semi-desert or open grassland to reedbeds and tropical forest but are perhaps most typical of grassy savannas and thorn scrub. The majority of them seek their food on the ground or in grass or other low vegetation but some of the parrot-finches are highly arboreal and feed on the seeds of wild figs. Their beauty, the demonstrative affection that most of them show towards their mates, their fascinating displays, the ease with which some of them can be bred in captivity and the readiness with which most of them will at any rate attempt to breed in that state and, less happily, the low prices (*much* less than the cost of a Canary or Budgerigar) for which many of them could until recently be purchased, have made them favourites with bird keepers of all kinds, serious aviculturists and behaviour students included. As a result much information on their behaviour and biology in captivity has been obtained. In this, as in most aspects of serious aviculture, the Germans early led the field and have continued far in front of most of their contemporaries elsewhere. More than a hundred years ago the justly famed Dr Russ successfully bred many species of estrildids in his birdroom and vividly described some of their behaviour, while, in more recent times, Germany's relative affluence has meant that some of her aviculturists have been able to combine their traditional expertise and interest in bird-keeping with the provision of near-ideal conditions for their captives without, apparently, having to worry much about questions of space and expense that so hamper aviculturists in some other lands.

As many other sympatric birds are both larger and more spectacular, the estrildids, until recently, had been relatively little studied in a wild state. Fortunately this is no longer true. Many detailed, interesting and important studies of estrildids in the wild have been made in the past couple of decades, notably (but not only) by Dr Klaus Immelmann in Australia, Dr Peter Kunkel in Zaïre and Dr Marie-Yvonne Morel in Senegal. Ornithologists working on estrildids in the field were usually able to 'get off to a flying start' through having the information which they or others had previously amassed from studies made on the same or allied species in captivity. The references will make it abundantly clear how much of our present knowledge of these birds derives from aviculturists.

In this book I have tried to give facts, so far as known, about all species of estrildids. It does not include any detailed anatomical descriptions or voice analysis but references to work on these subjects are given where possible. It is not intended as a comprehensive avicultural guide but, as some of my readers may be, or may at some time become, keepers of estrildids, I have, where possible, included some information on feeding and general care under the species' headings. There is also a short section dealing with some aspects of the keeping of estrildids. The first part of the book also discusses such subjects as behaviour, coloration, etc. which are, therefore, dealt with shortly and descriptively under the species' headings. In the species' section, forms believed to be most closely related to each other are placed together, at least to the limited extent to which this is possible in a linear arrangement. For each group, such as the typical waxbills or the parrot-finches, its general characteristics and the relationships of the forms within it are discussed first. Under the species' heading is given a description, together with a black and white drawing, except where the bird closely resembles some other species which is illustrated or when it is illustrated elsewhere in colour, and a synopsis of what is known of its behaviour and biology. Some displays and nestling mouth patterns are also illustrated.

The black and white drawings are sketches that I have done from photographs or from living birds, where this was possible. For a few, however, they had to be drawn from museum specimens. I have described size and shape in reference to nine species: the Goldbreast, *Amandava subflava*, the Avadavat, *Amandava amandava*, the Violet-eared Waxbill, *Uraeginthus granatina*, the Zebra Finch, *Poephila guttata*, the Spice Finch, *Lonchura punctulata*, Peters' Twinspot, *Hypargos niveoguttatus*, the Java Sparrow, *Lonchura oryzivora*, the Red-headed Bluebill, *Spermophaga ruficapilla* and the Black-rumped Waxbill *Estrilda troglodytes*. Outline sketches of these and the measurements from the individual specimens from which the sketches were made are given here.

Most of the references fall into two main categories, which are not mutually exclusive. There are those where part or all of the information given is derived from one or a few sources only or where some piece of information seems questionable as being, possibly, based on an isolated or misinterpreted observation. Secondly, for those species or subjects on which a great deal has been written, the references given are to papers which I have found of most interest or which appear to me to be particularly worth the reader's while to consult. The context should make the type of reference clear. An enormous amount has been written on some species, the Zebra Finch, for example. It should not therefore be concluded that any paper not cited in the references has necessarily been judged irrelevant or lacking in importance.

The distribution maps indicate the approximate geographical area inhabited by each species. It is of course to

Outline sketches for size and shape comparisons of (1) Java Sparrow (wing from carpal joint 69 mm, tail 44 mm, tarsus 17·5 mm, bill from feathering of forehead 16 mm). (2) Red-headed Blue-bill (w. 60·5 mm, t. 44 mm. tar. 20 mm, b. 13 mm). (3) Peters' Twinspot (w. 60·5 mm, t. 44 mm, tar. 20 mm, b. 13 mm). (4) Violet-eared Waxbill (w. 57 mm, t. 67 mm, tar. 17·5 mm, b. 11 mm). (5) Zebra Finch (w. 57 mm, t. 33 mm, tar. 15 mm, b. 10 mm). (6) Spice Finch (w. 58 mm, t. 39 mm, tar. 15 mm, b. 11 mm). (7) Black-rumped Waxbill (w. 50·5 mm, t. 37·5 mm, tar. 14·5 mm, b. 8 mm). (8) Goldbreast (w. 43·5 mm, t. 30 mm, tar. 2 mm, b. 7 mm). (9) Avadavat (w. 49·5 mm, t. 34 mm, tar. 14 mm, b. 10 mm).

be understood that any bird is only likely to be found in suitable habitat within the given range. Also that at any particular time a species is as likely to be increasing or decreasing in numbers, and consequently extending or contracting its range, as to be static in these respects. The distribution maps do not include areas to which the species have been introduced by man as, for example, the Common Waxbill, *Estrilda astrild*, in Portugal and Brazil. The dendrograms showing presumed or probable relationships are to supplement the text discussions not replace them. In this context 'presumed' means the presumption of the author and does not necessarily implicate others.

I have little hope that I have not overlooked some published information that should have been included. I know I have had to leave out much of interest because, for some species, the sheer amount of overlapping information made this necessary. Some may, perhaps justifiably, disagree with some of my opinions, but I have tried to present the evidence for both, or all sides where, as is sometimes the case with this much-studied family, there are differences of even informed opinion on such matters.

Apart from stimulating an interest in these birds I hope this book may encourage those aviculturists who keep estrildids to try to perpetuate in captivity not only the 'valuable' Australian finches but also some of the *at the moment* (written 1979) 'cheap' African and Asiatic species. Many of these are just as interesting and beautiful as any of the Australian finches and little or no more difficult to breed if some care is taken of them. Above all I hope it will encourage those who visit estrildid-rich lands to watch them in the wild. I feel sure that if those on safari tours in Africa turn their eyes from the warthogs and elephants to the firefinches round the campsite or the waxbills in the grass they will find that here at least there is truth in the saying: 'Small is beautiful'.

REFERENCES

Delacour, J. 1943. A revision of the subfamily Estrildinae of the family Ploceidae. *Zoologica New York Zool. Soc.* **28**: 69–86.

Mayr, E. 1968. The sequence of genera in the Estrildidae (Aves). Breviora, *Mus. Comp. Zool.* Cambridge, Mass., no. 287.

Nicolai, J. 1964. Der Brutparasitismus der Viduinae als ethologisches Problem. *Z. Tierpsychol.* **21**: 129–204.

Russ, K. 1879. *Die fremländischen Stubenvögel*, vol. 1. Hannover, Germany.

Sibley, C. G. 1970. *A comparative study of the egg-white proteins of passerine birds.* Bulletin 32. Peabody Mus. Nat. Hist., Yale University.

Steiner, H. 1955. Das Brutverhalten der Prachtfinken, Spermestidae als Ausdruck ihres selbstandigen Familiencharakters. *Acta 11 Congr. Internat. Orn.* Basel **195**: 350–355.

Ziswiler, V. 1965. Zur Kenntnis des Samenoffnens und der Struktur des hörnernen Gaumens bei körnerfressenden Oscines. *J. Orn.* **106**: 1–48.

Acknowledgements

While preparing this book I have had much help and encouragement from my friends and colleagues in the Sub-department of Ornithology of the British Museum (Natural History) and from many ornithologists and others elsewhere who have contributed valuable information or helpful discussion.

I am particularly indebted to Dr Luis Baptista, Mr C. W. Benson, Dr Fae Hall, Dr Colin Harrison, Dr Klaus Immelmann, Dr and Mrs Peter Kunkel, Dr Jürgen Nicolai and Mr Robin Restall. Also to Dr Gerhof Mees of the Leiden Museum and Dr Jan Wattel of University of Amsterdam for sending me on loan specimens of forms not represented in the British Museum skin collection.

1 Nomenclature: genera, species, subspecies and varieties

Here I shall try to define such scientific and popular terms as are likely to concern the average person interested in estrildids or other birds and to define the sense in which certain terms, which might otherwise be ambiguous to readers, are used in this book. Those wishing to delve at all deeply in avian taxonomy will, however, need to consult one or more of the works dealing specifically with the subject.

Estrildids belong to the order Passeriformes: the passerine birds. This order is, in an evolutionary sense, relatively recent and highly successful. The resultant large number of contemporary passerine species has been one factor that has caused ornithologists to divide this order into many different families. The differences between these passerine families are usually less marked and almost certainly less fundamental than those between other bird families. Also, as would be expected, the passerines include many species whose familiar affinities are in doubt or dispute.

The relationships of the estrildids have been discussed in the introduction. They are here treated as a separate family – Estrildidae – not as a subfamily – Estrildinae – within the weaver family Ploceidae.

Below the subfamily the term 'tribe' is sometimes used for groups of closely related genera. A term of more concern to the non-taxonomist is the genus (plural genera). A genus is a group of species that are related to each other and all of whose members appear to be more closely akin to other species within the same genus than they are to any species in other genera; for example the typical waxbills, genus *Estrilda*, or the parrot-finches, genus *Erythrura*. As would be expected, authorities often disagree as to what constitutes a genus, some (the 'lumpers') preferring where possible to recognise large genera, and others (the 'splitters') to put in the same genus only very close relatives. Unfortunately an almost equally good case can too often be made out for either course. It must be recognised that genera are, to a considerable extent, units of convenience and decisions as to whether to recognise a particular genus must often be arguable or arbitrary, or both. Naturally, for Nature has no regard for man's convenience, there are species that are intermediate between those in one genus and those in another. Some recent workers on estrildids in captivity, keenly observant of specific differences of behaviour, have tended to treat as congeneric only very closely related forms. This certainly avoids the likelihood of error run by the 'lumper' but inevitably leaves one with a lot of monospecific genera. I am myself inclined to err on the side of 'lumping' rather than 'splitting' but, as it seems to me undesirable to change the nomenclature un-

necessarily, I have been strongly biased towards accepting the genera recognised in the standard world list – 'Peters'' *Check-list of Birds of the World*, published by the Museum of Comparative Zoology, Cambridge, Massachusetts, USA unless there seemed to be an over-riding reason for not doing so. This may have resulted in too many African genera being recognised but the pros and cons of such decisions are set out in the introduction to each group.

The categories of subgenus, species-group and species subgroup are sometimes used to denote (in that order) degrees of relationship within a genus but they are not formal categories in the scientific nomenclature. Below them comes the superspecies, but this is, I think, best discussed after dealing with the species category. In the few cases where there is controversy about a specific name or its spelling, I have accepted that given in 'Peters'' *Check-list*.

The species is the basic category of classification in the sense that the species concept is more closely related to observable facts than most other categories. The term 'species' has been variously defined and most definitions have been objected to by someone on some grounds, good or otherwise. So far as birds are concerned, one might, I think, say that a species consists of a number (usually a very large number) of individuals, all of whom show more resemblances to each other than to any other species, interbreed freely where they come into contact with each other, and do not normally interbreed with individuals of other species. The Black-rumped Waxbill, Common Waxbill and Zebra Finch are, for example, obviously 'good' species. In scientific nomenclature a species is designated by a specific name, *not* capitalised, following the capitalised generic name – thus *Estrilda astrild* (the Common Waxbill), *Amandava amandava* (the Avadavat) and so on.

In different parts of its range a species of bird may, like man, show geographical variation. For example, the Zebra Finches of Timor have little or no barring on the throat and breast, unlike those of Australia. Such differing populations are termed races or subspecies. They are given a third scientific name (trinomial) which in the case of the first described or nominate form is a repetition of the specific name. Thus the Zebra Finch of Timor and nearby islands is *Poephila g.guttata*, the Australian Zebra Finch is *Poephila guttata castanotis* and so on.

The form of the species that was first described in some publication is usually called the nominate form or nominate race. Sometimes it is called the typical form because the first specimen so described is known as the 'type' of the species. Typical form (or race or subspecies) can, however, be misleading as it may wrongly suggest that the form first described is, somehow, more typical (using the word in its everyday sense) of its species than are others that simply happened to be discovered and described later.

Unless they are separated by natural barriers, such as the sea or areas of country unsuitable for the species to inhabit, subspecies intergrade with each other and many individuals – indeed all of them in some areas – will be intermediate in character. Also, of course, some sub-species are more distinct than others. Many of them get named by over-zealous taxonomists on account of very small average differences. Under the species' headings in this book I have in some cases described and named only the more distinct of such geographical races. By doing so it is possible to give a general idea of what the species looks like and the amount of difference it shows in different parts of its range. Any subspecies that has not been described here is very similar indeed to one or other of those that have.

Geographic races may in time come to differ so much from their parent stock that they evolve into new species. Usually (and possibly always) such speciation can only take place if they are isolated from other populations. This may come about in different ways. Some members of a species may invade an island whither others of their kind do not follow. A species may disappear from large areas of its range through alteration of habitat, leaving isolated populations separated by areas of country no longer suitable for them. If, after such a period of isolation, something happens to cause the two populations to come together again they may have become so different in appearance, voice or behaviour (or all three) that they will no longer interbreed. Each has in fact become a 'good' species.

They may, however, interbreed when they meet again but if the resultant 'hybrid' offspring are for any reason less viable than 'pure' members of both populations then selection will favour any characters that tend to prevent mating between the two stocks. Such characters as a tendency to prefer different habitats when breeding (which would tend to re-isolate the two stocks even though they were in the same general area) or the development of different colour patterns (which, by imprinting, would discourage pairing between the two) might be 'seized on' and developed by natural selection in such circumstances. In this way full specific status may be achieved only after a period during which there has been some interbreeding between the two reunited forms.

Where two similar forms, which seem clearly derived from a common ancestor, now occupy different geo-graphical areas and appear too distinct to be treated as races of one species, they are commonly given specific rank but within the same superspecies. A superspecies is, as its name suggests, a form whose geographical representatives have evolved to the point where they seem best considered as species rather than subspecies. Perhaps it would be more correct to say that they have evolved to a point between the category of species and that of subspecies (or race) but, in scientific nomenclature, are considered best treated as species and given specific names. Occasionally the term 'semispecies' is used for such members of the same superspecies but there is as yet no universally used particular designation for them in the scientific (Latin) terms. Sometimes the geographical representatives of a form have diverged considerably. In such cases they are not usually classed as members of a superspecies even although this is, or at least was, their relationship.

Naturally it is sometimes uncertain whether the geographical and still similar representatives of a form should be treated as species within a superspecies or as races of a single species. Where there is considerable doubt as to whether a form should be given specific or only subspecific rank I think it is preferable, in a book of this kind, to take the former course, to ensure that available information can be unambiguously attached to the form concerned. The status of the various forms is discussed in the introduction to the group to which they belong, where the taxonomy and relationships within each group are dealt with.

Where two closely-related species whose ranges over-lap or adjoin are very similar in appearance they are often termed sibling species. Needless to say there are different opinions as to what degree of resemblance must be shown for this term to be used. The term 'variety' is often incorrectly used in lay publications when species or race is meant. The word 'variety' should be used only for those aberrant individuals that differ markedly from the norm of their species, a white Zebra Finch, for example. The term 'colour morph' is often used for the differently coloured individuals of species that (within the same geographical area) have populations regularly containing two or more differently coloured forms, like the red-headed and black-headed colour morphs of the Gouldian Finch.

The term 'breed', which is often misleadingly used in the newspapers instead of 'species', means a well-established domestic form and is usually only applied to those that show some differences of shape rather than or as well of colour. Thus Scots Fancy Canaries or Pouter Pigeons are called breeds but white, fawn, pied and silver Zebra Finches are not so termed.

Throughout this book the terms 'group(s)' and 'form(s)' are used in a general sense as convenient. Their meaning in any particular case will be clear from the context.

2 Distribution and adaptive radiation

The distribution of the estrildids has been roughly outlined in the introduction. They occur naturally in the Ethiopian, Oriental and Australasian regions and also in New Caledonia, some of the Pacific islands and Madagascar (see map). The number of forms in each of the different areas differs greatly, with about 79 species in 18 genera in the Ethiopian region, 19 species in 3 genera in the Oriental, 36 species in 9 genera in the Australasian region, 5 species in one genus in the Pacific (including Micronesia and New Caledonia) and a single species in Madagascar.

From the above it will be clear that the greatest amount of differentiation has taken place in Africa. This in spite of the fact that small seed-eating birds of other families – weavers, finches, buntings and some larks – are well represented in Africa. The weavers, family Ploceidae, are indeed not only extremely numerous both in species and individuals, but are, like the estrildids, pre-eminently eaters of grass seeds. The large number of African forms is one piece of circumstantial evidence in favour of the general (but not universal) opinion that the estrildids originated in the Ethiopian region. The past climatic history of Africa has, as shown by Moreau, evidently been highly favourable for differentiation and consequent speciation, owing to the shiftings, shrinkings and spreadings of different types of habitat, and this might have caused explosive differentiation even in an immigrant group. Kunkel (1969) has, however, argued cogently, and I believe rightly, that their parasitisation by the whydahs and indigo-birds, *Vidua* spp., is very good evidence for the African origin of the estrildids.

It is fairly certain that the parasitic whydahs (under which term I here include also the indigo-birds) are most closely related to the euplectine weavers (Nicolai 1969) although they show astonishing resemblances to their estrildid hosts in the mouth markings, begging postures, food accepting technique and juvenile plumages of their young. Most of them are parasitic on a single estrildid species although the Pintailed Whydah, *Vidua macroura*, parasitises several (closely related) species of typical waxbills, *Estrilda*. It seems most probable, as Kunkel and Nicolai are both convinced, that the ancestral estrildid must have been parasitised by the ancestral viduine, before either of them had evolved the striking structural and behavioural characters that now distinguish their young from those of other passerines and which must, presumably, have evolved concurrently in host and nest parasite.

The whydahs are all birds of grassy savanna or steppe country in Africa. They now parasitise some (but not all) species of typical waxbills, *Estrilda*, the Violet-eared and Grenadier Waxbills, *Uraeginthus granatina* and *U. ianthinogaster*, and probably all firefinches, *Lagonosticta* (Nicolai, 1972) and the pytilias, *Pytilia* spp. In the course of their

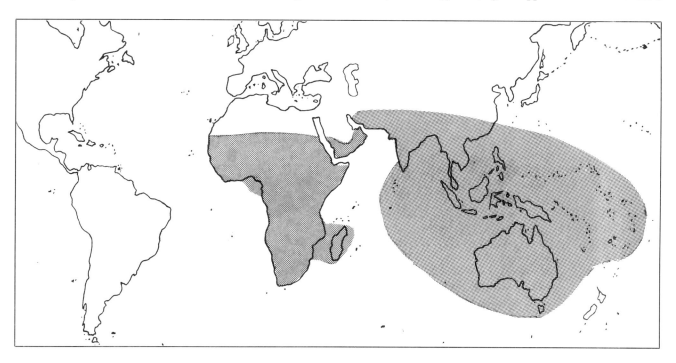

differentiation and speciation most forms of estrildids, or rather their ancestors, evidently managed to 'shake off' their viduine parasites. Probably in most cases this was due to their invading and learning to live in new habitats to which the parasite was unable to adapt. There are, of course, now many estrildids living in habitats suitable for whydahs, which are not parasitised by them. In their case other factors must have freed them from the parasite in the course of their evolution. In some, as Kunkel suggests, this may have been because at some period their numbers became too few to maintain viable stocks of their whydah, or through the latter having been unable to evolve mouth marking differences sufficiently in time with those of the host to prevent discrimination against its (the parasite's) nestlings. In others it may have been because at one time in their evolutionary history, their ancestors moved outside Africa or into unsuitable habitats within it, thereby ridding themselves of their parasitic whydah, and only at a later, parasite-less stage, re-established themselves in African savannah or steppe. Kunkel is of the opinion that this was the case with the African mannikins and probably also with the Goldbreast and the silverbills.

Kunkel instances two present-day examples of estrildids shedding their parasite by invading habitats unsuitable for it: the Pintailed Whydah, though it has here and there followed its host – the Common Waxbill – into grass-grown open slopes in the mountain bamboo forest, has not followed it into the *Panicum*-grown clearings in the rain forest of the Congo Basin. Similarly the indigo-birds have followed their hosts – the Red-billed and Dark Firefinches – west of the natural savannah into the cultivated savanna of central Ruanda but not into the highlands around Lake Kivu. Kunkel's hypothesis that the ancestral estrildid was a bird of grassland savanna or steppe carries, as he points out, an important implication. This is that the various scrub and forest inhabiting species that some authorities (e.g. Delacour, Steiner 1960) have considered the most primitive forms can hardly be so. Those peculiarities of structure, pattern or colour which they share cannot, therefore, be 'primitive' relicts but must have secondarily evolved, presumably in relation to their new habitats.

The African forms show the greatest amount of difference in size and shape within the Estrildidae. The smallest species are the Goldbreast and the Locust-finch, and the largest the seed-crackers and bluebills. The large form of seed-cracker also shows the greatest contrast in bill-shape (see plate 1, facing p. 96) between its enormous triangular bill and the slender, slightly-curved bill of the insectivorous ant-peckers, and the small, shallow but rather broad bills of some of the negro-finches, which are believed to be primarily insectivorous and frugivorous. The seed-eating forms have a range of bill shapes from short and stout to slender and sharply pointed. What is known of feeding habits in the wild suggests that relatively short, deep bills are often or usually correlated with mostly taking seeds direct from the growing plant. Slender, pointed bills may be adaptations for taking

considerable amounts of insects or for taking very small seeds from stony soil and the many crevices in its surface, as Immelmann's studies have shown is the case with the Painted Finch, or both. Most of the seed-eating species with relatively slender, sharply-pointed bills are mainly ground feeders.

In Africa estrildids are found in a variety of habitats, from arid steppe (with some bushes or small trees), open country and reed-grown marshes to primeval rain forest and montane bamboo jungle. The majority are, however, found in savanna, bush-grown steppe, forest edge or other places where there is abundant cover of bushes, scrub or long grass. Indeed, of the forest forms only Grant's Bluebill is, on present knowledge, a true inhabitant of the rain forest as distinct from being a bird of forest edge or second growth. Africa also alone harbours the most highly terrestrial forms, the ground-living quail-finches, *Ortygospiza*, which, never perching in trees or bushes and walking and running on the ground, show a more complete adaptation to life on the ground than do any Australian or Oriental forms.

Australia has evidently been the other main centre for adaptive radiation of estrildids. The differentiation of the Australian species has largely paralleled that in Africa except that no such aberrant or extreme forms as the ant-peckers or seed-crackers exist there, the most terrestrial species are less so than the quail-finches, and the difference in size between the largest and smallest Australian species is much less than between, say, a Red-headed Bluebill and a Goldbreast. This lesser diversity among Australian estrildids is a little surprising in view of the fact that, prior to recent introductions by man, no true finches, buntings, sparrows or weavers occurred in Australia. In general some (but not all) African genera with numerous included species tend to be represented, or perhaps it would be safer to say paralleled, in Australia by only one or two species. The affinities of all these forms are discussed in the introductions to each group of species further on.

Although Australia itself has under half the number of species of estrildids that are found elsewhere in the Australasian region, these latter show far less diversity, since they consist of 17 species of munias or mannikins – *Lonchura*, 2 parrot-finches – *Erythrura* and the monotypic genus *Oreosthruthus*. With the exception of the Avadavat and Green Avadavat, *Amandava amandava* and *A. formosa*, and 4 parrot-finches, all the estrildids of the Indo-Malayan region are also species of *Lonchura*. This genus almost certainly originated in either the Indo-Malayan or Australasian regions. The mannikins give the impression of being a relatively recent, still rapidly evolving and highly successful group. Indeed, the success of *Lonchura* species in such grass-grown habitats as there are in the Indo-Malayan and New Guinea regions may be one reason for the paucity of other estrildid genera in these areas.

Apart from recent introductions by man, only a few of the parrot-finches have been able to colonise New

Caledonia and some of the islands of the south Pacific. Here some of them have specialised in feeding on the seeds of wild figs. The interesting thing is how the first parrot-finches to arrive in forest-covered islands discovered this food. Probably the finding of split-open figs on the ground initiated this 'break through' to a new source of seed food. It also, incidentally, burdened them with physically stronger food competitors in the shape of other fruit-eating birds, especially the fruit doves of the genus *Ptilinopus*. Some of the parrot-finches have a wide range of food and include many different seeds, invertebrates and even fruit in their diet.

Mention has been made of the correlation between bill structure and feeding habits, but it is likely that social as well as alimentary pressures may have affected bill size. As in many other groups of birds, notably hornbills, toucans and parrots, the bills of the largest species of estrildids tend to be *proportionately* as well as actually larger than those of related smaller species. There is also a tendency for the larger-billed species to develop brightly coloured or conspicuously shiny bills even in groups where smaller species do not show such bill adornments to the same degree. It seems highly likely that in such species there has been selection for large conspicuous bills because of their intimidating or attracting functions in social situations as well as for their 'practical' use in feeding.

Allen's rule (that extensions of the body tend to be smaller in colder regions) appears to apply within the Estrildidae as montane forms tend to have proportionately smaller bills, as well as thicker plumage, than their congeners in lower (and warmer) regions.

Immelmann and Immelmann made comparative studies of the flight (as well as other aspects of behaviour) of African and Australian estrildids. They found that, in general, bush and tree frequenting species of scrub or savanna woodland usually fly only short distances, with a rather fluttering and only weakly (if at all) undulating flight. Species of open country and reedbed inhabiting species fly strongly, with marked undulations of the flight path, but when in flocks the reedbed species flew strongly on a level path with frequent quick, synchronised, sideways or upward turns. It is evident that the form of flight is adapted to the bird'e ecology and is not necessarily any indication of close relationship between species with similar flight styles.

Man's agricultural and sylvicidal activities, especially although not only where practised on a relatively small scale, often result in increasing food and suitable habitat for estrildids. It is, therefore, not surprising that many have become characteristic and abundant small birds of inhabited areas. Several species occasionally or locally nest in or around buildings and two, the Red-billed Firefinch over much of Africa and the Crimson Finch in parts of northern Australia, now habitually live around human dwellings and nest in nooks or crannies in or about them.

REFERENCES

Delacour, J. 1943. A revision of the subfamily Estridinae of the family Ploceidae. *Zoologica* **28**: 69–86.

Immelmann, K & G. 1967. Verhaltensökologische Studien an afrikanischen und australischen Estrildiden. *Zool. Jb. Syst. Bd.* **94**: 609–686.

Kunkel, P. 1969. Die Stammesgeschichte der Prachtfinken (Estrildidae) im Lichte des Brutparasitismus der Witwen (Viduinae). *Ardea* **57**: 173–181.

Moreau, R. E. 1966. *The bird faunas of Africa and its islands.* London.

Nicolai, J. 1964. Der Brutparasitismus der Viduinae als ethologsisches Problem. *Z. Tierpsychologie* **21**: 129–204.

Nicolai, J. 1967. Rassen und Artbildung in der Viduengattung *Hypochera. J.Orn* **108**: 309–319.

Nicolai, J. 1972. Zwei neue *Hypochera*-Arten aus West-Afrika. *J.Orn.* **113**: 229–240.

Steiner, H. 1960. Die Klassifikation der Prachtfinken, Spermestidae, auf Grund der Rachenzeichnungen ihrer Nestlinge. *J.Orn.* **101**: 92–112.

3 Plumage and coloration

Coloration of plumage and soft parts

The estrildids show a great variety of colours and patterns of plumage. Commonly they are relatively soberly clad in browns, greys, olive or other inconspicuous shades on their upperparts but with areas of brighter colour on head, underparts and rump. Only a few of them give the impression, however, of having highly developed cryptic plumage. Probably this is because their small size in itself makes them relatively inconspicuous from above if they 'freeze' in alarm, and because, in their covered nests, they are not exposed to view when incubating or brooding. A more or less streaked pattern on the upper parts, formed by the feathers having dark median and pale outer areas, is very common in weavers and buntings and also found in many of the true finches as well as in other birds. It is generally thought to be of particular use as protective coloration in open grassland although it is found also, but often in a less highly developed state, in many arboreal woodland birds. Although many estrildids feed among grass on the ground, this type of plumage pattern is only found in three species – the quail-finches, *Ortygospiza*. As these are terrestial birds of open country, that they alone among estrildids, should have developed this pattern is good circumstantial evidence of its protective value in such environments. In general, the most highly social species tend to be relatively dull in colour or at least to lack *extensive* areas of bright plumage.

As in other groups of birds, rich deep colours and especially deep and/or shining reds are commonest among forms that keep much to cover. There are, however, many bright and beautiful but usually lighter-coloured forms of semi-arid scrub. Even those species that have no bright primary or secondary colours often have striking markings and sometimes most delicately beautiful patterns of black and white. They usually have contrasting, white or pale areas on the rump. The juvenile plumage may be very similar to but paler than that of the adult or differ from it in lacking any well-defined markings and being of a nearly uniform and much paler hue or anything between these two extremes. Where the adults show sexual dichromatism which involves the male having brighter and more extensive areas of a colour also possessed by the female, this sexual difference is usually reflected to a lesser degree in the juvenile plumage. Where, however, the male possesses bright markings that are entirely lacking in the female, these are not usually shown at all by the juvenile; the Cut-throat is a well-known exception to this general rule.

As with other birds, all bright or conspicuously contrasted areas of plumage serve a social function. Usually they are either exhibited by special movements or postures in displays or they are shown automatically when the bird spreads its wings or tail or exposes its rump as it takes flight. In some cases areas of bright plumage with a social function may be, as it were, 'permanently on view' but are not made particularly prominent in any specific display; the white-spotted chestnut flanks of the male Zebra Finch are an example.

Extensive red areas tend to be found in forms which show considerable intra-specific aggression. In captivity such species often react with aggression or (in the case of females of dichromatic species) sexual responses to red coloured but often even unrelated species which are confined with or near them. It is of interest that whereas reds and yellows are widespread not only among estrildids but also in the true finches, the weavers and (yellow only) the old world buntings, the estrildids alone (among these groups) have some species with blue plumage. Even among them blue is a comparatively rare colour, being found in only three genera (*Uraeginthus*, *Erythrura* and *Chloebia*), of which only a few species have large and conspicuous areas of blue. I have here used the term 'blue' in its usual meaning and not to include the various shades of bluish, or even brownish grey called 'blue' by the breeders of domestic pigeons, canaries, fowls, cats, mice and dogs.

Red on the rump and upper tail coverts is widespread and may be a relatively primitive character within the Estrildidae. Steiner (1966) has shown that some species that do not themselves have red rumps, when crossed, produce hybrids with red or pink on the rump. All such crosses appear to involve, however, one parent with a dark and one with a white or yellow rump. The likeliest explanation seems to me to be that the dark-rumped parent does in fact possess some red pigment but this is masked by the dark melanin pigment and that the white or pale rump of the other parent is dominant (in the F_1 hybrids) over the melanin but not over the (hidden) red carotenoid pigments, thus allowing the latter to be visually expressed in the hybrids. See also the introductory section to the silverbills.

In some estrildids the sexes are alike in coloration or very similar but with the male slightly brighter. In others there is a marked sexual dichromatism so that the sexes are recognisable at a glance. Such sexually dichromatic forms include some in which both sexes have similar colours but the bright parts of the male are much brighter and/or more extensive, such as the Painted Finch and the Gouldian Finch, and others, such as the Avadavat and Zebra Finch, in which the male possesses bright colours or markings that are completely absent in the female. In some of these latter species the females appear to have an innate sexual response to the male colours.

As all estrildids build covered nests or breed in holes and, so far as is known, in all species both sexes share all parental cares, greater risks of predation on the incubating or brooding female cannot have influenced sexual dichromatism in them as it may have done in, for example, the true finches, which build cup-shaped or saucer-shaped open nests on which only the female sits. Sexual dichromatism in which the male (only) is largely red or brightly-coloured is usually found in relatively unsocial species, whereas most closely-flocking species are monomorphic. Otherwise there does not seem to be any consistent correlation between marked sexual dichromatism, or the lack of it, and any particular forms of behaviour, ecology or habitat. Many of the monomorphic or nearly monomorphic forms are highly social but so are some markedly sexually dichromatic forms. It does seem possible, however, that marked sexual dichromatism in (and only in) highly social forms may be connected with nomadism and/or opportunistic breeding during temporary and irregular periods of plenty. The marked sexual dichromatism of the Zebra Finch and the dichromatism *plus* dimorphism of the Pintailed Parrot-finch, as compared with other species of, respectively, *Poephila* and *Erythrura*, may be examples of this. It is possible, as I have elsewhere suggested for the same phenomenon in pigeons, that in such species there may be selective value in strong sexual dichromatism through its facilitating rapid pair formation. This idea is, on present knowledge, mere speculation, however.

In other cases we find closely related monomorphic and sexually dichromatic species with no evidence to suggest a likely reason for their difference. The pytilias (three species sexually dichromatic, two not), the negro finches (one dichromatic, three not) and the crimson-wings (two dichromatic, two not) are but some examples of this. The cordon-bleus well illustrate the three main trends of dichromatism or lack of it. In *U. angolensis* the sexes are either virtually alike or (racial difference) differ only in the female having less blue on her flanks. In the very closely related *U. bengalus*, the male has strikingly conspicuous dark red cheek patches, which are completely absent in the female. In *U. cyanocephala* both sexes are entirely shades of brown and blue (with some white) but the female usually has a paler red bill and her plumage colours are a very 'washed out edition' of the male's, with only a partially pale blue instead of an entirely bright blue head. Apart from the female of *U. bengalus* having an apparently innate sexual response to red markings (Goodwin), which must of course have evolved subsequently to or concurrently with her mate's acquisition of them, the three species do not, so far as at present known, show any differences that would account for their very different types and degrees of sexual dichromatism.

In some cases sexual dichromatism, or its absence, in reference to related sympatric species, may function as an isolating mechanism. However, even among the many more or less sympatric species one does not have a situation, comparable with the northern hemisphere ducks of the genus *Anas*, where sympatric sexually dichromatic species have very similarly coloured females but strikingly differently coloured males. Some sexually dichromatic estrildids, notably the Cut-throat, are not sympatric with any closely related or similar species. In one case, involving two members of a superspecies, there is circumstantial evidence to suggest that one function of sexual dichromatism is to facilitate quick and accurate pair formation. This is the remarkable early partial moult, involving only head feathers, of the juveniles of the Violet-eared Waxbill and the Purple Grenadier (Nicolai 1968, see also species sections dealing with these birds).

It seems likely that sexual dichromatism, or lack of it if it was the original condition of the proto-estrildid ancestor, has to do with intra-specific selection rather than to inter-specific or environmental factors. It is to be hoped that future studies on estrildids in the wild will throw more light on this subject.

The bills of estrildids are commonly bluish grey or black and bluish grey, the grey or bluish parts often with a high or opalescent sheen. All-black bills are also common. Many species, however, have bills that are entirely or partly red, pink, orange or yellow. Such brightly coloured bills seem to have evolved, presumably by separate mutations, in several different groups. In all such forms the bills of the young are dark and only gradually, from the base outward, become paler and brighter. In such bright-billed forms bill colour seems to provide important clues as to age and status in social, parental and sexual situations. In the Zebra Finch, young birds whose bills are still black are not normally either attacked or sexually molested and Immelmann (1973) found by experiments that this toleration of and lack of sexual interest in the young is dependent on their having black bills.

Rather surprisingly, Immelmann (1962, 1973) also found that, among some Australian species, bill colour apparently induced strong interspecific attraction between species with similarly coloured bills whereas the possession of almost identically sounding calls and close phylogenetic relationship did not have this effect. Thus he observed Zebra Finches with Star Finches and Masked Finches with Long-tailed Grassfinches in mixed flocks in spite of plumage differences which include great differences between the rump and tail colours of the different forms. In sexual contexts, however, bill coloration may serve as a species-specific isolating mechanism. This even proved to be the case when two naturally allopatric forms of *Pytilia*, which had been generally treated as conspecific, were brought together in captivity (Nicolai, 1968b).

REFERENCES

Goodwin, D. 1971. Imprinting, or otherwise, in some cross-fostered Red-cheeked and Blue-headed Cordon-bleus (*Uraeginthus bengalus* and *U. cyanocephalus*). Avicult. Mag. 77: 26–31.

Immelmann, K. 1962. Biologische Bedeutung optischer und

akusticher Merkmale bei Prachtfinken (Aves, Spermestidae). *Verh. DDeutsch. Zool. Ges.* (Saarbrücken, 1961) 369–374.

Immelmann, K. 1973. *Der Zebrafink*. In the Neue Brehm-Bücherei series, published by A. Ziemsen Verlag, Wittenberg Lutherstadt, Germany.

Nicolai, J. 1968a. Die isolierte Frühmauser der Farbmerkmale des Kopfgefieders bei *Uraeginthus granatinus* (L.) and *U. ianthinogaster* Reichw. (Estrildidae). *Z. Tierpsychol.* **25**: 854–861.

Nicolai, J. 1968b. Die Schnabelfärbung als potentieller Isolationsfaktor zwischen *Pytilia phoenicoptera* Swainson und *P. lineata* Heuglin (Fa. *Estrildidae*). *J. Orn.* **109**: 450–461.

Steiner, H. 1960. Atavismen bei Artbastarden und ihre Bedeutung zur Feststellung von Verwandtschaftsbeziehungen. Kreuzungsergebnisse innerhalb der Singvogelfamilie der Spermestidae. *Rev. Suisse de Zoologie* **73**: 321–337.

Plumage sequences and colour changes

According to species, young estrildids, when newly hatched, may be naked or clad in varying amounts of down on their upper parts. In these latter species conspicuous tufts of down still adorn the head (at the tips of true feathers) at fledging time. I fully agree with Ingram that the likeliest function of such down is to camouflage the nest cavity or to deceive predators as to its contents. Looking into the entrance of a nest I knew to contain healthy young cordon-bleus, *Uraeginthus* spp., I have often found it hard not to let my eyes be deceived by the amorphous downy blur.

At fledging, unless this has been premature, the young estrildid is clothed in its juvenile plumage but with the wing and tail quills not fully grown, although the bird is usually capable of flight. The adult plumage is usually acquired at the first moult although in a few species a plumage not quite as bright as that of the adult may, at least in some circumstances, first replace the juvenile dress. Usually the first moult starts within a few weeks of the young bird fledging and is completed before it is six months old. Failure to acquire full adult plumage for a year or more is usually, and probably always, caused by some adverse factors of captivity or possibly of parallel conditions (e.g. drought) in the wild. Russ, and others since, have convincingly described the acquisition of adult plumage as being by colour change, not moult, but this is certainly an error based on optical illusion. Especially in captive birds the first moult may proceed rather slowly; some feathers intermediate in character between the juvenile and adult dress may be produced; and newly emerged feathers may differ in colour (especially if they are red) from what they will appear a few weeks later. These factors in combination often give a strong impression of colour change without a moult when examination of the bird, or even careful daily examination of the floor of the birdroom or aviary, would show that a moult is in fact taking place. In captivity estrildids (and some other birds) sometimes have a juvenile plumage more similar to the adult dress than is normal. This is usually, perhaps always, due to some adverse factors having delayed feather growth in the nestlings. It is not, as some aviculturists like to think, a sign of the birds' vigour and fitness but rather the reverse.

Once the adult plumage is assumed there are no seasonal changes, other than those caused by wear and bleaching, except in the Avadavat, which alone among the estrildids, resembles most of the weavers in having a breeding and a non-breeding plumage. Very little is known about the moulting of estrildids in the wild except for Morel's fine and comprehensive study of the Red-billed Firefinch. She found that, at least in her study area in Senegal, adults of this species moulted only once a year (Morel, 1969). In captivity some species, or at least some individuals of them, may moult twice in a year (pers. obs.) but this may be due to some factor in their unnatural environment. Observations on ringed or otherwise individually known wild birds are needed.

It is well known that in captivity many of the true finches (and some other birds) that have red plumage, lose their red colours or replace them with some shade of pale straw yellow, dull gold or pale pinkish when they moult in captivity. In general this phenomenon is much less marked in the estrildids than in finches or weavers. If kept under good conditions most of them appear to retain their colours fully although if they are compared in the hand with a wild bird (or its skin), it will sometimes be seen that red markings are a little less bright or a little more orange in tone in the captive moulted or captive bred birds. The Avadavat does, however, usually show some and often marked deterioration of the red coloured areas which are replaced by coppery orange or even dull brownish orange although this process can sometimes be reversed and the bright red colour recovered if it is kept at a high temperature during the moult. The Star Finch (Graven) and the Pintailed Parrot-finch (Boosey) are said sometimes to replace red with yellow when they moult in captivity. I have myself noticed in the Goldbreast that captive-moulted and captive-bred birds are orange where the wild birds are (and in some cases they themselves were) red, and orange or golden-orange where wild birds are red-orange. In this species this apparent replacement of red pigment by orange and yellow also results in those parts of the plumage that look dark brown in the wild bird, looking olive green in life (although not or much less so after death) in captives.

A darkening of part or all of the plumage, caused by increased deposition of melanin pigment and/or its spread into normally pale or white areas sometimes occurs in captive birds. It is especially common in Avadavats and Goldbreasts that are kept in indoor aviaries and fed mainly on dry seed. It appears to be due to faulty metabolism caused mainly by insufficient supplies of vitamin D. Giving supplementary supplies of vitamins A and D, in addition to minerals and greenfood, and keeping the birds in a well-lighted room or enclosure where they have room to fly will usually cure affected birds even if they are kept indoors, although if at all possible they should also be given opportunities to expose themselves to the direct rays of the sun. With such treatment normally-coloured plumage will be produced at the next moult or, at latest, the next but one.

An odd change brought about by captive conditions is the shortening of the long, finely attenuated ends of the central tail feathers of the Long-tailed Grassfinch and the Gouldian Finch. Specimens bred in captivity appear never to grow central tail feathers as long as those of most wild conspecifics (Immelmann, 1965). The reason for this is quite unknown. It is found in birds that in other respects are equal to wild ones in plumage.

REFERENCES

Boosey, E. J. 1956. *Foreign bird keeping*. Iliffe Books Ltd., London.

Graven, N. 1957. Breeding the Star Finch or Ruficauda (*Bathilda ruficauda*). *Avicult. Mag.* **63**: 134–136.

Immelmann, K. 1965. *Australian finches in bush and aviary*. Angus and Robertson, Sydney.

Immelmann, K. 1973. *Der Zebrafink*. A. Ziemsen Verlag, Wittenberg-Lutherstadt. Germany.

Ingram, C. 1958. Camouflage in nestling birds. *Proc. 12th Int. Orn. Congress* (1958): 332–342.

Morel, M. Y. 1969. Contribution a l'étude dynamique de la population de *Lagonosticta senegala* L. (Estrildidae) a Richard-Toll (Sénégal). Interrelations avec le parasite *Hypochera chalybeata* (Müller) (Viduines). Doctorate thesis presented to the Faculty of Science of Rennes, France. Later printed (and published ?) as *Mémoires du Muséum National d'Histoire Naturelle*, Serie A, Tome LXXVIII.

4 Behaviour and biology

Feeding habits

As a group the estrildids are mainly seed-eaters. Many or most of them also take insects and/or some green food but only a very few aberrant forms are not known to take seeds and these latter have been little studied. Most estrildids even feed their nestlings partly or largely on seeds. Even some forms which, in captivity, usually feed their young mainly on insects, are known to give them considerable quantities of small seeds in a wild state. So far as is known a majority of them feed largely on seeds of grasses (some eating the seeds of such cultivated grasses as rice, millet and sorghums) although some are specialist feeders on the seeds of other kinds of plants, including the seeds of figs.

Ziswiler (1965), in a detailed comparative study, has fully described and illustrated the bill and palate structures and the correlated seed de-husking methods of the estrildids, finches and buntings. Some estrildids commonly or habitually swallow seeds whole and Ziswiler's studies show that those that do so have in many (possibly all) cases less marked structural adaptations for shelling seeds. Even some species which usually de-husk most of the seed they eat will, however, swallow some seeds whole. Although they are particularly liable to do this when very hungry (Ziswiler, pers. obs.) at least the cordon-bleus, in captivity, will often swallow some seed whole and shell some at the same meal, when they are showing no signs of any great degree of hunger. Possibly this is an artifact of captivity, prompted by the need for some element(s) present in the husk and otherwise lacking in their diet. Cardueline finches in the wild are, however, known to swallow some seeds whole (Newton, pers. obs. for the Goldfinch). Usually the seeds thus swallowed are either very small or unripe and soft, or both. Quite likely it will be found that even the normally seed-shelling species of estrildids, do at times swallow small or soft seeds whole in the wild.

Quickly as estrildids can de-husk seeds they can, as would be expected, swallow whole seeds much quicker. Shelling the seeds it eats thus forces the bird to spend more time eating than it would otherwise need to do. Presumably the more than compensating advantage is that the bird does not need to ingest so much un-nutritious matter as it otherwise would. That most *small* birds that are year round seed-eaters, and all small birds that feed their young nestlings on seeds, are de-husking species seems corroborative evidence for this. Apart from small doves, which feed their young squabs on crop milk, other partly seed-eating smallish birds, such as quail-thrushes,

dunnocks and larks, feed their young on insects.

The quail-finches, *Ortygospiza*, seek food entirely on the ground. Very many other forms are primarily ground feeders although they may sometimes take insects from leaves or twigs or seeds from a grass panicle within reach of a convenient perch. They normally, however, seek food on the ground, either picking up fallen seeds or reaching or (less often) jumping up to take seeds from low-growing plants. Some of them often dig in the substrate with the flicking side-to-side or down-and-flick-to-one side bill movements that are widespread in passerines and pigeons. Some will also break open lumps of earth with pick-axe-like blows of the closed bill.

Other species feed commonly or preferentially in vegetation, taking much of their food directly from the seeding plants. These are forms that can easily perch on sloping or even upright grass or reed stems as they feed from the panicle, many can hold panicles under foot while extracting the seeds. Most of the mannikins and typical waxbills come into this category. Some of these species have stout strong bills that enable them to bite out seeds from a panicle instead of seizing and tugging, with a twisting or shaking movement superimposed if they meet any resistance, as the weaker-billed forms do. Some of the parrot-finches, *Erythrura*, specialise in the seeds of wild figs, taking them both in the trees and from fallen fruit. They often use their feet to hold a fig while tearing it open and picking out the seeds.

The ant-pickers appear to specialise in feeding on worker ants although they also take other insects. The negro-finches, *Nigrita*, are apparently insect and fruit eaters but little is known in detail about their feeding habits. They appear to be largely arboreal. Other forms seek insects mainly in the same sort of places as they do their seed food except that some also catch flying insects – especially termites – on the wing, making short sallies from a perch to do so. Some of the ground-feeding species regularly wait at the nest entrances of those species of termites that are active outside by day or break open the covered surface runways of termites and eat the workers as they appear (Immelmann & Immelmann, 1967). The taking of aphids (greenfly) does not seem to have been recorded for wild birds but many almost surely must do so, in view of the immediate eagerness with which they take them from 'infected' plants or branches in captivity. Possibly this is because in the wild, the birds often take aphids from their usual food plants and so are thought to be taking seeds.

Insects are usually swallowed whole after being, unless very small, nibbled and more or less crushed in the bill. Some species hold sizeable caterpillars etc. by one end in the bill and beat them on the substrate with a sideways jerking movement of the head. This may result in the insect being broken or its legs broken off (pers. obs. for Blue-headed Cordon-bleu with grasshoppers). Mealworms may be decapitated and only the head eaten and/or have the soft contents squeezed out and eaten by repeatedly passing them through the bill; possibly some natural prey species may be similarly treated. The bill and tongue movements used in dealing with insects seem to be similar to, probably identical with, those used when shelling seeds (Kunkel, pers. obs.).

Estrildids do not seem to have been recorded taking mineral matter in the wild but it is almost certain that they must do so there as in captivity. Such behaviour is easily overlooked because it commonly takes up relatively little of the bird's time and mineral matter such as small bits of pulverised shell, salt-impregnated earth etc. may occur on the usual feeding areas.

REFERENCES

Immelmann, K. & G. 1967. Verhaltensökologische Studien an afrikanischen und australischen Estrildiden. *Zool. Jb. Syst. Bd.* **94**: 609–686.

Kunkel, P. 1959. Zum Verhalten einiger Prachtfinken (Estrildinae). *Z. Tierpsychol.* **16**: 302–350.

Newton, I. 1972. *Finches*. Collins, London.

Ziswiler, V. 1965. Zur Kenntnis des Samenöffnens und der Struktur des hörnernen Saumens bei kornerfressenden Oscines. *J. Orn.* **106**: 1–48.

Drinking, bathing, sunning, anting and preening

Most estrildids whose habits in the wild have been observed drink several times a day. A few such as the Violet-eared Waxbill, may, however, live for six months or more in areas with no surface water (Immelmann & Immelmann, 1967). All such species, that are known or believed to go without water for long periods in the wild, feed partly or largely on termites (and possibly some other insects) which presumably supply them with sufficient water. Experiments on captive birds (Cade *et al.* 1965) have shown that the Zebra Finch can survive for a long time without drinking. Possibly other arid country forms as yet, happily for them, untested, also have this ability. From the physiological adaptations that enable it to live without water for long periods, even when on a dry seed diet, it is clear that the wild Zebra Finch may be, and in the course of its evolution must often have been forced to endure thirst for long periods between the drying up of one source of water and its discovery of another. Normally, however, it keeps within easy flying distance of surface water and visits it to drink several times a day (Immelmann, 1973, pers. obs.). The same is true for some (and probably all) other arid country species that are mainly or entirely seed eaters (Immelmann & Immelmann, 1967).

The majority of estrildids usually drink, like most other birds, by dipping the bill into the water and then lifting the head. This widespread method, termed 'Schlucken' in German, is often said to involve only the scooping up of water in the lower mandible and the use of gravity to let it run down the throat. Some of the Australian estrildids, the Zebra Finch among them, keep the bill in contact with the water for a longer period and suck up water in a pigeon-like manner with peristaltic (and visible) movements of the oesophagus (Immelmann, 1973). This method not only looks but is pigeon-like, as Wickler has shown, by means of photography, that the throat movements of a drinking Long-tailed Grassfinch and a drinking Diamond Dove are identical.

This method of drinking is used by some (but not all) Australian forms that inhabit arid country, even by a few that do not usually live far from water. It is usually thought that its function is to enable the bird to imbibe the necessary amount of water more quickly, because it need not repeatedly lift its head, and that this is advantageous because a drinking bird is at risk from predators that tend to lurk around or suddenly appear at watering places. The fact that some dry country species drink in this manner whilst their believed closest relatives that inhabit wetter country do not, makes this hypothesis seem very likely. On the other hand, a bird with its bill lowered to the water for several seconds might seem as much at risk as one that took a little longer total time about drinking but kept raising its head and looking about as it did so. Possibly for this reason many arid country birds, including some estrildids and also sandgrouse (Cade *et al.* 1966), do not drink like pigeons but appear to have adapted to the need for haste by simply speeding up their 'dip and lift head' drinking movements.

It is sometimes suggested that a second advantage of the pigeon-like drinking is that it enables a bird to make use of drops of dew, rain on the surface of leaves or bark or other minuscule sources of water. As I have argued elsewhere (Goodwin, 1965) I do not think that the pigeon-like drinkers have much advantage here or, indeed, that there is so great a difference between the two drinking methods as is sometimes thought. Many birds that drink in the 'usual' way, will often drink drops of dew or rain from leaves or twigs or, under artificial conditions, a drop of water from the end of a slightly leaking tap or pipe. When they do so it certainly appears that the water is sucked in, not that the bird just scoops at it 'hit or miss', in which case most of the water drop would surely be lost. Moreover some (I suspect many) birds which drink in this way will use an apparent sucking, identical in appearance to that of a pigeon or Zebra Finch, if they are drinking from a very small and/or shallow area of water or other liquid. I have seen this pigeon-like method of drinking from cordon-bleus – *Uraeginthus angolensis*, *U. bengalus* and *U. cyanocephala*, the Goldbreast – *Amandava subflava*, and the Black-crowned, Black-rumped and Rosy-rumped Waxbills – *Estrilda nonnula*, *E. troglodytes* and *E. rhodopyga*. All these species usually drink by the dip and lift method but when the available liquid is, apparently, too shallow or too restricted in area, they put their bill tips into it and appear

Diagrammatic sketch of Cordon-bleu drinking spilled egg by suction.

to suck it up, with visible throat movements. I have seen this method most often when the birds have been drinking a shallow film of albumen from a broken egg or (*Estrilda* species) when drinking the 'honey dew' from aphid infested leaves but also when drinking very shallow or small amounts of water or milk. Under comparable conditions I have also seen this pigeon-like drinking from wild Blackbirds, *Turdus merula*, House Sparrows, *Passer domesticus*, and Domestic Fowls, *Gallus gallus*, but a Starling, *Sturnus vulgaris*, and a Rook, *Corvus frugilegus*, seemed unable to suck up water from a shallow film of it on a flat roof and a car park surface (respectively) until they turned their bills sideways on and flat against the wet substrate. From the above observations I incline strongly to think that when 'normally' drinking species dip their heads they do in fact suck as they scoop.

So far as is known all estrildids bathe in water and none, even of the arid country forms, dustbathe. Bathing takes place while the bird stands in shallow water with its feet on the bottom or gripping a submerged twig, reed or other object. As with other birds the preliminary stages usually involve much hesitation and apparent nervousness before the bird settles down to bathe seriously. This probably lessens the danger of the bird starting to bathe near a lurking predator. Bathing moods appear to be highly infectious, one estrildid starting to bathe will usually cause its mate, flock companions and at least in the case of captive birds, estrildids of other species to start to bathe. The same is probably true in the wild also, as it certainly is for many wild British passerine birds which habitually bathe in company with both their own and other species at communal bathing places. The reason for this high sociability when bathing is clearly because if there are several bathing birds, and others drying or about to bathe perched near, not only is an approaching predator likely to be quickly seen by somebody but each individual wet and temporarily flight-impeded bird has a better chance of *not* being the victim if it is one of several who are surprised by a predator than if it were bathing alone.

The bathing movements are the same as those of other passerines. Ducking of head and breast with a violent side-to-side shaking of the bill and upward flicking movements of the wings alternates with the head and foreparts being raised, the tail spread and lowered on the water and the wings beaten in and out of the water and flicked transversely over the back so that water is showered up over the body. During this phase the bird may tilt somewhat, first to one side and then to the other. Once determined bathing has begun, but not during the preliminaries, the plumage is erected so that the water can get between the feathers and, presumably, reach the skin. Some estrildids will also bathe on or in wet leaves or other vegetation, lowering themselves and then pushing their bodies forward along the wet surface. Like many other birds, they seem most eager to bathe and bathe more frequently when the air is humid than when it is dry.

After bathing the bird gets up onto some relatively safe perch to dry itself. The drying movements consist mainly of shaking and ruffling the plumage, vibrating the wing and tail tips together, drooping the wings with somewhat spread primaries, then vibrating them and making a rapid side-to-side movement of the tail. These drying movements are also used when the bird has accidentally got its plumage damp in rain, mist or wet foliage. In captivity (and possibly also when wild) some estrildids, among them *Estrilda troglodytes* and *Lagonosticta rubricata*, often perform the wing and tail drying movements for no cause that is obvious to the human watcher. Simmons (1964) has described bathing, preening and other aspects of feather care in birds in detail.

Preening and oiling are performed in the usual passerine manner (see Simmons, 1964, for details). So far as is known all estrildids scratch the head indirectly, the bird lowering one wing and then bringing the leg on that side up over the shoulder to the head. One use made of head scratching is to apply preen oil to the head feathers. The bird obtains oil from the preen gland, transfers some of it, by scratching the oily bill, to the foot and then scratches its head. Allo-preening, as the preening of one individual by another is now called, is always concentrated on the head and upper neck which cannot be reached by the bird's own bill. Allo-preening has, however, social as well as practical aspects and is discussed further in the section on display and social behaviour.

During preening previously applied preen oil, feather exudates and ectoparasites are removed and, usually, swallowed. It is probably true of estrildids, as it is known to be for some other birds, that sick individuals usually have more ectoparasites than do healthy birds and that individuals with deformed or injured bills nearly always harbour great numbers of ectoparasites. This indicates that one function of the normal frequent preening is to control the numbers of ectoparasites, even if they cannot be eliminated entirely. Like other passerines, estrildids clean their bills by stropping them vigorously against their perch. They also sometimes rub their faces against the perch, apparently to remove contaminating objects or to allay irritation.

Sunbathing is practised by estrildids as by many other birds. When sunning at fairly high intensity, the bird usually positions itself sideways on to the sun and erects its feathers, especially those on head, belly, flanks and rump. The oil gland is exposed by this feather erection. The bird leans a little to the far side, slightly droops the near wing and somewhat spreads its primaries. I have not seen in estrildids the posture with back to the sun and tail and (sometimes) both wings the spread that some other passerines show when sunbathing. The functions of sunning seem as yet uncertain, some of the evidence as to how far birds can compensate for dietary deficiencies by, apparently, ingesting irradiated preen oil from the feathers is conflicting (Kennedy). It has, however, been claimed that the action of sunlight (irradiation) on preen oil causes it to become a source of vitamin D (Simmons, 1964) and there is much circumstantial evidence suggesting that some such deficiencies, especially or perhaps only of vitamin D, can thus be made good. Sunning may also disturb ectoparasites and make them easier for the bird to capture; preening usually intersperses or follows sunbathing. Some sunbathing, especially when the bird adopts no special posture but merely sits quietly with somewhat fluffed out feathers, may serve simply to warm the bird. Although captive estrildids (in Britain) are usually keen to perch in the sun, at least for short periods, if not always to sunbathe actively, in really hot (even by British standards) weather they usually spend most of their time in the shade during the hottest hours of the day as many of them are known to do in their native haunts.

The now well-known habit of anting is widespread but not universal among passerine birds. It does not appear to be common in the Estrildidae but this may be due to its having been overlooked in the wild and to birds in captivity often being given no opportunity to indulge it. I have seen anting – of a type very like that of the Jay, with the ants not actually being picked up – from Goldbreasts and Avadavats (Goodwin, 1960, and species section), Kunkel (1967, and species section) repeatedly observed anting, but with millipedes, not ants, from captive Red-headed Blue-bills. I have also seen anting movements from cordon-bleus (Goodwin, 1971, and species sections) in response to the near proximity of millipedes and centipedes, and once in an apparent conflict situation by a bird prompted to feed young not its own.

There has been much dispute over the possible function of anting (see especially Simmons, 1957 and 1966) but it seems most likely that it serves to help to maintain the primary wing feathers in good condition and to discourage ectoparasites. The ventral ends of the primaries are the parts especially anointed with ant fluids by most birds when anting, and most exposed to the ants by species which do not pick up ants when so-doing; these are just the parts of the plumage least accessible to passerines when preening. Birds anting at high intensity do so with great apparent concentration and often give the impression of being less alert than usual to other stimuli. If this is truly so it may account for the relative infrequency of anting compared to other feather-care activities even among species that practise it. Simmons (1957) makes the pertinent suggestion that the active

anting movements of most passerines may be 'mere relics of a once more widespread anointing which proved harmful in some way'. This seems to me quite possible. Obviously there is much scope for aviculturists to experiment as to which estrildids 'ant' and in response to what stimuli (various ant species, millipedes, centipedes etc). Most useful of course would be to find which species ant in the wild and the circumstances in which they do so but it seems rather unlikely that such information will be obtained easily, if at all.

REFERENCES

Cade, T., Tobin, C. A. & Gold, A. 1965. Water economy and metabolism of two estrildine finches. *Physiol. Zool.* **38**: 9–33.

Cade, T. J., Willoughby, E. J. & Maclean, G. L. 1966. Drinking behaviour of sandgrouse in the Namib and Kalahari deserts, Africa. *Auk* **38**: 124–126.

Goodwin, D. 1960. Observations on Avadavats and Golden-breasted Waxbills. **66**: 174–199.

Goodwin, D. 1965. Remarks on drinking methods of some birds. *Avicult. Mag.* **71**: 76–80.

Goodwin, D. 1971. Anting by Red-cheeked and Blue-headed Cordon-bleus. *Avicult. Mag.* **77**: 88–93.

Immelmann, K. & G. 1967. Verhaltensökologische Studien an afrikanischen und australischen Estrildiden. *Zool. Jb. Syst. Bd.* **94**: 609–686.

Immelmann, K. 1973. *Der Zebrafink*. Neue Brehm-Bucherei series, Wittenberg Lutherstadt.

Kennedy, R. J. 1946. Sunbathing behaviour in birds. *British Birds* **62**: 249–258.

Kunkel, P. 1967. Zu Biologie und Verhalten des Rotkopfsamen-knackers, *Spermophaga ruficapilla* (Fam. Estrildidae). *Bonner Zool. Beiträge* **18**: 139–167.

Simmons, K. E. L. 1957. A review of the anting behaviour of passerine birds. *British Birds* **50**: 401–424.

Simmons, K. E. L. 1964. Feather maintenance, in *A new dictionary of birds* (edited by A. Landsborough Thomson): 284–286.

Simmons, K. E. L. 1966. Anting and the problem of self-stimulation. *J. Zool.* (London) **149**: 145–162.

Wickler, W. 1961. Über die Stammesgeschichte und den taxonomischen Wert einer Verhaltensweisen der Vögel. *Z. Tierpsychol.* **18**: 320–342.

Nesting, parental care and behaviour of young

All estrildids build enclosed nests with a side entrance although the few that sometimes or usually nest in holes then often let the top of the cavity suffice for overhead cover. Their nests vary considerably in size (relative to their builders) and strength of construction in different species. Most often they are built without any firm attachment to the vegetation in which they are sited, so that the nest can often be removed without damaging it. Some species, however, such as the Chestnut-breasted Finch, *Lonchura castaneothorax*, which nests among more or less vertical reed stems, incorporate surrounding vegetation into the nest walls, thus anchoring the nest more securely. The Painted Finch, which nests in clumps of Spinifex grass, first builds a platform of clumps of earth, bits of bark, small stones and similar materials. Presumably this is an adaptation which helps to prevent spinifex spines from penetrating the floor of the nest proper and injuring eggs or nestlings. Some species build long, downward-sloping tube-like extensions to the nest entrance. These may vary in length both between species and within a species. Such entrance tubes presumably function to make the nest chamber less easily found or less easily reached by some predators but they must make the escape of the brooding or incubating parent almost impossible if a predator does find the way in, without first alerting it. Probably this is why entrance tubes of appreciable length are not so widespread in the family as one might have expected them to be if they were always advantageous.

Some species of typical waxbills – *Estrilda* – 'decorate' the upper parts of their nests with conspicuous, and sometimes also odiferous objects. Some of them also regularly or usually build 'cock nests' or 'dummy nests' on top of or alongside the real nest. These two interesting behaviour patterns and their possible functions are discussed separately.

Grass stems, long fibres, thin roots and similar vegetation are the commonest nest materials used. Judging by their behaviour in captivity it would seem that most estrildids are not particularly fussy about the material for the main part of the nest and are usually willing to make the best of what is available. In some species the nest is unlined apart from rather finer stems etc. than are used for the outer parts, in others there may be a sparse or dense lining of soft materials, usually feathers or soft grass panicles. Immelmann (1967) has shown that there is no consistent correlation between the thickness and warmth-conserving qualities of the nest lining and the minimum outside temperatures. He suggests that one function of the white or pale feathers that many species like to line their nests with may be to match the white eggs so that they are not easily seen by a potential nest robber. The young of some species also have whitish down, as he points out. I have in the section on

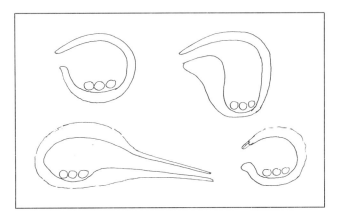

Diagrammatic interpretations of typical Estrildid nests, side view.

plumage sequences and colour changes said that I think nestling down – of whatever colour – may serve to make the young less recognisable as such. The preference for white feathers as a nest lining might also be, as many have suggested, because they reflect much light and make it easier for the parent to see to feed and tend the young inside the nest.

Most species carry grass stems or similar nest material in a characteristic way, holding a single stem by its firmest end or by a shred of fibre at that end (see sketches). Occasionally it may be carried by some side projection but never simply crosswise in the bill or several stems 'bundled' together in the way that most passerines carry nesting materials. Quite a number of species will 'bundle' feathers or other soft lining materials but others take only feathers which they can hold by the body end of the shaft and will not use any material, such as vegetable down, that has no firm end by which it can be held. The parrot-finches, the Gouldian Finch and the Quail Finch are known exceptions that carry all nesting materials 'bundled' (Kunkel, Ziswiler *et al.*).

Building estrildids, at least of those species in which the behaviour has been observed in detail, first assemble some

Male Red-cheeked Cordon-bleu carrying nest material by its firmest end.

Male Red-cheeked Cordon-bleu carrying nesting
material by its firmest end, in typical manner.

material at the selected site, then, standing or squatting
on this base, the bird builds up the sides around itself and
finally constructs the roof. The building movements have
been described and illustrated by Kunkel (1959). They
consist of taking pieces of material in the bill and pushing
them forcefully upwards (Wegschieben); pressing its
breast into the middle of the nest base and pushing strands

Male Red-cheeked Cordon-bleu carrying nest material
by a projecting piece of fibre at its firmest end.

of nesting material towards the perimeter (Ausmuldendes
Wegschieben); taking a strand of material and pulling it
from one side of the nest wall to the other, often turning
the head backwards over the shoulder at the end of the
movement (Seitwärtsziehen); stretching out from its
position in the centre of the future nest and lowering its
head to seize loose strands of material, pull them in
towards its body and fix them into the side of the nest
(Einziehen). Neither Kunkel nor I have seen an estrildid
lower itself onto its shoulders in the cup of the nest and
then scrape backward with the feet while depressing the
tail so it seems likely that estrildids do not have this
movement pattern, which is widespread, at varying
degrees of development, in other birds, or else use it only
very seldom. Kunkel noted that the shuddering, side to
side movement of the head and bill ('Einzittern' in
German), used by many passerines and pigeons when
trying to fix nesting material in place, appears not to be
used. I also have not seen it used by building birds but I
have seen it repeatedly and regularly from two species of
waxbills, *E. troglodytes* and *E. rhodopyga*, when fixing or
trying to fix 'decorations' to the top of the nest.

Avadavat with (left) several feathers 'bundled' in bill and
(right) with single feather carried in typical estrildid
manner (see text).

A few species often or usually take over old or
abandoned nests of other birds that build covered nests
with a side entrance, such as many weavers do.
Depending on the size of the interior they may then merely
reline it or virtually build a nest inside it. From the
readiness with which they accept covered, hole-in-side,
nest baskets in captivity it is possible that many species,
not at present known to do so, may occasionally make use
of other species' nests.

In species for which this behaviour is known, the male
usually takes the lead in searching for a nest site, with the
female closely following him. It seems that in many cases
the final decision as to the site depends on her responding
favourably when the nest-calling male has attracted her
attention to it. The male also collects much or all of the
material for the main structure of the nest which may be
built by him, mainly by the female, or by both. In some of
the species that use feathers to line the nest, both sexes
bring these even when the female does not otherwise
bring nesting material. This is probably because the grass
or other material for the main structure is almost always

superabundant whereas suitable feathers for the lining may be few or only fortuitously available, often depending on the chance of some bird with suitable plumage having been killed and plucked by a predator and it is, therefore, useful for either sex to snap up any suitable feather it finds. Immelmann (1962) found that in Western Australia only male Zebra Finches brought nesting material but in eight pairs that he watched in an arid part of Central Australia both sexes did so and the nests were more quickly built as a result, an apparent adaptation to the unpredictable local climate which makes it advantageous for birds to breed as quickly as possible when suitable conditions occur. In captivity females of species that do not usually collect material or build may do so if their mate is inadequate and does not perform his normal role.

Some species continue to build, or at least to incorporate materials into the nest, during incubation and many that do not, continue to bring feathers or other materials for the nest lining. Nesting or nest-lining material is often brought by a bird when it comes to take over from its mate. In some species (possibly all) that use feathers in the nest lining these seem to be most eagerly sought for near hatching time and while the nestlings are still very small. At such times one or more large feathers are often placed just inside in such a way as to screen the nest entrance or at least to impede a view into the nest.

A few species in the genera *Amandava*, *Lonchura*, *Emblema* and *Poephila* put pieces of charcoal inside their nests. It has been suggested that this may serve to absorb moisture from the substrate and/or the droppings of the young but nothing is known for certain of its function.

Some estrildids habitually roost in old nests of their own or other species and many of these build nests for roosting, although these are not so well constructed as breeding nests. In such species the young usually return to the nest to roost for at least the first few nights after fledging. Other species do not roost inside nests except when incubating or brooding. The habit of roosting in nests is sometimes acquired, young of species that do not normally do so, if reared by Bengalese Finches, may learn the habit from their foster parents.

In most (probably all) species the male and female both incubate and brood, in turn, by day, usually for periods of about one to one and a half hours at a time. Available observations suggest that in some species the females may take longer spells on the nest but some at least of such observations are based on captive birds. The few records that seem to suggest incubation only by the female may be based on incomplete observation or aberrant behaviour. In species which do not roost in nests, the female alone incubates and broods by night. It is likely that she also does in those species in which both sexes are inside the nest at night. Under captive conditions birds of either sex will often go onto the nest 'out of turn' if they see their mates have left the eggs or nestlings. Males whose mates have died suddenly, leaving them with hatching eggs or nestlings, and males which are homosexually paired, will sometimes incubate and brood at night. When changing

over at the nest many species, especially those whose nests have tube entrances, utter soft calls and the arriving bird does not enter the nest until it hears its mate answer. Clearly this behaviour serves to prevent the arriving bird coming to grief also should a snake or some other predator have entered the nest in its absence. The shells of hatched eggs are either eaten or carried out of the nest, possibly the extent to which the parent is or is not in need of lime may determine this rather than specific differences. In *Uraeginthus* either may occur.

Both sexes feed the young although, at least under captive conditions, if the female lays again before the young are independent, usually their father alone continues to feed them. As with other passerines, the adults clean their bills meticulously before feeding young nestlings. Nest hygiene is unrecorded for most species but the Bengalese Finch is known to eat the droppings of the young for the first week or so. From observations of nests I believe that the cordon-bleus, the Avadavat and the Goldbreast also do this and it is probable that most or all estrildids do. For the rest of the nestling period the young deposit their droppings on or in the interstices of the sides of the nest chamber where it soon dries and does not foul the plumage of the young. The construction of the nest and its materials probably facilitate this as if, in captivity, an impermeable wall forms one side of the nest, this may result in delayed drying of the faeces and consequent fouling of the nestlings' feathers (Goodwin, 1965).

Ziswiler (in Immelmann *et al.* 1963) found that when artificially incubated at a constant temperature of 38·5°C, various estrildids' eggs all hatched at $11\frac{1}{4}$ days but under natural or captive conditions the incubation period is usually from 12 to 14 days and sometimes longer. True incubation seems usually to begin with the third egg at the earliest. Many (and probably all) species normally lay an egg a day, in the early morning, until the clutch is complete.

Young estrildids beg in a prone posture with the neck turned through an angle of 90 to 160 degrees, and the open mouth turned upwards, often at an angle, towards the parent. In some species the tongue is lifted high above the floor of the mouth. In most the head is swung or oscillated like a pendulum from side to side during the begging. This form of begging may develop immediately or not until few days after hatching, the nestling at first simply turning its head up to beg without the peculiar twisting of the neck. Fledglings use a similar posture and most species do not use the fluttering wing movements otherwise so general with begging young passerines. This last is not, however, an absolute difference between estrildids and non-estrildids as such fluttering or quivering wing movements when begging have been seen, either regularly or occasionally, from the Green Twinspot (Kunkel, 1960), Pin-tailed Parrot-finch (Karl), Red-browed Finch (many authorities), Avadavat (many, including pers. obs.), Goldbreast (pers. obs., when begging at rather low intensity), and Black-rumped Waxbill (Herkner). I have also seen a suggestion of wing fluttering

Zebra finch, fledgling begging to parent. From a
photograph by Peter Kunkel.

at times from begging young of all three species of cordon-
bleus, *Uraeginthus*.

The remarkable begging posture is not, however, so
striking a difference between estrildids and other passerines as at first appears. At least a few estrildids, for
example, the Cut-throat (Hall, unpublished mss, Kunkel,
1959), the Dusky Twinspot and the Pin-tailed Parrot-
finch (Karl) do not (ever ?) use it but beg directly toward
the parent like the young of cardueline finches and most
other passerines. With the fledged young of many species,
the degree to which the typical estrildid posture is adopted
when begging depends on the degree of hunger or at least
eagerness for food of the young. Nearly sated Goldbreasts
and Avadavats may do little or nothing more than open
their mouths while maintaining a normal resting posture.
Even in forms, such as the cordon-bleus, in which the
begging behaviour seems more rigidly stereotyped, there
are slight differences of intensity according to hunger.
Also, in young able to fly, the begging is directed towards
the head of the parent. This is not readily apparent until one
happens to see a young bird begging from an adult below
it in the branches and notices that its head is then directed
downwards instead of upwards in the usual manner.

The young of the African mannikins, sub-genus
Spermestes, the Pictorella Finch, subgenus *Heteromunia*, the
Bicheno Finch, *Poephila bichenovii*, and the three species in
the genus *Amandava*, all partly spread and raise their wings
in a striking manner when begging. In the Avadavat and
Goldbreat, probably also in the other species that use this
wing movement, the wing further from the parent is
normally raised but if the parent approaches from directly
in front, then the fledgling raises both wings. It is very
striking to see one or both wings suddenly lifted vertically
but in fact, at least in *Amandava*, the movement is not an 'all
or nothing' affair and shows forms suggestive of the more
usual wing flutterings of other passerines. If a hungry
young Avadavat or Goldbreast is approached by its parent,
it crouches, twisting its neck and opening its bill in the usual

manner. It also partly opens its wings and flutters them,
then, as the parent comes up to it, the young bird suddenly
raises the far wing, or both if the parent is directly in front.
The wing or wings may be thrust out obliquely or horizontally rather than vertically. Occasionally the near wing
may be extended in spite of the parent's approach along the
same perch and the parent may then trip over it or perch on
it and unintentionally pin down its offspring in so-doing. If
the fledgling is tightly 'sandwiched' between two siblings
it makes no perceptible wing movements. Under these last
circumstances it does not seem impelled to accompany
even the most intense crouching and neck twisting with
any wing movements. It has been suggested that wing
raising when begging may serve to block the parent's view
of the other young, thus ensuring more food for the one
nearest to it, but there seems no evidence for this. It may
possibly happen if food is in short supply but when it is not,
the parent, who knows all its fledged young individually,
takes care to feed them all. In some species in which the
young beg with raised wings, the adults have hostile or
sexual displays in which the wings are raised in a similar
manner.

Estrildids feed their young by regurgitating food from
the crop. They never, even when being pestered as they
feed by flying young, give the young food that they have
not first swallowed. The feeding technique of parent
estrildids has often been described and Ziswiler (1967)
and Ziswiler *et al.* have also described the crop musculature that makes possible this method. Just before it feeds its
young, the parent appears to (and doubtless does) bring
up food into the upper part of its throat or back of its
mouth with peculiar side to side movements of its neck. It
then puts its bill into the young bird's mouth and
regurgitates more food with visible pulsating movements

Diagrammatic sketch of an estrildid (no particular
species) feeding a fledgling.

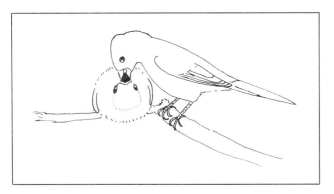

Male Blue-headed Cordon-bleu feeding fledged young.

of its throat and upper breast. It does not withdraw its bill when it regurgitates but keeps it in the fledgling's mouth and the latter, whose mouth is at right angles to its parent's, evidently grips to retain contact. When the parent wishes to feed a second young one it lifts its head and often has literally to shake off the first fledgling. The process is repeated with other young, two or more of the brood are fed at each feeding. Usually during the feeding the young bird's head stays very low but this appears to be because, although it is probably pushing upwards at the time, the strength with which it does so is less than that of the adult bearing down. I noticed, at first with surprise, that when a cock Avadavat adopted and fed fledgling Blue-headed Cordon-bleus, his head would be pushed up and back during the feeding act until he was almost literally 'lifted off his feet' by the upthrusting young Bluehead. I have here described the feeding of fledglings because I have not myself had clear views of the feeding of very small nestlings. As would be expected, and as Eisner's studies on the Bengalese Finch have shown, the feeding of small young is done in the same way except that the parent is naturally more restrained and gentle in its movements. As will now be clear the feeding behaviour of a parent estrildid differs strikingly from that of a cardueline finch such as the Canary, which also feeds from the crop but brings up a mouthful of food at a time and gives it to the young bird with only a brief mouth to mouth contact.

Nicolai suggests that the feeding method of estrildids requires specialised adaptive breathing techniques. He states that any attempt (of which innumerable have been made by bird keepers) to rear cardueline finches under estrildids, or *vice versa*, always fail through the young being choked when the foster parent attempts to feed them. Apart from cases where the intended foster parents, do not attempt to feed the strange nestlings. Certainly there can be no doubt that such attempts usually fail and possibly always do so. The only definite claim to the contrary I have seen is that of Teague who, in a list of birds that he had successfully fostered under Bengalese Finches, included three species of *Serinus* and the Cuban Finch, *Tiaris canora*. There is, however, evidence that young estrildids, at any rate once they are at the fledgling stage,

are able in some cases to take food from non-estrildid fosterers. *Die Gefiederte Welt* for 1970 (p. 40) published a photograph showing a Cuban Finch feeding a young Quail-finch, *Ortygospiza atricollis* and Goger described how a male Scaly-fronted Weaver, *Sporopipes squamifrons*, fed a young Red-cheeked Cordon-bleu that, after it left the nest, had been deserted by its parents.

The striking mouth markings of estrildids and parental reactions to them are discussed elsewhere.

As with other birds that have altricial young, estrildids seem to learn to recognise them as individuals when or shortly after they leave the nest. At least they usually readily accept a nestling of the same species and age as their own prior to the fledging of the latter but they will not usually feed strange fledglings. When two or more broods of cordon-bleus, *Uraeginthus*, fledged about the same time in my bird room, I have been surprised how unerringly the parents distinguished their own young. Nor, I feel sure, did they do so by their colour rings, the only way I could tell which was which. Knoblauch manipulated clutches of Zebra Finches in his bird room so that seven broods fledged in two and a half days, yet in spite of the horde of noisy young around them, the parents fed only their own. Knoblauch stated also that the young Zebra Finches begged only from their own parents. With cordon-bleus, *Uraeginthus* spp., I have repeatedly observed that at first the fledglings, when hungry, beg to any adult that comes near them but that within about 24 hours they learn to beg only from their parents, obviously because of the negative or even positively hostile response that they get from other adults.

That the parents know their own young individually and wish to feed them and only them, can be seen from the way in which they will sometimes persist in trying to tempt one of their sated offspring to accept more food and intersperse these attempts with an angry pecking away of other young of the same age that come up hungrily begging to them. It seems very seldom that parent estrildids *that have young of their own* will feed strange fledglings. In the only case I have known of this happening, the 'adopted' young fledged from a nest near to that of their adopters at a time when the latters' nest contained young nearly ready to fledge. Presumably in this instance the parents (Avadavats) were 'all set' to respond to the fledging of young.

Where several birds are kept in the same room or aviary, adoption of fledglings is, however, not at all uncommon. In my experience, with *Uraeginthus* and *Amandava*, it occurs invariably (1) or often (2), (3) and (4) under the following circumstances: (1) When a bird of either sex is in love with a bird who is paired to another. Under these circumstances the 'rejected lover' reacts as though the beloved's young were his or her own, often attempts to feed them in the nest in spite of attacks by the parents and always feeds one or more of the brood after they have left the nest. (2) By unpaired birds in breeding condition. (3) By cock birds whose mates have, for some reason or other, not co-operated with them successfully in breeding activities. (4) By homosexual pairs that have spent some time in fruitless nesting activities. In *Uraeginthus*, male homosexual pairs sometimes dispossess a heterosexual pair, incubate their eggs and rear the young. Although, unless imprinted on some other species, adopters prefer conspecific young, in default of them they often adopt the young of different species. I have known a female Green Avadavat adopt Zebra Finches, and a male Avadavat adopt Blue-headed Cordon-bleus. Knoblauch & Nicolai give many similar examples.

I have often noticed with cordon-bleus, as did Knoblauch with his Zebra Finches, that when a single youngster or the whole brood (as the case may be) is adopted by some other bird(s), their parents very soon cease to feed or show any particular interest in it or them. The seemingly obvious reason is that the young stop begging from their own parents and so no longer stimulate their parental responses. I do not, however, feel sure that this obvious explanation is the whole story as the parents do not otherwise *only* feed their young when they are pestered by them, on the contrary they repeatedly seek them out to feed them when they are quiescent and sometimes half sated. It will seem outrageously anthropomorphic to many of my readers to suggest even the possibility, at a simpler level, of some such state of mind as human parents in analogous circumstances might (if honest) express in such terms as 'Well, the kids are being well looked after, are'nt they?' or even a resentful 'Well, if they think more of strangers than they do of their own mother and father . . .' but I do not feel certain that it would be entirely wrong.

Presumably because the intention movements of feeding young are the same in most or all species, young estrildids, if at all hungry, quickly 'get the idea' when prospective foster parents of another species offer to feed them.

Estrildids will scold at a human or a non-human predator when they have young and, especially if they see their young caught or threatened, will make what appear to be intention movements of flying to attack but there seem few records of their actually doing so. Both Kunkel (1959) and I have observed that some species do not attempt to defend their young even when the latter are attacked or being maltreated by conspecifics or other estrildids no larger than themselves. As, at least in the case of cordon-bleus, the adults then mob the attacker from a little distance – just as they would a human handling their young – this can hardly be because they are indifferent. Possibly under natural conditions, nearly all nest predators are a potential danger to the adults also and so, at least in some species, natural selection has inhibited overt attacking of an enemy in this situation. The male of a pair of Avadavats living wild in Germany was, however, seen to attack a Wryneck that came near its nest (Ammersbach) so evidently this species at least sometimes attacks in defence of its brood. Further observations, especially of birds in the wild, would be of great interest.

In some species the parents lead the young back to the nest to feed them and/or to roost at night for at least a few nights after fledging. Other species do not do this but lead the young into cover or (when in captivity) to perches well above ground level. One or both parents go to the young, utter contact calls or alarm calls (depending on the circumstances) or make intention movements of feeding them, then hop or fly to or towards the place they wish the young to be. For those species whose young roost in the nest at night for a period after fledging, the nest must presumably be as safe or safer a roosting place for *each* of the occupants than would a roosting place outside it. It is then not surprising that some, although not all, of the species which do this build nests with long entrance tubes and sometimes with a 'cock nest' on top also.

Like other passerines, young estrildids, old enough to do so, will flee from the nest prematurely and try to scramble or flutter into cover if one of the brood is seized by a predator (or human) and screams in terror. Sometimes violent jarring of the nest or prolonged alarm calls by the parents will elicit this fleeing response.

It might be mentioned that although some estrildids are social even when breeding, and 'adoptions' and (less often) the feeding of recently fledged young by older young may occur in captivity, there is no evidence, for any species, of more than the two parents being involved with the rearing of a brood under natural conditions.

REFERENCES

Ammersbach, R. 1960. Tigerfinken (*Amandava a. amandava*) brüten in freier Waldbahn. *Gefiederte Welt* **1960**: 81–85.

Eisner, E. 1961. The behaviour of the Bengalese Finch in the nest. *Ardea* **49**: 51–69.

Goger, R. 1965. Freiwillige Ammendienste in der Voliere. *Gefiederte Welt* **1965**: 212–213.

Goodwin, D. 1960. Observations on Avadavats and Golden-breasted Waxbills. *Avicult. Mag.* **1966**: 174–199.

Goodwin, D. 1965. A comparative study of captive blue waxbills. *Ibis* **107**: 285–315.

Herkner, R. 1979. Erfahrungen mit meinen Grauastrilden. *Gefiederte Welt* **1979**: 43–45.

Immelmann, K. 1962. Beitrage zu einer vergleichenden Biologie australischer Prachtfinken (Spermestidae). *Zool. Jb. Syst. Bd.* **90**: 1–196.

Immelmann, K. 1967. Verhaltensökologische Studien au afrikanischen und australischen Estrildiden. *Zool. Jb. Syst. Bd.* **94**: 609–686.

Immelmann, K., Steinbacher, J. & Wolters, H. E. 1963. *Vögel in Käfig und Voliere: Prachtfinken*: 13–14.

Karl, F. 1964. Lauchgrune Papageiamadinen (*Erythrura prasina*). *Gefiederte Welt* **1964**: 2–4.

Knoblauch. D. 1968. Verhaltensweisen von Zebrafinken als Stubenvögel im Vergleich zu wildlebenden Zebrafinken. *Gefiederte Welt* **1968**: 227–231.

Kunkel, P. 1959. Zum Verhalten einiger Prachtfinken (Estrildinae). *Z. Tierpsychol.* **16**: 302–350.

Kunkel, P. 1960. Einiges über den grünen Tropfenastrild (*Mandingoa nitidula*) *Gefiederte Welt* **1960**: 131–132.

Kunkel, P. 1966. Bemerkungen zu einer Verhaltensweisen des Rebhuhnastrilds, *Ortygospiza atricollis* (Vieillot). *Z. Tierpsychol.* **23**: 136–140.

Nicolai, J. 1964. Der Brutparasitismus der Viduinae als ethologisches Problem. *Z. Tierpsychol.* **21**: 129–204.

Teague, P. W. 1936. Bengalese as foster-parents. *Avicult. Mag.* 1, 5th ser. 280.

Ziswiler, V. 1967. Der Verdauungstrakt körnerfressenden Singvögel als taxonomischer Merkmalskomplex. *Rev. Suisse Zool.* 620–628.

Ziswiler, V., Güttinger, H. R. & Bregulla, H. 1972. *Monographie der Gattung* Erythrura *Swainson, 1837 (Aves, Passeres, Estrildidae).* Bonner Zoologische Monographien, No. 2.

'Cock nests' and nest 'decorating'

Many of the typical waxbills, *Estrilda,* usually build an additional nest on top of or beside the one in which the eggs are laid. These have commonly been called 'cock nests' because of the mistaken belief that the cock roosted in them. The terms 'dummy nest', 'extra nest' and sub-nest (Boenigk's suggested English translation for his proposed term 'Nebennest') have also been used. I prefer to use the older and better-known term even if, like such generally accepted names as Muscovy Duck, Turkey, Marsh Tit and Cape Pigeon, it is technically a misnomer.

Diagrammatic sketch of section of nest and 'cock-nest' built in captivity by a male Rosy-rumped Waxbill. His mate, a Black-rumped Waxbill, did little or nothing towards the construction except for adding feathers etc. to the 'cock-nest'.
(The rise in the bottom line of the tube was caused by a 'bump' in the bird-room floor on which the nest was built).

My own observations of cock nests and the behaviour of their builders are restricted to observations on captive Black-rumped and Rosy-rumped Waxbills, *Estrilda troglodytes* and *E. rhodopyga* and descriptions of cock nests built by these species will be found in the species' sections. When discussing the subject here the facts and suppositions derive from *Estrilda* species only but it is highly likely that any explanation which is valid for them will prove equally so for any other species, if such there should prove to be, that also constructs cock nests *in the wild.*

Some of these species that build cock nests and at least

one that does not – the Lavender Waxbill (Munz) – habitually place such objects as white or glossy black feathers, bits of conspicuous paper and clumps of earth on top of the nest and in front of or inside the entrance of the cock nest (if one is present). At least three species, the Lavender Waxbill (Munz), Rosy-rumped Waxbill (pers. obs.) and Black-rumped Waxbill (pers. obs.), also use any dead nestlings and putrescent large-bodied dead insects they can find and carry for this purpose and show particular eagerness and excitement for such corpses. This behaviour has been termed both 'decorating' ('schmucken') and 'camouflaging' ('tarnen') by German writers (e.g. Kunkel, 1959) I shall here use the former, purely for convenience sake. 'Decorating' does not seem to have been recorded in the wild. No doubt the reason for this is that in the wild the materials used tend either to conceal the nest, or by calling attention to themselves divert attention from the nest beneath and, if they are noticed by the human finder, are thought by him to have got there adventitiously and so not recorded.

It is likely that the 'decorating' of the top of the nest may, according to the materials used, either genuinely camouflage the nest or else divert a potential predator, perhaps only some particular kind of predator, from discovering the nest beneath. I think that the latter must be the case at least with the three species known to use stinking dead nestlings and insect corpses. Before I had observed the use of small dead creatures I thought (Goodwin, 1964) that nest decoration was essentially nest-lining behaviour that had, in the course of evolution of these species, become redirected to the *outside* of the nest. I still think this is its most probable origin but it has clearly developed considerably and perhaps incorporated nest cleansing elements. At least the objects used for 'decoration' are mostly of a kind that are either used for lining nests (e.g. feathers) or are normally removed from them (bits of eggshell, dead nestlings etc.).

Cock nests usually differ from the real nest beneath or beside them by being smaller and/or not having progressed beyond the open-cup or partly domed stage. It is possible that, given adequate time, these latter would be completely roofed over but I think that selective pressures may have favoured the building of cock nests that do not get beyond a stage where the nest opening is more obvious and the nest chamber more readily visible than in the complete breeding nest. The Black-cheeked (Skead) and Rosy-rumped Waxbills, that are not known to line their breeding nests with feathers, place feathers inside and conspicuously just outside the entrance of their cock nests. With the Common and Black-rumped Waxbills, feathers may be used for both breeding nest and cock nest. In the Black-rumped and Rosy-rumped Waxbills (probably also in other species for which it has not been recorded), objects used for 'decoration', *including dead and putrid nestlings,* are also placed inside the cock nest or just outside its entrance.

Boenigk observed 11 pairs of Black-rumped Waxbills in a large aviary, of which 9 pairs built cock nests. He found that, with his birds, work on the cock nests only occurred when one of the pair was prevented from building by the deliberately or accidentally obstructive behaviour of its mate. This latter included times when the mate was incubating. I did not have the impression, when watching my captive birds of this species, that work on the cock nest was always the result of such thwarting, but I had not then read Boenigk's paper and did not watch particularly for this point. What I repeatedly observed, both in this species and *E. rhodopyga*, was that in any apparent conflict between the urge to incubate and fear or suspicion due to some disturbance, the birds would carry 'decorations' and lining material to the cock nest and fuss around it. Often a bird would, after much conspicuous movement outside it, go into the cock nest, only to come out and slip quietly and inconspicuously into the real nest after a minute or two. Very significant, I think, was the way in which pairs that had built in nest baskets on which they had been unable, in spite of frenzied efforts, to construct a cock nest, would adopt a nearby *Uraeginthus* nest in a similar basket as surrogate cock nest and, when alarmed or disturbed, fuss about it, carry feathers to it and so on, *not* around their own nest. Van Someren has vividly described how the males of wild pairs of the Common Waxbill, when disturbed by his presence, fetched feathers and pink grass-heads to their cock nests in a conspicuous and noisy manner. Other observers have remarked on the conspicuousness of the cock nests or have mentioned noticing a bird in them.

There has been much difference of opinion but as yet no good evidence from the wild as to the function, if any, of the cock nest. It has been suggested that the cock might roost in it (many authors) or that it might function to deceive predators (Belcher, Goodwin, Immelmann). Boenigk considers it 'just a functionless outcome of the strong nest-building drive' and Johnson, writing of the Common Waxbill, says 'the true purpose (of the cock nest) is to act as an overflow nursery into which some of the chicks move as they mature.' He gives no evidence for this statement.

It is fairly certain that the nest is not used as a roost by the cock bird or even as a resting place by day. The only evidence for this is the cock, or at least one of the pair, having sometimes been seen on or in the cock nest *by day*. Doubtless in such cases the bird was either working on it or had entered it as a result of being perturbed by the intruding human. Nor do captive male (or female) waxbills roost, or even *rest* by day, in their cock nests (Boenigk, Goodwin, Immelmann, Kunkel). As to the suggestion that some of the young move into the cock nest 'as they mature', perhaps the nestlings that are first to fledge or some that have mislaid their way back into the real nest, may at times gather or spend periods in the cock nest but I believe that if this happens it is more or less by chance. There can be no reason to suppose that the young would be any safer in the cock nest than they would be in the real one or in cover nearby and therefore this use of the cock nest, even if it sometimes occurs, can hardly have selective value.

Although, on one level, the cock nest is undoubtedly the 'outcome of a strong nest-building drive' I do not think Boenigk is right in concluding that it is a functionless one. Under captive conditions species with a strong nest-building drive, the Zebra Finch for example, sometimes indulge it with functionless or, so far as their breeding success is concerned, positively harmful results. The cock nest-building waxbills, however, construct their dummy nests *and when alarmed or suspicious act in a manner likely to call attention to them* as regularly in the wild as they do in captivity. I believe that the cock nest functions to mislead potential predators and thus to protect eggs and young *or the sitting parent*. Boenigkt argues against this suggestion on the grounds that the most important nest predators are likely to be snakes, lizards and small mammals which find their food primarily by scent and therefore would be hardly likely to be fooled. It seems to me that there are two answers to this claim. Firstly, the cock nest and the behaviour associated with it strongly suggest that it may function, inter alia, in relation to some predator that does hunt by sight. Secondly, the eagerness with which such rotting corpses as the bird can lift are taken to the cock nest suggest the possibility that these may serve as 'a red herring across the trail' in relation to creatures that smell out their prey. Holman (in Bannerman, 1949) suggested that the projecting grass stems at the entrance of the Orange-cheeked Waxbill's nest might serve to repel snakes and I have had the same impression when I pricked my finger trying to insert it into the entrance tube of a captive Rosy-rumped Waxbill's nest. Even if the cock nest only served to delay the entry of a predator this would probably allow the parent, alerted by activities overhead, to escape instead of being trapped together with its eggs or young by a snake or small mammal entering the real nest immediately upon arrival.

One creature that is not usually, if ever, misled by the cock nest is the parasitic Pin-tailed Whydah, *Vidua macroura*. As most of the cock nest building species are known or suspected to be parasitised by this whydah, it is possible that the cock nest originated as a means of deflecting the whydah from the real nest but that the parasite 'won out' in the course of evolution and the cock nest is now functionless, as Boenigk believes. I think, however, it is more likely that the cock nest is still functional and that its function is to mislead one or more probably several species of nest predator or to delay their entrance long enough to ensure that at least the adult is able to escape. Only studies in the wild will show whether I am right or wrong in this belief.

REFERENCES
Bannerman, D. A. 1949. *The birds of Tropical West Africa* **7**: 347, London.
Belcher, C. F. 1930. *The birds of Nyasaland*. London.
Boenigk, G. 1970. Verhaltensstudien zum Bau der 'Hahnennester' einiger Prachtfinkenarten (*Estrildidae*). *Beiträge zur Vogelkunde* **15**: 402–413.
Goodwin, D. 1964. Some aspects of nesting behaviour in *Estrilda*. *Bull. Brit. Orn. Club* **84**: 99–105.

Immelmann, K. & G. 1967. Verhaltensökologische Studien an afrikanischen and australischen Estrildiden. *Zool. Jb. Syst. Bd.* **94**: 609–686.

Johnson, P. 1977. *As free as a bird* Cambridge.

Kunkel, P. 1959. Zum Verhalten einiger Prachtfinken (*Estrildidae*). *Z. Tierpsychol.* **16**: 302–350.

Munz, K. 1979. Die Zucht des Schönburzels. *Gefiederte Welt* **1979**: 102–103.

Sclater, W. L. & Moreau, R. E. 1939. Taxonomic and field notes on some birds of north-eastern Tanganyika Territory. *Ibis* **3**, 13th ser.: 399–440.

Van Someren, V. G. L. 1956. Days with birds. *Feldiana: Zoology*, **38**: 492–495.

Schematic diagrams to show mouth pattern and light-reflecting gape tubercles of nestling Gouldian Finch. After drawings by Butler, 1898, and a photograph by Ziegler, 1963.

Nestling mouth patterns

Estrildid nestlings have strikingly patterned and coloured mouths. Most widespread is the 'domino pattern', as it is often called, in which the nestling has 5 black or very dark spots or patches on an otherwise pale palate and, in addition, 2 dark marks on the tongue, a dark, horseshoe-shaped mark on the inside of the lower mandible and conspicuously swollen and pale coloured gape flanges. In many forms bright or contrasting gape tubercles are present and these have evolved into light reflecting organs in the parrot-finches and the Gouldian Finch. This 5-spot pattern shows many minor variations both between groups and between species within groups. Many forms show a pattern of elongated marks or a single, more or less horseshoe-shaped dark marking on the palate. These patterns appear to have come about, in the course of evolution, by an extension and fusing together of the black spots of the domino pattern, which is generally believed, from its wide distribution, to be phylogenetically older. Extreme developments in this direction are the inclusive circular mouth markings of the African and Indian Silverbills and the double horseshoe pattern of the African mannikins. Other variations from the 5-spot pattern have involved the loss of some or most of the markings, as in the Java Sparrow and the Swee Waxbill. The more profusely spotted mouths of the avadavats and the Goldbreast, *Amandava* spp., may represent other development from the 5-spot pattern or possibly be representative of a yet older group.

In many cases close similarities of mouth markings undoubtedly indicates close relationship. Delacour, and later in more detail Steiner, based their classifications of the Estrildidae partly (Delacour) or mainly (Steiner) on this character. However, as Immelmann *et al.* (1963) point out, similar mouth patterns may have evolved independently, from the (presumed) original domino pattern, among relatively unrelated forms. Also striking differences, usually due to unilateral loss or diminution of some mouth markings, may exist between two closely related species. Extant descriptions and drawings suggest that there may even sometimes be minor individual differences within the same species but the apparent evidence for this may perhaps sometimes involve human error due to the false comparison of nestlings of different age or physical condition.

The ontogeny and histology of the mouth patterns of three species, the Bengalese Finch, African Silverbill and Blue-faced Parrot-finch, have been studied, described and their development illustrated by Glatthaar & Ziswiler.

The gape tubercles and/or swollen gape flanges invariably shrink and finally disappear not very long after the young leave the nest. The palate markings may last considerably longer (Kunkel & Kunkel) and they are retained in the adult in the cordon-bleus, the blue-bills and possibly some other forms.

Although the nestlings of many other passerines have brightly-coloured and a few have conspicuously patterned mouths, with one group of exceptions none of them at all closely resemble nestling estrildids. The exceptions are, of course, the parasitic whydahs and indigo-birds, *Vidua* spp., the mouth markings of whose nestlings very closely

Diagrammatic sketches to show variations in mouth patterns (but *not* in size and shape of mouths and bills), left to right Vinaceous Firefinch, Red-billed Firefinch, Avadavat, Chestnut Munia, Java Sparrow, African Silverbill.

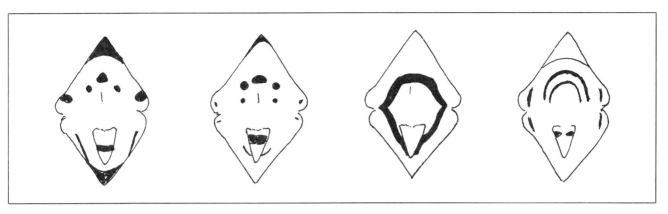

Diagrammatic sketches of nestling mouth patterns of (left to right) Red-cheeked Cordon-bleu, Dark Firefinch, African Silverbill, Bronze Mannikin.

resemble those of the young estrildids with whom they are reared.

Conspicuous colours or patterns of nestlings' mouths appear to have at least two and possibly four functions. The first is to serve as guides or markers for the adult feeding them, especially in the gloom of a covered nest. The second is, in conjunction with the begging movements and/or calls of the young, to provide a 'releaser' that elicits or stimulates parental feeding by the adult. It is probable that this second function is, in an evolutionary sense, largely correlated with competition between siblings. It is, of course, true that parent birds normally have a strong innate urge to feed their young and, in default of anything better, would certainly feed even a weakly begging nestling with a relatively inconspicuous (but visible) mouth. Such a one would, however, almost certainly be 'passed over' in favour of a vigorously begging, conspicuous-mouthed nestling.

The need for 'guidelines' for the feeding parent, or a conspicuous mouth to stimulate it, cannot, however, be responsible for the differences between the mouth markings of various estrildids. These involve not only the very striking differences between some (not all) of the major groups within the family but also the usually smaller but, even to human eyes, quite noticeable differences between some closely related species. It seems most likely these inter-specific differences have been brought about by natural selection because they themselves (and not some other feature with which they are genetically correlated) are or, in the recent evolutionary

history of the species, have been of use. The only obvious way in which they could be so is by enabling the parents to distinguish between their own nestlings and those of others. It seems that some, and possibly many estrildids have this ability and act upon it under appropriate circumstances but the evidence is conflicting or at least at first appears so.

Nicolai (1964 and 1969) gives several examples of captive estrildids of various species neglecting nestlings of other species, sometimes of quite closely related forms, when these have been put in their nests especially, although not only, when the nests also contained some of their own young. His very considerable experience of breeding estrildids in captivity convinced him that it is only in the absence of young of their own species that wild estrildids will rear the young of other forms. He pointed out that not even every pair of the domesticated Bengalese Finch will rear the nestlings of other species, at any rate if they also have, or can even hear young of their own species. Bengalese Finches are widely used for rearing rarer and more valuable species of estrildids and domesticated Zebra Finches will also often readily foster strange (estrildid) young. There are, however, cases of wild species rearing strange young even sometimes when these were hatched or placed among their own offspring. Wild-caught Zebra Finches readily reared Bengalese Finches, in spite of the extremely different mouth markings of their young. They also reared mixed broods of Bengalese and their own nestlings (Immelmann *et al.*, 1977). A pair that were probably wild-caught reared Orange-cheeked Waxbill (Gedney). When a pair of Long-tailed Grassfinches laid eggs in the nest of a pair of Avadavats, the latter reared the young grassfinches (again very different in mouth markings) even although, and to the detriment of two of, their own young which hatched at the same time (Herrmann). Baptista (pers. comm.) has had Bengalese Finches hatched and successfully reared both by Avadavats and by Grey-headed Silverbills. I have found that both Red-cheeked and Blue-headed Cordon-bleus will rear mixed broods of the two species, although admittedly in this case the differences are only slight (Goodwin, 1965).

Blue-headed Cordon-bleu – diagrammatic sketches of palate patterns of (left to right) a 3-day old nestling, an 8-day old nestling, an 18-day old fledgling (one of four, all same), and an adult female.

None of the species mentioned above as having reared strange nestlings with very different mouth patterns from those of their own nestlings are, however, parasitised by viduines and, with the possible exception of the two cordon-bleus, none seem likely to have been within recent evolutionary time. Nicolai (1969) found that the begging behaviour of the young Paradise Whydah is so emphatic and vigorous that if he placed parasitised broods (taken in the wild) under Bengalese Finches, only the parasites were adequately fed. On the other hand in the wild both the young Melba Finches and the young Paradise Whydahs were adequately nourished. Nicolai presumes, no doubt correctly, that this must be because the parent Melba Finches do distinguish to some extent the small differences between the mouth of the parasite and those of their own young and would descriminate in favour of the latter if the parasite did not manage to 'compensate' by its more vigorous begging and thus get equally nourished.

I think that selection for interspecific mouth pattern differences in the nestlings and (where it occurs) a fine parental responsiveness to it, must be connected with the past history of the estrildids and their viduine parasites (see also pp. 13–14). Although at the present stage of evolution the viduines seem to cause little or no harm to their hosts, it may not always have been so. Other and earlier viduines may have damaged the reproductive success of their hosts as, although probably not in the same ways, parasitic cuckoos, cowbirds and honeyguides do, and an ability to distinguish their own young may have been one factor that enabled some estrildids to dispose of their nest parasites. One might therefore expect such species as the Zebra Finch and the Avadavat, whose ancestors have probably been free of parasitic viduines for a very long period, not now to possess any strong instinct to reject or neglect young whose mouth patterns are 'wrong'. It is true that Immelmann *et al.* (1977) found that both white and normally-coloured captive Zebra Finches, when given mixed broods of white and normally-coloured nestlings, showed some preference for the latter. They fed both white and normal young but the normally-coloured nestlings were given rather more food and this was especially noticeable for the first few feeds of the day. When the young were equally hungry those with normally-marked mouths got preference. Immelmann *et al.* point out that under natural conditions, where the young are likely all to be quite hungry each time a parent arrives to feed them, the white ones would probably have fared worse. Here, although there was clear evidence of preference on the basis of mouth colour (for Immelmann *et al.* did not observe any differences of vigour and activity such as are sometimes noticeable between white and coloured forms of the same species), it was, of course a choice between a strikingly patterned mouth and one with *no pattern at all*. A very different situation from that of a choice between two mouths of equally striking and only slightly differing pattern.

It has also been suggested that, parasitism apart, there might be selection for specific discrimination in mouth patterns because of the possibility of an estrildid laying eggs in the nest of another species. This occasionally happens in captivity and may, but I should think seldom, happen in the wild. If such laying in the wrong nest was a significant cause of breeding failure one would, however, expect to find comparable differences, and powers of discrimination, in related species in many other groups of birds, for example the tits, which are known to sometimes incubate mixed clutches and rear the resultant broods (Perrins). It is, of course, possible that if mouth markings and an ability to distinguish them arose as a result of viduine parasitism, then the lesser hazards of the occasional mis-laying of a congener have, at least in some cases, 'kept them up to scratch'. My own opinion is that specific differences in the mouth patterns of estrildid nestlings, when correlated with parental ability to distinguish them from similar patterns of related forms, must have evolved in relation with and as a counter to nest parasitism in the past history of the forms concerned.

A possible fourth function of the conspicuous mouths of young passerines is worth mentioning here even although it does not apply particularly (and may not apply at all) to estrildids. In 1916 *Ibis* published a most interesting paper dealing with the mouth colours of young birds and illustrated with colour plates depicting 47 species, including two estrildids (Swynnerton). In it the author noted that he had been told by an African native, whose people ate various kinds of small birds, that the nestlings of many passerines had an unpleasant taste. This was the case even in some species of which the adults were highly palatable. He therefore suggested that in some birds the bright or conspicuous mouths of the nestlings might function as warning coloration and deter experienced predators, at least if these were not particularly hungry. Though this idea may sound rather far-fetched I think it is at least possible and should not be discounted. It might be at least one, if not the only reason why, in many species of birds, *frightened* nestlings gape towards the frightening object and adults often gape in defensive threat.

REFERENCES

Delacour, J. 1943. A Revision of the Subfamily Estrildinae of the Family Ploceidae. *Zoologica, New York Zool. Soc.* **28**: 69–86.

Gedney, C. W. (no publication date, probably late 19th century): *Foreign cage birds.* L. Upcott Gill, London.

Glatthaar, R. & Ziswiler, V. 1971. Ontogenie und Histologie der Rachenzeichnungen bei Prachtfinken, Estrildidae. *Rev. suisse de Zoologie* **78**: 1222–1230.

Goodwin, D. 1965. A comparative study of captive blue waxbills. *Ibis* **107**: 285–315.

Herrmann, A. 1970. Ammen- und naturliche Aufzucht von Spitzschwanzamadine. *Gefiederte Welt* **1970**: 25–26.

Immelmann, K., Steinbacher, J. & Wolters, H. E. 1963. *Vögel in Käfig und Voliere: Prachtfinken: 2–3.*

Immelmann, K., Piltz, A. & Sossinka, R. 1977. Experimentelle Untersuchungen zur Bedeutung der Rachenzeichnung junger Zebrafinken. *Z. Tierpsychol.* **45**: 210–218.

Kunkel, P. & I. 1975. Palate pigmentation in adults and subadults of some African Estrildidae, with special reference to the persistency of juvenile mouth-markings. *Ostrich* **46**: 147–153.

Nicolai, J. 1964. Der Brutparasitismus als ethologisches Problem. Prägungsphänomene als Faktoren der Rassen- und Artbildung. *Z. Tierpsychol.* **21**: 129–204.

Nicolai, J. 1969. Beobachtungen an Paradieswitwen (*Steganura paradisaea* L., *Steganura obtusa* Chapin) und der Strohwitwe (*Tetraenura fischeri* Reichenow) in Ostafrika. *J. Orn.* **110**: 421–447.

Perrins, C. 1979. *British tits*. Collins, London.

Steiner, H. 1960. Klassifikation der Prachtfinken, Spermestidae, auf Grund der Rachenzeichnungen ihrer Nestlinge. *J. Orn.* **101**: 421–447.

Swynnerton, C. F. M. 1916. On the colouration of the mouths and eggs of birds. *Ibis*, tenth series, **4**: 264–294.

Display and social behaviour

I shall here discuss in general terms some displays of estrildids, and some behaviour that they show in social contexts. This in order to avoid unnecessarily detailed repetition in the sections on individual species. Also to make clear the terminology used. Where alternative terms to the one chosen have also been widely used, these are given in brackets. Imprinting and species recognition are also dealt with here.

How far one should extend the term 'display' when dealing with social behaviour patterns is a moot point. Where relatively stereotyped postures and movements are directed towards another individual, as in the courtship display, it is clearly right to use the term. On the other hand one can hardly consider the particularly emphatic forms of the locomotion intention movements often seen in agonistic or sexual contexts to be 'displays' but some actions, such as allopreening and nest demonstration fall between the above extremes. As long as we recognise what particular behaviour patterns we are dealing with, it does not greatly matter how we mentally classify them.

LOCOMOTION INTENTION-MOVEMENTS (FLIGHT INTENTION-MOVEMENTS, TAIL FLICKING) Vertical, lateral or intermediate up and down or side to side flicking, jerking or wagging movements of the tail, sometimes also an upward flirt or flick of the closed or partly closed wings, are commonly shown by active estrildids (and other passerines). Their precise form and intensity varies between different groups and species; their intensity also according to the state of the individual bird. They appear to derive from the intention-movements of hopping or flying (Daanje, Kunkel, 1959) and are shown whenever the bird is even slightly motivated to hop or to take wing. They are often strongly emphasised in conflict situations such as when the bird appears torn between curiosity and fear as it examines some alarming object or creature, and in agonistic or sexual encounters.

FEATHER ERECTION (FLUFFING, RUFFLING, PUFFING-OUT THE FEATHERS) Feather erection, in which the plumage of some parts of the body are more erected than those elsewhere, so that certain areas appear enlarged and some particular markings or colours are often more prominently displayed, occurs in many sexual contexts. Typically the belly and flank feathers are most markedly raised. In lateral displays the feathers on the side towards the bird being displayed at are usually erected noticeably more than those on the opposite side, there being an immediate 'change of sides' in this respect if, as often occurs, the displaying bird hops around to the other side of the one it is displaying to.

Feather erection may be so extreme that the individual feathers are separated and visible (sometimes termed 'ruffled' as distinct from 'fluffed') or only to the extent that the feathers are not separated and the area concerned appears larger than normal but still presents a smooth continuous surface. Kunkel (unpublished manuscript) found that this latter type of feather erection is characteristic of forms that display with a grass stem or other nesting material in the bill, whereas the more extreme feather erection in display tends to be shown by species that do not hold a nest symbol in the bill. Kunkel even observed that in some species, such as the African Silverbill, which may display with or without nesting material held in the bill, the same individual will erect its plumage to a lesser or greater extent according to whether it is or is not holding the nest symbol.

Head and body feathers may also be erected in aggressive situations by threatening or fighting individuals, possibly when this happens it indicates some degree of conflict between fear and aggression. A general very full erection of the cover feathers, especially those of the head, is shown by the Blue-headed Cordon-bleu in its chasing flights.

Apart from such specific postures used in social situations, the degree of sleeking or fluffing of the plumage is, of course, of use in temperature control. Birds that are cold or ill fluff up their plumage, those that are hot sleek it down.

ANGLED TAIL (TAIL TWIST, INCLINED TAIL) In this the tail is held at an angle towards the other bird. This position of the tail is characteristic of the courtship and greeting displays of many forms. It is likely, as Kunkel suggests, that it derives from the position of the tail during copulation. Angled tail is often correlated with triangular head. The tail may be angled towards either side but always towards the object of sexual attraction. The orientation of the tail depends on that of the bird being displayed to; if a bird is displaying to another directly in front of it, it holds its tail quite straight. Angling of the tail in this manner occurs in some quite unrelated species, such as the Bullfinch, *Pyrrhula pyrrhula* and the Magpie, *Pica pica*.

TRIANGULAR HEAD This arrangement of the head feathers is difficult to describe although, in species that show it fully, unmistakable when seen. It seems to be brought about, as Kunkel states, by the feathers nearest to the bill being strongly sleeked down and those further back

Diagrammatic sketch of male zebra finch making the 'triangular head'. From a photo by Peter Kunkel.

progressively less so; the feathers on the cheeks and nape being strongly erected, those of the top of the head only very slightly. This gives the head a distinctive triangular shape, whether seen from above or from the sides, with the bill tip forming the apex of the triangle and often a suggestion of a ruff framing the face and forecrown. The cheek patches of such species as the Red-cheeked Cordon-bleu are well displayed frontally by this posture.

The triangular head is shown by many species of estrildids to a greater or lesser degree. It may accompany various actions and displays but always seems to be sexually motivated or, at any rate, not to occur unless sexual motivation is present. Kunkel (unpublished manuscript) thinks, however, that the triangular head may have been derived from the invitation to social preening and that it indicates some element of aggression.

TAIL QUIVERING (TAIL TREMBLING, TAIL SHIVERING) A quivering or tembling of the tail, in conjunction with a crouched posture with the tail slightly raised or horizontal, is characteristic of soliciting female estrildids – at least of species in which copulation has been observed. In some species it may also be used by both sexes in appeasing or greeting displays or by sexually thwarted males. Estrildids are unusual among passerines in that the

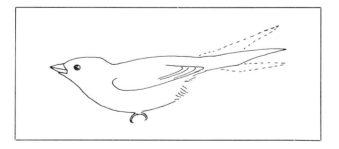

Blue-headed Cordon-bleu soliciting with quivering tail.

female does not quiver her wings when soliciting but does markedly quiver her tail. So far as I know the Corvidae are the only other family in which the females, or some of them, quiver the tail when soliciting. As I suggested (Goodwin, 1956 and 1976) tail quivering when soliciting might have evolved from a 'simple' trembling due to thwarted impulses to escape such as occurs in pigeons, humans and many other creatures.

MANDIBULATION This consists of a rapid opening and shutting of the mandibles. It may be ritualised at least to the extent of being slower and more emphatic than similar bill movements in other contexts. It occurs, in some species, in various sexual or agonistic contexts. Thus it may be incorporated with or intersperse greeting displays, nest demonstrations and, in rather divergent forms, the courtship display. It may also be directed at rivals after a fight or towards the mate after a disagreement. It is probable that, where they are retained into adulthood, the palate markings are made visible during mandibulation. In the cordon-bleus I have the impression that mandibulation is always linked with inhibited aggression but that the aggression is dying away rather than building up since a mandibulating bird is very much more likely to go over into more peaceful and appeasing behaviour than it is to become more aggressive. It is, however, possible that in some species no aggression, even inhibited, is correlated with mandibulation.

As in some other displays, there are differences of opinion as to the derivation of the bill movements used in mandibulation. Kunkel considers them to have been derived from the 'nibbling' movements used when feeding and when investigating nesting material. Güttinger (1970) believes them to be derived from the bill movements made when feeding young. That mandibulation occurs during nestcalling and when the pair are together on the chosen next site certainly lends weight to Güttinger's opinion as in this situation many birds show behaviour patterns derived from parental care. I am not sure which is correct. It might even be that mandibulation derives from different sources in different contexts or in different species.

CLUMPING (PERCHING OR SITTING IN CONTACT) The habit of resting side by side in contact with one or more others is common although not universal among estrildids. It is usually, but not necessarily, associated with allo-preening (q.v.). In many species adults usually clump only with their mates or (less often) still dependent young; probably in a natural state they never clump with individuals in other categories. In the most highly social species flock members clump freely with each other. Some species maintain individual distance and do not normally clump even with their own mates. In some sexually dichromatic species, the male colours inhibit males from clumping together even in situations where two females would do so. Where both sexes have bright and similar plumage, clumping and allo-preening are reduced or absent. Immelmann (1962) even observed that in the Star Finch,

Clumping estrildids.

in which there is much individual variation in the females, pairs in which the female had much red on her face indulged in less physical contact than pairs in which the female showed little red on the face. Kunkel's (unpublished mss) studies of firefinches, *Lagonosticta*, revealed that allo-preening between the members of a pair is inversely correlated with the (specific) amount of red in the female's plumage.

Under captive conditions many estrildids will clump freely with other species; even those that restrict their conspecific clumping to their mate will do so. Here it seems evident that sexual jealousy is the factor that prevents wider intra-specific clumping. Sexual jealousy appears only to be aroused by conspecifics of the same sex. Hence if, for example, a male or female Red-cheeked Cordon-bleu forms a clumping association with, say, a Goldbreast or Avadavat, its mate shows no aggressive response as he or she would do if a conspecific were involved and, indeed, is often drawn into the same clumping-partner relationship with the third bird.

With birds that are ill or very cold, any of the usual inhibitions may break down and clumping may occur regardless of the sex or status of the other bird(s). Species that normally maintain individual distance may also clump promiscuously and densely under such circumstances. This is true not only for estrildids but for many other birds. Probably the original function of clumping was the conservation of body warmth and it still sometimes serves this purpose. However, the fact that many tropical species which do not endure particularly cold nights clump, and some others, which live in habitats where the temperature at night is much colder than by day, do not do so if in health, suggests that at the present stage of evolution clumping is concerned more with maintaining or strengthening social bonds than with heat conservation.

ALLO-PREENING (MUTUAL PREENING, HETERO-PREENING, SOCIAL PREENING) This behaviour is common or habitual in many estrildids. In it the passive partner solicits (or submits to) being preened with erected head feathers and head turned with bill pointing away, head bowed or head tilted upwards. In species where special areas of plumage are displayed, such as the 'bibs' of the typical grassfinches, the preening invitation postures may be more ritualised and less prone to capricious momentary changes of position than in other species. The active bird preens the feathers of the other's head and upper neck, which it cannot reach with its own bill. Other parts of the plumage are preened only rarely and briefly. The preening does not consist only of passing feathers through the bill; the preener also often appears to pick up minute objects from between the feathers and swallow them. This is especially common when newly-fledged young are being preened by an adult, when the scurfy remnants of feather sheaths appear to be swallowed. The active partner also often picks at the tip, gape and commissure of the partner's bill, and apparently removes small objects. Although I have never been able to distinguish objects in the preener's bill – usually they are invisible to the human watcher – the swallowing movements of its throat are easily seen.

Inter-specific allo-preening: male Goldbreast preened by a male Red-cheeked Cordon-bleu.

As with clumping, allo-preening is in many species restricted to the mate and (less often) dependent young; some species allo-preen freely with others of their flock; and some do not allo-preen at all. In the majority of species there is a positive correlation between clumping and allo-preening but not in all. The Star Finch and Pintailed Parrot-finch do not normally clump but members of a pair allo-preen each other (Kunkel, unpublished mss). Kunkel found that in the crimson-wings, *Cryptospiza*, clumping was frequent but allo-preening did not seem to occur. Inter-specific allo-preening associations commonly occur among captive estrildids and, again as with clumping, the lack of inter-specific sexual jealousy allows a firmly paired bird to preen or be preened by an individual of another species without his or her mate being in any way angered or upset. Usually the weaker species or individual takes both the initiative and the subordinate role, soliciting preening and submitting to preening without, at first, attempting to preen back. When such an interspecific preening partnership has endured for some time (often for more than a year), however, the initially entirely subordinate individual may preen the other 'turn and turn about' as do members of a conspecific pair.

Allo-preening involves submission or appeasement on the part of the bird being preened and dominance or sublimated aggression on the part of the active partner (Goodwin, 1959, 1960, Harrison, 1962). Although the

Avadavats: bird on left soliciting allo-preening.

aggression involved often appears to be completely sublimated and the feelings of the preening bird entirely affectionate this is by no means always the case. A complete 'behavioural cline' obtains from aggressive attack to the most 'loving' forms of allo-preening. Allo-preening appears to serve, inter alia, to strengthen the personal bonds between mates or flock companions and/or to divert aggressive tendencies into a certainly harmless and probably useful form of activity. Although I was criticised for concluding when writing about allo-preening in pigeons (Goodwin, 1956) that *one* of its functions was the removal of ectoparasites and other foreign bodies, I am still of this opinion. It may not be a very important function, in view of the number of birds, even some estrildids, in which it does not occur; but that the allo-preening bird does remove and ingest particles can hardly be doubted by anyone who has closely watched this behaviour. It is even, I think, possible, that allo-preening had its origin in parental care since some birds – such as the Jay – which never allo-preen adults or fledgelings, clean and then preen the plumage of their nestlings if these have become soiled or wet in any way.

Although allo-preening expresses the dominance (probably only symbolically and momentarily in the case of mated pairs or other birds on personally friendly terms with each other) of the preener, it also indicates that its

aggressiveness has at least been sublimated to the extent that it will not attack or drive away the bird it preens. Weaker birds, especially when they have just been beaten in a fight, will sometimes go at once to stronger individuals and solicit allo-preening. They appear in such circumstances to derive some satisfaction from being preened. I have particularly noticed this with captive Goldbreasts that have formed allo-preening relationships with Cordon-bleus, or Blue-headed Cordon-bleus. The preener in such cases gives the preenee no help against its enemy then or in any future encounter but presumably the weaker bird must get some *feeling* of comfort, support or security from simply eliciting and submitting to this expression of dominance by the stronger. Perhaps it feels, at a simpler level (if that is possible), the same sort of mental comfort that many people derive from the emotional relationship (which they believe to be complementary or reciprocal) existing between themselves and a sacred crocodile, the one true God, or their favourite psychiatrist.

BILL-FENCING (BILL-PECKING) Estrildids often 'fight' by pecking at each others' bills in a rather formalised way. They seem to jab at the other bird's bill tip with the closed bill, appearing as if they were 'pulling their punches'. In my experience (and that of Kunkel, pers. comm.) this behaviour is shown between members of a pair or between male and female at pair formation. It does not occur in serious fights between same sex rivals. It indicates aggression which is inhibited but not to the same extent as in mandibulation which, in many species, usually follows mutual bill-pecking.

THREAT DISPLAY Threat display is poorly or not at all developed in most estrildids. It usually consists merely of the unritualised intention-movements of attack; the threatening bird crouches facing its adversary with lowered head, somewhat opened bill and spread or partly spread tail. Such rather more elaborate displays that I have seen or read about, such as an apparent deliberate display of the dark under-tail coverts by the Dark Firefinch (Goodwin, 1964) may well have been artifacts of captivity.

GREETING DISPLAY (RECOGNITION POSTURE, NODDING, BOWING) This display is performed by many species when the members of a pair come together after some little absence, by strange birds (sometimes) when meeting each other and, in some species by flock members when meeting after temporary separation. It commonly involves bowing or nodding movements, often in synchrony. Formalised, reduced or exaggerated bill-wiping movements may accompany the bowing or nodding. The greeting display seems to involve, at least initially, a high degree of excitement involving conflict between sexual attraction and fear or aggression. In firmly paired birds, of some species, the aggression, if present, often appears completely suppressed and the mood of the displaying birds entirely friendly.

NEST DEMONSTRATION AND NEST-CALLING When one of a

pair of estrildids, normally the male, has found a potential nest site, it attracts its mate's attention to it by characteristic behaviour. This involves (with minor specific and individual variations) uttering series of nest-calls, crouching on the site, usually with partly-spread tail feathers and

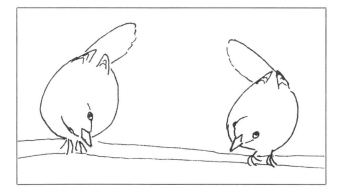

Greeting display of Dark Firefinch; pair approaching each other and bowing.

Greeting display of Dark Firefinch at highest intensity, as seen from above.

Java Sparrow in bowing phase of the greeting display.

mandibulating and/or making apparent intention movements of nest building. This behaviour is usually interspersed with hopping in and out of or around the site. When the female joins the male she shows similar but typically rather less intense behaviour, if she approves the site. If she does not, the male usually leaves it and searches for another.

In many (possibly all) species the male and female crouch together on the nest site and perform synchronous bowing movements and mandibulate. Güttinger (1970), who has seen this behaviour from all of the many species he has kept and closely observed, believes it derives from parental care of the young. This seems likely as the same is certainly true of some of the behaviour patterns shown by other birds, such as pigeons, in the same situation. These mutual activities are frequently broken off for a moment while one or other bird hops a little away, only to return immediately. Immelmann (1962), describing this behaviour in Australian estrildids, aptly says that the birds give the impression of doing this in order to have a 'reason' for repeated mutual greeting. All the above behaviour leads on to actual nest building. Specific differences, where known, are described under the species' headings.

COURTSHIP DISPLAY (INVERTED CURTSEY, STEM DISPLAY, NEST SYMBOL DISPLAY, BOWING DISPLAY) In this book I use the term 'courtship display' to cover a group of displays which are given to a mate or potential mate. They may differ in form between species and groups but usually have features in common and appear to be homologous. Although the courtship display is only one of the displays involved in the initial overtures of courting birds it is usually the most conspicuous, at any rate to human eyes. Like other behaviour patterns involved in 'courtship', it is also, in most species, commonly or regularly performed by the members of an established pair. The bird usually sings

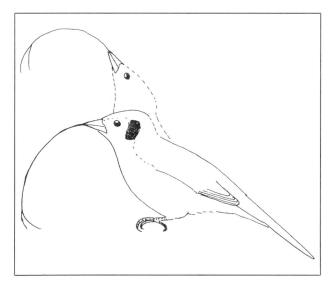

Diagrammatic sketches to show approximate highest and lowest positions of head in the courtship display of the Red-cheeked Cordon-bleu.

Diagrammatic sketches to show approximately highest and lowest positions of head in the courtship display of the Blue-headed Cordon-bleu.

at some time during its courtship display.

In many species the courtship display is the normal prelude to copulation although even in these by no means every such display ends in coition or attempts at it. In other species courtship display does not usually (if ever) lead immediately to copulation but appears only to mutually stimulate the birds and, presumably, to strengthen, re-affirm or intensify the bonds between them. In some the courtship display is performed only or usually

by the male alone (the female making appropriate responses in other ways); in others the female may sometimes or usually take part and perform the same movements. Kunkel (1959) uses the term 'Paarungsbalz' for courtship displays which (sometimes) lead immediately to copulation and 'Schaubalz' for those which do not but as the displays do not necessarily otherwise differ in form, and appear to be homologous, I prefer to use one term for both.

In the most widespread and therefore probably phylogenetically oldest forms of the courtship display, the displaying bird holds a conspicuous piece of nesting material and thrusts itself or bounces up and down with alternate stretching and bending of its legs. There is much specific variation as to the precise position and movements of the head in relation to the body. The up and down bobbing or thrusting – the 'inverted curtsey' of some authors – may also vary in precise form. The above basic pattern may be elaborated by the introduction of elements from juvenile begging or other behaviour patterns into the display or by the reduction or elimination of the up and down bobbing and the introduction of bowing movements. In most species the nest symbol used in the courtship display is identical with material that is most sought after for constructing or lining the nest but in at least one species, the Star Finch, this is no longer the case. In this species (*fide* Immelmann & Immelmann, 1967) conspicuous green or yellow grass stems are used to display with but soft, half rotten grass blades for building.

There have been, and are likely to continue to be, differences of opinion as to the derivation of these display movements. Both the upward stretching and (in other species) the bowing with material in bill are often, and I believe correctly, held to derive from the movement of fixing nesting material in (respectively) the roof or base of

Highest and lowest positions in the courtship display of the Black-rumped Waxbill.

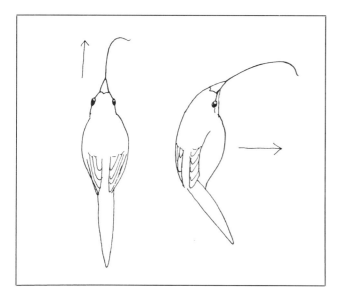

Cordon-bleu courtship display as seen from above. Left, to bird straight in front of the performer; right, to bird on its right side, note angled tail.

Diamond Sparrow, in lowered phase of courtship display.

the nest. Others, however, have thought that the bobbing or jerking movements might derive from intention-movements of flying up to mount the female and certainly, in at least one species – the Dark Firefinch (Goodwin, 1964) – the bobbing movements may develop into an upward flutter onto the female's back. A nice, although not unique example, of a display movement pattern virtually identical to movements used in at least two different situations, both of which (like the display) occur in reproductive contexts.

The holding of a piece of nesting material during the courtship display seems to be the primitive or original condition among the estrildids or their immediate ancestor. It appears to have been partially or completely lost, in the course of evolution, in several different groups. Courtship display without nesting material held in the bill is usually correlated with one or more of three ecological situations (Immelmann & Immelman, 1967). These are: displaying on the ground, the habit of often or usually nesting in holes or the old nests of other species, and being very highly gregarious. The selective pressures involved probably being, respectively, the difficulties of displaying with long conspicuous nesting material on the ground; a presumed general decrease in intensity of the nest building urge; and the desirability of avoiding display that by its extreme conspicuousness might arouse aggression from nearby conspecifics (Immelmann & Immelmann, 1967). It may be added that even the non-aggressive interest that some captive estrildids often show in the courtship displays of others have an 'off-putting' effect on the displaying birds (pers. obs.).

The courtship displays of different species show various degrees of intermediacy between those in which a nesting symbol is always held in the bill and those in which it

never is. In some species the same (individual) bird may display with or without nesting material; in others the symbol may be only briefly held during part of the display. This plasticity when the Estrildidae are considered as a whole is in strong contrast to the way in which such apparently obligatory symbol holders as, for example, the firefinches or the cordon-bleus, behave. These, although they may perform low intensity courtship display movements without a nesting symbol when alone, as they often do when singing, appear quite incapable of giving their courtship display in earnest unless they have nesting material in their bills. If they accidentally drop the nesting symbol or another bird snatches it from them, they cease their display at once. In some zoos and public aviaries captive birds are too often denied nesting material and other facilities. The 'reason' usually given is that straw, feathers or the like in the cages would look 'untidy' and give a bad impression to the visitors! Under such conditions the symbol-using estrildids (if physically not in poor shape) will sometimes use very 'sub-optimal' symbols. I once saw a cock Red-cheeked Cordon-bleu display with the small body feather of a Zebra Finch, an object it would never have used either to display or line its nest with except under such extreme deprivation. If a few

Green Avadavat: bowing display (courtship display).

Courtship posture of Bengalese Finch.

grass stems or large fluffy white feathers are surreptitiously introduced into their prison, the bored birds 'come to life' in an almost magical manner and at once indulge in a wild orgy of courtship displaying.

In some species the picking up and holding of nesting material is shown as a preliminary to courtship display, or in other reproductive contexts. It is not then usually possible to say whether this represents the last vestiges of a courtship-display with the nesting symbol, or the evolution of (so far as the nesting symbol is concerned) a new behaviour pattern.

PEERING (LISTENING, ZUHOREN IN GERMAN) This behaviour was first described in detail for the Spice Finch (Moynihan & Hall, 1954) and has been observed in many other estrildids, especially the highly social mannikins and silverbills (Immelmann & Immelmann).

Peering is a response to the undirected singing of one

Blue-billed Mannikin in courtship display (after Kunkel's 1965 drawings).

bird. The respondent, which is often the same sex as the singing bird and seldom its mate, flies or hops to the singing bird and stretches its neck till its head is close to that of the singer. It may stand either close beside or in front of the singing bird. It seems to be peering closely or listening to the other but the position of its head and tendency often to peck or poke the singer suggests aggressive tendencies. The singer usually tries to move his head away and often edges away along his perch but the peering bird follows, still peering and occasionally pecking or poking lightly at the singer's head or, but less often, he may peck the singer fiercely (Moynihan & Hall). Sometimes two or more birds may peer at the same singing individual although they then tend to get in each others' way. Moynihan & Hall observed that, in the Spice Finch, if the singer stopped as a result of the peering, it might invite the peerer to preen it, the two might clump together or they might fight. In some less social species at least, peering, or something very like it, may be shown (again seldom by the bird's own mate) as a response to the courtship display as well as to undirected singing.

Peering is sometimes thought to help flock cohesion among social species. Possibly it does so only in so far as it may, behaviourally, be a relatively peaceful alternative to a more positively aggressive response to the singing bird.

COMMENT ON THE DERIVATION OF DISPLAY MOVEMENTS ETC. In estrildids, and other birds, we see, as has been described above, many instances of displays or intra-pair behaviour patterns that appear to be built up largely of movements that are also shown in *other* reproductive contexts, such as nest building. In particular, behaviour patterns expressing apparent affection between two adults, not only in estrildids but in other creatures, man included, are similar or identical to those used in parental care. It is commonly, and I believe rightly, thought that such 'loving' behaviour of two adult birds, (or two people), and their feelings towards each other, of which the behaviour is the outward expression, have derived in the course of evolution from parental behaviour and feelings. In some species complementary 'infantile' behaviour and feelings have also become incorporated into the adult's behavioural repertoire.

When we go on to assume that these derived behaviour patterns must be necessary in order to stimulate the adults successfully to build, copulate, brood and feed their young we seem to be on slightly less firm ground. Since, if these various 'courtship' behaviour patterns evolved first as autochthonous behaviour patterns and only secondarily became incorporated into the inter-adult behaviour, this must imply that the birds *were* successfully copulating, building and rearing young *before* they began to behave in a parental (or infantile) manner towards their mates. We can of course argue, probably rightly, that the incorporation of the movements and (presumably) feelings already shown in other reproductive contexts into the inter-adult behaviour must, by its very existence, prove to have been of selective value to the species concerned but this is rather a circular argument. There is, however, some circumstantial evidence that this must be so. In many birds, although not so far as I know in any estrildid, we see that one sex now shows certain reproductive behaviour patterns *only* in their derived contexts and no longer in their original contexts. Thus, for example, the males of many pheasants feed the female but do not feed their chicks; the cock Blackbird, *Turdus merula*, and cock Canary, *Serinus canarius*, do not build but they mime nest building movements in their nest site demonstration displays.

SOME ASPECTS OF SOCIAL AND INTRA-PAIR BEHAVIOUR
Estrildids include forms, like the Melba Finch, which live in more or less territorial pairs, some, like the majority of munias or mannikins, that are highly social and others that show various intermediate stages between these two extremes. On the whole, however, they are gregarious rather than otherwise. Even the less social species may aggregate around sources of food or (more often) water in difficult times. In Australia some even form mixed species flocks (Immelmann & Immelmann) although more often, as with aggregations of different species of finches or pigeons in Britain, when two or more species appear to be mingled they are merely attracted to the same source of food, water or shelter and there is little or no interspecific sociality.

In the social species even breeding birds may regularly associate with other flock members. In some these social gatherings are facilitated by displays that were originally sexual in character (and may still be used in sexual contexts) but have secondarily become means of indicating or promoting friendly, or at least peaceable relations between flock members (Immelmann & Immelmann). The Immelmanns noted that, in many species, small groups keep together in spite of temporarily becoming merged with larger numbers of conspecifics around sources of food or water.

That estrildids are able to distinguish individuals both of their own and of other species has long been known to aviculturists who have kept and observed them. If twenty or more individuals of different (or the same) species have been kept together in a room or aviary for some time, all show intense curiosity (and conspecifics also often raping attempts or aggression) if a strange bird, of any of the species present, is placed among them. They gather round it, look at it closely and follow it when it moves. No such behaviour is shown if one of their number is caught, removed and then returned after a short while. This only evokes a very brief momentary interest which apparent individual recognition of the returned bird at once checks. The returned individual's own mate does, of course, show more excitement and intense greeting displays are usually performed by both members of the re-united pair.

The young often arouse considerable interest in adults other than their parents when they first leave the nest. Knoblauch (1966) has even seen such adults attempt to lead to safety young that had got into difficulties. I have not myself seen birds other than the parents (except in cases of adoption) show more than unhelpful alarm calling in such situations.

Ephemeral quarrels over food that is much liked and in limited supply and more lasting and embittered vendettas between sexual rivals are common among captive estrildids. One individual may, especially in the case of inter-specific allo-preening partnerships, dominate another over a long period. However, nothing like the 'classic' peck-order hierarchy, so common in man, and, it is said, regularly materialising in Domestic Fowls, *Gallus gallus*, in confinement, seems to develop among estrildids, even in captivity.

In most estrildids the pair is the basic social unit. The pair bond is usually strong and probably endures for life in the wild as it usually does in captivity. Even in many social species the members of a pair keep more closely together than either does to any other members of the group. Some or most of the highly social forms that live in reedbeds and/or grassland, such as many of the munias or mannikins, and typical waxbills and the Goldbreast show no especially close contact between members of a pair (outside the breeding period) when the flock is in flight or actively seeking food. The Immelmanns found, however, that at least in flocks of the Common Waxbill, Goldbreast and Quail Finch, when the birds were resting they did so in pairs. It is possible, however, that in such forms the bond between the members of a pair is less strong than it is in species in which the pairs never seem to 'merge their identity' with that of the rest of the flock. In my, admittedly very limited and non-experimental, experience, homosexual male pairs of Blue-headed and Red-cheeked Cordon-bleus (1 of each) and male (2) and female (1) pairs of Cordon-bleus, remain firmly paired in spite of the later presence of surplus and willing potential mates of the opposite sex. On the other hand when I introduced a homosexual male pair of Black-rumped Waxbills into a bird room containing, of their own species, only a homosexual female pair (both pairs originated in erroneous attempts to pick a male and a female from several specimens in dealers' cages!), the two pairs remained mutually hostile for some months but when all four went out of breeding condition, they formed a flock, clumped and allo-preened indiscriminately and, when they came again into breeding condition, each paired with a bird of the opposite sex.

Apart from their mutual reproductive activities the members of a pair keep within sight or hearing of each other and, in many cases, regularly clump and allo-preen. As with other birds, estrildids can distinguish the contact calls and songs of their mates from those of other conspecifics. Pair formation has been little studied in the wild in most species and its usual sequence may perhaps sometimes be distorted or 'telescoped' in captivity. In some of the more social forms it is known, even in the wild, to be initiated within the flock by a male courting a female who attracts him, wherever they happen to be. With cordon-bleus I have often had the impression that, were my birds free, individuals ready to pair would probably move conspicuously from their group to display with a symbol at a little distance, whither they would be followed by any bird wishing to pair with them. The Immelmanns were in fact able to confirm that this is so in the wild with *Uraeginthus angolensis*, and also with some of the firefinches, *Lagonosticta*.

Driving the female away from the close proximity of potential sexual rivals also probably occurs in some forms, as it does with the cordon-bleus in captivity (Goodwin, 1965).

In normal pairs greeting and courtship displays, copulation and, in the many species that practise them, clumping and allo-preening are characteristic intra-pair behaviour patterns that are mainly or solely directed at or performed with the bird's mate.

In many species of estrildids (and other birds), males may respond with attempts to copulate not only to soliciting females but also to individuals that are ill (especially if not able to balance well), newly introduced into the bird room or aviary, or crippled. At least in some of the species in which the sexes are alike or at least not markedly different in appearance, both sexes are treated similarly under such conditions and very often all the usual (between paired individuals) preliminaries to copulation are dispensed with and the bird simply tries to 'rape' the other (Goodwin, 1965, Kunkel, 1967, Morris, 1957, Moynihan & Hall; 1954). In *U. angolensis* in captivity, but only very rarely with the two other cordon-bleus, males may attempt to copulate with newly-fledged young. There appears to be no common visual pattern that can be responsible for eliciting copulation attempts in all the above cases, many of which have little in common with the 'normal' copulatory situation. A sick and 'wobbly', fluffed-out hen estrildid or pigeon, even more the posture and movements of a Mallard Duck threatened with rape, are indeed the antithesis of the appearance and behaviour of a soliciting female. Kunkel (1967 and pers. comm.) has suggested that in the firefinches, in which attempted rape of strange females commonly leads to aggressive attacks on them, the male is impelled by both aggressive and sexual impulses. The same has been suggested as the reason for the lack of introductory displays and frequent rough treatment of the unwilling female that characterise many of these 'extra-marital' copulation attempts. I am inclined to think that the aggression is a secondary result of the thwarting of the male's attempts at copulation. The lack of introductory displays and (when it occurs) rough treatment of the female are probably because the male only feels sexually, not in any way emotionally attracted to her. Comparable differences of sexual behaviour as shown towards loved and unloved individuals are not uncommon in man. I am inclined to think that males in breeding condition may respond with copulation attempts whenever they recognise an 'inability to resist', whether this inability is due to readiness to mate, as in the soliciting female, or physical weakness, as in a sick bird. This suggestion will seem far-fetched to some readers but is, I think, worth their consideration. It must be emphasised that raping assaults on strange females are usually only performed by males that already have mates of their own. Unpaired males (if healthy) almost always respond to the appearance of strange females by courting them, *not* by attempting to rape them.

Despite the close bonds and apparent affection between the members of a pair in most species, estrildids appear never to help their mate against an enemy. Even if the bird is being roughly treated by another of its own species and cries out in distress, its mate makes no attempt to assist it (Kunkel, 1959, pers. obs.). This is in striking contrast to the way in which both sexes zealously 'protect' their mates from any sexual advances by conspecifics of the same sex as themselves. Birds of some (possibly most or all) other families behave similarly. It is true that protection of its mate from conspecific enemies would involve a bird attacking individuals of its own species but the opposite sex but many birds are not inhibited from this in other contexts. I have never seen any attempt to help or defend clumping or allo-preening partners, nor, since the mate itself is not helped would one expect them to be. I have, however, read of one observation or rather series of observations to the contrary and, as they seem remarkable, they seem worth giving fully. Knoblauch kept nine Red-cheeked Cordon-bleus in a room together with two pairs of Black-rumped Waxbills and one pair each of Zebra Finches, Lavender Waxbills, Goldbreasts, Green Avadavats, Swee Waxbills and Red-billed Firefinches. He found that, although his Red-cheeked Cordon-blues (like mine) quarrelled among themselves, if any one of them was threatened by a bird of a different species, they would at once all sink their differences and band together for mutual defence ('sie schützen sich gegenseitig vor dem Angreifer'); he does not, however, give details. I have not myself seen any such behaviour – predator mobbing apart – from my own Cordon-bleus but these have not been kept with any species larger or more aggressive than themselves.

Kunkel (1959) found that his estrildids would sooner or later desert a sick mate, apparently when and because it could no longer adequately fulfil its role. With cordon-bleus, my experience has been that only severe and obviously terminal illness (sometimes) elicits desertion by the mate. Though, to look at the matter from a 'bird's eye view', it is probably more a case of the sick bird, by its apathy and lack of response, 'deserting' its healthy mate than the other way round. Mates that show no interest in any reproductive activities but still clump and allo-preen, or that are crippled, are not deserted. Whether such fidelity would, or could, obtain in the wild seems doubtful. If it did it would be biologically disadvantageous to the 'faithful' and fit mate but probably not for long as a sick or crippled tiny bird is not likely to survive for any length of time.

Kunkel (1959) observed that the removal or sudden death of a bird elicited great apparent distress, with searching behaviour and loud contact calling, from its mate. I confirmed this from my own experience, as I thought, when writing on cordon-bleus (Goodwin, 1965). Later, however, I read Knoblauch's paper on the estrildids in his bird room, in which he states that, in contrast to the mate's behaviour whenever he caught and removed a bird, when one died *in sight of its mate* the latter showed no evident reaction. It was as if it realised and accepted the fact of death. One one occasion an exhausted young House Sparrow was brought to him. He put it in a cage in his bird room, where it rested still in a corner. Naturally the inquisitive estrildids at once came all around the cage looking at the strange bird. Suddenly they all at once lost interest and dispersed. On looking to see the reason, Knoblauch found that the Sparrow, although still in the same position, was now dead.

On reading this I was at first inclined to disbelieve it but then I recalled, though admittedly not very clearly, one or two deaths among my birds that I could not remember as having elicited the usual signs of distress from the mate and wondered whether I had formerly erred by mentally including as 'sudden death' cases where I had in fact myself removed the sick bird *before* its death. The number of cases that I have been able to observe since then have been too few to be 'statistically significant', only one to three for each species, but so far as they go, and much to my surprise, they confirm Knoblauch's observations. Where a bird (species involved are Red-cheeked and Blue-headed Cordon-bleus, Goldbreast and Avadavat) has died *in sight of its mate*, the latter has shown little or no reaction. Certainly none of the frenzied contact calling that is shown if the mate is caught and removed. It certainly seems as if the bird that has seen its mate die somehow knows it is gone for good and beyond recall. Whether in such a situation the bird really is, as it appears to be, less distressed than the agitated calling bird whose mate has been removed, is perhaps uncertain. In man we know that grief is not always measurable by the outward display of it.

Whether the above different reactions to the death of and to removal of the mate are usual, apply only to certain species, or even only to some individuals of certain species is as yet unknown. If they are, in any species, normal, it is puzzling that they should have evolved. Under natural conditions it would be seldom, I should think, that an estrildid *dies* (as distinct from being killed) in sight of its mate, so that though it might well be advantageous for it then to waste no time or energy in fruitless distress or vain contact calling, one would have thought the situation too rare to have exercised much selection pressure. On the other hand the nearest natural parallel to the owner removing a bird from room or aviary would surely be the taking of a bird by a predator. Such a bird, in the wild, would be most unlikely to escape or return, so to search and call for it would be in vain. They might perhaps lead to a more speedy meeting with a potential replacement for the lost mate but, on the other hand, they might well attract the attention of the returning predator.

SPECIES RECOGNITION, SEXUAL RECOGNITION, AND IMPRINTING
Estrildids in captivity (as, of course, in the wild) form intraspecific, heterosexual pairs; provided that they have the opportunity to do so and were themselves reared by their own parents. The members of such pairs may, as has been said, form unilateral or mutual allo-preening partnerships with estrildids of other species (and either sex) but these associations are not sexual in character and do not affect the bird's relationship with its mate. In default of a reciprocating conspecific of the opposite sex, many estrildids will form homosexual pairs in captivity. Species in which the sexes look alike seem more prone to do this than those which are sexually dichromatic but in at least one of the latter – the Red-cheeked Cordon-bleu – males will readily do so. It is only if no conspecific of *either* sex is available that interspecific pairs are formed except in some very closely related and similar species or species in which the female reacts strongly and positively to specific male colours, as does the female of the Red-cheeked Cordon-bleu, for example. In the latter case the female may more readily pair, or try to pair, with a male of another species that shows the 'right' colours than to a female of her own species. One factor that is probably important in facilitating homosexual and interspecific pairing in captivity is that the enforced proximity of the birds means that they will see and hear displays *which are performed by both sexes and/or in similar form in different species* given by such biologically 'unsuitable' prospective mates, which they would seldom or never do under natural conditions. The very strong personal bonds that, at least in many species, exist between the members of a pair, are such that, once an interspecific or homosexual pair is firmly bonded, the later presence of a willing opposite sex conspecific will not usually entice either partner to break the pair bond that it has already formed. This bond is a purely personal one; if the mate is lost the survivor, given a choice, will pair with a mate of its own species and the opposite sex.

Every naturally reared estrildid (or other bird) reacts sexually, and usually also in all other social contexts, only or preferentially to its own species. Many (not all) species of birds do not, however, recognise their own kind instinctively or else, as is the case in some ducks (Schutz) and probably also the Zebra Finch (Immelmann, 1972), innate species recognition can be obliterated or suppressed by conditioning in early life. They appear to learn the characteristics of their species from their parents and sometimes also from their siblings or other members of their species with whom they associate in early life. Particularly the kind of creature towards which the bird's future sexual activities will be exclusively or preferentially directed is determined then. This learning when restricted to a definite early period, is called 'imprinting'. For many species it is known that birds other than the parents or foster parents only affect imprinting when the fosterer is a human or some other species very unlike its foster children, or when the young birds are early deprived of their parents' company. For example, in the Zebra Finch (Immelmann, 1972) young reared singly by hand become imprinted on man, whereas if a group of young are hand-reared they imprint on their siblings and respond normally to conspecifics when adult. On the other hand if young Zebra Finches are reared by Bengalese Finches then their siblings have no such effect and they later react sexually to Bengalese Finches only, if given a choice.

In birds, such as ducks and partridges, which have active young who follow the mother or both parents (according to species) and leave the nest when from one to three days old, the sensitive period for learning what creature to follow is early and brief. Common Partridges, *Perdix perdix* (Lorenz), and Pheasants, *Phasianus colchicus* (pers. obs.), less than a day old will no longer accept a Domestic Fowl or Golden Pheasant as foster mother. The sensitive period for the sexual imprinting comes later, is of longer duration and is subject, in some cases, to some individual variation. There is much variation between different groups and species, even in the relatively few in which the point has been studied, as to the time and duration of the sensitive phase for sexual imprinting. In the Zebra Finch numerous and careful experiments by Immelmann and his colleagues (Immelmann, 1972, and other references in the specific section) have shown that sexual imprinting is possible only between about the thirteenth and fortieth days of age. Social experience outside this period has no effect whatsoever on subsequent sexual preferences.

Sexual preferences caused by imprinting are usually, and perhaps always, unaffected by the bird's sexual or reproductive success or lack of it. Male Zebra Finches, that had been imprinted on Bengalese Finches, and which after their sensitive period were never allowed to associate with Bengalese but kept paired with hen Zebra Finches for periods of from nine months to seven *years*, still preferred to court Bengalese Finches to Zebra Finches when their mates were removed and they were given a free choice of hen Bengalese and hen Zebra Finches equally unknown to them as individuals (Immelmann, 1972). This in spite of their having successfully reared many broods of young with conspecific mates and never having mated with a Bengalese. In the case of the bird that had been paired with a hen of its own species for seven years, its age was certainly greater than that usually reached by a Zebra Finch in the wild, so there can be no doubt that imprinting lasts for life in this as in other species for which the matter is known.

Schutz's work on ducks has shown that in some (probably all) species in which only the male is brightly coloured and distinctive, such as the Mallard, females usually recognize males instinctively and show sexual preference for males of their own kind no matter what species they have been reared by or with. Males on the other hand, if reared by other species of waterfowl (or reared with them, being cared for by humans) usually become imprinted on this other and 'wrong' species and, when adult, show sexual behaviour only towards them. On the other hand in ducks such as the Chilian Teal, in which both sexes are nearly alike and are cryptic in colour,

both sexes become sexually imprinted on other species if they are reared alone with or by them. Although I have done no deliberate experiments in the matter, I have had a few instances of accidental cross-fostering in Red-cheeked and Blue-headed Cordon-bleus which suggest that a similar state of affairs may exist in this group of estrildids. Of one male and four female Blue-headed Cordon-bleus reared by Red-cheeked Cordon-bleus all except one female were firmly imprinted on the foster species, even though they were reared and kept in a room with adults of both species and, in the case of three of the hens (including the one which proved not to be imprinted on Red-cheeked Cordon-bleus), were also fed by a male of their own species from the day they fledged. In complete contrast, two female Red-cheeked Cordon-bleus that were reared by Blue-headed Cordon bleus, responded sexually only to males of their own species (Goodwin 1971). Subsequent to this, another female Blue-headed Cordon-bleu was reared by Red-cheeks, responded for her first two years of life only (so far as I saw) to male Red-cheeked Cordon-bleus, who ignored or repulsed her, but then paired to a male Blue-headed. Shortly after she had done so a male Red-cheeked Cordon-bleu, who had been reared by Blue-heads, became old enough to pair and began to court her. She responded to some extent but the personal bond with her conspecific mate kept her from deserting him. As, however, neither of the males showed jealousy of the other, as they would have done of a conspecific rival, a kind of threesome developed. When resting the female Blue-head was usually clumped between her conspecific and her Red-cheeked mate, one on either side. All her several broods of young were, however, pure Blue-heads, so it is possible that the Red-cheeked male never actually copulated with her.

In view of the complete imprinting on the foster species in three out of five female Blue-heads, and the one male, it seems at first surprising that the two female Red-cheeked Cordon-bleus fostered by Blue-heads showed sexual responses only to their own species. Assuming they were a fair sample, albeit such a small one, I think the answer parallels the findings of Schutz for ducks and is explicable by the different types of sexual dichromatism of the two species. Although his entirely blue head and richer brown upperparts make the cock Blue-headed Cordon-bleu very different in appearance from the hen, this difference is one of the relative brightness of the colours and the extent of blue on the head. In the Red-cheeked Cordon-bleu, however, the crimson cheek patches of the male are a conspicuous badge of his sex no nuance of which is shown by the female. Extrapolating from what is known to obtain in ducks (Schutz) is seems likely that the female Red-cheeked Cordon-bleu could more easily have evolved an innate response to the male's red markings, alternatively, that such innate sexual recognition would be less liable to obliteration by imprinting than in the case of the Blue-head. Although I have only had one male Red-cheeked Cordon-bleu reared by Blue-heads, this bird *was* imprinted on his foster species.

An interesting feature of the imprinted *Uraeginthus* was that both the male Red-cheeked Cordon-bleu that was imprinted on Blue-heads and the male Blue-head that was imprinted on Red-cheeks, reacted sexually to both males and females of the species on which they were imprinted whereas the imprinted female Blue-heads made sexual advances only to male Red-cheeked Cordon-bleus. In the case of the male Red-cheek the likeliest explanation is that there is some innate recognition of the red markings as male characters so that neither sex of the fosterers supplied the 'right' clues for any sex identification. The difference in the behaviour of male and female Blue-heads is, unless it was fortuitous, which is possible with such a small sample, more puzzling. It suggests at least the possibility that females of this species have the potentiality for sexual recognition based on a conspicuous character of their (foster) father's plumage.

Whether imprinted on the 'wrong' species or not, the males of both the Blue-headed and Red-cheeked Cordon-bleus distinguish well between the very similarly coloured females of the two species. On several occasions when I saw an imprinted female Blue-head solicit a male Red-cheek (three different individuals) she was attacked by him. The attacks were violent and the males did not make the 'triangular head' as they do in all sexual contexts. Nevertheless it is difficult to account for these furious attacks other than by some kind of sudden frustration and I suspect that, possibly at what would in humans be called a subconscious level, the male Red-cheeked Cordon-bleus *were* sexually aroused by the soliciting display (which is identical in both species) and their being inhibited from responding sexually because of the female's 'wrong' specific characters caused them to get angry and attack.

Where, as in the case of most domesticated birds, a species exists in differing colours, young become imprinted on the colour of their parents and later prefer mates of the parents' colour, regardless of their own. This is known to be the case in Domestic Fowls (Lill & Woodgush), Domestic Ducks (Schutz), Domestic Pigeons (Goodwin, Warriner) and Zebra Finches (Immelmann *et al.* 1978).

That, even in birds which imprint firmly and regularly under appropriate, or perhaps better inappropriate conditions, there is nevertheless some innate recognition of, or at least tendency to respond most readily to their own species seems clear from the following facts. In all species in which the point has been investigated (and less thoroughly tested and/or less numerous observations suggest that the same is true for others) the young birds imprint most easily and completely on related and similar species, less so on those that are less like their own kind. This has already been indicated in discussing the effect of siblings in connection with imprinting. Very clear evidence for this in Zebra Finches came from some careful experiments of Immelmann. He found that when Zebra finches were reared by mixed species pairs, each consisting of a cock Zebra Finch paired to a hen Bengalese Finch or *vice versa*, they almost always showed sexual preferences for their own species. This was regardless of whether the foster-mother or foster-father was the conspecific 'parent'.

Some estrildids evidently imprint less easily or completely than do Zebra Finches and Blue-headed Cordon-bleus. Vetterli (1970) found that with Blue-faced Parrotfinches and ten other species (not specifically named in his paper), if the young and their Bengalese foster parents were kept in an aviary with others of the former's species, they did not in later life show sexual preferences for Bengalese Finches but behaved normally. This was in contrast to the behaviour of his Zebra Finches which, like Immelmann's, imprinted firmly on their fosterers under the same conditions.

Under natural conditions imprinting insures that the young bird will recognise and in adult life react sexually towards its own kind. One of its functions seems to be to reinforce or supplement innate species-recognition. This is probably of importance where the birds in question are very similar in general appearance to allied and sympatric species, such as the females of some of the firefinches and (though they only overlap in restricted areas) the cordon-bleus, or both sexes of some of the mannikins. Imprinting is also likely to be a relevant factor in speciation since, as Immelmann (1972) in a very comprehensive but lucid and succinct paper, points out it may lead to a very precise recognition of the future sexual partner and is quickly adaptable to any change in the species-specific characteristics.

REFERENCES

Daanje, A. 1950. On locomotory movements in birds and the intention movements derived from them. *Behaviour* 3: 48–98.

Goodwin, D. 1956. Further observations on the behaviour of the Jay. *Ibis* 98: 186–219.

Goodwin, D. 1958. The existence and causation of colour-preferences in the pairing of feral and domestic pigeons. *Bull. B.O.C.* 78: 136–139.

Goodwin, D. 1959. Observations on Blue-breasted Waxbills. *Avicult. Mag.* 65: 117–128.

Goodwin, D. 1960: Observations on Avadavats and Golden-breasted Waxbills. *Avicult. Mag.* 66: 174–199.

Goodwin, D. 1964. Observations on the Dark Firefinch, with some comparisons with Jameson's Firefinch. *Avicult. Mag.* 70: 80–105.

Goodwin, D. 1965. A comparative study of captive blue waxbills. *Ibis* 107: 285–315.

Goodwin, D. 1971. Imprinting, or otherwise, in some cross-fostered Red-cheeked and Blue-headed Cordon-bleus. *Avicult. Mag.* 77: 26–31.

Goodwin, D. 1976: *Crows of the World.* London & Cornell, USA.

Güttinger, H. R. 1970. Zur Evolution von Verhaltensweisen und Lautäusserungen bei Prachtfinken (Estrildidae). *Z. Tierpsychol.* 27: 1011–1075.

Harrison, C. J. O. 1962. An ethological comparison of some waxbills (Estrildini) and its relevance to their taxonomy. *Proc. zool. Soc. London* 139: 261–282.

Immelmann, K. 1962. Beiträge zu einer vergleichenden Biologie australischer Prachtfinken (Spermestidae). *Zool. Jb. Syst.* 90: 1–196.

Immelmann, K. 1972. Sexual and other long-term aspects of imprinting in birds and other species. *Advances in the study of behaviour* 4: 147–174.

Immelmann, K. & Immelmann, G. 1967. Verhaltensökologische Studien an afrikanischen und australischen Estrildiden. *Zool. Jb. Syst.* **94**: 609–686.

Immelmann, K., Kalberlah, H. H. Rausch, P. & Stahnke, A. 1978. *Sexuelle* Prägung als möglicher Faktor innerartlicher Isolation beim Zebrafinken. *J. Orn.* **119**: 197–1212.

Knoblauch, D. 1966. Meine Prachtfinken und ihr zusammenleben als Stubenvögel. *Gefiederte Welt* **1966**: 144–146.

Kunkel, P. 1959. Zum Verhalten einiger Prachtfinken (Estrildinae). *Z. Tierpsychol.* **16**: 302–350.

Kunkel, P. 1967. Displays facilitating sociability in waxbills of the genera *Estrilda* and *Lagonosticta*. *Behaviour* **29**: 237–261.

Lill, A. & Woodgush, D. G. M. 1965. Potential ethological isolating mechanisms and assortative mating in the domestic fowl. *Behaviour* **30**: 16–44.

Lorenz, K. 1935. Der Kumpan in der Umwelt des Vogels. *J. Orn.* **83**: 137–213 and 289–413.

Morris, D. 1957. The reproductive behaviour of the bronze mannikin, *Lonchura cucullata*. *Behaviour* **11**: 156–201.

Moyniham, M. & Hall, F. 1954. Hostile, sexual and other social behaviour patterns of the spice finch (*Lonchura punctulata*) in captivity. *Behaviour* **7**: 33–76.

Schutz, F. 1965. Sexuelle Prägung bei Anatiden. *Z. Tierpsychol.* **22**: 50–103.

Vetterli, F. 1970. Meine liebsten Vögel, die Japanische Mövchen. *Gefiederte Welt* **1970**: 214–215.

Warriner C. C. 1960. *Early experience in mate selection among pigeons.* University Microfilms Inc., Ann Arbor, Michigan, USA.

Voice

I begin this section with an attempt to justify my decision not to include sound spectrograms (sonagrams) in this book. Sound recording and the interpretation of sonagrams is not a field in which I am competent and I have therefore thought it better to give verbal descriptions of calls together with, where possible, references to papers or books in which they are illustrated in sonagrams.

Although the use of sonagrams is admittedly essential in any detailed comparative study of bird sounds, I have found that, deplorable though the fact may be, there are many others like myself to whom a verbal description of a call conveys more than a sonagram does. Nor apparently, are sonagrams always perfect instruments. Nicolai (1964), who has great experience in sound recording of birds emphatically states that in some cases sound spectrograms only imperfectly reproduce the variety and nuances of estrildid calls and that distinctly differing calls that 'neither the bird nor an experienced observer could confuse' ('die weder Vogel noch geschulter Beobachter jemals verwechseln würden') may look almost identical on a sonagram.

Calls of many estrildids are illustrated by sonagrams in an important paper on the structure and function of estrildid calls by Güttinger & Nicolai; in Güttinger's earlier paper on the evolution of estrildid behaviour patterns and vocalisations; and, for the Australian grassfinches, by Zann. As a painless, indeed very pleasant and entertaining introduction to the understanding of sonagrams *and* other aspects of the study of bird vocalisations, R. Jellis' book and accompanying record can be warmly recommended.

The vocalisations of estrildids, or other birds, are not part of a language in the specifically human meaning of that word but are rather comparable with our involuntary exclamations and expressions of anger, fear, delight and other emotions. They do indeed convey information to others, often enable the caller to obtain information from them, and serve important functions in the life of the individual and its species, but they are probably seldom, if ever, uttered with insight or intent. The motivation of any utterance seems to be a particular (presumed) mood or emotional state of which that call or song is the outward expression. Because a call is thus linked with a particular emotional state of the caller rather than with any deliberate intent to convey information or achieve some other specific end, it may sometimes be uttered in quite 'useless' situations. Useless, at least, except in so far that simply 'expressing its feelings' may be of value to the bird.

For example, the function of the contact calls of the cordon-bleus is to maintain or re-establish contact between paired or related individuals or flock members and perhaps also to alert them to be ready to respond to possible danger. Its motivation, however, would seem to be a degree of alarm, uneasiness or apprehension. In most situations it is clearly functional and often appears to be uttered deliberately and with insight (Goodwin, 1965). Some (not all) of the cordon-bleus I have kept have, however, also regularly uttered contact calls as a reflex-like response to the sound of the telephone handpiece (in another part of the house) being replaced in its holder. Also, presumably because the two calls seem to represent expressions of different *intensities* of similar feelings, the same cause may elicit contact calls from one cordon-bleu and alarm calls from another. Under wild conditions, natural selection has insured that calls are not normally given in situations in which they could be misleading or harmful. The contact calls of the cordon-bleus furnish an excellent example of this. A cordon-bleu that is ill or *badly* frightened never utters its contact call. In this situation in which one might expect the bird would be most eager to contact its mate, parents or companions it avoids doing so. Obviously this inhibition has evolved to protect related individuals from unnecessary and useless risks.

The songs of estrildids are mostly rather quiet, sometimes partly inaudible or nearly so to human ears and usually short and not very musical, although some species have loud and musical song phrases. In some species only the male sings, in others both sexes do but the female usually sings less often than the male and has a shorter song. As in other passerines, the young bird indulges in much seemingly inconsequential and 'rambling' warbling and reiteration of various call notes before finally producing and concentrating on its adult song. The characters of estrildid song have been described in detail by Hall who gives sonagrams of the songs of twenty-three species of the genera *Lonchura*, *Emblema*, *Poephila*,

Avadavat, singing (left) with head feathers partly erected; (Right) with head feathers sleeked making the 'triangular head'.

Aegintha, *Amandava*, *Estrilda* and *Amadina*. In many species there is much individual variation between the songs even of wild caught individuals (Immelmann, pers. obs.).

The songs of estrildids are primarily sexual in character and seem usually to have no aggressive or territorial connotations. Only a few species sometimes sing in aggressive contexts (Wolters). Song is an integral part of the courtship display of most species but it is also uttered as what has been termed 'solitary song' or 'undirected song'. This undirected song tends, even in social species, to be given especially when the singer is at a little distance from others (Harrison). Paired birds seldom sing (except during courtship display) when very near to their mates. At least in captivity the males of some species appear often deliberately to go out of sight of their mates 'in order' to sing (Nicolai, pers. obs.). In some species the song phrase is also used by the male as a contact call (Nicolai, 1962).

I do not think that a rigid distinction can be drawn between courtship song and undirected song. The actual song phrases are similar or identical in the two situations; the plumage of the undirected singer usually shows at least some indication of the arrangement characteristic of courtship display and this differential feather erection is often intensified if a sexually attractive conspecific approaches. Low intensity courtship display movements may also be performed by the singer (Goodwin, 1965, Wolters). In many species a singing bird is attractive to others and elicits approach and 'peering' from them (see section on Display and social behaviour). In some, probably most, species, the song is learned from a parent (or foster parent). Immelmann in a detailed study of song development in the Zebra Finch, Spice Finch and African Silverbill found that in these species the song is learned from the father or foster father. There is an innate basic outline of the song as a sequence of notes with an approximate duration. This template is characterised by much individual variation and is completed or, if the young bird is reared by a different species, covered over by a song template acquired in early life. The sensitive period for the acquisition of song elements starts before the young bird produces any kind of song and closes during

the early phases of its juvenile song, although the (previously) acquired song patterns are only perfected some weeks later. This early period for the completion of song learning is very different from the situation in many non-estrildid passerines (Immelmann, 1969, Jellis) and is probably correlated with the early sexual maturity of estrildids.

In the Avadavat but not, so far as I know, in other estrildids, vocal mimicry of the songs of other species that have *not* stood *in loco parentis* to the singer, may occur (Delacour, Goodwin, 1960), at least in captivity. In some species of estrildids song may be innate. This seems to be the case at least with the Yellow-winged Pytilia (Güttinger & Nicolai). A male of this species who was reared under Bengalese Finches prefaced his song with some Bengalese notes, but the song itself was unadulterated and identical to that of a wild male.

Although, as has been shown, song may be learned, all other estrildid vocalisations appear to be innate. Even individuals that have been fostered by and/or are paired to mates of other species utter (apart from song) only the normal calls of their own kind and do not attempt to imitate the calls of their mate or foster parents (Güttinger & Nicolai). They do, however, either learn or intuitively comprehend the significance of the calls of a non-conspecific mate and respond appropriately to them, answering them, when appropriate, with the corresponding innate call(s) from their own species' repertoire.

Estrildid calls are often rich in nuances and minor variations (Kunkel, pers. obs.), which probably allow very precise expression and understanding of the caller's moods. Güttinger & Nicolai found that all species they investigated had at least four quite distinct calls: the contact call, the begging call of the young, the nest call and the alarm call. Many species possess other calls in addition to these. The similarity or otherwise of calls that have the same function and appear to be homologous is not always a reliable guide to relationships. The alarm calls of the two closely related cordon-bleus, *Uraeginthus angolensis* and *U. bengalus* are very distinct to human ears; very similar-sounding but probably not homologous alarm calls are given by Peters' Twinspot and some of the parrot-finches. Güttinger & Nicolai give several other similar examples.

Contact calls, as has been said, function to maintain or re-establish contact between members of a pair or flock. Many estrildids have two forms of contact call (as distinct from giving the same call at differing intensities), the close contact call (locomotion intention call, flight-intention call; in German: 'Stimmfühlungslaut') and the distance contact call (identity call, contact call, long call; in German: 'Distanzruf'). The former seems often motivated by the intention to move or fly rather than any concern with loss of contact, but, whatever its motivation, its function appears to be to keep individuals in contact and probably also more or less to synchronise their activities. The distance contact call, which might perhaps as fittingly be termed *the* contact call, is often very different in character. Its motivation, at least in the estrildids best known to me, has been discussed above, its function is certainly that of a 'contact call' in the truest sense.

The function of the nest call is to attract the attention of the mate to a prospective (or already chosen) nest site and, probably, also to entice it to join its partner and perform mutual ceremonies which reinforce the bond between them. In some species at least it is very similar to and may derive from the begging calls of the young. It has in common with begging for food that it is an appeal to another bird to perform some specific behaviour. In some species, such as the Blue-headed Cordon-bleu, more than one type of call may be used by a nest-calling bird under similar, but probably not truly identical, conditions.

In some estrildids a special call, often similar to and perhaps derived from the nest call, is given by one or both partners when changing over at the nest. It is most common in species whose nests have a tubular entrance that conceals the interior from view and its function appears to be to let the arriving bird know that all is well and it can safely enter the nest.

The alarm call is given in various situations, all of which appear to involve considerable excitement *and* thwarting or conflict. Most often the conflict appears to be between escape and some other impulse. Sometimes alarm calls, usually at rather low intensity, appear to be given merely in annoyance and, because fear and danger are not always involved, the alarm call is sometimes given other names such as the 'excitement call' (Harrison), 'Erregungsruf' by some German writers. However, alarm, in the usual human sense of that word, usually appears to be one component of the situation eliciting the alarm calls of estrildids (and other birds) in most circumstances. The function of the call, under natural conditions, is to call the attention of conspecifics, particularly inexperienced young, to the presence of a predator or some other danger.

Captive, and presumably also wild estrildids react appropriately to the alarm calls of many other birds. This may be due to and is certainly reinforced by learning but there may perhaps be some innate or intuitive recognition of alarm calls (and of screams of fear) of other species. My cordon-bleus not only react to the alarm calls of House Sparrows and Blackbirds in the garden outside their room, but also utter alarm calls if they see a Jay, *Garrulus glandarius*, in the garden. As the Jay does not resemble any species likely to threaten them or their nests in Africa, they presumably took their cue from the behaviour of breeding Sparrows and Blackbirds and thus learnt to regard Jays with alarm. They show no such reaction to the sight of a Feral Pigeon or Wood Pigeon, unless it flies close and presents a hawk-like appearance.

Well-feathered nestlings and recently-fledged young of many (perhaps all) estrildids utter screams of apparent terror when seized in the hand. Usually the bird gives one or two screeches and then falls silent (if held carefully), but manipulation of it for ringing may cause almost continuous screeching. Exceptionally a young bird may screech if cornered and unable to escape although more usually in this situation it is either silent or utters alarm calls *until* the moment that it is seized. Under natural conditions such fear screaming is the response of a young bird when seized by a predator. Other nestlings respond by jumping out of the nest and attempting to flee, adults by intense alarm calling and mobbing of the 'predator'. In most species adult birds do not scream in fear when held or do so only very rarely. Possibly if roughly handled or seized by a hawk or other natural predator they might, however, do so, as do adult thrushes, *Turdus* and Starlings, *Sturnus vulgaris* in such plight.

The function of the fear scream is to enable (with luck) some of the brood to escape when a predator has discovered the nest. In such circumstances if it caught one nestling it would be bound to return for the others and the doomed bird's scream of terror may at least save some of its siblings. In some species of birds, such as the Mallard, a captured young one may actually be rescued alive by its parent (pers. obs.) but there is no evidence for any effective defence of their young by estrildids. The motivation of fear screaming seems to be terror. As anyone who has had much to do with birds or other animals will know, screams of terror, however much they differ between species, are instantly recognisable for what they are and are usually very 'upsetting' to any person not directly benefitting from the death or capture of the creature calling out.

Some estrildids have a specific threat call and the cordon-bleus have a call that is given in sexual chases and appears to be largely aggressive in character.

REFERENCES

Delacour, J. 1935. Les Bengalis rouges. *L'Oiseau* **3–4**: 376–388.

Goodwin, D. 1960. Observations on Avadavats and Golden-breasted Waxbills. *Avicult. Mag.* **66**: 174–199.

Goodwin, D. 1965. A comparative study of captive blue waxbills (Estrildidae). *Ibis.* **107**: 285–315.

Güttinger, H. R. 1970. Zur Evolution von Verhaltensweisen und Lautäusserungen bei Prachtfinken (Estrildidae). *Z. Tierpsychol.* **27**: 1011–1075.

Güttinger, H. R. & Nicolai, J. 1973. Struktur und Funktion der Rufe bei Prachtfinken (Estrildidae). *Z. Tierpsychol.* **33**: 319–334.

Hall, M. F. 1962. Evolutionary aspects of estrildid song. *Sym. Zool. Soc. London* **8**: 37–55.

Harrison, C. J. O. 1962. Solitary Song and its Inhibition in Some Estrildidae. *J.Orn.* **1962**: 369–373.

Immelmann, K. 1969. Song development in the Zebra Finch and Other Estrildid Finches. *Bird Vocalisations* (ed. R. A. Hinde), Cambridge University Press.

Jellis, R. 1977. *Bird Sounds and their Meaning.* BBC, London.

Kunkel, P. 1959. Zum Verhalten einiger Prachtfinken. *Z. Tierpsychol.* **16**: 302–350.

Nicolai, J. 1962. Anmerkung 1 (comments on Harrison's note). *J.Orn.* **1962**: 373–375.

Nicolai, J. 1964. Der Brutparasitismus der Viduinae als ethologisches Problem. *Z. Tierpsychol.* **21**: 129–204.

Wolters, H. E. 1962. Anmerkung 3 (comments on Harrison's note). *J.Orn.* **1962**: 377–379.

Zann, R. 1975. Inter- and Intra-specific Variation in the Calls of Three Species of Grassfinches of the Subgenus *Poephila* (Gould) (Estrildidae). *Z. Tierpsychol.* **39**: 85–125.

5 Estrildids in captivity

Some avicultural notes

As has been said in the Introduction, this book is not intended to be a complete avicultural guide. The present chapter consists merely of a few personal observations and opinions which, however, may prove of some use or interest to would-be keepers of estrildids. Some subjects, on which I am ill qualified to comment, such as medicines and the desirability or otherwise of giving antibiotics, which are widely used as prophylactics and cures on the continent, but are not always readily available to the ordinary person in Britain and the actual construction of aviaries or bird rooms, are deliberately omitted.

Except when otherwise indicated, general remarks here can be taken as applying with certainty only to species that I have kept. I am, therefore, listing here those species and in brackets after them the approximate number of years that I kept them. Cordon-bleu or Blue-breasted Waxbill (10 years), Red-cheeked Cordon-bleu (17 years), Blue-headed Cordon-bleu (18 years), Avadavat (16 years), Goldbreast (21 years), Dark Firefinch (2 years), Jameson's Firefinch (7 years), Kulikori Firefinch (3 years), Black-rumped, Rosy-rumped and Black-capped Waxbills (4 years, two of the Black-rumped for about 8 years) and Java Sparrow (3 years). Of these the first 6 species but not the others, repeatedly bred successfully. Most of the other species nested but did not rear young. The remarks here on wild foods and soft foods taken by my birds do not, however, refer to the Java Sparrows.

ADVICE AND WHERE TO FIND IT When I was in the Australian outback I was introduced to a man who was interested in bird-keeping. His very small aviary was empty when we met. The reason was soon explained, his methods were to catch birds that appealed to him in appearance (unfortunately for themselves these had apparently included such species as the beautiful Australian chats, *Epthianura*), put them in his aviary, give them dry commercial packet bird seed and water and see whether they would live or die. Some of the allegedly 'expert' advice one reads on the ease with which estrildids (and other birds) may be kept sometimes strikes me as not much farther advanced in ethics and conception. English and American works on bird-keeping often give the impression that all most estrildids need is dry seed and a little greenfood now and then. Such species as the domesticated Bengalese and the Zebra Finch may live under such a regime but many others will not, at least not for any length of time.

Whereas English sources, or some of them, often tend to give the impression that estrildids are not, and should not be allowed to be, 'any trouble' to keep, German works tend to the other extreme and seem to assume that their readers, beside being blessed with unlimited wealth, are able to spend all day with their birds, and yet active enough to run energetically around collecting various wild foods. Such fortunate people are indeed ideally fitted to keep estrildids (or any other creatures that they fancy), but those with less time and money need not despair of moderate success. The introductory section on keeping estrildids in Immelmann *et al.* (1963) can be thoroughly recommended to all who can read German, even if it may seem here and there, at least to the English reader, to advocate the ideal rather than the practically possible. Nicolai's two fine books on bird-keeping (1963a, 1963b) can be similarly recommended. Only in one matter am I doubtful of advice given by Immelmann *et al.* This is that sick birds should, medicines apart, be fed only on dry seed. I may be wrong but I cannot see how a diet which is said to be inadequate to maintain a fit bird can be adequate to restore a sick one to health. A less up-to-date and possibly for that reason less daunting German work is that of Dr Russ who lived in the 'dark ages' before much was known about nutrition, vitamins and so on. His advice is correspondingly simple and no doubt in some respects and for some species quite inadequate, but he had considerable success. In any case he is very well worth reading for his ability to convey vividly his interest in the birds he kept and his delight in their charm and beauty.

References to other useful books or articles, that I have found, are given under the species' headings. When evaluating the likely worth of any advice it is helpful if one knows how long one's mentor has successfully kept the species in question and with what success. If possible it is a good idea to get into personal communication with aviculturists who keep the species one wants to know more about. A visit to them and their birds should be made at the first opportunity, on the basis of which it will be easy to judge whether one should heed their advice or not. An advertisement in some avicultural or ornithological journal is one way in which one may be able to get in touch with such persons.

Bird-feeding

INTRODUCTORY COMMENTS Much scientific work has been done on the nutritional needs of man but one has only to look at a few of the dozens of diets recommended to us by as many highly qualified experts to know that 'doctors differ', at least in their interpretation of the evidence. After man, few creatures' dietary needs have been more studied than those of the Domestic Fowl yet no one can say that our modern intensively kept and scientifically fed chickens are, on average, in anything remotely approaching such good condition as most of those kept by our ignorant fore-fathers or by relatively primitive peoples in remoter parts of the world today. So the fact that little or no scientific work has been done on the needs of most estrildids in captivity need not unduly dishearten one. Nor, of course, should it be assumed that what we do know necessarily represents complete, final or absolute knowledge of the subject. 'The proof of the pudding is in the eating', *and* in its effects on the eater. If the reader's birds thrive, breed successfully and their young breed in due course, then their food must be adequate. If not then some deficiency in the diet is probably, although not certainly, at least part of the cause. Where available, information on foods taken in captivity has been indicated for each species under the species' headings, but the following remarks are, I think, generally applicable.

SEEDS In the wild many estrildids preferentially or usually take seeds that are not fully ripe ('half ripe' is the usual term but the precise stage preferred doubtless differs with the species of both birds and seeds) and even the fully ripe and already shed seeds, that the ground feeders largely take, are seldom so dry and hard as the kiln-dried seeds commercially available. These latter may for some species, and possibly under certain conditions for most species, be more difficult to digest. I do not, however, think that, in general, their free use is to be condemned, provided they are not made the sole available food. Even when offered soaked seed and other foods many estrildids (all the species that I have kept) still take large quantities of dry seed, while everyone who has done much feeding of wild birds will know that many species will readily eat the ordinary commercially available dry seeds (of kinds suitable for them) even at times when they are not suffering from any shortage of natural foods. This is true of at least some estrildids, notably the Australian Red-browed Finch, as well as for seed-eating birds of several different families in Europe and North America.

It is usually wise to offer a variety of seeds although one or more of the following are likely to be taken in greatest quantity by most estrildids: the small Panicum or Indian Millet, White Millet, Japanese Millet and Canary Seed. These should all be available ad lib. at least unless none have been taken over a period of a year or more. Birds' appetites may change, probably in correlation with their dietary needs, and it should not be assumed that just because a seed or other food is not eaten in the first few months it is offered that it never will be. Similarly most species will feed largely on one or two seeds – very often Panicum and White Millets – but will take small amounts of other foods. Ornithologists often talk about the 'important' foods of a species, meaning those that it takes in considerable quantity, but aviculturists should bear in mind that foods that are only taken in small quantities may be just as important for the bird's health. The mixtures of seeds and,

it is usually claimed, other additives, that are sold under such titles as 'foreign finch tonic seed' usually contain at least some seeds that many species like although sometimes containing others, particularly Red Millet, that they do not. It has always puzzled me why Red Millet is so often included in 'mixtures' of seeds. Hungry Feral Pigeons apart, I have never seen any bird eat it, certainly none of the estrildids I have kept has ever done so, and Immelmann *et al.* warn, rightly in my opinion, that it is unsuitable for them. There is, however, little fear of the birds taking harmful seeds if they have an ample choice. Some claim that if the small waxbills are allowed to eat the larger kinds of millet this will eventually cause their deaths. Certainly, like their owner, they will die sooner or later but, provided they are not forced to take White Millet or Japanese Millet through *lack* of Panicum, I doubt if their deaths are ever likely to be due to over-large seeds. I am, of course, speaking now of adult birds. If through lack of natural foods such as tiny, and relatively soft, wild seeds and/or insects, some small estrildids feed their newly hatched young on large or even on Panicum millet it will certainly kill them. Some of the seeds found in commercial grass seed mixtures may be taken and so long as one is sure that the seed does not contain harmful chemicals, grass seed mixtures can be freely offered as an addition to the menu.

It is usual to place seed in hoppers or other containers so contrived that only a small amount of seed is exposed at a time. As with so many modern human afflictions, the commendable if sometimes misguided reason for this is hygiene. The seed in such containers cannot be contaminated by the birds' excreta. Some of it can, however, and usually will be dropped and, as it falls more or less beneath the birds feeding at the hopper, be both fouled and eaten by birds below, that are hungry because a stronger or more dominant individual is keeping them away from the feeder. In my opinion, when several or many birds are kept in an aviary or bird room, it is best to put the seed either in *large, shallow* containers, lined with clean newspaper or better the white soft paper of 'kitchen rolls' or even to just put it on the floor. In either case choose areas least likely to be much fouled and preferably put each kind of seed separately. After a little experience one can soon adjust things so that, if economy is necessary, only about say a third or less more than is normally eaten is put down daily. On the following day all the seed not eaten can easily be swept up, or if on dishes emptied out into a dust pan, and fed to wild birds in the garden. If one has not got a garden visited by seed-eating birds then give it to the pigeons and sparrows in the nearest town or park. Thus nothing will be wasted. Above all do not attempt to make your captive birds eat *all* their seed. Some of even the best seed is likely to be defective – as germination tests will prove – and it is false economy not to allow a pretty wide margin in this matter. The above remarks about putting seed or seed containers on the floor does not, of course, apply if one has species or individuals that are extremely reluctant to feed at floor level.

Millet sprays are an expensive way of giving seed but some species like pulling the seeds from them. I have found the species I have kept would freely take seed from sprays that had been soaked *and were still moist*, but not from dry sprays, and that, except possibly when feeding young, they took ordinary soaked seed just as readily.

Seed can be soaked by placing it in a vessel of (initially) slightly warmed water that is placed in a warmish or at any rate temperate rather than cold room. Within an hour or so diastase is produced and this dissolves the starch in the seeds into the more easily digested dextrine (Baptista, pers. comm.). The soaking seed should be put into a sieve and rinsed under a running tap twice or more times per day. After the first 12 hours or so it is better placed in a shallow vessel with only enough water to keep it wet or just covered. After about three days sprouts (the rootlets, not as some think, the growing shoots) appear. At this stage, Dr Baptista tells me, the food value is a little less but some bird-keepers prefer to give it to the birds at this stage. I have found that those species I have kept much prefer seed that has soaked only 12 to 36 hours to that with sprouts clearly showing. Soaked seed can be slightly dried in a cloth or it can simply be scattered on clean white fabric or paper on a dish. The birds, in my experience, are only eager for it while it is still at least slightly moist. It is probably a good thing to supply soaked seed (as well as dry) daily but it may be rather time-consuming to do so and I have found that with birds that are not breeding and are getting greenfood and some animal food there is no difference in their condition whether getting or not getting soaked seed daily. I take care to supply it daily (if at all possible in small quantities several times daily) to any that are feeding nestlings or recently fledged young.

One way of supplying vitamin D (and A) is to add cod-liver oil (I use a brand sold in the local chemists which is also said to contain added Vitamin E) to either dry or soaked seed. A few drops to about a small handful of seed, well mixed in. With birds that are able to expose themselves to plenty of direct sunlight and are getting a varied diet it is probably unnecessary, but I should always advise giving such oil-treated seed once or twice a week to birds kept indoors, or in wintertime. I speak, of course, of birds kept in Britain or similar climates, not in the tropics. Oil-treated seed or rather the oil in it is rendered ineffective after exposure of some hours to daylight so what is left should always be cleared away and put out for the wild birds at latest on the morning after it has been given.

GREENFOOD Strictly some of the foods to be discussed here should have come under the previous heading as it is the ripe or yet unripe seeds that are usually the main parts eaten from at least much of the 'greenfood' given to captive birds. I am, however, using the term in its usual avicultural sense to include all parts of various wild or cultivated green plants that are fed to captive estrildids.

Few leaves, shoots, buds or seeds are known to be poisonous to estrildids and it is tolerably certain that they will not take sufficient of such as may be to harm them, except, possibly, under very unusual circumstances. One need, therefore, have few worries about offering any plants to the birds, at least provided that species about which one may have any doubts are offered together with others known to be palatable or harmless, so that there is no likelihood of the birds eating harmful vegetation because they have no other to hand.

Of plants of which the half ripe or nearly ripe seeds, and sometimes also the buds and flowers (perhaps mainly to get at the embryo seeds) are eaten, three of the very many that I have tried stand out as pre-eminent favourites. They are the Common Knot-grass, *Polygonum aviculare*, Chickweed, *Stellaria media* and Annual Meadow Grass, *Poa annua*. The first of these usually flowers and seeds in late summer, on rather dry open areas, especially dusty cart tracks, footpaths and the more badly trodden parts of football fields and similar places. Chickweed and Annual Meadow Grass commonly grow in disturbed soil in gardens, on stubble fields after harvest and often spring up under trees in the early spring before the leaves shade out the light. There are several similar and allied species of knot-grass and chickweed which are also eaten (though most not quite so keenly). All can be offered to the birds, as can any flowering or seeding grasses, experience will show which, if any, are never eaten by any particular species. If millet is scattered or sown in one's garden, some of it may grow and, if it does, the 'unripe' seeds are liked by many estrildids.

Apart from seeds in various stages of ripeness, estrildids often take pieces of leaf and especially the growing tips of young grass and other green shoots. Whole growing shoots of seedling grasses, up to about an inch long may be mandibulated and swallowed. Of plants whose leaves, or bits of them, are readily eaten, Dandelion, Chickweed, Lettuce, Clover and of course young grass may be mentioned as being usually obtainable. An excellent way of obtaining greenfood, or some of it, for a varied selection is best when possible, is to sow grass seed in shallow dishes which are placed in the birdroom or aviary when the grass shoots are about half an inch or so high. After a day or two the dish can be removed and if put aside for a week or two the grass will often recover and can be used again. It has been claimed that greenfood grown indoors or in a greenhouse (and the grass treated as above will not grow outdoors in winter) is likely to be deficient in nutrients. I do not know if this is so, but it is certainly better than no greenfood at all which, in winter, is often the only alternative. Some greenfood should be offered to the birds daily if possible and, with the help of home-sown grass, it usually *is* possible even if one lives in a town and is away from home most of the day. Above all the bird-keeper should not stop providing greenfood just because his birds do not eat much of it or even if they do not eat any of it for some weeks or months.

Most estrildids (and many other birds) take pieces of leaf or other greenstuff, and seeds from seed heads of some plants and grasses, by seizing with the bill and then giving a backward jerk to tear off a piece (or pull out the seed).

This they are easily able to do with a naturally growing plant or shoot but are often quite unable to do if greenfood is simply put on the floor of the aviary or (worse) hung suspended. Greenfood should therefore either be given clamped firmly between two bricks or between a brick and the floor or otherwise firmly secured in a place convenient for the feeding bird, as will usually have to be the case for chickweed, lettuce etc.; or else turves or heavy sods of earth complete with the growing grass and/or weeds can be placed in the aviary. These latter will often stay green for a couple of days or so and may regenerate if placed outside in the garden after use.

Some writers on foreign bird-keeping recommend hanging up bunches of greenfood and often go on to say how these are especially appreciated by the typical waxbills and the mannikins. The true situation is that these species, which habitually feed among growing vegetation in the wild, are experts at clinging to swaying stems and can hold food underfoot are able, albeit often with considerable difficulty, to feed from a hanging bunch of grass or other greenfood, whereas purely ground-feeding species, like firefinches, cannot or can only do so with difficulty and very ineffectively. Greenfood should therefore, always be placed on the floor, on some spacious ledge or table or, for species or individuals reluctant to go to floor level, tied or otherwise fixed firmly to or near perches. One of the sad facts of man's recent progress is that, in contrast to such life-enhancing earlier discoveries as electricity, field glasses, and hot-water bottles, almost every post-1946 innovation has either brought more sorrow and worry than happiness or, as in the case of supersonic flight, has brought a minimal increase of happiness to a very few at the cost of a great deal of misery to very many. The one exception I can think of is the plastic bag, for which the bird keeper has cause to be grateful. A few plastic bags, and bits of string to tie them up with, slipped into his pocket, travel bag or rucksack and the aviculturist is able to gather any useful greenstuff that he passes and keep it fresh in the bag for up to several days.

LIVE FOODS Two forms of live food for birds can be widely purchased, but neither is ideal for estrildids. Blowfly (*Calliphora*) maggots are bred in large quantities for the use of anglers and can be bought at many tackle shops. Unfortunately, as a rule only the last instar (or near it) maggots are sold, which are too big and tough to be easily, or in some cases at all, dealt with by the smaller estrildids. Also they are often bred in the carcases of ex-battery hens and there have been some nasty cases of losses of captive birds by disease caused through their use. In summer they can easily be produced by some modern equivalent of Isaac Walton's classic advice for breeding them: 'Take a dead cat or kite and let it be fly-blown . . .'. The RSPB will probably look askance if any of my British readers kill a Kite for this purpose, however, and whatever carrion is used the process is apt to be messy and smelly. Though if one does breed them one can at least take them when

suitably small and make sure they are more or less clean by keeping them in a vessel of bran or sand for a few days before giving them to the birds. Buying them has the additional disadvantage in that they are not usually obtainable during the coarse fishing close season from mid-May to mid-June.

Mealworms are also available commercially but at a pretty high price. There is much difference of opinion as to their suitability for estrildids. Some advocate fairly free use of small or cut-up mealworms but most of the more experienced and successful German breeders of estrildids are convinced that the hard chitinous exoskeletons of mealworms are harmful to many estrildids and recommend that they should be cooked before giving them to the birds. The exact methods are not always stated but are clearly usually similar to those of Kühner, who recommends stewing the mealworms for about five minutes in water at 'cooking heat' (I presume this means not quite at boiling point), then beheading them and removing the last 3 mm of the tail end before cutting them in two and giving them to the birds.

Whiteworms (Enchytreae), unlike mealworms, are extremely easy to breed in quantity at home. They are eaten readily by many species. The only difficulty is in first purchasing a 'culture' in which some of the worms are still alive. Too often the shops that sell them, mostly those dealing with tropical fish, will be found to have let all the worms in the culture dry up or starve before sale. Books on fish-keeping usually give very long-winded, complicated and time-consuming recipes for breeding whiteworms, involving esoteric mixtures of loam, garden soil, leaf-mould etc. and the use of sheets of glass. None of this is necessary as I have proved, having bred the creatures successfully and plentifully for over 16 years. All you need do is to buy one or more (preferably about three, if you want to have a constant and plentiful supply) large plastic washing-up basins. Buy also some sphagnum peat, or one of the peat-like types of bulb fibre, from a gardening shop. The peat itself is cheaper and more pleasant to use, if it can be obtained. Fill the basin or basins with peat that has been mixed with water until it is wet but of a crumbly, not sloppy consistency. Buy some whiteworm culture from a tropical fish shop. Make sure that at least some of the whiteworms in or on the clay or other substrate of the culture are still alive.

With a large spoon, which is best kept handy on top of the peat in the basin, scoop out one or more hollows in the peat. Put in each a dollop of rather wet milk-sop (bread and milk mixture) and a spoonful or so of the culture. Cover up both whiteworms and milk-sop with the peat; if this last is not done, mildew will grow on the exposed parts of the bread-and-milk. Place the plastic bowls under the bed in the spare room or in any similar place in a fairly cool but not freezingly cold room. Keep the substrate moist. After a week or so, have a look and if the milk-sop is largely gone add some more. Within a month you will have large numbers of whiteworms. They can be fed to the birds by putting spoonfuls, or better, handfuls of peat and worms and spreading it on a clean part of the aviary floor. When waxbills have young and you have to leave them for most or all of the day, you can also put one or two heaps of peat and worms, which will not dry out so quickly and will keep them busy digging about in it.

When they begin to dry out the whiteworms gather into a tight ball and many estrildids will not then take them, though I have seen cordon-bleus, rather hesitantly pull individual worms from such a ball. These balled-up worms will recover if wetted and put back into the basin, making sure they are buried near or with food. The substrate that has been put in the aviary should not go back into your culture but be thrown on the garden, new peat being added in its place.

Whiteworm cultures of this sort very seldom go wrong and, if they do, can easily be thrown away and a new start made. Occasionally those once abundant but now (in Britain) rather rare creatures the Fruit Fly, *Drosophila* sp. and the House Fly, *Musca domestica* (or perhaps some other fly like it, I am no entomologist) will also lay in the culture and their small maggots form a very welcome addition to the birds' diet. They do not, however, continue to thrive and multiply but the whiteworms go on and on, breeding prolifically at cost of very little care.

Green aphids (greenfly) are much liked by many estrildids although the grey, greenish grey and black species are evidently distasteful and are not eaten by them. In the spring anyone with roses in his garden will be able to procure some greenfly from his own rosebuds. Buds that can be spared or that are going to be pruned anyway, can be cut off and simply given to the birds to pick the aphids off them; otherwise the greenfly can be brushed off with a *soft* paint brush into a container and tipped out for the birds. Greenfly may also be found on the buds and growing shoots of some other garden plants. There is some competition by the garden birds, at least in London, where insect food for the House Sparrows and Blue Tits is in short supply, but ladybirds are the real enemy. Both the handsome adult beetles and their ugly grubs have great appetites for aphids and once the grubs have been produced in numbers, usually in London about mid-May to mid-June, depending on the weather, the surviving greenfly become too few and scattered to be worth collecting. Unlike the greenfly they feed on, the ladybirds and their larvae are distasteful to estrildids and to most other birds.

The budding and flowering panicles of *Poa annua* and many other grasses are often heavily infested with greenfly. Any such grasses one finds should be cut, put into one of the handy plastic bags already mentioned and carried home for one's birds. Stinging Nettles are often a wonderful source of greenfly. Unlike other plants they cannot, of course, be searched to any extent by wild birds and so, unless or until the ladybirds breed up to massive numbers, they often support large numbers of greenfly for many weeks on end. The most heavily infested plants usually stand out by looking relatively pale and anaemic. To collect them for the birds you need a large plastic bag (about 18 inches (45 cm) deep is ideal) and a pair of sharp scissors. Grip the nettle by the top of its stem or rather by the buds or flowers there and cut it off at a convenient length, including all the most greenfly-covered leaves. Then still holding it by the tip, lift it gently loose (the more gently it is moved the fewer aphids will drop off) and lower it into the plastic bag. It is much easier if you wear gloves and have a friend to hold the bag open, but can be managed without getting very badly stung on one's own and gloveless. The leaves of the nettles in the bag keep the sides of it from crushing the greenfly even if it is placed in a rucksack. To feed the greenfly to the birds, take the nettles two at a time into the aviary and, holding them by their basal ends, beat them against each other or brush them with a soft brush to dislodge the aphids. Be very careful not to leave any leaves or even broken bits of leaf on the floor as small birds suffer considerable pain if they tread on them and get stung. I imagine serious injury might result if, as a result of pecking at or among nettle leaves, they got stung in or near the eye, but, having seen a waxbill's evident pain when its foot was stung, I have taken care to avoid similar or worse mishaps since.

The larvae and pupae ('eggs') of ants seem to be a very favourite food with almost all birds that are offered them in captivity although, except by occasional accident, only relatively few species take them in the wild. The large Wood Ant, *Formica rufa*, is locally abundant in Britain in heath and pine country. It is said to be eaten by the Green Woodpecker, *Picus viridis*, but I have never seen a Green Woodpecker anywhere near a Wood Ants' nest, only (and regularly) at those of the smaller meadow ants. The pupae of the Wood Ant are collected commercially in Austria, in parts of which this insect is almost unbelievably abundant. German aviculturists go to great pains to buy large supplies and keep them in their deep freezes for use during the winter (Nicolai, 1965a) but the process of preparation is rather long and time-consuming. Estrildids are afraid of the Wood Ant and probably would be justified in their fear as the ant's biting and acid-squirting can be quite painful even to man. If, therefore, pupae or larvae of this ant are given, great care must be taken that the adults do not accompany them.

My own experience with ant pupae etc. for estrildids mainly involves the Yellow and the Black Meadow Ant, *Lasius fuscus* and *L. niger*, possibly also similar species that I may have confused with them. The nest of the former is commonly found (at least in southern England) in fields, pastures and grassy or thyme-covered banks; that of the latter sometimes in fields but more often on banks, at grassy road sides and similar places. In towns it often occurs in numbers, making its nests under concrete, tarmac, paving stones etc. although sometimes (if unmolested) in sunny garden borders or against the garden fence. Whole nests can be dug up and flung into the aviary, but a less wasteful procedure is to arm oneself with a spoon or small trowel and a suitable container, whenever, on a sunny morning, one is likely to find or pass nests of either species. At such times the pupae or

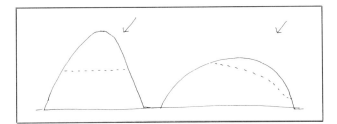

Diagrammatic outline sketches of above ground portions of nests of the ants *Lasius fuscus* (right) and *Lasius niger* (left). Arrows show direction of sun's rays. On a fine morning most pupae will be at levels of and/or above dotted lines.

grubs will have been brought up near the top of the nest to warm up and nests containing plenty of pupae, or at least the parts of them above ground, will have a peculiar 'fresh' or friable look, hard to describe but experience will soon teach its appearance. If, first getting the container ready, one inserts the spoon just below the surface of the top of the nest one will soon find the pupae and/or larvae and be able to spoon them up, often with relatively few ants with them. The nest of the Black Ant tends to be more conical and the pupae more concentrated in it than in the Yellow Ant. At some times there may be no pupae but lots of the winged alates and these also the birds will eat, though not always quite so eagerly. Often by the afternoon of a *hot* day the ants will have taken their pupae down below ground level again. So it is best to hunt for them in the morning, after about two hours sunshine in the fairly early morning is ideal.

Whilst on both humanitarian and conservational grounds it is a good idea to try to avoid a great many ants being collected together with their younger stages and the nest substrate, some are bound to be and are desirable. They seem to cause only minor discomfort even to small estrildids, which soon learn to avoid them or quickly pick them off. Moreover, if you have collected more than can be at once used, the ants will look after their larvae and pupae, to some extent. If all are put into the aviary, with some clods of grass, the ants will usually take the pupae not immediately eaten and hide them under the clods, which can then be removed later to expose them again to the birds. The adults will also be used for anting by *Amandava* species. If they are kept with the pupae in containers or on the dry floor of an indoor bird room, they can be fed and given moisture by supplying them with bits of bread, sponge or cloth that have been saturated in a solution of honey and water.

Termites, at least the workers, are by all accounts an excellent food for estrildids and are taken by many of them in the wild. They do not, unfortunately, occur in Britain so I can give no advice on their collection and use. Those overseas readers who can obtain them regularly and in quantity should have little trouble in successfully breeding species that feed their young on insects.

Though I have here concentrated on a few kinds of live food which I have found obtainable readily (or in the case of ants not so readily as in former years) in England, many other invertebrates can be offered and there is little doubt that, other things being equal, the greater the variety the better. The 'top spit' of earth and/or dead leaves etc. from woodland, hedgerows or even the 'wilder' parts of the garden, often contain many invertebrates that estrildids will eat and, even if they only find a few, many species will get valuable exercise and interest in searching for them. Obviously one should avoid areas that may have been sprayed with poisons or defaecated on by numbers of House Sparrows or other wild birds. Smooth green or brown caterpillars and grasshoppers, if not too large, may be mentioned as creatures that are much liked and sometimes (though in my experience not very often) available in quantities.

SOFTFOODS, EGGFOOD ETC. The main function of these, at least so far as estrildids are concerned, is to supply a substitute for insect food that may not be readily obtainable and/or proteins or other substances that may not be otherwise present in the diet.

There are many foods on the market that are, or so their makers claim, scientific, complete and suitable for all kinds of birds; sometimes all three of these claims being made for a particular food, sometimes only one or two. I have tried several of these foods and, while they may be all that is claimed for them, none of my estrildids have ever eaten any of them. However, that is no proof that no estrildids ever would eat them, and there is not likely to be much danger in offering such foods provided that no reliance is placed on them unless or until they are seen to be freely eaten. Nicolai (1965a), however, warns that some of these foods contain a great deal of horse fat which may in time cause serious digestive troubles. Under no circumstances should they replace other foods to the extent of the latter not being offered.

There are various recipes for eggfood. The commonest is hardboiled egg forced through a sieve and mixed with about the same proportion of powdered plain biscuit or bread. I use egg only, putting an egg in cold water, bringing it to the boil or to near boiling point and then letting it simmer for about 12 to 15 minutes. I do not add any bread or biscuit to the egg after forcing it through a clean gauze strainer and mixing it up with a fork, as I have found that if it is mixed with bread or biscuit my estrildids will not eat it. Nor is there any point in trying to force them to do so as they are clearly getting enough farinaceous food in their seed. Some writers on bird nutrition claim that unadulterated egg is too 'rich' and will cause liver trouble, but I have never had any adverse results that I know of from using it. The situation may be different with species that are rearing their young primarily on eggfood. The species I have kept have never eaten much of it, although observation shows that most individuals eat a little most days, even when not breeding. Even so one egg makes a two days' supply, of which less than a third is eaten, for about 20 small estrildids. I put the prepared egg in two shallow, rounded dishes, one of which is kept in the fridge until needed the following day. In such shallow rounded dishes it tends to dry rather than go sour. I remove the surplus each evening, or at first light the following day if I am not home before dark, and give it to the garden birds. It is eagerly eaten by Starlings, House Sparrows, Blackbirds, Song Thrushes, Feral Pigeons and Woodpigeons. No doubt those lucky enough to live in the country where more birds visit their gardens, would find other species take it also. I also give my estrildids milk-sop. Although very little of it is eaten, some is and also some of the milk is drunk from it. The surplus can be fed to wild birds, or used for whiteworm cultures.

My earliest attempts to get my estrildids to eat eggfood or milk-sop failed completely. Later, however, I achieved it by putting a dish of each in the bird room daily and also, since birds are often reluctant to try large masses of stuff as food, sprinkled a few odd morsels of each around the dishes and over the seed in the big seed tray. After many weeks of this regime, each week when cleaning out the room, I left the birds without food for about 30 to 45 minutes. Care was taken that they had already had at least an hour of light to feed before this was done. When I put back the water containers, I put eggfood and milk-sop in also, scattered morsels of the former in the (empty) seed tray and of the latter on the clean paper around the dish.

The birds flew down expecting food. The first few times only one or two pecked half-heartedly at egg or milk-sop. Within a few weeks, however, several of the birds were eating it. In all cases I was careful not to keep them without seed for more than at most half an hour after the soft foods had been put in. Once a few individuals started to eat eggfood or milk-sop, others soon started to do so. This was not, however, a matter of sudden learning. Often a bird would show definite interest when it saw another waxbill, *especially one of the same species*, eating soft food and investigate the food itself, but I did not see an instance in which such an apparent first try led to immediate acceptance, as it sometimes does with pigeons. In species of which I had both wild-caught and captive-bred individuals, the latter *all* started to sample soft foods before *any* of the former did so, although all took them eventually. Of the species I have kept, only Avadavats and firefinches, *Lagonosticta* spp., absolutely refused eggfood and milk-sop under any circumstances, but the number was not sufficient to be sure that this was a specific rather than an individual phenomenon.

GRIT AND MINERALS A number of birdwatchers, among them some very accomplished ornithologists, imagine that birds only take mineral matter as 'grit' to assist the grinding up of their food in the gizzard. A little detailed observation of wild birds would show that much of the mineral matter they eat could be of little use for such a purpose. Very often, birds that are supposedly taking 'grit' from roads or tracks, are in fact taking seeds or insects that have blown or fallen on them. Seed-eating birds do take some grit that appears to function as an aid to grinding up the seeds they swallow, but the greater part of the mineral matter they ingest seems to be taken in order to obtain calcium, salt or other minerals for assimilation.

I always supply my birds not only with sand, one of the commercially obtainable 'mineralised' grits (said to contain a great variety of minerals), and cuttlefish bone, but also with crushed dried eggshell and salt. Some people give cuttle bone as, except for grit, the sole source of calcium (apart from what may be in the food), but I think this is unwise as it may lead to the birds ingesting too much salt or other matter in attempting to get enough calcium. The eggshells can be sterilised, or virtually sterilised by heating them (but not until they burn brown) or by dunking them for a few moments in boiling water and then drying them. They can then be put between two sheets of clean paper and pulverised with a hammer. The resultant mixture of powdered and broken shell is best placed in 'finger pinch' little piles on several different clean parts of the floor and ledges in the aviary, as there may be competition for them. I find that, even though they have grit and cuttle bone ad lib., if my estrildids have no eggshell for five or six days they at once fly down and eat it eagerly. Some authorities recommend merely roughly crushing the dried eggshells but from observation I do not think such small and relatively weak-billed species as cordon-bleus and Goldbreasts can adequately break up large bits of eggshell.

Salt, except what may have been available in the grit or cuttle bone, I did not supply until 1977. By an odd coincidence at the same time as one of my hen Blue-headed Cordon-bleus had either mysteriously lost or been plucked of most of her head feathers, I read a paper (Schmidt) which showed that feather-plucking in captive parrots was at least in some cases not due to all the many and conflicting causes usually supposed, but to lack of sufficient salt in the diet. Schmidt had found that a solution of salt water best suited parrots so afflicted but that small passerines would pick up individual grains of table salt. I decided that it could do no harm to offer my birds a sprinkling of salt and, although I have only on a very few occasions seen them take any, I have continued to do so. The balding hen Blue-headed Cordon-bleu did, in fact, regrow her feathers within a few weeks, but I am not convinced that in her case the salt was responsible for the cure or its lack for the trouble. Further studies (Scher-nekau, 1979) have confirmed that lack of salt is often, and possibly always the cause of feather-plucking in captive parrots, such birds being almost always ones that have *not* been allowed tit-bits of human foodstuffs.

There is a widespread belief that salt is harmful to certain birds and some laboratory experiments appear to have confirmed this. As to the first, this belief is based, I think, on the human tendency to seek the cause of avian or human ills in something that the unfortunate creature *has* eaten or indulged in rather than its being due (as it far more often is) to the *lack* of something that it was deprived of. As to the second, what happens to a bird forced to drink salt solutions or go without sufficient water, and often under very stressful laboratory conditions, can, I think, be considered of no relevance as to the safety of offering salt on a 'take it or leave it' basis to birds that have ample supplies of unsalted water.

Charcoal is recommended by some authorities. It can be purchased from food dealers or, I suppose, one can easily make it at home by burning small bits of wood, as I did when I was breeding Avadavats which, like some of the grassfinches, put charcoal in their nests. However, I have never seen any of the species I have kept eat it so I do not bother to supply it.

WATER TEMPERATURE It is obvious that few wild estrildids can ever drink or bathe in really cold water. I always, therefore, make sure that no water given to my birds is ice-cold and that bathing water is at least luke-warm.

The holiday stand-in

The aviculturist who does not forgo all holidays or other periods away from home is bound to be faced with the problem of who is going to care for his or her birds at such times. If there is a husband, wife, brother, other relative or friend living in the same house or nearby, the problem may be easily solved, or it may be rendered more difficult because people who feel they 'ought' to volunteer for or be asked to perform the task may be quite unfitted to do so. 'How unfitted? Surely any fool can feed a few waxbills for a week?' I can imagine the reader thus mentally responding. It is not, however, a matter of intelligence or the ease or difficulty of the task but of the person's attitude towards birds. If the prospective stand-in *likes* birds and feels sympathetically towards them, then, given willingness and ability to read the written instructions left for them there is no need to worry as to their IQ or ornithological knowledge.

On the other hand, many people do not feel any sympathy with birds or other non-human creatures and, in their hearts, they feel that care and food are wasted on them. Some bird-keepers may delude themselves into thinking that such people will, nevertheless, look after the birds properly because they love, are indebted to or are being paid well to do so by the aviculturist himself. But, in most cases such people will not and *can not* care properly for the birds temporarily in their charge. They may honestly intend to care for the birds for love of their owner, for payment or for some other reason. But they will not. No one can give of what they do not have. Similarly, few people can really be in doubt as to which of their friends have this feeling for living birds and which do not. If one has to go away one should make every endeavour to see that one's birds are being cared for in one's absence by a person of the first type.

Cages, and letting birds out of them

No one who can keep his birds in a suitable birdroom or aviary is likely to want to keep them in cages for any length of time, but sometimes it may be necessary temporarily to do so, and some people may be so unfortunate as to have so little space available that they are forced to.

The late Duke of Bedford (the avicultural one) wrote that most parrot cages on sale seemed to be deliberately designed to cause the maximum discomfort to the bird and the maximum inconvenience to its owner. The same is certainly true of very many of the cages for small birds, especially those for Budgerigars, that are now commercially available. Apart from their being too small (especially for the Budgerigars for which many of them are intended) and too cluttered up with various gadgets, the smaller estrildids can get through the wires of most 'ordinary' bird cages. The unsuitability of cages of glass or glass substitutes will be obvious to anyone with any knowledge of birds. Those who are accomplished 'do-it-yourselfers' will, no doubt, wish to make themselves any cages they need. For those who, like myself, are not, I recommend trying to get in touch with a professional or amateur cage-maker and getting him to make you some cages. These should be as large as possible. Their size and shape can depend on where in the room they have to be fitted. For example, normally one would make cages about twice as long as wide or high but to fit a recess near the window of one of my rooms I had a cage made that is about two and a half times as high as it is long or deep.

Have the cage made not with the usual very shallow floor tray but with a deep tray with sides about 3 inches (7 cm) deep, so that clods of grass etc. can be put on it and the tray still easily pulled out. As well as the usual small doors into which one can just get one's arm, most of the front should consist of another door which can be easily opened or closed and easily fastened open. Ideally cages should be so situated that by opening the window of the room at appropriate times part (but not all) of the interior of the cage will be in direct sunlight. Cages may be all wire or with wire fronts only or any intermediate condition. It is, however, important that they are well lit and, unless the birds are quite tame, the far side from that on which the owner or any other person in the room will usually be, should either be of some opaque substance or close to the wall. If the far wall is of wire or other transparent material, the birds may try to fly through it and possibly injure themselves, if they can see an open area beyond it, if alarmed by a person on the near side.

Cages should be fitted up, not cluttered up, with perches of natural twigs and branches of various thicknesses and/or with reeds, tussocks of rank grass etc. according to species. If it is necessary to have lights and human activity in the room after dark, then a cloth should be fixed so that it can be lowered over the cage without disturbing the inmates while it is still dark, before the lights are put on. If sources of fairly concentrated heat or light need to be provided in or close to the cage, this should be at one end of it so that the birds can retire to a less brightly lit or warmly heated part if they wish. Let the birds quite alone for a few hours after they are first put in the cage so that they can get used to it, rest, feed and drink, before anyone uses the room. If one is keeping them, say, in one's bedroom, one will find at first that they show alarm at one's movements about the place. If, however, one *takes no notice of their reactions*, they very quickly become habituated. Unless they are showing social reactions to humans (usually this will only be birds that were hand-reared) trying to re-assure frightened birds by approaching and talking or whistling to them may have the opposite effect.

If the birds have to be kept in cages permanently or for any length of time, one will naturally want to allow them at least fairly frequent periods at liberty in the room or in two or more adjacent rooms as the case may be. Apart from enabling them to take more exercise than they could in a cage and giving them more to interest them, this often enables some of their behaviour patterns to be shown more fully than would be possible in a cage. It also, in my experience, may result in birds nesting (often siting the nest inside the cage) that would not, or at least did not do so as long as they were permanently confined. As it is not desirable or possible to have the birds free in the room the whole time (else one has it as a birdroom and no need for cages from the first), the aim will usually be to be able to let the birds out at convenient times but have them go back into the cage without trouble.

I have found the following method successful with cordon-bleus, Dark Firefinches, Java Sparrows and some non-estrildid species such as the domestic Canary. The birds should be thoroughly used to the cage and its surroundings, so far as they have been able to see these from inside. This can best be judged by their behaviour, but, in general, one can estimate that they should have been in the cage about five or six days before releasing them. Care must be taken that all possibilities of fatal accidents have been fore-seen and prevented. No open windows, unguarded fires, vessels of water, tangles of thread etc. Estrildids like most (but not all) birds will quickly learn that window glass cannot be flown through, but the first time it is advisable to screen the glass with twigs or place many perches crossing in front of it so that the birds are less likely to fly hard against it before they learn its nature. If the glass is screened with netting, curtain or similar material (not really advisable), it is important to make many sizeable holes in it so that the birds cannot be trapped behind it. One or more *conspicuous* perches must be fixed so that they project well into the room, but their ends are inside or adjacent to the open part of the cage, the *large* front door of which should be opened and fastened back. There should be food and water conspicuously just inside the cage or even fastened (a millet spray if the birds like spray millet) to one of the perches that project outside.

Though no doubt interesting it is not a good idea to stay and watch the birds come out. Unless one is a rather phlegmatic person one is bound to get nervy and worried at the apparent dis-orientation of a bird or impatient at its hesitation, and even if one's nervousness does not 'rub off on them', the birds are likely to be made anxious by one's attention being fixed on them. Much better to open the cage door after having made all ready, at about three or four hours before dusk, and then resolutely leave the room and *do not go back to it until it is quite dark*. In all probability one will find the birds roosting on the curtain rail or somewhere else in the room. With the aid of a torch catch them gently, put on the light, put them back in their cage, leave the light on for half an hour or so, to give them time to feed (in case they have not been back and fed after first leaving the cage), then dim the light (or partly cover the cage) to let the birds settle down. After this has been done two or three times the birds will probably be found to have gone back to roost in the cage of their own accord. If they have not, the next time touch or push them so that they take fright and fly from their roosting perches in the dark before catching them and returning them to the (im-mediately lighted) cage. This, done a couple of times, will usually result in them going back into the cage to roost of their own accord. If it does not then you will just have to resign yourself to picking them from their roosts and putting them back each time, which is very little trouble. In such case lightly rub your hands with flour (brushing it off before catching your birds) as otherwise contact (even brief and light as it should be if you place your hand round the roosting bird to gently enclose it) with even an apparently unsweaty palm and fingers will sooner or later mar the birds' plumage.

Once you are sure that the birds are coming back to the cage for food, you can of course, if due precautions about windows etc. have been taken, let them out at any time of day. There will then also be no harm in your using the room. You will find that, being able to get further from you and, according to their specific habits, take refuge at a higher level or behind or under furniture, has a calming effect on them. In general, other things being equal, the larger the enclosure in which captive birds are kept, the tamer they become. Statements to the contrary are usually based on the mistaken notion that inability to get far away, poor health or a state of extreme hunger are synonymous with tameness.

KNOCK BEFORE YOU ENTER When birds are kept, whether free or in cages, inside a room with a solid door so that they cannot see their owner's approach, they are often much alarmed when he enters. The remedy for this is always to warn the birds when you are about to open the door and come among them. All that is needed is always to whistle the same phrase, rattle the door handle or make some other noise, *that one does not make in other contexts*, a moment before one enters. The birds very soon learn, are prepared for one's entry and, even if a little alarmed are not surprised or startled by it. If I remember rightly both Gedney and Dr Russ adopted this plan and no doubt many other aviculturists, like myself, thought of it inde-pendently but it is not a point I have seen mentioned in modern books on aviculture.

CLAW GROWTH AND CATCHING These two subjects come easily under one heading as to clip their claws is likely to be the commonest reason that captive birds have to be caught at otherwise awkward or unsuitable times. Some estrildids in captivity, even when in apparently good health, suffer from excessive growth of the claws. This trouble is usual with species which, in the wild state, perch a lot on abrasive reed- and grass-stems, and is usually assumed, probably rightly but I know of no scientific proof, to be due to lack of such abrasive perches. Many of the munias or mannikins, the Avadavat and the Goldbreast are among the species usually affected. If, as happens all too often in zoos and public aviaries, the bird's owner does nothing, the overgrowth of the claws reaches a state where the bird cannot perch or scratch itself without discomfort or difficulty. It is also very liable to injure itself through getting its overgrown claws caught up in wire netting or among twigs. Before this stage is reached it is likely to have had difficulty in copulating and been liable to puncture its eggs accidentally. If some (not all) of the perches are of abrasive materials this may possibly prevent or lessen the trouble but as a rule the only remedy is to catch the bird and clip its claws as soon as they are seen to be overlong and/or beginning to cause the bird *slight* difficulty. If the bird is held carefully in a good light it is very easy to clip the claws with a pair of sharp scissors, taking care of course not to cut the 'quick', that is the blood vessel inside the basal half (approximately) of the claw. If the foot is held to a good light this blood vessel is easy to see and one can cut clear of it.

Ideally one should catch up the bird for this or any other purpose with the greatest possible speed and without disturbing others housed with it. In practice this is not usually possible with estrildids or with other small seed-eating species which cannot usually be quickly lured into a trap or to the hand by a proffered titbit. Picking them by hand off their roosting place after dark is only feasible in the case of a pair or two that are at large in a furnished room, as previously described. If attempted in a birdroom or aviary it will cause a general panic with distress and possible injury. One method sometimes recommended is to spray the bird one wants to catch with water, from a handspray, until it is too wet to fly properly and can be easily and quickly caught. I think this method would only work if the birds were thoroughly used to seeing one, spray in hand, squirting water in their vicinity. When I tried it, I found the sight of the spray in use scared the birds at least as much as the sight of a net, the bird I wanted to catch quickly and repeatedly avoided the spray of water and I succeeded only in soaking the walls of the room and myself. So I went back to the 'bad old' method of catching the birds in a butterfly net with well-padded rims. This does cause alarm or even panic but so long as the birds never see you with the net (or anything the least like it) except on the occasions when you have to catch one or more of them, they do not show such fear of you *without* the net, even only a few minutes after they have panicked at the sight of you with it. Even the caught birds very soon recover. I have, in emergencies, caught and clipped the claws of Goldbreasts and Avadavats that were building or

incubating and it has not caused the birds to discontinue either activity.

REFERENCES

Gedney, C. W. (circa 1890?) *Foreign cage birds*. L. Upcott-Gill, London.
Immelmann, K., Steinbacher, J. and Wolters, H. E. 1963. *Vögel in Käfig und Voliere: Prachtfinken*: 16–24.
Kühner, P. 1967. Zur Ernährung der Prachtfinken. *Gefiederte Welt* **1967**: 175–176.
Nicolai, J. 1965a. *Vogelhaltung – Vogelpflege*. Kosmos, Stuttgart.
Nicolai, J. 1965b. *Käfig- und Volierenvögel*. Kosmos, Stuttgart.
Russ, K. 1879. *Die fremländischen Stubenvögel*, vol. 1. Hannover.
Schernekau, J. 1979. Nochmals zur Salzfütterung bei Papageien. *Gefiederte Welt* **1979**: 39
Schmidt, U. 1977. Erfahrungen mit Federfressen. *Gefiederte Welt* **1977**: 48–51.

Fostering

It is a common but fortunately not universal avicultural practice to rear valuable or difficult estrildid species more easily or in greater numbers than would otherwise be possible by giving their eggs or young to Bengalese Finches or, less often, to Zebra Finches to hatch and/or rear. I have no practical experience of this although I have had a few cases in which birds were accidentally reared by other species through mixed clutches of eggs or pairs of male birds taking over nests with eggs from their parents.

With such species as Gouldian Finches fostering enables much larger numbers of young to be produced and in other instances a handy pair of Bengalise may prevent the loss of a clutch of deserted eggs or deserted nestlings. There are, however, drawbacks and dangers. Especially that strains of birds with defective parental instincts may be thus perpetuated. See also the next section on 'Domestication, and that on imprinting in the section on display and social behaviour.

Domestication and perpetuation of captive stocks

These two subjects seem best discussed in the same section because I believe that long-term maintenance of captive stocks of any estrildid is unlikely to be achieved unless some degree of domestication precedes it.

The *Concise Oxford Dictionary* defines the word 'domestic' as 'tame, kept by or living with man' and 'domesticate' as 'to naturalize, to make fond of home, to bring under human control, to tame'. These definitions evidently mean that to a strict grammarian the naturalized Starlings flying free in Australia and North America, a wild hawk that has been caught and trained for falconry, or a Cordon-bleu that has been caught wild in Africa and put in a birdroom can be termed domestic. In ordinary speech the word is usually applied to birds or other creatures that are kept and bred by man and whose numbers have been maintained generation after generation without the need to introduce 'fresh blood' by means of wild-caught individuals. I have used the terms 'domestic' and 'domesticated' in this sense only in this book. Among estrildids the Bengalese Finch, the Zebra Finch and the Java Sparrow can be considered domesticated; the Gouldian Finch and the Long-tailed Grassfinch seem to be on the way to that state.

Nicolai (1959), in discussing the Canary, which he believes to be an exception, stated that as a general rule species of birds that have been domesticated are those members of their groups which are both most adaptable under wild conditions *and* easiest to keep and breed in captivity. The second of these attributes is certainly nearly always the case, at least to the extent that the wild forms of domesticated species are among the most easily bred in captivity of their genus but I doubt if the first always is. I should think for example that under free conditions the Pheasant, *Phasianus colchicus* and the Wood Pigeon, *Columba palumbus* are likely to be rather more, not less adaptable than the Red Jungle Fowl, *Gallus gallus*, and the Rock Pigeon, *Columba livia*. What we do find, as I discussed more fully (Goodwin, 1965) in a book now out of print, is that all domestic birds with the exception of that very special case the Cormorant, *Phalacrocorax carbo*, are species that can subsist very largely on grain (or other cultivated seeds) or grass. Our domestic cage birds (and the Domestic Pigeon) are all species that can rear their young without insects or other invertebrates. It is no accident that, out of all the many species of doves and parrots that have been kept (and sometimes bred) in captivity in past and present centuries, the only four to have been domesticated – the Rock Pigeon (ancestor of all our Domestic and Feral Pigeons), the African Collared Dove, *Streptopelia roseogrisea* (ancestor of the Barbary Dove or Blonde Ringdove and its white form the 'Java Dove'), the Diamond Dove, *Geopelia cuneata*, and the Budgerigar, *Melopsittacus undulatus* – are all naturally species of arid country where they feed mostly on seeds picked up from the ground. The Zebra Finch, the only (as yet) fully domesticated Australian passerine, shares its range and habitat with the Diamond Dove and the Budgerigar and is, like them, a seed-eater. The Java Sparrow and the White-backed Munia are also seed-eaters and (although little studied in the wild) also appear to feed in part on ripe seeds picked up from the ground.

Little is apparently known (see species sections for details and references) of the precise dates when the Java Sparrow and Bengalese Finch were first bred in captivity. The former was probably and the latter certainly domesticated in China. Possibly at some past time the beautiful wild-coloured Java Sparrows may have been sufficiently rare and valuable in China to induce people to breed them systematically. It is perhaps rather more likely that it was the first white or pied mutants to be obtained whose rarity and value stimulated systematic captive breeding and consequent domestication, as the first *domesticated* Java Sparrows to be imported into Europe were white and pied. In both North America and Australia domestic Java Sparrows of the wild 'blue' colour pattern

can now be had as well as white and pied specimens. In Australia all such blue domesticated birds are said (Brown, 1963) to have been derived from (heterozygous) white forebears. Gedney, who visited a Java Sparrow breeding establishment in Japan in the nineteenth century, found that those who ran it believed in the sort of pre-natal influences that, so the Bible tells us, were successfully used by Jacob to increase his heritage. The breeding Java Sparrows there were kept in white cages, with white dishes and perches in white-painted rooms, supposedly to increase the chances of their producing pure white offspring.

In Britain, so far as I am aware, only white and pied *domestic* Java Sparrows have ever been obtainable. Surprisingly they seem never to have been and are not now so widely kept as the more noisy and no more beautiful Zebra Finch or the much less beautiful Bengalese. I think that, owing to climatic or some other adverse factors they have not proved so easy to breed generation after generation as in other lands. About thirty years ago when (in Britain) a pair of wild Java Sparrows were sold relatively cheaply, forty times as much was asked for one domesticated white specimen. Russ, who bred the white form very successfully in his birdroom in the last century, remarked on the high price it then fetched in Germany.

The Bengalese Finch, or rather its wild ancestor, seems an odd species to have been domesticated as it has neither beautiful colours nor an attractive song. Presumably its tameness and the ease with which it could be kept and bred endeared it to its original keepers. The same qualities, especially the way in which (most) Bengalese will court, build nests or tend their young (e.g. Cooper) in full view of a nearby human watcher makes it a favourite of some people despite its plain appearance. Nowadays, and in the recent past, however, the greatest numbers of Bengalese have been and are kept not for any appreciation of their intrinsic virtues but for the purpose of hatching and rearing the young of more costly estrildids, notably the Gouldian Finch.

Much more is known about the history of the Zebra Finch in captivity. It is not certain (Immelmann) when the bird was first imported into Europe. Dr Russ, writing in the late 1870s, says that until a few years before ('bis vor wenigen Jahren') Zebra Finches had only been occasionally obtainable. He waxes enthusiastic over the bird's tameness and beauty and the ease with which it can be kept and bred although he admits that it has an unpleasing voice and lacks the grace and agility of the African waxbills. Dr Gedney, writing I think at about the same period (his book has no publishing date), clearly implies that the demand for the Zebra Finch in England exceeded the supply as he says that dealers had then recently taken to calling the Goldbreast 'Zebra Waxbill' in the hope that gullible buyers would confuse it with the more valuable and rare Zebra Finch.

Thus it seems that a combination of factors was responsible for the popularity of the Zebra Finch: its attractive appearance, its hardiness, the ease with which it could be bred in captivity and the fact that, at least in the early years of its captivity, surplus home-bred birds could be readily sold at a profit. The situation was (and for that matter was until very recently) different with most of the usually imported African and Asian estrildids which, besides being less easy to breed in captivity, were available in numbers at such rather horrifyingly low prices that there could be no question of selling home-bred birds at a price that would cover the cost of rearing them, much less show a monetary profit. Apart from its feeding habits predisposing it to domestication, the Zebra Finch in its wild state often habitually drinks water very heavily contaminated by the droppings of its own species and of other birds (pers. obs.). It is probable therefore that it is naturally more resistant to diseases that can be spread in this way than are some other species, and this would also have pre-adapted it to cope with one 'occupational hazard' of captivity.

A common feature of domestic birds (with some exceptions which I shall mention) is that they show strong and efficient parental behaviour. They are not merely, like so many species, willing to *begin* nesting in captivity but, 'given half a chance,' will bring the attempt to a successful conclusion. The reason is, of course, that there has been intense selection for individuals that would *successfully* rear young under the conditions imposed by man. Among estrildids the long-domesticated Bengalese Finch is an extreme example of this, as, in another family, is the Barbary Dove, both species which were (and to a large extent still are) kept and bred in small cages for very many generations. It has often been stated that some breeds and strains of the Domestic Fowl have lost their parental behaviour through being bred for egg production. This may be the case (though I have seen no proof) with the battery birds now kept in the more technically 'advanced' parts of the world but it was certainly *not* true of Domestic Fowls in England at least up to the late 1940s, nor is it of those kept in many parts of the world, including some of the remoter parts of Britain, today. On the contrary, due doubtless to countless generations of intense if unde-liberate selection for parental behaviour, the Domestic Hen, alone among birds so far as I am aware, would not only 'go broody', that is indulge in incubation behaviour, even on an empty nest but even 'stay broody' and resume incubation after being removed from her home and placed upon eggs in completely strange surroundings. Certainly there were so-called 'non-sitting breeds' – Minorcas, Leghorns and other breeds deriving originally from the Mediterraenean areas – which would not usually do this but even most of them *would* go broody if allowed to accumulate a clutch of eggs.

Where, however, man has been able to solve any problems of parental neglect by fostering eggs, then we do find domestic forms with reduced or defective parental behaviour. This commonly obtains in domesticated ducks of Mallard origin, it having been the custom for many hundreds of years to place duck eggs under Domestic

Fowls or (in the far East) to hatch them by artificial heat. More recently, of course, both Duck and Fowl eggs have usually been hatched in incubators in the West too. Egypt has always been instanced, incidentally, as a country where Domestic Fowls' eggs were habitually hatched in crude but effective incubators but, though this was true, I found during my time there in the Second World War, that the use of broody hens also for this purpose was common and widespread. Where particular strains or breeds of Domestic Fowls, Canaries or Pigeons have been highly valued it has often been the practice to 'maximise' their production by fostering their eggs under less valuable conspecifics. This seems in some cases to have already led to deterioration of parental instincts in the 'valuable' kinds but this is difficult to evaluate as the artifical 'points' for which show specimens of many breeds are selected are in fact deformities that in some cases may and in others are known to make effective parental behaviour difficult or impossible.

Those who make a practice of farming out the eggs of their Gouldian Finches or other valuable estrildids to the care of Bengalese Finches should therefore realise that apart from the question of imprinting (discussed in the section on display and social behaviour) they may perpetuate defective parental behaviour in this way. Some will think, and some but rather fewer will argue that the greater number of, say, Gouldian Finches that can be produced by this method more than outweighs its drawbacks. It is a fair and in some ways reasonable argument. After all Domestic Ducks have been per-petuated for at least about two thousand years during which most of them hatched under Domestic Fowls; anyone who can afford to buy and keep Gouldian Finches is going to have no difficulty in obtaining and maintaining some Bengalese Finches to foster them. My own opinion is that it would be better to concentrate on trying to perpetuate only those Gouldian Finches which *will* hatch and rear their own young in captivity. The ideal ought to be to produce Gouldian Finches that will rear young in captivity as freely and successfully as the Bengalese do, an aim that is not likely to be achieved if every egg laid by behaviourally defective parents is fostered out. I must admit, however, that this opinion is based largely on the interest and pleasure which I obtain from observing any birds I keep perform their complete breeding cycle and some may consider these as trifling or sentimental reasons. I will say no more on this subject except to point out that those breeders who believe in letting their Gouldian (or other) Finches rear their own young yet cannot resist keeping some Bengalese to 'save' deserted or neglected eggs or young are also selecting *against* effective parental behaviour in their birds. Because while one pair of 'naturally' breeding Gouldian Finches are hatching and rearing one brood, a pair that will not sit on their eggs will have laid two or three, perhaps even four clutches of eggs. So it is obvious which parental type will be 'selected' for.

If one excepts domestic poultry and such other birds as may be bred for purely commercial purposes, it is, I think, correct to say that there are three main reasons why people keep birds. I propose to define and discuss them briefly here.

Firstly, the one now considered most respectable in the eyes of contemporary arbiters of morality in such matters, is the keeping and breeding of rare or endangered species for conservational reasons. The aim is to perpetuate captive stocks and disseminate them as widely as possible in order that even if the wild birds die out their species will not, and/or to produce captive stocks which can be re-introduced to parts of their natural range that are now lacking or depleted of wild birds of the species. Sometimes the idea of introducing stocks to *new* prospective home-lands is also mooted but this is apt to engender controversy among the conservationists themselves. So far as I am aware the Hawaiin Goose, *Branta sandvicensis*, is the only species in which the first two of the above aims seem to have been largely achieved although devoted work to this end is currently in progress with others. So far as estrildids are concerned there seems to be no evidence that any species *that is commonly and successfully bred in confinement* is in danger of extinction in the wild. A few species are very local and may possibly be in danger but, on present evidence, I doubt if it would be justifiable on conservational grounds to catch numbers of them for captive breeding programmes.

Secondly, there are those people who, for one reason or another, are enchanted by the natural beauty and interest of the estrildids (or other birds) which they keep and perpetuate for the pleasure they obtain from them. This pleasure may be scientific – making a study of the birds, aesthetic appreciation of their beauty, a sentimental attachment to them or a mixture of all three. Whichever it is, the keeper is likely to wish to maintain stocks of the species as close to the wild type as possible. If this is not kept in mind as a desirable aim (and sometimes even if it is) there may well be slight divergences in coloration and size (I am not now talking about colour mutations) from the original. There will certainly be some minor behavioural differences linked with selection for those birds which proved most adaptable to captivity. This latter is not, I think, to be deprecated as it may well be an essential pre-requisite of establishing reasonably large and successful captive stocks. I am, of course, here talking about abundant species where there is no question of any need or moral obligation to re-introduce captive stock to the wild. It might, however, be mentioned, since the contrary has been often stated or implied, that, provided there has been neither deliberate selection for abnormal characters nor breeding from sickly individuals because of the value (whether monetary or otherwise) of their young, and that large numbers have been bred and maintained, even long-domesticated stocks of some birds and mammals have very successfully 'gone wild.' Feral Pigeons almost throughout the world and the feral Fowls and feral Guinea-fowls of many tropical and subtropical islands are examples.

It is not known for certain whether white, pied, dilute-coloured and other mutations occur more often under captive conditions than in the wild. What is certain is that, whereas in the wild any conspicuous freaks tend to be eliminated by predators or other environmental factors, under captive conditions they may be and often are selected *for*. People always hanker after rarities even if, like white Peacocks, they do not compare in beauty with the normal birds. For the most part, and certainly with all the colour mutations of domesticated or wild estrildids in captivity, such colour varieties always involve the loss or partial loss of some marking or pigment (or both) possessed by the normally-coloured bird. So long as, *and only so long as*, good stocks of the normally-coloured forms are maintained, the breeding of colour varieties is not likely to be inimical to the preservation of birds very similar if not always identical to the wild original.

The case is, in my opinion, very different with the third main reason for keeping birds, which is the keeping and/or breeding of birds in order to compete with them at bird shows. People who do this are usually termed 'bird fanciers' in contradistinction to 'aviculturists' although, unfortunately, some people and the media are apt to confuse the two. Quite apart from objections which may be made to the risks to the birds that are sometimes involved in their being 'shown' and the bad impression that shows often give to many lay visitors who wrongly imagine that the birds are permanently kept in the little cages in which they are exhibited, I believe that 'the fancy' and all it stands for is entirely inimical to the interests of all who keep birds for the reasons previously discussed.

This is because the 'standards of excellence' on which the birds are judged at shows are arbitrarily drawn up by fanciers for fanciers. Initially, where wild species are concerned, the show standards usually merely mean that a bird a little larger than average will win against one of normal size if both are equally bright and healthy. Since the show standard also demands that the bird be in good plumage and general condition, it is at this stage often seen, even by non-fanciers, as encouraging good aviculture by penalising degenerately small or dull-coloured specimens. If show standards remained static at that point little harm (from the point of view of those who like natural-looking birds) would be done but they do not. Writing, approvingly, of the show standards for the Bengalese Finch, Buchan all too truly says: 'It is generally accepted [by fanciers] that the ideal should be just out of reach and consequently . . . each one [of a class of birds at a show] will fall short of the ideal in one respect or another'. This outlook is, of course, responsible for the way in which show standards become ever more exaggerated. In the Zebra Finch and Bengalese Finch this has only led, so far, to a demand for birds a little larger and heavier in build than the wild prototypes. The probable future development for these two species can, unfortunately, be deduced from what has happened (at least in Britain) to the Budgerigar. From being a dainty, lively, active, easily-kept and exceptionally small parakeet which charmed by its diminutive size as well as its other qualities, it has, through the Budgerigar Fancy's standards demanding what fanciers evidently considered 'bigger and better' specimens, led to the modern 'British' Budgerigar having become a much larger bird with a bulging head. It is less active and hardy and, to all who do not subscribe to the fancier's evaluation, a much less attractive bird.

In the case of the Domestic Pigeon and the Canary, birds still approximating to the wild type in shape were being bred in countless thousands throughout the world, even though more divergent breeds have been developed, before showing on a big scale began in the latter half of the last century so the results were less all-embracing. Breeds were 'improved' out of all recognition, for example the Norwich Canary was changed from a neat, active bird of a naturally (or at least genetically) rich golden-yellow hue, to a huge, heavy, beetle-browed parody of its former self which needed to be colour-fed with pepper to obtain the orange colour now in demand. However, different breeds were bred to different standards and, though condemned as 'worthless' by fanciers, so many 'common pigeons' and 'ordinary song canaries' remained that it was, and still is, possible to obtain or breed specimens approximating somewhat to the wild ancestral types if not facsimiles of them. This is not possible where the numbers of a species in captivity are smaller, its value is judged on how closely it approximates to show standards and where there is only a 'single standard' for it. It will probably not be possible, since the export of wild birds from Australia is now forbidden, ever to see again in our aviaries Budgerigars of the type that enchanted in our youth those of us who are no longer young. I therefore feel strongly that all non-fanciers who keep estrildids, even if only Zebra Finches or Bengalese, should not only refrain from showing their birds or attempting to breed them 'to show standards' but should endeavour to persuade others to set more value on birds that closely resemble the wild ancestral forms than on those which have been magnified or monstrified to conform to the fanciers' whims.

Although in theory it would be perfectly feasible, I am not sure whether in practice it will prove possible to maintain viable stocks of as-yet undomesticated estrildids in captivity for an indefinite period if, as may well happen, the African and Asian countries follow Australia's example in forbidding their export. Very many species have been bred successfully in many countries, especially in Germany where at least one large and well-equipped research institute was for many years (and perhaps still is) largely devoted to the breeding and study of these birds. There are, however, some adverse factors that might well prevail against long-term success in this sphere. Both individuals and institutions, often for justifiable reasons, are apt to suffer from (or rejoice in) the 'off with the old

love and on with the new love' syndrome, which may result in stock being dispersed into less competent hands. Old age, ill health and other personal disasters may likewise bring a captive breeding stock of some estrildid (or other bird) quickly to an end. The very wealth of species available makes it more difficult for the successful breeders of a particular species to find others equally interested in it to whom they can give surplus stock. One must not, however, be too pessimistic. If, as I think likely to happen, the number of species available becomes reduced in the next ten years or less, this might well make more likely widespread keeping, of at least some of those species still available.

In the past some individuals have succeeded against severe odds. Teague in England and Rübner on the continent (I presume in Germany) managed to maintain stocks of, respectively, Gouldian Finches and Blue-headed Parrot-finches right through the difficult war years when, in general, most *wild* tropical species in captivity died out through lack of suitable food, warmth or care. I think, all the same, that unless a species is being bred by at least several different people and preferably in several different countries also, the chances of maintaining stocks of it are slight. In some species of estrildids, as of other birds, of which the extinct Passenger Pigeon was perhaps the most notable example, a species of which wild-caught individuals, and sometimes the first few generations of captive-bred birds, breed freely and apparently successfully in captivity, may become largely or wholly infertile in later generations and so die out. It is not known why this happens in some species and yet not, obviously, in others, which have become domesticated. Inbreeding is certainly not always the cause. Rübner's parrot-finches were necessarily very inbred but, after thirty years, they were healthy, hardy and as fertile as their wild-caught ancestors.

REFERENCES

Brown, R. E. B. 1963. Java Sparrows. *Avicult. Mag.* **69**: 329.

Buchan, J. 1976. *The Bengalese Finch.* Published by Isles d'Avon, Bristol.

Cooper, G. R. 1973. Bengalese for me. *Foreign Birds* **39**: 150.

Gedney, C. W. (circa 1890?). *Foreign cage birds.* L. Upcott Gill, London.

Goodwin, D. 1965. *Domestic birds.* London.

Immelmann, K. 1973. *Der Zebrafink.* Wittenberg-Lutherstadt.

Nicolai, J. 1959. Verhaltensstudien an einigen afrikanischen und paläarktischen Girlitzen. *Zool. Jb.* **87**: 317–362.

Rubner, I. H. 1961. Dreifarbige Papagaiamadinen. *Gefiederte Welt* **1961**: 75–76.

Russ, K. 1879. *Die fremlandischen Stubenvögel,* vol. 1. Hannover.

Teague, P. W. 1946. Further notes on the breeding of Gouldian Finches. *Avicult. Magazine* **53**: 12–13.

6 The estrildid finches

The ant-peckers

The ant-peckers, *Parmoptila*, look more like warblers than estrildids. They were variously placed with the warblers, tits and flower-peckers until Chapin, in a masterly paper on relationships of weavers and estrildids (then both included in the same family), argued conclusively that the mouth pattern of their nestlings and their nesting habits showed them to be aberrant estrildids.

The ant-peckers have a slender bill with the area round the nostrils depressed, a slightly curved culmen ridge and an arched central part of the cutting edge of the upper mandible. Unlike as this bill is to those of more typical estrildids, the gap is largely bridged, as Chapin points out and illustrates, by the bills of the negro-finches, *Nigrita*. A further peculiarity of *Parmoptila* is its brush tongue. This has been described (Moreau *et al.*) as follows: 'its tip is narrowly cleft to about one third of the length of the tongue and both the edges and the two tips are thickly set with short fimbriae'.

Brush tongues are characteristic of birds that feed in part on nectar or, and perhaps more particularly, on pollen. The ant-peckers are not known to take such food. So far as is known they are insectivorous and feed largely on ants. Apparently they take the worker ants which, unlike the sporadically appearing winged sexual forms, are eaten by very few birds. It would be interesting to know whether the fimbriated tongue is of use in feeding on ants or, if not, what its function is.

In their coloration the ant-peckers are not very similar to any other estrildid species to my eyes although others (e.g. Delacour) have seen a resemblance in colour pattern to that of the Brown Twinspot. Their bill shape and their nests suggest that, as Chapin suggested, their closest relative may be the negro-finches.

All forms of *Parmoptila* have been treated by some workers (e.g. Delacour, Immelmann *et al.*, Traylor) as races of a single species, *P. woodhousei*. The two main groups are allopatric but specimens of each have been taken at localities fairly near to each other on the Middle Congo, suggesting that their ranges may possibly overlap (Hall & Moreau). They also show plumage differences that might serve as isolating mechanisms. I provisionally, therefore, follow Hall & Moreau in recognising two species.

REFERENCES
Chapin, J. P. 1917. The classification of the weaver-birds. *Bull. Amer. Mus. Nat. Hist.* **37**: 243–280.
Delacour, J. 1943. A revision of the Subfamily Estrildinae of the Family Ploceidae. *Zoologica, New York Zoological Society*, **28**: 69–86.
Hall, B. P. & Moreau, R. E. 1970: *An atlas of speciation in African passerine birds.* British Museum (Natural History) London.
Immelmann, K., Steinbacher J. & Wolters, H. E. 1975. *Vögel in Käfig und Voliere: Prachtfinken*: 524–525.
Traylor, M. A. 1968. In *Peters' check-list of birds of the world.* Museum of Comparative Zoology, Cambridge, Mass.

Ant-pecker *Parmoptila woodhousei*

Cassin, 1859, *Proc. Acad. Nat. Sci. Philadelphia* 11, p. 40.

DESCRIPTION Between Spice Finch and Avadavat in size but very different from either in appearance owing to its slender, warbler-like bill. It has a brush tongue (Moreau *et al.*). The wings are rather rounded and the tail rather short. Forehead dark brownish red. Rest of upperparts a slightly reddish and rather dark earth brown with paler shafts and reddish buff tips to the feathers on crown, nape and wing coverts and, to a very slight extent, elsewhere. Wing quills and tail, except for fringes of outer webs, without the rufous tinge. Under wing coverts golden-buff with obscure darker markings. Lores dusky. Rest of face, including ear coverts and throat, chestnut. Rest of underparts pale buff, more or less spotted with drab (Most individual feathers on the breast have olive drab, interrupted cross bars and dusky fringes; lower down the cross bars mostly become complete; on the belly and under tail coverts the dark markings are sparser and more crescentic; on the flanks the feathers are basically dark with buff cross bars and/or crescentic markings). Irides dark brown to brownish red. Bill blackish. Legs and feet flesh-coloured to pale greyish brown.

The female lacks the brownish red forehead but her forehead feathers are conspicuously tipped with reddish buff. The juvenile is duller brown above and dark reddish buff with obscure dusky cross-bars below, except for the tibial feathers and under tail coverts, which have a pale buff ground colour. The nestling has white tubercles in the gape (Chapin). Probably its mouth markings are similar or identical to those of *P. rubrifons jamesoni* (q.v.).

The above description is of nominate *P. w. woodhousei* from south-east Nigeria, the Camerouns, Gabon and western Congo. *P. w. ansorgei*, from northern Angola is slightly larger and less reddish, more olive, in tone on the upperparts.

See plate 1, facing p. 96.

FIELD CHARACTERS Small warbler-like bird with chestnut throat, dull brown upperparts and pale, dark-spotted underparts. Male also has reddish forehead.

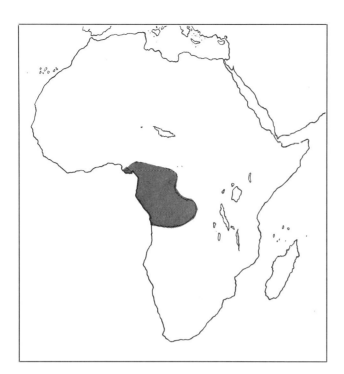

DISTRIBUTION AND HABITAT Tropical Africa in south-eastern Nigeria, southern Camerouns, Gabon, western Kasai and adjoining Leopoldville province of Zaire, north-western and north-eastern Angola. Inhabits forest undergrowth, secondary forest, forest edge and bush- or shrub-grown open areas.

FEEDING AND GENERAL HABITS So far as known feeds largely on ants although also taking some other small insects (Bates, Bannerman, Chapin). In the wild small species of ants seem to be taken but six captive birds (in Europe) preferred Wood Ants, *Formica rufa*, to the smaller meadow ants, *Lasius* spp. (Mitsch). These captives also ate greenfly, spiders, small moths, small beetles and some other insects but refused house flies, fruitflies and mealworms. They would eat about 30 ants in a couple of minutes when hungry. While ants could be supplied fairly frequently (for seven months) they kept in apparently good health but soon died when live ants were no longer available.

In the wild sometimes, possibly usually, in small parties but the captive birds were not at all sociable towards one another, or towards other estrildids kept with them, although they did not fight. They needed a temperature of 24°C; at 22° they showed clear signs of distress by their fluffed out plumage and apathy. They roosted singly on branches, never in boxes, baskets or the nests of weavers or estrildids.

NESTING The large, roundish nest, up to 20 cm (8 in.) in depth, is (always?) placed in the fork of a branch of a tree or shrub. It is built of grass and dead leaves, sometimes with a little moss on the outside, and lined with fine fibres from plantain leaves (Chapin, and other authors whose accounts appear to derive from his). The side entrance

sometimes has a porch over it (Bannerman). Sometimes nets are made almost entirely of fibres (Bates). Eggs 3 or 4 (Chapin).

VOICE Apparently unrecorded so presumably the species is rather quiet.

DISPLAY AND SOCIAL BEHAVIOUR No information.

OTHER NAMES Flower-pecker Weaver-finch

REFERENCES
Bannerman, D. A. 1953. *The birds of West and Equatorial Africa.* Oliver and Boyd, Edinburgh, London
Bates, G. L. 1930. *Handbook of the birds of West Africa.* John Bale, Sons and Danielsson Ltd. London.
Chapin, J. P. 1954. The birds of the Belgian Congo. *Bull. Amer. Mus. Nat. Hist.* **75B**.
Mitsch, H. 1973. Der Ameisenpicker – ein Aussenseiter under den Prachtfinken. *Gefiederte Welt* **1973**: 35–37.
Moreau, R. E., Perrins, M & Hughes, J. T. 1969. Tongues of the Zosteropidae (White-eyes). *Ardea* **47**: 29–47.

Red-fronted Ant-pecker   *Parmoptila rubrifrons*

Pholidornis rubrifrons Sharpe and Ussher, 1872, *Ibis*, p. 182.

DESCRIPTION As previous form, *P. woodhousei*, with which it may be conspecific, except as follows:

Forehead and forecrown bright red. Face, sides of neck, hind crown and nape olive-brown with pale buff shaft streaks and feather tips, giving a spotted effect. Upper parts olive-brown with buff tips to the wing coverts. Top of throat ('chin') buffish; rest of underparts chestnut. Female like female of *P. woodhousei* but with a spotted, not chestnut, throat. The ground colour of the feathers of the underparts tends to be paler, almost white, and the dark markings on the feathers to be smaller, so that the female's underparts appear a little paler and more brightly spotted than in most females of *P. woodhousei*. Juvenile probably like that of *P. woodhousei*, mouth markings of nestlings almost certainly identical with those of the following race.

The above description is of nominate *P. rubrifrons* from Liberia and Ghana (Gold Coast), *P.r. jamesoni*, from the forests of the upper and middle Congo differs in the male having his face and chin chestnut like the rest of his underparts. Irides red or brownish red and legs and feet yellowish buff. These soft part colours probably apply to nominate *rubrifrons* too but are based on Chapin's description of *jamesoni*. The nestlings have three small yellowish tubercles at each side of the gape, set in black skin. Their mouths are pale yellow with five black spots on the palate and a black crescent on the inside of the lower mandible, under the tongue.

FIELD CHARACTERS Small, warbler-like bird, dull brown above with speckled (*rubrifrons*) or chestnut (*jamesoni*) face, *bright* red forehead and chestnut breast and underparts. Female olive brown above and pale, spotted or speckled darker, below.

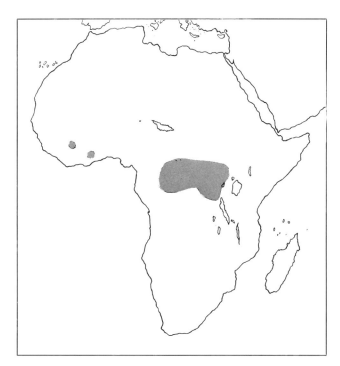

DISTRIBUTION AND HABITAT Denkera, Ghana; Mount Nimba, Liberia and the Congo Forest from Lukeola and Ubangi River east to the forest of western Uganda. Inhabits forest and scrub at the forest edge (Chapin).

FEEDING AND GENERAL HABITS Known to feed on ants, their larvae and pupae, and also on other insects (Chapin). Usually in pairs or family parties. Once an adult male was collected from a mixed bird party. When seeking food examines both live foliage and clumps of dead leaves. Has not been seen on the ground.

NESTING Nest has not apparently been found. It is probably identical to that of the previous form, *P. woodhousei* (q.v.). Specimens in breeding condition have been collected in February, May and September.

All the above information on habits, nesting etc., derives from Chapin's observations on *P. rubrifons jamesoni*.

VOICE No information.

DISPLAY AND SOCIAL BEHAVIOUR No information.

OTHER NAME Red-fronted Flower-pecker Weaver-finch.

REFERENCES
Bates, G. L. 1930. *Handbook of the birds of West Africa*. London
Hall, B. P. & Moreau, R. E. 1970. *An atlas of speciation in African passerine birds*. British Museum (Natural History) London.
Chapin, J. P. 1954. The Birds of the Belgian Congo. *Bull. Amer. Mus. Nat. Hist.* **75B**.

The negro-finches

The negro-finches, *Nigrita*, are a group of four species which differ considerably from other African waxbills and also among themselves. They have rather slender to (one species) very slender bills, which are usually somewhat flattened and expanded around the nostrils. This is, presumably, an adaptation to their feeding habits as they appear to eat mainly small insects and fruit. They are boldly patterned in grey and black; grey and chestnut; or black, white and brown. One species, *N. canicapilla*, has its wings spotted with white. These markings are terminal spots at the apex of the feather, as in the Asiatic Avadavat, *Amandava amandava*, not a pair of spots, one on each side of the rhachis, as in the similar-appearing spotted areas of the twinspots. Nothing appears to be known of the displays of the negro-finches but their nests and more especially the mouth patterns of their nestlings (Steiner) show their estrildid affinities. These nestling mouth patterns and what little else is known of them suggest that their closest relatives are probably such genera as *Cryptospiza Pyrenestes* and the even more atypical *Parmoptila* (Steiner).

The Grey-headed Negro-finch, *N. canicapilla*, and the Pale-fronted Negro-finch, *N. luteifrons*, are widely sympatric. They are similar in colour but differ in size, in the colour of their foreheads and in the white-spotted wings of *N. canicapilla*. These latter characters probably serve as species recognition marks and it is noticeable that the wing spots are much reduced in one form of *N. canicapilla*, the western race *N.c. emiliae*, whose range nowhere overlaps that of *N. luteifrons*.

The Chestnut-breasted Negro-finch, *N. bicolor*, is a slightly slimmer and slightly longer-tailed bird and differs from its congeners in its dark chestnut face and underparts. Its range widely overlaps those of the other three species. The White-breasted Negro-finch, *N. fusconota*, appears even more distinct from all its congeners than any of them is to the others. It has a much more slender bill and a longer and much more strongly graduated tail. Wolters places it in the subgenus *Percnopis*. However, although a very distinct form its affinities seem undoubtedly with the other *Nigrita* species.

Their allopatry and specific differences in size and bill shape make it likely that there are well defined ecological differences between the species of *Nigrita*. That so far there is little positive evidence of this merely reflects the comparative lack of information on them.

REFERENCES
Immelmann, K., Steinbacher, J. & Wolters, H. E. 1963. *Vögel in Käfig und Voliere: Prachtfinken:* 59.
Steiner, H. 1960. Klassifikation der Prachtfinken, Spermestidae, auf Grund der Rachenzeichnungen ihrer Nestlinge. *J. Orn.* **101**: 92–112.
Wolters, H. E. 1964. On the relationships and generic limits of African Estrildinae. *Ostrich supplement* **6**: 75–81.

Grey-headed Negro-finch   *Nigrita canicapilla*

Aethiops canicapillus Strickland, 1841, *Proc. Zool. Soc. London*, p. 30.

DESCRIPTION Slightly larger than Peter's Twinspot but with much longer, less rounded wing and long, slender bill, narrow and slightly hooked at the tip, widened and flattened at the base and with curving culmen. Tail rounded. Forehead, face, sides of neck and entire underparts dense black. A white line forms a border between the black forehead, face and neck and the slightly silvery grey crown, nape, and hind neck. Mantle and back a similar grey to the crown. Lower back and rump greyish white, most of the feathers with obscure greyish subterminal bars. Longest upper tail coverts dark grey, fringed whitish, others as rump. Tail black. Wings black with conspicuous white spotting, due to white spots at the tips of the coverts and inner secondaries. Under wing coverts mainly silvery white. Irides orange-red or red in life, yellow or cream after death (Chapin). Bill black. Legs and feet dark grey, dark brown or blackish. Sexes alike but females have on average smaller bills. Juvenile a general dark smoky or brownish grey, paler on the rump and with blackish wings which show only faint and dingy spotting. The irides of a recently fledged juvenile were grey and its bill dark grey with white gape tubercles still showing. The nestling has five black spots on the palate, a black crescent in the lower mandible and four white tubercles at each side of the gape, two at the base of each mandible (Immelman *et al.*). The Van Somerens, however, described a nestling as having yellow tubercles and only three at each side, one at the base of the upper and two at the base of the lower mandible.

The above description is of nominate *N.c. canicapilla*, from Fernando Po, southern Nigeria and the Cameroons south to Mayombe and east to the eastern Congo. *N.c. emiliae*, from western Africa from Guinea to Ghana, is smaller in size (wing averaging around 65 to 67 mm as against 69 to 73 mm), has the rump only slightly paler grey than the back and the white line dividing the black and grey parts of the head only slightly indicated. The spots on the lesser wing coverts are smaller and silvery grey not white, those on the median and greater coverts and inner secondaries are usually grey fringes rather than spots so that the wings appear lightly spotted and laced with silvery grey, not boldly spotted with white as in the nominate form. The juvenile is like that of the nominate race but has only faint brownish lacing on the wing coverts. *N.c. angolensis*, from north-western Angola and Kasai, possibly also Manyema, is very like nominate *N.c. canicapilla* and with equally boldly spotted wings but is darker grey on the upperparts. *N.c. schistacea*, from southern Sudan, Uganda, Kenya and northern Tanzania, is also the same size as nominate *N.c. canicapilla* but a darker grey on hind crown, mantle and back, and usually has smaller and less numerous wing spots. *N.c. diabolica*, from Mount Kenya through the Aberdares to the Crater Highlands and Kilimanjaro, is like *N.c. schistacea* but smaller (wing averaging around 63 to 68 mm) and has sooty grey upperparts and *dull* black underparts. *N.c. candida*, from the Kungwe-Mahare Mountains, western Tanzania, resembles *N.c. schistacea* but has the crown and nape whitish grey like the rump.

See plate 1, facing p. 96.

FIELD CHARACTERS Small black bird with grey upperparts and conspicuous whitish rump. At close quarters the white spotting on the black wings is striking except in the westernmost race, *emiliae*. Black, not whitish, forehead and white spots on wings distinguish it from the smaller Pale-fronted Negro-finch, *N. luteifrons*.

DISTRIBUTION AND HABITAT Tropical Africa, north to Guinea and south to north-western Angola in the west and to southern Sudan and western Tanzania in the east. See also under 'Description', and map. Inhabits open forest, forest edge, second growth, gallery forest and also plantations and other tree-grown cultivated areas.

FEEDING AND GENERAL HABITS Feeds mostly above ground, at varying heights in trees or creepers. Known to take small fruits, including some species of figs and a mulberry-like fruit, and caterpillars (Chapin, Immelmann *et al.*, Mackworth-Praed & Grant). Probably also takes many other insects and Bates found that the fleshy pericarp of the oil palm nut was eaten by it in West Africa. Insects and small seeds (possibly from fruits?) have been found in stomachs of birds collected (Van Somerens). Captive birds ate a soft food made from artificial nectar, grape sugar, ant pupae and egg yolk, and also soft newly-moulted mealworms, wax moth larvae, and fruit flies. Two individuals took no seed at all (Kleefisch), two others ate small quantities of maw seed and soaked millet but fed mostly on other foods (Ponweiser).

Less sociable than most estrildids but sometimes seen in small parties and will join mixed bird-parties foraging through the trees (Mackworth-Praed & Grant). Two captive birds (sexes unknown) did not associate together (Ponweiser). Often 'tame' and inquisitive towards man (Mackworth-Praed & Grant).

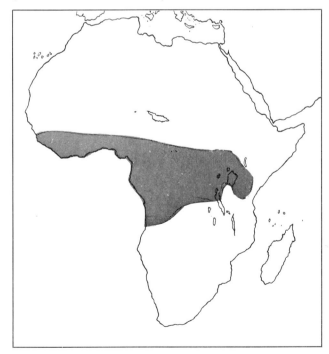

NESTING The nest is sited in a tree, usually about 3 to 15 metres above ground. Sometimes at the end of a branch and possibly with a preference for spiny or densely foliaged trees. It is large and roundish, about the size of a football, built of fibres, grasses or similar materials, sometimes also of dead leaves or moss, and lined with grass panicles or other softer materials. The nest has a side entrance, usually near the top of one side. Eggs 4 to 6.

Recorded breeding in September in Liberia; in November in Fernando Po; in September to December and in February and August in Nigeria; in March, April, June and July in Cameroun; in May in Gabon; in March in Angola; in March to November in Congo (Zaïre) and from March to July and in October in Uganda (Chapin, Immelmann *et al.*, Mackworth-Praed & Grant, the Van Somerens).

VOICE The only vocalisation described seems to have been a 'complaining whistle' ('Klagender Pfiff') and a short song of soft whistled notes which Bates transcribed as 'ki-yu ki-yu, weh-weh-weh' and others similarly. Ponweiser apparently heard no other call, and especially notes that he heard no contact calls from his captive birds.

DISPLAY AND SOCIAL BEHAVIOUR No information.

REFERENCES

Bates, G. L 1930. *Handbook of the birds of West Africa.* London.

Chapin, J. P. 1954. The birds of the Belgian Congo. *Bull Amer. Mus. Nat. Hist.* **75B.**

Immelmann, K., Steinbacher, J. & Wolters, H. E. 1963. *Vögel in Käfig und Voliere: Prachtfinken:* 61–64. Aachen, Germany.

Kleefisch, T. 1974. Seltenheiten auf dem Vogelmarkt. *Gefiederte Welt* **1974**: 65–66.

Mackworth-Praed, C. M. & Grant, C. H. B 1973. *African handbook of birds.* ser. 3, vol. 2. Longman Group, London.

Ponweiser, H. 1974. Ein seltener Prachtfink, der Graunacken-schwärzling. *Gefiederte Welt* **1974**: 141–142.

Van Someren, V. G. L. & G. R. C. 1949. The birds of Bwamba. *Uganda Journal,* **13**, special supplement.

Pale-fronted Negro-finch   *Nigrita luteifrons*

Nigrita luteifrons J. & E. Verreaux, 1851, *Rev. Mag. Zool.* (Paris), ser. 2, **3**, p. 420.

DESCRIPTION Similar to the previous species, *N. canicapilla*, in shape except for somewhat shorter tail and bill and more strongly curved culmen but smaller in size (about size of Spice Finch but very different in shape). Forehead pale buff to straw yellow or yellowish white, shading to pale grey on crown. Rest of upper parts a clear grey, a little darker on the mantle and back than elsewhere and palest, sometimes nearly whitish, on the rump and upper tail coverts. Wing coverts and inner secondaries a dark blackish grey, rest of wings and tail black. Under wing coverts mostly silvery grey. Face, including line above eye, ear coverts, and all underparts intense black. Irides of specimens from Oguma and Congo said to be red, of specimens from elsewhere pale grey, brownish white or cream-coloured (Chapin, Rand *et al.*, specimens in British Museum). It is uncertain whether this represents geographical variation in iris colour or post-mortem changes such as have been described (Chapin) for *N. canicapilla.* Bill black. Legs and feet fleshy brown to greyish brown.

The female differs from the male in having all her head and underparts a clear grey except for a black patch around each eye and a pale buff tinge on the forehead. A female collected by Chapin had yellow irides. Others said to have had pale grey or whitish eyes. The juvenile is like the female but a duller grey and tinged with buff on the underparts. Mouth markings similar to those of the Grey-headed Negro-finch (q.v.).

The above description is of nominate *N.l. luteifrons* from the African mainland. *N.l. alexanderi,* from Fernando Po, averages slightly larger in size, has a proportionately larger bill and the pale yellowish buff of its forehead is brighter and extends well on to the crown. Irides said to be black (Mackworth-Praed & Grant).

FIELD CHARACTERS Male a small compact black bird with clear grey upperparts and pale forehead. Female all grey except for black 'goggles' and blackish wings and tail. Lack of white spots on the wings and pale, not black, forehead, distinguish it from the Grey-headed Negro-finch.

DISTRIBUTION AND HABITAT Tropical Africa in southern and south-eastern Nigeria east through the southern Camerouns and Zaïre (Congo) to western Uganda, and south through Gabon and Zaïre to north-western Angola. Also on Fernando Po. Inhabits forest but usually in secondary growth, tree- or shrub-grown clearings and forest edge.

FEEDING AND GENERAL HABITS Scale insects are sometimes, perhaps usually, a major food. Other (unidentified) insects, the pulpy husk of the oil palm fruit and unidentified fruits and seeds have also been found in the crops or stomachs of collected specimens (Bates, Serle).

Seeks food largely, perhaps entirely, above ground in trees and shrubs; sometimes visits flowers and catches insects in flight (Mackworth-Praed & Grant, Serle). Usually seen singly or in pairs (Serle).

NESTING The nest is sited in trees or bushes. Most descriptions seem to derive from nests described by Rand

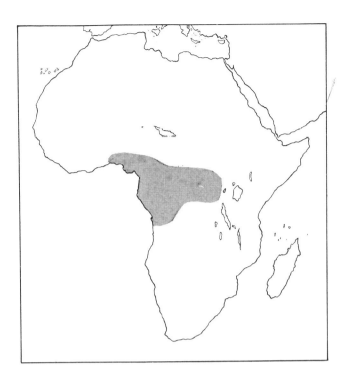

et al. and Serle (1954) respectively. The former was in a bush about 2·5 metres from the ground and was made of grass, oval in shape, with an entrance high in one side. Serle's nest was about 3·5 metres high in the middle of the bushy top of a garden hedge. It was about 130 mm in diameter with a side entrance about 35 mm across. It was made of dry green moss and a few grass stems, lined with seeding grass panicles and contained 4 eggs. Recorded breeding in October in Fernando Po, in June in Cameroun, and in March and April in Gabon (Mackworth-Praed & Grant, Rand *et al.*).

VOICE The (contact?) call of the male (and female?) is a faint musical whistling 'choo'. His song is a simple sweet phrase on a descending scale (Serle, 1965). Perhaps this latter is the same as the 'beautiful song' that both sexes of a pair uttered whenever they came to the nest to feed their young and to the sound of which the young at once reacted by starting to beg vocally (Rand *et al.*).

DISPLAY AND SOCIAL BEHAVIOUR No information.

REFERENCES

Bates, G. L. 1930. *Handbook of the birds of West Africa.* London.

Chapin, J. P. 1954. The birds of the Belgian Congo. *Bull. Amer. Mus. Nat. Hist.* **75B**.

Mackworth-Praed, C. M. & Grant, C. H. B. 1973. *African handbook of birds.* ser. 3, vol. 2.

Rand, A. L., Friedmann, H. & Traylor, M. A. 1959. Birds from Gabon and Moyen Congo. *Feldiana: Zoology* **41**: 221–410.

Serle, W. 1954. A second contribution to the ornithology of the British Cameroons. *Ibis* **96**: 47–80.

Serle, W. 1965. A third contribution to the ornithology of the British Cameroons. *Ibis* **107**: 230–246.

Chestnut-breasted Negro-finch   *Nigrita bicolor*

Pytelia bicolor Hartlaub, 1844. *Syst. Verz. Naturh. Samml. Ges. Mus.* (Bremen), Abth., **1**, p. 76.

DESCRIPTION Similar to previous species, *N. luteifrons*, in size and shape but it has a longer, although less massive, bill with a less curved culmen and rather longer and more graduated tail. Crown, nape and upperparts dark slaty grey, a little browner in tone on the wing quills and darker, nearly black, on the upper tail coverts. Tail dull black with obscure greyish tips to outer feathers. Underwing coverts pale silvery grey with a buffish tinge. Forehead, face and all underparts a very dark, slightly purplish chestnut. Irides red or reddish brown; eye-rims bluish grey. Bill black. Feet and legs dark brown.

The female is a slightly paler and more brownish slate above and all her chestnut parts are lighter (although still quite dark) and of a purer chestnut, less purplish tone. The juvenile is a general dull brownish grey, tinged with buffish chestnut on the underparts. Mouth markings of nestlings are probably identical to those of the next race (q.v.).

The above description is of nominate *N.b. bicolor*, from Sierra Leone east to Ghana. *N.b. brunnescens*, from the more eastern parts of the species' range, is slightly larger (wing length 57 to 65 mm as against 53 to 59 mm). The male is more brownish grey above, the colour of its upperparts being very similar to but darker than that of the female of nominate *bicolor*, and slightly duller and less purplish in tone on the chestnut areas. Sexual differences are comparable to those described for *N.b. bicolor*. Chapin describes the mouth markings of the nestlings as consisting of four little lemon-yellow tubercles in each corner of the gape; the palate mostly lemon yellow, with five black dots, the posterior pair very small; tongue and most of floor of mouth flesh-coloured, with a blackish mark across the tongue and a blackish crescent inside the lower mandible.

FIELD CHARACTERS Small dark bird. Slate grey or brownish grey above with chestnut face and underparts and blackish tail. No pale or white markings.

DISTRIBUTION AND HABITAT Tropical Africa from Sierra Leone, and perhaps also south-eastern Senegal, east to eastern Zaïre and western Uganda. South to south-western Angola. Also on Principe Island. Inhabits forest edge, forest clearings and secondary growth. Also at times in primary forest (Chapin).

FEEDING AND GENERAL HABITS Known to eat small caterpillars and other small insects (Bates, Chapin). Bates found that it also ate the oily pericarp of the oil palm nut. Has, on at least two occasions, been observed taking the small white eggs of the tree frog, *Chiromantis rufescens*, from the frothy mass on the branches, in which they are laid (Forbes-Watson, pers. comm.). Usually seen singly or in pairs at varying heights above ground in trees or shrubs but Chapin also saw it on the ground on or near roads

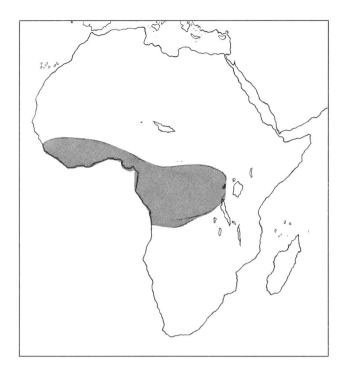

through forest. Said to sometimes accompany mixed bird parties (Bannerman).

NESTING A nest found by Bates had an outer framework of dried leaves and a more compact inner layer of the tops of *Panicum*. It contained 5 eggs. Chapin saw a male of the species building with dried leaves. Bannerman says the nest is built of fine grasses and the clutch size is 2. Although not indicated, it seems likely that this refers only to one nest, or very few, as the clutch size given suggests either an unusually small or else an incomplete clutch.

VOICE Said to have a 'low, sweet and mournful' little song which is given from high in the tops of trees (Bannerman).

DISPLAY AND SOCIAL BEHAVIOUR No information.

REFERENCES
Bannerman, D. A. 1953. *The birds of West and Equatorial Africa*, vol. 2. Edinburgh and London.
Bates, G. L. 1930. *Handbook of the birds of West Africa*. London.
Chapin, J. P. 1954. The birds of the Belgian Congo. *Bull. Amer. Mus. Nat. Hist.* **75B**.

White-Breasted Negro-finch   *Nigrita fusconota*

Nigrita fusconotus Fraser, 1843, *Proc. Zool. Soc. London* **1842**, p. 145.

DESCRIPTION About size of Avadavat but with rather long, strongly graduated tail and slender bill, somewhat broadened and flattened near base of upper mandible and with only a very slight curve to the culmen ridge. The bill is much slenderer than those of the Grey-headed and Pale-fronted Negro-finches.

Top of head (including the area around the eyes and the upper part of the cheeks), hind neck, lower rump, upper tail coverts and tail black, with glossy bluish or purplish fringes to the feathers of the crown, nape, lower rump and upper tail coverts. Mantle, back, inner wing coverts and inner secondaries dull brown with a slight yellowish tinge, shading to a more definite tawny brown on the lower back and upper rump. Rest of wings brownish black except for the lesser wing coverts which are mostly dark purplish with brownish centres to the feathers. Under wing coverts silky white. Throat and lower part of face silky white, often with a creamy tinge, shading to greyish white or very pale grey on the rest of the underparts, except for the median area of the belly which is often more creamy white than greyish white. Irides dark brown. Bill black. Legs and feet slate grey, grey or greenish grey.

Sexes alike but possibly with females averaging a little lighter brown above and less greyish on the underparts. The juvenile has the parts of the head that are black in the adult dull brown, its rump and tail are blackish brown and the greyish white underparts more or less tinged with dull buff.

The above description is of nominate *N.f. fusconota*, from south-eastern Nigeria to Uganda and western Kenya and south to northern Angola, central Zaïre and Fernando Po. *N.f. uropygialis*, from further west in the species' range, has the lower back and upper rump pale yellowish fawn, contrasting with the dull brown, dusky-fringed feathers of its back and mantle. Its legs and feet are (always?) dark brown.

FIELD CHARACTERS Small, warbler-like rather than finch-like, bird, with glossy black head, and tail contrasting with white throat and underparts and brown back. Upper part of rump conspicuously pale in western race.

DISTRIBUTION AND HABITAT Tropical Africa in south-eastern Guinea, Ghana, Nigeria east to Uganda and western Kenya, and south to northern Angola and central Congo (Zaïre). Also on Fernando Po. Inhabits forested regions but mainly or especially in partly cleared areas and secondary growth. Locally in gallery forest.

FEEDING AND GENERAL HABITS Known to eat small caterpillars and other small insects, small orange-

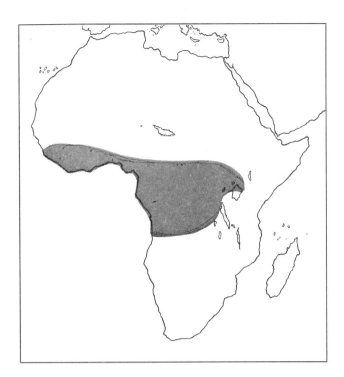

coloured berries, the oily pericarp of oil palm nuts, other (unidentified) fruits and small seeds. This data all derives from the crop or stomach contents of collected specimens and it is possible (since they were not identified) that the seeds may have been from fruits that the birds had swallowed.

Has usually been encountered in pairs or small parties. Seeks food at varying heights in trees, shrubs and bushes. Appears not to have been seen on the ground although sometimes feeding in branches very near it (Bates, Chapin, Mackworth-Praed & Grant, the Van Somerens).

NESTING The nest is placed in a tree or shrub or in the angle of a palm frond. It is built of fibres, bast, dry grass, dead leaves, moss or similar materials with a side entrance near the top. One nest, found by the Van Somerens, was made entirely of the fine bark fibres of a vine. Eggs 3 to 6. Recorded breeding in February in Ghana, in November in Fernando Po, in January in Nigeria, in June in Cameroun, from June to September in north-eastern Congo (Zaïre), in March in northern Angola and in July and August in western Uganda (Chapin, Immelmann *et al.*, the Van Somerens).

VOICE The song has been described as 'beginning with a trill which slows down till ends with separate notes of chip chip chip' (Bates) and as 'a simple, sweet phrase with only a brief pause after each delivery. The pitch rises and then falls, the notes becoming staccato and softer till they die away' (Serle).

DISPLAY AND SOCIAL BEHAVIOUR No information. The song is apparently regularly given from a song perch at the top of a tree (Bates, Serle) and also when moving about seeking food (Serle). These observations suggest the

possibility of the warbler-like shape being correlated with (for an estrildid) rather unusual behaviour, but much more information is needed.

REFERENCES
Bates, G. L. 1930. *Handbook of the birds of West Africa*. London.
Chapin, J. P. 1954. The birds of the Belgian Congo. *Bull. Amer. Mus. Nat. Hist.* **75B**.
Immelmann, K., Steinbacher, J. & Wolters, H. E. 1963. *Vögel in Käfig und Voliere: Prachtfinken*: 59–61.
Mackworth-Praed, C. M. & Grant, C. H. B. 1973. *African handbook of birds*, ser. 3, vol. 2. Longman Group, London.
Serle, W. 1965. A third contribution to the ornithology of the British Cameroons. *Ibis* **107**: 230–246.
Van Someren, V. G. L. & G. R. C. 1949. The birds of Bwamba. *Uganda Journal* **13**, special supplement.

The olive-backs

The olive-backs, *Nesocharis*, are a distinct group of three forms, characterised by their boldly-patterned olive-green, bluish grey and black plumage. They have rounded wings, medium-length to very short tails and bills that are either thick (two forms) or rather slender (one form) but agree in being sharp-pointed with a suggestion of a hook to the upper mandible and in having a curved culmen. They are very agile and acrobatic when seeking food. Two are largely insectivorous, the other, so far as known, is a food specialist on the seeds of a composite.

Delacour included *Nesocharis* in his enlarged conception of *Estrilda*. Immelmann *et al.* (1963) considered it most probably related to the Negro-finches, *Nigrita* but later (1975) favoured a closer relationship with the Swee Waxbill, *Estrilda melanotis*. The latter's olive back and (some forms only) black face give it some resemblance to *Nesocharis* but I think possibly a rather superficial one. The olive and grey shades of the Swee Waxbill are not identical with or very close to those of *Nesocharis* and the latter shows no trace of the fine cross-barring of *E. melanotis* and other *Estrilda* species. Steiner includes it in his tribe Cryptospizae, together with *Cryptospiza*, *Parmoptila*, *Nigrita* and *Pyrenestes*, largely on the similarity of the mouth markings of the nestlings. I think he is probably right and that this group, perhaps particularly the *Cryptospiza* species, are most nearly related to *Nesocharis*.

The Grey-headed Olive-back, *Nesocharis capistrata*, occurs in the same general areas as the other two forms though it does not seem to have been taken at identical localities (Hall and Moreau). It has a much more extensive range than either of its congeners. Shelley's Olive-back, *N. shelleyi*, and the White-collared Olive-back, *N. ansorgei*, are completely allopatric and both have, so far as known, relatively small ranges which are widely separated from each other. They have an almost identical colour pattern and Friedmann treats them as conspecific. As, however, they differ in bill shape and tail length and also in feeding habits, *shelleyi* being apparently largely insectivorous and *ansorgei* specialising on one kind of seed only (see species sections), I prefer to treat them as species within the same superspecies.

REFERENCES

Delacour, J. 1943. A revision of the subfamily Estrildinae of the family Ploceidae. *Zoologica*, New York Zoological Society **28**: 69–86.
Hall, B. P. & Moreau, R. E. 1970. *An atlas of speciation in African passerine birds*. British Museum (Natural History), London.
Immelmann, K., Steinbacher, J. & Wolters, H. E. 1963 and 1975. *Vögel in Käfig und Voliere: Prachtfinken*: 54 and 520.
Steiner, J. 1960. Klassifikation der Prachtfinken, Spermestidae, auf Grund der Rachenzeichnungen ihrer Nestlinge. *J. Orn.* **101**: 92–112.

Shelley's Olive-back   *Nesocharis shelleyi*

Nesocharis shelleyi Alexander, 1903, *Bull. Brit. Orn. Club*, **13**, p. 48.

DESCRIPTION About size of Avadavat. Considerably smaller than *N. capistrata*, and with a proportionately much shorter tail and more slender bill. Entire head glossy black. Sides of neck and hind neck bluish grey, at the sides (but not at the nape) separated from the black of the head by a narrow whitish line. Breast, mantle and back a deep yellowish olive-green, often with a strong golden tinge. Rump and upper tail coverts similar but even more strongly suffused with yellowish or golden. Wing coverts, inner secondaries, outer webs of outer secondaries and outer fringes (except near their ends) of outer webs of primaries a slightly duller yellowish olive than the back. Rest of wings greyish black. Tail black. Under wing coverts silvery white. Underparts below the breast bluish grey like hind neck. Irides brown. Bill bluish grey, tipped with black or darker grey. Legs and feet grey to greyish brown.

The female has the underparts entirely bluish grey. The olive-green of her upperparts, especially on the rump, is usually less yellowish, and never so richly golden in tone as that of the brightest males. I have only been able to examine two juveniles, sexed by their collector as a male

and a female. They were like the adult female in coloration but duller; the olive-green areas less yellowish and the grey of the underparts with a tinge of brownish olive. They are said to have had black irides, bluish grey, black-tipped bills and dark slate legs and feet.

The above description is of nominate *N.s. shelleyi*, from Fernando Po and Mt Cameroon. *N.s. bansoensis*, from Mt Manenguba and the Bamenda and Banso Highlands, Cameroun, averages a little larger (wing length about 45–48 mm as against 42–44 mm) and is a little darker in both the grey and the olive-green parts of its plumage (not lighter on the grey parts as sometimes mistakenly stated). Sexual differences are similar to those of the nominate form.

FIELD CHARACTERS Very small yellowish olive and bluish grey bird with black head and short black tail. Grey on neck and underparts (and breast of female) distinguish it from weavers and finches with otherwise somewhat similar coloration.

DISTRIBUTION AND HABITAT (arrowed on map) Fernando Po, Mt Cameroun, the mountain ranges of Cameroun and (*fide* Mackworth-Praed & Grant) perhaps also the Obudu Plateau of Nigeria. Inhabits mountain forest, chiefly its edge, and also bush-grown mountain savanna (Eisentraut, 1963, Immelmann *et al.*).

FEEDING AND GENERAL HABITS Takes small insects and also small (unidentified) seeds (Bates, Immelmann, Mackworth-Praed & Grant). Seeks food in an agile, tit-like manner in trees, bushes and grass (Eisentraut, 1963, Immelmann *et al.*). Can hang by one foot (Mitsch).

Four captive birds preferred aphids (greenfly) but also ate wax moths, spiders and caterpillars. Two of them took

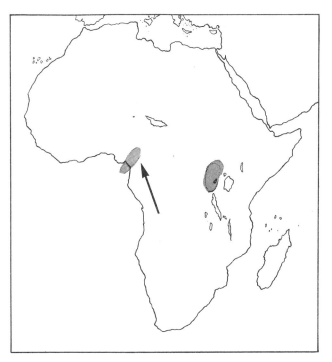

a little ripe or over-ripe peach, apricot and tangerine. None of them would touch seed of any kind or artificial soft foods (Mitsch).

NESTING Sometimes, and probably most often, uses old (or commandeered?) nests of weavers and sunbirds, which it lines thickly with vegetable down but one pair nested in a clump of moss, making the usual vegetable down lining within it (Eisentraut, 1963 and 1968, Mackworth-Pracd & Grant). Three young were in the moss nest (Eisentraut, 1968) and 3 eggs in another (Immelmann *et al.*).

VOICE High-pitched 'needle-sharp' but loud notes and very soft notes have been recorded (Bannerman, Mitsch).

DISPLAY AND SOCIAL BEHAVIOUR Four captive birds, three males and a female, were very sociable, allo-preening each other and clumping together (Mitsch).

OTHER NAMES Fernando Po Olive-back, Little Olive Weaver.

REFERENCES
Bannerman, D. A. 1953. *The birds of West and Equatorial Africa*, vol. 2. Oliver & Boyd, Edinburgh & London.
Bates, G. L. 1930. *Handbook of the birds of West Africa*. John Bale, Sons & Danielsson, London.
Eisentraut, M. 1963. *Die Wirbeltiere des Kamerungebirges*. Hamburg & Berlin.
Eisentraut, M. 1968. Beitrag zur Vogelfauna von Fernando Poo und Westkamerun. *Bonn. Zool. Beitr.* **19**:49–68.
Immelmann, K., Steinbacher, J. & Wolters, H. E. 1963. *Vögel in Käfig und Voliere: Prachtfinken*: 58–59.
Mackworth-Praed, C. M. & Grant, C. H. B. 1973. Handbook of African birds, ser. 3, vol. 2.
Mitsch, H. 1967. Meisenastrilde. *Gefiederte Welt* **1967**: 45.

White-collared Olive-back   *Nesocharis ansorgei*

Pytelia ansorgei Hartert, *Bull. Brit. Orn. Club* **10**, p. 26, 1899.

DESCRIPTION Very like the previous form, *N. shelleyi*, but slightly larger, with much longer tail and much deeper, rather Bullfinch-like bill. Coloration and colour pattern like those of *N. shelleyi* (q.v.) but with the white line bordering the black cheeks more pronounced and continuing round in front to form a white collar between the black throat and the olive breast. Sexual differences as in the previous form, *N. shelleyi* (q.v.). Irides dark brown. Bill black, bluish grey right at base. Legs and feet dark grey. The mouth markings of the young have been described by J. P. Chapin as: 'gape wattles like those of *Estrilda*, a little curved ridge and two balls, all vivid light green-blue, separated by black skin. On the palate there seemed to be only one median black spot'.

FIELD CHARACTERS As for Shelley's Olive-back (q.v.) but average length, not very short, tail and stouter bill.

DISTRIBUTION AND HABITAT (arrowed on map) Eastern Congo (Zaire) and Uganda: in the eastern Ituri and the Toro district of Uganda south of Lake Kivu and Rwanda (Ruanda-Urundi). Inhabits marshy areas, streamsides, clearings and forest edge, always near water.

FEEDING AND GENERAL HABITS The only known food is the seeds of the composite *Melanthera scandens* (syn. *M. brownei*), the minute seeds of which are shelled and most of the husk discarded (R. T. Chapin, Friedmann). Dr Peter Kunkel (pers. comm.) found that, in the Kivu area where he studied this olive-back, these seeds were eaten throughout the year. He found it impossible to persuade captive birds to take any other food.

Agile and tit-like when feeding; will cling with the left foot to a stem while holding the ball-like seed-head in its right foot and picking out the seeds (R. T. Chapin).

Usually in pairs or family parties. Never in large flocks (R. T. Chapin).

NESTING Uses old or abandoned nests of weavers. Both sexes carry in vegetable down and grass panicles to line the egg chamber of the selected weavers' nest. May

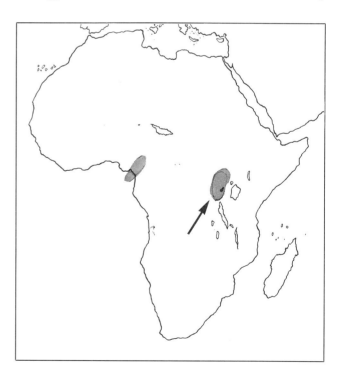

sometimes nest in vegetation as a pair were seen carrying material into a drooping bunch of dead Hagenia flowers. Eggs 2 to 3. The breeding season lasts from November to July (R. T. Chapin).

VOICE 'Little lisping calls' (R. T. Chapin) and trilling calls (Kunkel, unpublished mss) have been described. The male's song (possibly individually variable) is described by R. T. Chapin as 'a weak but pleasant little trill, introduced by two short notes' and by Kunkel (unpublished mss) as a series of hardly modified trilling call notes.

DISPLAY AND SOCIAL BEHAVIOUR Kunkel (unpublished mss) saw a greeting display very like that of the Lavender Waxbill. The pair stood in an upright posture, with their bodies turned a little away from but their heads turned towards each other. They had the feathers of the lower breast, belly and flanks fluffed out and angled tails, the female remained still but the male nodded or bowed towards her about 20 times. He sang between bows and made a symbolic bill-wiping movement at every fourth or fifth bow. A short bout of mutual bill pecking followed.

OTHER NAMES Olive Weaver-finch.

REFERENCES
Chapin, J. P. 1954. The Birds of the Belgian Congo. *Bull. Amer. Mus. Nat. Hist.* **75B**.
Chapin, R. T. 1959. The behaviour of the Olive Weaver-finch *Nesocharis ansorgei. Ostrich supplement* **3**: 230–232.
Friedmann, H. 1968. The Olive Weaver-finch *Nesocharis ansorgei ansorgei. Bull. Brit. Orn. Club* **88**: 135–138.

Grey-headed Olive-back   *Nesocharis capistrata*

Pytelia capistrata Hartlaub, 1861, *J. Orn.* 9, p. 259.

DESCRIPTION About size of Spice Finch but plumper, softer-feathered and with shorter bill. Bill pointed at tip but deep and broad at base with curved culmen. Wings rounded, tail medium length and slightly rounded at end. Face, including lores, ear coverts and a very narrow area at front of forehead, greyish white to pale silvery grey. Throat and a narrow band extending upward behind the ear coverts, black. Most of forehead, crown, nape, hind neck and sides of neck, breast and median part of belly a clear, slightly bluish grey. Flanks bright yellow, tinged with green (the visible areas of the individual feathers are olive-centred but with broad bright yellow fringes). Ventral area and under tail coverts pale grey, tipped with yellowish green. Upperparts a bright yellowish olive-green except for the tips and inner webs of the wing quills and the normally concealed parts of the tail feathers which are dark grey. Under wing coverts yellowish buff. Irides deep red to reddish brown. Bill black. Legs and feet dark grey, blackish or dark brown. There is a colour photograph of the species in *Die Gefiederte Welt* for April 1978.

Sexes alike but in worn plumage the feathers of the green parts look darker and duller but their tips paler and yellower, giving a somewhat scaly or streaky effect. The juvenile is like the adult but both the green and grey areas are duller and darker. Its bill is at first whitish but with the tip, and the edges of the lower mandible, greyish and grey legs and feet. The yellow flank patch is replaced by olive.

See plate 1, facing p. 96.

FIELD CHARACTERS Small grey and yellowish olive bird with black throat and whitish, black-edged cheeks, giving it a somewhat tit-like look, and bright yellow flanks.

DISTRIBUTION AND HABITAT Tropical Africa, from Gambia, Portuguese Guinea and Ghana through central Nigeria and the Cameroons to north-eastern Congo (Zaire), western Uganda and extreme southern Sudan. Inhabits bush- and tree-grown areas near swamps and in savanna, riparian woodlands, wood edge and also (*fide* Bannerman) closed forest.

FEEDING AND GENERAL HABITS Recorded taking the seeds of wild figs (Bates), grass seeds, small insects and small snails (Chapin) and ants (Serle). Unidentified seeds, some from fruits, also found in the crops and stomachs of collected specimens.

Seeks food in trees and shrubs, foraging among the leaves and twigs in an active, acrobatic manner suggestive of foraging tits, *Parus* (Chapin, Serle). Also seeks food on the ground (*fide* Mackworth-Praed & Grant).

NESTING The only known nest appears to be one found by Chapin. The bird was building and the nest was built of dry weed and grass stems. It had a side entrance rather high up and the whole nest measured about 18 cm from top to bottom. It was unlined and obviously not finished. It was sited about 3 metres high in a row of thick bushes.

VOICE The song has been described as a pleasant 'chwee-chwee-chwee-chwi', not loud and descending in scale

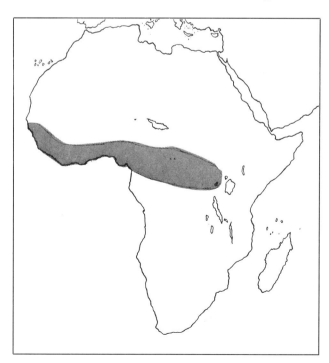

(Chapin). No other calls appear to be known and Chapin comments that the species is usually silent.

DISPLAY AND SOCIAL BEHAVIOUR   No information.

OTHER NAMES   White-cheeked Olive-back, White-cheeked Waxbill.

REFERENCES
Bannerman, D. A. 1953. *The birds of West and Equatorial Africa.* vol. 2. London
Bates, G. L. 1930. *Handbook of the birds of West Africa.* London.
Chapin, J. P. 1954. The Birds of the Belgian Congo. *Bull. Amer. Mus. Nat. Hist.* 75B.
Mackworth-Praed, C. W. & Grant, C. H. B. 1973. *African handbook of birds*, ser. 3, vol. 2.
Serle, W. 1940. Field observations on some northern Nigerian birds. *Ibis* Jan. 1940: 1–47.

The Cut-throat and the Red-headed Finch

The Cut-throat, *Amadina fasciata*, and the Red-headed Finch, *A. erythrocephala*, are the only species in their genus and stand clearly apart from all other estrildids. They are rather thick-set, strong-billed birds whose plumage is predominantly in shades of brown with complex barred and spotted patterns. Although they usually hop, both species can and do walk, run or 'polka-step' for short distances (Immelmann & Immelmann). They are birds of arid country and are almost (but not quite) entirely allopatric. They are sometimes treated as members of a superspecies and although they seem perhaps to have diverged rather far for such treatment are certainly geographical representatives.

Amadina has usually been regarded (Delacour, Mayr, Morris) as a very distinct and distant offshoot of the mannikins, *Lonchura et al.*, but Güttinger believes it to be an endemic African form and most closely related to *Pytelia*. He shows that *Amadina* agrees with *Pytelia* in their nestlings both having the inside of the lower half of the mouth black in colour and being clad in a considerable amount of down; and in some aspects of voice and behaviour. The plumage *patterns* also show some similarities, if allowance is made for the different coloration, and the males of both genera have red on the head. Some of these characters are, admittedly, shared by other African estrildids.

There is on the other hand, little except the large, deep bill of *A. erythrocephala*, to link *Amadina* with *Lonchura* and I concur with Güttinger in thinking that he is right in believing it most closely allied to *Pytelia*

REFERENCES
Delacour, J. 1943. A revision of the subfamily Estrildinae of the family Ploceidae. *Zoologica* 28: 69–86.
Güttinger, H. R. 1976. Zur systematischen Stellung der Gattungen *Amadina, Lepidiopygia* und *Lonchura* (Aves, Estrildidae). *Bonn. zool. Beitr.* 27: 219–244.
Immelmann, K. & G. 1967. Verhaltensökologische Studien an afrikanischen und australischen Estrildiden. *Zool. Jb. Syst. Bd.* 94: 609–686.
Mayr, E. 1968. The sequence of genera in the Estrildidae (Aves). *Breviora* 287: 1–14.
Morris, D. 1958. The comparative ethology of grassfinches (Erythrurae) and mannikins (Amadinae). *Proc. Zool. Soc. London* 131: 389–439.

Cut-throat   *Amadina fasciata*

Loxia fasciata Gmelin, 1789, *Syst. Nat*; 1 (2), p. 859.

DESCRIPTION   A little larger than Spice Finch with proportionately larger and broader head, slightly shorter bill, much longer and more pointed wings and tail only slightly rounded at the end. Forehead, crown and nape pale sandy brown or sandy fawn with a slight pinkish tinge and delicate crescentic black bars (usually two) across each feather. Mantle and back similar but the pink tinge more pronounced and the black bars taking roughly the form of broad inverted 'Vs' (or, better, the rough silhouette of a more or less schematised and headless bird in flight!), only one such bar present on many or most feathers, and it may be reduced to a small black dot. On the lower rump and upper tail coverts the black bars usually form broad subterminal bars and the ends of the feathers are pale buff to creamy white. Wing coverts a darker and more greyish brown with black subterminal bars, usually in the inverted V shape, and broad pinkish fawn tips. Scapulars and inner secondaries similar but with the black bars usually restricted to the outer webs. Outer secondaries and primaries dusky greyish brown with narrow pinkish fawn outer edges and tips. Under wing coverts pinkish fawn. Central tail feathers brownish black, usually with very small white apical spots which soon wear off. Outer tail feathers broadly tipped with white; outer webs of outermost pair entirely white.

Upper throat and front of face creamy white. A broad bright but rather dark red band across the lower throat extends up the sides of the face to above the ear opening. This red band is narrowly bordered at the lower sides, and sometimes right across the lower edge, by black-tipped feathers. Otherwise the upper breast immediately beneath the red band is creamy white, shading to pinkish fawn on the breast. On the lower breast and upper part of the abdominal area there is a patch of dull chestnut, broadly enclosed at the front and sides by conspicuous pale spotted plumage whose individual feathers have extensive white or very pale tips which are backed and partly enclosed by the blackish V-shaped subterminal markings. Flanks pinkish fawn, with narrow blackish fringes to the feathers forming a delicate barred or scaly pattern. Lower belly and ventral areas pale fawn to whitish. Under tail coverts with extensive whitish tips backed by blackish crescentic subterminal bars and greyish bases. Bill pale horny grey, pinkish grey, grey and pinkish or bluish grey, sometimes darker on culmen. Iris brown, reddish or light brown; 'grey and red' once recorded. Legs and feet pale flesh-coloured. Brownish legs and feet often recorded but perhaps due to staining.

The above description is of birds in fairly new plumage. In worn plumage the pink tinge is lost and the bird is paler and more sandy. In very worn plumage it may appear *darker* owing to partial or complete abrasion of the pale feather ends. There is also much minor individual and/or micro-geographical variation.

Female has no red on throat and face, being pale fawn, speckled with blackish (blackish tips to feathers) where the male is red. Her underparts are primarily pale fawn, with blackish markings on sides of breast and flanks; these sometimes extend right across the breast. Some females show a slight 'suggestion' of the male's belly patch and spotted surround. The juvenile male is nearly intermediate in pattern between male and female but has the red band conspicuously present although it is paler than in the adult. The tips of its wing coverts and inner secondaries are paler and more sandy in tone than those of the adult. Juvenile female like adult but with paler feather tips as in juvenile male.

The unfeathered nestlings have dark greyish skin, profuse pale down on head and upperparts, a five-spot palate pattern, blackish lower half of the mouth and swollen pale yellow gape flanges. There are splendid photographs of them in Güttinger (1976).

The above description is of nominate *A.f. fasciata*, which is found from Senegal and Gambia east to the south-eastern Sudan and north-western Kenya. *A.f. alexanderi*, from southern and western Eritrea, Ethiopia, Somalia, Kenya and Tanzania, appears darker, duller and greyer. This is due to the black markings on its upper parts being usually broader and the parts of the feathers behind the subterminal black markings duller and greyer. The black markings on the under parts also tend to be both broader and more extensive, usually being present over the upper breast. Because of this the chestnut patch and surrounding spotted plumage is less conspicuous. The form found further south in the species' range, *A.f. meridonalis*, is like *A.f. alexanderi* but usually even darker and tends to have a proportionally slightly smaller bill. The races intergrade where they meet and all show differences due to wear and individual variation.

Cut-throats are prone to induced melanism under adverse captive conditions.

See plate 7, facing p. 256.

FIELD CHARACTERS Social, 'sandy speckly', sparrow-like small birds with white tips to outer tail feathers. 'Cut-throat' of male diagnostic, possessed at all ages and seasons. Owing to the species' sociability and strong pair bond females will rarely be seen alone.

DISTRIBUTION AND HABITAT Africa, in arid country north of the tropical forest areas, from Senegal and Gambia east to Sudan and Eritrea and south in eastern Africa to the western Transvaal, northern Orange Free State and Mosambique. Inhabits dry acacia savanna, semi-desert or desert country with some trees or bushes and available surface water, mopane woodland, cultivated areas and villages.

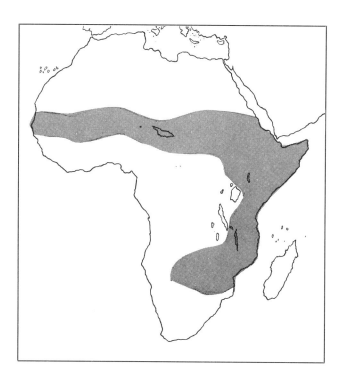

FEEDING AND GENERAL HABITS Known to eat grass (and other?) seeds and termites. Probably takes other insects and some green food, when available. Mackworth-Praed & Grant include 'corn' among its foods but give no further details. In captivity often readily takes not only millets and canary seed, eggfood and insects but also commercial soft food mixtures, and even fruit (Knoblauch, Immelmann). Will often *successfully* rear young in captivity on only dry and soaked seed, greenfood and eggfood with little or no insect food.

Usually in flocks, small or large but sometimes in single pairs, or single individuals when mate on nest, when breeding (Lynes). Comes to water, at least in Somalia, in the middle of the day (Archer & Sudman). Usually hops on ground but can walk or run short distances (Kunkel). In captivity often aggressive to other birds when breeding and its natural nesting behaviour (q.v.) makes it very liable to investigate the nests of species weaker or less bold than itself and often to throw out eggs or young. Although the resultant destruction is due to the folly or ignorance of the bird-keeper in question, he is apt to try to shift the blame onto the bird as when Perkins (1897) started an informative article on his breeding of the species with the words: 'I do not intend to write an eulogy on the Ribbon Finch, for my deliberate opinion is that it is a hateful little bird.' It was, incidentally, bred in captivity as early as 1790, by Vieillot.

NESTING Nest built in a tree, shrub or bush, sometimes in a hole in a tree or building. Very often makes use of old, deserted or commandeered nests of other species, especially of weavers, Ploceidae. In such cases it usually adds only feathers or other lining material. Nests built by the Cut-throat itself are rather rough-looking roundish

---

78 *Estrildid finches of the world*

structures of grass stems and similar materials, sometimes with a short funnel entrance, and lined with feathers, if these are available. Sometimes nests colonially. In captivity Knoblauch found that pairs which had not bred were greatly excited by and interested in the sound of the begging calls of nestlings of a pair that did breed and, shortly after this, all the other pairs nested. Subsequently all the Cut-throats in the aviary began and ceased breeding in synchrony. Güttinger found that breeding pairs defended the immediate vicinity of their nests against conspecifics. Knoblauch found that his Cut-throats were peaceable among themselves even when breeding but even non-breeding individuals would drive birds of *other* species from Cut-throats' nests. This unusual behaviour may be of use in the wild to enable them to acquire the nests of other species and/or to prevent their reconquest by the original builders or other species (such as *Amandava subflava*) that may be competing for them.

Both sexes incubate in turns by day, the male usually bringing a piece of nest-lining material when he comes to take over. At least in captivity both sexes roost in the nest at night. Incubation period 12–13 days. Young fledge at 21–23 days and are fed by the parents for about 21 days after fledging (Güttinger, Immelmann). The young do not twist their necks in the usual estrildid manner when begging (Hall, unpublished mss; Kunkel).

Recorded breeding in January, February, August and September in the Sudan; in May, November and December in Danakil, Abyssinia; in July in Turkana, Kenya; May to August in the Kenyan Highlands; March to May in Malawi and in September and November in West Africa. Breeds at the end of the wet season and in the dry season (Mackworth-Praed & Grant, Immelmann *et al.*).

VOICE Contact calls (and possibly some others) are rather sparrow-like chirping notes but appear not to have been studied in detail. Hall (in her unpublished manuscript) also records a nest call 'resembling the sound made by a squeaking door', 'low monosyllabic notes' that are uttered by a pair together at the nest site while neck-stretching and mandibulating; a 'loud and plaintive "kee-air"' uttered during or in intervals of active flying around by nesting birds; a loud shrieking attack call when defending the nest area; and a buzzing hiss that is sometimes given with the defensive display (q.v.).

The song is usually described as low pitched and ventriloquial, with a humming or buzzing sound but Hall (unpublished mss.) describes that of the male as 'a fruity warble which may be repeated several times without a break' and that of the female as 'low, toneless warbling sounds'. The male sings both undirected song and in display. When singing the bird usually more or less erects the feathers of its head and underparts and turns its head from side to side.

The young have a two-syllabled begging call which are described by Hall (unpublished mss) as a series of 'aa' notes repeated rapidly and interrupted by a more high-pitched 'whee', thus 'whee a aa a aa a aa whee a a aa . . . .'.

Güttinger (1976) gives sound spectrograms of the song and begging calls and Hall (1962) of the songs of this and many other estrildids.

DISPLAY AND SOCIAL BEHAVIOUR In courtship display the male assumes an upright posture and faces the female. He may make the triangular head or erect his head feathers more evenly. Most of his body plumage is erected but to differing degrees, so that the dull chestnut belly patch and its white-tipped surround are prominently displayed. He then performs what Morris (1954, 1958) terms the 'inverted curtsey', bobbing up and down by alternately stretching and bending his legs. He sings at the female (though the display may start in silence) and usually turns his head and the upper part of his body jerkily from side to side through an angle of about 90 degrees as he does so (Kunkel, 1959). Sometimes he holds a piece of nesting material in his bill during part or all of the display but quite often he does not. Copulation may follow the display if the female is willing and solicits in the usual way with quivering tail. Male Cut-throats are more apt to 'go through the motions' of the Courtship display when alone than are most male estrildids. Hall (unpublished mss) has also seen female soliciting and copulation follow the male's approaching the female in a horizontal posture, with ruffled plumage, and striking her under her chin with closed bill, and inside the nest following the nesting display in which both birds extend their necks forward and mandibulate together. In captivity, and perhaps also when wild, male Cut-throats often attempt to rape unwilling females, chasing them and seizing them by the nape or neck.

Eisner, in a paper on the Bengalese finch, seems to have described what seems primarily a defensive threat display used by incubating or brooding birds. Most of the plumage is erected but the head feathers sleeked down, the bill is held open and the bird moves 'with slow, rhythmic and sinuous side-to-side movements in an S-wave of chest, neck and head, the carpal joints sometimes being raised on the side opposite the direction in which the head is turned at that moment.' The display aroused a strong subjective response in her and she found it distressing to watch. Hall (unpublished mss) observed the same display, which may be accompanied by a buzzing hiss, used in (defensive?) threat display away from nests.

'Peering' occurs in response to song, the bird's mate usually driving off any other individuals who are also interested (Güttinger). Allo-preening is very common between mates but otherwise infrequent. Mandibulation and bill-fencing are also common. The locomotion-intention movements of the tail are less frequent and less pronounced than in most estrildids (Kunkel, 1959).

OTHER NAMES Ribbon Finch, Cut-throat Finch, Cut-throat Weaver.

REFERENCES
Eisner, E. 1961. The behaviour of the Bengalese Finch in the nest. *Ardea* **49**: 51–69.

Güttinger, H. R. 1976. Zur systematischen Stellung der Gattungen *Amadina*, *Lepidopygia* und *Lonchura* (Aves, Estrildidae). *Bonn. zool. Beitr.* **27**: 218–244.

Hall, M. F. 1962. Evolutionary aspects of estrildid song. *Symposia Zool. Soc. London* no. 8: 37–55. (Also unpublished manuscript on estrildid behaviour.)

Immelmann, K., Steinbacher, J. & Wolters, H. E. 1973. *Vögel in Käfig und Voliere: Prachtfinken*: 481–496.

Knoblauch, D. 1973. Bandfinken in der Vogelstube. *Gefiederte Welt* **97**: 26–28.

Kunkel, P. 1959. Zum Verhalten einiger Prachtfinken (Estrildidae) *Z. Tierpsychol.* **16**: 302–350.

Lynes, H. 1924. On the birds of North and Central Darfur. *Ibis* **6**, 11th ser.: 648–719.

Mackworth-Praed, C. W. & Grant, C. H. B. 1960. *African handbook of birds*, ser. 1, vol. 2.

McLachlan, G. R. & Liversidge, R. 1957. *Roberts birds of South Africa*.

Morris, D. 1954. The courtship behaviour of the Cut-throat Finch. *Avicult. Mag.* **60**: 169–178.

Morris, D. 1958. The comparative ethology of grassfinches (Erythrurae) and mannikins (Amadinae). *Proc. zool. Soc.* **131**: 389–439.

Perkins, S. 1897. The nesting in captivity of the Ribbon Finch. *Avicult. Mag.* **3**: 61–63.

Red-headed Finch   *Amadina erythrocephala*

Loxia erythrocephala
Loxia eryocephala (sic) Linnaeus, 1758, *Syst. Nat.* ed. 10, 1, p. 172.

DESCRIPTION Similar in proportions to previous species, *A. fasciata*, except for thicker, deeper bill with more steeply downward-sloping culmen. Also larger, nearly as large as Java Sparrow.

Forehead, crown, nape, face and throat dark blood red; in worn plumage turning to a rusty orange-red on the nape and to some extent elsewhere. Sides of neck, hind neck, mantle and back soft brownish grey. Rump delicately barred, the individual feathers grey with a narrow blackish bar, then a broader buff bar, then a narrow black subterminal bar and finally a buffish white tip. The rather long upper and under tail coverts are similar but with a very conspicuous buffish white tip to each feather, backed by a black subterminal bar, and the markings posterior to it obscure. Central tail feathers dark greyish brown at base shading to nearly black at tip. Outer tail feathers tipped with white and the outermost pair also white on the outer webs. Wings brownish grey, the coverts and inner secondaries with buffish white tips and blackish subterminal bands, forming a spotted pattern and two spotted bars across the folded wings. Outer secondaries and primaries brownish grey with buffish fringes to the outer webs. Under wing coverts mainly buff. Sides of lower neck and lower throat pale brownish grey. Breast delicately barred creamy white and blackish, the barred feathers intergrading in pattern with those of the lower breast, belly and flanks, which, in the living bird, give a beautiful spangled pattern, on a light chestnut background, the individual feathers being barred black

and white with broad white subterminal bands, fringed black at the tips and edged at the sides with pale chestnut, or cinnamon. In the centre of the belly there are often many nearly spotless chestnut feathers. There is a creamy white area just before the vent. Irides brown. Bill pinkish horn, reddish horn or pinkish. Legs and feet pinkish flesh colour.

Female has either no red at all on the head or a faint wash of it caused by rusty orange tips to some of the feathers, usually only on the crown and nape. Her underparts are paler than the male's, with less prominent barring, and spotting confined to the flanks. No chestnut except for a tinge on the flanks, central area of belly creamy buff and unmarked. Juvenile male paler and more buffish or sandy on the brown upperparts and with a pale, rusty orange head. Some young males show no reddish on the head and others very little, at fledging time and Immelmann *et al.* (1975) state that it is only young whose development has been retarded which show reddish head feathering at fledging. Otherwise intermediate in colour pattern between adult male and adult female. Juvenile female like adult but paler and buffier and with barring on the underparts less distinct. Nestlings as in the previous species, *Amadina fasciata*.

See plate 1, facing p. 96.

FIELD CHARACTERS Small brownish, thick-billed bird with red head (male) and conspicuously barred and spotted underparts and white tips to outer tail feathers.

DISTRIBUTION AND HABITAT Southern Africa in Angola north to Luanda and southern Huila, Southwest Africa, southern and central Botswana (Bechuanaland), southwestern Rhodesia, Cape Province, Natal, Transvaal and

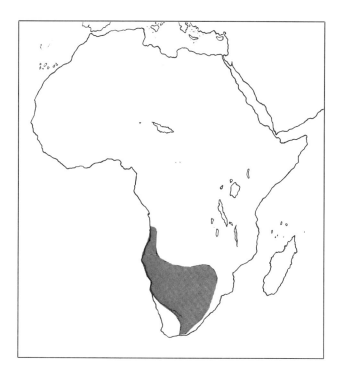

Griqualand. Inhabits dry savannas and semi-desert country with trees and bushes but appears dependent on surface water being available. Often around human habitations.

FEEDING AND GENERAL HABITS Feeds on the ground. Known to take seeds of grasses and Harvester Termites, *Hodotermes mossambicus*.

Highly social. Usually in small flocks of up to 30, sometimes in larger flocks. Sometimes in pairs but commonly two or three pairs prospect for nest sites together and nest close to each other. Breeding birds join the main flock to feed and rest when "off duty".

Both hops and walks on the ground (The Immelmanns, 1967). Flight over a distance strong and undulating (The Immelmanns, 1967).

In captivity its behaviour and needs are apparently very similar to those of previous species, *A. fasciata* (q.v.). Some have found it less aggressive and less prone to interfere with other birds' nests (Immelmann *et al.* 1975) but in view of its nesting habits it would seem unwise to chance keeping it with weaker species that one hoped to breed from.

NESTING So far as known always nests either in the old (or sometimes commandeered?) nests of other birds, chiefly weavers and sparrows, or in holes of buildings. Often several pairs will breed close to each other in old nest chambers of the Sociable Weaver, *Philetairus socius*.

Eggs 3 to 8, usually 4 to 6. Parental behaviour and nest defence display as in the previous species, *A. fasciata* (q.v.). Incubation period 12 to 14 days, young fledge at 20 days, both records for captive birds in Europe (Hall, unpublished mss and Scheeder, 1962). Breeds from March to September (McLachlan & Liversidge).

Immelmann & Immelmann (1967) describe how when seeking a nest site the pair, with the male leading, cautiously approach suitable nests of other species, especially nest chambers in the underside of the nest mass of the Sociable Weaver. They are at once driven away by the occupant(s) of nests in use and, presumably as a consequence, show much hesitation before entering an unoccupied nest.

VOICE Hall (unpublished manuscript) states that all the calls and the song are very similar to those of the Cut-throat (q.v.) but 'deeper and fruitier'. Immelmann *et al.* (1975) describe the call note (Lockruf) as a sparrow-like 'shep' or 'tshep' (my anglicisations) given in a quicker series on taking wing than at other times. The alarm call is a sharp 'tek' or 'tak', and there is a hissing anger note (Wutlaut) like that of the Zebra Finch. The song is described as whirring or buzzing ('schnurren') and soft. A sound spectrogram of it is given by Hall (1962).

DISPLAY AND SOCIAL BEHAVIOUR As previous species, *A. fasciata*, so far as known but the displays do not seem to have been described in detail. The Immelmanns observed pair formation take place gradually within the flock, initiated by the male repeatedly singing at a chosen female. When the two birds clump together and allo-preen each other the pair can be considered firmly established.

OTHER NAMES Red-headed Weaver Finch.

REFERENCES

Hall, M. F. 1962. Evolutionary aspects of estrildid song. *Symposia Zool. Soc. London* no. 8: 37–55. (Also unpublished manuscript on estrildid behaviour.)

Immelmann, K & G. 1967. Verhaltensökologische Studien an afrikanischen und australischen Estrildiden. *Zool. Jb. Syst. Bd.* **94**: 609–686.

Immelmann, K., Steinbacher, J. & Wolters, H. E. 1973 and 1975. *Vögel in Käfig und Voliere: Prachtfinken*: 497–510.

McLachlan, G. R. & Liversidge, R. 1957. *Roberts birds of South Africa.*

Scheeder, F. 1962. Rotkopfamadinen (Amadina erythrocephala L.). *Die Gefiederte Welt*, Sept. **1962**: 168–169.

Teschemaker, W. E. 1906. The breeding of the Red-headed Finch. *Avicult. Mag. new ser.*, vol. **4**: 354–357.

The pytilias

The forms in the genus *Pytilia* are medium-sized African estrildids whose second primaries are emarginated on both webs with a rather sharp notch or cut away effect on the inner web, and rather slender bills. All have red rumps and tails, red, orange, golden or green wings, barred underparts and mainly grey or grey and greenish body colour. They keep much to trees and scrub but feed on the ground. They are parasitised by the paradise whydahs, formerly placed in the genus *Steganura*, which is now usually included in *Vidua*.

The relationships of *Pytilia* are uncertain but it seems likely to be more closely related to *Amadina* than the very different appearance of the adult birds would at first suggest. Although these differ in coloration, the patterns of their plumages are rather similar, and there is a very close resemblance in the appearance and mouth patterns of their nestlings (see especially Steiner). The Green Twinspot, *Mandingoa nitidula*, shows a considerable resemblance to *Pytilia melba* in colour pattern and, in view of their different habitats and ecologies (so far as known) this seems more likely to be due to relationship than convergence.

Within the genus *Pytilia*, the Melba Finch or Green-winged Pytilia, *P. melba*, appears to stand further apart from the rest than any of them do to each other. It has a longer tail than any of its congeners, much lighter and brighter shades of red, yellow and green in its plumage and is altogether a more colourful bird. It has a wide range in Africa and shows considerable geographical overlap (Hall & Moreau) with *P. afra* although, on the whole, it is a bird of more arid areas. It is of interest that *P. afra*, the species with which it overlaps, is the one most like it in colour pattern although, except for its golden-orange wings, duller and darker.

The Orange-winged Pytilia or Red-faced Finch, *P. afra*, and the Yellow-winged Pytilia, *P. hypogrammica*, are

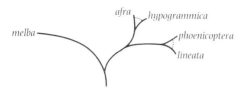

Presumed relationships of *Pytilia* species. See text for discussion. Dotted lines connect members of the same superspecies.

allopatric and clearly close relatives. They differ chiefly in *P. afra* being predominantly greenish in body colour and having a red bill and *P. hypogrammica* being predominantly grey and having a black bill. '*Pytilia lopezi*' is a red-winged form of *P. hypogrammica*. Delacour treats them as conspecific but others, such as Traylor in *Peters' Check-list*, given them specific rank. In view of Nicolai's findings on *P. phoenicoptera* and *P. lineata* (see further on) I prefer to give *afra* and *hypogrammica* specific rank within the same superspecies.

The Aurora Finch or Red-winged Pytilia, *P. phoenicoptera*, and the red-billed form that replaces it in Abyssinia have usually been treated as races of a single species. They are alike in colour and plumage pattern but have differently coloured bills, black in *P. phonoecoptera* and red in *P. (phoenicoptera) lineata*. Nicolai found that captive birds of the two forms behaved as different species and did not interbreed. Even when there was an excess of males of *phoenicoptera* and an excess of females of *lineata* neither form showed any sexual interest in the other. As their calls and displays are similar or identical it was presumably the different bill colour that functioned as an isolating mechanism. It is likely that it would be at least equally effective under natural conditions, should the two even come together in the wild, so I think they are best treated as members of a superspecies rather than as conspecific.

REFERENCES

Delacour, J. 1943. A revision of the subfamily Estrildinae of the family Ploceidae. *Zoologica, New York Zool. Soc.,* **28**: 69–86.

Hall, B. P. & Moreau, R. E. 1970. *An atlas of speciation in African passerine birds.* British Museum (Natural History) London.

Nicolai, J. 1968. Die Schnabelfärbung als potentialler Isolationsfaktor zwischen *Pytilia phoenicoptera* Swainson und *Pytilia lineata* Heuglin (Familie:Estrildiae). *J. Orn.* **109**: 450–461.

Peters, J. L. 1968. *Check-list of birds of the world.* Cambridge, Mass.

Melba Finch   *Pytilia melba*

Fringilla melba Linneaus, 1758, *Syst. Nat.* ed. 10, **1**, p. 180.

DESCRIPTION About size of Peter's Twinspot but slimmer in shape and with a much more slender bill. Inner web of outer primary of adult indented near tip. Forehead, malar region and throat dark orange-red to deep vermilion. Rest of head, including lores, sides of face, nape and neck, medium grey, paler and browner in worn plumage. Lores greyish buff. Mantle, back, upper part of rump, wing coverts, inner secondaries and outer webs of other wing quills yellowish olive-green. Rest of wing quills brownish. Underwing coverts obscurely barred pale and darker grey. Lower rump and upper tail coverts light carmine to orange-red. Two central tail feathers and outer webs of most others carmine red. Inner webs of most tail feathers blackish brown. Outer webs of the outermost pair light drab. Breast greenish gold to yellowish green with white and dark spotting 'showing through' the lower half (approximately). This effect is caused by feathers that are barred white and dark grey, with the end bar taking the form of two large white spots with a dark surround, and decomposed greenish gold tips. Lower breast and flanks barred dark grey and dull white; centre of lower belly and ventral area buffish white. Under tail coverts buffish white to buff, sometimes with a faint trace of darker barring. Irides dark red, orange-red, light red or reddish brown. Bill scarlet, carmine or crimson with ridge of culmen usually dusky, blackish or dark reddish; sometimes with a dark median streak and tip to the lower mandible. Legs and feet brown, yellowish brown or greyish brown.

The female has no red on her head, which is grey, whitish grey beneath the eyes and on the lores. Her throat is dull white barred with light grey. Towards the breast the grey bars become darker and more clearly defined and the barring on the flanks approaches (but does not equal) that on the male for darkness and clarity. Rest of plumage as male's. Bill dark brown with usually some pink or red at base of lower mandible.

Juvenile of both sexes light greyish drab above, tinged with olive on the back and a more definite yellowish olive on the outer fringes of the wing quills. Buffish olive fringes to coverts and inner secondaries. Parts of rump and tail, that are red in adult, dull rusty orange. Sides of face greyish buff. Underparts greyish buff to buff, except for white patch anterior to vent, with faint traces of darker barring. Irides greyish brown. Bill at first dark. Legs and feet paler and greyer than adult's. The juvenile male acquires his red face at an early stage in the first moult. In South Africa (*fide* Skead) this moult always starts with the head feathers but in some specimens I have seen from elsewhere breast and flank feathers are as far advanced. Nestling dark with sandy-white down (Skead). Mouth pattern apparently somewhat variable (see pictures in

Steiner & Immelmann *et al.* and colour plate in Nicolai (1964)) but always involving a conspicuous central black spot on palate, two blue spots at either side, whitish gape tubercles, a pale-tipped dark or partly dark tongue and blackish lower part of mouth. There may be racial or individual variation in nestling down colour as Nicolai (in Immelmann *et al.*, 1963) describes nestlings as having dark grey down. There are photographs of nestlings, fledglings and adults in Nicolai's 1964 paper on whydahs.

The above description is of nominate *P.m. melba* from Cabinda, Lower Congo, southern Katanga, western Malawi (Nyasaland), Zambia, Rhodesia and parts of South Africa. Also in western Transvaal, Orange Free State, northern Cape Province and southern South West Africa. *P.m. grotei*, from north-eastern Tanzania south to Mosambique, differs in having the red on the throat spreading over much of the breast, only the sides and lower edge of the breast being greenish gold. The olive on its upper parts tends to be more strongly tinged with gold. *P.m. belli*, from western Uganda, south through Kivu and Rwanda to both northern shores of Lake Tanganyika, Lake Rukwa, western Tanzania and islands in Lake Victoria, is very similar to *P.m. grotei* but perhaps averaging more golden on the upper parts. *P.m. percivali*, from south-western Kenya and northern Tanzania, has a red throat and golden breast as in nominate *P.m. melba* but both the red and the gold are paler and there are no partly concealed spots on the breast, the corresponding feathers being barred in pattern like the rest of the underparts (except as otherwise described for *P.m. melba*). *P.m. soudanensis*, from southern and eastern Sudan and adjacent Abyssinia through northern and eastern Kenya to Somalia and the lowlands of southern and eastern Abyssinia, is similar to nominate *P.m. melba* but often has the red of the throat more or less suffusing the gold of the breast. Its wing coverts may be suffused with red, as is sometimes the case with *P.m. belli* and *P.m. grotei* also. There is often an extensive whitish area on the belly and the creamy buff under tail coverts have faint darker bars. Bill sometimes pink.

P.m. citerior, which occurs in the arid thorn bush zone from Senegal and Guinea east to Bahr el Ghazal and Kordofan, is paler than other races. The red on its head and throat is a bright, light vermilion and is joined by a stripe of red running over and behind the eye. The area immediately under the eye and the lores are also red. The grey and green upper parts are a little paler than in other forms and tend to bleach more. Its underparts are lightly cross-barred with narrow greyish and/or greenish brown bars on the white feathers. Its breast is a bright golden yellow with no suffusion of red, contrasting with the light vermilion throat. The female is also paler than those of other races.

Some other subspecies have been described by zealous taxonomists but all are very similar indeed to one or other of those described above.

Nicolai's studies suggest the possibility that the forms with red above the eye and those with grey above the eye

may have reached specific level. He found both forms living side by side at Kisangiro and Lembeni, Tanzania.

FIELD CHARACTERS Green and grey small bird with barred flanks and underparts and red rump and tail. Male also has bright red face and golden-yellow or red and golden breast. Longer-tailed than other pytelias. Further distinguished from *P. afra* by lack of orange on wing and, in the male, by lack of grey band below its much brighter red throat. From *P. lineata* also by its (melba's) green back and from *P. phoenicoptera* by all these characters and its red bill.

DISTRIBUTION AND HABITAT Tropical Africa and part of southern Africa but not in the western and central African rain forest areas. See map and racial distributions (under 'Description').

Inhabits dry acacia thornland, dry and fairly open woodland with some scrub or bush cover, thorn scrub bordering watercourses, semi desert or desert edge with thorn cover, and grassland or cultivated areas with interspersed bushes or patches of thorn scrub.

FEEDING AND GENERAL HABITS Feeds on the ground, taking seeds and termites. In central Transvaal, Skead found that seeds of grasses of the genera *Urochloa* and *Sporobolus*, and termites, were the major foods although seeds of *Alternanthera pungens* and of the grasses *Rhynchelytrum repens*, *Setaria verticillata* and *Panicum maximum* were also taken. Probably other small insects are eaten should the bird come across them when looking for seeds or termites. When feeding, the Melba Finch habitually turns over debris and breaks open termite galleries (Skead).

Skead found it only in pairs except in the case of dependent young still with their parents and aggregations at neutral feeding or drinking places. The Immelmanns (1967) also found it living in territorial pairs. This is

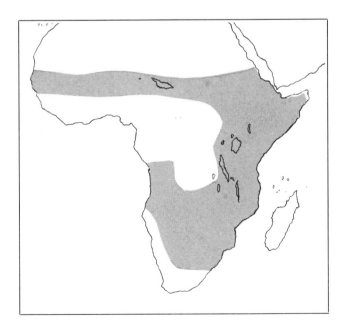

corroborated by its behaviour in captivity and it is possible that the small flocks in which some observers (e.g. Hoesch) have usually seen it have been birds at 'neutral' feeding or drinking places or temporary flocking due to adverse local conditions.

In captivity the male (unless ill) is highly aggressive towards conspecifics of the same sex and towards related species that show red on the head or bill. Some individuals, and probably most when closely confined, may also attack related species that do not have red on the face or unrelated species that do.

Melba Finches are generally agreed by those who have kept them (I have not) to be difficult and delicate when they first arrive, most probably due to lack of sufficient (or any) animal food between their capture in Africa and eventual sale in Europe or elsewhere. Some writers on bird-keeping have implied that, once in good condition, Melba Finches only need a few maggots and mealworms daily (in addition to seed, minerals etc) to keep them so but such writers do not seem to have successfully bred them and Immelmann *et al.* (1963) state that they need a rich variety of insect food throughout the year, which must consist only in small part of mealworms and these either cooked or newly moulted, that whiteworms and fruitflies are usually refused, that eggfood, even if taken by the adults will not suffice for any young they are rearing, and that they need to be kept at a temperature of 20 to 22°C. Aviculturists of modest means would seem well advised to leave this species alone.

NESTING Nest in a thorn or other bush or small tree, usually from 0·5 to 5 metres above ground. Dome-shaped or roundish, of grass and other vegetation, lined with feathers. Skead found that, as with many estrildids, a platform was initially built. On this and round it the birds built an outer shell of strong, dry grass stems. Green grass panicles were used for the main body of the nest and strips of broad grass blades, especially of *Panicum maximum*, often added to the outside of the nest, which was lined with feathers. One nest examined contained 8 Guineafowl feathers and 22 of Domestic Fowl. Only males were seen to collect material in the wild (no birds seen actually building) and only the male of a captive pair was seen either to bring materials or to build (Skead).

Eggs 3 to 6. Incubation period (in captivity) 12–13 days. Young fledge at about 21 days and are able to feed themselves 14 days after fledging (Immelmann *et al.*, 1963). Male and female incubate in turn by day and both spend the night in the nest (Immelmann *et al.*). Lynes, however, noted that with wild birds in the Sudan, he never found a female incubating by day. He implies that he visited nests at different times of day but does not go into details.

Wild Melba Finches in central Transvaal fed their young with grass seeds as well as with termites from the first day (Skead) but in captivity only insect food, preferably ant pupae and/or greenfly will be fed to the young at first (Immelmann *et al.*). Possibly with this and other estrildids, various soaked grass seeds might be offered to breeding birds with good results.

The Melba Finch is parasitised by the Paradise Whydah, *Vidua paradisaea*, and the Broad-tailed Paradise Whydah, *V. orientalis*. The former exploiting the forms with grey around the eye and the latter the more northernly forms that have the eye surrounded by red (see Nicolai, 1964 and 1977).

Skead found that in South Africa the species might breed from November to June, with a peak in February and March as a rule but with the peak always *after* the heaviest rains and in the latter part of the rainy season and extending into the dry season. The period between breeding seasons was 5 to 6 months. Recorded breeding in Zambia from January to April, in Malawi and Mosambique February to June, in Tanzania in April, in Nigeria in August and September, in Sudan in October, November, February and May to July, in Abyssinia in May and June and in Uganda and Kenya from March to May (Mackworth-Praed & Grant).

VOICE The following is derived from Nicolai (in Immelmann) who found considerable geographical variation in the vocalisations of this species.

The contact call of nominate *P.m. melba* is a hard to pinpoint, thin 'see-eh'. The alarm call, also used in any form of excitement is transcribed by Nicolai as 'geeb' (my anglicisation) and by Skead as 'wick'. The song of the male is longer than that of most estrildids, each strophe lasts upwards of sixteen seconds, begins with a sound like a drop of water falling onto the surface of water, followed by a long and then a short whistled note, then by gurgling and trilling sounds which end with three fluting notes. The strophe is usually repeated several times. The female also sings but her song is less loud and shorter. A soft version of the song functions, in this species, as a nest call.

In *P.m. citerior* the noticeably different song consists of a series of single 'veet' notes, a strophe of two whistled notes that vary in pitch and two short gurgling strophes. When the male loses contact with his mate he calls her with a series of notes ('Rufstrophe').

Sound spetrograms of the contact calls of *P.m. damarensis* (treated here, as in *Peters' check-list*, as a synonym of *P.m. melba*) and of *P.m. citerior* are given in Güttinger (1973).

The young have a two-syllabled begging call (Güttinger, 1976).

DISPLAY AND SOCIAL BEHAVIOUR Courtship display takes place on the ground. Male and female hop around each other with angled tails, the male meanwhile holding a feather or grass stem in his bill and singing.

To entice the female to the nest or a proposed nest site, the male raises and quivers his tail and utters a soft version of his song.

Allo-preening appears not to be recorded. The Immelmanns (1967) failed to see it during intensive observations of wild birds in southern Africa.

OTHER NAMES Green-winged Pytilia, Melba Waxbill.

REFERENCES

Güttinger, H. R. 1976. Zur systematischen Stellung der Gattungen *Amadina, Lepidopygia* und *Lonchura* (Aves, Estrildidae). *Bonn. zool. Beitr.* **27**: 218–244.

Güttinger, H. R. & Nicolai, J. 1973. Struktur und Funktion der Rufe bei Prachtfinken (Estrildidae). *Z. Tierpsychol.* **33**: 319–334.

Hoesch, W. & Niethammer, G. 1940. Die Vogelwelt Deutsch-Sudwestafrikas. *J. Orn.* **88**: Sonderheft.

Immelmann, K. & G. 1967. Verhaltensökologische Studien an Afrikanischen und australischen Estrildiden. *Zool. Jb. Syst. Bd.* **94**: 609–686.

Immelmann, K., Steinbacher, J. & Wolters, H. E. 1963. *Vögel in Käfig und Voliere: Prachtfinken*: 25–38. Aachen, Germany.

Lynes, H. 1924. On the birds of North and Central Darfur. *Ibis* **6**, 11 the ser., 648–719.

Mackworth-Praed, C. W. & Grant, C. H. B. 1960. The African handbook of birds, ser. 1, vol. 2. London.

Nicolai, J. 1964. Der Brutparasitismus der Viduinae als ethologisches Problem. *Z. Tierpsychol.* **21**: 129–204.

Nicolai, J. 1977. Der Rotmaskenastrild als Wirt der Togo-Paradieswitwe. *J. Orn.* **118**: 175–188.

Skead, D. M. 1976. Ecological Studies of Four Estrildines in the Central Transvaal. *Ostrich*, suppl. no. 11.

Orange-winged Pytilia   *Pytilia afra*

Fringilla afra Gmelin, 1789, *Syst. Nat.,* **1** (2) p. 905.

DESCRIPTION Very slightly smaller than previous species, *P. melba*, but with proportionately much shorter tail, slightly shorter and less slender bill and shorter, denser body plumage. First primary sharply emarginated on both webs. Forehead, face, cheeks and upper part of throat blood red to deep crimson, sometimes with a dulled or speckled appearance owing to the grey feather bases being partly exposed. Crown and nape dull olivaceous grey with darker feather centres giving a faintly spotted effect. Mantle, back and those parts of the inner secondaries that are visible when the wing is folded, dark yellowish olive to dark greenish gold. Rump and upper tail coverts crimson, the tips of the feathers of a different texture and, especially when worn, of a paler and brighter red. Central tail feathers and outer webs of all but the outermost pair carmine red. Inner webs of most tail feathers and outermost pair dull brown to blackish, sometimes with a small buffish mark at the feather tip but more often not in adult birds. Lesser and median wing coverts as back but often with a more orange tinge and with paler tips to the feathers. Primary coverts and tips and inner webs of primaries blackish brown. Golden-orange fringes to the greater wing coverts and outer webs of outer secondaries and primaries form a bright band and patch on the folded wing. Under wing coverts mainly pale golden-buff. Sides of neck and a band across lower throat and upper breast medium grey. Breast dark yellowish olive, often with an orange tinge, with faint, more or less crescentic whitish cross bars on the feathers. Rest of underparts, except for a yellowish white ventral patch, similar but with the whitish bars wider and more prominent. Under tail coverts dark olive with broad pale buff to whitish tips. Irides orange, orange-red, brownish red or red. Bill light crimson, light dull red or pink with dark brown, blackish brown or pinkish brown basal half (approximately) of upper mandible. Legs and feet pale whitish flesh colour to fleshy brown.

Female has no red on her grey head. Upper throat whitish with faint greyish bars. Underparts grey, tinged with olive, and barred with dull white. Golden-orange areas on wings tending to be a little less bright than male's. Bill brownish pink or dull reddish, basal part of upper mandible dusky brown.

Juvenile very like adult female but duller and browner above, paler and buffier below with less distinct barring and those parts of the tail that are red in the adult of a dark rusty orange. All of the few specimens I have examined have buffish or off-white tips to most of the tail feathers. Some juveniles are greyer, others more buffish in plumage tone. This appears to be an individual not a sexual difference. The unfledged nestling is very like that of the previous species, *P. melba*, with long down on its upperparts. There is an excellent photo of it in Nicolai (1964). The mouth pattern of the nestling perhaps varies geographically, individually or with age. Many examined by Nicolai (in Immelmann, 1963) had no dark spot on the middle of the reddish palate but only a violet spot on either side, but those (presumably) examined by Steiner (1960) had a blackish central spot on the palate, similar to that of the nestling *P. melba*.

FIELD CHARACTERS Small, rather squat-shaped bird, mainly dark olive gold and greyish with conspicous orange patch on wings and red rump and tail. Short tail and conspicuous orange on wings distinguish this species from the Melba Finch, greenish or yellowish back and orange (not red) on wings from *P. phoenicoptera*, same and red bill from *P. lineata*. For differences from the allopatric *P. hypogrammica* see that species.

DISTRIBUTION AND HABITAT Africa in eastern and southern Abyssinia, southern Sudan and northern Uganda and the adjoining Congo region south through Kenya and Tanzania to Malawi, northern Mosambique, north-eastern Transvaal, west through Zambia and Rhodesia, Katanga and Kasai to central Angola; lower Congo from Cabinda to Kwamouth, and Zanzibar.

Inhabits thorny thickets near water, open woodland, the edge of gallery forest, grassland with bushes and trees and sometimes Mopane woodland. Tends to choose better-watered, less arid areas than those favoured by *P. melba* but with some overlap.

FEEDING AND GENERAL HABITS Feeds mainly and perhaps entirely on the ground. Known to take grass seeds. Almost certainly also takes termites and, probably, other insects and seeds as well. Usually in pairs or family parties; sometimes in small, loose flocks when not breeding. Often

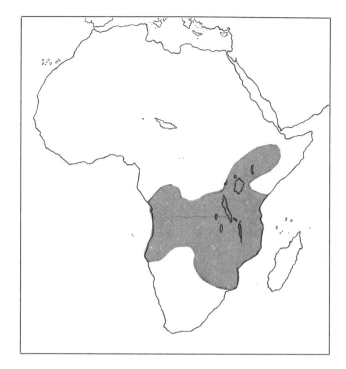

perches well up in trees. Flight strong, and it often flies at a good height, unlike *P. melba*.

In captivity it seems able to survive longer on an all-seed diet than can *P. melba* but (*fide* Nicolai, 1965) needs a plentiful supply of animal food if it is to be *kept* in health. Breeds readily in captivity if a good supply of fresh ant pupae can be provided for it to feed its young (Nicolai, 1965) and it is one of the many estrildids that are very easy to breed in captivity in warm countries where unlimited supplies of termites can be obtained. However, the fact that it has often been reared successfully under Bengalese Finches (Immelmann) and even by its own parents in aviaries where maggots were the only form of live food supplied (Restall) suggests the likelihood that in a wild state the young may in fact be fed partly on vegetable food, probably green or very small seeds.

NESTING The nest is a rather frail or at least frail-looking roundish structure of dried grass stems, and sometimes other vegetation, usually lined with only a slight pad of feathers (Vincent). It is placed in a tree, bush, shrub or palm at from about 1 to 3 metres above ground. Eggs usually 3 or 4, sometimes 5. Both sexes incubate in turn by day and both roost in the nest. Incubation period 12–13 days. Young fledge at about 21 days. They can feed themselves about 14 days after fledging but may be fed by the parents for some time after this. The above information on fledging times etc. is from captive birds (Immelmann *et al.*). In captivity, and possibly also when wild, the female often starts to lay before the roof of the nest is complete.

Recorded breeding from January to May in Rhodesia, Zambia and Katanga; March to June in Malawi (Nyasaland); April and May in south-eastern Congo, April to June in Tanzania and Zanzibar and specimens in breeding condition collected in June in southern Abyssinia.

This species is parasitised by the Broad-tailed Paradise Whydah, *Vidua obtusa*.

VOICE Both distant and close contact calls are very suggestive of the cheepings of a young Domestic Chick and very variable in tone, emphasis and degree of loudness. The song is comprised of three strophes. It begins with a long series of two- or three-syllabled rattling notes; then follows a series of soft fluting notes and finally a short, crackling 'kay'. The fluting strophe of the song is strongly sexually motivated and it is also used as a nest call. The above information is from Nicolai (1964 and Immelmann *et al.*). Sound spectrograms of contact calls are given in Güttinger & Nicolai (1973).

DISPLAY Immelmann (1963) describe the courtship display as similar to that of *P. melba*. Male and female hop around each other with angled tails. The male utters the fluting song strophe and the female a call sounding like 'dooeet' (my anglicisation). The male intersperses this with tail quivering. Finally, if stimulated, the female solicits with quivering tail and the male mounts and copulates. Kunkel (unpublished mss) has repeatedly seen courtship display, always on branches, in which the male, with nesting material in his bill, jumps up and down, throwing back his head. He quivers his tail and, between the jumps, quickly turns a little to one side or another. Copulation was not seen to follow.

When nest-calling the male utters the fluting song strophe and raises and quivers his tail.

OTHER NAMES Red-faced Finch, Yellow-backed Pytilia.

REFERENCES
Chapin, J. P. 1954. The birds of the Belgian Congo, pt. 4. *Bull. Amer. Mus. Nat. Hist.* **75**B.
Güttinger, H. R. & Nicolai, J. 1973. Struktur und Funktion der Rufe bei Prachtfinken (Estrildidae). *Z. Tierpsychol.* **33**: 319–334.
Immelmann, K. Steinbacher, J. & Wolters, H. E. 1963 and 1973. *Vogel in Kafig und Voliere: Prachtfinken*: 39–45, and 516.
Mackworth-Praed, C. W. & Grant, C. H. B. 1960. African handbook of birds ser. 1, vol. 2. London and New York.
McLachlan, G. R. & Liversidge, R. 1957. *Roberts birds of South Africa*, revised ed. Cape Town.
Nicolai, J. 1964. Der Brutparasitismus der Viduinae als ethologisches Problem. *Z. Tierpsychol.* **21**: 129–204.
Nicolai, J. 1965. *Käfig und Volierenvögel*. Kosmos, Stuttgart.
Restall, R. L. 1975. Finches and other seed-eating birds. London.
Steiner, H. 1960. Klassifikation der Prachtfinken, Spermestidae, auf Grund der Rachenzeichnungen ihrer Nestlinge. *J. Orn.* **102**: 92–112.
Vincent, A. W. 1949. On the breeding habits of some African birds. *Ibis* **91**: 660–668.

Yellow-winged Pytilia   *Pytilia hypogrammica*

Pytelia hypogrammica Sharpe, 1870, *Ibis*, p. 56.

DESCRIPTION Very similar in size, shape and colour pattern to the previous species, *P. afra*, with which it forms a

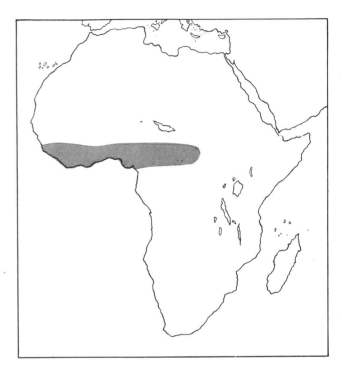

superspecies. In appearance it differs from *P. afra* as follows: red of face, rump and upper tail coverts a little lighter and brighter, scarlet rather than crimson. Mantle, back and inner secondaries a darkish medium grey. Parts of wings that are golden-orange in *P. afra* are usually a deep, slightly greenish, yellow-gold but may be greenish yellow or (less often) predominantly orange-red. Under wing coverts barred white and grey. Underparts with no olive or yellow tinge, uniformly grey on throat and upper breast and delicately barred elsewhere with dull white. Under tail coverts blackish grey with white tips. Irides red. Bill black. Legs and feet flesh-coloured to fleshy brown.

Female like female of *P. afra* (q.v.) but with mantle and back brownish grey like crown and nape. Wings as male but none of the many specimens I have seen showed any red or orange tint in the golden parts of the wing. One female, no. 1966.16.4230, in the British Museum (Natural History) collection has a narrow superciliary stripe of red-tipped feathers. Juvenile very like female but duller and the grey parts of a more brownish grey. Nestling like that of *P. afra* (Nicolai).

Pytilia lopezi Alexander was based on an individual male of this species, the bright parts of whose wings are orange-red. A male collected by Serle in Enugu – BM(NH) no. 1966.16.4227 – is intermediate in wing colour between more typical specimens of the species and the type of *P. lopezi* and has, in addition, a patch of red-tipped feathers on its breast. The red-winged form would appear to be a colour morph or (less probably) a local race. Six young bred from a pair of '*lopezi*' all had red wings like their parents (Matzinger).

FIELD CHARACTERS Small thick-set grey 'finch' with red face (male) or all dull grey head (female), red rump and tail and golden yellow or orange-red wings.

Shorter tail, grey back and breast, and black bill distinguish it from *P. melba*; usually golden yellow or orange wings, and in male the red face, from *P. phoenicoptera*.

DISTRIBUTION AND HABITAT Western Africa from Sierra Leone and the Ivory Coast east to central Oubangi-Shari. Inhabits savanna woodland and derelict cultivated areas. In Nigeria Nicolai found it a bird of the derived savanna and southern Guinea savanna.

FEEDING AND GENERAL HABITS Feeds mainly, and perhaps entirely, on the ground. Known to take grass seeds, which are certainly a major food, also termites and other insects. A captive pair ate mainly small kinds of millet but also took canary seed and soaked niger and lettuce seed. They were very fond of ant pupae and fed their young entirely on these for the first few days (Eckl).

Usually in pairs or family parties. When not feeding often perches well up in trees. Flight undulating and very fast. When disturbed by man it commonly flies to a distance, often out of sight (Nicolai).

This species is little known in aviculture but Eckl found it relatively hardy and less sensitive to changes of temperature than many estrildids. His birds reared their young on fresh ant pupae for the first few days but later also fed them with dry millet. They were in an aviary with an outside flight so may have caught a few other insects. Matzinger successfully bred both yellow-winged and red-winged forms in smallish indoor aviaries. He gave them ant pupae, grass seeds, chickweed and soaked millet.

NESTING The nest is sited in a bush, shrub or tree from 0·5 to 4 metres above ground. It is roundish and loosely built with the usual side entrance. Several nests found by Nicolai were built only of grass panicles and lined with feathers, but one found and examined in detail by Serle had three clearly defined layers: an outer one of broad grass strips, an intermediate one of grass stems and a lining of flowering grass pannicles and a few guineafowl feathers.

Eggs usually 3, sometimes 4. Incubation period 12–14 days (Eckl, Matzinger, Nicolai), young fledge at 16–17 days (Nicolai, Eckl). Both sexes incubate in turn by day. Breeds in the dry season. Nests have been found from

October to January (inclusive). In his study area Nicolai found the breeding season was interrupted and many nests and young destroyed by the local habit of setting fire to large areas of the countryside as soon as it was dry.

Parasitised by *Vidua togoensis* (Nicolai, 1977).

VOICE Nicolai says the vocalisations of this species are very like those of *P. phoenicoptera* (q.v.). Sonagrams of the contact call are given by Güttinger & Nicolai). Eckl describes the song (?) given by the courting male as a repeated 'vee-vee-vee' (my anglicisation). The song is innate (Güttinger & Nicolai).

DISPLAY AND SOCIAL BEHAVIOUR Eckl repeatedly saw a courtship display, on the ground, in which the male, by the side of his mate and with angled tail, bowed repeatedly to her or hopped around her bowing and uttering the 'vee-vee-vee' notes. He only saw copulation on one occasion. Then the birds were perched and the male, in an erect posture, sang and bowed to the female. She responded by soliciting with quivering tail and mating took place. Burkard saw mutual bowing between male and female. He describes courtship display in which the male, with nesting symbol in his bill, jumps up and down, letting go of the perch momentarily and throwing up his head as he does so.

OTHER NAMES Golden-winged Pytilia, Red-faced Aurora Finch.

REFERENCES
Burkard, R. 1964. Die Balz des Rotmaskenastrilds. *Gefiederte Welt* **1964**: 85–86.
Eckl, G. 1974. Die Erstzucht des Rotmaskenastrilds (*Pytilia hypogrammica* Sharpe). *Gefiederte Welt* **98**: 42.
Güttinger, H. R. & Nicolai, J. 1973. Struktur und Funktion der Rufe bei Prachtfinken (Estrildidae). *Z. Tierpsychol.* **33**: 319–334.
Matzinger, H. 1979. Die zucht des rotflügeligen Rotmasken-astrilder. *Gefiederte Welt* **1979**: 101–102.
Nicolai, J. 1977. Der Rotmaskenastrild (*Pytilia hypogrammica*) als Wirt der Togo-Paradieswitwe (*Steganura togoensis*). *J. Orn.* **118**: 175–188.
Serle, W. 1957. A contribution to the ornithology of the eastern region of Nigeria. *Ibis* **99**: 371–418.

Aurora Finch   *Pytilia phoenicoptera*

Pytilia phoenicoptera Swainson, 1837, *Birds W. Africa*, **1**, p. 203, pl. 16.

DESCRIPTION Similar in size and shape to previous species but perhaps a little shorter-feathered on head, and bill proportionately averaging a very little longer, giving it a rather thin-headed appearance. Head and body (where not otherwise stated) a medium pure grey, palest on the throat and darkest on the back, with darker centres and pale fringes to the feathers on the forehead and fore-crown, and delicately barred with dull white on lower breast, belly, flanks and under wing coverts. Under tail coverts dark grey, broadly tipped with white. In some individuals the lower flanks and under tail coverts are

suffused with red and, exceptionally, the under tail coverts may be tipped with rose pink instead of white. Wings dark brownish grey with outer fringes of outer secondaries and basal two-thirds of primaries (approximately), small feathers along edge of carpal joint, and visible parts of the lesser, median and greater wing coverts, scarlet to crimson red, sometimes fading to orange-red in worn plumage. Rump and upper tail coverts scarlet to crimson. Central tail feathers and outer webs of all other tail feathers, except the outermost pair which are entirely drab brown, carmine to crimson. Inner webs of all but outermost and central pairs of tail feathers brownish black. Iris red. Bill black, sometimes with a greyish area at base of lower mandible. Legs and feet pale brown to brownish flesh.

Female brownish grey to greyish brown where male is pure grey. She is also rather paler (as well as browner) on the underparts and with the (less conspicuous) barring extending up over the entire breast. Her red parts are often less bright but in both sexes there is much individual variation as well as that due to wear. Juvenile like female but paler and browner, tinged buff and with buff, not white, barring on underparts. Red areas dull orange-red. Bill at first greyish.

Individuals with red face masks, like those of *P. afra* and *P. hypogrammica*, have been bred in captivity (from normally-coloured parents) but do not seem to have been seen in the wild (Immelmann *et al.*, 1975).

FIELD CHARACTERS Small grey (male) or brownish grey (female) 'finch' with red rump, tail and wings. Red (not yellow or orange) wings distinguish it from all normally-coloured individuals of other *Pytilia* species. Lack of any red on head (in normally-coloured examples) distin-guishes male from males of all other pytilias and, as these birds are usually in pairs or family parties, adult males are likely to be seen if any of the species are.

DISTRIBUTION AND HABITAT Northern tropical Africa in the semi arid zone from Gambia and Portuguese Guinea east to Nigeria, northern Cameroons, Bahr el Ghazal, equa-torial Sudan, north-eastern Congo and northern Uganda.

Inhabits open woodland, savanna, clearings in or edges of thicker woodland or bush and bamboo thickets, cultivated areas and around villages.

FEEDING AND GENERAL HABITS Seeks food on the ground. Known to take grass seeds and termites. Usually in pairs or family parties. Sometimes in association with other estrildids or the Grey Singing Finch, but probably this represents more or less fortuitious aggregations at feeding or drinking sites. When not feeding spends much of its time, or at least seems to have been most often observed, in trees.

In captivity it appears to be the most easy of the pytelias to keep and breed although Immelmann *et al.* recommend that it be kept in a temperature of not less than 20°C. It is usually tame towards its owner, nests freely and is never provoked or frightened into deserting by examination of

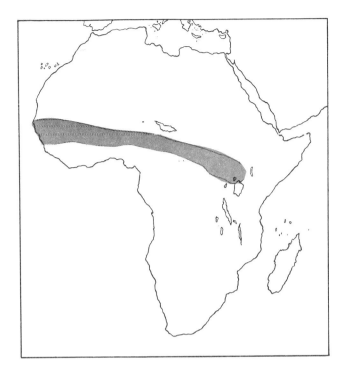

its nest (Cotterel, Nicolai, Russ). Ideally it needs unlimited supplies of fresh meadow ant pupae or larvae to rear its young and will hardly ever fail to do so successfully if these can be supplied. Even in a wild state, however, some seed is fed to the nestlings (Bannerman) and Cotterel was successful in breeding Aurora Finches when a limited amount of mealworms and grasshoppers were the only insects supplied.

When alarmed often crouches still with raised tail (Immelmann *et al.*, 1963).

NESTING Nest similar to that of other pytilia species (q.v.). It is sited usually near the top of a bush or small tree at about three-quarters of a metre to two metres high. Three or 4 eggs have comprised the clutch in most nests so far examined. Incubation period 12–13 days (Russ, Immelmann *et al.*). Young fledge at about 21 days. These times all of captive birds in Europe. Both sexes share incubation and brooding by day in the usual way. Male often, probably whenever he can find one, brings a feather when he comes to take over a spell of incubation.

There is much circumstantial evidence that this species is parasitised by the whydah, *Vidua (Steganura) interjecta* (Nicolai, 1977).

VOICE Nicolai describes the distance (contact) call as fluting or whistling in tone. Immelmann *et al.* (1963) describe a call, whose function they do not state, as a ventriloquial-sounding 'eek' or lkyerk', and a soft 'geegee-geegee' (hard 'G') which is uttered during copulation.

The song evidently shows a good deal of either individual and/or geographical variation. Nicolai (1968) describes it as beginning with a repeated series of rattling notes, followed by a double note whose second part is

drawn out into a croaky whistle ('krächzend-flotend klingt'). Aurora Finch songs heard by Immelmann *et al.* (1963) and Cotterel seem to have been, respectively, better and worse (to human ears) than those heard by Nicolai. The former describe the song as a melodious fluting strophe, the latter as like 'the gutteral creakings of some small unoiled machine'.

DISPLAY AND SOCIAL BEHAVIOUR Russ, who was the first person to breed and study this species in captivity, described courtship display in which the male, with angled tail, bobs up and down as he hops around the female, bowing, until she joins in the 'dance'. He noted that first the displaying male and then the female would utter a penetrating, monosyllabic 'tseet tseet' (my anglicisation). Russ does not say if his birds held a piece of nesting material in the bill during this display but Nicolai (1968) says this species has a typical courtship display dance with nest material held in the bill and notes that at each upward movement the bird's feet let go of the branch.

In captivity this species is very un-aggressive, in strong contrast to the Melba Finch. More than one breeding pair can be successfully kept in the same aviary (Nicolai, 1968).

OTHER NAMES Red-winged Pytilia, Aurora Waxbill.

REFERENCES

Bannerman, D. A. 1949. *The birds of tropical West Africa*, vol. 7. London.
Cotterel, R. 1960. Breeding the Aurora Finch. *Avicult. Mag.* **66**: 161–164.
Immelmann, K., Steinbacher, J. & Wolters, H. E. 1963 and 1975. *Vögel in Käfig und Voliere: Prachtfinken*: 48–54 and 517–520. Aachen, Germany.
Mackworth-Praed, C. W. & Grant, C. H. B. 1973. *African handbook of birds*, ser. 3, vol. 2. London.
Nicolai, J. 1968. Die Schnäbelfarbung als potentialler Isolations-faktor zwischen *Pytilia phoenicoptera* swainson und *Pytilia lineata* Heuglin. *J. Orn.* **109**: 450–461.
Nicolai, J. 1977. Der Rotmaskenastrild (*Pytilia hypogrammica*) als Wirt der Togo-Paradieswitwe (*Steganura togoensis*). *J. Orn.* **118**: 175–188.
Russ, K. 1879. *Die Fremdländischen Stubenvögel*, vol. 1. Hanover, Germany.

Red-billed Aurora Finch   *Pytilia lineata*

Pytelia lineata Heuglin, 1863, *J. Orn.* **11**, p. 17.

This form is usually treated as a race of the Aurora Finch, *P. phoenicoptera*. For reasons for treating it separately here see introduction to group.

DESCRIPTION As previous form, *P. phoenicoptera*, except as follows: barring on underparts broader, coarser and more conspicuous. Bill bright red. Iris brown in the only specimen, an adult male, for which I can find this information recorded. Nicolai noted that his captive specimens of this form had shorter bills, brighter red on their wings and were a paler grey. The rather small series of skins in the British Museum (Natural History) do not show these differences which may, perhaps, have been individual rather than specific (or racial) in character. I have not seen an adult female of this form, it is said to be like that of *P. phoenicoptera* except for having a red bill which is, however, paler than the male's and with a dark area at the base of the upper mandible (Nicolai). Juvenile like that of *P. phoenicoptera* but its bill soon starts to turn pinkish and then red.

FIELD CHARACTERS Small, short-tailed grey (male) or brownish grey (female) 'finch' with red wings, rump, tail and bill and barred underparts.

DISTRIBUTION AND HABITAT Abyssinia: in the western and north-western regions and in the south-eastern highlands (Urban and Brown). Presumably in similar habitats to those favoured elsewhere by *P. phoenicoptera*.

FEEDING AND GENERAL HABITS As *P. phoenicoptera*, so far as known, but very little information.

NESTING I can find no information on wild birds. In captivity as *P. phoenicoptera* (Nicolai). Langberg (in Restall) successfully bred it on a diet of seeds, various soft foods, mealworms and mosquito larvae.

VOICE As *P. phoenicoptera* (Nicolai).

DISPLAY AND BEHAVIOUR As *P. phoenicoptera*, so far as known. Nicolai said the males of his captive birds performed courtship display more often than his males of *P. phoenicoptera* although the displays were the same.

OTHER NAMES Red-billed Red-winged Pytilia, Red-billed Aurora Waxbill.

REFERENCES

Nicolai, J. 1968. Die Schnabelfärbung als potentialler Isolationsfaktor zwischen *Pytilia phoenicoptera* Swainson und *Pytilia lineata* Heuglin (Familie: Estrildidae). *J. Orn.* **109**: 450–461.

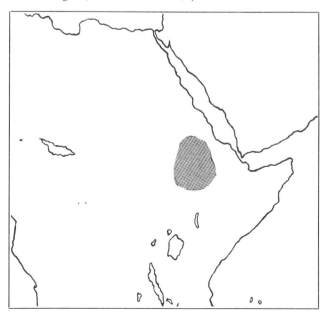

Restall, R. L. 1975. *Finches and other seed-eating birds.* London.
Urban, E. K. & Brown, L. H. 1971. *A check-list of the birds of Ethiopia.* Addis Ababa, Ethiopia.

The twinspots

The twinspots form a group of medium- to large-sized waxbills who take their name from the 'paired' white spots, one on either side of the shaft of the feather, on the sides of the lower breast and flanks; sometimes also elsewhere. They vary in colour but the males always, and both sexes usually, have some red in their plumage. Most of them show marked sexual dichromatism. They all live in or near dense or thorny cover and feed on the ground. Their vocabulary includes relatively complex and often melodious songs. Nothing that is known of their behaviour contradicts the likelihood of their all being fairly closely related. They, and some other forest and forest-edge forms probably related to them, have usually been considered as primitive. Kunkel has, however, argued that it is much more likely that estrildids evolved in grassland habitats and that forest and brush-haunting species are the derived forms, not *vice-versa*, and I think he is right.

Both recent and earlier workers on the group have concluded that the twinspots are related to each other but have disagreed as to how closely and whether or not some are closer to other 'non-twinspot' species. Currently (Traylor, in *Peters' Check-list*), they are distributed among the genera *Hypargos*, *Euchistospiza*, *Clytospiza* and *Mandingoa*. Hall and Moreau also recognise these genera but with reservations as to the wisdom of so doing.

Opinions differ as to whether these genera are 'well-differentiated' (Mayr) or 'poorly-differentiated' (Hall & Moreau). I am of the latter opinion and would prefer to include all, *Mandingoa* possibly accepted, in the genus *Hypargos* and only refrain from doing so for the following considerations: firstly it is possible that some of the twinspots may yet prove to be more closely related to species within other genera, such as *Cryptospiza*, and *Lagonosticta*, than they are to *all* other twinspots (see further on). Secondly genera are, as has been said largely units of convenience and therefore it seems desirable, in a work of this kind, to recognise the genera used in the world check-list unless one feels reasonably convinced that it is best not to do so. I have therefore here recognised four genera of twinspots although, like Hall and Moreau, with some misgivings.

The genus *Hypargos* contains Peters' Twinspot, *Hypargos niveoguttatus*, and the Rosy Twinspot, *H. margaritatus*. These two very similar species are allopatric throughout most of their respective ranges, but occur together in parts of Mozambique. Usually, but apparently not always, they are found in different habitats. They are

Possible relationships of twinspots, crimson-wings and firefinches. See text for discussion.

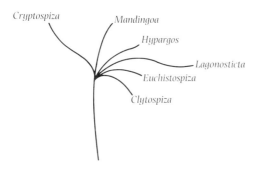

probably fairly closely related to *Euchistospiza* and they may be nearer to the blue-bills, *Spermophaga*, and the firefinches, *Lagonosticta*, than they are to the similarly patterned but very differently coloured Green and Brown Twinspots.

The two species in the genus *Euchistospiza* both have a well-developed first (outermost) primary, an allegedly primitive but quite possibly adaptive character that they share with the Brown Twinspot and the blue-bills. Both are largely dark grey in colour and they are completely allopatric. In appearance the Dusky Twinspot, *E. cinereovinacea*, seems to connect *Hypargos* with the firefinches, *Lagonosticta*, and has often been placed in the latter genus (e.g. by Sclater). The 'twin' spots on its crimson flanks are small and bar-shaped, very suggestive of those of some *Lagonosticta* species. Dybowski's Twinspot, *E. dybowskii* has pronounced spots on its black flanks; its rather short tail and red back suggest possible relationship with the crimson-wings, *Cryptospiza*, but Wolters (1966), who has seen individuals of both in life, thinks its closest affinities are with *E. cinereovinacea*.

The Brown Twinspot, *Clytospiza monteiri*, also has a large outermost primary and has often been treated as congeneric with the two previous species (Delacour, Steiner). It has, however, a rather distinct colour pattern and its courtship display seems marginally closer to that of *Hypargos*, with which it is allopatric. It seems best therefore to maintain it as a monotypic genus unless all the twinspots, probably together with the crimson-wings and blue-bills, are to be 'lumped' in a single genus, a proceeding which might have much to commend it.

The Green Twinspot, *Mandingoa nitidula*, has been sometimes placed in *Hypargos* (e.g. Delacour), sometimes in *Cryptospiza* (Bates). It has a more pointed wing and shorter tail than either. Its head coloration and pattern is very like that of the Red-faced Crimson-wing, and its general colour pattern also suggests a possible relationship with *Pytilia*. Of the species included here the Green Twinspot seems perhaps the most likely to have its closest relatives outside the 'twinspot' group.

REFERENCES

Bates, G. L. 1930. *Handbook of the birds of West Africa*. London.
Delacour, J. 1943. A revision of the subfamily Estrildinae of the family Ploceidae. *Zoologica, New York Zool. Soc.* **28**: 69–86.
Hall, B. P. & Moreau, R. E. 1970. *An atlas of speciation in African passerine birds*. British Museum (Natural History) London.
Kunkel, P. 1969. Die Stammesgeschichte der Prachtfinken (Estrildidae) im lichte des Brutparasitismus der Witwen (Viduinae). *Ardea* **57**: 172–181.
Mayr, E. 1968. The sequence of genera in the Estrildidae (Aves). *Breviora* **287**: 1–14.
Sclater, W. L. 1930. *Systema Avium Aethiopicarum*, pt. 2. British Ornithologists' Union, London.
Steiner, H. 1960. Klassifikation der Prachtfinken, Spermestidae, auf Grund der Rachenzeichnung ihrer Nestlinge. *J. Orn.* **101**: 92–112.
Traylor, M. A. 1968. *Peters' check-list of birds of the world*. Cambridge, Mass.
Wolters, H. E. 1966. *On the relationships and generic limits of African Estrildinae*. Proceedings of the second Pan-African Ornithological Congress 1964, Ostrich Supplement no. 6.

Peters' Twinspot   *Hypargos niveoguttatus*

Spermophaga niveoguttata Peters, 1868, *J. Orn.* **14**, p. 133.

DESCRIPTION See p. 9 for shape and measurements. Wing rounded, tail longer in proportion than in *Lagonosticta* species, between rounded and graduated in shape though not appearing so when folded. Forehead, crown and upper part of nape dark to medium greyish olive-brown, nearly clear grey in worn plumage. Centre of hind neck, mantle, back, wing coverts and those parts of the wing quills that are visible when wing is folded, deep reddish brown to slightly reddish olive-brown, usually a little paler on the primaries which tend to fade more. Some individuals have the upper parts suffused with red. Rest of wing quills dull sepia brown. Under wing coverts silvery white. Lower rump and upper tail coverts wine-red to crimson, sometimes a brighter red in worn plumage. Central tail feathers, except at the tips and at the base where concealed by the tail coverts, and outer webs of same areas of the outer tail feathers, wine-red to dark crimson, rest of tail feathers brownish black. Face, including area above eye, breast and sides of neck deep crimson to carmine, often becoming a brighter and lighter hue in worn plumage. Rest of underparts black, boldly spotted with white on the sides of the lower breast and flanks. Most of these spots are in pairs on either side of the vane of a feather. Sometimes a reddish suffusion on the spotted feathers at the sides of the breast, affecting only the black parts of the feathers. Irides dull brown to reddish brown; the conspicuous and rather wide bare eye-rims are pale blue. Bill shining greyish blue, greenish blue or purplish blue with black or bluish black culmen ridge, tip and cutting edges; sometimes only around the nostrils and the base of the lower mandible are bluish and the rest black. Legs and feet slate grey to greyish brown.

The female is a paler and buffish grey on the head, her face is greyish with buffish lores. The brown of her upper parts is lighter and more yellowish, although variable; the red of her rump and tail lighter and duller than that of the male. Her throat and breast are buff, usually strongly suffused with pinkish red or carmine (red tips to buffish feathers), on lower throat, breast and sides of neck, more often than not the breast looks predominantly reddish. Her underparts below the breast are sooty grey to medium grey, usually suffused with buff. She has white spots similar to those of the male and these, being edged with black, are very conspicuous in spite of the otherwise greyish background. Bill bluish black or dark grey with base, or base of lower mandible only, greyish blue. Irides, eye-rims and legs as in male.

The only juvenile of this species that I have seen, an unsexed specimen (which I suspect is a male) is similar to the female on the upper parts except that the top of its head is browner. Breast and sides of neck reddish brown, shading to dark reddish buff on the flanks. Centre of belly, ventral regions and under tail coverts greyish black with buffish feather fringes. The description of juveniles given by Immelmann *et al.* suggests similar but perhaps slightly paler and less reddish specimens, perhaps a sexual or geographical difference. Newly-hatched nestlings are flesh-coloured with some greyish down but darken to dark grey or black in their first day of life. The nestling has 3 dark spots on the palate, only a trace of the usual dark crescent in the under mandible, unmarked tongue and pale yellowish orange gape swellings (Immelmann *et al.*, 1964).

Geographical variation exists but is, in my opinion, slight, and I have therefore preferred to give a composite description which covers geographical and individual variation and changes due to wear. Clancey (1961) has, however, described several races which Immelmann *et al.* (1964 and 1976) consider valid.

See plate 3, facing p. 128.

FIELD CHARACTERS Small, but not tiny, 'finch' with brown upperparts, deep red face and breast (male) or greyish face and rosy buff to carmine breast (female). Black (male) or greyish (female) underparts, *boldly spotted with white* at sides, are diagnostic. Bright pale blue eye-rims conspicuous if bird seen fairly close.

The bold white spots (not tiny dots or flecks) on the black or grey sides distinguish it from all species except Dybowski's Twinspot, which has dark grey breast and red back; the Green Twinspot, which has green upperparts and the female Red-headed Bluebill, which has bright red face and breast, spots all over its grey underparts and proportionately very much larger bill.

DISTRIBUTION AND HABITAT Tropical Africa from eastern Zaïre (Congo) and eastern Angola to Kenya and Mozambique (see map) but rather sporadically distributed within this wide range. Locally found up to about 1800 metres but usually at low elevations. Inhabits bushy cover along water-courses, bush-grown gullies, grassy and bushy areas at forest edge and similar places. In north-eastern Tanzania Moreau found its favourite haunts were bushes, not necessarily very dense, that were 'smothered' with rank grass. Most often found near water but sometimes in quite dry thorn bush (Immelmann *et al.*, 1964, Mackworth-Praed & Grant, McLachlan & Liversidge, Sclater & Moreau, Vincent).

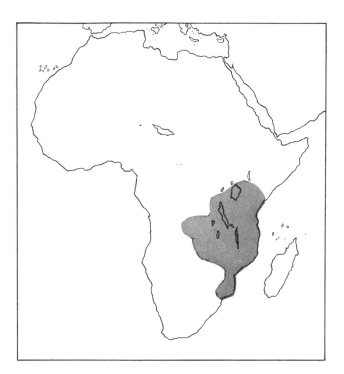

FEEDING AND GENERAL HABITS Known to take grass seeds, picked up from the ground, and presumably also takes some insects and possibly seeds of other plants. Usually in pairs or small groups, the latter probably most often family parties. Seeks food on the ground. Often feeds on paths, roads and small open spaces but otherwise keeps in or close to cover. Not very frightened of man and often found close to human habitations. In captivity usually quite tame and not at all nervous or panicky, but may react with distress and desertion if its nest is looked into (Nicolai).

In captivity readily takes panicum millet (often other millets and canary seed also) soaked or sprouted millet, greenfood and half ripe seeds of grasses and chickweed. Said to need insect food all the year round (eggfood and soft foods are usually refused) and especially when rearing young when, if possible, fresh ant pupae should be given (Immelmann *et al.* 1964). Immelmann *et al.* recommend a temperature of 22°C to 25°C for newly-imported birds and that it should never be kept at temperatures of below 20°C. There is, however, at least one record (Drake) of the species not only surviving but successfully rearing young without artificial heat and with the provision of very little in the way of insect food.

NESTING Nests on the ground or in a bush, shrub or tree at no great height. The nest is roundish, built of grass, fibres, rootlets and similar materials and lined with feathers. It sometimes has a short entrance tube and in one instance an only partly covered cock's nest was built on top of the real one (Sclater and Moreau). This latter nest was 15 cm (6 inches) long and had an entrance tube 6 cm (2½ inches) long. In captivity it usually prefers to nest on the ground, among cover, although sometimes in a bush, shrub or basket above ground. When nesting on the ground the bird first makes a little 'scrape' by repeatedly making a short jump forward when on the site and thus clearing away loose substrate and/or ground debris. Will use grass and coconut fibres and, by choice when available, small rootlets. The nest is lined with feathers and may have a short entrance tube or merely a few drooping pieces of material hanging over and partly obscuring the entrance. Only the male normally brings material for the outer part of the nest although the female may bring feathers for the lining. Immelmann *et al.* (1964) state that the femals does the actual building (with material brought by the male) but perhaps further observations are needed before it can be concluded that the male does not build also.

Three to six eggs. Incubation period 12 to 13 days (Immelmann *et al.*, 1964). Harrison & Dormer record incubation periods of 16 days but perhaps this involved nests in which there was a check in incubation. Young fledge at about 21 days, sometimes they return to the nest to roost for a further night or two but sometimes (and perhaps more often) they do not. Both sexes share parental care in the usual way. The bird coming to take its turn on the nest usually brings a feather or other piece of nesting material (Harrison & Dormer).

VOICE The close contact call is a soft and very variable 'tseet' or 'tsee-et'. The distance contact call is similar but louder, longer-drawn out and more emphatic. A rapid-tempo trill, very similar to the trilling call of the Purple Grenadier, seems also to be used as a distance contact call. The alarm call is a harsh 'tschee'. The nest call begins with the close contact call and then follows a quick series of notes that could be transcribed as 'beetbeetbeetbeet', repeatedly interrupted by contact calls. The song begins with a trill, which is followed by series of both pure and gurgling whistled or fluting notes (Nicolai, in Immelmann *et al.*, 1964, my anglicisations).

DISPLAY AND SOCIAL BEHAVIOUR The courtship display has been described in detail by Harrison & Dormer. The male with a feather or other nest material in his bill and spread and partly angled tail, dances around the female, uttering a faint song sequence. He performs a bobbing movement, the head being alternately pointed upward at an angle of about 70 degrees and bowed to about 30 degrees every second during the display. He starts with his head in the elevated position and body low to the ground. He next bows, then throws it up and at the same time hops about half an inch off the ground. His head is then slowly lowered to the slightly bowed position and the sequence repeated. He does not hop until his head is in the lowest position, so that he can throw it up again simultaneously with the next hop. The hen may remain quiescent or, occasionally, perform slow hops, without nesting material in the bill. If the female responds by soliciting with quivering tail, copulation follows.

Harrison & Dormer state that in the wild this species indulges in a form of communal display. Toward evening, a number of pairs congregate in a patch of thick undergrowth. Here the males hop around, keeping several yards apart, and display, as if to each other, uttering a sharp 'chip' followed by a long musical trill on a descending scale. The females simply sit and watch.

Allo-preening is common between members of a pair. Pairs in breeding condition are, in captivity, often aggressive not only towards conspecifics but also towards related or similarly-coloured species.

OTHER NAMES Peters' Spotted Firefinch, Red-throated Twinspot.

REFERENCES
Chapin, J. P. 1954. The birds of the Belgian Congo. *Bull. Amer. Mus. Nat. Hist.* **75B**.
Clancey, P. A. 1961. Miscellaneous taxomic notes on African birds XVI–XVII. *Durban Mus. Novit.* **6**: 79–118 (97–104).
Drake, K. 1935. The breeding of Peter's Spotted Firefinch (*Hypargos niveoguttatus*). *Avicult. Mag.* 4th ser., **8**: 198–199.
Harrison, C. J. O. & Dormer, B. P. 1962. Notes on the display and behaviour of Peter's Twinspot and the Brown Twinspot. *Avicult. Mag.* **68**: 139–143.
Immelmann, K., Steinbacher, J. & Wolters, H. E. 1964 and 1976: *Vögel in Käfig und Voliere: Prachtfinken*: 126–137 and 539–540.
Mackworth-Praed, C. W. & Grant, C. H. B. 1963. *African handbook of birds*, ser. 2, vol. 2. Longman, Green and Co. Ltd. London.
McLachlan, G. R. & Liversidge, R. 1957. *Roberts birds of South Africa.* Cape Town.
Nicolai, J. 1965. *Käfig- und Volierenvögel.* Kosmos, Stuttgart, Germany.
Sclater, W. L. & Moreau, R. E. 1933. Taxonomic and field notes on some birds of North-Eastern Tanganyika Territory. *Ibis* 13th ser., **3**: 309–440.
Vincent, J. 1936. The birds of Northern Portuguese East Africa. *Ibis* 13th ser., **6**: 48–125.

Rosy Twinspot   *Hypargos margaritatus*

Spermophaga margaritata Strickland, *Ann. Mag. Nat. Hist.*, **13**, p. 418, pl. 10.

DESCRIPTION Very similar to the previous form, *H. niveoguttatus*, but is more slender in build and slightly smaller and longer-tailed. The plumage pattern is almost or quite identical but coloration differs as follows: Face, sides of neck and breast a beautiful deep mauvish pink, a little darker and redder over the eyes than elsewhere. Top of head light to medium sandy brown, rest of upper parts a light to medium reddish brown with a sandy tinge. Parts of rump and tail that are red in Peters' Twinspot, are dark mauvish pink. Spots on sides of breast and flanks not white but a delicate pale but bright shell pink. Irides dark brown; eye-rims mauvish pink and less conspicuous than those of Peters' Twinspot (Immelmann *et al.*, 1976). Clancey states that the eye-rims are cobalt blue but his picture shows the male with pinkish and the female with blue eye-rims. Bill dark greyish blue. Legs and feet dark grey or blackish.

The female is a slightly less reddish brown on her

upperparts. Her face and throat are light greyish brown, shading to clear grey on the breast. Sides of breast and flanks black, boldly spotted with white (not pale pink as in the male). Median area of belly white or buffish white, shading to barred white and greyish on the under tail coverts. Eye-rims a mixture of bluish and pinkish (Immelmann *et al.*, 1976), perhaps sometimes blue, as shown by Clancey.

I have not seen a juvenile specimen. Burkard, who bred this species in captivity, describes it as greyish brown above, tinged with red on the rump and tail. Light brown on the breast and whitish grey on the belly. The mouth markings consist of 3 black spots on a yellow area of the palate; the gape tubercles are blue, the rest of the mouth and the tongue reddish. Young nestlings are naked except for some down on the head. Burkard gives a photograph of a recently fledged juvenile.
See plate 3, facing p. 128.

FIELD CHARACTERS Pink (not deep red) face and breast and grey (not reddish or buffish) breast distinguish male and female, respectively, from Peters' Twinspot. Conspicuous pale pink (male) or white (female) spots on black sides of breast and flanks distinguish it from all other species.

DISTRIBUTION AND HABITAT South-eastern Africa from the Save River, Mozambique, to Lake St Lucia, Zululand. Found in coastal thickets of bushes and palms, acacia thickets and, in the Lebombo Mountains, thick growth at the edge of forest. Commonly in drier habitats than those frequented by Peters' Twinspot.

FEEDING AND GENERAL HABITS Usually in pairs or small parties. Seeks food on the ground. Known to take seeds, probably also takes insects and some green food. In

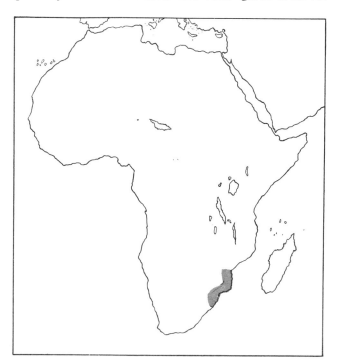

captivity will take panicum millet, canary seed, soaked and sprouted millet, ant pupae and sometimes artificial foods. Burkard's pair apparently reared their young at least partly on fresh ant pupae (Burkard, Immelmann *et al.*, 1976).

General behaviour and needs in captivity probably similar to previous species but apparently at first much more delicate and requiring great care (Burkard).

NESTING I can find no record or description of wild nests. A captive pair built a nest in a half-open box in an exposed position in the aviary, although there were bushes and reeds in which they otherwise spent most of their time. They laid 4 eggs and reared 3 of the young (Burkard, his paper is illustrated with photographs of the nest and a fledgling).

VOICE Apparently at least some calls are distinct in sound from those of the previous species (Immelmann *et al.*, 1976). Contact call (close?) a soft 'seesee'. Alarm call a short trilling 'rrrrree' (Burkard), possibly the long, high-pitched, ringing 'tseerrrr' said to be given in excitement (Immelmann *et al.*, 1976) is a variant of the same call. The begging of nestlings sounded like a very rapidly repeated 'veeveeveevee . . .' (Burkard). The song is a short, not very loud, stereotyped strophe, resembling that of the Red-billed Firefinch (Immelmann *et al.*, 1976).

DISPLAY AND SOCIAL BEHAVIOUR Little information. Probably similar to that of Peters' Twinspot. Allopreening is said to be less often performed (Immelmann *et al.*, 1976) but this might be based on individual rather than specific differences.

OTHER NAMES Pink-throated Twinspot, Verreaux's Twinspot.

REFERENCES
Burkard, R. 1968. Uber die Zucht einiger seltener Prachtfinken. *Gefiederte Welt* **1968**: 148–150.
Clancey, P. A. 1964. *The birds of Natal and Zululand.* Oliver and Boyd, Edinburgh and London.
Immelmann, K., Steinbacher, J. & Wolters, H. E. 1964 and 1976: *Vögel in Käfig und Voliere: Prachtfinken*: 137–140 and 540–541.
McLachlan, G. R. & Liversidge, R. 1957. *Roberts birds of South Africa.* Cape Town.

Dybowski's Twinspot *Euchistospiza dybowskii*
Lagonosticta Dybowskii, Oustalet, 1892, *Naturaliste*, p. 231.

DESCRIPTION About size of Spice Finch but very different in shape, with denser plumage, more slender bill and rounded and broader tail. Head, neck, hind neck and breast dark grey. Wings dark greyish olive-brown, the median and secondary coverts often have white terminal spots or narrow bars which are set off by black marks contiguous and posterior to them. Under wing coverts dark grey with white tips, giving a barred or speckled effect. Mantle, back, rump and the long upper tail coverts, which cover rather over half the tail, deep lustrous crimson red. The bases of these red feathers are grey but the grey is usually concealed unless plumage is missing or disarranged. Tail black with a varying but usually small amount of dark red on the fringes of the outer webs of most feathers. Underparts below the breast black, conspicuously and boldly spotted with white except along the median line of the belly, the ventral area and under tail coverts. The white spots are oval to rectangular in shape and 'paired', one each side of the vane of the feather. Irides dark red; eye-rims purplish red, but paler, even flesh pink in young adults (Kujawa). Bill black. Legs and feet dark greyish brown to brownish black.

The female is a little smaller than the male and a slightly lighter grey on head, breast etc. The red on her back and rump is duller than the male's. Her belly and flanks are grey and although the white spots are bordered both anteriorly and posteriorly with black, they are less strikingly contrasting than the male's. Irides sometimes (perhaps usually) brown; eye-rims grey, yellowish grey in young adults (Kujawa). Juvenile dark grey with small rust-brown spots on back and rump, no white spots on underparts. Irides grey with paler grey eye-rims. Bill dark grey, at first paler at base and whitish at gape. Legs and feet greyish flesh (Kujawa, whose paper is illustrated with photographs of both juveniles and an adult). In captivity full adult plumage has been obtained by about 8, or at latest 10, weeks old (Pensold, 1974). Young nestling has blackish grey skin and grey down on head and back. Mouth markings consist of 5 dark spots on palate, a dark mark at base of each mandible, two dark spots on the tongue and a dark crescent inside lower mandible; picture in Immelmann *et al.* (175) and Kujawa.

See plate 3, facing p. 128.

FIELD CHARACTERS Small dark grey (male) or medium grey (female) bird with red back and rump and profuse bold white spots on its black (male) or black and grey (female) flanks. Any two of the above characters, in combination, distinguish it from all sympatric species.

DISTRIBUTION AND HABITAT West Africa, in eastern Sierra Leone and from the Cameroons through Oubangi-Chari to the upper Uele and adjacent parts of Sudan. Has been found in grass-grown rocky places, cultivation at the bases of granite hills, the borders of gallery forest and grassy plateaux on high mountains (Bannerman, Chapin, Mackworth-Praed & Grant, Immelmann *et al.*, 1963).

FEEDING AND GENERAL HABITS Known to seek food on the ground and to take grass seeds and small insects but otherwise little recorded of its habits in the wild. Detailed observations on it in captivity have been published by Kujawa and Pensold. It habitually digs for food, flicking the substrate to either side with its bill. When seeking insect food it notices the slightest movement in the substrate up to about two metres away and at once dashes to the spot and digs eagerly.

In captivity it has been successfully fed on mixed millets

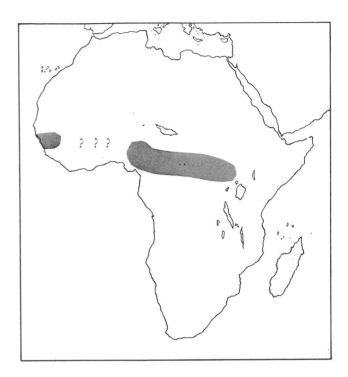

and canary seed with some niger seed and such insect foods as cut-up and cooked mealworms, small live mealworms and crickets, ant pupae, bee grubs, and green aphids (greenfly). Flowering and seeding chickweed, Rye Grass and Annual Meadow Grass are sometimes also eaten. Eggfood is sometimes readily taken. Wild-caught birds often at first refuse many foods, even some kinds of live insects, that are new to them. As with some other birds, pairs that have once bred *successfully* in captivity may be less selective in the matter of rearing foods for subsequent broods and captive-bred individuals are usually much more ready to sample strange foods than are wild-caught birds (Pensold, 1968b and 1974). Like other ground-feeding birds this species is often reluctant to take food from a dish and to ensure that sufficient food and sufficient variety of food is taken, it should be strewn on the floor or (in the case of egg food etc.) placed in *small* dishes, dotted about on the floor.

Probably lives in pairs and is territorial under natural conditions as in captivity adult males attack juveniles as soon as they start to show adult plumage and young males fight each other fiercely as soon as they are sexually mature, which they are at an early age (Pensold, 1974). Kujawa noted that his birds preferred to rest and preen on perches from 0·5 to 1·5 metres high and always in a position where they could not have been seen by any creatures looking down from above.

NESTING I can find no records of wild nests; the following is derived from Pensold's and Kujawa's observations of birds breeding in captivity.

The nest may be built in a shrub, shelter of reeds, branches or etc. or (rarely) in a nest box. Pensold (1974) found his birds usually chose to nest on the floor in some corner where he had placed a heap of materials to encourage them. The nest is roundish, built of grass, fibres and similar material, usually or always on a base of coarser materials, and lined with feathers. The nest is built mostly, perhaps entirely, by the male. Nests built on the floor have an entrance tube 7 to 9 cm long, those built above ground do not (Pensold, 1974). Eggs usually 4 to 6, sometimes 3. Both sexes incubate and brood in the usual manner. The parents usually utter the alarm call when coming to feed well-grown young. Broods of three or more young are brooded for 7 to 9 days, but if there is only a single nestling the female will brood it at night till it is 14 or 15 days old (Pensold, 1974). The young beg in the usual estrildid manner but fledglings may (when nearly satiated or in a state of anxiety?) simply stretch their heads straight towards the adult (Kujawa, Pensold, 1974).

VOICE The alarm call is a loud 'tset-tset-tset' or 'tsit-tsit-tsit'. A softer, run-together 'tsit-tsit' may be a close contact or locomotion intention call. The song of the male is complex and variable. Individuals vary their songs and there is also considerable variation between the song repertoire of individuals. The same bird in its song commonly produces phrases suggestive of the rolling trill of a Canary, the deep notes of the Nightingale and the fluting phrases of the Blackbird's, *Turdus merula*, song. Song is given when alone, most often when perched in cover, and in display. The female also sings, especially if unpaired and alone, her song is softer than but otherwise like the male's. The young utter a loud begging call from an early age.

DISPLAY AND SOCIAL BEHAVIOUR The courtship display usually takes place on the ground. The male, holding a stem or feather in his bill, hops around the female with head held up at a steep angle, belly feathers erected and the tail partly spread. Either the song or series of softer notes may be uttered. The female may also perform this display. It is (sometimes) followed by copulation (Kujawa, Pensold, 1974).

OTHER NAMES Dybowski's Dusky Twinspot.

REFERENCES
Bannerman, D. A. 1953. *The birds of West and Equatorial Africa*, vol. 2. Oliver and Boyd, Edinburgh and London.
Chapin, J. P. 1954. The birds of the Belgian Congo. *Bull. Amer. Mus. Nat. Hist.* **75B**.
Immelmann, K., Steinbacher, J. & Wolters, H. E. 1963 and 1975. *Vögel in Käfig und Voliere: Prachtfinken*: 74–77 and 526–528. Aachen, Germany.
Kujawa, W. 1965. Die Erstzucht des Dybowskis Tropfenastrild *Euchistospiza* dybowskii (Oust.). *Gefiederte Welt* **1965**: 222–225.
Mackworth-Praed, C. W. & Grant, C. H. B. 1973. *The African handbook of birds*, ser. 3, vol. 2. Longman Group Ltd, London.
Pensold, R. 1968a. Erfahrungen bei der Zucht von Dybowskis Tropfenastrilden. *Gefiederte Welt* **1968**: 181–182.
Pensold, R. 1968b. Nachtrag zu 'Erfahrungen bei zer Zucht von Dybowskis Tropfenastrilden'. *Gefiederte Welt* **1968**: 224–225.
Pensold, R. 1974. Beobachtungen bei der Haltung und Zucht des Dybowskis Tropfenastrild. *Gefiederte Welt* **1974**: 109–110.

Dusky Twinspot   *Euchistospiza cinereovinacea*

Lagonosticta cinereo-vinacea Sousa, 1889, *Jorn. Sci. Math. Phys. Nat. Lisboa*, ser. 2, **1**, p. 49.

DESCRIPTION Slightly smaller than the previous species, Dybowski's Twinspot, and with proportionately longer tail and shorter bill. Head, neck, breast, mantle and back dark grey to blackish grey. The wings are a similar and only slightly more brownish grey but the exposed parts of the wing feathers become markedly browner with wear. Some feathers of the wing coverts, inner secondaries and lower back may have their tips more or less tinged with dark red. Rump and upper tail coverts wine-red to deep crimson. Tail black. Sides of lower breast and flanks wine-red to dark scarlet, delicately freckled or spotted with white. The individual spotted feathers have black or very dark grey basal areas, then two 'paired' white dots or interrupted bars between and beyond which the feather is red. Median part of lower breast, belly, ventral area and under tail coverts black. Irides dark reddish brown to deep red; eye-rims red. Bill slaty black, sometimes with a mauve sheen. Legs and feet dark grey to greyish black. Sexes said to be alike although the two adults sexed as females, that I have examined, both have the black on the underparts less intensely black than in specimens sexed as males. Immelmann *et al.* say it appears that females always have brown and males red irides, if this is so then one of above-mentioned females is wrongly sexed as its irides were described as 'crimson' by the collector.

The juvenile is dark brownish grey, usually with some brownish red suffusion on the sides of the breast and flanks, and the red on rump and upper tail coverts paler and duller than the adult's. Irides brown with pale grey or whitish eye-rims. Bill black, whitish at gape in fledgling. Legs and feet brownish. Mouth markings of nestling similar to previous species. There is a good photograph of fledglings in Baars' paper.

The above description is of nominate *E.c. cinereovinacea* from the high plateau of western and central Angola. *E.c. graueri*, from the highlands of eastern Congo to western Uganda is said to be darker on both the red and grey parts of its plumage. I have not seen an adult specimen of this race, the single juvenile I have seen is like those of the nominate form.

See plate 3, facing p. 128.

FIELD CHARACTERS Small dark grey and black bird with dark red rump and dark red, white-speckled flanks. Lack of any red on dark grey head and breast distinguishes it from all sympatric and (more or less) similar species.

DISTRIBUTION AND HABITAT The high plateau of western and central Angola and the highlands of eastern Zaïre (Congo) from Lake Chahafi south through Rwanda and west of Lake Tanganyika to Marungu and the Impenetrable Forest in western Uganda. Has been found in bush-grown highland grass savannahs, grass-grown mountain gulleys and in thickets in (probably in clearings or at the edge of) the Rugege Forest. Most often at altitudes of about

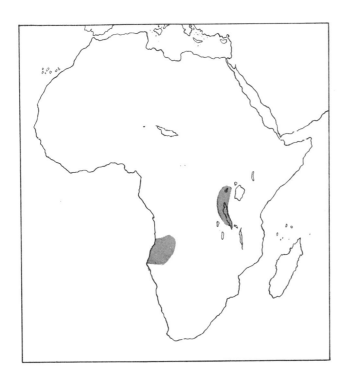

1500 to 1850 metres (5000 to 6500 feet) (Chapin, Immelmann *et al.*, 1963, Mackworth-Praed & Grant).

FEEDING AND GENERAL HABITS Said to eat grass seeds and to associate in pairs or small parties. I can find nothing else recorded of its habits when wild. A pair that bred successfully in captivity (Baars, Wolters) were provided with a great variety of seed, greenstuff and insects, but always eagerly searched, presumably for small wild insects, in fresh woodland soil that was daily given to them.

NESTING A nest built in captivity was round with a large side entrance and no entrance tube (photograph of it in Baars). It was built among twigs and reeds fixed to a wall, about a metre high, although similar and higher sites were available. Only the male collected material and built. Three eggs were laid. Prior to the laying of the third egg the male spent much time in the nest by day, but during incubation proper he only relieved his mate for short spells (Baars). Possibly this was an artefact of the captive conditions with unlimited food. Incubation period 13 days (Immelmann *et al.*, 1975, in reference to the same pair and nest). Young fledged at 21 days. Both parents roosted together in the nest during incubation and until the young left it. The young did not crouch and twist their necks in the usual estrildid manner when begging (Baars, Immelmann *et al.*, 1975).

VOICE The close contact has been written as 'tsyip tsyip', it is intensified, as a distance contact call (also uttered in mild alarm) to a louder 'tsvilip', often repeated. The begging call of the young is a loud 'visvisvisvisvis . . .'. The song, given in the courtship display, consists of varying series of not very loud or striking notes (Wolters, my anglicisations).

DISPLAY AND SOCIAL BEHAVIOUR In the courtship display the male, with a grass stem or other nesting material in his bill, jumps around his mate on the ground or, but apparently less often, beside or in front of her on a perch. When on the ground his tail is spread and in contact with the substrate (Burkard, Wolters).

REFERENCES
Baars, W. 1967. Nochmal: Erstzucht des Schiefergrauen Astrildes. *Gefiederte Welt* **1967**: 81–82.
Burkard, R. 1968. Über die Zucht einiger seltener Prachtfinken. *Gefiederte Welt* **1968**: 148–150.
Chapin, J. P. 1954. The birds of the Belgian Congo. *Bull. Amer. Mus. Nat. Hist.* **75B**.
Immelmann, K., Steinbacher, J. & Wolters, H. E. 1963 and 1975. *Vögel in Käfig und Voliere: Prachtfinken*: 78–79 and 528–529. Aachen, Germany.
Mackworth-Praed, C. W. & Grant, C. H. B. 1973. *The African handbook of birds*, ser. 3, vol. 2. Longman Group Ltd, London.
Wolters, H. E. 1965. Erstzucht des Schiefergrauen Astrilds (*Euchistospiza cinereovinacea*). *Gefiederte Welt* **1965**: 225–226.

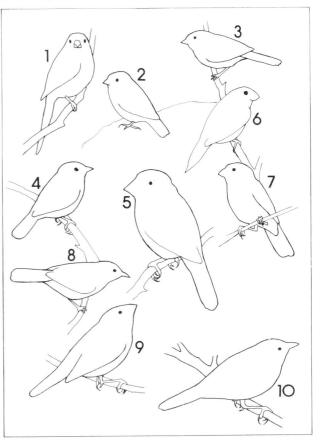

Plate 1 Some African estrildids, to show diversity.
(1) Violet-eared Waxbill, *Uraeginthus granatina*; (2) Locust Finch, *Ortygospiza l.locustella*; (3) Black-rumped Waxbill, *Estrilda troglodytes*; (4) Green Twinspot, *Mandingoa n.nitidula*; (5) Black-bellied Seed-cracker, *Pyrenestes o.ostrinus*; (6) African Silverbill, *Lonchura cantans*; (7) Grey-headed Olive-back, *Nesocharis capistrata*; (8) Ant-pecker, *Parmoptila w.woodhousei*; (9) Red-headed-Finch, *Amadina erythrocephala*; (10) Grey-headed negro-finch, *Nigrita c.canicapilla*.

MWWoodcock

MWWoodcock

Brown Twinspot *Clytospiza monteiri*

Pytelia monteiri Hartlaub, 1860, *Proc. Zool. Soc. London*, p. 111, pl. 161.

DESCRIPTION About size of Peters' Twinspot but with more rounded wing with longer first primary (about half the length of the second), slightly shorter and broader tail and proportionately rather more slender (and hence longer looking) bill. Entire head dark slate grey except for a bright vermilion or orange-red median stripe from the middle to the lower throat. Mantle, back and wings a dull dark earth brown. Underwing coverts barred chestnut and white. Rump and upper tail coverts dark orange-red. Tail brownish black. Breast and underparts rich chestnut-brown, sometimes tinged with red on the ventral area and under tail coverts, spotted and barred with white. On the upper breast and upper flanks there are, on most feathers, two paired roundish white spots and sometimes two smaller and fainter spots nearer the base of the feather. The spots intergrade into bars, usually two on each

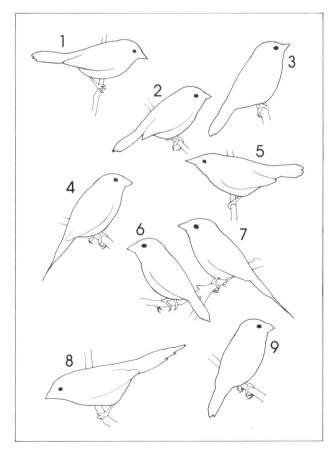

Plate 2 Some Australian estrildids to show diversity. (1) Red-browed Finch, *Aegintha temporalis*; (2) Bicheno Finch, *Poephila bichenovii*; (3) Beautiful Firetail, *Emblema bella*; (4) Gouldian Finch, *Chloebia gouldiae*; (5) Painted Finch, *Emblema picta*; (6) Pictorella Finch, *Lonchura pectoralis*; (7) Long-tailed Grassfinch, *Poephila acuticauda*; (8) Crimson Finch, *Neochmia p.phaeton*; (9) Chestnut-breasted Finch, *Lonchura c.castaneothorax*.

feather, on the belly, lower flanks and under tail coverts. Irides usually blood red or dark red, sometimes reddish brown; eye-rims bluish. Bill black, greyish blue at base. Legs and feet fleshy brown.

The female has no red on the throat but a dull white median stripe that extends right up to the base of her lower mandible. The orange-red of her rump, the chestnut of her underparts and the grey on the sides of her head are paler than the male's. Juveniles are a lighter and less greyish brown on the upper parts with the head a more brownish grey. The underparts are a duller and paler chestnut brown without white markings apart from indistinct whitish barring on the belly, ventral area and under tail coverts. The rump and upper tail coverts are dark rusty orange. Young males have the grey of the head and the chestnut of the breast darker than young females (Neff, 1975, apparently corroborated by differences in unsexed juveniles in the British Museum collection). Three-day-old nestlings have dark skin and quite profuse pale down. Their mouth markings consist of five black spots on the yellow palate, a black band, narrowing centrally, across the flesh-coloured tongue and a black crescent inside the lower mandible. The swollen bilobed gape flanges are described as white by Neff (1975) and as white externally and yellow inside by Chapin & Immelmann *et al.* There is a black spot on the inside of the gape, at the base of each mandible. Good photographs of nestlings and a juvenile are given in Neff's 1977 paper.

See plate 3, facing p. 128.

FIELD CHARACTERS Small dark grey and dark brownish bird with red rump and blackish tail. Chestnut-brown, white-spotted breast and underparts diagnostic. Tail noticeably fan-shaped when spread.

DISTRIBUTION AND HABITAT Tropical Africa, in savannas north and south of the equatorial forest, from western Cameroons (Bamenda) east to southern Sudan north to near Bussere and western Kenya in the Nyanza Province. Inhabits savanna with tall grass and bushes; also forest edges and clearings and cultivated areas provided grass and cover are available (Chapin, Immelmann *et al.*, Mackworth-Praed & Grant).

FEEDING AND GENERAL HABITS Feeds largely (probably entirely) on the ground, where it moves with long quick hops, in a horizontal stance. Known to take grass seeds, insects including termites, and spiders, but little else recorded of its habits in the wild. In captivity it will take various millets and (some individuals) canary seed. Sometimes takes soaked spray millet and chickweed (Immelmann *et al.*, 1963) but Neff (1975, 1977) found that his birds took little greenfood or soaked seed except when rearing young, and recommends the periodical addition of multi-vitamin supplements (1975) *and* the regular addition of vitamin A supplements (1977) to its diet. When rearing young, however, his birds eagerly took ant pupae, whiteworms and the half-ripe seeds of various unidentified grasses, and home-grown millet. Individuals

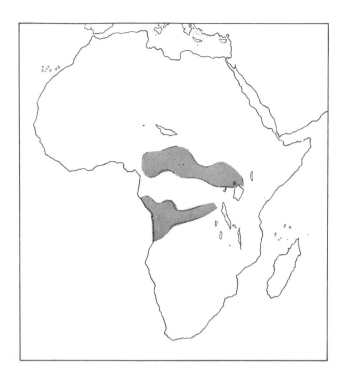

watched by Burkard swallowed seeds whole without first shelling them.

In captivity tends to be nervous and shy and to keep much to cover. Prone to over-growth of the mandibles and to hyper-growth of leg and foot scales. Neff (1975) describes medical treatment for these troubles which can be minimised, but not entirely prevented, by diet as recommended above and keeping the birds in a large enclosure.

NESTING Chapin found the Brown Twinspot breeding in old nests of *Lonchura cucullata* and other (unidentified) species. These old nests had been re-lined with hair, feathers, soft vegetable material and, in every case, also with some cast snake skin. Myres (in Mackworth-Praed & Grant) describes small domed nests of grass, presumably built by the Twinspots themselves.

In captivity, however, the species builds a complete nest for itself (summary of his own and others' observations in Neff, 1975), among twigs or bushy cover, on the remains of an old nest, or on a rough platform of grass etc. placed for it; once in a box. Various materials may be used but Neff (1975) found that, when ample choice was given, the nest was always mainly built of broad blades of grass and wheat, and thickly lined with feathers. Grass that was still green was always preferred when available. Throughout incubation and brooding of the nestlings, the male takes feathers and pieces of *green* grass into the nest. The large side entrance of the nest is always screened or 'closed' by a feather while eggs or young are being brooded.

Only the male collects material but, if the female is in the nest she may take feathers from him and position them. Up to 5 feathers may be carried at a time. The nest may be round or more or less elongated in shape according to its

site. Eggs 4 to 6. Incubation period 13 days; young fledge at 19–21 days (Neff, 1975 and 1977). When wild breeds at the end of the rains and beginning of the dry season. In Uelle district, Zaïre, from August to December; in Uganda from June to October and in southern Sudan in September (Chapin, Immelmann *et al.*, 1963).

VOICE The close contact call is a repeated 'vay, vay, vay . . .' which is intensified and tends to be uttered in longer series as a distance contact call. Recently fledged young utter a loud 'eek, eek, eek' to enable the parents to locate them as they hide in cover. The alarm call is a hard-sounding, *Sylvia*-like 'tek'. The song of the male, which seems to be given, or at least to have been heard, only in courtship display, is a variable series of notes, hard to describe and unlike the song of any other estrildid. Harrison & Dormer liken it to the 'crackling' of Bishops, *Euplectes* spp. The above is derived mostly from Neff (1975).

DISPLAY AND SOCIAL BEHAVIOUR The courtship display is like that of Peters' Twinspot except that the male's movements are more jerky and less graceful. With a feather or grass blade in his bill, he performs long hops around or half around the female. His tail is usually spread and angled towards her, his head alternately pointed upwards at an angle of about 70 degrees and bowed towards the female at an angle of about 30 degrees. The male sings during this display. Neff's (1977) description implies that, at least in some cases, display may occur without nesting material in the bill or that it may be held only at the beginning of the display. The female may perform the same movements in synchrony with her mate or remain passive. If she solicits, in the usual manner with quivering tail, copulation follows (Neff, 1977).

Allo-preening is frequent between the members of a pair.

OTHER NAME Monteiro's Twinspot.

REFERENCES
Burkard, R. 1962. Plauderei über einige seltene Prachtfinken. *Gefiederte Welt* **1962**: 185–186.
Chapin, J. P. 1954. The birds of the Belgian Congo. *Bull. Amer. Mus. Nat. Hist.* **75B**.
Harrison, C. J. O. & Dormer, B. P. 1962. Notes on the display of Peter's Twinspot and the Brown Twinspot. *Avicult. Mag.* **68**: 139–143.
Immelmann, K., Steinbacher, J. & Wolters, H. E. 1963 and 1975. *Vögel in Käfig und Voliere: Prachtfinken*: 71–74 and 525. Aachen, Germany.
Mackworth-Praed, C. W. & Grant, C. H. B. 1973. *African handbook of birds*, ser. 3, vol. 2. Longman Group Ltd, London.
Neff, R. 1975. Der Braune Tropfenastrild. *Gefiederte Welt* **1975**: 181–184.
Neff, R. 1977. Über den Braunen Tropfenastrild. *Gefiederte Welt* **1977**: 122–123.

Green Twinspot   *Mandingoa nitidula*

Estrelda nitidula Hartlaub, in Gurney, 1865, *Ibis*, p. 269.

DESCRIPTION About size of Zebra Finch but different in

shape (see sketch) with smaller head, more slender bill, short tail and rather pointed wing. Face orange-red on lores, around eyes, anterior parts of ear coverts and bright orange on upper parts of throat. Rest of head, breast and upperparts, except where otherwise stated, darkish olive green. Inner web of wing quills and tips of primaries blackish. Rump and upper tail coverts tinged with golden or rusty orange. Central tail feathers olive green with black shafts; outer tail feathers blackish with olive green fringes on the outer webs and paler, greenish grey tips. Lower breast, flanks and belly black, boldly spotted with white (mostly paired white spots, one either side of the vane of the feather). Toward the median line the ground colour tends to be tinged with greenish grey and the spots less extremely prominent. Ventral area, extreme lower flanks and under tail coverts buffish olive. Irides dark brown or brown; eye-rims narrow and probably greyish blue as in *M.n. chubbi*. Bill black with tips of both mandibles and sometimes a more extensive area on lower mandible red, sometimes bill is entirely blackish. Legs and feet brownish flesh, purplish brown or purplish grey.

The female has the face deep yellowish buff to orange-buff with a lighter buff upper throat. The olive green of her rump and upper tail coverts have only a slight yellow or golden tinge. The spotted feathers of her underparts are largely grey but the white spots are edged with black. Plumage otherwise as male, but eye-rims probably yellowish brown. The juvenile is a general greyish olive above, greener on rump and tail and a medium drab grey, without spots, on the underparts. The only male juvenile of this (the nominate) race that I have seen had no green tinge on the breast but perhaps this is an individual variation or wrongly sexed as male juveniles of other races have an olive green wash on the breast. The face and upper part of the throat are buff or greyish buff. Nestlings are at first yellowish flesh coloured, later grey, with long (6 or 8 cm) whitish grey down on head, back and shoulders. They have three pale blue tubercles, edged inside with black, at each corner of the gape, one on the upper and two on the lower mandible. There are three large and two very small black spots on the flesh-coloured palate. The tongue has two black dots joined by a brownish band (Immelmann *et al.*). Diagram of nestling's mouth in Proebsting.

The above description is of nominate *M.n. nitidula*, from northern and central Tanzania west to southern Katanga and northern Zambia and south to Natal, Pondoland and eastern Rhodesia. *M.n. chubbi*, from southern Abyssinia and south-eastern Sudan through Kenya to the south-east shore of Lake Victoria, the Usambara Mountains of Tanzania and Zanzibar and Pemba Islands is brighter in colour. The male has the face deep orange-red or tomato red, his breast may be tinged with gold, strongly suffused with deep orange-red or something between these extremes and his rump and upper tail coverts are usually a deep rusty orange. The female has the breast suffused with buff. The juvenile is greener above than that of the nominate form and juvenile males are strongly washed

with olive green on the breast. The western race of the species, from Sierra Leone and Liberia east to Uganda and south to north-western Angola and Kasai, *M.n. schlegeli*, has a considerably larger bill. Its face is deep scarlet or dark tomato red, its breast a deep red to greenish golden-orange. The olive green of its upper parts has a strong golden tinge and may be suffused with rusty orange, especially on the hind neck. Eye-rims red. Bill black with tip, and cutting edges of mandibles shining red. Its female usually has some golden tinge (less than the male's) on the green upper parts and her breast is mainly greenish gold or rusty buff. Her eye-rims are greyish blue. The juvenile resembles that of *M.n. chubbi*. The form from Fernando Po Island, *M.n. virginiae*, has a strong orange tinge on its upper parts and an entirely red bill.

See plate 1, facing p. 96.

FIELD CHARACTERS Small olive-green bird with red, orange or buff face and most of underparts boldly spotted with white on a black background. Combination of green upperparts and white-spotted black underparts diagnostic. The Melba Finch, *Pytelia melba*, has a rather similar colour pattern but is paler both on the red and green parts (though brighter), its underparts are usually more barred than spotted and never on a black ground and it has *a longer and red tail and red rump in both sexes*.

DISTRIBUTION AND HABITAT Africa from Sierra Leone, Liberia and Ghana, south to north-western Angola and Kasai, east to Uganda, south-eastern Sudan and southern Abyssinia, and south through Kenya, Tanzania, Zambia, Malawi, and Mozambique to eastern Rhodesia, Natal and Pondoland. Also on Fernando Po, Zanzibar and Pemba Islands. Inhabits thickets, including coastal palm thickets,

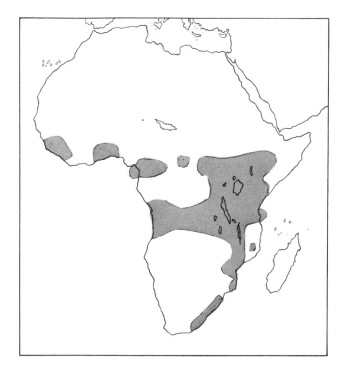

secondary forest, bushy cover along streams, forest edge and sometimes dense grass and the undergrowth of exotic conifer plantations. When in dry country, always in evergreen cover near water. Up to 2000 metres in eastern Africa and to 1200 metres in the Cameroons.

FEEDING AND GENERAL HABITS Seeks food on the ground, often in clearings, on paths or in cultivated plots or fields but keeping near to cover and fleeing quickly into it if frightened. The western form often takes cultivated rice, picking up fallen grains before and after harvest (Chapin) and has been recorded feeding on scraps of cassava and oil palm husk (Bannerman, Bates). The eastern race is known to take grass seeds (Vaughan). Probably grass seeds and small insects are taken by all forms of the species. Usually seen in small parties or pairs.

In captivity needs a plentiful supply of insect food as well as dry and soaked seed (Immelmann *et al.*, Karl, Knöckel, Nicolai, Neff, Proebsting), Karl who successfully kept and bred both western and eastern races of this bird in captivity, found that the large-billed western form was fond of paddy rice both dry and soaked. Some of his pairs reared their young largely on fresh ant pupae and whiteworms, refusing mealworms and fruit flies but one, at a time when ant pupae were unobtainable, successfully reared two broods largely on mealworms, which had been smeared with a liquid vitamin supplement and of which they ate only the heads. Captive birds usually take the winged females of meadow ants, *Lasius* spp. very eagerly. Some individuals will readily take hard-boiled egg (Neff). Except when it first arrives in Europe this species is much less sensitive to cold than many African estrildids and can be kept successfully in an unheated outdoor aviary during the summer months. Immelmann *et al.* recommend, however, that it should not be kept at a temperature allowed to drop below 15°C.

Very agile among twigs and branches and can half hop, half run lengthwise along vertical branches. At such times its plump shape and tail held slightly upwards give it a Wren-like appearance. On the ground it both hops and uses a 'polka-step'. Locomotion intention movements consist only of a slight upward jerk of the tail, which is usually carried horizontally (Kunkel, 1960).

NESTING Descriptions of wild nests, that I have read, all seem to derive from Vaughan's account of a single nest found on Pemba Island. This was 'a large untidy domed structure'. It was 'decorated' with a cast-off snake skin and built about 3 metres high in a mangrove tree at the edge of mangrove forest. Clutch size in the wild is usually said to be 3 eggs but I cannot find the source of this, unless it is McLachlan's and Liversidge's reference to a clutch of 3 laid by *captive* birds. The latter usually, however, lay 4 to 6 eggs in a clutch (Immelmann *et al.*, Neff, Proebsting).

In captivity this species will nest either in large nest boxes or in bushes or similar cover. The large and massively built nest is made of grass stems, coconut or sisal fibres, bast, fine roots and similar materials and the nest chamber lined with feathers or with moss and

feathers. The side entrance has a diameter of about 4 centimetres and usually no entrance tube. There may be racial variation here as tube-less nests, in captivity, may all involve *M.n. schlegeli* and Neff had a pair of *M.n. chubbi* which built a nest with a 10 centimetre-long entrance tube. The male brings material for the nest. It has sometimes been implied that only the female does the actual building but Neff and Proebsting observed both sexes building, with material brought by the male. Occasionally the female may bring material for the lining (Karl).

Both sexes incubate in turn by day and both roost in the nest at night. The male of a pair of *M.n. schlegeli* relieved the incubating female about 6 times per day but never for periods of more than half an hour (Karl). In one instance two females paired to the same male and successfully bred, the two hens (which had probably been paired to each other before the male was introduced) laying in the same nest and incubating together except when relieved by their mate (Knöckel). Young birds may breed when only about 10 weeks old and still partly in juvenile plumage.

Incubation period 12 to 13 days. Young fledge at 21 days but at first return to the nest to roost. Both adults and well-grown young make a snapping noise as an apparent defensive threat when they are inside the nest and feel menaced by the approach of some creature outside it.

The above information on captive breeding is derived from Immelmann *et al.*, Karl, Knöckel, Neff and Proebsting.

VOICE Except where otherwise stated, the information here refers either certainly or probably to the race *M.n. schlegeli*.

The contact call is a drawn out melodious 'tseeeht', prefaced by shorter notes – 'tak' or 'tek' with a somewhat lip-smacking tone. At high intensities, as when paired birds are separated, the 'tseeeht' call is increased in length and loudness (Proebsting). Sometimes, as close contact and locomotion intention calls, only the 'tak' notes are used (Immelmann *et al.*, 1963). The excitement (= alarm?) calls are a sharp melodious 'tsit-tsit' and 'tsit-terrerr' but Neff recorded the alarm call of the race *M.n. chubbi* as a sharp 'terr' and Kunkel had a single male of *M.n. schlegeli* which apparently used a series of 'tek' calls in alarm. A melodious trill is uttered as a greeting between mates and variants of it in other situations, such as when changing over at the nest or arriving at the nest with building material.

The song of the male appears to be subject to some variation but always to include series of fluting or whistling notes, usually drawn out and sometimes dropping in pitch, and trilling notes, prefaced and/or interjected with the kissing or lip-smacking 'tak' notes. The descriptions of Neff and Proebsting do not suggest any significant differences between the songs of *M.n. chubbi* and *M.n. schlegeli* but Immelmann *et al.* (1976) transcribe a song of *M.n. virens* (treated here as a synonym of *M.n. chubbi*) which also included silvery, bell-like notes. The song is given during courtship display and also, but apparently less often, by the male when perched near the female but not actually displaying (Kunkel) in this way.

DISPLAY AND SOCIAL BEHAVIOUR Courtship display takes place above ground in a bush, tree or etc. The male, with a piece of nesting material held in his bill, performs upward bobbing movements (inverted curtseys) in which his feet do not leave the perch and his head is held nearly vertically during the upward thrust. His head and tail are angled towards the female if she is to one side of him. Should the female not be near the male at the start of the display, she usually flies to him as soon as he begins to sing. She may solicit on the spot and copulation follow (Proebsting) but more often, if stimulated, she flies to the nest, enters it, and is followed by the male. Further song is often then heard from inside the nest and the nest's movements suggest that copulation takes place there (Karl, Neff).

Kunkel once observed a male singing at a sick female whom he was perched beside. He turned his head from side to side and slightly raised and quivered his wings.

Allopreening and clumping appear to occur rather seldom as a rule (Knöckel, Kunkel) but some birds freely indulge in both (Proebsting).

Knöckel found his birds very peaceable. Seven kept together behaved as a loose flock and showed no aggressiveness although neither flock members nor the members of pairs within the flock, clumped when at rest.

OTHER NAMES Green-backed Twinspot, Schlegel's Twinspot.

REFERENCES
Bates, G. L. 1930. *Handbook of the birds of West Africa.* John Bale and Danielsson, London.
Bannerman, D. A. 1953. *The birds of West and Equatorial Africa,* vol. 2. Oliver and Boyd, Edinburgh and London.
Chapin, J. P. 1954. The birds of the Belgian Congo. *Bull. Amer. Mus. Nat. Hist.* **75B**.
Immelmann, K., Steinbacher, J. & Wolters, H. E. 1963 and 1976. *Vögel in Käfig und Voliere: Prachtfinken*: 79–89 and 529–530.
Karl, F. 1961. Die Erstzucht des Grünen Tropfenastrild (*Mandingoa nitidula schlegeli*). *Gefiederte Welt* **1961**: 1–3.
Kunkel, P. 1960. Einiges über den Grünen Tropfenastrild (*Mandingoa nitidula*) *Gefiederte Welt* **1960**: 131–132.
McLachlan, G. R. & Liversidge, R. 1957. *Roberts birds of South Africa.* Cape Town.
Neff, R. 1964. Haltung und Zucht der Grünen Tropfenastrilds der Rasse *Mandingoa nitidula chubbi*. *Gefiederte Welt* **1964**: 239–241.
Proebsting, F. 1964. Der Grüne Tropfenastrild *Mandingoa nitidula schlegeli*, seine Haltung und Zucht. *Gefiederte Welt* **1964**: 81–83.
Sclater, W. L. & Moreau, R. E. 1933. Taxonomic and field notes on some birds of North-Eastern Tanganyika Territory. *Ibis* 13th ser., **3**: 399–440.
Vaughan, J. H. 1930. The birds of Zanzibar and Pemba. *Ibis* 12th ser., **6**: 1–48.

The crimson-wings

The crimson-wings, *Cryptospiza*, are a group of medium-sized waxbills with rounded wings and rather short rounded tails. They are olive and red or grey and red in colour and in all the back and rump are red. They are montane species and their distribution suggests that in the relatively recent past they may have been more widespread.

The Red-faced Crimson-wing, *Cryptospiza reichnenovii* and the Abyssinian Crimson-wing, *C. salvadorii*, are best treated as members of a superspecies, as Hall and Moreau suggest. They are allopatric throughout most of their respective ranges and present evidence (Woosnam, in Ogilvie-Grant) indicates that where both occur in the same geographical area they inhabit different altitudes. *C. reichenovii* occurs in two widely separated populations which show, however, only very slight racial differences. The Dusky Crimson-wing, *C. jacksoni*, and Shelley's Crimson-wing, *C. shelleyi*, are at least geographically sympatric with each other and with the other two species. There is not yet sufficient field information as to whether or to what extent they are ecologically separated.

It seems most likely that the crimson-wings' closest relatives are the twinspots, blue-bills and seed-crackers. The resemblances of colour pattern between Dybowski's Twinspot, *Euchistospiza dybowskii*, and *Cryptospiza* and between the head patterns of the Green Twinspot, *Mandingoa nitidula* and the Red-faced Crimson-wing, have been discussed in the introduction to the twinspots (p. 90). The crimson-wings form, however, a relatively well-differentiated group and certainly merit generic rank unless all the twinspots, the blue-bills, and possibly also the seed-crackers, are placed in a single genus; a solution that might have much to commend it in spite of the difficulties of defining such a genus.

REFERENCES
Hall, B. P. & Moreau, R. E. 1970. *An atlas of speciation in African passerine birds.* British Museum (Natural History) London.
Ogilvie-Grant, W. R. 1910. Zoological Results of the Ruwenzori Expedition 1905–6. *Trans. Zool. Soc. London* **19**: 253–459.

Red-faced Crimson-wing *Cryptospiza reichenovii*

Pytelila reichenovii Hartlaub 1874, *Ibis*, p. 166.

DESCRIPTION Slightly smaller than Peters' Twinspot in body size but cobbier in shape with proportionately smaller bill, shorter wings and much shorter tail. Plumage soft and dense. Patch at each side of head, including lores and area around eye, deep scarlet. Mantle, back, rump, most of those parts of the wing coverts that are visible when the wing is folded, outer webs of inner secondaries and ends of some of the flank feathers, a rich carmine or deep blood-red. Primary coverts, secondaries (except where otherwise described above) and primaries greyish

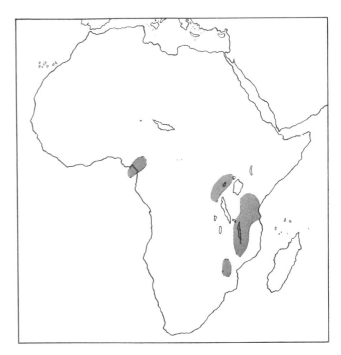

black, tinged with olive on the outer webs. Tail dull black. Rest of plumage dark yellowish olive shading to a rather darker and less yellowish hue on head and nape and greenish buff on the throat. Irides dark brown, eye-rims red or pinkish but narrow. Bill black. Legs and feet brown, dark brown or greyish brown.

The female has the face patch buff, not red, and perhaps averages a little paler on the underparts and a very little less bright red on the upperparts. Juvenile like female but with the buff face patch less clear and the upper parts, except for the rump and upper tail coverts, appearing only washed with dull carmine red (carmine tips to olive feathers). Young males began to show red feathers on the face about 3 weeks after fledging (Sieberer.) The nestling has five black spots on the yellow palate. Its tongue has two black spots and there are two black spots on the inside of the lower mandible on at either side of the tongue. Gape with four iridescent tubercles, outlined in black, on each side, three in the base of the upper and one in the base of the lower mandible (Immelmann *et al.*). Fledglings have swollen gape flanges of lower mandibles varyingly developed, sometimes yellow and conspicuous (Sieberer). Sieberer's paper is illustrated with photographs of juveniles.

The above description is of nominate *C.r. reichenovii* from the Cameroons, Fernando Po and the escarpment of Angola at Gabela, Cuanza Sul. *C.r. australis*, from the eastern part of the species' range, although separated by great distances (see map) from the nominate race, hardly differs from it, being merely, on average, a very little lighter in both the olive and red parts of its plumage.

FIELD CHARACTERS Small, short-tailed 'finch' with red back and rump, black tail and conspicuous red (male) or buff (female) patch around eye. The red or buff eye patches on an otherwise dark olive head distinguish this from other crimson-wings, the only species with which confusion is likely. Juveniles probably not specifically identifiable in the field unless with their parents.

DISTRIBUTION AND HABITAT Mountain forest in western Africa in the western Cameroons, from Bamenda to Mt Cameroon, including Kupé Mountain (Eisentraut), Fernando Po; the escarpment of Angola at Gabela, Cuanza Sul; and the Obudu Plateau in eastern Nigeria; and eastern Africa in the mountain forests from Ruwen-

zori and Kibale to eastern Kivu; Mt Kungwe, The Usambara Mountains, Iringa, Njombe and Poroto Mountains Tanzania, and Malawi and nothern Mozambique; eastern Rhodesia and the Nyika Plateau of Zambia (Dowsett). Usually at elevations between about 1000 and 2100 metres but as low as about 200 metres in the Usambaras, near Amani (Sclater and Moreau).

Inhabits areas with thick undergrowth, tree ferns or other low cover. Possibly presence of some grasses desirable or essential. Thus often, and perhaps mainly, near or at the forest edge, along streams or near paths or other small openings. On Ruwenzori, and perhaps elsewhere, in rough open country, old cultivation and millet fields below the forest line (Woosnam, in Ogilvie-Grant). Probably there was abundant dense cover in all these latter places.

FEEDING AND GENERAL HABITS Known to take grass seeds. Moreau found that, at Amani, seeds of the grass *Setaria chevaleri* were a main food and the birds also ate fragments of pounded maize (and were trapped by the natives when coming to take this latter food). In parts of Zaïre takes the small green, bean-like seeds of balsams, *Impatiens* sp. (Kunkel, *in litt.*). Presumably other foods, including insects, are also eaten. Usually seen in small parties on or near the ground. Moreau found that, around Amani, they usually kept within the forest shade and never ventured more than 90 metres (100 yards) from cover.

In captivity it is not very clear which of the commercially available seeds are taken most readily as successful keepers of this species seem, wisely, to have offered a great variety. It will also eat seeding grasses and chickweed and soft food as well as such insect food as ant pupae, whiteworms, gnat larvae and small mealworms. When they had young a pair searched every nook and crevice of their aviary for spiders (Sieberer). Although a good supply of varied insect food is desirable when young are being reared, Sieberer found that, when he was unable to supply so much insect food as he had for their first brood, his pair reared their second brood largely on soaked seed, chickweed and small mealworms. The young of the second brood did not grow so fast as those of the first but were in no way defective.

Has been seen to beat lumps of soft food on the ground in much the same manner (to judge from description) as that used by cordon-bleus with a large insect, eating the bits that broke off (Sieberer). Captive birds have been seen 'anting' with large millipedes but not with ants (Kunkel). Very fond of bathing. In captivity it is usually tame and calm and does not desert or become much alarmed if its nest is looked into.

NESTING Accounts of wild nests in the standard works all seem to derive from that of Moreau (in Sclater & Moreau) who found nests usually 5 to 6 metres (15 to 20 feet) above ground in tree ferns, *Cyathea usambarensis*, or saplings of the forest pawpaw, *Cylicomorpha parviflora*, both of which have thorny stems. The nest is an 'oblate spheroid' with a wide porched entrance pointing slightly upward. One examined in detail was made of skeletonised leaves and lined with feathery seed heads of a grass, *Panicum* sp., and the horsehair-like mycelium of a fungus, probably a species of *Merasmius*. Other nests, not examined closely, appeared to be made mainly of grass.

Nests built in captivity have been in boxes and baskets (Schassmann & Sieberer, photographs in the latter), built of coconut fibres, grass stems and similar materials and the egg chamber lined with feathers or moss and feathers. Schassmann describes the nest as like that of the House Sparrow, Sieberer's photographs show a projecting porch of stems or similar materials, apparently continued beyond the entrance of the short entrance tube. Broods of 3 and of 4 young have been produced in captivity. The nest is built mainly by the male and may be completed in 2 days (Sieberer). Both sexes incubate and brood in turn in the usual way. Sieberer's birds, when they had young in the nest, changed over 5 or 6 times in the late afternoon and evening, for periods of only 10 to 15 minutes at a time. No doubt this is an adaptation to finding a large supply of insect food to feed the young to repletion before nightfall. Young fledge at about 21 days and are fed for another 10 to 12 days, almost entirely by their father. Change over at the nest is usually silent but sometimes the brooding or incubating female will utter soft murmuring notes, which always result in the male going at once to the nest.

For the first few evenings after fledging the parents call the young back into the nest to roost but, at least in captivity, not all the brood heed the parents and some roost outside the nest (Sieberer). Fledged young beg (always?) in a finch-like manner, stretching their necks straight towards the parent (Sieberer).

VOICE Utters a sharp chirping 'tsit' and also a loosely strung together series of notes (Immelmann *et al.*). The song is soft and variable. Moreau (in Sclater and Moreau) describes it (from many captive specimens) as only audible for about 9 metres (ten yards), individually variable and consisting of four long drawn notes, descending in scale and each followed by a staccato chirp. Nicolai (in Immelmann *et al.*, 1963) likens the song to that of the Green Twinspot and notes that the end strophe is a two-syllabled whistling phrase with a complaining ('klag-endes') tone.

The song is given during the courtship display and also when perched near to the mate or fledged young, possibly also when perched alone.

DISPLAY AND SOCIAL BEHAVIOUR The most detailed description of the courtship display, that I have found, is that of Kunkel in his unpublished mss. It is very similar to that of the *Estrilda* species. With the feathers of the belly, lower breast and flanks somewhat raised, angled tail and head slightly turned towards the bird being displayed to, the displaying bird performs upward thrusts of head and body by alternately stretching and bending its legs. The head is held upwards stiffly, not thrown back beyond the line of the body on the upward movement. This display may be performed with or (less often) without nesting material in bill. Both male and female give this display, the male usually accompanies it with song, the female displays in silence (Kunkel). The display may terminate with copulation (Sieberer) but often does not. On a few occasions Sieberer saw an apparent display in which the male, perched beside his mate and with body and head held steeply upward, sang at her. She sometimes responded by adopting a similar stance but also quivering her tail. The male also sang in this way to his flying but still dependent young, who would then gather round him and listen attentively.

The greeting display is similar to that of typical waxbills, *Estrilda* but newly paired and pairing birds although otherwise adopting a posture similar to that of the Lavender Waxbill in its greeting display: upright, with breast and belly feathers partly erected, head turned slightly towards the partner with feathers arranged to make the 'triangular head', and tail angled towards the partner, do not then bow but simply hop sideways towards each other (Kunkel, unpublished mss.).

OTHER NAMES Reichenow's Crimson-wing, Red-eyed Crimson-wing.

REFERENCES
Dowsett, R. J. 1970. On a collection of birds from the Nyika Plateau, Zambia. *Bull. Brit. Orn. Club* **90**: 49–53.
Eisentraut, M. 1968. Beitrag zur Vogelfauna von Fernando Po und Westkamerun. *Bonn. Zool. Beitr.* **1968**: 49–68.
Immelmann, K., Steinbacher, J. & Wolters, H. E. 1963 and 1976. *Vögel in Käfig und Voliere: Prachtfinken*: 94–97 and 531–533.
Kunkel, P. 1967. Zu Biologie und Verhalten des Rotkopfsamen-knackers. *Bonn. Zool. Beitr.* **18**: 139–168.
Ogilvie-Grant, W. R. 1910. Zoological results of the Ruwenzori Expedition 1905–6. *Trans. Zool. Soc. London* **19**: 253–459.

Schassmann, A. 1970. Etwas über die Zucht meiner Reichenow's Bergastrilde *Gefiederte Welt* **1970**: 87–88.

Sclater, W. L. & Moreau, R. E. 1933. Taxonomic and field notes on some birds of North-Eastern Tanganyika Territory, pt. 5. *Ibis* **1933**: 399–440.

Sieberer, O. 1972. Geglückte Zucht von Reichenows Bergastrild (*Cryptospiza reichenovii*). *Gefiederte Welt* **1972**: 142–146.

Abyssinian Crimson-wing *Cryptospiza salvadorii*

Cryptospiza salvadorii Reichenow, 1892, *J. Orn.* **40**, pp. 187, 221.

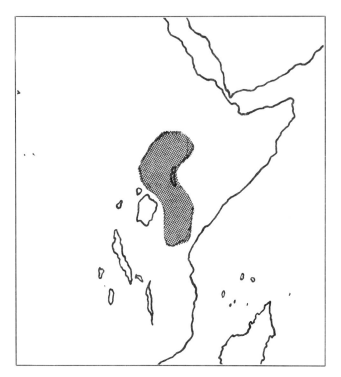

DESCRIPTION Very similar to the previous species, *C. reichenovii*, from which it differs as follows: No red (male) or buff (female) on face, these parts being greyish olive with, in the male, blackish lores. The tone of the head is slightly greyer and the underparts are a slightly paler and usually more greyish olive, the throat more noticeably buff or greyish buff and the under wing coverts buffish. Eye-rims greyish and inconspicuous. Sexes nearly alike except that the female has buffish lores and her red parts are a shade paler and with a slightly more orange tinge. Juvenile bears same relation to adult as that of *C. reichenovii* (q.v.). Haeflin (1980) gives photographs of juveniles and half-grown nestlings.

The above description is of nominate *C.s. salvadorii*, from central Abyssinia to Mount Varaguess in northern Kenya. *C.s. ruwenzori*, from the Ruwenzori Mountains of western Uganda and eastern Kivu, has the head and nape of a less olivaceous, more definitely grey hue and the underparts lighter and greyer. It tends also to have a slightly smaller bill. *C.s. kilimensis*, from south-eastern Sudan south through Kenya to northern Tanzania, is more or less intermediate between the other two. It intergrades with *C.s. kilimensis* on Mt Elgon. Further races have been described but seem best treated as synonyms of one or other of the above, whose differences are slight enough.

FIELD CHARACTERS Small dull grey or greyish olive 'finch' with red back and rump. Lack of any red or buff on head (except for buffish throat, and lores of female) distinguish it from adults of the otherwise very similar Red-faced Crimson-wing. Juveniles not identifiable from other juvenile crimson-wings in the field.

DISTRIBUTION AND HABITAT Mountains of central Abyssinia, south-eastern Sudan, northern Kenya and Uganda west and south to eastern Kivu, and northern Tanzania. Said to occur at all elevations (Mackworth-Praed & Grant) but on Ruwenzori, Woosnam found it at heights of 2000 to 2500 metres (7000 to 8500 feet), above the range of the Red-faced Crimson-wing (Ogilvie-Grant). Inhabits mountain forest, forest edge, thickets along streams and rivers and bamboos. Sometimes in riparian thickets in savanna country.

FEEDING AND GENERAL HABITS Known to take seeds of some grasses of the genus *Setaria* (Van Someren) and of balsams of the genus *Impatiens* (Kunkel, pers. comm.). Comes out to feed in openings in the forest and at its edge but at once flees into thick cover if disturbed. Van Someren noted that the birds he watched feeding took seeds from bent-over lower sprays of seeding grass, that were partly hidden among foliage, and thus did not fully expose themselves. Haeflin, who successfully bred this species in an indoor aviary, provided ant pupae, eggfood, soaked millet and greenfood, as well as dry seeds. Has been seen 'anting' with large millipedes in captivity (Kunkel 1967).

NESTING Between ball-shaped and oval, built of grass and tendrils with a side opening toward the upper part, placed 2 to 4 metres (6 to 12 feet) above ground in a small tree or among creepers. Most other descriptions of nests seem derived from or to agree with that of Van Someren, given above, but Mackworth-Praed & Grant describe it as being covered, over the grass and tendrils, with moss and Belcher describes a nest, also spherical with a large upward-directed side entrance, as built of skeletonised leaves on a foundation of wet moss with inside dry grass panicles and a lining of feathers. Eggs 3 to 5, said to be sometimes spotted with minute grey spots (Mackworth-Praed & Grant) but this requires confirming. Recorded or probable breeding dates are June and July on Mt Elgon, also December and January; August to October in the Kenya highlands, probably also March or April, and February on Mt Kilimanjaro (Mackworth-Praed & Grant).

VOICE Presumed contact call has been described as a low-pitched 'chip-chip' (Van Someren) or 'Tsheep-tsheep' (Immelmann *et al.*, my anglicisation). The song, given during the courtship display is probably merely a variant of this, it is described by Burkard as 'tsig-tsig' or 'tseeg-

tseeg'. He also, however (in Immelmann *et al.*, 1963), describes another or perhaps the true song as a soft melodious but almost plaintive 'dee-goo-goo-day-dee' (my anglicisation).

DISPLAY AND SOCIAL BEHAVIOUR Courtship display and greeting display as Red-faced Crimson-wing (Kunkel, unpublished MS.). Kunkel's birds, when performing the courtship display, did not let go of the perch but Burkard's birds did so, thus performing small leaps. Presumably there is individual or intensity difference here and further observations are needed. On one occasion Kunkel saw a female lift and quiver her wings when performing the greeting display.

OTHER NAMES Salvadori's Crimson-wing, Crimson-backed Forest Finch.

REFERENCES

Belcher, C. F. 1930. *The birds of Nyasaland.* Crosby, Lockwood and Son, London.

Burkard, R. 1968. Über die Zucht einiger seltener Prachtfinken. *Gefiederte Welt* **1968**: 148–150.

Haeflin, H. 1980. Über die Zucht des Salvadoris Bergastrilds (*Cryptospiza salvadorii*). *Gefiederte Welt* **1980**: 144–145.

Immelmann, K., Steinbacher, J. & Wolters, H. E. 1963 and 1976. *Vögel in Käfig und Voliere: Prachtfinken*: 90–94 and 530–531.

Kunkel, P. 1967. Zu Biologie und Verhalten des Rotkopfsamenknackers. *Bonn. Zool. Beitr.* **18**: 139–168.

Mackworth-Praed, C. W. & Grant, C. H. B. 1960. *African handbook of birds*, ser. 1, vol. 2.

Ogilvie-Grant, W. R. 1910. Zoological results of the Ruwenzori Expedition 1905–6. *Trans. Zool. Soc. London* **19**: 253–459.

Van Someren, V. G. L. 1939. The birds of the Chyulu Hills. *Journal of the East African and Uganda Natural History Society* **14** 15–129.

Dusky Crimson-wing   *Cryptospiza jacksoni*

Cryptospiza jacksoni Sharpe, 1902, *Bull. Brit. Orn. Club* **13**, p. 8.

DESCRIPTION Similar in size and shape to the Red-faced Crimson-wing but very slightly larger and plumper in shape and with proportionately slightly shorter bill. Forehead, crown, face, sides of neck, mantle, back, rump, upper tail coverts, outer webs of inner secondaries and lower flanks dark rich crimson red. Under wing coverts mainly dark buff. Some or most of the feathers of the nape, centre of hind neck and inner greater coverts tipped with red, commonly so much so that these parts appear predominantly red. Rest of plumage dark grey. Irides dark brown, eye-rims pink or reddish (yellowish recorded for one individual—Immelmann *et al.*, 1963) and somewhat serrated-edged. Bill black. Legs and feet olive brown to blackish brown.

The female is like the male but has the nape, sides of hind neck and centre of the crown dark grey and the red parts of her plumage, especially on the face, are a rather lighter red with a definite orange tinge. From descriptions, and the one male individual I have seen, the juvenile

resembles the female but has no red on the head, only a trace on the flanks and the red on its upperparts is duller. Nestlings have a yellowish white palate with 3 large dark or black spots and behind them two smaller and often obsolescent dark or black spots (Chapin, Immelmann *et al.*, 1963).

FIELD CHARACTERS Small, plumpish bird with red face and mainly red upperparts and mainly dark grey below. Dark grey, not olive, underparts distinguish from other crimson-wings but confusion probably easy if birds are glimpsed in shade of thick cover. Red on head and lack of spots on flanks distinguish from dusky twinspots.

DISTRIBUTION AND HABITAT: Mountains of eastern Congo (Zaïre) from west of Lake Edward south to Kivu, Rwanda (Ruanda-Urundi), and adjacent parts of Uganda. Inhabits forest and bamboo growth, at about 1500 to 3000 metres (5000 to about 10000 feet). Usually in areas with dense undergrowth; often at forest edge or in or near openings in the forest (Chapin, Mackworth-Praed & Grant, Woosnam in Ogilvie-Grant).

FEEDING AND GENERAL HABITS Known to take seeds, including some of grasses (Chapin), the small green, bean-like seeds of balsams, *Impatiens* (Kunkel, pers. comm., Van Someren) and possibly also cultivated millet (Woosnam, in Ogilvie-Grant). One (only) of seven collected by Chapin had eaten eight tiny snails (Chapin). Probably also takes insects as in captivity it is said to need a considerable amount of animal food such as ant pupae, fruit flies and mealworms. Captive birds also ate a protein-rich soft food, half ripe grass seeds, soaked seed and greenfood but hardly touched dry seed (Immelmann *et al.*, 1963).

Usually seen in pairs. Sometimes, and possibly most often, feeds outside or in openings of the forest in grassy or

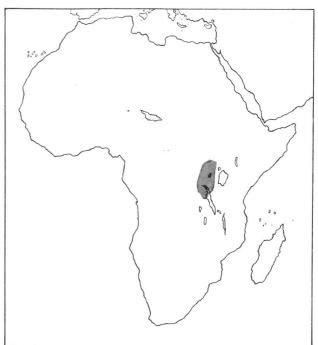

weed-grown places but flees quickly into cover when disturbed. Woosnam (in Ogilvie-Grant) often found it in dense undergrowth in dark parts of the forest, far from the edge. In captivity has been seen 'anting' with large millipedes (Kunkel).

NESTING No information. Probably similar to that of the Red-faced Crimson-wing (q.v.).

VOICE Burkard (in Immelmann *et al.*, 1963) describes the usual (probably contact?) calls as a sharp 'pee' or 'tsit' and a soft, trilling 'geegeegeegee'. The song is simple and consists essentially of only slightly modified call notes (Kunkel, unpublished MS.). Burkard describes it as incorporating a high-pitched 'peeee' and a rather deep but not loud, drawn-out 'gay' or 'gooayoo'.

DISPLAY AND SOCIAL BEHAVIOUR The courtship display and the greeting displays are like those of the Red-faced Crimson-wing (Kunkel, unpublished MS.) although copulation has not actually been observed in this species.

OTHER NAMES Jackson's Crimson-wing, Jackson's Hill Finch.

REFERENCES
Chapin, J. P. 1954. The birds of the Belgian Congo. *Bull. Amer. Mus. Nat. Hist.*, **75B**.
Immelmann, K., Steinbacher, J. & Wolters, H. E. 1963. *Vögel in Käfig und Voliere: Prachtfinken*: 97–99.
Kunkel, P. 1967. Zu Biologie und Verhaltens des Rotkopfsamenknackers. *Bonn. Zool. Beitr.* **18**: 139–168.
Mackworth-Praed, C. W. & Grant, C. H. B. 1973. *The African handbook of birds*, ser. 3., vol. 2.
Ogilvie-Grant, W. R. 1910. Zoological results of the Ruwenzori Expedition 1905–6. *Trans. Zool. Soc. London* **19**: 253–459.
Van Someren, V. G. L. 1949. *The birds of Bwamba*. Special supplement to the Uganda Journal, vol. 13.

Shelley's Crimson-wing   *Cryptospiza shelleyi*

Cryptospiza shelleyi Sharpe, 1902, *Bull. Brit. Orn. Club* **13**, p. 21.

DESCRIPTION Larger than the other crimson-wings (wing about 65–67 mm as against 50–60 mm) and with the bill having a somewhat swollen appearance. Head (excepting

throat), hind neck, mantle, back, rump and upper tail coverts carmine red. Wings dark brownish or greenish black, sometimes washed with red on the coverts and inner secondaries. Under wing coverts greenish buff. Tail dull black. Throat and most of underparts yellowish olive, strongly tinged with rusty orange on the flanks and blackish olive on the under tail coverts. Bill pinkish red to deep red, pinkish at extreme base. Irides very dark brown, eye-rims reddish pink. Legs and feet dark brown. The female has an olive head; reddish fawn immediately around the eyes in the only specimen I have examined (the type). Bill reddish, shading to horny brown at base of upper mandible and on culmen ridge and at base of centre of lower mandible. Juvenile said to resemble female, but is possibly duller. There is a close-up photograph of a live (but tethered) male in Lippens & Wille.

FIELD CHARACTERS Small red and yellowish olive bird with blackish wings and tail. Red or partly reddish bill (if visible) distinguish it from all other crimson-wings. Red head distinguishes male from all others except Dusky Crimson-wing, from which it can be told by its yellowish olive, not dark grey, throat and breast.

DISTRIBUTION AND HABITAT Mountain forests from Ruwenzori, and western Uganda to Kivu and south-western Rwanda (Ruanda-Urundi). Inhabits dense undergrowth or its immediate vicinity but there is little information about it.

FEEDING AND GENERAL HABITS Known to eat the tiny seeds of balsams of the genus *Impatiens* (Kunkel, pers. comm., Van Somerens). A bird collected by Chapin contained remains of both seeds and insects. Kunkel found that wild-caught birds readily took the seeds of *Impatiens* but could

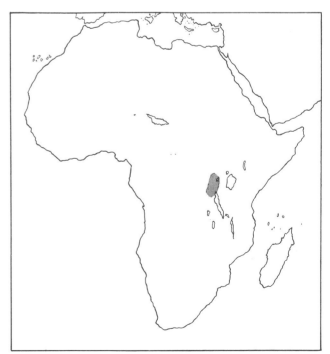

not be induced to take millet when *Impatiens* seeds were unavailable (pers. comm.).

Has been seen seeking food on the ground (Chapin). Keeps much to cover and difficult to watch or shoot. Sometimes associates with other species of crimson-wings (Van Somerens).

NESTING No information.

VOICE The Van Somerens describe a series of twittering notes, rising and falling in pitch.

DISPLAY AND SOCIAL BEHAVIOUR No information.

OTHER NAME Red-billed Crimson-wing.

REFERENCES
Chapin, J. P. 1954. The birds of the Belgian Congo. *Bull. Amer. Mus. Nat. Hist.*, **75B**.
Lippens, L. & Wille, H. 1976. *Les oiseaux de Zaïre.* Tielt, Belgium.
Van Someren, V. G. L. & G. R. C. 1949. *The birds of Bwamba.* Special supplement to the Uganda Journal, vol. 13.

The blue-bills

The blue-bills, *Spermophaga*, take their English name from their large bluish and red bills which have a mother-of-pearl-like sheen. They have rather rounded wings with a well-developed first (outermost) primary, a feature usually believed to be a primitive character and which they share with the dusky twinspots, *Euchistospiza*, and the Brown Twinspot, *Clytospiza*. In plumage pattern they greatly resemble the seed-crackers, *Pyrenestes*, and the red parts of their plumage are of a similar glossy texture to those of the latter. They also much resemble them in their swollen-looking bluish or whitish eye-rims although this character is shared, to some extent, by other probably related genera, such as *Hypargos*.

Kunkel's detailed study of the Red-headed Blue-bill, *S. ruficapilla*, has shown that this species (and in all probability this applies to other *Spermophaga*) agrees with the cordon-bleus, *Uraeginthus angolensis*, *U. bengalus* and *U. cyanocephala* in many details of behaviour. As the two genera differ considerably in habitat and ecology it is likely that these similarities indicate phylogenetic affinity, as they can hardly be due to convergence. It seems probable that *Spermophaga* and *Uraeginthus* are more closely related than their differing size and coloration would at first suggest. It might be remarked that the red areas of *Spermophaga* approximate quite closely to the rather similarly textured blue areas of *Uraeginthus* and that one of the latter, *U. bengalus*, does have some glossy red in its plumage. I am inclined to think that *Spermophaga* is rather more closely related to *Pyrenestes*, in spite of the latter's not sharing its large outer primary, than to any other genus but with *Hypargos* and probably also *Uraeginthus* also fairly near.

The Red-headed and Red-breasted Blue-bills, *S. ruficapilla* and *S. haematina*, are allopatric except in a small area around Yambuya (Hall & Moreau). They are not known to differ in ecology. *S. ruficapilla* has a completely isolated and well-differentiated eastern race which may possibly have reached specific status.

Grant's Blue-bill, *S. poliogenys*, shows a wide geographical overlap with both *S. ruficapilla* and *S. haematina* but is usually found in different habitat and is, presumably, ecologically separated.

REFERENCES
Hall, B. P. & Moreau, R. E. 1970. *An atlas of speciation in African passerine birds.* British Museum (Natural History), London.
Kunkel, P. 1967. Zu Biologie und Verhalten des Rotkopfsamen-knackers, *Spermophaga ruficapilla* (Fam. Estrildidae). *Bonn. zool. Beitr.* **18**: 139–168.

Red-headed Blue-bill *Spermophaga ruficapilla*

Spermospiza ruficapilla Shelley, 1888, *Proc. Zool. Soc.* London, p. 30.

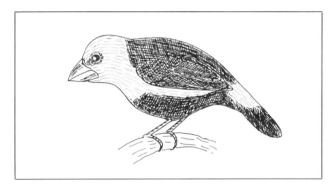

DESCRIPTION A large, large-billed estrildid with rather rounded wings. Tail between rounded and a blunt wedge-shape when spread. Head (except for a small blackish area immediately in front of and above the eyes), breast and upper flanks a shining deep scarlet red, sometimes a little darker and duller on nape and top of head, where dark feather bases may show. Upper tail coverts a slightly darker and less bright red. Rest of plumage black, slightly glossy on back, wings and tail. Irides dark brown to reddish brown; eye-rims narrow and dark bluish immediately in front of and behind the eye, broader and bluish white above and below the eye (Kunkel, 1967). The large bill is silvery blue, light blue or purplish blue with a mother-of-pearl sheen and the tip and cutting edges of the mandibles pink or red, sometimes, perhaps only in youngish birds, orange at tip of lower mandible. Legs and feet dark brown, dark olive or blackish. The palate markings of the adult are similar to those of the nestling and consist of three black, yellow-rimmed spots on a yellowish grey palate (Kunkel and Kunkel).

The female has the red areas less brilliant and tinged with orange. Her upperparts, where black in the male, are dark slate-grey. Her underparts, where not red, are dark grey, spotted and barred with white. On the lower breast and upper flanks the grey feathers have two paired white spots, lower down these develop (or degenerate) into broken bars and then to cross bars on the belly, ventral area and under tail coverts, where some individuals show buffish or (less often) pink suffusion. Her eye rims are bluish, only slightly paler, and not so wide as the male's, above and below the eye (Kunkel, 1967a) and her bill less bright. Juveniles are dark dull grey, tinged with reddish brown on face and breast and with rusty carmine tips to the upper tail coverts. Some have ill-defined cross-barring on the belly and flanks. Young males are sometimes and perhaps usually darker than young females and not barred below (Chapin) but some young females may be equally dark and unbarred (Kunkel, 1967a). Bill leaden grey with tip and cutting edges yellow. Newly hatched young are yellowish flesh with a few down feathers on the upper parts. Melanin pigment begins to appear in the bill on the second day. Nestlings have a shining yellow mouth with three black spots on the palate. There are three yellow tubercles at each side of the gape. On the sixth day two small black marks develop on the inside of each mandible, near its tip (Kunkel, 1967a). The first moult begins a few days after fledging but proceeds slowly and takes more than two months to complete (Kunkel, 1967a). There are photos of adult and nestling in Kunkel, 1967b.

The above description is of nominate *S.r. ruficapilla*, from most of the species' range. The isolated race, *S. ruficapilla cana*, from the East Usambara Mountains of Tanzania, has those upperparts that are black in nominate *S.r. ruficapilla*, a dark-medium slate grey (not so dark as that of the female *S.r. ruficapilla*) tinged with brown on the primaries and underparts. The red areas are lighter, almost vermilion, but equally shining, and the grey of the mantle spreads up on to the nape to a varying extent. Eye-rims whitish. Bill shining purple at base and on culmen ridge shading to red at tip and along the cutting edges of the mandibles. Sexual differences comparable to those described for the nominate race but the female is more barred than spotted below.

FIELD CHARACTERS   Black or dark grey finch-like bird with red head, breast, flanks and upper tail coverts and a large shining bluish, red-tipped bill. Female with belly and lower flanks spotted and/or barred with white. Red head distinguishes male from Red-breasted Blue-bill, *S. haematina* and the female from it and from Grant's Blue-bill. *S. poliogenys*. Male of *S. poliogenys* is very similar to male of present form in colour pattern but has brilliant red not dark red upper tail coverts *and rump* and is a lighter and even more vivid red on head and breast. Black, not red, tail and less massive and red-tipped bill distinguish it from *Pyrenestes* species.

DISTRIBUTION AND HABITAT   Northern Angola to southern Kasai; north-eastern Congo east to southern Sudan, Uganda and western Kenya south to Baraka on the west shore and the Kungwe mountains on the east shore of Lake Tanganyika. An isolated, and racially distinct population in the East Usambara mountains of Tanzania. Inhabits dense cover and its near vicinity at the edge of

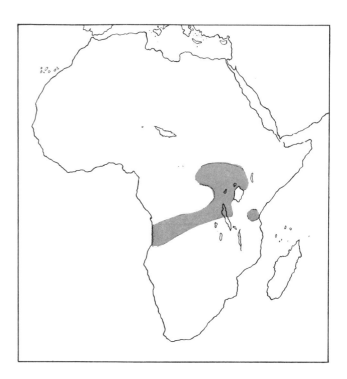

forest, secondary growth, bushy forest clearings, riverside thickets, damp overgrown valleys and depressions in plantations or otherwise cultivated areas and the intermediate zone between cultivation and mountain forest. Often in damp places but not or not often in real marshland. In some areas up to about 2100 metres or more, in others at low elevations (Kunkel, 1967a and b, Chapin). The race *S.r. cana* is recorded as inhabiting forest undergrowth (Sclater & Moreau) but possibly is also mainly a bird of secondary growth and forest edge.

FEEDING AND GENERAL HABITS   The nominate form is known to take seeds of *Ipomenea* (Convolvulaceae), *Indigofera* (Leguminosae), the small tare-like seeds of another (unidentified) leguminous plant (Kunkel, 1967a and b) and of the sword grass, *Imperator* (Van Somerens). Insects, including weevils, other small beetles and termites, are also eaten (Chapin, Kunkel). The race *cana* is said to take exclusively grass seed, especially that of *Olyra latifolia* (Sclater & Moreau) but confirmation of this is needed. In captivity the nominate form will take a variety of foods. Ripe and half-ripe dari, various millets, hemp, the seeds of the garden composite, *Tithonia diversifolia*, greenstuff such as chickweed and lettuce, ant pupae, whiteworms, crickets, wax moth larvae and other insects (Burkard, Kleefisch, Kunkel, 1967a). Kunkel's birds eagerly ate eggfood made of hard-boiled egg without any bread or biscuit added. Seeds are (always?) swallowed whole, without de-husking (Kunkel, 1967a). In captivity, and probably also in the wild, the nestlings are fed mainly or entirely on animal food.

Seeks food on the ground but sometimes also in vegetation. When feeding on seeding sword grass, has been seen to alight about the middle of the stem, which bent under the bird's weight so that it rested on the surrounding plants, when the bird sidled along the stem to feed from the panicle (Van Someren). Breaks up clumps of earth or termite nest with hard, downward directed blows of its bill and lifts and moves aside dead leaves but does not use side to side bill flicking as do many estrildids (Kunkel). Feeds much on weed-grown open land, fallow cultivation and clearings but usually keeps near to cover and flees into it at the least alarm. In captivity at first wild and shy but may soon become quite tame though apparently much individual variation (or variation due to subtle differences in its treatment) in this. Sometimes holds nesting material under one foot (to re-arrange it in bill) but in a rather inefficient way, placing the material on the perch and then moving the near foot outwards so that it may (but does not always) clamp it to the perch (Kunkel, 1967a).

Most often encountered singly, in pairs or small parties. In captivity pairs in breeding condition become extremely aggressive to conspecifics but show no aggression towards other species unless these closely resemble them in coloration *and* plumage pattern (Kunkel, 1967a). Usually holds itself in a horizontal, rather crouching posture. Flight rather direct and more slow and fluttering than that of Estrilda species (Kunkel, 1967a). Spends much time on the ground or perched in low cover. Can perch on nearly or quite vertical stems of branches but cannot cling, hang and stretch about among vegetation like, for example, the typical waxbills. The locomotion-intention movements involve upward and downward flicking of wings and tail very similar to those of blue waxbills; at high intensities the tail is partly spread and swung jerkily from side to side (Kunkel, 1967a). A male of the race *S.r. cana* flicked its wings only through a very small angle and made *only* side to side tail movements (Moreau & Moreau); probably this was an individual rather than racial difference. Bathes freely and captive birds usually did so when it rained, especially when a heavy shower began to slacken off. They anted with large millipedes but not with ants (Kunkel, 1967a).

NESTING I can only find two records (Chapin and the Van Somerens) of wild nests. One, incomplete, was at the base of an oil palm, the other, which was about 2·5 metres high in a tree and contained 3 young, was described as a large untidy structure of coarse grass and ferns, lined with finer grasses. In captivity (Kunkel, 1967a and b, Kleefisch) a roundish nest is built of coarse materials such as coarse grasses, dead leaves, fern, roots and moss and lined with fine grasses, coconut or similar fibres and feathers. There is no entrance tube but long pieces of material often or usually hang down from the side entrance. Large pieces of material are carried singly by one end but small and soft materials are 'bundled' (Kunkel, 1967a). Nest built mainly or entirely by the male but the female also brings materials for lining it (Kunkel, 1967a). Kleefisch found that his birds always built several nests, usually three, at the same time but Kunkel's breeding pair apparently did

not; which is the normal or most usual behaviour remains, therefore, uncertain.

Incubation by Kunkel's birds started always with the last egg, not before. Both sexes incubate in turn by day but the hen spends more time on the nest than her mate. As usual, she alone sits at night.

Incubation period 17 to 18 days; young fledge at 20 days (Kunkel, 1967a). The fledged young are called or led into cover by their parents but not back to the nest. Both sexes care for the young although, if the parents nest again while the young are still dependent their mother ceases to feed them before she begins to lay. Kleefisch found that when his birds were feeding young in the nest, they invariably flew first to one of the unused nests at the opposite end of the aviary so that anyone not knowing the situation might have been misled as to the whereabouts of the nestlings. As Kunkel's birds appear to have done nothing like this, further observations are needed to discover whether this behaviour (and the pre-requisite building of more than one nest) is usual or common and what circumstances elicit it.

VOICE The distance contact call has been described as 'tseet' or 'seet' (my anglicisation) by Kleefisch and, for the race *cana*, as an 'uninflected squeak' by Moreau & Moreau. The alarm call of the two races would appear also similar or identical, a hard 'tshak' or 'tshake' (Kleefisch) for the nominate race and "a single Stonechat-like clacking note" for *cana* (Moreau & Moreau). The nominate form of the species has two forms of song, both prone to a good deal of variation. The first was described by Kleefisch as seven whistling or fluting notes, the first four rising and the last three falling in pitch, and by Kunkel (for a different individual) as a loud sequence of long drawn fluting notes ending in a trill. This song is given by males in, or coming into, breeding condition and in the early stages of nesting. The second form of song is very variable and consists of a medley of trilling, whistling, rattling and kissing sounds, not loud but often with a markedly guttural tone (Kleefisch, Kunkel). It is given during the courtship display. Presumably this second song is the (only) one recorded for the race *S.r. cana*, which Moreau & Moreau describe as 'a most queer and laboured . . . succession of clinks, clucks and kissing noises, only audible at a distance of a few yards'.

DISPLAY AND SOCIAL BEHAVIOUR The courtship display usually takes place on the ground or on low perches. The male partly fluffs out the feathers on his belly, flanks and back and sleeks down those on his head and neck, so that he has a hump-backed appearance. The tail is angled towards the mate but, unlike what occurs in most estrildids, the flank feathers are not more fully fluffed out on the side nearest to her. The male holds a piece of grass, a leaf or other nesting material in the usual way. He bows to one side towards the female till his bill is about 45 degrees below the horizontal and then throws back his head till it is about 70 degrees above it. He does not bounce up and down by flexing and stretching his legs during the head movements or at any time in the display. The second type of song is uttered. Copulation may follow the display but does not (ever?) do so until the female is about to lay; it is preceded by the male pecking at his mate's head, nape and back and/or by her soliciting with quivering tail. In what was apparently the only successful copulation to have been so far described, the male clung, fluttering, to the female's back for a considerable time, like a male Goldbreast, and afterwards hopped around her, bowing. Incomplete versions of this display, in which no nesting material is held and/or no bowing and lifting of the head shown are frequent. The display has never been seen given by the female (Kunkel, 1967a).

Bill fencing occurs in minor aggression between mates or parents and their flying young. Mandibulation occurs as an appeasing behaviour in similar contexts. When greeting each other after a short absence, mates angle their tails towards each other and often slightly spread them.

Allopreening does not occur and clumping is rare except between recently fledged young. When not breeding members of a captive pair seem little interested in each other and probably do not stay together in the wild. Other birds of the same sex are peacefully tolerated, or at least ignored, by non-breeding birds but attacked by those in breeding condition.

OTHER NAMES Red-headed Blue-billed Weaver, Red-headed Forest Weaver.

REFERENCES

Burkard, R. 1962. Die Zucht des Rostbrustsamenknackers. *Gefiederte Welt* **1962**: 41–42.

Chapin, J. P. 1954. The birds of the Belgian Congo. *Bull. Amer. Mus. Nat. Hist.* **75B**.

Kleefisch, T. 1967. Nochmals: Rotkopfsamenknacker. *Gefiederte Welt* **1967**: 156–157.

Kunkel, P. 1967a. Zu Biologie und Verhalten des Rotkopfsamen-knackers, *Spermophaga ruficapilla* (Fam. Estrildidae). *Bonn. Zool. Beitr.* **18**: 139–168.

Kunkel, P. 1967b. Lebensraum, Haltung und Zucht des Rotkopfsamenknackers. *Gefiederte Welt* **1967**: 82–84.

Moreau, R. E. & W. M. 1937. Biological and other notes on some East African birds. *Ibis*, 14th ser. **1**: 321–345.

Sclater, W. L. & Moreau, R. E. 1933. Taxonomic and field notes on some birds of North-Eastern Tanganyika Territory, pt. 5. *Ibis* **1933**: 399–440.

Van Someren, V. G. L. & G. R. C. 1949. *The birds of Bwamba.* Uganda Journal **13**, special supplement.

Red-breasted Blue-bill   *Spermophaga haematina*

Loxia haematina Vieillot, 1805, *Ois. Chant.*, p. 102, pl. 67.

DESCRIPTION Similar in size and shape to previous species, *S. ruficapilla*, but with the bill averaging a little less deep and with a slightly straighter culmen. Median part of throat, breast and flanks a deep but shining scarlet red. Rest of plumage intense black. Irides dark brownish red to dark brown; eye rims pale blue. Bill shining pearly blue or blue and blackish, with red tip. Legs and feet brownish black, greenish black or dark olive. The female has the red

on throat, breast and flanks a little lighter and slightly tinged with orange. Her face, including ear coverts and forehead, are dull red or dark orange-red. Her upper parts are dark leaden grey, except for dark orange-red upper tail coverts and a variable amount of dark red suffusion on crown, nape, hind neck and basal halves of the tail feathers. Her underparts, where not red, are spotted and barred with white on a dark grey ground. There is much individual variation in detail but, in general, the feathers of the lower breast tend to have a blackish-edged white subterminal spot or band, those of the flanks (where not red) to have two paired spots and the belly and under tail coverts to be more definitely barred and to have a buffish suffusion on the basal parts and fringes of the feathers. The under wing coverts are similarly barred. Irides dark brown. Red tip to bill usually less extensive than in male.

The juvenile male is a dark dull grey with dark dull orange upper tail coverts and the feathers of the breast tipped or suffused with dark rusty orange. The juvenile female has less reddish tinge on the breast and a strong trace of pale cross barring on the underparts. Newly hatched nestlings are pale flesh-coloured with pale grey down on head, back and shoulders. They have swollen yellowish-white gape flanges that, by an indentation, are divided into two on both mandibles. There are 3 dark spots on the yellow palate and another dark spot in each corner of the upper mandible (just at gape) and a half moon-shaped dark mark on the inside of the lower mandible near the tip. There are good photographs of nestlings of different ages in Neff's (1978) paper. Juveniles (in captivity) are in adult plumage by three months old (Neff).

The above description is of nominate *S.h. haematina*, from the south bank of the river Gambia south and east to Ghana. In *S. haematina pustulata*, from southern and central Nigeria, east through the southern Cameroons to the Uele, Manyema, Lualaba and Lower Congo, the male has the face and ear coverts red, or very strongly suffused with red, the upper tail coverts bright red and the shining red of the breast and flanks a slightly lighter shade than in the nominate form. The red tip of his bill extends back in a red stripe along the cutting edges of both mandibles. The female has an orange-red face and bright red or orange-red upper tail coverts. Nestlings (always?) have two dark streaks on the inside of the upper mandible near the tip (Kleefisch, 1974). Kleefisch (1976) gives excellent photographs showing the sexual differences in the juvenile plumages of this race. *S.h. togoensis*, from South Togo to south-western Nigeria, is intermediate between the above-described races. Females are usually more like those of *S.h. pustulata* but males, although having red upper tail coverts and red along the cutting edge of the bill, have black faces. The races intergrade and birds from many areas are intermediate.

FIELD CHARACTERS Black forehead and crown distinguish male from males of other blue-bills. Reddish, not grey, face distinguishes female from female of *S. poliogenys*, predominantly grey, not red, crown and nape from *S.*

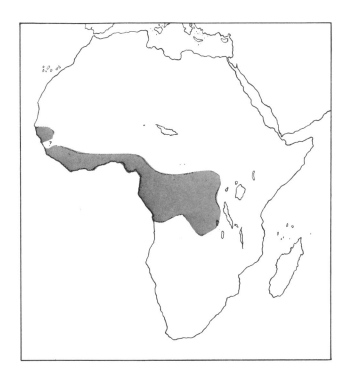

ruficapilla. Field characters in reference to other birds as for previous species (q.v.).

DISTRIBUTION AND HABITAT Tropical western and west-central Africa (see racial ranges, given above, and map). Habitats similar to those of previous species, *S. ruficapilla* (q.v.).

FEEDING AND GENERAL HABITS Has been recorded eating cultivated rice, various seeds (not identified), insects, spiders and the husk of the oil palm fruit (Chapin, Serle). Seeks food at least partly, and probably mostly, on the ground. Feeding and general behaviour as the previous species, *S. ruficapilla*, except where otherwise indicated.

In captivity it refuses large and hard seeds. Soaked or sprouted wheat and oats are eaten but of dry seed only small seeds such as various kinds of millet and canary seed. These latter seeds should, however, also be given soaked. Half-ripe spray millet, seeding grasses and chickweed and other greenstuff are taken, especially by captive-bred birds. Eggfood is usually eaten readily. Most who have successfully bred this species emphasise that a plentiful and specifically varied supply of insects must be given, which can include wax moths and their larvae, House Fly maggots, and pupae, small grasshoppers and crickets, whiteworms, newly moulted mealworms, smooth caterpillars etc (Burkard, Kleefisch, Neff). Neff found, however, that a free supply of insects, especially mealworms, appeared to cause liver troubles if given to non-breeding birds and that half-ripe seed and soaked seed is of most importance. He found that young were reared successfully when these were supplemented only with ant pupae.

Usually in pairs or family parties (Chapin). The wing

flicking locomotion intention movements accompany almost any activity, at higher levels of excitement the tail is flicked also. Males frequently bill wipe as an apparent displacement activity (Neff). Wild caught birds often remain wild, shy and suspicious but captive-bred birds, except for an obligatory nervous period for the first few days after fledging, are tame and calm (Neff).

NESTING Placed in a bush or shrub, usually low down between a half and two metres above ground. The nest is roundish, about the size of a soccer ball, with a side entrance which either lacks or has only a suggestion of an entrance tube. It is built of grass panicles, stems, dry leaves, fern fronds and other materials, lined with vegetable down and sometimes feathers. 3 to 6 eggs. In the Cameroon mountains birds in breeding condition have been found in late October, December and January and a female about to lay was collected in Cameroon in early August (Immelmann *et al.*).

In captivity it will build with a variety of materials, strips of grass, grass stems, fibres, millet sprays, leaves, small roots etc. Nest lined with softer materials, fine fibres and whitish feathers. Carries materials bundled (but probably takes long stems by one end as does *S. ruficapilla*). Neff observed that it was always the *right* foot that was used to hold down tangled fibres while the bird pulled out individual strands with the bill. Males that are unpaired will build complete nests. Probably, but not certainly, the nest is usually or always built (except for some of the lining) by the male, as in previous species. Neff's birds usually laid 4 eggs per clutch. Incubation period 14 to 16 days (Burkard, Kleefisch, 1978, Neff). Both sexes incubate by day, the male spending as much (Neff) or more (Burkard) time on the eggs as the female, who alone incubates at night. This apparent difference in the amount of time spent on the nest by day between the male of this species and that of the Red-headed Blue-bill is more likely to be due to individual differences or to be an artefact of captive conditions than a true specific difference. Kleefisch found that the young were not brooded at night after the fifth or sixth day and that it was necessary to increase the temperature of the bird room to about 25°C from the fifth to the twelfth day.

Young in captivity have fledged at 18 (Kleefisch, 1974) and 22 days (Neff) old. Fledged young may return to the nest to roost for the next few nights and subsequently roost in other old nests (Neff) or they may never return to the nest once having left it (Immelmann *et al.*, Kleefisch). Probably the availability of other cover for roosting is a factor here. Young begin to feed themselves 2 or 3 days after leaving the nest and are independent about 12 days later (Kleefisch, Neff).

VOICE This section and that on display is derived from Neff (1978) and Burkard (1962, and in Immelmann *et al.*, 1964 and 1976) unless otherwise indicated.

The locomotion-intention and close contact call is a short 'tsip' or 'tsip-ip' etc, sometimes a more drawn-out 'tsee'. A Blackcap-like 'tak' appears also to be used as a contact call. The alarm call begins as a relatively slow 'tsip-tsap . . .' and becomes faster until the notes run into each other. A ticking call and a 'strong tak tak' (my anglicisations) are also used as alarm calls. All alarm calls are accompanied by violent wing and tail flicking.

There are two forms of song similar to, perhaps allowing for individual differences identical with, those of the previous species, *S. ruficapilla* (q.v.). The second of these, the display song, is very like that of the Brown Twinspot. Both sexes sing, the female usually less often and less loudly than the male.

Neff also describes a song of excitement ('Erregungs-gesang'), composed of notes derived from alarm calls and given in response to apparently alarming stimuli, such as his catching another bird in the same aviary. This excitement, or perhaps better alarmed, song, may, however, go over into trilling or other notes characteristic of other songs (Kleefisch, 1974).

DISPLAY AND SOCIAL BEHAVIOUR   Neff describes one display in which the male, with nesting material in his bill and uttering the fluting song, bobs up and down like a displaying *Estrilda* and rhythmically opens his wings. If the female flies to him he drops the nest symbol, mandibulates, spreads his wings at the shoulders in an 'heraldic eagle' manner and throws his head back so that his red breast is fully displayed, meanwhile vibrating his tail.

In a second form of (courtship?) display the male flies suddenly to the ground, and hops with emphatic bounds around a bundle of fibres or other nesting material. After 3 to 5 such leaps a number of fibres are gathered in the bill. He then makes 2 or 3 more such hops, flies to a perch, throws back his head and gives his display song (q.v.). While singing he keeps his head up, raises his wings like a singing Starling, *Sturnus vulgaris*, and vibrates his tail. The female usually sits near but copulation does not (ever?) follow.

Immelmann *et al.* (1964) describe a courtship display in which the male, with a long grass stem in his bill, hops slowly to and fro in front of the female.

It is difficult to be sure if the displays of this species differ as much from those of the related *S. ruficapilla* as the above descriptions suggest. I suspect that detailed comparative studies might show that the main constant difference was the lack of a bowing component in the present species. This would correlate with it having the bright red colour confined to the breast and flanks and not also on the forehead and crown as in the Red-headed Blue-bill.

Social behaviour as described for previous species, including the lack of clumping and allo-preening. Perhaps even more aggressive, at least in captivity, to other individuals of the same sex.

OTHER NAMES   Bluebill, Red-breasted Forest Weaver.

REFERENCES

Burkard, R. 1962. Die Zucht des Rostbrustsamenknackers. *Gefiederte Welt* 1962: 41–42.

Chapin, J. P. 1954. The birds of the Belgian Congo. *Bull. Amer. Mus. Nat. Hist.* 75B.

Immelmann, K., Steinbacher, J. & Wolters, H. E. 1964 and 1976. *Vögel in Käfig und Voliere: Prachtfinken*: 115–122 and 535–536.

Kleefisch, T. 1974. Kafigzucht des Rostbrustsamenknackers (*Spermophaga haematina*). *Gefiederte Welt* 1974: 144–149.

Kleefisch, T. 1976. Weiteres über Rostbrustsamenknackers (*Spermophaga haematina pustulata*). *Gefiederte Welt* 1976: 89–90.

Neff, R. 1978. Der Rostbrustsamenknacker (*Spermophaga haematina*). *Gefiederte Welt* 1978: 1–8.

Serle, W. 1957. A contribution to the ornithology of the eastern region of Nigeria. *Ibis* 99: 371–418.

Grant's Blue-bill   *Spermophaga poliogenys*

Spermospiza poliogenys Ogilvie-Grant, 1906, *Bull. Brit. Orn. Club* 19, p. 32.

DESCRIPTION   Very similar to the previous species, *S. haematina*, but bill perhaps averaging a little less thick. Head, face, breast, flanks, rump and upper tail coverts a very bright glossy red (shining light scarlet or deep vermilion). Area immediately adjacent to the front and upper part of the eye, hind crown, nape, mantle and upper back shining bluish black. Rest of plumage intense black. Irides brown; eye rims pale blue to bluish white. Bill pink or red merging into a shining metallic blue area at the base and around the nostrils on the upper mandible and a rather larger blue area at the base of the lower mandible. Bill has a mother-of-pearl appearance as in other blue-bills. One, collected when moulting, had the bill entirely metallic blue except for the tip and cutting edges of the lower mandible and a small patch in front of each nostril. Legs and feet dark olive to olive brown. There is a close-up coloured photograph of a live (but tethered) male in Lippens & Wille.

The female has the head, face and most of the upperparts dark grey, with a bluish sheen on mantle and back. Her rump and upper tail coverts are bright shining red, like the male's. Throat and upper breast bright orange-red. I have not seen a juvenile of this species. Immelmann *et al.* and Mackworth-Praed & Grant describe it as brownish grey with red upper tail coverts and state that the juvenile female is distinguishable by having ill-defined spotting on the underparts. A juvenile female had a yellowish palate with three black spots, a dusky ring, interrupted at the top, around the tongue and a dark crescent on the inside of the lower mandible (Chapin). The palate markings, in dark grey on yellowish, are retained in the adult (information on labels of specimens in the British Museum collection).

FIELD CHARACTERS   Black nape and more extensive and more brilliant red on rump might serve to distinguish male from male Red-headed Blue-bill but only if a good view were obtained. Female distinguished from females of other blue-bills by entirely grey face which contrasts with the bright red throat and breast. Field characters otherwise as Red-headed Blue-bill (q.v.).

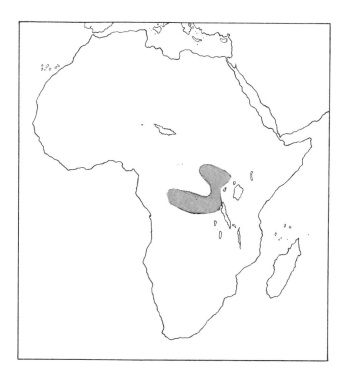

DISTRIBUTION AND HABITAT Congo (Zaïre) from the mouth of the Oubangi east to Lake Albert and Kivu, and the Bwamba forest in Uganda. Inhabits virgin forest and, but less often, secondary growth.

FEEDING AND GENERAL HABITS Twelve birds collected by Chapin had all eaten seeds, many of them rather large, oval seeds (not identified). Three of them had also eaten insects and one a spider. A single specimen collected by Kunkel (pers. comm.) had also eaten seeds.

Usually found in uncut forest where it moves about actively among the lower undergrowth and patches of *Phrynium* plants. Sometimes hops about on the ground in damp places. Occasionally found in secondary growth but seldom comes out even at the edges of clearings. Adults are very wary of man, immatures less so. All the above is derived from Chapin.

NESTING No information. Adults in breeding condition have been collected in January, February, May and September (Chapin).

VOICE Burkard (in Immelmann *et al.*) heard a repeated, melodious 'tyee-dyeeu' (my anglicisation) from captive adults; Chapin a hoarse 'chip' from a wild juvenile.

DISPLAY AND SOCIAL BEHAVIOUR A captive pair appeared to be very closely attached to each other, in contrast to pairs of the other two *Spermophaga* species. They always moved about, fed and bathed together, and clumped closely when at rest. Allo-preening was, however, seldom performed and then in a rather perfunctory or symbolic manner (Burkard, in Immelmann *et al.*).

OTHER NAME Grant's Forest Weaver.

REFERENCES
Chapin, J. P. 1954. The birds of the Belgian Congo. *Bull. Amer. Mus. Nat. Hist.* **75B**.
Immelmann, K., Steinbacher, J. & Wolters, H. E. 1964. *Vögel in Käfig und Voliere: Prachtfinken*: 113–115.
Lippens, L. & Wille, H. 1976. *les oiseaux de Zaïre*. Tielt, Belgium.
Mackworth-Praed, C. M. & Grant, C. H. B. 1973. *African handbook of birds*, ser. 3, vol. 3.

The seed-crackers

The seed-crackers, *Pyrenestes* (formerly usually spelled *Pirenestes*) are remarkable for their large and apparently highly specialised bills and correlated jaw musculature (Sushkin). They are usually, and probably rightly, placed in a group of species which includes *Cryptospiza* and *Spermophaga* (Delacour, Steiner, Wolters). *Pyrenestes* is rather like *Cryptospiza* in coloration but their colour patterns differ and the bright shining red feathers of the seed-crackers are very different from the subdued red of *Cryptospiza*. Their mouth patterns, however, and what has been recorded for their behaviour, agree well enough. The colour patterns, and the gloss and texture of the red parts of the plumage of *Pyrenestes* and *Spermophaga*, are much alike but, as Immelmann *et al.* point out, *Pyrenestes* does not have the (supposedly primitive) rather long outermost primary of *Spermophaga* (and some other African genera); their bills are very differently shaped and the females of the two genera are quite differently patterned ('ganz anders gezeichnet'). However, *Pyrenestes*' unique bill gives no clue to its relationships and the differences between the female's pattern and that of *Spermophaga* involves only the spotted underparts of the latter, a character absent in adult males and poorly developed or vestigial in juveniles, so possibly not of great phylogenetic importance. I think that *Pyrenestes* may be as close to *Spermophaga* as it is to any other genus.

Three species of seed-crackers are usually recognised although White treats them all as races of one species and may be right to do so. The Crimson Seed-cracker, *Pyrenestes sanguineus*, differs from the Black-bellied Seed-cracker, *P. ostrinus*, only in the male being brown like the female on those parts where the male of *P. ostrinus* is black. The Lesser Seed-cracker, *P. minor*, is slightly smaller and less extensively red in colour. No significant differences of voice or behaviour between any two of the above forms has been recorded. Hall and Moreau were aware of no geographical overlap between any two forms but Brunel claimed to have found *P. ostrinus* and *P. sanguineus* both breeding in the same marshes near Bingerville, Ivory Coast. This may indicate that these two forms have certainly reached specific level but other explanations are possible. For example, morphs resembling *sanguineus* might occasionally occur among (otherwise) *ostrinus* populations or vice versa.

I here treat *P. sanguineus*, *P. ostrinus* and *P. minor* as species, which can be considered as members of a superspecies (for any overlap that exists involves only a relatively very small area). This is, however, done mainly for convenience, in order that available information can be attached unambiguously to the relevant form. Further observations, especially in the Bingerville area, are needed to ascertain if the three forms are best treated thus or as races of a single species.

A peculiarity of all three species is that among each forms with large bills and others with small bills occur and are connected by intermediates. The differences in bill size are to some extent correlated with differences in body size but are relatively greater. In the Crimson Seed-cracker birds with markedly differently-sized bills do not appear to have been found in the same place. In the British Museum (Natural History) specimens from Sierra Leone include a large-billed female from Rokupr (width of lower mandible at base 18 mm, length of culmen 16 mm); 5 males and 2 females from Bo and a male from Mange and one from Benguema with medium-sized bills (width 14·5 mm to 16·5 mm, length 11 mm to 14 mm) and a small-billed pair from near Kaulahun (width 14 mm in both, length 11 and 11·5 mm).

In the Black-bellied Seed-cracker, *P. ostrinus*, there is some geographical overlap but within it the different forms are thought to be ecologically isolated (Chapin, 1924 and 1954). In the Lesser Seed-cracker, *P. minor*, large-billed and small-billed forms occur together (Vincent).

Presumably the forms with differently-sized bills evolved in isolation from each other as a result of different feeding habits. In *P. ostrinus* there is some circumstantial evidence that larger and harder seeds are habitually taken by the large-billed birds (Chapin 1924 and 1954). Chapin suggests that alteration of the habitat by man has been the cause of their (presumed) former geographical isolation breaking down in some areas. It is, however, interesting that comparable differences in bill size should have evolved in *each* species without, in any case, being correlated with any difference of coloration. In both *P. sanguineus* and *P. ostrinus* races, based on bill-size differences and differences in range (partial only in *P. ostrinus*) have been described (see species accounts) and are usually recognised, as in *Peters' check-list*. Provisionally this seems, as Traylor (in *Peters' check-list*) argues, the best way to treat them. It must, however, be emphasised that, at least taxonomically, they differ from each other in precisely the same way as do the small-billed and large-billed forms of *P. minor*, which have not been racially separated because they show no geographical separation. Further field observations on the genus are much needed but, in view of geographical and political considerations, are perhaps unlikely soon to be undertaken.

REFERENCES

Chapin, J. P. 1924. Size-variation in *Pyrenestes*, a genus of weaver-finches. *Bull. Amer. Mus. Nat. Hist.* XLIX: 415–441.
Chapin, J. P. 1954. The birds of the Belgian Congo. *Bull. Amer. Mus. Nat. Hist.* 75B.
Delacour, J. 1943. A revision of the subfamily Estrildinae of the family Ploceidae. *Zoologica, New York Zool. Soc*, 28: 69–86.
Hall, B. P. & Moreau, R. E. 1970. *An atlas of speciation in African passerine birds.* British Museum (Natural History), London.
Immelmann, K., Steinbacher, J. & Wolters, H. E. 1963. *Vögel in Käfig und Voliere: Prachtfinken*: 101.
Steiner, H. 1960. Klassifikation der Prachtfinken, Spermestidae, auf Grunde der Rachenzeichnungen ihrer Nestlinge. *J. Orn.* 101: 92–112.
Sushkin, P. P. 1927. On the anatomy and classification of the weaver-birds. *Bull. Amer. Mus. Nat. Hist.* 57: 1–32.
Traylor, M. A. 1968. *Peters' check-list of birds of the world.* Cambridge, Mass.
Vincent, J. 1936. The birds of Northern Portuguese East Africa. *Ibis* 13th ser., 6: 48–125.
White, C. M. N. 1963. *A revised check-list of African flycatchers, tits, tree creepers, sunbirds, white-eyes, honey eaters, buntings, finches, weavers and waxbills.* Lusaka, Zambia.
Wolters, H. E. 1957. Die Klassifikation der Webefinken (Estrildidae). *Bonn. zool. Beitr.* 2: 90–129.

Black-bellied Seed-cracker   *Pyrenestes ostrinus*

Loxia ostrina Vieillot, 1805, *Ois. Chant.*, p. 79, pl. 48.

DESCRIPTION About size of Red-headed Bluebill but with even larger and differently shaped bill which is very deep and broad at the base, especially of the lower mandible but coming to a point at the tip and with straight gonys and culmen ridge either straight or with a very slight concavity near the base. A marked notch near the base of the upper mandible. Tail between roundish and wedge-shaped.

Head, neck, breast, flanks, rump and upper tail coverts a glossy deep bright scarlet red, slightly darker on the head than elsewhere. Central tail feathers and outer webs of outer tail feathers dull crimson or carmine but looking lighter when seen against the light. Inner webs of outer tail feathers and underside of tail dull black. Rest of plumage coal black. Irides dark dull red to reddish brown; eye-rims bluish white to white, only visible and very conspicuously widened above and below the eyes. Bill metallic bluish black with the base of the lower mandible at the sides and the basal half of the top of the upper mandible bluish grey except for a narrow black line along the flattened centre of the culmen. Legs and feet yellowish brown to brownish horn-coloured.

The female has the head red but the upper breast, nape and flanks are warm olive brown with a variable amount of red tips and suffusion. Rump, upper tail coverts and tail as male's but inner webs and underside of tail sepia, not black. Rest of plumage warm olive brown. Irides brown to dark brown. Bill as male's but without the paler patch at base of culmen. The juvenile is a general dark dull olive brown with those parts of the rump and tail, that are red in the adult, dark rusty orange. Irides dark greyish brown, eye-rims yellow. Bill blackish. Mouth markings of nestlings five dark spots on the yellow palate, the posterior pair very small. Three light yellow tubercles in each corner of the gape between the first and second and at the base of the third the skin is blackish, and between the second and third there is a small additional pale yellow papilla. Also a dark bar across the tongue and a dark crescent on the inside of the lower mandible (Chapin, 1954).

The perplexing situation in regard to the 'races' of this species and its congeners have been discussed in the introduction to the genus. The above description is of nominate *P.o. ostrinus* which is found along the northern edge of forest from Abidjan, Ivory Coast and Ghana through southern Nigeria and Cameroons to north-eastern Congo and Uganda. Also on the coast from Spanish Guinea to lower Congo and in north-western Angola, Kasai, western Katanga and north-western Zambia. There is a close-up coloured photograph of a live (but tethered) male of this form in Lippens & Wille. In the last three areas it co-exists with the other two 'races'.

P. ostrinus frommi (syn. *P.o. maximus*) is larger and larger-billed; wing about 70 to 76 mm as against about 64 to 70 mm; width of under mandible at base about 17 to 21 mm as against about 14 to 17 mm. It is found locally in savannas alongside gallery forest from Togo to central Nigeria and Cameroons, Oubangi-Chari, upper Uele District and adjacent Sudan, one record for Uganda. South of the forest in south-western Tanzania, north-eastern Zambia, southern Katanga and Kasai. Two specimens from Stanleyville in the middle of the Congo forest (Traylor, in *Peters' check-list*).

P.o. rothschildi is smaller and smaller-billed; wing about 59 to 64 mm, width of lower mandible at base about 12 to 14 mm. It occurs in clearings in forest from Ghana through southern Nigeria and Cameroons east to the eastern borders of Congo (Zaïre) and south to northern Angola, Kasai, Zambia and Katanga, overlapping the other two 'races' on the northern and southern boundaries of its range.

See plate 1, facing p. 96.

FIELD CHARACTERS Small finch-like bird with large to huge triangular bill. Male red with black back, wings and belly; female mainly brown, with red head, rump and tail. Male distinguished from Red-headed Bluebill by red tail and lack of red tip to differently-shaped bill. Female distinguishable from female bluebills by red tail and unspotted brown underparts; from crimson-wings by brown, not red or partly red, mantle and by much larger bill.

DISTRIBUTION AND HABITAT Western and central Africa, from Abidjan and Ghana (Gold Coast) east to north-eastern Zaïre (Congo) and Uganda and south to northern Angola and south-western Tanzania and eastern Zambia. See also under 'Description' heading, and maps. Inhabits forest clearings, forest edge and savannas near gallery forest. Found in or near thick cover; often near water or in damp places. Some correlations between habitat and bill size have been given under 'Description'; but see also introduction to group. (Rand, Chapin, and Van Somerens).

FEEDING AND GENERAL HABITS Feeds on and/or near the ground, at once fleeing to cover with quick direct flight

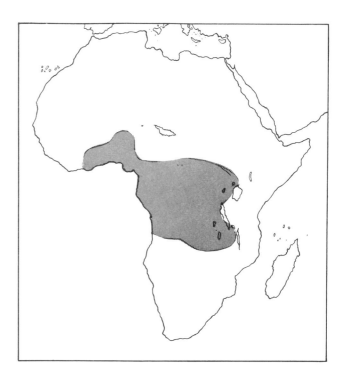

when disturbed (Chapin, 1954). Soft seeds, unidentified but from which a husk may have been removed, unripe rice, spiders, pieces of green leaf and on one occasion seeds of a sedge, *Scleria* sp. have been found in the crops of collected specimens of the small-billed form, *rothschildi* (Chapin, 1924, 1954). The large-billed forms are known at times to take the hard-shelled, nut-like seeds of sedges, probably of the genus *Scleria* (Bates, 1911) and it is considered probable (Chapin, 1924, 1954) that this is their major food. Chapin (1954) found a communal roost of the form *rothschildi* in long grass in an old rubber plantation.

NESTING The nest is placed from 1 to 8 metres above ground in a tree, creeper, screw pine or other growth. It is large, roundish with the usual side entrance, built of strips of palm leaf, grass stems, fern fronds and similar materials and lined with fine grass or grass panicles. Strands of material may hang from the entrance. Eggs 3 to 5. Both sexes incubate. Appears to breed during the rainy seasons. Has been found breeding, or in breeding condition in September in southern Sudan; from March to May and in September and October in Uganda; in January and February in Gabon and in July and November on the Ivory Coast (Bates, Chapin, 1954, Immelmann *et al.*, Mackworth-Praed & Grant).

VOICE Chapin (1954) heard a short pleasant warble from an adult male, a low metallic 'peenk' from a juvenile and a chattering from both adults and young. A captive male (Burkard, in Immelmann *et al.*) uttered a pleasing, finch like song: 'dee-oh-la-dee-day' and variants. Immelmann *et al.* describe a presumed alarm call as 'terr', probably the chattering heard by Chapin was a variant of this.

DISPLAY AND SOCIAL BEHAVIOUR A captive male bobbed slowly up and down with a long stem held in his bill; presumably this represents the courtship display or part of it. Rand observed a display or pursuit flight in which the pair flew at a great height, in undulating flight, the male about 6 metres (20 feet) behind the female.

OTHER NAMES Rothschild's Seed-cracker, Large-billed Seed-cracker, Notch-billed Weaver.

REFERENCES

Bates, G. L. 1911. Further notes on the Birds of Southern Cameroon. *Ibis* 9th ser., **5**: 581–631.

Chapin, J. P. 1924. Size-variation in *Pyrenestes*, a genus of weaver-finches. *Bull. Amer. Mus. Nat. Hist.* **XLIX**: 415–441.

Chapin, J. P. 1954. The birds of the Belgian Congo. *Bull. Amer. Mus. Nat. Hist.*, **75B**.

Immelmann, K., Steinbacher, J., & Wolters, H. E. 1963 and 1964. *Vögel in Käfig und Voliere: Prachtfinken*: 105–112.

Lippens, L. & Wille, H. 1976. Les oiseaux de Zaïre. Tielt, Belgium.

Mackworth-Praed, C. W. & Grant, C. H. B. 1973. *African handbook of birds*, ser. 3, vol. 3.

Rand, A. L., Friedmann, H. & Traylor, M. A. 1959. Birds from Gabon and Moyen Congo. *Fieldiana: zoology*, **41**: 223–410.

Van Someren, V. G. L. & G. R. C. 1949. *The birds of Bwamba.* Special supplement to the Uganda Journal 13.

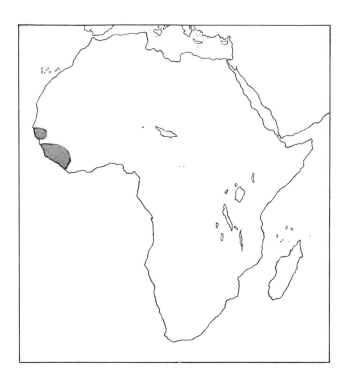

Crimson Seed-cracker   *Pyrenestes sanguineus*

Pirenestes sanguineus Swainson, 1837, *Birds W. Africa* **1**, p. 156.

DESCRIPTION Similar in size, shape, plumage pattern to the previous form, *P. ostrinus*, with which it may be conspecific (see pp. 113–14) and like it exhibiting size differences that are correlated with proportionately greater differences in the size of the bill. All the parts that are black in males of *ostrinus* are a warm darkish olive brown, sometimes tinged with red on the upper parts and sometimes with black fringes on the feathers of the underparts, thus showing an approach to *ostrinus*. Irides dark brown. Other soft part colours as in *P. ostrinus* (q.v.). Female and juvenile like those of *P. ostrinus*.

The large-billed forms are usually separated racially as nominate *P.s. sanguineus*. They have been obtained or recorded from Gambia to Portuguese Guinea, Bouaké on the Ivory Coast and Rokupr, Sierra Leone (female, no. 1937.1.3.40) in the British Museum (Natural History) collection. Small and medium-billed forms are usually put together under the name *P.s. coccineus*. They occur in Sierra Leone, Liberia and (*fide* Traylor) have been recorded from Bingerville, Ivory Coast.

Nestlings have yellow mouths with 3 black marks on the palate and 2 black stripes about 1 mm long near the end of the inside of the upper mandible. In the gape, at each corner, there are 3 golden yellow tubercles (Fritz).

FIELD CHARACTERS Brown back and belly distinguish male from the (probably conspecific) male of *P. ostrinus*. Otherwise as *P. ostrinus* (q.v.).

DISTRIBUTION AND HABITAT West Africa. Recorded from Gambia, Portuguese Guinea, Sierra Leone, Liberia and the Ivory Coast from the Basse Côte to north of Korhogo (Brunel & Thiollay). Further observations from the Ivory Coast are needed to confirm whether this form and *P. ostrinus* are truely sympatric there as has been claimed (Brunel). Appears to have been most often observed in thick cover in or near marshes and in flooded rice fields but habitat probably essentially as in previous form, *P. ostrinus* (q.v.).

FEEDING AND GENERAL HABITS Little recorded. Has been encountered, presumably feeding, in flooded rice fields and on paths through cover. Apparently wary and shy of man in the wild and a captive pair were very shy for the first year or so of their aviary life (Fritz). In all probability its habits and food will prove closely similar or identical to those of *P. ostrinus* (q.v.). Captive birds kept by M. & T. Silzer took ant pupae, whiteworms, mealworms and other insects when feeding young but at other times fed mostly on canary seed and millet. In captivity the claws are apt to overgrow (Mohr).

Fritz offered his captive birds a variety of food but, when not breeding, they only took soaked and sprouted millets and green food. He implies, however, that they also took ant pupae, oats soaked in milk and eggfood when they were rearing young. Mohr's specimens took mostly dry millets.

NESTING Nest like that of *P. ostrinus*. The few found seem to have been built mostly of reeds but this no doubt due to local availability of material. Nest said to have been found (in same area as nests of *P. ostrinus*!) in November near Bingerville, Ivory Coast (Brunel) and birds in breeding condition collected in August and September in Sierra Leone (Mackworth-Praed & Grant).

A captive pair (which did not breed until they had been 3 years in captivity) built a nest of reed blades and coarse grass, about 15 centimetres in diameter. The following information is derived from this captive pair: 3 to 4 eggs. Both sexes incubate in turn by day and both roost in the nest at night. Incubation period 16 days; young fledge at 24 days and are then able to fly. Roost in nest for some nights after fledging. They began to feed themselves after 2 days and were independent 10 days after leaving the nest. The parents keep the nest clean (method not recorded) until 11 days after hatching but not thereafter.

VOICE The courtship song has been described as long and melodious (Fritz). Rand describes a male as 'singing merrily' in flight (see under 'Display'). No other information but calls will doubtless prove similar or identical to those of *P. ostrinus*.

DISPLAY AND SOCIAL BEHAVIOUR A captive male was seen to display on a high perch, hopping up and down and singing with a long stem held in his bill. Both male and female of a pair were seen to display on ground, turning in a circle, each hopping up and down with a stem in its bill and each singing (Fritz).

Rand watched a display or pursuit flight in which the birds dashed up into the sky. The female, in erratic and undulating flight, made a circle of about 180 metres (600 feet) back to the swamp; the male followed about 15 metres (50 feet) behind her, singing at short intervals.

REFERENCES

Bannerman, D. A. 1953. *The birds of West and Equatorial Africa.* Oliver and Boyd, Edinburgh and London. vol. 2.

Brunel, J. 1955. Observations sur les oiseaux de la basse Côte d'Ivoire. *Oiseau* **25**: 1–16.

Brunel, J. & Thiollay, J. M. 1969. Liste preliminaire des oiseaux de côte-d'Ivoire. *Alauda* **37**: 315–337.

Fritz, H. 1977. Erstzucht des Karmesinastrildes (*Pirenestes sanguineus*) *Gefiederte Welt* **1977**: 121–122.

Mackworth-Praed, C. W. & Grant, C. H. B. 1973. *African handbook of birds*, ser. 3, vol. 3.

Mohr, H. 1974. Kurzmonographie der Gattung *Pirenestes. Gefiederte Welt* **1974**: 213–215.

Rand, A. L. 1951. Birds from Liberia. *Fieldiana: Zoology* **32**: 561–653.

Silzer, M. & T. 1980. Geglückte Zucht von Karmesinastrilden. *Gefiederte Welt* **1980**: 21–22.

Traylor, M. A. 1968. In *Peters' check-list of birds of the world.* Museum Comp. Zool. Cambridge, Mass. USA.

Lesser Seed-cracker   *Pyrenestes minor*

Pyrenestes minor Shelley, 1894, *ibis*, p. 20.

DESCRIPTION As previous form, *P. sanguineus*, but averaging, in both small-billed and large-billed forms, a little smaller and smaller-billed. Forehead, crown, face (including ear coverts), throat, median part of upper breast, rump and upper tail coverts a deep but bright scarlet red. Tail as in *P. sanguineus* (q.v.) Rest of plumage olive brown, a little paler and often tinged with buffish or greyish on the underparts. In worn plumage the general tone is greyish brown with pale brown fringes to the outer webs of the wing quills. The red on the upper breast may partially extend to the lower breast and upper flanks, where some feathers may be tipped or marked with red. Irides brown or dark brown. Eye rims possibly less conspicuous than in other forms of *Pyrenestes* as collectors appear neither to have recorded them on labels nor in accounts they have written of their collections. Legs and feet dark brown.

The female has the red on the head restricted to the forehead, face (including area just above the eyes but not the posterior parts of the ear coverts) and throat. Some females also show traces of red on the upper breast. Juvenile like that of *P. ostrinus* (q.v.) but a lighter shade of olive brown.

Small-, intermediate- and large-billed forms occur in the same localities (Vincent).

FIELD CHARACTERS Small olive brown bird with red head, rump and tail and large, deep, triangular blackish bill. Red tail and unstreaked back distinguish it from Cardinal Quelea and Red-headed Quelea; brown (not red) back and red throat from Shelly's and Dusky Crimson-wings.

DISTRIBUTION AND HABITAT The Uluguru Mountains and Pugu, eastern Tanzania to Malawi and Mozambique. Inhabits bushy cover along water courses (Vincent) and forest edge (Mackworth-Praed & Grant).

FEEDING AND GENERAL HABITS Little information, probably as other forms of *Pyrenestes*. Has been encountered in pairs in or near thick, low cover. Known to eat seeds (Immelmann *et al.*, Mackworth-Praed & Grant, Vincent).

NESTING Said to make a large untidy nest with a side entrance (Mackworth-Praed & Grant). Probably identical in nesting habits to other *Pyrenestes*.

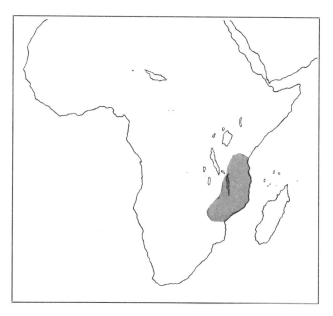

VOICE A sparrow-like 'zeet' and a sharp clicking 'qap' (Vincent) and a trilling song strophe (Immelmann *et al.*) are the only calls I can find recorded.

DISPLAY AND SOCIAL BEHAVIOUR No information.

OTHER NAME Nyasaland Seed-cracker.

REFERENCES

Immelmann K., Steinbacher, J. & Wolters, H. E. 1963: *Vögel in Käfig und Voliere: Prachtfinken*: 101–103. Aachen, Germany.
Mackworth-Praed, C. M. and Grant, C. H. B. 1960. *African handbook of birds* ser. 1, vol. 2. Longman, Green and Co., London.
Vincent, J. 1936. The birds of Northern Portuguese East Africa. *Ibis*, 13th ser., **6**: 48–125.

The firefinches

The firefinches, *Lagonosticta*, are a group of small African waxbills in which the males, and sometimes also the females, usually have a considerable amount of red in their plumage and small white dots or tiny bars at the sides of the breast. In fact only one race of one species lacks red (except on the rump and tail) and only one species lacks the white dots. Despite their name, the reds in their plumage are crimson, wine-red or pink rather than any shade that could be described as 'fiery'. They have rather short, rounded or bluntly wedge-shaped tails, a tendency to a crouched posture and feed on the ground. Owing to their small size and the possession of similar small white spots by the Lavender Waxbill, they have sometimes been placed in the genus *Estrilda*. It is, however, likely that the white spotting of *E. caerulescens* is due to convergence. The firefinches differ from the Lavender Waxbill, and other *Estrilda* species, in many points of voice and behaviour. They agree more closely in both these and in taxonomic characters (size excepted) with the twinspots of the genera *Hypargos* and *Euchistospiza*. These seem to be their closest relatives and they are probably nearer to other genera such as *Spermophaga*, *Pyrenestes* and *Uraeginthus* than they are to *Estrilda*. They are parasitised by the indigobirds or combassous, *Vidua* (formerly *Hypochera*) spp. (Nicolai, Payne).

The Red-billed or Common Firefinch, *L. senegala*, is the archetypal firefinch to many people because it is a tame and common bird around human habitations over much of Africa and has been imported in numbers into Europe as a cage and aviary bird from the late eighteenth century onwards. As firefinches go it is, in fact, a rather distinct species. Its nearest relatives are probably the Brown Firefinch, *L. nitidula*, and the Bar-breasted Firefinch, *L. rufopicta*. These two replace one another geographically and seem best treated as members of a superspecies as their voice and plumage differences seem too great to regard them as conspecific.

The Dark or Blue-billed Firefinch, *L. rubricata*, and Jameson's Firefinch *L. rhodopareia*, are somewhat similar in appearance but differ in voice and in the shape of the

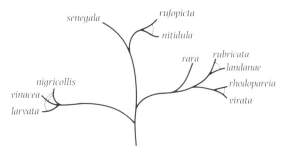

Probable affinities within the genus *Lagonosticta*. See text for discussion. One dotted line connects members of a superspecies, two dotted lines distinct races of the same species.

second (outermost) primary. Their ranges overlap widely on the map but they usually occur in different habitats. The recently discovered firefinch from the Chad area seems, on present evidence (Erard and Roche), best treated as a race of *L. rhodopareia*.

The Landana Firefinch, *L. landanae*, appears to be allopatric with *L. rubricata* and is very similar to it in appearance. It is quite likely that they will prove to be conspecific. As, however, very little is known about it, and its partly red bill might well serve as an isolating mechanism in reference to *L. rubricata*, I prefer to treat them, provisionally, as forming a superspecies.

The Kulikoro Firefinch, *L. virata*, is very like *L. rubricata* in appearance but it lacks the attenuated second primary and in voice, and what is known of its habitat choice, it agrees more closely with *L. rhodopareia*. Compared to both *rubricata* and *rhodopareia* it shows only slight sexual dichromatism, the female being nearly as red as the male. In captivity this red coloration of the female initially aroused aggression from and hindered pair formation with males of both Dark and Jameson's Firefinches (Goodwin, 1964 and 1969). *L. virata* has been variously treated as a race of *L. rubricata* (Traylor) or of *L. rhodopareia* (Goodwin, 1969, Hall & Moreau). Hall and Moreau record both *L. rubricata* and *L. virata* from the same area. Even if this record involves an error of identification or a specimen of *rubricata* well outside its normal range, I think the differences given above argue against treating *L. virata* as a race of *L. rubricata*. It is, in my opinion, closest to *L. rhodopareia* and is clearly its geographical representative. As, however, observations on captive birds suggested that, if the two came together under *natural* conditions, they would probably not interbreed, I prefer, at least provisionally, to treat *virata* as forming a superspecies together with *rhodopareia*.

The Black-bellied Firefinch, *L. rara*, is a particularly beautiful species and the only one that normally lacks the characteristic white dots in its plumage. Hall and Moreau treat it as forming a superspecies with *L. rhodoparareia*; the two are allopatric and the females of each have a red loral stripe, a character they share with *L. virata* and *L. senegala*. It has, however, an attenuated outer primary like *L. rubricata* and I think there is insufficient evidence to link it more closely with *L. rhodopareia*.

The Vinaceous, Black-faced and Masked Firefinches are a very distinct group, characterised by the black face masks of their males, which are absent in the females. They are allopatric. The predominantly pink Vinaceous Firefinch, *vinacea*, and the predominantly grey Black-faced Firefinch, *nigricollis* differ, so far as is known, in nothing except coloration and are best treated as races of a single species, *L. vinacea*. For convenience I have, however, dealt with them separately in the species' section. The Masked Firefinch, *L. larvata*, is more strongly differentiated and I concur with Immelmann *et al.* (1976) in thinking it best given specific rank but within the same superspecies as *L. vinacea*.

REFERENCES

Erard G. & Roche, J. 1977. Un nouveau Lagonosticta du Tchad meridional. *Oiseau Rev. Fr. d'Orn.* **47**: 335–343.

Goodwin, D. 1964. Observations on the Dark Firefinch, with some comparisons with Jameson's Firefinch. *Avicult. Mag.* **70**: 80–105.

Goodwin, D. 1969: Observations on two Jameson's Firefinches. *Avicult. Mag.* **75**: 87–94.

Hall, B. P. & Moreau, R. E. 1970. *An atlas of African Passerine birds*. British Museum (Natural History), London.

Immelmann, K., Steinbacher, J. & Wolters, H. E. 1976. *Vögel in Käfig und Voliere: Prachtfinken*: 550–551.

Nicolai, J. 1972. Zwei neue *Hypochera*. Arten aus West-Afrika. *J. Orn.* **113**: 229–240.

Payne, R. B. 1973. *Behaviour, mimetic songs and song dialects, and relationships of the parasitic indigobirds (Vidua) of Africa*. Orn. Monographs no. 11. Published by the American Ornithologists' Union.

Red-billed Firefinch   *Lagonosticta senegala*

Fringilla senegala Linnaeus, 1766, *Syst. Nat.*, ed. 12, **1**, p. 320.

DESCRIPTION About size of Avadavat or very slightly smaller, with proportionately slightly more slender proportions, more slender bill and only slightly rounded tail. Top of head, mantle and back a slightly reddish light earth brown, more or less strongly washed with rose-red, carmine or dull scarlet. The red colour is usually confined to the tips and fringes of the feathers. It is most extensive on the forehead and hind neck, which are predominantly red, and least extensive on the hind crown and nape which are usually mainly brown. Wings a slightly darker brown with a varying amount of red on the fringes of the wing coverts. Under wing coverts buffish brown. Rump, upper tail coverts and a varying amount of the outer webs of all but the outermost tail feathers deep rose-red, dull scarlet or a slightly mauvish red. Rest of tail dull black except for the outermost pair of feathers, which are dull brown. Face, sides of neck and most of the underparts rosy red, purplish red, dull scarlet or some intermediate shade. Sides of breast spotted, to an individually varying degree, with small white dots. Some of the feathers involved have two more or less 'paired' white dots, one on either side of the shaft, others have only one. Occasional unspotted

individuals occur (Morel, 1969). On the belly and lower flanks the red merges into buffish brown on the ventral area. Under tail coverts buffish brown to greyish drab, sometimes with paler fringes and sometimes tinged with red. Apart from individual variation, birds in worn plumage often lose most of the red feather tips of the upper parts and so look much browner. Iris brown to brownish red. Eye rims yellow and conspicuous. Bill red or pink with culmen ridge and ridge of lower mandible (gonys) black or very dark. Legs and feet brown to brownish flesh-coloured. Palate markings similar to those of nestling (M. Y. Morel, 1969). In Senegal (and probably elsewhere) adults moult only once a year (Morel, 1969).

Female has red stripe from base of lower mandible to, and often over, the eye, and sometimes a red suffusion on feather tips at the side of the face and sides and front of neck. Her rump, upper tail coverts and tail are coloured like the male's. Otherwise her entire upper parts are a slightly buffish earth brown or drab, slightly darker on the wings. Underparts light yellowish drab, brighter and paler buff on the centre of the belly and ventral area. White spots on breast larger than those of male (commonly nearly twice as large) and usually more profuse, often extending right across the breast and further down the flanks. Eye rims paler than the male's and sometimes whitish or silvery grey. Bill sometimes paler than male's but otherwise similar. Juvenile like female but with no red on the face, no white spots on the underparts and an entirely black bill. The young nestling is yellowish orange with profuse whitish down (Morel, 1964). Its mouth markings consist of three black spots on the pale palate, a black half-moon under the unmarked, yellow-topped tongue, a white tubercle at the base of each upper and lower mandible and a purplish blue tubercle at each side in the gape between the (Payne gives superb colour photographs of a nestling's mouth and there are black and white photographs in Morel, 1969 and in Immelmann *et al.*). Morel (1969) gives detailed descriptions of nestlings from 1 to 18 days old.

A variety in which the normal red colour is replaced by a light, bronzy orange and which has a yellow bill has been observed and collected on several occasions. A pair of such birds, that bred in captivity, produced only orange young (Boosey 1961).

The above description is of nominate *L.s. senegala*, from Gambia and Senegal south and east to Sierra Leone, Ghana and Nigeria. *L.s. rhodopsis*, from extreme northern Senegal and Mali east to the Suden, the lowlands of western Eritrea and Abyssinia below 1000 metres (3000 feet) is slightly paler and more yellowish on the brown and buff parts of its plumage. In *L.s. brunneiceps*, from the highlands of Eritrea and Abyssinia above 1000 metres (3000 feet), the male is very like nominate *L.s. senegala* but averages a little brighter red and with fewer, and in many individuals no white dots on the sides of the breast. The female is of a more greyish, less buffish brown, both above and below and tends to be less profusely spotted on the breast. The irides of this form are often, or perhaps usually, bright orange or reddish. *L. senegala somaliensis*, from central Somalia and adjacent south-eastern Abyssinia through the coastal lowlands of Kenya to Usambaras and Dar-es-Salaam, Tanzania, is very like *L.s. brunneiceps* but a little paler in both sexes, though without the yellowish tone of *L.s. rhodopsis*. *L.s. ruberrima*, from Uganda and adjacent parts of the Congo, south to western Tanzania, to Rungwe and Iringa and west through Kivu, Katanga and extreme northern Zambia to Kasai and the north-eastern corner of Angola, has the upper parts predominantly pinkish wine-red to carmine so that, except in very worn plumage, brown shows only on the nape and wings. Its belly and under tail coverts are of a darker, more greyish brown than in the previously-described forms. Its white breast dots are small and often sparse but I have seen no specimen in which they were not present and clearly visible. The female is similar to that of *L.s. brunneiceps* but sometimes of a more buffish hue. She usually has some red suffusion on her face, throat and lesser and median wing coverts; sometimes also on her breast, flanks and upper parts. *L.s. rendalli*, from southern Angola, north on the coast to Benguella, Damaraland, east to Zambia and southern Tanzania and South Africa in eastern and nothern Cape Province, Orange Free State and the valley of the Orange River, is quite like nominate *L.s. senegala* but has the brown on its lower parts a little more buffy and extensive, the red averaging a rather paler tone, and very little red on the upperparts except on the forehead and wing coverts (and, of course, the usual red on rump, upper tail coverts and tail). The white dots often spread right across the breast. Its irides are bright brownish red to orange-red. The female is also like that of the nominate form but perhaps a little less buffish in tone and more profusely spotted on the breast. There is much individual and possibly also micro-geographical variation and some zealous systematists have recognised more races than those listed above.

See plate 3, facing p. 128.

FIELD CHARACTERS Tiny, 'tame' bird, usually in pairs or small parties. Male predominantly red, female brown with some red on face and rump. Its mainly red bill distinguishes it from all other firefinches except *L. landanae* in which the male has dark greyish brown back, female rosy buff breast and both a blackish ventral area and under tail coverts; *L. rufopicta* which is mainly dark brown and both sexes of which have a mauvish red face and breast, and very profuse white marks which form delicate bars rather than dots; and *L. nitidula*, in which both sexes have mauve-pink faces, throats and upper breasts, the latter profusely spotted with white, and the rest of the plumage cold greyish brown. The present species, *L. senegala*, is nearly always the commonest firefinch around human habitations..

DISTRIBUTION AND HABITAT Tropical and southern subtropical Africa. Widely distributed but absent from some tropical forest and desert areas. See map, and under 'Description' for countries inhabited. Appears to be

naturally an inhabitant of dry areas where there is abundant Acacia scrub or other cover, and surface water. In Senegal, M. Y. Morel found its natural habitats were inundation zone woodlands dominated by *Acacia nilotica*, *Zizyphus mucronata*, and *Salvadora persica*; bushy savanna dominated by *Acacia tortilis*, *A. senegal* and *A. seyal*; and along the edges of lakes with *Typha* sp. and *Tamarix* sp. In Zambia also areas dominated by *Acacia nilotica* are the most favoured of natural habitats (Payne). Over much of its present range it is, however, primarily a bird of cultivated areas, villages and towns, being found around human dwellings in many places where the natural vegetation is of types not inhabited by it. Is not able to live in built-up parts of modern towns, presumably owing to shortage of suitable food. Sedentary or indulges only in short local movements (Morel, Payne).

FEEDING AND GENERAL HABITS So far as I know, M. Y. Morel's study of this species in Senegal is by far the most comprehensive yet made. Her findings largely agree with less complete observations made by others elsewhere. In this and the following sections the information is based largely or mainly on her (1969) study except where otherwise indicated.

Feeds mainly on the ground, occasionally from a perch conveniently near to a seed-head. Picks up most of its food from the ground but will seize and shake stems or panicles to dislodge seeds and make little jumps after flying termites. Feeds largely on the seeds of grasses. In Senegal, seeds of *Panicum aphanorum*, *P. subalbidum*, *P. longijubatum*, *Setaria* sp., *Pennisetum asperifoliom*, *P. violaceum*, *Digitaria velutina*, *Dactyloctenium aegyptium*, *Enicochloa colona*, *Chloris pilosa*, *C. pulsa*, *C. prieuri*, and *Sporobolus coromandelianus* are all eaten. In Zambia also feeds mostly on grass seeds, especially of *Setaria* spp. and *Enicochloa colonum*. Takes spilled cultivated grains, especially millets, but also fragments of larger grains, such as rice. In at least one case (M. Y. Morel 1969) whole grains of rice had been eaten. Will freely enter huts and houses in search of food. Cheesman, writing of the species in Dangila, Abyssinia, says 'I have often seen women grinding the small millet (teff) in their huts surrounded by these little crimson birds, which were picking up small pieces on each side of the grinding stone well within arm's reach of them.'

Takes some green vegetation, plucking a fragment from a leaf in the usual estrildid way by gripping and then making a backward jump. Termites and other small insects are eaten but M. Y. Morel found that, in the area where she studied it, insects were taken rarely and irregularly and the diet of both adults and nestlings was almost entirely seeds. She found, however, that even in Senegal, commercially available seeds would not suffice for successful breeding in captivity unless insects (termites) were also given. In Zambia Payne found that seeds comprised at least 90 per cent of the nestlings' diet.

Usually in pairs or in small parties when not breeding but at all times several or many pairs or individuals may gather at a food source. Appears to be usually highly sedentary but, at least in Buluwayo, ringing showed that non-breeding groups may move around, staying in an area for several days, then departing, only to return a few weeks later, their place having been taken by others of their species meanwhile (Harwin). Seeks shade in hot weather and will not then seek food in the open during the hotter hours of the day. When breeding only the area immediately around the nest is usually defended.

Locomotion intention movements usually involve only a usually rather deliberate and unharried up and down movement of the tail (Russ, Kunkel, 1959). Harrison (1956, 1962) observed jerky side to side tail movements by excited birds. Bathes and sunbathes in usual passerine manner. Roosts on the branches or twigs of trees and shrubs, or sometimes on some perch in a building, not in old or disused nests. In captivity roosting in nests or nest baskets etc may be induced by too cold a temperature or by artificial light being left on after the Firefinches want to go to sleep.

In captivity (in Britain or western Europe) usually very delicate on arrival and at all times sensitive to sudden falls of temperature. It is unwise and unkind to attempt to over-winter it in an unheated room, much less in an outdoor aviary. Immelmann *et al.* recommend a minimum temperature of 18°C. Birds that have been allowed to fly at liberty during the summer, which they usually safely can be in a garden not frequented by cats or Sparrowhawks, should be caught up and brought inside *before* the nights start getting cold in early autumn. If fit breeds quite freely in captivity. It was bred by Vieillot in the eighteenth century and by Russ and others in the nineteenth. Immelmann *et al.* advise that besides dry and soaked seeds, it should be given ant pupae, whiteworms, fruitflies

and cooked, cut-up small mealworms when rearing young. Kessner, however, successfully bred it in cages, giving only seed, greenfood, a commercial food for insectivorous birds and a few small mealworms.

Circumstantial evidence suggests that the species suffers heavy predation. In her study area, M. Y. Morel thought Genets, *Genetta senegalensis* and Domestic Cats were important predators. The Pheasant Cuckoo, *Centropus senegalensis*, Shikra Hawk, *Accipiter badius* and Red-collared Falcon, *Falco chiquera* were among its bird predators. Domestic Fowls sometimes take newly fledged young and in some areas the bird is captured in large numbers for sale to other countries as an aviary bird. Annual mortality of adults, in the Richard Toll area, Senegal, was from 70–75 per cent (M. Y. Morel, 1964) and was similar for both sexes.

M. Y. Morel found that all birds moulted at some time during the period from February to August, the moult of individuals taking 3·5 months or more to complete (wing and tail quills included). Juveniles began to moult when about 6 weeks old but whereas those hatched in August took about 270 days, those hatched in February and March only 170 days to complete the moult to adult plumage. The moult of juveniles was also concentrated in the period February to August when available food was decreasing but day length and temperatures increasing. Almost all juveniles, whenever hatched, had attained adult plumage by the onset of the new breeding season in August.

Payne found that in Zambia the moult usually began after breeding had finished. Its average duration was 3·5 to 4 months.

NESTING Will nest in a great variety of sites: a hole, nook or niche on or in a building, especially in the thatched roofs of some types of native huts; in a bush or shrub, among the leaf stalks of palms or plantains, among tangled roots, in a hole in a bank or on the ground in a hoofprint or some other recess or among rank vegetation. Not usually more than 4 to 5 metres above ground and commonly less. Nest roundish, rather loosely constructed, with a large side entrance that occasionally has a suggestion of an entrance tube or at least of the upper part of one. There are photographs of several nests in Morel (1969). The nest is made of dry grass stems and panicles, sometimes also, or alternatively, of fibres, rootlets, dead leaves or other materials. In captivity Asparagus fronds are often much liked (Russ). The building bird collects materials near to the nest site, which commonly results in well-camouflaged nests. The nest is lined with feathers and for these the bird must, of necessity, often go greater distances than it does for the rest of the nesting material. Probably there is a preference for white or pale feathers but the dark grey, white-spotted feathers of Guineafowl and other dark feathers are often taken. Only the male collects nesting material and builds (M. Y. Morel, 1969, Harrison, 1956), the female rarely, and perhaps in most cases never, even bringing feathers for the lining.

Nests in holes and niches may be more or less cup-shaped and open at the top and such nests have also been found in sites on the ground and elsewhere (M. Y. Morel, 1969). Possibly open-topped nests are usually (or always?) built only when the configuration of the site, or material available, did not permit completing the usual roofing over of the nest. Old nests may be relined and used again, sometimes by their builders, sometimes by another pair.

Eggs 3 to 6, commonly 3 or 4. Up to 8 eggs recorded but this probably due to eggs from a previous clutch remaining in the nest, as sometimes happens (M. Y. Morel, 1969). Both sexes incubate and brood in turn in the usual way. Incubation period 11 to 12 days. Young fledge at 18 days and are fed for about 8 days more by their parents, or by their father alone (Immelmann et al., M. Y. Morel, 1969). This species is regularly parasitised by an indigo-bird or combassou, Vidua chalybeata. The latter often or usually enters the nest, in spite of some mild opposition, and lays while the Firefinch is also in the nest (G. Morel, 1959). More than one Combassou may parasitise the same nest. The harmful effects of parasitism are greatest when the parasite's egg or eggs have been added to a Firefinch clutch of 4 or more. With 3 egg clutches it is thought (Morel, 1969) the extra egg and nestling may have an over-all beneficial effect. The average number fledged from successful non-parasitised nests was 2·6 young Firefinches, from successful para-sitised nests 2·1 young Firefinches and 1 young Com-bassou (M. Y. Morel, 1969).

At Richard Toll, Senegal, breeding took place mainly from August to May, with October to December (in-clusive), the period immediately after the rains, the most favoured, presumably because seeds are then very plentiful and the temperature and insolation lowest, permitting more constant activity. In Zambia Payne found that most pairs bred from March to May, in the late rains and early dry season. Has been found breeding in the Hoggar Mountains in April, in Nigeria from November to January, in Sudan in July and August, in Abyssinia in September and October, in Kenya from March to July and September to February (thus in both the rainy and dry seasons, as in Senegal), in Tanzania from March to July, in Malawi from February to October and in December, in southern Congo (Zaïre) from December to March, in Rhodesia from January to August and in South Africa from November to April (Immelmann et al., McLachlan & Liversidge). Up to five successive broods may be reared by the same pair (M. Y. Morel, 1969).

VOICE The vocalisations of this species have been described and discussed by Harrison (1956), Nicolai (1964) and Morel (1969). These authors are broadly in agreement in their transliterations and opinions on motivation and function of the various calls although Morel's list is the most extensive. The information here is derived from the above authors except where otherwise indicated.

The locomotion intention or close contact call is a soft but high-pitched 'dwee', 'uee' or similar. It is constantly given as the bird goes about its everyday activities and especially whenever it flies or is about to fly.

The distance contact call is just an emphasised, louder and rather longer-drawn version of the same (Nicolai, 1964). It serves to keep individuals in touch, or to reunite them when they are at a distance and/or out of sight of each other, it is not usually given when the 'out-of-sight' partner is very close and its mate knows where it is.

The distress call (M. Y. Morel, 1969) is possibly a variant of the distance contact call. It is described as plaintive, long-drawn, high-pitched and far carrying. It is uttered when the parents return to a nest and find that their young have been removed by a predator.

The attacking call is a thin, short cry, only audible at close quarters but distinct from the close contact call (M. Y. Morel, 1969).

The alarm call (excitement call of some authors) is a low-pitched, abrupt 'tzet', 'chuk' or 'clŏŏk' which may be repeated several times in fairly rapid succession but is never run together to form a continuous sound. It is given as a response to the sight of a predator or interference or trespass by a rival. Also in some situations where danger or distress may appear not to be present but where (in my opinion) at least some degree of tension or conflict is involved, as for example, when a bird comes to take over from its mate on the nest. It is often or usually accompanied by a side to side jerking of the tail (Harrison, 1956).

The nest call is a rapid series of soft notes, run together with a continuous churring undertone to them (Harrison, 1956). They are uttered by either sex, apparently to entice its mate to join it in the nest or on an actual or potential nest site. As the cock usually takes the lead in site selection and nesting, he is much more often heard to utter them than is the hen.

The begging call of young nestlings is very soft and whispering. Older nestlings and still dependent fledged juveniles beg with two repeated notes. The first is a 'tset' similar to the alarm note, followed immediately by 'tet', thus 'tset-tet, tset-tet'. The pause between the two syllables is constant or nearly so but that between the two pairs of syllables shortens in correlation with the intensity with which the call is uttered. The begging of an excited brood produces a medley of sound in which the individual notes are hardly distinguishable (Nicolai, 1964).

The song is melodious but simple. It consists of a strophe of from 2 to 6 soft, fluting notes which rise slightly in pitch towards the end of the strophe, giving a slightly interrogative tone. The strophe is always prefaced by a single note similar to or identical with the alarm note 'tset' or 'chuk'. There is considerable individual variation but not sufficient to cause any difficulty about specific identification of the song. Some males always use the same strophe, others may vary their song and sometimes utter strophes of two, sometimes of 3 or more notes. When singing, the male usually goes through the motions of the courtship display or some suggestion of them. Often he holds a piece of nesting material in his bill and turns slowly from side to side as he sings (M. Y. Morel, 1969).

Song is given by the male when alone, either through bereavement or when his mate is momentarily out of his sight. Morel & Harrison never heard males sing while performing the courtship display but Immelmann *et al.* say, and Kunkel (1969) seems to imply, that some males sing during this display. There is evidently individual, or possibly geographical, variation in this.

Under natural conditions females seldom, if ever, sing. Captive females may sing if alone, although the sight of a male nearby (even if they cannot reach it) will inhibit them from singing (M. Y. Morel, 1969).

A single note that Harrison describes as a click-like 'stip' is uttered in the bowing final phase of the courtship display, at least on those occasions when the display has otherwise been silent.

Payne gives sound spectrograms of the song and calls, and of their imitations by the Combassou.

DISPLAY AND SOCIAL BEHAVIOUR The courtship display was described by Vieillot (1790) and subsequently by Harrison (1956), Kunkel (1959) and Morel (1969). The male takes a feather or piece of grass etc. by one end in his bill and either approaches a female or by wing-whirring flights, conspicuous hopping to and fro, or starting to display alone, attracts her to him. When she is beside him he angles his tail, which may be partly spread, towards her and, with upraised head, bobs rather slowly up and down, pushing upwards in a series of vigorous jerks in which his feet sometimes or usually either leave the perch for a moment or else sounds suggesting this are made by unclenching and reclenching his toes. If the display takes place on the ground, the male may hop around the female as he displays. From three to seven upward movements are followed by a deep bow towards the female so that the feather is presented to her at or just below the level of her breast. The symbol is then dropped. M. Y. Morel (1969), when she saw a displaying male close to from above noticed that, when he dropped the feather, the male's head was positioned towards the female like that of a begging fledgeling and his bill was open so that his mouth markings must have been visible to her.

In the nominate form of the species, *L.s. senegala*, copulation, when it occurs, usually follows on from the courtship display. The female solicits with quivering tail and the male makes ritual pecks at her head and nape, then mounts and copulates. Sometimes the female may, however, solicit without any immediately preceding display from the male (M. Y. Morel, 1969) and sometimes copulation may be initiated by the male simply hopping up to the female with angled tail and pecking at her nape. Kunkel (1959) found that with his captive Red-billed Firefinches from eastern and southern Africa this was the usual procedure, and although the males often performed the courtship display this was never immediately followed by copulation or attempts at it. In captivity already paired males react to strange females by attempts to mount and copulate without any previous display.

Pair formation (of wild birds in Senegal) is initiated by the male picking up a feather or stem, approaching a female or juvenile male (usually one of a feeding group on the ground) and performing the courtship display at it. If the bird is a female wanting to pair she shows interest, stays, and the two fly off, and remain together after the display. Individuals not sexually interested move away when a male with display material in his bill approaches them (although sometimes another male will try to rob him of the feather). Although the pair bond is normally strong, M. Y. Morel (1969) had proof (from ringed birds) of occasional 'divorces', even of pairs that had bred together, and the re-pairing of both birds to other individuals. She also found that males largely in the buffish brown juvenile plumage and males lacking the white breast dots were apparently able to obtain mates without difficulty.

In the greeting display head and tail are angled towards the other bird, bows are made towards it, involving a 'curtsey'-like lowering of the body. Contact calls and slight lateral movements accompany or intersperse the 'curtseying' (Kunkel, 1967).

Allo-preening and clumping is common between mates and recently fledged siblings. Wild pairs do not tolerate attempts at either by a third individual. Allo-preening and clumping partnerships with other species may develop under captive conditions.

OTHER NAMES Senegal Firefinch, Common Firefinch, Little Ruddy Waxbill.

REFERENCES

Bannerman, D. A. 1953. *The birds of West and Equatorial Africa*, vol. 2. Oliver & Boyd, Edinburgh and London.

Boosey, E. J. 1961. Breeding results at Keston Foreign Bird Farm during 1960. *Avicult. Mag.* **67**: 63–66.

Cheesman, R. E. & Sclater, W. L. 1936. On a collection of birds from north-western Abyssinia. *Ibis* 13th ser., **6**: 163–197.

Harrison, C. J. O. 1956. Some fire-finches and their behaviour. *Avicult. Mag.* **62**: 128–141.

Harwin, R. M. 1959. Observations from a Buluwayo Garden. *Ostrich* **30**: 97–104.

Immelmann, K., Steinbacher, J. & Wolters, H. E. 1964. Vögel in Käfig und Voliere: Prachtfinken: 151–172. Aachen, Germany.

Kessner, B. 1958. Prachtfinken in Kafigen. *Gefiederte Welt* **1958**: 214–215.

Kunkel, P. 1959. Zum Verhalten einiger Prachtfinken. *Z. Tierpsychol.* **16**: 302–350.

Kunkel, P. 1964. Prachtfinken im Kivuhochland. *Gefiederte Welt* **1964**: 141–142.

Kunkel, P. 1967. Displays facilitating sociability in waxbills of the genera *Estrilda* and *Lagonosticta* (fam. Estrildidae). *Behaviour* **39**: 237–261.

McLachlan, G. R. & Liversidge, R. 1957. *Roberts birds of South Africa*, Cape Town.

Morel, G. 1959. Le parasitisme de *Lagonosticta senegala* (L.) par *Hypochera chalybeata* (Müller). *Ostrich* Supplement 3: 157–159.

Morel, M. Y. 1964. Natalité et mortalité dans une population naturelle d'un passereau tropical: le *Lagonosticta senegala*. *Terre et Vie* **3**: 436–451.

Morel, M. Y. 1969. Contribution a l'étude dynamique de la population de *Lagonosticta senegala* L. (Estrildides) à Richard-Toll (Sénégal). Interrelations avec le parasite *Hypochera chalybeata* (Müller) (Viduines). Doctorate thesis presented to the Faculty of Science of Rennes, France. Later printed (and published?) as *Mémoires du Muséum National d'Histoire Naturelle*, Serie A, **LXXVIII**.

Nicolai, J. 1964. Der Brutparasitismus der Viduinae als ethologisches Problem. *Z. Tierpsychol.* **21**: 129–204.

Payne, R. B. 1973. *Behaviour, mimetic songs and song dialects, and relationships of the parasitic indigobirds* (Vidua) *of Africa.* Orn. Monographs no. 11. Published by the American Ornithologists' Union.

Payne, R. B. 1980. Seasonal incidence of breeding, moult and local dispersal of Red-billed Firefinches in Zambia. *Ibis* **122**: 43–56.

Russ, K. 1879. *Die Fremlandischen Stubenvögel*, vol. 1. Hannover, Germany.

Vieillot, L. P. J. 1790. *Histoire naturelle des plus beaux oiseaux chanteurs de la zone torride.* Paris.

Bar-breasted Firefinch   *Lagonosticta rufopicta*

Estrilda rufopicta Fraser, 1843, *Proc. zool Soc. London*, p. 27.

DESCRIPTION Very similar to previous species, *L. senegala*, but plumper in shape with a more graduated, broader-looking tail and proportionately slightly larger bill. Feathers of forehead immediately behind upper mandible dark pinkish red to carmine. Rest of forehead, crown, nape, mantle, back and wings a rather dark, dull, earth brown. Lesser and median wing coverts often, hind neck, mantle, back, greater coverts and secondaries rarely, more or less suffused or tipped with wine-red or carmine. Under wing coverts buff. Lower part of rump and upper tail coverts wine-red. Tail brownish black with a variable amount of wine-red on the basal two-thirds of the two central feathers and the outer webs of all others except the outermost pair. Face, including lores, stripe over eye and ear coverts, dull scarlet to wine red, often brighter on lores and over eye than elsewhere. The red of these areas shades to a usually slightly lighter and more mauvish red or mauvish pink on throat and breast, which becomes paler and mixed with greyish brown on belly and flanks. The feathers of the breast and some of those on the upper flanks have small white marks, emphasised by a deepening of the reddish colour immediately posterior to them. Most of these white marks are 'paired' and in shape form small bars rather than spots, giving a delicately 'broken-barred' effect in life. There is, however, much individual variation in the size, shape and profuseness of the white markings. Ventral area and under tail coverts greyish buff. Irides brown to blackish, eye-rims silvery grey to whitish. Bill pink to purplish red, sometimes duller or paler at base and with culmen ridge and part or all of ridge of lower mandible dark horn to black. Legs and feet pinkish brown to dull flesh-coloured.

The female is like the male except that she sometimes (not always!) has the red of her face and breast a little paler. Juvenile a general dull brown, somewhat paler below and suffused with pink or pale carmine on the breast. Rump and tail like adults' but duller. Bill dark. Feet and legs purplish or greyish. Mouth markings similar to allied species, with only 3 palate spots (Nicolai).

The above description is of nominate *L.r. rufopicta*, from the western part of the species' range. *L.r. laterita*, from southern Sudan, north-eastern Congo, Uganda and south-western Abyssinia is a poorly differentiated race. It is usually slightly more greyish brown above, a slightly paler and more mauvish pink on cheeks, face and breast, and with the white breast marks almost always shaped as bars and often extending unbroken across the feathers.

FIELD CHARACTERS Tiny mauvish red and brownish bird with white barring or freckling on breast. Distinguished from *L. senegala* by both sexes having similar amount of red on head and breast (in *L. senegala*, brown female contrasts with red male). Red bill distinguishes it from all other sympatric firefinches.

DISTRIBUTION AND HABITAT Tropical Africa in Senegal, Gambia, Sierra Leone, Ghana (Gold Coast), Nigeria, northern Cameroons, central Oubangi-Chari, northern Congo, southern Sudan and part of Uganda. Inhabits grass savannas and thick cover along streams and rivers; also often in villages and about other human habitations. Generally in rather damper areas than those frequented by *L. senegala*.

FEEDING AND GENERAL HABITS Little detailed information available. Feeds largely, and probably entirely, on the ground. The crops of five collected by Chapin all contained only small seeds, including in one case eleusine millet. Sometimes in small flocks of 6 to 20 individuals (Chapin, Serle, Weekes). Said to associate with other small birds but this might merely refer to aggregating at sources of food.

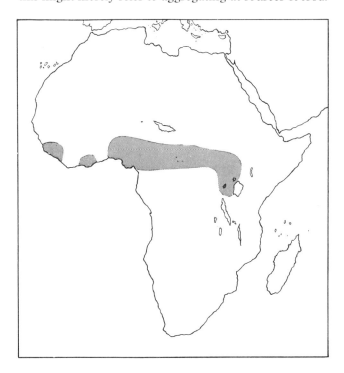

Locomotion-intention movements involve side-to-side but not up-and-down tail movements (Harrison, 1956, 1962). Often 'tame' and confiding around human habitations. In captivity at first shy and timid (unlike *L. senegala*) but perhaps only so when given insufficient cover. Feeding requirements in captivity probably similar to those of *L. senegala*. Hybrids between it and *L. senegala* are fertile both *inter se* and with both parent species (Steiner, in Immelmann *et al.*).

NESTING A nest found by Weekes, in September, in the Sudan, was in tall grass, about 60 cm (two feet) high. It was of the usual roundish type with side entrance, built of fine grass, scantily lined with feathery grass panicles and contained 4 well-incubated eggs. Similar nests were found by Serle in July and October in northern Nigeria were in tussocks of grass a few inches above ground and were lined with feathers. Harrison's captive male built nests of coarser materials than those chosen by *L. senegala* and lined them with fine grass, not using feathers although these were freely available. Parasitised by an indigo-bird which was named as a new species by Nicolai (1972).

VOICE 'Musical twittering' heard from wild individuals (Weekes). Harrison (1956, 1962) made detailed studies of a captive male's vocabulary. Its contact call was short, sharp, high-pitched and rather piercing and unpleasing. When flying to and fro, it kept up a continual succession of call notes, quite distinct and of varying pitch but following in rapid succession. The alarm call was almost exactly like that of *L. senegala* but perhaps slightly lower in pitch and more nasal in tone. The song was vigorous and rather harsh, composed of apparently unrelated high metallic, and low nasal notes. It consisted of variations on one or two recurrent phrases. It was uttered when the bird was alone and also during courtship display.

DISPLAY AND SOCIAL BEHAVIOUR Courtship display as previous species but lacking the final low bow towards the Female (Harrison, 1956, 1962). This, however, is based on a single individual that was paired to a female of a different species so further observations are desirable.

OTHER NAME Speckled Firefinch.

REFERENCES
Chapin, J. P. 1954. The birds of the Belgian Congo. *Bull. Amer. Mus. Nat. Hist.*, **75B**.
Harrison, C. J. O. 1956. Some fire-finches and their behaviour. *Avicult. Mag.* **62**: 128–141.
Harrison, C. J. O. 1962. An ethological comparison of some waxbills (Estrildini) and its relevance to their taxonomy. *Proc. zool. Soc. London* **139**: 261–282.
Immelmann, K., Steinbacher, J. & Wolters, H. E. 1964. *Vögel in Käfig und Voliere: Prachtfinken*: 145–151. Aachen, Germany.
Nicolai, J. 1972. Zwei neue *Hypochera* – Arten aus West-Afrika. *J. Orn.* **113**: 229–240.
Payne, R. B. 1973. *Behaviour, mimetic songs and song dialects, and relationships of the parasitic indigobirds (Vidua) of Africa.* Orn. Monographs no. 11. Published by the American Ornithologists' Union.
Serle, W. 1938. Observations on the breeding habits of Nigerian Estrildine weaver-birds. *Oologists' Record* **18**: 40–45.
Weekes, J. T. 1948. The nesting habits of some southern Sudan birds. *Ibis* **90**: 116–118.

Brown Firefinch   *Lagonosticta nitidula*

Lagonosticta nitidula Hartlaub, 1886, *Bull. Mus. Nat. Hist. Belg.* **4**, p. 145, pl. 4, fig. 2.

DESCRIPTION Very similar to the previous species, *L. rufopicta*, but appreciably larger (wing 51–56 mm as against 44–51 mm). Upper parts (except, sometimes, for a few pinkish feathers on front of forehead) a rather dark greyish brown, slightly darker on the wings and slightly greyer on head, rump and upper tail coverts. Underwing coverts mainly bright buff. Tail darker greyish brown, central feathers nearly black when fresh. Face, including lores and areas immediately above and behind eyes, dark mauvish pink, sometimes with the grey feather bases more or less showing, giving a freckled effect. The mauvish pink deepens to mauvish red, or even to nearly crimson, on the breast, which is conspicuously spotted with white. The white markings mostly consist of small, nearly rectangular paired spots, one on either side of the feather shaft but, at least on some individuals, some of these are fused and form a more or less continuous bar across the feather. Some greyish feathers at the sides are backed by a dark mark posterior to and adjacent to them. On the lower breast the red or pink shades into slatey grey or buffish grey, and to greyish brown on belly and lower flanks. Ventral area and under tail coverts pale buffish. Iris dark brown to reddish brown; eye-rims bluish white. Bill pink, red or purplish red with culmen ridge and central ridge of lower mandible (gonys) blackish or bluish grey. Feet and legs brownish to grey.

The female has all the pink areas paler and more mauvish, and the mauve pink of her breast does not usually extend so far down as that on the male. The buffish and greyish areas of her underparts also tend to be paler. Juvenile a rather less greyish brown above. Throat and breast brownish grey shading to dull buffish brown on belly and flanks. No pink or red anywhere. Bill at first dark. Gape tubercles of nestling pale yellow (Benson). Mouth markings of nestling very similar to those of *L. senegala* and *L. rufopicta* but with 5 palate spots (Nicolai) and the blue gape tubercles of these represented by a violet-blue area in the gape between the large pale yellow or whitish tubercle at the base of each mandible (picture in Neff).

The above description is of specimens of *L.n. nitidula*, in the British Museum (Natural History) collection, from Zambia (N. Rhodesia), Zaïre (Congo) and central Angola. The populations from Botswana to the Zambesi Valley above Victoria Falls have been racially separated as *L.n. plumbaria* (Clancey). I have not seen specimens of this form, which is said to be paler and greyer both above and below.

FIELD CHARACTERS Small dull greyish brown bird with

mauve-pink or mauve-red, white-spotted breast and mainly red bill. Lack of any red on rump or upper tail coverts at once distinguishes it, especially when seen in flight from above or behind, from all other firefinches and from the much larger and brighter Peters' and Pink-throated Twinspots.

DISTRIBUTION AND HABITAT Central and eastern Angola to southern Kasai, Katanga, Botswana (Bechuanaland) and Zambia (Northern Rhodesia). Inhabits thickets near water and reed beds, with adjacent more open areas. Locally around human habitations.

FEEDING AND GENERAL HABITS Little information from the wild, where it appears a rather uncommon species, though perhaps sometimes overlooked. Has been observed in small flocks which appear usually based on some fairly thick cover but come into open places to feed. In captivity (and probably when wild also) entirely a ground feeder, digging in and scattering the substrate with its bill in search of food. Especially prone to seek food on *damp* earth. Will take all kinds of millet that have been soaked or are germinating (Neff); also seeding grasses, chickweed, ant pupae and whiteworms. Animal protein seems of vital importance for it. Once acclimatised it is not very sensitive to cold but Neff states it should be kept in a temperature not less than 15°C and recommends a temperature of about 18°C in winter and 20–25°C in summer.

Locomotion-intention movements involve up and down, vertical not lateral tail movements. In captivity it is at first shy and nervous, so much so that it is quite unsuitable for caging and must always be kept in a bird room or aviary with plenty of cover. All the behavioural information on this species is derived from Neff's observations on his captive birds except where otherwise indicated.

NESTING All accounts of nesting in the wild, that I have read, seem to derive from Benson's (1959). A dome-shaped nest with side entrance, lined with Domestic Fowl feathers, was found 'built into the inside of the grass shelter of a pit-latrine' on 10 September at Kabeti, Zambia. It contained 3 fresh eggs. A brood of 3 well-feathered young were found in the old nest of a sunbird on 24 February near the Lukanga/Kafue confluence. In each case one of the parents was obtained and identified.

Neff bred from and studied two pairs in captivity and the following is condensed from his observations. Always takes over the nest of some other species. If the latter are still in possession they are not physically attacked but the persistent intrusion of the male Brown Firefinch often succeeds in making them desert. The amount of further building and whether both coarse and fine, or only fine, materials are used depends on the state of the newly-acquired nest. In all cases nests are thickly lined with feathers, white feathers being preferred. Both sexes build but only the male searches for and brings material. Usually a few loose stems are left projecting around the entrance and may give the false impression of an entrance tube.

Eggs 3 to 7. Both sexes incubate and brood. At night the male roosts in thick cover near to the nest. Incubation period 12 to 13 days. Young fledge at 18 to 19 days. For the first few days the young beg with upstretched heads and side to side movements of the neck but change at 5 to 7 days old to the typical estrildid begging posture.

Apparently parasitised by an indigo-bird, which was named as a new species by Nicolai (1972).

VOICE Possibly some individual and/or geographical variation. Burkard described the contact calls of his birds as suggestive of the chirping notes of the Goldbreast or of sparrows: 'weet, weet-weet' etc. but Neff never heard sparrow-like chirping from his birds. He transcribed the close contact call as 'tseeb tseeb-sa-seeb' and the distance contact call as a sharp 'tdrrr'. When taking flight a note like 't-trrr' or 'tsa-trr' is uttered. Alarm call a hard 'trrrt-t-t, eet-eet-, trr-trrrt' or 'trrr-tk-tk-tk'. Anger call, used when flying to attack another bird: 'ta-ree' or 'tsa-ree'. Neff lists two main song variants: 'tseekedeetseeeedeetsweee' and a series of interposed close and distant contact calls: 'tsee drr, tsee-tsee-tsee, dr drr'. The songs of Burkard's specimens was a short, repeated, chirping strophe: 'weet-weeheet' or 'weet, weet, weeheet'. Young males sing the usual mixed medley of all the species' notes (Neff).

DISPLAY The courtship display in this species (Neff) has two distinct and separate phases, each apparently comparable to one part of the courtship display of, for example, the Red-billed Firefinch. One is a pre-copulatory display, the other not. In the latter, the male, usually with a feather or stem in his bill, fluffs out his breast feathers, bounces up and down on his perch (without his feet

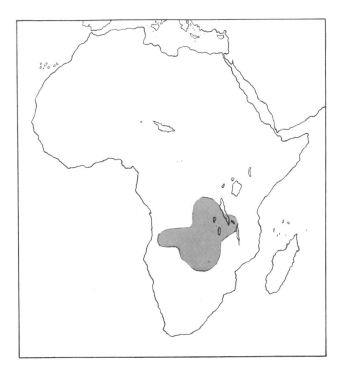

leaving the perch) and turns his head from side to side. Sometimes he sings during the display, sometimes not. In the pre-copulatory display, the male flies noisily to and fro with a feather in his bill. He lands beside the female and bows towards her so as to show her the feather from below (her) eye level. He utters calls that Neff transcribes as 'tsooeeleep tskooeep' (my anglicisations). After 3 or more bows the male drops the feather and pecks two or three times at the female's nape. She then solicits with quivering tail and the male mounts and copulates.

OTHER NAME Brown Twinspot (has been used by at least one bird dealer, causing confusion with the species properly so named).

REFERENCES

Benson, C. W. 1959. *Some additions and corrections to a check list of the birds of Northern Rhodesia.* Occasional Papers of the National Museum of Southern Rhodesia, no. 23b.

Burkard, R. 1960. Ein Erstimport der grosse Pünktchen-Astrild. *Gefiederte Welt* **1960**: 183–184.

Clancey, P. A. 1962. Miscellaneous taxonomic notes on African birds 19. *Durban Mus. Novit.* **6**: Part 15.

Mackworth-Praed, C. W. & Grant, C. H. B. 1973. *African handbook of birds,* ser. 3, vol. 2. Longman Group, London.

McLachlan, G. R. & Liversidge, R. 1957. *Roberts birds of South Africa.* Cape Town.

Neff, R. 1966. Der Grosse Pünktchenastrild. *Gefiederte Welt* **1966**: 21–23.

Nicolai, J. 1972. Zwei neue *Hypochera* – Arten aus West-Afrika. *J. Orn.* **113**: 229–240.

Black-bellied Firefinch   *Lagonosticta rara*

Habropyga rara Antinori, 1864, *Coll. Uccelli,* p. 72.

DESCRIPTION About size of Avadavat, or slightly larger, with proportionately longer bill and larger tail. Outermost primary slightly emarginated. Tail somewhat graduated (but appearing rounded) with broad central feathers. General colour a soft deep mauvish wine-red above and very dark mauve-pink on breast and flanks, which have no white spots. Lores and immediately around eyes a little darker and less mauvish shade of red, rump and upper tail coverts usually a little brighter than the back. In worn plumage brown feather bases may show and to some extent suffuse the red of the upper parts. Wings, except for faint wine-red fringes to the lesser and median coverts, dark dull brown. Underwing coverts and much of the undersides of the primaries silvery buff. Tail black with some wine-red on fringes of the central feathers. Centre of extreme lower breast, belly and under tail coverts, black. Irides dark brown to blackish; eye rims greyish. Bill black with basal half or two-thirds of sides of lower mandible pink, red or whitish. Legs and feet slate grey to blackish.

The female has the head, nape and hind neck a rather dark and slightly brownish grey except for a dark wine-red loral stripe from bill to eye and a paler, brownish grey to buffish, throat. Mantle and back dull earth brown, usually

strongly suffused with dull wine-red but variable, and shading to a definite wine-red on rump and upper tail coverts. Wings as male's but not quite so dark. Tail as male's but a less intense, browner, black. Breast and flanks a light, dull, pinkish carmine, sometimes suffused with buff. Centre of lower breast and belly buff, shading to dull black on ventral area and under tail coverts. Juvenile dull brown, paler on belly and buffish on under tail coverts. Upper tail coverts dull carmine. Male juveniles sometimes (possibly always but too few examined to be certain) have the brown parts suffused with dull red. Immelmann *et al.* describe the nestling as having 5 black spots on a cream to (at back) reddish palate, a black crescentic mark on the inside of the lower mandible, two black marks on the tongue that often join together across it, the corner of the gape purple with two white tubercles on either side. Possibly there is some variation in the gape colouring, either individual, geographical or dependent on the precise age of the nestlings as Burkard describes young and few days old as having at each corner of the gape 2 small turquoise blue tubercles and a larger red tubercle behind them. Their skin was reddish and they had very little down.

The above description is of nominate *L.r. rara,* from the highlands of northern Cameroon, Sudan, Uganda, Kenya and northern Congo (Zaïre). *L. rara forbesi,* see plate 3 facing p. 128 from Nigeria and eastern Sierra Leone, is much brighter, having the red parts of the plumage a warm, rich crimson and all the wing coverts and inner secondaries broadly edged with dark red. Its black areas also tend to be a more intense black. Its female has the belly dark greyish, not buff, tends to be slightly more suffused with red on the back, and has the rump and upper tail coverts a brighter red. The only juvenile of this race that I have seen is buffier in colour than those of nominate *L.r. rara* but this might possibly be an individual difference.

FIELD CHARACTERS Very small bird, mauve-red or dark crimson, with black tail and belly (male) or dull reddish and greyish with red rump and black tail. Very similar to other firefinches but, if well seen, male distinguished by red mantle and back from all species except *L. senegala,* which is smaller and a lighter red. Reddish back, grey head and partly pink under mandible separate female (if seen clearly!) from otherwise very similar females of most other firefinches.

DISTRIBUTION AND HABITAT Highlands of northern Cameroons to southern Sudan, northern Uganda and adjacent parts of Kenya, the northern edge of the Congo (Zaïre) and locally in Nigeria, eastern Sierra Leone and south-eastern Senegal (Morel, in Immelmann *et al.,* 1976). Inhabits savanna and grassland; commonly in native cultivation and farmland (Serle).

FEEDING AND GENERAL HABITS Seeks food on the ground. Known to feed largely on small seeds but also takes both worker and winged termites and probably other small insects (Chapin, Serle). In captivity will take panicum

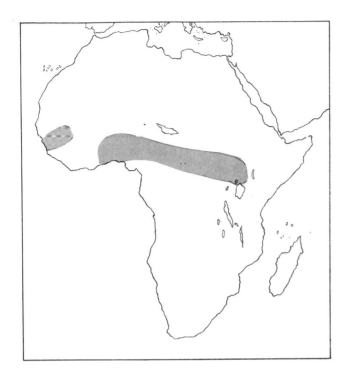

et al.). The song is variable. It usually consists of three distinct strophes. First come four or five low-pitched, plaintive notes: 'peeeh' or similar; then a somewhat Greenfinch-like trilling of variable length, then a fluting or whistling 'tyee-tyee-tyee' or 'tew-tew-tew' very like that of *L. rubricata* (Nicolai, in Immelmann *et al.*, Harrison). Payne gives a sound spectrogram of the alarm call of this species and its mimicry by the indigo-bird parasitic on it.

DISPLAY AND SOCIAL BEHAVIOUR In the courtship display, which is preceded (always?) by the male flying to and fro in undulating flight with a stem or feather in his bill, the male hops around the female on the ground, his head held obliquely upward with the symbol in his bill and his spread tail dragging on the ground (Burkard, Immelmann *et al.*). The female responds by quivering her tail (Burkard) or, occasionally, by making similar hops to those of the male (Macke, in Immelmann *et al.*). In the descriptions I have read it was not stated whether, if the female is responsive, the display is followed by copulation but perhaps this was implied.

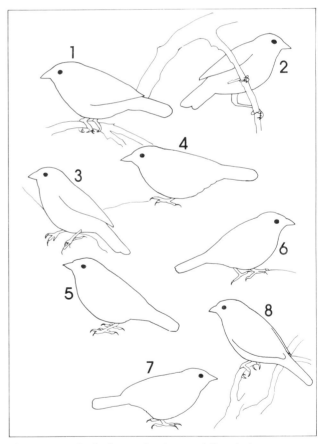

Plate 3 Some firefinches and twinspots (all males).
(1) Peters' Twinspot, *Hypargos niveoguttatus*; (2) Brown Twinspot, *Clytospiza monteiri*; (3) Rosy Twinspot, *H. margaritatus*; (4) Dybowski's Twinspot, *Euchistospiza dybowskii*; (5) Dusky Twinspot, *E. cinereovinacea*; (6) Vinaceous Firefinch, *Lagonosticta v.vinacea*; (7) Black-bellied Firefinch, *L. rara forbesi*; (8) Red-billed Firefinch, *L. senegala*.

and spray millets, sometimes also white millet, seeds of some grasses, seeding and flowering chickweed and some green vegetation. Insect food, preferably ant pupae and/or greenfly seems usually essential for successful rearing of young. Eggfood is sometimes readily eaten. Nicolai (in Immelmann *et al.*) says it is essential daily, whenever insects cannot be supplied, as animal protein is necessary even for non-breeding birds. Cotterel, however, found that his birds, which were in an outdoor aviary, took ant pupae and other insect food only when they had young.

Found in pairs, singly (probably only when mate is on nest or has been recently killed) and in small parties. Sometimes associates with *L. rubricata* (Serle). In captivity, and probably also when wild, prefers to roost low down in thick cover.

NESTING The nest is placed low down in a thick clump of grass; sometimes in a bush, tree, heap of debris or the thatch of a hut (Serle, Mackworth-Praed & Grant, Immelmann *et al.*). Like that of other firefinches, roundish with side entrance, built of grass blades, stems and panicles, sometimes also rootlets or other vegetation, and lined with feathers. Eggs 3 to 4. Both sexes incubate and brood in usual way. Has been found breeding from September to November (inclusive) in northern Congo (Chapin), from August to November in south-eastern Sudan, and in late July and early October in Nigeria (Immelmann *et al.*).

VOICE The alarm call had been described as a repeated sharp 'chek' (Harrison), 'chew' (Cotterel) or 'tseeay' (Nicolai, in Immelmann *et al.*). Harrison describes the contact call as a single, rather nasal 'keeyh' or 'squeer'. The nest call is a soft 'tya-tya-tya' (Nicolai, in Immelmann

MWWoodcock

MWWoodcock

Clumping and allo-preening are common between the members of a pair.

REFERENCES

Burkard, R. 1968. Über die Zucht einiger seltener Prachtfinken. *Gefiederte Welt* **1968**: 148–150.

Chapin, J. P. 1954. The birds of the Belgian Congo. *Bull. Amer. Mus. Nat. Hist.* **75B**.

Cotterel, R. 1962. Breeding the Black-bellied Firefinch. *Avicult. Mag.* **68**: 27–29.

Harrison, C. J. O. 1962. An ethological comparison of some waxbills (Estrildini) and its relevance to their taxonomy. *Proc. zool. Soc. London* **139**: 261–282.

Immelmann, K., Steinbacher, J. & Wolters, H. E. 1964 and 1976. *Vögel in Käfig und Voliere: Prachtfinken*: 197–204, and 550.

Payne, R. B. 1973. *Behaviour, mimetic song and song dialects, and relationships of the parasitic indigobirds* (Vidua) *of Africa*. Orn. Monographs no. 11. Published by the American Ornithologists' Union.

Serle, W. 1957. A contribution to the ornithology of the eastern region of Nigeria. *Ibis* **99**: 371–418.

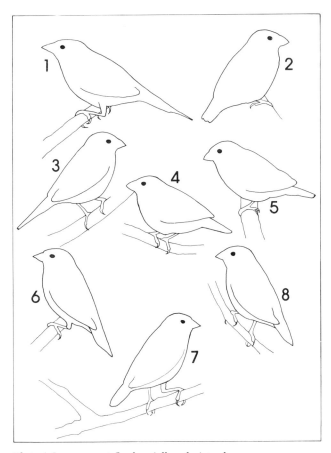

Plate 4 Some parrot-finches (all males) to show variation within the genus.
(1) Pin-tailed Parrot-finch, *Erythrura p.prasina*; (2) Royal Parrot-finch, *E. cyaneovirens regia*; (3) Red-headed Parrot-finch, *E. psittacea*; (4) Peale's Parrot-finch, *E. pealii*; (5) Mindanao Parrot-finch, *E. coloria*; (6) Green-faced Parrot-finch, *E. viridifacies*; (7) Green-tailed Parrot-finch, *E. hyperythra intermedia*; (8) Three-coloured Parrot-finch, *E. tricolor*.

Dark Firefinch   *Lagonosticta rubricata*

F. (ringilla) rubricata Lichtenstein, 1823, *Verz. Doubl. Zool. Mus. Berlin*, p. 27.

DESCRIPTION Similar to previous species, *L. rara*, in size and shape but bill averaging a little thinner and tail a very little longer. Outermost (second) primary emarginated on inner web. Top of head and nape a rather dark dull grey with a slight mauvish tinge that is only visible in certain lights. Mantle, back and wing coverts a dark dull slightly olivaceous brown that does not contrast at all strongly with the grey head. Wing quills a very slightly darker brown. Underwing coverts intermixed dull grey and buffish. Rump, upper tail coverts and basal half (approximately) of outer webs of all tail feathers, except the outermost pair, deep carmine to wine-red. Rest of tail brownish black. Lores and adjacent area immediately over (but not beyond) eye a darkish but bright red, shading to pinkish, intermixed with grey and/or buffish on face and ear coverts and a soft pinkish crimson or pinkish carmine on throat, breast and most of underparts. Small shining white spots at sides of breast and on upper flanks. Most of these are single spots on one side of the feather but on some birds a few paired spots may be present. Centre of belly sooty grey, shading to sooty black on ventral area and under tail coverts. Irides dark brown to blackish. Eye-rims probably as other races (q.v.). Bill with upper mandible dark grey or blackish, shading to black at tip, lower mandible black or blackish at tip, pink at base. Legs and feet greyish horn, greyish brown or blackish.

The female has the upper parts a paler shade of dull brown, the top of her head may be brown like the back or a lighter and more mauvish or pink-tinged grey that that of the male. The carmine of her rump and tail is slightly duller. Red loral area lighter than male's and lower edge of it buffish or reddish buff and extending under the eye. Sides of head mauvish grey, more or less suffused with pink. Red of throat, breast and flanks much lighter than in male, a soft pale rosy carmine. Centre of lower breast and belly buff. Ventral area and under tail coverts blackish brown.

Juvenile dull brown above and dull yellowish brown below with some dull wine red on the rump and upper tail coverts. Bill at first short and dark. Nestling dark and naked except for a little whitish down. Five black spots on a whitish ground on the palate, a black bar across the tongue, a black crescent on the inside of the lower mandible and a white gape with bluish tubercles at the base of each mandible. See also remarks on young of following race.

The above description is of nominate *L.r. rubricata*, from South Africa in central Cape Province east and north through Natal to the eastern Transvaal and southern Mosambique. *L.r. haematocephala*, from further north in Mosambique, extreme eastern Zimbabwe, Zambia, southern Katanga and eastern and southern Tanzania, has the head and nape a beautiful dark mauvish pink. The red of its lores contrasts less or not at all with the pinkish red of the face. The red on its breast and underparts tends to be darker and richer than that of nominate *L.r. rubricata*, often appearing a deep ruby red in the living bird. The back is a slightly warmer, almost slightly reddish shade of brown and the black of the ventral area and under tail coverts more intense. Its eye-rims are rose-pink. Its bill bluish grey to steel blue with the tips and cutting edges of the mandibles, sometimes also the culmen ridge, blackish. The female is very like that of the nominate form but has a dark mauvish pink head and nape, less extensive buff on the belly but with the usually rather deeper rosy carmine underparts often strongly suffused with buff. Her eye rims are a paler and duller pink, more or less intermixed with brownish buff. The juvenile is like that of the nominate form but perhaps less buffy, more brown below. I noticed that my captive juveniles could be sexed as soon as they left the nest by the males showing, in a good light, a very faint rosy flush on the breast. All these birds were, however, bred from a single pair so I am not sure how far this sexual distinction is valid for the race or species as a whole. Nestlings from the same pair showed considerable minor differences in mouth markings, due either to age or individual variation (Goodwin).

L.r. ugandae, from the drier parts of the Cameroons east through northern Congo and Uganda to south-eastern Sudan, central Abyssinia, central Kenya and northern Tanzania is similar to *L.r. haematocephala* but averages a little darker and the male often has the crown and nape intermixed with dull brown. Occasional males of this race (and possibly also others) may lack the white breast spots. In *L.r. polionota*, from former Portuguese Guinea east to Nigeria, the male is a darker and greyer brown on the back and this colour extends over the top of the head which is not or only faintly tinged with red. The red of his rump, face and underparts is darker and more intense than in other races. The female is, however, very like those of other forms and, like most of them, has a dark pinkish head.

The above described races are those recognised in the current edition of *Peters' check-list of birds of the world*. Some workers on the group recognise further races but this seems unnecessary as they represent intergrades between two or more of the above.

There are a few specimens of this species in the British Museum (Natural History) that have been sexed by their collectors as females but are in coloration identical to typical adult males. I believe that these are more likely to represent errors in sexing than genuine females in full male plumage.

FIELD CHARACTERS Small red (male) or buffy-red (female) bird with dark brown back, red rump and black tail. Distinguishable (if good view obtained) from *L. rara* by brown, not red, back and female by pinkish head and white spots at sides of breast; from *L. rufopicta* by lack of white barring or freckling *right across* breast; from *L. rhodopareia* by darker general colouring (both sexes) and from *L. senegala* by darker coloration and grey and

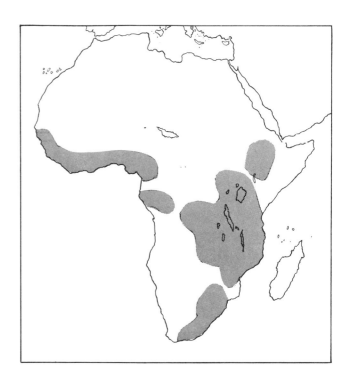

blackish, not red, bill and female by same *and* by her pinkish head and rosy breast and flanks.

DISTRIBUTION AND HABITAT Western, central, eastern and southern Africa. See map and 'racial descriptions'. Inhabits edges of forest and savanna woodland, thick cover along streams, densely grown valleys in hill country, bracken/briar association on hillsides, and thorn tree scrub with tall grasses. Apparently needs a combination of fairly low cover and some grass. Occasionally around villages, usually only where *L. senegala* is not present. Not found in open savanna, open grassland or rain forest.

FEEDING AND GENERAL HABITS Feeds largely on seeds of grasses, and possibly of some other plants. Also takes termites and other small insects. When seeking food flicks aside loose substrate with its bill and often breaks up clumps of earth or debris by drawing itself up to its full height and striking downwards with its closed bill. In captivity will eat the usual millet seeds. Immelmann *et al.* say that animal food is essential for it at all times and in default of insects eggfood should be given. My own birds showed little interest in insects except when they were rearing young and would not touch eggfood. Still, it would always be advisable to offer small insects such as green aphids (greenfly), ant grubs or pupae, whiteworms and any other available small insects. I have, however, successfully bred this species at a time when I could obtain nothing in this line except whiteworms and mealworms, of which latter only the head and a small part of the upper body was actually eaten (Goodwin).

Usually in pairs or small parties, the latter probably usually parents with dependent young. Often feeds on paths, roads or small open areas close to suitable cover. If disturbed by man tends to dive or dodge into low cover instead of flying up (Van Someren). I found similar behaviour in captive birds. Sometimes 'tame' or indifferent to man in the wild. A wild caught pair that I had were rather timid and shy (but never 'panicky', once they were allowed to fly free in the upstairs rooms of my house). They became much tamer once they had reared a brood of young. Very quickly becomes 'at home' and learns its way about a room or rooms of a house, hopping under beds and into cupboards and flying confidently from one room to another. When they had young, my pair discovered the mealworm supply in a box in the linen cupboard and proceeded to help themselves.

NESTING Nests in bushes, shrubs, grass clumps, heaps of brushwood, piles of debris at the foot of trees and similar places, usually from about 0·5 metre to 2·5 metres above ground but sometimes at ground level. Nest roundish, built of grass, rootlets, fibres etc. The nest is of the usual firefinch type with side entrance and when in a more or less 'open' position in a bush or shrub it is usually about 15 cm (6 inches) in diameter and with coarse grass blades on the outside, but if tucked into a grass clump or nook among dense debris much less material is often used (Van Someren, Vincent). I found the same with captive birds. When a pair nested in an enclosed nest-basket they used only a few fine grass stems at the sides. When the same pair nested on a bookshelf in the room they built a complete and fairly thick-walled nest. Van Someren noted that when the nest is built in a mass of debris there is usually a little 'ramp' of material just below the entrance, which often reveals it to the knowing searcher. The nest is lined with feathers, often only a very few (Vincent) but this probably represents lack of available feathers. Van Someren found that a 'bait' of feathers was a sure means of making the birds betray the whereabouts of their nests and my captive birds always had their eggs lying in a thick bed of feathers. A nest found by Serle in Nigeria had a small 'porch' over the entrance. Material for the outer part of the nest is brought, and at least in some cases mostly put in place by the male but both sexes bring feathers for the lining. As with other estrildids that use them, feathers are added during incubation and while the young are small as well as, and perhaps more eagerly than in the period before incubation.

Eggs 3 to 5. Both sexes incubate in turn by day, only the female at night, as usual. One or other of a captive pair were often on the nest by day from the morning the first egg was laid but the eggs were first covered at night on the day that the third had been laid. In a captive pair, that I made all-day observations on when they had young two days old, the male went on the nest seven times between 3.00 am and 15.40 pm, usually spending about 20 minutes on the nest on each occasion. Possibly the shorter spells of the male were an artefact of captivity, caused by food not having to be searched for. When approaching the nest to incubate the male would utter the trilling twitter

(see 'Voice'). Sometimes the female would utter whistling calls before he entered the nest but more often she did not. When the male had entered the nest a soft twittering was uttered by one or both, then the female would slip out. Very often she would at once utter whistling calls from a perch. Whenever she did so the male would come out of the nest, fly to her, perform a greeting display with her and then return to the nest. When the female relieved the male she never uttered whistling calls but once the young hatched and until they were about 7 to 8 days old, the female uttered alarm calls immediately after leaving the nest (whether anyone was in sight or not). These did not cause her mate to come out of the nest. Incubation period probably 11 days. In the wild young said usually to fledge at about 15 days old (Van Someren). Captive-bred young in England fledged at 16 days. They were first seen to feed themselves *competently* at 27 days and their father was last seen to feed them when they were 32 days old (Goodwin). As with other species the parents are very upset if recently fledged young are in the open and try to lead them to cover or (perhaps only in the case of captive birds) back into the nest, though I never saw young that had fledged actually return to the nest. Hofwegen records captive young at once going back into the nest each evening when the male uttered a 'warning whistle' but I saw nothing like this with my birds.

Usually breeds at the end of the wet and early part of the dry season. Has been recorded breeding from early February to June (Immelmann *et al.*, Vincent) in southern Congo; November to April in South Africa (McLachlan & Liversidge); from January to May in Zambia; February to June in Malawi (Nyasaland), in June in eastern Angola, March to May in Mozambique and August to December in northern Congo.

VOICE Except where otherwise indicated, this section is based on my observations of a few captive specimens of *L.r. haematocephala*. There may be geographical, as there are certainly minor individual variations in the song and some of the calls. Most other less detailed descriptions agree fairly well and the more divergent accounts probably stem from *L. virata* (q.v.) being confused with or treated as a race of this species.

The alarm call is a loud, hard 'tchit, tchittick!', 'tchittick-ik' etc, very suggestive in tone of the scolding of a Wren, *Troglodytes troglodytes*, although in tempo more like the much less loud 'ticking' of a Robin, *Erithacus rubecula*. The more apparently distressed (but not the more fearful, see under) the bird is the louder, harder and more rapidly run-together the alarm calls. Where fear appears to be the dominant emotion the bird is inclined to give single 'tchits' or 'ticks' rather than the more usual series of notes. The alarm call was given by my captive birds: when a bird was alarmed by my close presence or by the appearance of a strange person (if one attempts to capture, or otherwise much frightens a *caged* individual, it utters the single, hard 'tchits'); by the parents when their young were approached by a human or if one of them cried out in fear or fluttered against a window pane; by adults with dependent young (either fledged or in the nest) when, looking out of the window, they saw a cat (and once when they saw a Jay) in the garden; whenever a bird flew from one room to another, when I was standing in the doorway so that it had to pass within a few centimetres of me, it would give a brief burst of alarm calls at the moment that it passed me; by a bird taking wing when I had put it off its nest; and by the female (but not the male) immediately after coming out of the nest (where the male had relieved her) when it contained chipping eggs or young under about a week old. Here the call seems to indicate conflict between the desire to incubate or brood and the need for food or exercise.

What I called the trilling call is a drawn-out trill with a rising inflection. It is usually monosyllabic and variable in length and loudness but always with a strong 'r' sound running through it and an excited-sounding tone. It might be written as 'trrrrrrrrrr-t' or 'trrrrrrrrrrrrr' and bears some resemblance to both the probably homologous trilling call of the Java Sparrow (q.v.) and the shivering trill of the Wood Warbler, *Phyllocopus sibilatrix.* When given at high intensity it is uttered with widely opened bill and a marked quivering of the whole body; when it is given at lower intensity this quivering may only be noticeable in the tail where it is, of course, always most conspicuous.

This self assertive call seems basically aggressive although when used between members of a pair it often seems to indicate sublimated or inhibited aggression. When the pair trill *together* at another bird it may function to increase the emotional bond between them. It was given by my captive birds in the following situations: by a male, or by both sexes of an established pair, on catching sight of another Dark Firefinch; when another Dark Firefinch (whether mate or rival) flew into the room where it was living (sometimes it was given when a cordon-bleu flew into the room, no doubt because this supplied some of the same stimuli as a flying Dark Firefinch); by rival males prior to or 'between rounds' of a fight and by the victor when the vanquished flew away; in answer to the same call from another Dark Firefinch, whether mate or rival; by a male in response to contact calls of a female or if she approached him when he did not, apparently, want her immediate presence – in such case he usually hopped or sidled away from her as he trilled; by either of a pair as it took wing after a greeting display with its mate; during greeting displays but, in this situation, it was only given at low intensity.

What I term the trilling twitter is similar in phrasing to the alarm call but much less loud, lacking the hard tone and with an 'r' sound in it. It could be written: 'trittit!', 'trittittit!' or similar. It is probably the call termed the contract trill (Kontakttriller) by Immelmann *et al.* It combines some elements of both the trilling call and the alarm calls but seems to express a lesser degree of excitement. It is uttered in many circumstances where there is a mild degree of excitement involving the presence of other Dark Firefinches. It may be given when two birds come together; as a response to the trilling call of another bird out of sight and by the male as he approaches the nest to take over incubation or brooding. In this situation, and perhaps also in some others, it functions as a close contact call.

When a fledgling is seized in the hand it often gives an unpleasant husky screech. Adults and independent juveniles seldom utter this sound, sometimes they do so, however, in a rather deeper tone than a fledgling does. The function of this call (which under natural conditions is, presumably, given when the bird is seized by a predator) is to induce escaping behaviour in others of the brood and to alert the parents.

A captive-bred young male uttered a rather similar-sounding, drawn-out, husky screech 't'skaaaaa' or 't'schair' when he was hopping or (more often) flying towards females in whom he was sexually interested but not firmly paired to. He adopted much the posture of the courtship display *whilst flying* and uttered this screech with wide-open bill. He showed this behaviour towards another's mate (when he was unpaired), and later towards a female *L. virata* during the early stages of courtship. He did not screech in this manner at his first mate (his sister, whom he had always known) or to his second mate *after* they were firmly paired.

The nest call is a very soft, repeated 'tŭ-tŭ-tŭ-tŭ . . .' or 'tĕh-tĕh-tĕh-tĕh-tĕh . . .'. It is given by the male (and probably also at times by the female) in the usual situations. It may be interspersed with a very soft form of the trilling twitter.

The soliciting call is very similar to the nest call but usually uttered rather more rapidly and with a more excited tone. There are some apparent differences between the soliciting calls of males and females but too few birds were observed to be sure that these slight differences were sexual not individual. This call is given by the soliciting female if the male is not immediately at hand or not immediately responsive. It is sometimes given by the male when he is about to mount the female and also, more especially, when he wishes to mount her and she is being uncooperative.

I termed display calls several calls uttered (at times) when giving the courtship display or in song (q.v.) but not heard in other contexts. They are: a clear, high-pitched 'pee' or 'week', a squelchy-sounding 'squeh', a husky 'fwit' which is vocal but rather like the sound made by the wings in the greeting display (q.v.), a soft, husky whispering or muttering which, like the squelchy-sounding note, may be punctuated by a click similar in sound to the bill-snapping of the Java Sparrow.

Any or all of these calls may be given by the displaying male in any sort of order but if he only utters one note, or repetitions of one note, during a bout of courtship display, then it is usually either the squelchy 'squeh' or the high-pitched 'pee' call.

The contact calls are loud and even within a few, mostly related, captive individuals showed marked individual differences. A wild-caught male uttered as contact calls any of three distinct strophes, that appeared not to differ in motivation or function. These were a loud, ringing 'chew-chew-chew-chew . . .' with an almost Nightingale-like tone and richness, a slightly less musical but equally loud 'chwee-chwee-chwee . . .' and a more Canary like 'chub-chub-chub-chub . . .' The contact calls of one of this bird's captive-bred sons could have been transcribed with the same letter combinations but were harsher in tone. As in other species contact calls seem often (perhaps always) motivated by some slight degree of fear or uneasiness and may be given in what appear to be slightly fear-provoking situations even when the mate is present and nearby although typically they are given in the mate's (visual) absence or in response to contact calls from another bird.

Besides a 'chwee-chwee-chwee . . .' very like that of the male, the female has whistling notes that appear to belong to the contact call repertoire. A wild-caught female had three of these: a long-drawn, thin, high-pitched, plaintive whistling 'feeeeeeeeeeeeeeeee', somewhat suggestive of the flight display call of the Golden Plover, *Pluvialis apricaria*, a slightly louder and slightly less plaintive series of upwardly inflected two-syllabled whistles: 'feeeú-feeeú-feeeú-feeeú . . .' and a shorter, quicker 'feeú-feeú-feeú always given in series of three and suggestive of the whistling of a Nuthatch, *Sitta europea*. One of her daughters had similar but individually distinct series of contact calls. When these calls are given by a female alone in a room, I have not been able to find any differences in the situation correlated with the three different forms of the whistling calls. At other times the single, plaintive 'feeeeeeeeeeeeeee' seems to express a greater degree of fear or disquiet. It is not given in response to contact calls of another bird, in which situation the tri-syllabic form (see above) or the male-like 'chwee-chwee-chwee-chwee . . .' is uttered.

The song of the male consists of repetitions from his repertoire of calls, given in varying and apparently arbitrary sequence. The only exception is the alarm call which I never heard from birds that appeared to be unequivocally singing. The pitch and intensity of some notes may be varied or the singing male may give them in somewhat different forms. Thus the high-pitched 'pee' may be given as several notes strung together: 'pee-pee-pee-pee' in a very musical and poignant tone suggestive of the 'Tereus!' notes in the song of the Nightingale, *Luscinia megarhynchos*; the trilling call may end in a liquid bubbling sound and so on. There are two main types of singing, one loud and the other *sotto voce*, but every degree of intergradation between the two occurs. When singing loudly the bird usually utters each note two or more times in a series, when singing quietly a note will often be uttered only once at a time.

In both forms of song there is a characteristic pause after each note or series of notes and usually the singer does not immediately repeat the same note or series of notes after a pause. The bird may sing while perched, standing on the ground, or hopping about. He tends to hold his head high, and to look around in the pauses, although he may use them for feeding. As with other estrildids he often indulges in courtship display movements, usually at low intensity, when singing alone. In loud song, the staccato bursts of vehement short phrases or single notes, with silent pauses between, is very suggestive of the Nightingale's song.

Visual isolation is the commonest situation eliciting song which cannot, in this species, always be clearly distinguished from contact calling (see above). The loud song is only rarely, but the softer variants are quite often, given within sight of conspecifics. I once, however, saw and heard a male utter loud song when two of his flying young were perched on either side, both in actual physical contact with him.

Immelmann *et al.* record a soft 'tsyee' or 'tshyeek' (my anglicisation) as the close contact call and a song that also seems to consist of a repetition of series of the various call notes, but without marked pauses between the strophes, from birds that were probably *L.r. ugandae* or *L.r. congica*.

Payne gives a comprehensive series of sound spectrograms of the vocalisations of this species, and of their mimicry by the indigo-bird parasitic on it. The song is on the Kosmos record no. 75–09325, published in Stuttgart, Germany.

DISPLAY AND SOCIAL BEHAVIOUR The greeting display is very striking when performed at high intensity. The two birds approach and bow towards each other. As they bow their tails come well above the horizontal. There is sometimes some quick movement of the tail but most of the time it is angled towards the partner so that when the two come really close their tails overlap (see sketch p. 39). The bows are sometimes in synchrony, but more often not, and alternate with a rather upright stance in which the heads are still turned towards one another. As the bird bows it slightly lifts its still folded far wing and slaps it down again on its rump, making a soft but clearly audible 'thuk' or 'fwut' sound. Often, when she bows, the hen seems to try to bring her head across the male's breast in front of and below his head and, but less often, the male appears to try to do this. Particularly in the early stages of pair formation the male's head is usually held a little higher than the female's during the head-up phase and if one head is lower at the climax of a synchronous bow, it is the female's.

The greeting display is given when members of a pair come together after a brief absence. It is, as usual with other species, shown particularly intensely during pair formation and at such times is especially likely to be prefaced with bill pecking or mandibulation and often one bird will suddenly break off and fly away (always into *another* room if they are free in a house) uttering the trilling call as it goes. I have also seen the greeting display given by a recently independent male juvenile to his father when the latter performed courtship display by himself.

The courtship display is very like that of the Red-billed Firefinch. The male takes a feather, piece of grass or other nesting material and grips it by its firmest end. He holds his head rather upright (but its position can vary somewhat) and has his head feathers sleeked down but belly and flank feathers partly raised. The tail is usually slightly depressed and is angled towards the female if she is on one side of him but straight if she is in front of him. The male then bobs up and down with a slight upward and backward throw of his head. He may utter any or several of the display calls (see under 'Voice'). Sometimes, but relatively seldom, he brings his head right down and bows in front of the female's breast. Occasionally the wings may be raised and fluttered during the courtship display. Usually the male drops his symbol just before he begins to flutter his wings but he continues the up and down body movements which may become more intense and culminate in an upward jump and flutter on to the female and an attempt to copulate.

If the female responds to the courtship display by soliciting the male will mount and copulate. At other times copulation may be initiated by the female soliciting with the usual crouched posture and quivering tail, without any apparent immediate stimulus from the male, or the male may take the initiative by approaching the female or hopping persistently after her, uttering the soliciting call and attempting to mount her. In the latter circumstances apparently successful copulation may take place without any signs of her readiness from the female other than her crouching still when the male mounts. Under all circumstances the male, before mounting, pecks at the female's head and nape and (but far fewer pecks) down to her rump, in much the same manner that male cordon-bleus do. If coition is, apparently, achieved, brief mutual bill pecking follows but this does not take place after unsuccessful attempts. In captivity males that are already paired attempt at once to copulate with any strange female put in their aviary, without any previous display. As the female does not co-operate, these attempts fail (Kunkel).

I twice saw a wing raising display (?) from young that had just become independent. In one case a juvenile female was in a room hitherto strange to her and appeared rather alarmed. Her father, who was thoroughly familiar with this room, flew in, alighted on the opposite side of the room to her and uttered contact calls. She at once flew and alighted near to him, crouched with head and tail slightly raised and fully lifted first one wing and then the other. On the same day a male juvenile of the same brood was in the room where he had been reared. His father went into a small cage in a corner of the room and uttered the nest call from a twig platform inside. The young male at once flew to him, landed on top of the cage, and gave the same crouching and wing-lifting as its sister had done shortly before. I never saw any similar display from adults.

I have seen adults briefly preen the heads of their fledged young but I have not seen adults allo-preen each other and on the few occasions when I saw a female try to allo-preen her mate (on each occasion when he was drying after a bath and had his head feathers fully erected) she

was repulsed. Dependent young may huddle against each other or a parent but I found that close clumping together was not common even between members of a pair although at night, and by day when not breeding, they would often perch in contact. Immelmann *et al.*, however, infer close clumping is usual between mates so probably there are individual or racial differences here.

Mandibulation, bill-fencing and bill pecking occur in the usual situations. Threat display usually consists, if at all, merely in the intention movements of attack, crouching with lowered, forward pointing head, open bill and spread or partly spread tail. If a male inside a cage and one outside it are defying each other, one or both may twist its tail diagonally so that the black under tail coverts are exhibited toward the rival. The tail is held straight during this manoeuvre, not angled towards the other as in sexual displays. I did not, however, see this display except under these unnatural conditions.

OTHER NAMES Blue-billed Firefinch, Ruddy Waxbill, African Firefinch, African Crimson Finch.

It is unfortunate that the name African Firefinch, originally (but not often) used in avicultural and bird-dealing circles for any and all of the *Lagonosticta* species, most usually *L. senegala*, to distinguish them from the Australian Crimson Finch, has been used in some regional works for *L. rubricata*, as all *Lagonosticta* species are native only to Africa and in most parts of that continent *L. senegala* is by far the best known.

REFERENCES

Chapin, J. P. 1954. The birds of the Belgian Congo. *Bull. Amer. Mus. Nat. Hist.* **75B**.

Goodwin, D. 1964. Observations on the Dark Firefinch, with some comparisons with Jameson's Firefinch. *Avicult. Mag.* **70**: 80–105.

Immelmann, K., Steinbacher, J., & Wolters, H. E. 1964. *Vögel in Käfig und Voliere: Prachtfinken*: 172–188. Aachen, Germany.

Kunkel, P. 1967. Displays facilitating sociability in waxbills of the genera *Estrilda* and *Lagonosticta* (family Estrildidae). *Behaviour* **29**: 237–261.

McLachlan, G. R. & Liversidge, R. 1957. *Roberts birds of South Africa*. Cape Town.

Payne, R. B. 1973. *Mimetic songs and song dialects and relationships of the parasitic indigo-birds (Vidua) of Africa*. Orn. Monographs no. 11. Published by the American Ornithologists' Union.

Serle, W. 1938. Observations on the breeding habits of Nigerian estrildine weaver-birds. *Oologists' Record* **18**: 40–45.

Van Someren, V. G. L. 1956. Days with birds. *Feldiana: Zoology* **38**. Published by the Chicago Natural History Museum, Chicago, U.S.A.

Vincent, A. W. 1949. On the breeding habits of some African birds. *Ibis* **91**: 660–688.

Landana Firefinch   *Lagonosticta landanae*

Lagonosticta landanae Sharpe, 1890, *Cat. Birds Brit. Mus.* This form may be conspecific with *L. rubricata*. See introduction to the group for reasons for treating it separately here.

DESCRIPTION Very similar to *L. rubricata haematocephala* (q.v.) but averages very slightly smaller and is a little brighter on the red parts, especially on the lores and above the eye. Bill with upper mandible dark steely grey, sometimes tinged with pink, and lower mandible pink to purplish red with dark tip. Birds with the upper mandible largely pink or reddish have been recorded but it appears (Chapin) that this may be sometimes, possibly always, due to post-mortem colour change. Legs and feet dark greenish slate.

FIELD CHARACTERS As for *L. rubricata* (q.v.) except for pink or red under (and possibly sometimes also upper) mandible which might make confusion of male with male of *L. senegala* more easy but females of the two quite different.

DISTRIBUTION AND HABITAT Cabinda and Lower Congo south through western Angola to the escarpment of Cuanza Sul and upper Cuanza River. Found in savannas along the edge of secondary or gallery forest (Traylor).

FEEDING AND GENERAL HABITS Apparently not recorded, probably as *L. rubricata.*

NESTING Said to breed in the late rains and early dry season (Traylor) but I can find no description of the nest – which is probably identical to that of the previous (and possibly conspecific) form *L. rubricata.*

VOICE No information.

DISPLAY AND SOCIAL BEHAVIOUR No information.

OTHER NAMES Pale-billed Firefinch.

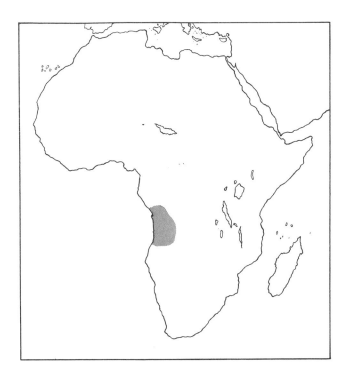

REFERENCES

Chapin, J. P. 1954. The birds of the Belgian Congo. *Bull. Amer. Mus. Nat. Hist.* **75B.**

Mackworth-Praed, C. W. & Grant, C. H. B. 1973. *African handbook of birds,* ser. 3, vol. 2. Longman Group, London.

Traylor, M. A. 1963. *Check-list of Angolan birds.* Lisbon, Portugal.

Jameson's Firefinch *Lagonosticta rhodopareia*

E.(strelda) rhodopareia Heuglin, *J. Orn.* **16**: p. 16.

DESCRIPTION Very like the Dark Firefinch, *L. rubricata*, but a very little smaller and also slimmer, with proportionately slightly longer tail, and the outermost (second) primary not emarginated on its inner web. Lores, feathers just above eye and a very few right at the top of the throat, at base of lower mandible, light scarlet. Face, breast and most of underparts a deep soft slightly mauvish rose-pink. Commonly a few tiny white dots on flanks and sides of breast but many birds lack these. Top of head and nape a slightly darker pink and with the brownish grey feather bases showing through to a varying extent. Mantle and back a reddish light earth brown, strongly suffused with rosy pink to mauvish red. Wings a slightly darker brown with reddish fringes to the coverts. Under wing coverts buffish and silvery. Rump, upper tail coverts and fringes of basal halves (approximately) of outer webs of tail feathers rosy carmine to wine-red. Rest of tail, ventral area and under tail coverts dull black. Irides dark brown or brown; eye-rims pinkish and not very conspicuous. Bill bluish grey with blackish or dark grey tip, culmen ridge and cutting edges; the upper mandible is usually a darker shade of grey than the lower and sometimes largely blackish. Legs and feet dark grey.

The female has her lores a paler red than the male's but looking bright against the dull greyish pink or mauvish pink of her face and head. Her back is less suffused with red than the male's, her rump and tail similar to his. Her breast and underparts appear mainly a light but variable rosy buff, most of the feathers being buffish with more or less pale dull pink or dull mauvish pink tips. The feathers of her ventral area and under tail coverts are dark grey with buff fringes. The juvenile is brown above, buffish brown below, rump and tail like adult's but duller. Just fledged young had the mouth red with five black palate spots on a whitish ground. The gape flanges were violet and blue, with no definite tubercles; the bill black and grey. Two-day old nestlings had two violet tubercles on a red base at the corners of their mouths. They had dark skin and only a little down on their heads (Burkard). Payne gives excellent colour photographs of the mouth of a nestling.

The above description is of *L. rhodopareia jamesoni*, the best known race of the species, which is found in southern Kenya, easter and southern Tanzania west to Katanga, southern Kasai and Zambia, and south to Ngamiland, lower Cunene River, Transvaal and Zululand. In nominate *L.r. rhodopareia*, from southern Abyssinia (and, formerly at least, in parts of Eritrea), south-eastern Uganda and northern Kenya, the male is brighter and deeper red on the rump, face and underparts, deep scarlet or light crimson rather than pink, and a darker brown, less suffused with red, on the mantle, back and wings. The female differs from that of *L.r. jamesoni* in being darker and redder on the breast, a darker red on the lores, a darker brown above and having much less pink suffusion on her grey or greyish brown face and crown.

I have not seen a male of *L.r. ansorgei*, from Cabinda and lower Congo south through western Angola to Huila. It is said (Immelmann *et al.*) to be a brighter red than other forms. The female has the red loral patch both brighter and more extensive than those of *rhodopareia* or *jamesoni* and is usually brighter below but has no red suffusion in the brown of her head and back.

A female firefinch very like a female of *L. rhodopareia* but with a greyish head clearly demarcated from its pinkish throat and with the brown of its mantle and back much more strongly suffused with red, was collected by Dr J. Brunel in the Baibokoum region, in southern Chad, on 16 April 1973. I was kindly shown this specimen by Mr C. W. Benson, to whom it was sent, and thought it most likely represents a previously undescribed race of *L. rhodopareia*. Subsequently both sexes of this form were obtained. Males were (Erard & Roche) very like males of *L. rhodopareia* but with grey crown and nape and chestnut mantle and back. Erard & Roche provisionally treated this form as a race of *L. rhodopareia*, *L.r. bruneli*. So, later, did Brunel *et al. L. virata* also may be conspecific with *L. rhodopareia*; for reasons for treating it separately here, see p. 118.

FIELD CHARACTERS As Dark Firefinch (q.v.) but paler and pinker both above and below (male) or paler (female). Very like D.F. but in areas of possible overlap paler. Habitats typically differ also. Differences from other sympatric firefinches essentially as for Dark Firefinch

DISTRIBUTION AND HABITAT Central Africa south of the equatorial forest, eastern and south-eastern Africa. Will possibly be found also in the Chad area (see under 'Description', last paragraph) and is replaced in parts of western Africa by the possibly conspecific *L. virata*. Habitats chosen are similar to those of the Dark Firefinch but usually in drier areas though the two occur together in some places (Chapin, Immelman *et al.*).

FEEDING AND GENERAL HABITS Similar to those of Dark Firefinch, so far as known, but little recorded of its behaviour in the wild. Feeds on grass seeds picked up from the ground. Probably also takes small invertebrates and some greenfood. One captive pair reared young on soaked seed, refusing ant pupae (Johnson). Others who have successfully bred this species found fresh ant pupae essential as a rearing food (Immelmann *et al.*).

NESTING Nest and nest sites similar to those of Dark Firefinch (Chapin, Goodwin, Mackworth-Praed & Grant, McLachlan & Liversidge, Vincent). Materials gathered and nest built largely, perhaps entirely, by the male. Both sexes

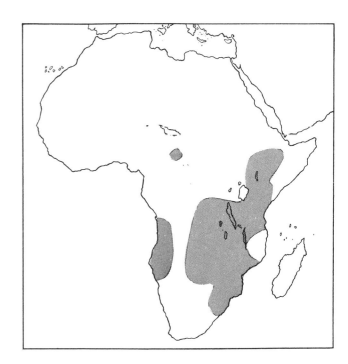

share incubation and care of the young in usual way. Has been found breeding from November to June in South Africa and Rhodesia, in March and June in Malawi, in February and March in Zambia and from January to March in Tanzania. In general nests at the end of the rains and in the early part of the dry season.

VOICE Immelmann *et al.* state that the calls and song of this species are similar to those of the Dark Firefinch but I found some differences between the vocalisations of a male *L. rhodopareia jamesoni* and those of several males (and females) of *L. rubricata haematocephala* kept at the same time (Goodwin, 1964). The alarm call sounded quite differently from that of the Dark Firefinch, being a hard rattling trill – 'trrrrrrrr' 'trrrr-trr-trrt' etc, very like the aggressive trill of *L. rubricata*. It was, however, recognised as an alarm call by my Dark Firefinches as they responded to it (if at all) by uttering their alarm calls *not* their (similarly sounding) trilling call. The locomotion intention calls of this male *jamesoni* were a very soft 'tsit, tsit' which intensified into a repeated 'ti-ti-ti-ti' (the 'i' pronounced as in 'bit' in both cases). A soft 'chu' or 'teu' was sometimes given in apparent threat or defiance. His distance contact calls consisted of series of very sweet musical notes strung together and uttered either rather rapidly: 'we-we-we-we-we-we . . .' or more slowly and poignantly: 'weet-weet-weet-weet-weet . . .'. Usually in a burst of calling he would give both fast and slow variants, the latter were very suggestive of one of the phrases in the song of the Woodlark, *Lullula arborea*. A long, thin, plaintive, whistling 'feeeeee', repeated three or four times, was sometimes given by this male when he was performing the courtship display alone. It usually resulted in his mate (a female *L. virata*) flying to him. His usual display notes were a squelchy 'squeh' and a husky 'fwit', like those of the Dark Firefinch but less loud. His nest call was like that of *L. rubricata* but a little huskier. When singing, the bird went through most of his repertoire in the same manner as my Dark Firefinches did. Nicolai describes the song (= my contact calls?) of other individuals of this species as like that of *L. rubricata* but in lower tempo and characterised by a long Canary-like trill. The 'songs' of both species are available, at least in Germany, on the Kosmos-Schallplatte (record) no. 75–09325 (Nicolai). Payne gives sound spectrograms of many calls of this species. Brunel *et al.* give sound spectrograms of the calls of the races *jamesoni* and *bruneli*.

DISPLAY AND SOCIAL BEHAVIOUR The courtship display of my male *L.r. jamesoni* was exactly like that of males of *L. rubricata haematocephala*, including the occasional wing fluttering. The Jameson's Firefinch, however, adopted a rather crouched, less upright body stance throughout the display but I am not sure whether this was a specific or individual difference. At each upward thrust the feet leave the ground or perch, and very often the squelch note was uttered. When displaying on the ground (as my male often did) his position changed with each jump, first to one facing a little to one side of his original position and with the next upward jump compensating or rather over-compensating so that he then landed facing slightly to the other side. The greeting display of this male was like that of the Dark Firefinch (as were those of two female *L. virata*, which he was paired with at different times) except that the wing slapping component was seen only very seldom and at low intensity.

REFERENCES

Brunel, J., Chappuis, C., & Erard, C. 1980. Data on *Lagonosticta rhodopareia bruneli*. *Bull. Brit. Orn. Cl.* **100**: 164–170.

Burkard, R. 1968. Über die zucht einiger seltener Prachtfinken. *Gefiederte Welt* **1968**: 148–150.

Chapin, J. P. 1954. The birds of the Belgian Congo. *Bull. Amer. Mus. Nat. Hist.* **75B**.

Erard, C. & Roche, J. 1977. Un nouveau *Lagonosticta* du Tchad meridional. *Oiseau Rev. Fr. d'Orn.* **47**: 335–343.

Goodwin, D. 1964. Observations on the Dark Firefinch, with some comparisons with Jameson's Firefinch. *Avicult. Mag.* **70**: 80–105.

Goodwin, D. 1969. Observations on two Jameson's Firefinches. *Avicult. Mag.* **75**: 87–94.

Immelmann, K., Steinbacher, J. & Wolters, H. E. 1964. *Vögel in Käfig und Voliere: Prachtfinken*: 189–197. Aachen, Germany.

Johnson, F. 1936. Breeding of Jameson's Firefinches. *Avicult. Mag.*, 5th ser. **1**: 50–52.

Mackworth-Praed, C. W. & Grant, C. H. B. 1960. *African handbook of birds*, ser. 1, vol. 2.

McLachlan, G. R. & Liversidge, R. 1957. *Roberts birds of South Africa*. Cape Town.

Nicolai, J. 1965. *Käfig- und Volierenvogel*. Kosmos, Stuttgart, Germany.

Payne, R. B. 1973. *Behaviour, mimetic songs and song dialects, and relationships of the parasitic indigobirds* (Vidua) *of Africa*. Orn. Monographs no. 11. Published by the American Ornithologists' Union.

Vincent, A. W. 1949. On the breeding habits of some African birds. *Ibis* **91**: 660–688.

Kulikoro Firefinch *Lagonosticta virata*

Lagonosticta rubricata virata Bates, *Bull. Brit. Orn. Cl.* 1932: **53**: 7

DESCRIPTION Similar to previous form, *L. rhodopareia*, with which it may be conspecific but slightly larger and longer billed. Coloration very like that of *L. rubricata polionota* but less bright and it has a narrower head and more slender, longer-looking bill and the second primary is not emarginated on the inner web. Feathers of front of forehead with dull red tips. Rest of top of head, nape, mantle and back dark dull grey; wings dark brownish grey. Under wing coverts greyish with a silvery sheen. Rump and upper tail coverts deep scarlet. Tail brownish black, all but the outermost pair of tail feathers have the basal half or rather more of their outer webs fringed with dull scarlet or carmine red. Lores, area immediately above eye and a small area at base of bottom of lower mandible, deep scarlet. Rest of face, throat, breast and most of underparts a deep, soft, pinkish crimson. Very small dull white dots at sides of breast and on upper flanks (possibly absent in a minority of individuals as in some other firefinches). Tibial feathers and centre of belly dull grey. Ventral area and under tail coverts black. Irides dark brown to black. Bill slate blue with black tip, the upper mandible usually darker than the lower and sometimes mainly blackish. Legs and feet dark grey, greyish black or dark brown.

The female, unlike females of related species, resembles the male except that the pinkish crimson of her face and underparts is a little paler and duller although not strikingly so. The juvenile (*fide* Burkard) is grey with red on rump and tail like that of the adults but duller. Nestlings a day or two old are described (Burkard) as having dark grey skin, whitish down, and two large and one small gape tubercles (colour not stated).

FIELD CHARACTERS Very small red and dark greyish bird. Could only be confused with other firefinches, of which the only sympatric species is *L. senegala*, whose red bill (both sexes) and predominantly light brown plumage (females and juveniles) at once distinguish it.

DISTRIBUTION AND HABITAT Mali, along the Upper Niger River from Bamako to Mopti. Inhabits areas where bushes and grass grow among rocks in rough country (Bates).

FEEDING AND GENERAL HABITS As previous species, *L. rhodopareia*, so far as known. Grass seeds are probably its main food and are the only one recorded for wild birds (Bates). In captivity it has similar needs and tastes to Jameson's and Dark Firefinches.

NESTING I can find no record of wild nests. A female with a brood patch and whose ovaries showed she had recently laid eggs was shot near Mopti in December (Bates). Two captive females, one of whom I had for about a year paired to a male Dark Firefinch and the other for three years paired to a male Jameson's Firefinch, were never seen to do any building or lining of nests. I repeatedly noticed that

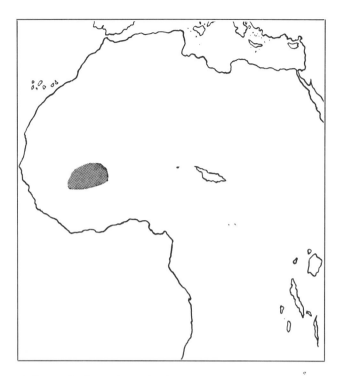

if the male brought a feather for the lining when the female was inside the nest she never tried to take it from him, as a female blue waxbill usually does when her mate brings a feather while she is sitting. A pair of *L. virata* kept by Burkard built a roundish nest with a large side entrance about 50 cm high in a fir tree. The many clutches laid by my two hens and a clutch laid by Burkard's were all of 4 eggs. Parental behaviour as in other firefinches (Burkard, pers. obs. of females only).

VOICE Except where otherwise indicated, this section is based on my own observations on two captive females and Harrison's (1957, 1963 and pers. comm.) observations on two males, one of which (which one it is unfortunately not certain) was undoubtedly and the other most probably of this form although at the time (before one, whose skin had been kept after death, was critically compared with museum skins) both were thought to be *L. rubricata polionota* (Harrison, 1957). One of these males was paired to a female *L. rubricata*.

The alarm call is a rattling trill, like that of *L. rhodopareia* but louder, deeper-pitched and harsher, sometimes with a suggestion of a 'ch' sound 'welling up' in the middle of a trill. I wrote it as 'chrrrrrrr', 'choorrrrrr', 'choorrrr(ch)rrrrrr(ch)rrrr-rrrr' and variants. Harrison noted that in his males the pitch became higher with the intensity of the calling. Burkard, however, describes the alarm calls of his pair as a sparrow-like 'tshek' repeated at short intervals.

Contact calls of males were described as low-pitched, nasal, slightly harsh 'kyew' or 'kyah' (Harrison, 1957) that of females as a harsh 'kew' (pers. obs.) both subject to much minor variation. One of my females uttered a long, plaintive 'feeeeeeeeeeeeeeee' and, less often, a two-syllabled

'feeee-eeeee' as distance contact calls. They were very similar to the homologous calls of the female Dark Firefinch (q.v.) but even more plaintive and drawn-out, almost eerie in tone and astonishingly like a common call of the Sun-bittern, *Heliopyga helias*, the long-drawn, single version having the same sad, haunting quality as the Sun-bittern's call. The same calls of my other female were less drawn out and (perhaps only because of that) less plaintive. The nest call of the male is described by Harrison as a faint, persistent, clucking note. I heard a soft 'chew' or 'teu', very like that of my male Jameson's firefinch and used in similar threat or defiance contexts.

The song of one of Harrison's males consisted only of 'a long-drawn toneless trill'; the other had a melodious, high-pitched song of short, loud phrases that were frequently repeated. Burkard records that both male and female of his pair uttered a similar song, consisting of series of whistling notes in a Canary-like tone. Neither of my two hens ever (to my knowledge) sang in this manner.

DISPLAY AND SOCIAL BEHAVIOUR The courtship display is similar to that of *L. rubricata* and *L. jamesoni*. Burkard noticed that his birds never spread the tail in display (as *L. rubricata* usually does to some extent) and his hen also gave this display, though never when the male was performing it. I did not see courtship display from either of my two hens. The greeting display is like that of the Dark Firefinch and Jameson's Firefinch, as with the latter, the lifting and slapping down of the closed wing seems to occur less often than in *L. rubricata*.

Burkard did not observe allo-preening in his pair though he noted that a fledgling submitted to allo-preening from a Brown Firefinch which had adopted it, nor did I observe allo-preening by my two females.

OTHER NAMES Grey-backed Firefinch, Blue-billed Firefinch, Dark Firefinch. (It is unfortunate that owing to having often been mistaken for or considered conspecific with *L. rubricata*, or considered conspecific with *L. rhodopareia*, it is uncertain in most cases which references in the literature apply in whole or part to *L. virata*.)

REFERENCES
Bates, G. L. 1934. Birds of the southern Sahara and adjoining countries in French West Africa. *Ibis* 13th ser. **4**: 685–717.
Burkard, B. 1961. Die Zucht des Graurückenastrildes. *Gefiederte Welt* **1961**: 94–95.
Goodwin, D. 1964. Observations on the Dark Firefinch, with some comparisons with Jameson's Firefinch. *Avicult. Mag.* **70**: 80–105.
Goodwin, D. 1969. Observations on two Jameson's Firefinches. *Avicult. Mag.* **75**: 87–94.
Harrison, C. J. O. 1957. Notes on the Dark Firefinch. *Avicult. Mag.* **63**: 128–130.
Harrison, C. J. O. 1963. Jameson's Firefinch and Dark Firefinch. *Avicult. Mag.* **69**: 42.

Vinaceous Firefinch   *Lagonosticta v. vinacea*

Estrelda vinacea Hartlaub 1857, *Syst. Ornith. West-afrika*, p. 143.

DESCRIPTION About same size and shape as previous species, *L. virata*, but bill a little larger. Second (outermost) primary somewhat emarginated on inner web. Top of head medium grey, shading into rosy mauvish pink on the hind neck. Mantle, back, most of wing coverts and outer webs of inner secondaries a slightly darker and duller mauvish pink shading into rosy crimson or carmine on the rump, upper tail coverts, two central tail feathers and outer webs of most other tail feathers. Rest of tail feathers black except for the outermost pair which are all dark drab. Wing coverts on upper (outer when wing closed) edge of wing, primaries and outer secondaries dark greyish brown, primary coverts a less greyish brown. Under wing coverts silvery buff. Face and throat black. Sides of neck and most of underparts a beautiful soft rosy mauvish pink, spotted with small white dots on the sides of the breast and flanks, some of these spots are single and some 'paired'. Ventral area and under tail coverts dull black. Irides dark red to reddish brown with (*fide* Immelmann *et al.*) bluish grey eye rims. The bill and leg colours are either locally or individually variable or else some records are erroneous, perhaps due to post-mortem changes. Three adult males and a female in the British Museum (Natural History) collection are said to have had bills that were dark olive green on the upper mandible, pale olive green on the lower, with dark or black tips and cutting edges, and pale olive green legs and feet. A live captive pair also had bills and legs of this colour (Cotterell). Two other male specimens are said to have had bills with black upper and purplish lower mandibles and black legs and feet. Immelmann *et al.* state that the bill is bluish grey with a black tip and the legs and feet brownish grey.

The female lacks the black face mask. Her head and face are light brownish grey slightly to strongly tinged with rosy pink. Her upperparts are browner, and usually paler than the male's, her rump and tail a little duller. Her throat is buff, greyish buff or pinkish buff. Her breast and flanks a soft dull rosy pink or mauvish pink, often suffused with buff, shading to buff on the belly and ventral area. Under tail coverts dark pinkish buff. White spots at sides like male's but a little less bright. There is much minor variation in depth of colour and amount of pink both above and below. The juvenile is a general dull brown with the red on rump and tail duller than the adult's. The nestling has five black spots on the palate, a black crescent on the inside of the lower mandible and two black marks on the tongue. It has a bluish white tubercle at the base of each mandible and between them in the corners of the gape a violet blue tubercle which is separated by dark skin from the lower of the bluish white tubercles (Immelmann *et al.*); sketch of mouth markings in Steiner (1960).

See plate 3, facing p. 128.

FIELD CHARACTERS Very small mauvish pink bird with black face mask, grey crown and reddish rump and tail (male) or pinkish brown and buffish (female). The only firefinches sympatric with it are the Red-billed and Dark Firefinches, from which the black face of the male and lack

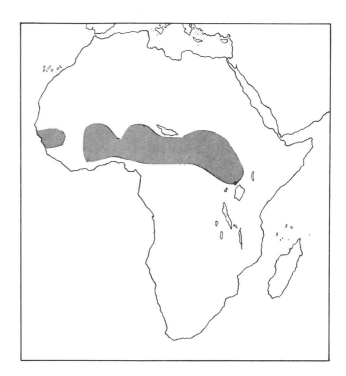

of any red on the greyish face of the female at once distinguish it.

DISTRIBUTION AND HABITAT Senegal, Gambia and former Portuguese Guinea to Bamako in Mali. Inhabits areas where there are bamboo thickets or clumps and surface water. Has become much less common and more localised in Gambia in synchrony with and presumably as a result of the decrease of bamboo (Bannerman, Cawkell & Moreau).

FEEDING AND GENERAL HABITS Little information on this form in the wild, presumably feeds mainly on grass seeds and small insects. In captivity will take millet and is very eager for insect food when rearing young, when it will take (for its size) rather large spiders as well as small insects (Wharton-Tiger). Appears usually to be delicate in captivity, although it has been kept and bred outside during an English summer (Wharton-Tiger). Immelmann *et al.* recommend that it be first kept in a temperature of 22 to 25°C and subsequently never at a temperature of below 18 to 20°C and that it must be given insect food throughout the year as well as both dry and soaked seed and greenfood.

NESTING Nesting in the wild does not seem to have been yet described (April 1978) but sites and nests are probably similar or identical to those of the grey form next dealt with (q.v.). In captivity it builds a ball-shaped (Immelmann *et al.*) or barrel-shaped (Cotterell) nest of grass stems, coconut fibres etc, lined with feathers and with a small side entrance. Usually it is sited in a bush, clump of grass or heather, bundle of twigs or similar place, only rarely in a box or basket (Immelmann *et al.*). Eggs usually 4, sometimes 5. Incubation period 11–12 days. Young fledge at 18–20 days (perhaps earlier in the wild?) and are fed for 9 or 10 days after. Both sexes share parental cares in the usual way.

VOICE The locomotion intention and close contact call is a shrill, shrew-like 'seesee' (Harrison) or 'tspeettspeet' (Immelmann *et al.*). The distance contact call is a louder, more piercing version of it. The alarm call is a series of hard notes run together 'dwit-it-it' or similar, very suggestive of the alarm call of the Red-cheeked Cordon-bleu (Harrison, Immelmann *et al.*). The song is soft and plaintive; it consists of two more short strophes of repeated, clear notes (Harrison, Immelmann *et al.*). It is available (at least in Germany) on the Kosmos record no. 75–09325 (Nicolai). Harrison also records a 'squelch' note, similar to but fainter than that of *L. virata*, which is uttered during courtship display. Payne gives sound spectrograms of some calls of this form and of *L.v. togoensis*.

DISPLAY AND SOCIAL BEHAVIOUR The courtship display is like that of the Dark Firefinch. It usually takes place on the ground and involves the male hopping around the female as he displays. The display may be silent (Immelmann *et al.*), the 'squelch' note may be uttered with the upward movement of the head (Harrison) or the bird may sing (Immelmann *et al.*). In the latter case (*fide* Karl, in Immelmann *et al.*) the display is never directly followed by copulation. Harrison notes that the upward head movement of the courtship display makes the black bib appear momentarily larger and more striking. Like many other species the Vinaceous Firefinch often indulges in courtship display movements when alone and with no material in his bill.

OTHER NAMES Black-faced Firefinch, Vinaceous Waxbill.

REFERENCES

Bannerman, D. A. 1953. *The birds of West and Equatorial Africa,* vol. 2. Oliver & Boyd, Edinburgh and London.

Cawkell, E. M. & Moreau, R. E. 1963. Notes on birds in the Gambia. *Ibis* **105**: 156–178.

Cotterell, R. 1964. Breeding the Vinaceous Firefinch. *Avicult. Mag.* **70**: 106–108.

Harrison, C. J. O. 1962. An ethological comparison of some waxbills (Estrildini) and its relevance to their taxonomy. *Proc. zool. Soc. London* **139**: 261–282.

Immelmann, K., Steinbacher, J. & Wolters, H. E. 1964. *Vögel in Käfig und Voliere: Prachtfinken*: 205–215. Aachen, Germany.

Nicolai, J. 1965. Käfig- und Volierenvögel. Kosmos, Stuttgart, Germany.

Payne, R. B. 1973. *Behaviour, mimetic songs and song dialects, and relationships of the parasitic indigo-birds* (Vidua) *of Africa.* Orn. Monographs no. 11. Published by the American Ornithologists' Union.

Wharton-Tiger, Mrs. 1933. Breeding the Vinaceous Fire-finch. *Avicult. Mag.* 4th ser. **5**: 437–439.

Black-faced Firefinch   *Lagonosticta vinacea nigricollis*

Lagonosticta nigricollis Heuglin, 1863, *J. Orn.* **11**, p. 273.

DESCRIPTION Size, shape and plumage pattern as previous form (q.v.) but coloration differs as follows: Upper parts, except for rump and tail, a rather dark slaty grey, usually a little paler on the crown and nape than on the mantle and back. Wings a similar but slightly browner grey. Underparts pale grey, usually with some mauvish pink suffusion on the breast and flanks. Rest of plumage, including black face and white spots at sides of breast, as in *L.v. vinacea.* Irides brown or dark brown, eye rims light bluish. Bill grey to greyish blue, with darker tip and cutting edges. The female is a much more brownish grey above and has the throat and central part of the breast and belly and under tail coverts dark or pale buff. The juvenile is mainly drab brown with dark buffish belly. Rump and tail like adults' but a duller red.

The above description is of *L. vinacea nigricollis*, from the eastern Cameroons and Oubangi-chari to Bahr-el-Ghazal, northern Uganda and the upper Uelle district of Zaïre (Congo). *L.v. togoensis*, of the interior savannas from Ghana to Nigeria and (possibly only as a non-breeding visitor) Darfur, Sudan, averages a very little paler grey on head and underparts and a shade more brownish on the mantle and, if the specimens in the British Museum (Natural History) are a fair sample, often with little or no pink suffusion. It is, however, a rather poorly differentiated race, especially when allowance is made for the appreciable individual differences and those due to plumage wear.

DISTRIBUTION AND HABITAT Tropical Africa from Ghana, Nigeria, eastern Cameroons and the Oubangi-Chari east to Darfur, Sudan, Bahr-el-Ghazal, the upper Uelle district of Zaïre (congo) and northern Uganda. Inhabits grass savannas, neglected and abandoned cultivated areas and farmland.

FEEDING AND GENERAL HABITS Seeks food on the ground, flying into trees or scrub when alarmed. Known to take small seeds (species not stated), termites and other small insects (Chapin). Seen in pairs, singly (mate on nest?) and in small parties (Bannerman). Appears not to have been kept in captivity, or if so not written about, but its behaviour and needs are probably identical to those of previous form.

NESTING Published accounts that I have read all derive from Serle, who, in 1937, found two nests, containing clutches of 3 and 4 incubated eggs, in July and August in northern Nigeria. One nest, which was roundish, of withered grass, lined with fine grass tops and a few feathers, was two feet above ground in a pile of brushwood in open farmland; the other (not described so presumably similar) was in a small bush in a marshy hollow in savanna grassland.

VOICE Probably very similar to or identical with that of previous form but more information needed. Chapin says that it has a lisping and weak 'call note' and a song like that of the Dark Firefinch. Bannerman says it utters a 'loud, clear song'. Payne gives sound spectrograms of some calls of *L.v. togoensis.*

DISPLAY AND SOCIAL BEHAVIOUR No information, probably as that of previous form, the Vinaceous Firefinch.

OTHER NAMES Grey Firefinch, Grey Black-faced Firefinch.

REFERENCES

Chapin, J. P. 1954. The birds of the Belgian Congo, pt. 4. *Bull. Amer. Mus. Nat. Hist.* **75B**.

Lynes, H. 1924. On the birds of North and Central Darfur. *Ibis* **1924**: 648–719.

Payne, R. B. 1973. *Behaviour, mimetic songs and song dialects, and relationships of the parasitic indigo-birds* (Vidua) *of Africa*. Orn. Monographs no. 11. Published by the American Ornithologists' Union.

Serle, W. 1938. Observations on the breeding habits of Nigerian estrildine weaver-birds. *Oologists' Record* **18**: 40–45.

Masked Firefinch   *Lagonosticta larvata*

Amadina larvata Rüppell, 1840, *Neue Wirbelt.*, *Vögel*, p. 97, pl. 36, fig. 1.

DESCRIPTION Very like the Vinaceous Firefinch, with which it may be conspecific (see p. 119) but averaging a very little larger and slightly longer in tail and bill. Coloration suggestive of that of the South African form of the Black-cheeked Waxbill but plumage pattern different. Forehead and crown dark grey to greyish black. Face, including ear coverts and throat, black. Feathers of sides of hind crown, sides of neck, hind neck and upper mantle varyingly, but usually extensively, tipped with wine-red or carmine. Rest of mantle, back and wings dark slate grey, becoming browner in worn plumage. Rump, upper tail coverts, all but the ends of the two central tail feathers and much of the outer webs of most other tail feathers, rich wine-red, fading to rusty carmine with wear. Rest of tail black. Breast and flanks wine-red, sometimes, especially on the flanks, mixed with slate grey owing to the grey basal parts of the feathers showing to some extent. Small white dots, some single, some paired and all accentuated by a contiguous posterior dark mark, on sides of lower breast and flanks. Centre of lower breast dark grey shading to black on belly, ventral area and under tail coverts. Irides brown, eye-rims light blue. Bill dark slate blue to bluish black, under mandible paler. Legs and feet dark bluish grey. These soft part colours are based on only a few specimens so further information is needed.

The female has the upper parts dark brownish slate to medium dull greyish brown. Rump and tail like male's but not quite so deep a red. Face and ear coverts may be dark grey like the crown, greyish buff or buff. Throat dark greyish buff to buff, breast similar but tinged with pink and shading to buff on the belly and dark slightly pinkish drab on the flanks. White dots as in male. Ventral area and under tail coverts dark buffish drab to sooty grey. One female in the British Museum (Natural History) collection has wine-pink tips to some of its neck feathers. I have not seen a juvenile of this form or description of one.

FIELD CHARACTERS Male a small dark greyish bird with black face and wine-red breast, hind neck, rump and tail.

Female dark brownish grey with some (usually dark) buff below and wine-red rump and tail. Darker colouring and black face distinguish male from other firefinches; dark colouring and much shorter tail from Pink-bellied Black-faced Waxbill. Female darker and duller than those of other firefinches; wine-red rump and tail and (if visible) white dots on sides distinguish it from other darkish and nondescript small birds.

DISTRIBUTION AND HABITAT Western Ethiopia and eastern Sudan from Gallabit in the north to Boma Hills in the south. Inhabits bamboo growth at 1000 to 1500 metres (3000–5000 feet), the grassy banks of woodland streams and grassy savanna woodland (Cave and Macdonald, Mackworth-Praed & Grant).

FEEDING AND GENERAL HABITS Apparently little known. Said to occur in small parties and occasionally in large flocks (Mackworth-Praed & Grant).

NESTING No information.

VOICE No information.

DISPLAY AND SOCIAL BEHAVIOUR No information.

OTHER NAME Black-faced Firefinch.

REFERENCES

Cave, F. O. & Macdonald, J. D. 1955. *Birds of the Sudan*. Edinburgh and London.

Mackworth-Praed, C. W. & Grant, C. H. B. 1960. *The African handbook of birds*, ser. 1, vol. 2.

Urban, E. K. & Brown, L. H. 1971. *A checklist of the birds of Ethiopia*. Addis Ababa, Ethiopia.

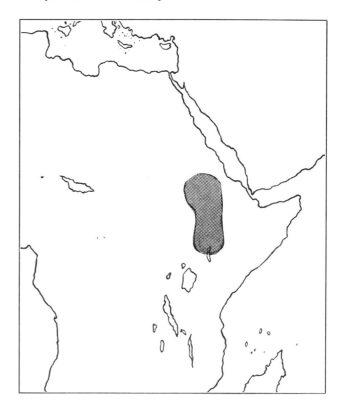

The blue and purple waxbills

The waxbills in the genus *Uraeginthus* are characterised by their blue rumps and otherwise partly blue or partly purple plumage. They are shapely birds with rather long, graduated or wedge-shaped tails. They vary from rather smaller to slightly larger than the one of them – the Violet-eared Waxbill – which is used (see p. 9) for size comparison. They have sometimes been included with the typical waxbills in the genus *Estrilda*, notably by White (1963) but they differ from the typical waxbills (and more closely resemble genera which White maintains) in their feeding habits, their inability to hold objects under the feet or to bite off grass stems, their nests and some of their plumage characters. Kunkel (1967) found that the behaviour of *Spermophaga ruficapilla* agreed in many details with that of *Uraeginthus* species and it seems likely that the bluebills, *Spermophaga*, may be their closest relatives, in spite of the considerable differences of size and coloration. So far as the latter is concerned, as Kunkel points out, there are similarities of plumage pattern between the two genera and also in plumage texture. There is a closer correlation in hue and texture between the red feathers on the head or underparts of *Spermophaga* species and those on the red cheek patches of *U. bengalus* than between the former and the non-lustrous red feathers of the firefinches, *Lagonosticta*.

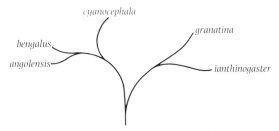

Presumed affinities within the genus *Uraeginthus*. See text for discussion.

The blue waxbills or cordon-bleus include three species: the Red-cheeked Cordon-bleu or Red-cheeked Blue Waxbill, *Uraeginthus bengalus*, the Cordon-bleu or Blue-breasted Waxbill, *U. angolensis*, and the Blue-headed Cordon-bleu or Blue-headed Waxbill, *U. cyanocephala*. It must be mentioned that English aviculturists and bird-dealers use the name 'Cordon-bleu', without qualification, for *U. bengalus* (only) so that confusion is possible with records where no description or scientific name is given. *U. angolensis* and *U. bengalus* are very closely related but in some areas occur together without interbreeding so they are best treated as full species (Hall & Moreau, 1970). The occasional occurrence (not always in areas of actual or potential overlap) of males with apparently anomalous or intermediate facial colour patterns seems more likely to be due to individual variation than to hybridisation. In discussing this question, Immelmann *et al.* (1964) state that there is a variant specimen of *U. bengalus*, in the Koenig Museum, in Bonn, that besides the normal red cheek patch has red edgings on some of the feathers on its lower throat and breast. As Chapin (1954) has pointed out, the females of the two forms differ, even though much less conspicuously than the males. In captivity, and doubtless also in the wild, females of *U. bengalus* show a positive and apparently innate sexual reaction to the red face patch of the male (Goodwin, 1965, 1971 and later obs.). They react to the males of *U. angolensis* (but not to the *red*-billed males of *U. cyanocephala*) as they do to females of their own species.

The Blue-headed Cordon-bleu, *U. cyanocephala*, is more different from the two previous forms than they are from each other. Although much closer to them than it is to the other two *Uraeginthus* species, it shows some degree of intermediacy in its slightly larger size, the much greater relative paleness of the female, and the head pattern of most juvenile females, which much resembles that of *U. granatina*. It has a relatively limited range in eastern Africa and although it overlaps geographically to some extent with *U. bengalus* it is usually a bird of rather more arid country. When both species are kept together in captivity, the males (provided they have been reared by their own kind) show no sexual interest in females of the other species. The blue waxbills are mainly ground feeders, taking seeds and small insects.

The purple or purple and chestnut waxbills number only two species, the Violet-eared Waxbill, *Uraeginthus granatina*, and the Purple Grenadier or Purple Waxbill, *U. ianthinogaster*. They are allopatric and might be considered as members of a superspecies, although perhaps better as geographical representatives as they have diverged considerably in colour patterns and voice. They are sometimes put in a separate genus of their own, *Granatina*, but this seems needless 'splitting' of genera as their affinities are clearly, and comparatively closely, with the three blue waxbills. They tend to inhabit more arid country but otherwise their habits are very similar although they appear to be rather more insectivorous. In captivity in Europe they are more delicate than the blue species. Each of them is parasitised by a Whydah, whose range nearly coincides with theirs (Hall & Moreau).

REFERENCES

Chapin, J. P. 1954. The birds of the Belgian Congo, pt. 4. *Bull. Amer. Mus. Nat. Hist.* **75b**.

Goodwin, D. 1965. A comparative study of captive blue waxbills (Estrildidae). *Ibis* **107**: 285–315.

Goodwin, D. 1971. Imprinting, or otherwise, in some cross-fostered Red-cheeked and Blue-headed Cordon-bleus. *Avicult. Mag.* **77**: 88–93.

Hall, B. P. & Moreau, R. E. 1970. *An atlas of speciation in African passerine birds.* British Museum (Natural History) London.

Immelmann, K., Steinbacher, J. & Wolters, H. E. 1964. *Vögel in Käfig und Voliere, Prachtfinken*: 216–267.

Kunkel, P. 1967. Zu Biologie und Verhalten des Rotkopfsamen-knackers, *Spermophaga ruficapilla* (Fam. Estrildidae). *Bonner Zoologische Beiträge* **1967**: 139–167.

White, C. M. N. 1963. *A revised check list of African flycatchers, tits, tree creepers, sunbirds, white-eyes, honey eaters, buntings, finches, weavers and waxbills.* Lusaka, Zambia.

Red-cheeked Cordon-bleu *Uraeginthus bengalus*

Fringilla bengalus Linnaeus, 1776, *Syst. Nat.* ed. 12, **1**, p. 323.

DESCRIPTION About size of Avadavat but slimmer and with a rather long tail that is wedge-shaped when spread. Inner web of second primary emarginated but not markedly so. Face, including the area immediately above the eye, throat, breast and flanks a beautiful light bright blue which may, however, appear anything from pale silvery blue to deep cornflower blue according the angle and intensity of the light. Rump and upper tail coverts a slightly duller blue. A large, more or less bean-shaped patch of dark crimson on the cheeks, involving most of the ear coverts. Central tail feathers a rather dark greenish or greyish blue, brighter at the fringes of the feathers, outer tail feathers dull grey with some blue on the outer webs. Top of head and rest of upperparts (except where otherwise stated above) a rather light, slightly reddish brown, darker and duller on the tips and inner webs of the primaries. Centre of lower breast and belly and under tail, coverts pinkish buff. In life, but not in a study skin, a trace of a paler area, corresponding to the white belly patch of *U. cyanocephala*, is usually visible if the bird is viewed from below. Bill greyish pink, fleshy pink, purplish pink or reddish, with blackish tip and cutting edge of the upper mandible. Irides light brown, medium brown or reddish brown. Narrow and rather inconspicuous pale yellowish orbital skin. Legs and feet pale fleshy brown to horn brown.

Female has no red on cheeks. She is usually a little paler and duller with some admixture of brown in the blue of the lower throat and sides of breast. The juvenile male is like the adult female but has the blue areas paler, duller and usually a little less extensive. The juvenile female is similar but usually with the blue areas less extensive than in her brothers. Recently fledged juveniles have dark greyish irides, darker fleshy brown legs and feet, short black bills and a small dark blue tubercle at the base of the upper mandible at each side of the gape. The dark pigment is lost from the base of the bill outwards, for a period the young have strikingly bi-coloured bills. Nestling at first reddish, with fawn down which soon fades. Three black spots and a dark central line on the whitish palate, black band across tongue and a long triangular black crescent in the lower mandible. In an 8 day old nestling the gape tubercles were not yet developed. The palate markings of the nestlings are retained in adulthood. In captivity (in England) juveniles attain adult plumage at about 3·5 to 4·5 months old.

The above description is of nominate *U.b. bengalus*, from Senegal west to Eritrea and south to western Kenya and Uganda. *U.b. ugogoensis*, from northern and western Tanzania, is a slightly duller brown above and the female has the brown at the sides of the neck extending more forwards, under the blue ear coverts. The form from coastal Kenya and Tanzania, *U.b. littoralis*, is said (van Someren, 1922) to be slightly smaller and the male to

have a smaller red facial patch. *U. bengalus brunneigularis*, shown on plate 8, facing p. 257, from the highlands of Kenya east of the Rift Valley, from Mount Kenya south to Simba, averages a little larger than nominate *U.b. bengalus* and the female has the entire head brown except for a blue tinge on the throat and, in some individuals, a violet tinge on the ear coverts. Almost the exact opposite of this is seen in *U.b. katangae*, from southern Kasai, extreme eastern Angola south to Cazombo, Katanga and Zambia, in which the female has a bright blue face but her underparts are buffish brown except for a very slight blue tinge on the breast. Both sexes of this race have the brown on the upper parts duller and darker even than in *U.b. ugogoensis*. Some of the above races intergrade and there is also individual variation apart from differences due to plumage wear.

See plate 8, facing p. 257.

FIELD CHARACTERS Red on cheeks of male distinguish him from *U. angolensis*, this and his brown crown from *U. cyanocephala*. Brown and light blue plumage distinguish both sexes from all other small sympatric birds.

DISTRIBUTION AND HABITAT Tropical Africa from Senegal and Guinea east to Eritrea and south to coastal and western Tanzania, Cazombo, Katanga and northern Zambia.

Inhabits thorn scrub, savanna, dry woodland, cultivated areas with bushes or shrubs, gardens, villages and roadsides. Often in very arid country but only if surface water is available. Locally may live in mangroves if these are adjacent to good feeding areas.

FEEDING AND GENERAL HABITS Feeds mostly on the ground. Known to take seeds of grasses and termites; probably takes some other seeds and other small invertebrates.

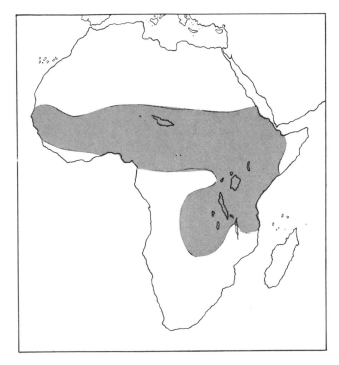

Flying termites, and no doubt other flying insects, often taken in the air by a short sally from a perch. Large prey (*pers. obs.* on captive birds with grasshoppers and caterpillars) are held in the bill and beaten on the ground or perch. Seeks concealed food by flicking loose earth etc to one side with the bill. Will also apparently stab with closed bill at a lump of earth, the movement ending with a sideways flick to remove the broken piece.

In captivity, given a choice of seeds, feeds largely on the small panicum millet but some individuals also eat a lot of white millet and take a little small canary seed. Although most seed is de-husked, a certain amount of panicum and white millet is often swallowed whole. Fond of seeding and flowering Annual Meadow Grass, *Poa annua*, Knot-grass, *Polygonum aviculare* and Chickweed, *Stellaria media*. At times will eagerly take the tips of growing young grass and tear and eat bits from the leaves of lettuce, dandelion, Knot-grass and Chickweed, if the plants are clamped between bricks or under some heavy object so that it can do this. Pupae, larvae and the winged males and females (but not the workers) of meadow ants, *Lasius fuscus* and *L. niger*, green aphids (but not black or grey aphids), small green caterpillars, and very small centipedes are taken eagerly, especially when the birds are feeding young. Whiteworms and small maggots less keenly. If they are used to eating it, some pairs will feed eggfood and milk sop to their young but, if obtainable, a plentiful supply of insect food should be given to ensure that young are successfully reared. I have, however, had broods of healthy young of this and of the Blue-headed Cordon-bleu reared when only whiteworms, eggfood, milk sop, soaked seed (millets and a commercial grass seed mixture) and flowering and seeding Chickweed could be supplied. Kühner recommends mealworms (cooked for 5 minutes in water at 'cooking heat', then beheaded and be-tailed before feeding them to the birds) and egg yolk when ant pupae cannot be had. Fiebig bred the species successfully with no additions to a seed and greenfood menu except a commercial 'eggbiscuit' damped with water. Captive birds take much mineral matter, especially crushed baked eggshell (see p. 57) when rearing young or laying. They will often eagerly drink the albumen from cracked or broken eggs. When thus taking very shallow or small amounts of liquid they use a pigeon-like sucking instead of their usual 'dip and then raise head' drinking method.

Usually in pairs or small flocks in which the pair is the basic unit. Sometimes in larger flocks but these are probably most often mere aggregations at good feeding or safe resting places. Single birds sometimes seen, these are probably usually individuals whose mates are on the nest, have been recently bereaved, or have temporarily lost contact with others. Sometimes associates with other small estrildids but most probably these associations are usually a chance 'sharing' of resources.

Hops on the ground. I have not seen the flight of this species in the wild or read a description of it. In a room with which they are familiar the flight is swift and fairly straight but with a suggestion of the bounding curves in which many passerines usually fly. Flying in steep up and down bounds or curves and hovering over the selected perch before alighting, from which the species gets its German name of 'Butterfly Finch' is only shown if the bird is in a strange place and/or afraid to alight or unsure which way to fly. Does not roost in nests except when incubating or brooding nestlings. An upward flicking or throwing of the tail is a common movement. It has a lateral as well as a vertical component but the latter is usually most emphasised. At high intensity the closed or only slightly opened wings are jerked up as well and the whole body violently moved. These appear to be locomotion intention movements and are shown whenever the bird is at all restless or excited, provided that they are not precluded by the need to adopt other specific movements or postures. They are commonly used when alighting near any other bird who arouses sexual impulses but can hardly be considered as a display.

Anting movements in response to and occasional brief apparent attempts to ant with millipedes and centipedes have been observed but never with ants (Goodwin, 1971b and subsequent obs.).

Crouching and 'freezing' in apparent alarm has been seen a few times in captive birds but less often than in *U. angolensis* (q.v.)

NESTING Nest sited in a bush or tree, often among thorns and usually from 1 to 9 metres high. Sometimes builds in the old nest of a weaver, less often in some niche in or on a building. In some areas the nest is usually built near an active wasps' nest. It is rounded and smallish, with a side entrance, built of grass stems and panicles, sometimes also rootlets, stems of other plants and fibres. In Nigeria Serle (in Bannerman, 1949) found that most nests had an enveloping outer layer of fine roots. Sometimes lined or partly lined with white or pale-coloured feathers, sometimes (Lynes) only with soft grass panicles, fine stems and other vegetable matter. Nest lining material is added during incubation and for the first few days after the hatching of the young. Captive birds take white and pale feathers to the nest with greatest keen-ness shortly before, during and for the first day or two after the hatching of a brood. Some of these feathers are almost always arranged so as to make it difficult or impossible to see anything else when one looks into the nest entrance and may, perhaps, have some protective function in reference to certain potential nest predators. It would be interesting to know whether nests without feathers in the lining represent geographical or individual preferences, lack of suitable feathers in the habitat, or nests examined early in the incubation period before the impulse to collect and add feathers has reached its fullest peak. In captivity, and probably also when wild, the male brings most or all of the material for the main structure of the nest and builds it into place himself unless, as often happens, the female at the site takes it from him to build with. Both sexes collect and bring back materials to line the nest with. Under exceptional circumstances the female is, however, capable of building an entire nest without any help from her mate (Goodwin, 1965). All nesting material is carried, a single piece at a time, by one end or (less often) by some knot in or projecting from the stem. A firm end (or projection) to hold seems essential; thus although soft fluffy feathers, flowering heads of grass (with a hard stem) and so on are taken, entirely soft and flaccid materials such as bits of wool and vegetable down are not used.

The clutch consists of 3 to 6, rarely 7 eggs. The eggs (in captivity) are laid in the early morning at daily intervals. Judging from the growth state of broods of various sizes, effective incubation begins usually with the third egg. Both sexes take turns of incubation and brooding by day but only the female does so at night. Goger noted that when one of his birds came to relieve its mate on the nest it always uttered soft notes, which the mate answered, the relieving bird then slipped into the nest and its mate came out. I have not often heard these notes when watching nest relief but this might be due to a hearing failure on my part. The incubation period is 11 days (Immelmann *et al.*). All young that I have bred in captivity have fledged at 17 to 19 days old and (a few defective specimens excepted) could fly quite strongly on leaving the nest. Periods of as long as 20 to 21 days in the nest have, however, been recorded (Immelmann *et al.*). Young about to fledge spend some time looking out of the nest, and giving contact calls, which are answered by their parents, before 'taking the plunge' or rather flying *up*wards to some perch above nest level. Nestlings a few days old have fawnish down on head and upperparts. Their bills are then grey, darker at base and bluish at the commissure. This description is, however, based on only a few captive broods.

Both parents feed the young after fledging unless, as often happens in captivity and possibly in the wild also, they have begun another nest, in which case the female usually ceases to feed them when or shortly before she begins to lay. In such cases the male continues to care for the flying young even if he is taking turns at incubating the next clutch of eggs. Immelmann *et al.* state that, in captivity, the adults neglect their young if they start another nest but this has not been my experience either with this species or with its two close relatives. If, however, fledged captive young are 'adopted' and fed by another pair or individual then (and in my experience *only* then) will their father cease to feed them *if* he and their mother have another nest. The parents of newly-fledged young in captivity (and doubtless in the wild also) show great anxiety if the young are in an exposed position on the ground or otherwise appear to be in danger. A parent, usually the male, will often fly down repeatedly to such a fledgling, alight beside it, sometimes make intention movements of feeding it, and fly back up onto a perch until the young bird follows or hides itself in some cover. Once they have left the nest the young do not usually return to it (never in my experience) and the adults make no attempts to induce them to do so. Indeed once the young are showing clear signs of readiness to leave the nest, the parents appear eager to encourage them to do so.

In captivity young begin to feed themselves effectively about 7 days after fledging and the parents usually feed them until at least 5 to 7 days later. Experimental pecking at and mandibulating any seed-like or seedhead-like objects (and much else) begins, however, even before fledging; when the young bird is peering from the nest entrance. The young receive food in the usual crouching estrildid begging posture with twisted necks. They make side to side movements of the head as they beg with open mouths and lifted tongues. Although the begging posture is more stereotyped than in *Amandava*, it can vary in intensity. In young able to fly the begging is always directed towards the adult. If, for example, a young one is begging from an adult *below* it in the branches, its head is then directed downwards not upwards in the usual manner.

Young that have left the nest are individually recognised, perhaps by voice, perhaps visually as a result of the intense interest and concern of the parents with each individual young one when it leaves the nest. If eggs or nestlings of *U. cyanocephala* of the same age are placed among those of *U. bengalus* the parents will rear both species together and, in spite of the differences in the begging calls of the young and their different gape markings (blue tubercles present in *U. bengalus*, absent in *U. cyanocephala*), will not discriminate between them after fledging. Strange young, even if of similar age to its own flying young, are seldom or never fed but are ignored or repulsed. A bird vainly trying to persuade one of its own sated fledglings to accept more food will often angrily peck at a fledgling from another brood that begs from it. Under captive conditions 'childless' individuals will sometimes adopt the fledged young of others, and if they are vainly 'in love' with one of their parents will usually do so. The same is true of *U. angolensis* and *U. cyanocephala* (Goodwin, 1965).

VOICE The song is a short and rather squeaky strophe that varies individually and possibly geographically. Also the same individual may utter different song variants (Immelmann *et al.*, pers. obs.) 'te'tchee-wa-tcheee', 'ssee-deedelee-deedelee-ssee-ssee' are transcriptions (Immelmann's and mine) of two songs. Song usually accompanies the stem display (q.v.). It is also given when the bird is alone, either temporarily or through being unpaired or bereaved. The removal of the female elicits frequent song, alternating with high intensity contact calling from the male. When singing alone the bird usually adopts a posture or makes movements suggestive of those of the stem display. The song of the female is variable and tends to be shorter than that of the male. Except when displaying I have not seen a male of this species sing when beside or very near his mate but females occasionally do so, usually, and perhaps always, only if the male has given inadequate sexual responses.

Young birds utter much inconsequential sounding warbling, in which the variety of sounds seems greater than in the adult song and all the calls may be interjected.

When restless and apparently ready or eager to fly, a not very loud but rather sharp 'tsit-tsit-tsit' or 'zip-zip' is uttered. These calls are also given with much vehemence just before and at the moment of taking wing, not just if the bird intends to fly from one branch to another but when, from its restlessness or as the result of some disturbance, it seems likely that it would fly some distance were it free. This call probably functions to maintain contact between birds that are close to one another but moving about and more particularly to indicate intention of flying to a distance and to arouse a similar mood in the companion(s). Other individuals within hearing often respond with the same calls and restless movements but this seems to be a result of the mood spreading, one does not have the impression of a purposive response as one sometimes does with the contact call.

The contact call is a high-pitched, squeaky but somewhat sibilant 'tsee-tsee-tsee', 'tseu-tseu', or similar; typically given in series of 2 or 3 notes run together and then a pause, but sometimes singly. It is subject to some variation and usually has an urgent and interrogative tone. It is given under many circumstances whose common factor usually seems to be that a mild degree of alarm, uneasiness or apprehension has been aroused. It is given in response to any loud and *unusual* noise, in response to the sudden absence, invisibility or illness of the mate, and in response to the contact calls of other individuals especially to those of the mate, offspring or parent(s) or, in the case of unpaired birds, to those of a stranger of the opposite sex. If a captive Cordon-bleu flies into a strange room it gives this call amost immediately after alighting. If it is put into a strange cage or enclosure, it utters contact calls as soon as it has got over its first fright and immediately following the period during which it usually utters a few alarm calls. The contact call is also given during the greeting ceremony, usually by the bird that takes the initiative. A bird which is *badly* frightened or that is seriously ill never gives contact calls, even if its mate is uttering them frantically within hearing. The same is true of some, and probably most or all other birds. Obviously there has been strong selection against giving contact calls in situations where they would entice related (and other) conspecifics into danger or persuade them to waste time and energy keeping company with an inevitably doomed individual. The contact call is also given by fledglings when looking out of the nest prior to their first emergence from it and by their parents in reply to them.

The function of the contact call appears to be to maintain contact between individuals, especially between mates or members of the family in which the young are still dependent or partly so. Also, perhaps, to alert other conspecifics to be ready to look out for and respond to any possible danger.

The begging call of well-grown nestlings and dependent juveniles is a repeated, high-pitched, squeaky cheeping with a querelous nagging tone and the first note or two of a series usually shorter than the rest: 'tchĕ-tchēē-tchēē-tchēē-tchēē' or 'chĕ-chĕ-chēē-chēē-chēē-chēē.' It tends to be speeded up in extreme eagerness or excitement and is then very similar in sound to (and possibly homologous with) the chasing call of the adult male. Often there is some rise and fall in pitch but this is much less marked than in *U. cyanocephala*. The begging call intergrades with the slightly hoarse-sounding version of the contact call given by the young. Fledged young usually give contact calls when at a little (or great) distance from the parent and go over to begging calls as they approach close to it.

The nest call may be uttered by either sex but more often by the male. It is a nagging repetitive squeaky cheeping that I cannot with certainty distinguish from the begging call. While giving it the bird crouches in a potential nest site, looks repeatedly towards its mate or prospective mate and accompanies or intersperses its calling with movements that appear to be intention movements of building but are sometimes also similar to the head movements of begging juveniles. Sometimes a much softer series of calls, a soft 'pwĕ-pwĕ-pwĕ-pwĕ . . .' are given in place of the louder calls and the latter are usually or always superseded by such softer calls when the partner comes right up to the nest site or enters it alongside the mate.

The threat call is a sharp but somewhat squeaky 'Chik-chik-chik . . .' subject to much variation in tone. It is usually given in an horizontal or near horizontal position, facing a conspecific enemy. It may be followed by attack and, if not, usually goes over into longer and more nagging-sounding notes that soon become (to my ears) not distinguishable from loud nest-calling and which are accompanied by similar up and down head movements. Loud, harsh, singly uttered (but often repeated) 'chiks' are often used in apparent alarm or possibly to express a less degree of alarm than that expressed by the alarm call (q.v.). They often preface and form part of the alarm call or, are followed by, contact calls.

The alarm call is a rapid, chattering 'che-che-che-che' in which the individual notes can be heard plainly in spite of the rapidity with which they are run together. In tempo it is thus very similar to the rapid, chattering alarm call used by the Song Thrush, *Turdus philomelos*, when mobbing predators, or the alarm chatter of the Magpie, *Pica pica*. It is given in many situations, all of which appear to involve thwarting or conflict. Most often between two (or more) incompatible impulses. Typical situations in which it is given are: (1) by a bird whose fledgling(s) appear to it to be in danger, given with particular vehemence if a young bird cries out in fear; (2) by a cornered fledgling, unable to escape by flight, as it sees the hand closing on it; (3) at the sight of a predator. It may, however, also be given, usually at lower intensity, in situations apparently involving only annoyance, as by an individual that has failed to catch a flying insect it has chased. The function of the alarm call appears to be primarily to alert conspecifics, especially the mate or dependent young, to the presence of actual or potential danger.

A shrill but slightly husky, repeated screech or scream is sometimes given by fledglings when handled. Usually the bird gives one or two screeches and then falls silent. Occasionally an adult female will screech when handled but I have never known an adult male do so. Probably both adults and young would usually or always screech if painfully seized by a real predator. The screech elicits intense fear responses from other fledglings (including 'exploding' from the nest by young up to 2 or 3 days younger than the normal fledging age) and alarm calling from their parents.

The buzz screech is very like the fear screech in sound but usually huskier, longer drawn out and has a suggestion of a buzzing sound permeating it. The buzz screech is typically given by a bird of either sex when flying with a grass stem or other nesting material with which it intends to display. If a Cordon-bleu carrying nesting material utters the buzz screech in flight it is sure to display with it on alighting. The converse does not hold good, very often a bird will fly with a stem or feather and then display with it without having uttered the buzz screech in flight. A bird that has been disturbed by outsiders when displaying, if it flies off carrying the symbol to display elsewhere, usually utters the buzz screech as it flies. I have heard the buzz screech uttered during hostile encounters but only on rare occasions.

The buzz screech has a strongly attractive effect. If the bird is paired its mate almost always flies at once to land beside it when it alights. When a female gives the buzz screech in flight, several males commonly fly after and alight beside her. This suggests a sexual difference in the sound of the buzz screech which has eluded my ears.

Field studies are needed to discover in what situations the buzz screech is used in the wild and hence to deduce its function. I suspect it may function to entice the mate, or a prospective mate, away from the vicinity of other birds that have interfered with courtship or are likely to do so, and also to advertise the presence of an unpaired bird that is ready to pair.

The chasing call is given during sexual chases or 'driving' (see under 'Display and social behaviour') and in rather less intense form it may be given as an apparent alternative to song especially by an unpaired male or one separated from his mate. In the latter situation it is always followed by or alternates with the song. The chasing call consists of a single rather loud, harsh note, followed by a series of similar but usually less drawn out notes. It is subject to much minor variation and always sounds 'exasperated' to human ears. It may derive from the begging calls of fledged young. When a very hungry juvenile flies after its father uttering the begging call in flight both sound and actions are very similar to those of an adult male chasing a female. This is more marked in the present species, in which the chasing call, like most others, is higher pitched and more squeaky in tone, than in *U. cyanocephala*.

The above information is based mainly on study of captive birds (Goodwin, 1965, Immelmann *et al.*, 1964)

but none of the field observations I have read in any way contradict it. Sonagrams of alarm and contact calls are given in a paper by Evans (1972). I believe that, at comparable intensities, there are sexual differences in most calls that my ears cannot register with certainty. I have, however, definitely noticed that the alarm and contact calls of females are sometimes (and perhaps always) higher pitched than those of males.

DISPLAY AND SOCIAL BEHAVIOUR The triangular head is characteristic of sexually motivated displays. A sexually aroused bird always angles its tail towards the other individual if the latter is to one side of it. Mandibulation, in which the palate markings are made visible frontally, is performed in many social situations in which the common factor seems to be inhibited aggression. Fear, sexual attraction, a personal bond or fatigue may each, in different cases, be the inhibiting factor.

In the courtship display the male holds a piece of nesting material, preferably a long piece of grass or a white feather, by one end, or less often by some projection or knot. He perches near or beside the female with his flank feathers somewhat erected, but so as to present a smooth, not ragged contour, on the side nearest her. His tail is angled towards her and his head may be slightly turned towards her. If she is directly in front of him his tail is in line with his body. He then bobs up and down, as he rises he throws back his head (see sketch p. 39). He holds the nesting symbol and usually sings during the display. His feet do not appear to leave the perch completely but to rise up a little and the toes to unclench a little at each upward movement. An audible sound, presumably the foot coming again into full contact with the substrate, follows each bounce and is especially noticeable if the bird is performing on a dry branch or the newspaper covered floor of my birdroom. Often the male may hop around the female as he displays, especially if she is on the ground or on a ledge. Sometimes the male starts to display alone on a perch, he is then often unnoticed by his mate until he begins to sing, which he usually does after two or three upward movements, when she at once flies to him and he then directs the display at her.

The female also gives the courtship display but usually only when she has no mate or when her mate appears to be behaving inadequately. A paired female in such a situation may display alone or fly to her mate and direct the display at him. Females that are unpaired may perform the movements of the courtship display without a symbol in the bill, males and adolescent birds may perform low intensity display movements while singing without a symbol. I have, however, never seen a *Uraeginthus* of either sex deliberately approach another bird to give this display without first securing the symbolic material.

The courtship display in *Uraeginthus* is a pre-copulation display in so far as it often elicits soliciting from the female. Even when the female is herself giving the courtship display she may go over to soliciting. If she solicits in response to his display the male invariably performs some of the normal preliminaries to copulation and usually copulates. The female, when she solicits with crouched posture and quivering tail in the usual estrildine manner, most often does so in response to the courtship display from the male but sometimes to his mere approach to her with 'triangular head' and angled tail, to his starting precopulatory pecking without prior display, or even without previous discernable (to the human watcher) stimulus from him. When soliciting the feathers around the cloaca are parted and the lips of the cloaca open and shut rapidly, as with other birds. The male responds to the female's soliciting by pecking with apparently closed bill at her head and nape. He appears to peck quite hard but must, I think, 'pull his punches'. Pecking rapidly, he works down to the female's rump and cloaca, few, or no pecks being administered to the areas between nape and rump. The pecking appears quite savage but the female responds with more intense soliciting and consequent fuller exposure of her cloaca to the male. The male then mounts, sometimes giving a further peck or two at his mate's head as he does so. As he manouvres into position he beats his wings, presumably to maintain balance. Sometimes the wing fluttering continues throughout an apparently successful copulation but more often the wings suddenly cease to beat and are held spread or partly spread but drooping and still. As this happens there is a pulsating movement of the male's rump and tail suggesting that this sudden cessation of wing beating coincides with the orgasm. The length of time during which the cloacae of the pair are in apparent contact is longer than in any other birds I have seen copulate except the Anatidae. After copulation the male may regain the female's back and then hop or fly off or he may fall or fly downwards off her. If he alights beside her bill-fencing and/or mandibulation between them usually follows.

Apart from interference by other birds (in captivity), copulation attempts may break off owing to the female ceasing to solicit and showing mild aggression or the male failing to complete the act in spite of her encouragement. In these latter cases (and sometimes as a prelude to final success) the male may 'leapfrog' over the female or hop on and off her back several times between bouts of sexual pecking. After such abortive attempts the male may crouch in the soliciting posture and the female may then peck his nape, rump and cloaca. I have never seen the female attempt to mount the male and he does not quiver his tail although I once saw a male do so, when perched normally, in response to his mate repelling his advances. I have seen attempts to copulate with recently fledged young and with sick adults on only a very few occasions with this species, so this is discussed in the section on *U. angolensis* in which such behaviour, in captivity, seems more frequent.

I have only seen occasional and usually low intensity versions of the submissive courtship display and the dominant greeting display from *U. bengalus* so these are discussed also under *U. angolensis*.

The greeting display is performed when members of a pair meet each other again after a temporary separation or, in captivity, when the light goes on in the bird room in the morning and the members of a pair see each other again. It is also shown by unpaired individuals towards others to whom they are sexually attracted. One bird approaches the other (or the approach may be mutual) with the triangular head and angled tail. It lowers its head and either makes a formal bill-wipe on the perch towards the other or, rather more often, bows as if it would bill wipe but without actually doing so. These bows or bill wipes may be interspersed with turning slightly away as the head is lifted. Usually both birds (but only the active one if the other is unresponsive) utter contact calls, usually as only a single or double call, seldom as a series. Appeasing, sexual or aggressive behaviour may follow the greeting display, especially in the case of birds meeting each other for the first time. Kunkel (1949) found that the homologous display of *Estrilda caerulescens* occurred in situations in which the aggressive tendency was in conflict with some other impulse but in the blue waxbills sexual attraction seems to be the constant factor although it may be in conflict with fear or aggression or both (or neither). It is never shown towards individuals that are regarded with obvious hostility.

In sexual chases the male pecks at the female and, as she flies off, chases her with his body plumage fluffed out and uttering the chasing call. In captivity such behaviour is usually (and I suspect in the wild always) directed at the bird's own mate or at a female he is sexually interested in and who has already shown signs of interest in him. The commonest cause of such a sexual chase is when another male interferes with the performance of the courtship display or otherwise approaches the pair. It probably functions, like the 'driving' of pigeons (Goodwin, 1956) to remove the female from the presence of possible rivals. In *U. bengalus* this behaviour seems less strongly ritualised than in *U. cyanocephala*. More often than in the latter species, the male of *U. bengalus* may drive his mate from another male without plumage erection or uttering the chasing call.

The members of a pair usually rest and roost clumped side by side. Healthy adults of this and other blue waxbills clump with and allo-preen only their own mates, individuals with which they are desirous of pairing and (to a lesser extent) their dependent young. Under captive conditions they will, however, often respond to allo-preening invitations from other small estrildids such as *Amandava subflava* and *A. amandava*.

Females appear to have an innate response to the red cheek patches, or at least to a combination of red and blue on the head of the male. In strong contrast to similarly treated females (and males) of *U. cyanocephala*, two females of this species, reared by a pair of *U. cyanocephala*, showed no imprinting to the foster species (Goodwin, 1971). Wild-caught females responded sexually to (disinterested) males of *U. cyanocephala*, presumably reacting to the combination of red bill and blue head, but showed no interest in males of the more closely related *U.*

angolensis, even when these actively courted them (Goodwin, 1965). As is the case with some pigeons, females that are eager to pair may respond sexually to aggressive attacks from a male, even although these differ even more from his normal courting behaviour than is the case with pigeons. Possibly because of this response to red on the head, females of *U. bengalus* do not readily form homosexual pairs in captivity. Males often do but usually through having first formed a mutual bond as juveniles *before* they grew their red cheek feathers. Males of *U. bengalus* distinguish between the very similar appearing females of *U. angolensis* (and still more the obviously different females of *U. cyanocephala*) and those of their own species. Only in default of a willing conspecific partner will they, in captivity, pair readily with females of *angolensis*, rather less so with those of *cyanocaphala*.

OTHER NAMES Cordon-bleu, Red-cheeked Blue Waxbill, Red-eared Waxbill (an early name, later usually applied to *Estrilda troglodytes*).

REFERENCES

Bannerman, D. 1949. *The birds of tropical West Africa*, vol. 7. London.

Evans, S. M. 1972. Specific distinctiveness in the calls of Cordon Bleus (*Uraeginthus* spp., Estrildidae) *Anim. Behav.*, **20**: 571–579.

Fiebig, O. 1967. Schoa-Schmetterlingsfinken, Haltung and Zucht. *Gefiederte Welt* **91**: 152–153.

Goger, R. 1951. Meine ersten Erfahrungen mit der Zucht der Schmetterlings-finken. *Gefiederte Welt* **1961**: 29–31.

Goodwin, D. 1956. The significance of some behaviour patterns of pigeons. *Bird Study* **3**: 25–37.

Goodwin, D. 1965. A comparative study of blue waxbills (Estrildidae). *Ibis* **107**: 285–315.

Goodwin, D. 1971a. Imprinting, or otherwise, in some cross-fostered Red-cheeked and Blue-headed Cordon-bleus. *Avicult. Mag.* **77**: 26–31.

Goodwin, D. 1971b. Anting by Red-cheeked and Blue-headed Cordon-bleus. *Avicult. Mag.* **77**: 88–93.

Immelmann, K., Steinbacher, J. & Wolters, H. E. 1964. *Vögel in Käfig und Voliere: Prachtfinken*: 216–234.

Jackson, F. J. 1938. *The birds of Kenya Colony and the Uganda Protectorate*. vol. 3. London.

Kühner, P. 1967. Zur Ernährung der Prachtfinken. *Gefiederte Welt* **91**: 175–176.

Lynes, H. 1924. On the birds of North and Central Darfur. *Ibis* **6** (11th ser.): 648–719.

Mackworth-Praed, C. W. & Grant, C. H. B. 1960. *The African handbool of birds*, Ser. 1, Vol. 2, 2nd ed. London.

van Someren, V. G. L. 1922. Notes on the birds of East Africa. *Novit. Zool. Tring* **29**: 1–246.

Cordon-bleu   *Uraeginthus angolensis*

Fringilla angolensis Linnaeus, 1758, *Syst. Nat.*, ed. 10, **1**, p. 182.

DESCRIPTION Like Red-cheeked Cordon-bleu but a little less slender in shape and slightly shorter-tailed and with inner web of second primary rather more more sharply emarginated. Male coloured like male of *U. bengalus* but with no red on the face, the brown of the upper parts of a colder, more greyish tone, and the bill mauvish grey or silvery grey with blackish tip and cutting edge. Many collectors have recorded birds with red or purple bills but further information on this point is needed as the bills of dead birds very quickly turn a reddish purple colour (pers. obs.). It is often said that males of this species and *U. cyanocephala* are a brighter blue than males of *U. bengalus*. I could never see any noticeable specific differences though I kept all 3 species flying in the same room. The female has the blue a little paler than the male's and confined to the face, throat, and breast. In life the partly white feathers of the ventral region are usually so disposed as to form a rectangular white patch, clearly visible from below, between legs and vent. Juvenile male like adult female but duller and paler with, at fledging time, a shorter and black bill with a dark violet-blue tubercle at either side of the gape. Juvenile female similar but with the blue plumage a little less extensive. Mouth markings of nestling similar to those of Red-cheeked Cordon-bleu.

The above description is of nominate *U.a. angolensis* from Angola. *U.a. damarensis* is treated as a synonym of it by some authorities but specimens from Damaraland, that I have examined, are paler. The populations from Ngamiland, Barotseland west of the Zambesi and western Zimbabwe have recently been separated (Wolters, 1963) under the name *U.a. cyanopleurus*. They resemble *U.a. damarensis* but the female has blue on the flanks as well as on the breast. *U.a. niassensis*, shown on plate 8, facing p. 257, from the rest of the species' range, has a slightly longer and more pointed tail and is a warmer brown above (in both these points more resembling *U. bengalus*). Its female has the flanks as well as the breast blue, only very slightly less brightly and extensively so than the male.

See plate 8, facing p. 257.

FIELD CHARACTERS Combination of very small size and light blue and brown plumage distinguishes from all sympatric species except *U. bengalus*, the males of which have red cheek patches.

DISTRIBUTION AND HABITAT Southern and south-central Africa in Cabinda, Angola, Zaïre (Congo), Damaraland, Barotseland, Caprivi Strip, Ngamiland, Botswana (Bechuanaland), southern-eastern southern Kasai, Tanzania, Zambia, Zimbabwe, Mozambique, Transvaal and Natal. Introduced on São Tomé and Zanzibar.

Habitats much as previous species and like it often in cultivation and around human habitations (Benson & Benson). Especially characteristic of dry Acacia – thorn-veld (Skead 1975). Does not appear to have been recorded in mangroves, may occur at forest edge. Not always dependent on the presence of surface water (*fide* the Immelmanns, 1967). Requires a combination of bushes, scrub or small trees for cover and areas of bare ground or short grass for feeding (Clancey, Hall & Moreau, Heinrich, Immelmann *et al.*, McLachlan & Liversidge, Stark).

FEEDING AND GENERAL HABITS Very much as *U. bengalus* (q.v.). Feeds mainly on the ground but often catches flying

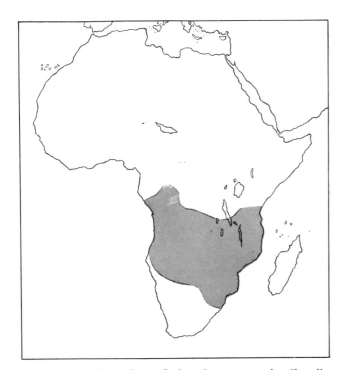

insects by taking short flights from a perch. Skead's (1975) studies showed that, in central Transvaal, seeds of the prostrate weed *Portulacea oleracea* and of the grasses *Urocloa mosambicensis* and *Sporobolus* sp. were major foods. Also taken were the seeds of *Verbene bonariensis* and *Alternanthera pungens* and of the grasses *Panicum laevifolium*, *Panicum maximum*, *Tricholaena monachne*, *Rhynchelytum repens*, the fallen, small, undeveloped fleshy fruits of the Witgat Tree, *Boscia albitrunca* and termites. Nestlings were fed largely on green seeds and termites. In the parts of South Africa and Zimbabwe where they studied it the Immelmans (1967) found that during the dry season *U. angolensis* fed almost entirely on grass seeds but at the beginning of the rainy season gradually changed over to a diet of termites. Feeding behaviour and preferences in captivity are identical with those of *U. bengalus* (Goodwin, 1959, 1965). Usually in small flocks within which only members of a pair maintain close contact though other individuals are usually within hearing. Quite often in larger flocks when not breeding and sometimes in pairs. Roosts, and rests by day, in bushes or trees, each pair usually alone in a tree or bush or at least some distance from others in it (the Immelmanns, 1967). Has been found roosting in old nests of the Masked Weaver, *Ploceus velatus* (Skead 1975).

Skead describes it as having a 'short and jerky' flight over short distances, from bush to bush, and a 'more undulating' flight over longer distances but the Immelmans (1967) say that even in the open its flight has only a suggestion of the bounding curves common to many other passerines. Hops on the ground.

Crouching in a horizontal posture with legs strongly bent was often seen from captive birds in response to large flying birds, usually Wood Pigeons, *Columba palumbus*, passing outside the window of the room in which they (the Cordon-bleus) were kept. It was also sometimes shown by an *angolensis* of either sex if I *suddenly* entered the room when it was just outside its nest entrance, never if it was perched elsewhere. Presumably this response is given in response to flying birds of prey in the wild.

NESTING Much as previous species. Nest made of grass and grass panicles, including flowering panicles of green grass, and lined with feathers. I found that nests of captive birds of this species usually contained many more feathers than those of *U. bengalus* and *U. cyanocephala* nesting in the same bird room under identical conditions. Often or perhaps most commonly semi-colonial but with each nest usually in a separate bush or clump of bushes (Immelmanns, 1967, H. H. Parker *in litt.*, Skead, 1975). Sometimes, however, perhaps when eagerness for a site near a wasps' nest overcomes aversion to close neighbours, two or more nests may be in the same bush. Gray (1945) found three active nests in one acacia tree. Two were each within two or three inches of a wasps' nest, which was between them. Of nineteen nests found by Gray in northern Malawi (Nyasaland) all were within 5 to 45 centimetres (two to eighteen inches) of a wasps' nest; the wasps involved belonged to three genera, *Polistes*, *Icuria* and *Belanogaster*. Nesting material is usually obtained in the immediate vicinity of the nest but the birds will travel several hundred metres to obtain white feathers (Immelmann). Although white and pale-coloured feathers are preferred, dark or spotted feathers are sometimes used, when they are the only ones available (Vincent, 1936, *pers. obs.*).

Three to six eggs. Building, laying and parental behaviour as *U. bengalus* (q.v.). Wild birds observed by Immelmann defended the area immediately around the nest but my captive birds (unlike my captive *U. bengalus*) defended only the nest entrance, only their personal enemies were driven from the nest's vicinity.

Skead (1975) found that in central Transvaal most breeding took place from January to June, the breeding peak occurring one or two months after the main rains. At this time green seeds and termites are plentiful.

VOICE The song is individually variable, usually rather like that of *U. bengalus* but purer, sweeter and less squeaky and sibilant in tone. 'Chreu, chreu, chittywoo, weeoo, wee!' and 'Chre-chreu, chre, chre, chittyweeoo!' were attempts to paraphrase the songs of two males.

The flight-intention calls are not, to my ears, distinguishable from those of *U. bengalus*. The contact call is essentially similar but usually distinguishable by being very much sweeter and less squeaky and sibilant in tone. The begging and loud nest calls are also similar to those of *U. bengalus* but less sibilant and squeaky-sounding. The threat call is likewise less squeaky but not always clearly distinguishable from that of *U. bengalus*.

The alarm call is, however, quite different to human ears, being a short, rattling call in which the individual notes (presumably) composing it cannot be picked out. In this it is comparable to the alarm notes of the Mistle Thrush, *Turdus viscivorus* or to the noise made by a wooden rattle. The fear screech of fledglings is a little huskier and less shrill than that of *U. bengalus*. I am not able to distinguish the buzz screech of this species from those of *U. bengalus* and *U. cyanocephala*. I have not heard the chasing call from *U. angolensis*.

All calls are used in the same situations as described for *U. bengalus*. My observations were on birds of the nominate race but such descriptions as I have found by others do not suggest any significant geographical variation in voice.

DISPLAY AND SOCIAL BEHAVIOUR As in the previous species, *U. bengalus*, except where otherwise stated here. Unpaired males leave the flock and give the stem display alone, which attracts unpaired females to them. Probably the same behaviour is shown by *U. bengalus* and *U. cyanocephala*, as their behaviour in captivity suggests, but it seems only to have been definitely noted in the wild for this species, by the Immelmanns (1967). The dominant greeting display (Goodwin, 1965) was seen often from captive birds. The bird hops or flies to the one eliciting the display, either landing beside it in a rather upright posture or actually bumping into it, usually delivering a peck at the other's head as it does so; but this peck appears to be given with closed bill and to be harmless as with the pre-copulatory pecks. Then the displaying bird, which always shows triangular head and angled tail, may hop around the other, especially if they are on the ground.

The submissive courtship display was also seen often from captives of this species though less often and only at low intensities from *U. bengalus* and *U. cyanocephala*. It is perhaps questionable whether it ought to be considered a display, as it is not very stereotyped, but it is convenient to do so and, when given at high intensity, it is very striking. The bird adopts a crouching, horizontal posture, lowers its head or (if on the ground) stretches it forward. The head feathers are erected as when soliciting allo-preening. The head is usually inclined away rather than towards than, towards the other bird and is often twisted or tilted in a way suggestive of, although less marked than, the head-twisting of begging juveniles. The wings, or the far wing only if the displaying bird is pressing up against its mate, are partly opened and violently fluttered, there is frequent or constant mandibulation. The mantle feathers may be erected. The tail is not usually aligned in any special way but may be angled *away* from the bird displayed to. Low intensity variants in which there is only slight extension and movement of one or both wings are more common and grade into a simple crouching and offering of the head (for allo-preening) without wing movements or mandibulation.

This display was seen most often and most intensely from young birds courting their first prospective mates. It is commonly shown mostly or only by the male but when a female is taking the initiative she will give this display more often than the male involved. It is seldom seen, especially at high intensity, between members of a pair that have been together some time. A male that was homosexually paired to a one-legged male did, however, give this display often during the 18 months that they were paired but was never seen to do so to a female with whom he paired after the cripple's death.

This display seems to be appeasing and submissive towards the individual at whom it is directed. A strong element of inhibited aggression is, however, involved. This is shown by the occurrence of mandibulation and the raised mantle feathers. Also, when this display is given at high intensity it is always immediately followed by an attack on an actual or potential rival or, in default of such, on some convenient scape-goat. This overt aggression is, however, never directed at the bird which has elicited the submissive courtship display. The latter, if not indifferent, responds with domineering or mildly aggressive behaviour of various kinds; the dominant greeting, allo-preening, mandibulation or (sometimes as a first response) pecking.

Ritualised sexual chases were not observed from captives of this species. In captive birds attempts to copulate forcibly with newly fledged young birds were frequent. These were only made when a young bird had only recently fledged, especially if it huddled still or was balancing unsteadily on a perch. Rape may also be attempted with sick birds, if they totter or move unsteadily (Goodwin, 1965). Males that attempt to copulate with a fledgling are immediately and fiercely attacked by its father. This behaviour is clearly homologous with the impulse to attack any copulating conspecifics and at most perhaps intensified by parental feelings. The mother never interferes with such assaults on her young and, surprisingly, I have never seen either sex attack a conspecific (or other waxbill species) that was aggressively attacking its offspring. Once a male *U. cyanocephala* dragged a protesting fledgling *U. angolensis* from its nest, flung it to the floor and flew down and pecked it there but the parents made no attempt to defend it. They behaved precisely as they would have done had I been handling a screaming fledgling, mobbing with alarm calls and flight intention movements but not attacking (though they mobbed the Blue-head from a closer distance). This was certainly not due to their being normally in any way overawed by the other species. Similar failure of other estrildids to protect their young has been noted (Kunkel, 1959). It is possible that some of the small estrildids do not actively defend their young under any circumstances because under natural conditions almost all the vertebrate nest enemies of these tiny birds are too dangerous for the adult to risk attacking.

In captivity some males readily courted females of *U. bengalus* but were not accepted by them.

OTHER NAMES Blue-breasted Waxbill, Blue Waxbill.

REFERENCES

Benson, C. W. & F. M. 1977. *The birds of Malawi*. Limbe, Malawi.
Clancey, P. A. 1964. *The birds of Natal and Zululand*. Edinburgh.

Goodwin, D. 1959. Observations on Blue-breasted Waxbills. *Avicult. Mag.* **65**: 194–169.

Goodwin, D. 1965. A comparative study of captive blue waxbills (Estrildidae). *Ibis* **107**: 285–315.

Gray, W. J. 1945. Some notes on the nesting of certain birds in northern Nyasaland. *Ostrich* **16**: 49–54.

Heinrich, G. 1958. Zur Verbreitung und Lebensweise der Vögel von Angola. *J. Orn.* **99**: 309–421.

Immelmann, K., Steinbacher, J. & Wolters, H. E. 1964. *Vögel in Käfig und Voliere, Prachtfinken*: 234–241.

Immelmann, K. & G. 1967. Verhaltensökologische Studien an afrikanischen und australischen Estrildiden. *Zool. Jb. Syst. Bd.* **94**: 609–686.

Kunkel, P. 1959. Zum Verhalten einiger Prachtfinken (Estrildinae). *Z. Tierpsychol* **16**: 302–350.

McLachlan, G. R. & Liversidge, R. 1957. *Roberts' birds of South Africa*. Cape Town.

Skead, D. M. 1975. Ecological studies of four estrildines in the Central Transvaal. *Ostrich* suppl. no. 11.

Vincent, J. 1935. The birds of Northern Portuguese East Africa. *Ibis* 13th ser., **5**: 485–529.

Wolters, H. E. 1963. *Uraeginthus angolensis cyanopleurus* subsp. nov. *J. Orn.* **104**: 185–190.

Blue-headed Cordon-bleu
Uraeginthus cyanocephala

Estrilda cyanocephala Richmond, 1897, *Auk*, **14**: 157.

DESCRIPTION Very slightly larger than *U. bengalus* (q.v.) and resembling it except as follows: Head appears proportionately rather larger and rounder, with a slightly stouter bill with a slightly less curved culmen. Usually carries itself a little more upright. Entire head blue like the face, breast and flanks. Brown of upper parts of a warmer, more reddish tone. Centre of lower breast and under tail coverts a warm buffish brown with which the rectangular fluffy white ventral patch contrasts strongly. This latter feature is very conspicuous when looked at from below. Bill crimson, scarlet or deep pink at base, darkening to very dark red or blackish at the tip. Irides light chestnut, brownish red or red. Legs and feet a paler dull flesh colour or fleshy brown than those of *U. bengalus*.

Female paler than male in both the blue and brown areas, the sexual difference in depth of colour being more marked than in *U. bengalus*. The blue on the sides of her head extends to above the eye but the top of her head is brown, usually with some blue on the forehead and sometimes with a few blue or blue-tinged feathers on the crown. Blue on the flanks usually less extensive than in the male, sometimes with only a little blue in this region. Bill usually paler than male's but sometimes as deep a red as even red-billed males.

Juvenile male like adult female in plumage but duller and often with the blue less extensive. Juvenile females often have only the cheeks blue but some of them have blue on the breast and forehead also. In captivity (in England), juveniles attain adult plumage at about 4·5 to 5·5 months old. Nestlings have mouth markings similar to those of *U. bengalus* and *U. angolensis* but lack the blue or violet gape tubercles. Young nestlings have pinkish flesh skin and pale reddish fawn down. At fledging time the juvenile has the bill grey at the base and black at the end, not all black as in *U. bengalus* and *U. angolensis*. The legs and feet of those I have bred have been dull fleshy grey or dull mauvish grey at fledging, soon becoming browner and paler, but Grunder observed young with blue (=bluish grey?) legs and feet. Irides dark greyish. In all three species the fledgling's eye looks dark and lustrous with the iris not readily distinguishable from the pupil at a little distance.

See plate 8, facing p. 257.

FIELD CHARACTERS Entirely bright blue head distinguishes male from *U. bengalus* (and all other small birds). Females and juveniles probably not distinguishable from *U. bengalus* except at very close quarters or when in company with adult male(s).

DISTRIBUTION AND HABITAT Northern Kenya, southern Somalia and adjacent regions of Abyssinia, south through eastern Kenya to Dodoma and Kilosa in Tanzania. Inhabits arid country with bushes and/or trees, usually acacias or thorn scrub.

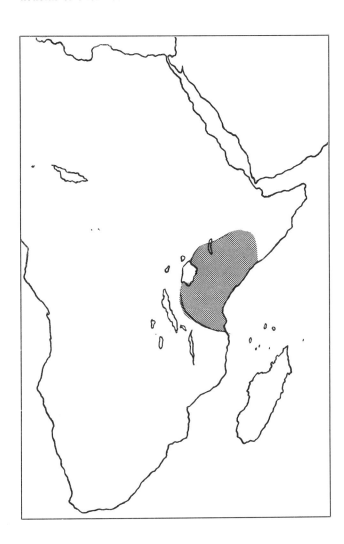

FEEDING AND GENERAL HABITS Feeding habits as *U. bengalus*
so far as recorded. In captivity tends to take a larger
amount of white millet but its tastes are otherwise as those
of the Red-cheeked Cordon-bleu (q.v.). Known to take
grass seeds picked up from the ground and termites. Often
knocks open the earthen tunnels, that termites build up
acacia saplings, in order to get at the insects (Moreau &
Moreau). In captivity swallows rather more (not all) of the
panicum millet and white millet that it eats without first
shelling it.

Usually in pairs or small parties, sometimes in association with *U. bengalus* (Beals 1966, Evans 1972),
occasionally in larger flocks. Anting movements, usually
brief or abortive, have been seen from captive birds in
response to millipedes and centipedes (Goodwin, 1971).

This species and *U. angolensis* are often said to be
hardier, or less delicate, in captivity than is *U. bengalus*. My
limited experience has been that there is no difference
between them if they are initially healthy but that it was
easier to purchase specimens of *U. cyanocephala* and *U.
angolensis* that were not *already* ill than was the case with
U. bengalus. I suspect that because the two former species
fetched higher prices and were not ex/imported in such
vast numbers, they usually got less harmful treatment
between being caught in Africa and sold in Europe.

NESTING Wild nests have been described as being oval or
barrel-shaped with the entrance low down at the side,
made of grass and always placed within a foot or two of a
hornets' nest in bushes or low trees. Four to six eggs.
Recorded breeding from November to January, in March
and April, and in June in northern Tanzania and in
February in Kenya (Mackworth-Praed & Grant, 1960,
Thomas 1960).

When coconot fibres were available to my captive birds
they used fewer feathers in the nest lining, in a few nests
which I examined in detail, there was a distinct inner part
of fibres and a few feathers in the bottom part of the nests.
Incubation period about 11 days. Newly hatched young
have reddish skin and the *fawn* down (which soon fades) of
a more reddish hue than that of *U. bengalus*. Young (in
captivity) usually fledge at 18 days, less often at 17 or 19
days. They are, like their congeners, able to fly *up*wards
from the nest when they first leave it.

VOICE The song is variable but it is uncertain whether or
not major variations are geographical rather than
individual. It is less squeaky in sound than the song of *U.
bengalus*, delivered at a slower tempo than those of either
U. bengalus or *U. angolensis* and is a mixture of sweet and
plaintive notes and others that are husky and rather
harsh. I paraphrased the song of one male as: 'Teu, skurr!
tsee-ee-wee-see-see, skurr, teh-teh'; the opening not very
plaintive and sweet, the immediately following 'skurr'
harsh and husky, then a jumble of soft notes followed by
another harsh note and then two long, sweet notes at the
end. The songs of females are similar to but usually shorter
than those of males. The differences between the songs
of two wild-caught males (which had very similar songs)

and those of another bought from the same dealer a year
later were, to my ears, at least as different as between the
latter's song and those of *U. bengalus* and *U. angolensis*.
Song and other calls are, except where otherwise stated
below, used in the same situations as by *U. bengalus* (q.v.).

The contact call is rather lower in pitch than in the
other cordon-bleus, neither so squeaky as that of *U.
bengalus* nor so sweet-sounding as that of *U. angolensis*. A
version in which two notes are given together, the first
very short – 'tse-tseeuu' is common, especially from
females. In spite of their great similarity and the amount of
variation shown, the contact calls of this species and *U.
angolensis* are almost always readily distinguishable.
Those of *U. bengalus* are somewhat intermediate in sound
although usually more squeaky than either.

The begging call is less loud than in the two previous
species, more sibilant and 'silvery' in tone and running up
and down the scale in a manner that makes it very
suggestive of the begging calls of fledged young tits, *Parus*
spp. When given at very high intensity by young
approaching independence the begging call is very similar
to and perhaps the precursor of the chasing call of the
adult male.

One form of nest call, is a high pitched 'chee-chee-chee'
and (more often) softer variants. This is doubtless the
homologous nest call to those of *U. bengalus* and *U.
angolensis*. Rather more often, however, *U. cyanocephala*
nest calls with a soft, throaty-sounding 'tchet-tchet' or
'Tchrut-tchrut' or, at lower intensity, a very soft 'inward
sounding' ticking note. These calls do not differ, to my
ears, to the same sounds when used in threat. A male that
is uttering the first type of nest calling usually changes
over to the 'tchet' or 'tchrut' notes when his mate or
prospective mate comes right up to the nest or nest site.

In threat the 'Tchet' or 'tchrut' calls may be given
rather louder and in quicker tempo than is usual when
nest-calling. The threat calls of females tend to be higher
pitched and to differ less than do the male's from the
homologous threat calls of *U. bengalus* and *U. angolensis*.

The alarm call is a harsh, emphatic 'Tchek-tchek-tchek'
the number of 'tcheks' and the emphasis with which they
are given varying greatly but with each component
'tchek' note always quite distinct, the general tempo being
much the same as in the 'chink' alarm call of the
Blackbird, *Turdus merula*. Thus in this species the alarm
call only differs from the threat call in being given rather
more loudly, harshly and emphatically.

The fear screech of handled fledglings is similar to but
rather higher in pitch than those of *U. bengalus* and *U.
angolensis*. The buzz-screech is like that of its congeners. It is normally used in the same situations as by *U.
bengalus* (q.v.) but I have heard it given on a few occasion
by males driving other birds from their nest site. The
chasing call is huskier and less squeaky in sound than that
of *U. bengalus*. It usually consists of a preliminary single,
loud, harsh note followed by a string of similar but less
loud and less drawn-out notes strung together, and has an
exasperated tone; 'tchaa! tcheh-tcheh-tcheh-tcheh-

tcheh'. It is subject to much variation and sometimes the initial note may be shorter instead of (as is more usual) longer than the string of notes that follow it. It is given as an alternative to song perhaps more often and regularly than by *U. bengalus*. Usually the bird giving it in song equivalent partly erects its body plumage and makes the triangular head. Evans (1972) gives sonagrams of alarm and contact calls of this species.

DISPLAY AND SOCIAL BEHAVIOUR As in *U. bengalus* (q.v.) except where otherwise stated here.

The courtship display differs from that of *U. bengalus* and *U. angolensis* in that the head tends to be more turned towards the bird displayed to, it is thrown less far back in the upward movement and comes further down in the forward movement (see sketch p. 40). One has the impression that *U. cyanocephala* is bowing or nodding whereas the other two species appear to throw up their heads. The difference is, of course, correlated with the head adornments, *U. bengalus* and *U. angolensis* having brightly coloured cheeks but *U. cyanocephala* also a blue forehead and crown and red culmen to display.

In this species driving or sexual chasing seems to be more frequent and more highly ritualised. When chasing the female the male usually erects his head and body feathers to such an extent that he gives the impression of a bright blue ball flying after her. Sometimes I have had the impression that, although other contour feathers appeared simply to be erected, the triangular head was made when chasing. Once, when two captive females were fighting on the floor of the bird room, the mate of one of them came close, looked at them as they grappled fiercely, then darted at them, *pecked his own mate* and, having thus separated them, drove her off, flying after her with erected plumage and giving the chasing call. Possibly the behaviour of the females suggested a sexual assault sufficiently to arouse the male's jealousy, his behaviour was clearly that which he would have used to separate his mate from another male and not a case of coming to her assistance in a fight.

Both sexes of this species imprint readily, although not always irrevocably, on *U. bengalus*, if they have been reared by them. If, by accident or design, they hatch or are given mixed broods of both species, they will rear them, both in the nest and after fledging without showing discrimination, in spite of the differences in voice and appearance of the young.

OTHER NAMES Blue-headed Waxbill, Blue-capped Cordon-bleu.

REFERENCES
Beals, E. W. 1966. Sight additions to the avifaunal list of Ethiopia. *Jl. E.Afr. nat. Hist. Soc. natn. Mus.* **25**: 227–228.
Evans, S. M. 1972. Specific distinctiveness in the calls of cordon bleus (*Uraeginthus* spp.; Estrildidae). *Anim. Behav.* **20**: 571–579.
Goodwin, D. 1962. Some notes on my Blue-headed Waxbills (*Uraeginthus cyanocephalus*). *Avicult. Mag.* **68**: 117–128.
Goodwin, D. 1965. A comparative study of blue waxbills (Estrildidae). *Ibis* **107**: 285–315.
Goodwin, D. 1971a. Imprinting, or otherwise, in some cross-fostered Red-cheeked and Blue-headed Cordon-bleus. *Avicult. Mag.* **77**: 26–31.
Goodwin, D. 1971b. Anting by Red-cheeked and Blue-headed Cordon-bleus. *Avicult. Mag.* **77**: 88–93.
Grunder, A. 1963. Blauköpfige Schmetterlingsfinken. *Gef. Welt* **1963**: 49–50.
Immelmann, K., Steinbacher, J. & Wolters, H. E. 1964. *Vögel in Käfig und Voliere: Prachtfinken*: 216–234.
Mackworth-Praed, C. W. & Grant, C. H. B. 1960. *The African handbook of birds*, ser. 1, vol. 2, 2nd ed. London
Moreau, R. E. & W. M. 1939. Observations on some East African birds. *Ibis* (14) **3**: 296–323.
Thomas, D. K. 1960. Notes on birds breeding in Tanganyika. *Tang. Notes and Records* **55**: 225–243.

Violet-eared Waxbill   *Uraeginthus granatina*

Fringilla granatina Linnaeus, *Syst. Nat.* ed. 12, **1**, p. 319.

DESCRIPTION Rather slender in shape but with quite large bill and strongly graduated and long tail (see p. 9 for measurements). A cobalt blue band across the front of the forehead extends into a narrow 'eyebrow' over each eye. Cheeks and ear coverts a bright but very delicate shade of violet-purple. Throat and a stripe from the base of the upper mandible to the eye black. Wings dull greyish brown with faint reddish brown or reddish fawn fringes to most feathers. Lower belly blackish. Lower rump and upper tail coverts deep shining cobalt blue. Under tail coverts a similar but less bright blue. Tail black, tinged with blue on fringes of feathers. Rest of upper and under parts a deep chestnut except on the lower mantle and back which are usually paler and browner. Bill usually bright red, sometimes purplish red. Irides and eye rims red or orange. Legs and feet dark purplish grey, slate grey or blackish.

Female very much paler all over than male. Blue on forehead less extensive, much paler and tinged with purple where it extends over the eye. Purple on face paler and less brilliant. Blue on rump less bright and no blue on under tail coverts, which are pale buff. Most of forehead, crown and nape pale chestnut or warm brown, shading to dull greyish brown on mantle and back. Wings like male's. Underparts pale creamy buff to brownish buff, paler on throat and under tail coverts and often darkening to light reddish brown on the breast. Much minor individual variation. Soft parts as male's but often paler.

Recently fledged juvenile like female but duller, with buffish brown or greyish brown head and no red, purple or blue except for a little dull purplish blue on the rump and upper tail coverts. Bill and eye rims blackish, iris brown.

The young nestling has blackish skin and long, whitish down. Its palate is largely orange and its tongue orange or yellow crossed with a black band. The palate pattern is of the 5-spot type but with the 2 lower spots small or absent. It has blue gape tubercles (Hoesch & Niethammer, Immelmann *et al.*).

Nicolai (1968) was the first to describe the remarkable early partial moult of this species (and *U. ianthinogaster*). When between 24 and 35 days old the juvenile sheds the feathers of all (and only those) parts of the head that are purple, blue or black in the adult. At the completion of this moult (which is very quick as all the feathers involved are shed and grow at the same time) both sexes have their faces coloured like those of adults of the same sex but are otherwise in juvenile plumage. The complete moult to adult dress does not take place until several weeks later.

See plate 1, facing p. 96.

FIELD CHARACTERS Combination of small size, long tail and predominantly chestnut (male) or buffish (female) plumage with red bill and touches of purple and blue at once distinguish it from all sympatric species. From its allopatric relative, *U. ianothinogaster*, the lack of blue patches (male) or white spots (female) on the underparts would identify it.

DISTRIBUTION AND HABITAT Southern Africa in Angola, Botswana (Bechuanaland), Zambia, Zimbabwe, Mosambique and South Africa. Inhabits dry thorn scrub, tangles of thorn and other cover along streams and dry river beds, open Acacia and other woodland, usually with some thorn undercover, and sometimes equivalent cultivated areas. Often in waterless country.

FEEDING AND GENERAL HABITS Feeds largely on the ground but also quite often in bushes, trees or other vegetation. Will (*fide* Skead, 1975) hold grass panicles under foot while feeding from them. Skead, who made a detailed study of the species in central Transvaal, found that in winter seeds of the prostrate weed *Portulaca oleracea* and of

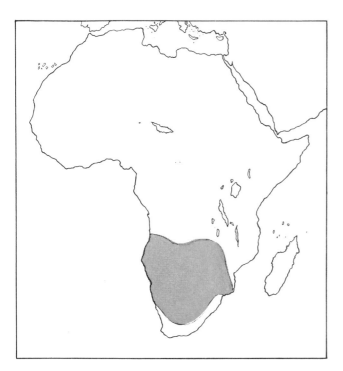

grasses of the genus *Aristida* were major foods. Seeds of *Alternanthera pungens* and of the grasses *Tragus beteronianus*, *Panicum laevifolium*, *P. maximum*, *Urochloa mosambicensis*, *Brachiara nigropedata*, *Digitaria argyrograpta*, *Tricholaena monachne*, *Rhynchelytrum repens*, *Setaria perennis*, *Cenchrus siliaris*, *Chloris pycnothrix*, *Egrarostis lehmanniana*, *E. barbinodis* and *Trichoneura grandiglumis*. Nectar of *Aloe davyana*, the small underdeveloped fruits of *Boscia albitrunca*, and flowers of the grasses *Urochloa* and *Rhynchelytrum* and termites were also taken. Small green caterpillars are also eaten and, probably, any small soft-bodied insects of non-poisonous species.

The Immelmanns (1967) found that in the area they studied it termites were the main food during the dry season and circumstantial evidence suggested that it habitually went without drinking for many weeks and perhaps for the entire dry season. It will, however, often come to water when available.

Usually in pairs, single birds (mate sitting or recently killed?), or family parties. Two or more families of recently-fledged young may associate (Payne). Occasionally in larger parties or in company with *U. angolensis* or other waxbills. Such associations are probably usually fortuitous although in Mashonaland Irwin found it 'invariably' in association with *U. angolensis*. The Immelmanns found that each pair kept within an area of several hundred square metres, from which intruding conspecifics were promptly driven out. In captivity more than one pair cannot be kept in the same aviary as (unless they are ill) they will not tolerate other conspecifics or the closely related *U. ianthinogaster*; very often they will not even tolerate the less closely related cordon-bleus.

This is apparently one of the most delicate of waxbills in captivity, requiring a varied assortment of animal food at all times and being much more sensitive to low temperatures, temperature changes and humidity than are most African estrildids, even although in a wild state it is found where the night temperatures often drop to below freezing point. It is therefore the more notable that the first specimen brought alive to Europe, a male that was given in 1754 to the Marquise de Pompadour, was kept alive by her for three years. Doubtless she had a happy combination of wealth, ample spare time and real fondness and feeling for birds, *all* of which are likely to be needed by anyone wishing to keep this species with success.

NESTING Nest usually 60 cm to 2 metres (2 to 6 feet) above ground in a thorn or (less often) some other bush or shrub. It is rounded with a side entrance that often has a slight porch projecting above it. It is built of grass stems or similar materials and lined with feathers. Phillips (1907) found that captive birds used green grass, torn up by the roots, in preference to dry grass and preferred rather large, curled feathers to smaller ones. A large feather is often so placed that it blocks or obscures the nest entrance (Hoesch & Niethammer). In captivity Phillips (1907) found that the male collected the materials and did most of the building, the female only occasionally building with materials her mate had brought. Two to five eggs. Both sexes incubate and brood by turns in the usual way. The male is said always to bring a feather when he comes to take over a spell on the nest (Immelmann *et al.*) but probably this depends on his being able to find one readily. Incubation period 12–13 days, young fledge at 16 days (Immelmann *et al.*, 1964). Found breeding in South Africa and Zimbabwe from January to May, as late as June in the northern Transvaal, and in January and February in Zambia. Regularly parasitised by the Shaft-tailed Whydah, *Vidua regia* – of 15 nests found by Skead, 5 had been parasitised.

VOICE The fullest description of the voice of this species, that I have read, is by Nicolai (in Immelmann *et al.*, 1964) from which the following is taken except where otherwise indicated.

The male has a twittering song, which ends in fluting tones and suggests the song of the Swallow, *Hirundo rustica*. He is particularly prone to sing at dusk. In aggressive threat he utters a harsh 'chay-chay-chay'. Phillips (1907) may perhaps refer to a variant of this when he writes: 'the murder-call is "psis" or "psit" uttered loudly and continuously (by the male pursuing a non-resisting rival). The excitement (and mobbing?) call is like the hard "tsek" of the Common Firefinch, *Lagonosticta senegala*. A varying series of these excitement calls is used by the male as a greeting to the female and answered by her with an individually varying, sonorous strophe of 8 or 9 notes that is characterised by having 2 clear, fluting notes in the middle and at the end. There is also a short call "tsyeet" (my anglicisation throughout), perhaps the same as the low, repeated "tsit" described by Phillips (1906) and from the latter's description evidently a flight-intention call. He also describes a "squee" or "squwish", uttered by the male only; and (1907) soft and sweet "rolling" notes, used, together with building movements, when enticing the female to the beginnings of a nest he has built, and a wagtail-like "chissick" used as "a note of warning of the presence of a stranger or any strange or dangerous object or creature".'

DISPLAY AND SOCIAL BEHAVIOUR I have not found any detailed description of the courtship display but it is almost certainly similar or identical to that of the Purple Grenadier (q.v.) and, as in that species, the female often joins the display as Phillips (1906) writes '... when dancing to one another, or one to the other, ... with something in the bill held at one end after the approved waxbill fashion, they often dance on the ground, and so are able to go round and round one another ...' Other displays seem not to have been described although the species has often been bred in captivity. Its territorial behaviour has been noticed under the 'General Habits' section above.

OTHER NAMES Grenadier Waxbill, Grenadier.

REFERENCES

Clancey, P. A. 1964. *The birds of Natal and Zululand.* Edinburgh and London.
Hoesch, W. & Niethammer, G. 1940. Die Vogelwelt Deutsch – Südwestafrikas. *J. Orn.* **88**: Sonderheft.
Immelmann, K. & G. 1967. Verhaltensökologische Studien an afrikanischen und australischen Estrildiden. *Zool. Jb. Syst. Bd.* **94**: 609–686.
Immelmann, K., Steinbacher, J. & Wolters, H. E. 1964. *Vögel in Käfig und Voliere, Prachtfinken:* 253–267.
Irwin, M. P. S. 1953. Notes on some birds of Mashonaland, Southern Rhodesia. *Ostrich* **24**: 37–49.
Mackworth-Praed, C. W. & Grant, C. H. B. 1963. *African handbook of birds,* ser. 1, vol. 2. London.
McLachlan, G. R. & Liversidge, R. 1957. *Roberts birds of South Africa.* Cape Town.
Nicolai, J. 1965. *Käfig- und Volierenvögel.* Kosmos, Stuttgart.
Nicolai, J. 1967. Die isolierte Frühmauser der Farbmerkmale des Kopfgefieders bei *Uraeginthus granatinus* (L.) und *U. ianthinogaster* Reichw. (Estrildidae). *Z. Tierpsychol.* **25**: 854–861.
Payne, R. B. 1970. The mouth markings of juvenal *Vidua regia* and *Uraeginthus granatinus.* *Bull. Brit. Orn. Club.* **90**: 16–18.
Phillips, R. 1906. The Violet-eared Waxbill. *Avicult. Mag.* New Series **4**: 295–306.
Phillips, R. 1907. Further notes on the Violet-eared Waxbill. *Avicult. Mag.* New Series **5**: 325–339.
Skead, D. M. 1975. Ecological studies of four estrildines in the Central Transvaal. *Ostrich* suppl. no. 11.

Purple Grenadier   *Uraeginthus ianthinogaster*

Uraeginthus ianthinogaster Reichenow 1879.

DESCRIPTION About size of previous species or slightly larger; less slender and with proportionately slightly shorter tail. Looks a less elegant and (in my eyes) less beautiful bird. Face immediately above, around and below eyes deep bright blue, less bright and tinged with mauve at the lower periphery. Rest of head, neck and throat a deep rufous or chestnut brown, not quite so dark as that of *U. granatina*, shading into reddish earth brown on the mantle

and back. Wings darker dull brown, most feathers edged dull rufous. Lower rump and upper tail coverts deep bright slightly mauvish blue. Under tail coverts dark greyish with mauvish blue feather tips. Tail black, often strongly tinged with purplish blue on the feather fringes. Breast and underparts, except for the dull greyish ventral area, a deep shining purplish blue, marked with chestnut brown. The chestnut markings usually take the form of an irregular band across the lower breast, often with some subsidiary blotches lower down. The blue colour is on the ends of the feathers so its amount is also affected by wear. Some individuals have the underparts below the throat uniformly blue or nearly so but most have a patchy appearance, suggesting some domesticated variety rather than a wild species. Bill red or pinkish red, often with a purplish sheen, often with the base or greater part of the upper mandible dusky or blackish. Irides and eye-rims red, yellow irides once recorded. Legs and feet dark greyish to black.

Female a paler and duller rufous on head and neck. Blue around eyes less extensive and of a pale mauve hue, sometimes with some of the small feathers white or partly white. Brown of back a little greyer than male's. Ventral area and under tail coverts barred fawnish and dull grey. Rest of underparts pale reddish brown, a little deeper on the breast than elsewhere. Dull white subterminal marks on the feathers form a spotted and barred pattern on breast, belly and flanks. Soft parts as male's but perhaps averaging paler.

Juvenile male like adult female but a little paler and duller with no white markings on the underparts or mauve on the face. Juvenile female similar but paler. Bills of juveniles dusky or blackish, legs and feet paler than adult's. There is an early partial moult of the head feathers, as in *U. granatina* (q.v.), at which the young acquire the blue (male) or pale mauve (female) feathers round the eyes.

Nestling very like that of previous species. Nicolai (1969) gives a fine close up photo of a nestling, showing its mouth.

The above description is of the nominate form from central, eastern and southern Kenya and part of Tanzania. *U.i. hawkeri*, from the south-eastern Sudan, southern Abyssinia, Uganda and northern Kenya, is a little paler on the brown and chestnut parts and the male's back is more reddish brown. *U.i. roosevelti*, from Western Kenya is a little darker than nominate *U.i. ianthinogaster*, the feathers around the female's eyes are usually of a darker mauve and her underparts may be washed with mauve. The races all intergrade and there is much individual variation.

There has been much disagreement as to how many races of this species, and which, should be recognised. I here follow Mackworth-Praed & Grant (1960) whose decisions in the matter, though not the latest, seem to me the best.

FIELD CHARACTERS Combination of purplish blue and chestnut plumage and red bill (male) or deep blue rump and blackish tail (both sexes) separate it from all sympatric species. From the allopatric *U. granatina* by largely blue breast and underparts (male) or white spotting and barring on underparts (female).

DISTRIBUTION AND HABITAT Northern Somalia, southern Abyssinia, south-eastern Sudan, north-eastern Uganda, Kenya and Tanzania south to Iringa. Inhabits arid country, usually in thick thorn scrub or aloes but sometimes in more open bushy country.

FEEDING AND GENERAL HABITS Feeds at least in part on the ground, commonly in open areas near cover but little recorded of its feeding or other habits in the wild. Known to take grass seeds but probably takes termites and other insects also. In captivity takes some species of insects, small spiders and whiteworms eagerly and also takes some green food (Immelmann *et al.*).

Usually in pairs or small parties in the wild, single birds frequently seen. These latter are probably birds whose mates are on nest or who have been recently bereaved.

In captivity its behaviour and care are very similar to that of and for the Violet-eared Waxbill (q.v.) but it appears to be rather less delicate. It is usually peaceable towards other small birds except other *Uraeginthus* species which, cordon-bleus included, are often persistently attacked.

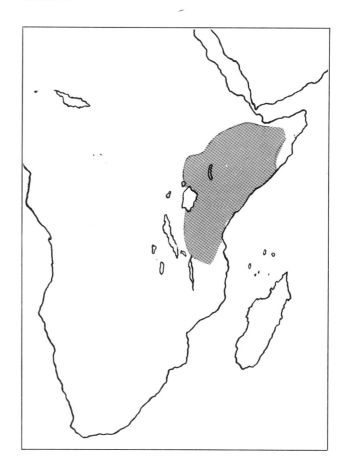

NESTING A loosely put together roundish nest with side entrance, lined with feathers and placed low down in a bush or shrub. Three to five eggs, in captivity usually four. Has been recorded breeding in March and April in southern Kenya and in December, January and February in northern Tanzania. Is parasitised by Fischer's Whydah, *Vidua fischeri*. In captivity, and probably in a wild state also, both sexes build. The male continues to bring feathers to line the nest throughout incubation. Both sexes incubate in turn by day but the hen only at night.

VOICE Calls and song quite distinct from those of *U. granatina*. Has two very different types of song. One consists of nine musical, far-reaching notes and functions to contact and call the bird's mate back to it. It is used by both sexes. The other, uttered only by the male consists of a strophe beginning with soft crackling and buzzing sounds and ending in a trill. Excitement and greeting calls similar to those of *U. granatina* but softer, the female's answering greeting is a short strophe which differs in sound and structure from that of *U. granatina*. Evans (1972) recorded a high-pitched rattling alarm call which was commonly used and a more rarely used (presumed) alarm call that consisted of a 'series of more easily distinguishable segments'. He gives sonagrams of these and other calls of the species. The above information, and that following on display is Immelmann *et al.* (1964) except where otherwise stated. A record on sale in Germany (Kosmos-Schallplatte no. 75-09325) gives both songs and calls (Nicolai, 1965). Nest call a series of very soft sounding notes, repeatedly interspersed with short contact trills.

DISPLAY AND SOCIAL BEHAVIOUR Courtship display similar to that of the cordon-bleus but usually performed on the ground. The male holds a stem or feather in his bill and, as he bobs up and down, begins to sing and to bow his head alternately to either side at an angle of about 45 degrees. The female alights beside him and either gives the greeting display with tail twist and head towards him or also begins to display. Copulation appears only to have been seen following occasions when the female joined in the display. Only when the female is relatively or quite disinterested does the male fly after her among the branches with material in his bill and display at her (Nicolai in Immelmann *et al.*, 1964). Nest-seeking and nest-calling behaviour as in cordon-bleus.

OTHER NAME Purple Waxbill.

REFERENCES

Archer, G. & Godman, E. M. 1961. *The birds of British Somaliland and the Gulf of Aden*, vol. 4. Edinburgh and London.

Boosey, E. J. 1958. Breeding of the Purple Grenadier Waxbill (*Granatina ianthinogaster*) at the Keston Foreign Bird Farm. *Avicult. Mag.* 64: 164–166.

Evans, S. M. 1972. Specific distinctiveness in the calls of cordon-bleus (*Uraeginthus* spp.: Estrildidae). *Anim. Behav.* 20: 571–579.

Immelmann, K., Steinbacher, J. & Wolters, H. E. 1964. *Vögel in Käfig und Voliere: Prachtfinken*: 245–253. Aachen, Germany.

Mackworth-Praed, C. W. & Grant, C. H. B. 1960. *African handbook of Birds*, ser. 1, vol. 2. London.

Nicolai, J. 1965. *Käfig und Volierenvögel*. Stuttgart.

Nicolai, J. 1969. Beobachtungen an Paradieswitwen (*Steganura obtusa* Chapin) und der Strohwitwe (*Tetraenura fischeri*) Reichenow in Ostafrika. *J. Orn.* 110: 421–447.

Schwarz, H. 1964. Purpurgranatastrilde und ihre Brut. *Die Gefiederte Welt* 1964: 55–57.

The typical, swee and lavender waxbills

The genus *Estrilda* includes all those species that are commonly thought of as more or less typical waxbills. Among them are the Common, Black-rumped and Orange-cheeked Waxbills, which were early imported into Europe and whose sealing wax-like red bills inspired their English name.

Most species of *Estrilda* show a fine dark and light barred pattern, which may be very distinct or only faintly indicated, on part or most of their adult plumage. They feed mainly on the seeds of grasses and obtain much of their food direct from the growing plants; they are extremely agile and they habitually hold objects under foot when feeding or manipulating nesting material. They build rather large nests with a tubular entrance and, usually, a cock's nest on top or alongside the real nest. The Swee Waxbill, *Estrilda melanotis* and the lavender waxbills, *E. caerulescens*, *E. perreini* and *E. thomensis* diverge in some respects from this general picture but I concur with Traylor (in *Peters' check-list*) in thinking that, as they are most closely allied to other *Estrilda* species, they are best included with them in that genus.

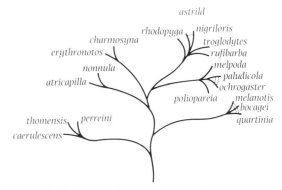

Probable affinities within the typical waxbills, genus *Estrilda*. See text also. Dotted lines connect members of a superspecies, two dotted lines very distinct races of the same species.

The Common Waxbill, *Estrilda astrild*, Black-lored Waxbill, *E. nigriloris*, Rosy-rumped Waxbill, *E. rhodopyga*, Black-rumped Waxbill, *E. troglodytes*, and Arabian Waxbill, *E. rufibarba* form a species group of very similar and clearly closely-related forms. They are all mainly brownish or greyish in colour, a pattern of fine cross-barring on most of the plumage and a conspicuous red or (one form only) black eye-stripe. All build rather large, compact nests with an entrance tube and a cock's nest on top or (less often) alongside it. There is considerable geographic overlap between *E. astrild* and *E. rhodopyga*, although where both occur there seems usually to be habitat and/or altitudinal differences between them. With this exception members of this species group are mainly, but not entirely, allopatric in distribution (Hall & Moreau). There is strong circumstantial evidence, but as yet no proof, that all the African forms share the parasitic attentions of the Pin-tailed Whydah, *Vidua macroura*.

The Black-lored Waxbill is clearly closely related to the Common Waxbill, from which it differs most strikingly in its shorter and black, not red, eye-stripe. It has, so far as is known, only a very small range and is entirely surrounded by *E. astrild*, with which it is completely allopatric. That *E. nigriloris* has derived from *astrild* stock seems almost certain and some ornithologists have treated it as a race of *E. astrild*. However, the very differently coloured face might well act as an isolating mechanism, should the two ever come into contact and we have in the genus the example in *E. nonnula* and *E. atricapilla* of two forms very similar in appearance, and almost certainly of recent common ancestry, that behave as good species where they are (now) sympatric. I prefer, therefore, to treat *E. astrild* and *E. nigriloris* as members of a superspecies rather than as conspecific though admitting that further and more detailed studies might prove this a wrong decision.

The Arabian Waxbill, *E. rufibarba*, has sometimes been treated as a race of the Black-rumped Waxbill, *E. troglodytes*, which it resembles in its mainly black rump and tail. This is a rather striking common character but in some other features *E. rufibarba* more closely resembles other members of the *astrild* species group. Thus in its very pronounced cross-barring it is closer to *E. astrild* while (more importantly, I think) in its relatively large and mainly dark but parti-coloured bill and in the lack of any pink or red tinge on its underparts it is closest to the Rosy-rumped Waxbill, *E. rhodopyga*. These four species (and *E. nigriloris*) are all closely allied and, on its presently known characters, *E. rufibarba* seems to me as likely to represent some stock ancestral to both *E. troglodytes* and *E. rhodopyga* (and possibly also *E. astrild*) as to be a race or representative of *E. troglodytes*. I therefore follow Hall & Moreau in treating it as a separate species.

The Orange-cheeked Waxbill, *E. melpoda*, and the Fawn-breasted Waxbill, *E. paludicola*, are very similar in plumage pattern and coloration. They are found in similar habitats and are mainly allopatric but occur together in part of the Middle Congo and have been collected at the same place in two other areas (Hall & Moreau). Where they co-exist, and throughout most of their respective ranges, they differ most obviously in *E. melpoda* having a bright orange and *E. paludicola* a nondescript greyish face. The very distinct north-eastern race of the Fawn-breasted Waxbill, *E. paludicola ochrogaster*, shows some approach to *E. melpoda*, in having a golden-buff face, sometimes deepening almost to orange around the eyes, but its coloration is otherwise less like that of *E. melpoda* than that

of other races of *E. paludicola*. It is possible that it may be nearing or even have reached specific level but on present knowledge it seems best treated as a race of *E. paludicola* and the latter and *E. melpoda* as distinct but closely related species.

The Anambra Waxbill, *E. poliopareia*, is sometimes treated, as by Traylor in *Peters' Check List*, as a race of *E. paludicola*. It is known only from a relatively small part of southern Nigeria, where it co-exists with *E. melpoda*, but is far from the nearest areas where *E. paludicola* is known to occur. Superficially it is most like *E. paludicola ochrogaster*, the form of *paludicola* geographically furthest from it, but differs from *E. paludicola ochrogaster* and from those forms of *E. paludicola* that are geographically nearest to it as follows: it has a deeper, blunter-looking bill; its rump and upper tail coverts are bright orange-red to bright vermilion instead of scarlet to orangy-carmine (*ochrogaster*) or scarlet to rosy carmine (other forms of *paludicola*); the ventral patch is entirely buff, not tinged or tipped with rose-red or pink; the upper flanks and sides of the breast of the male are usually washed with dull red; and the irides are (always?) cream-coloured not red or reddish brown. I concur with Hall & Moreau in thinking that, on present evidence, *E. poliopareia* is best given specific rank. Hall & Moreau point out that it and the *astrild* species-group are allopatric and say they are not convinced that its affinities may not be with this group rather than the *melpoda* species-group. This may be so but I think that its characters do indicate that it is most closely related to *E. melpoda* and *E. poliopareia* and I therefore include it in the same species-group with them.

The Black-crowned Waxbill, *E. nonnula*, and the Black-headed Waxbill, *E. atricapilla* have, despite their names, an identical and 'cap-like' distribution of black on their heads. They are otherwise very similar although *E. atricapilla* is a little darker, has more extensive and brighter red on its flanks and an entirely black instead of black and red upper mandible. Over much of their respective ranges they are allopatric but they occur together in parts of the Cameroons and the Congo and where they do so show no apparent differences of habitat or ecology being found feeding together on the same plants in the same forest clearings. Possibly more detailed studies might show that there are some ecological differences or possibly their co-existence is temporary and may eventually end with one displacing the other through competition.

The Black-cheeked Waxbill, *E. erythronotos* and the Pink-bellied Black-cheeked Waxbill, *E. charmosyna*, seem to form a link between the *astrild* species group and the *nonnula* species-group on one hand and the *caerulescens* species-group on the other. In most characters they are nearer to the former two groups but in some aspects of their voice and behaviour show approach to the lavender waxbills (Kunkel, 1967), with which they are allopatric. *E. erythronotos* occurs in two widely separated areas (see map) in southern and eastern Africa. The east African populations of *E. erythronotos* are very similar to *E. charmosyna*, the males differing chiefly in the former being slightly darker and less suffused with pink and in having a blackish belly patch while the females, which are greyer and paler, are even more alike each other. The differences, however, appear to be constant, in eastern Africa, *charmosyna* is said to inhabit dryer areas (Hall & Moreau), though *erythronotos* is characteristically a bird of dry acacia scrub in the southern parts of its range and the two occur together extensively in southern Kenya (Williams & Traylor, in Immelmann *et al.*). Dr Jürgen Nicolai (pers. comm.), who studied both species in the Athi River District of Kenya in April and May 1980, observed no ecological differences between them. Further information is needed but on present evidence it seems likely that they have reached specific level and they are therefore treated as separate species here.

The Lavender Waxbill, *E. caerulescens*, the Black-tailed Lavender Waxbill, *E. perreini*, and the Cinderella Waxbill, *E. thomensis* are a very distinct group that in plumage, and in *E. caerulescens* in proportions also, appear to connect the more typical waxbills with the firefinches, *Lagonosticta*. These resemblances may be due to convergence as in their behaviour, however, they more resemble the other *Estrilda* species (Harrison, Kunkel, 1959) and seem better included in *Estrilda* (as they are in *Peters' Check List*) than placed in the separate genus *Glaucestrilda* Roberts. Apart from their unusual mainly bluish grey coloration and lack of the typical *Estrilda* cross-barred pattern, they seem to be more arboreal and insectivorous than other *Estrilda* species. Some may prefer to emphasise their distinctness by giving *Glaucestrilda* subgeneric rank but I see no necessity for this.

The Swee or Yellow-bellied Waxbill, *Estrilda melanotis*, differs from other *Estrilda* species in its shorter, only slightly rounded tail (which often appears square-ended when folded), partly green coloration and in having, in some populations, a more striking and marked degree of sexual dichromatism. It has sometimes been put in the monotypic genus *Coccopygia* but is now usually included in *Estrilda*. I think this is a right decision as, in spite of its unique characteristics, it has more in common, both behaviourally and in plumage characters, with the other species included in *Estrilda* than it has with those in other genera.

The Swee Waxbill is found in three main populations, which are allopatric. In southern and south-eastern Africa there is a strongly sexually dichromatic population in which the male (only) has a black face and both sexes have buff bellies. To the east and north (see map) there is a population in which both sexes have grey heads and yellow bellies. Far from both, in Angola, is a population in which the males have black faces, like the southern form, but both sexes have yellow bellies and are, apart from their sexual dichromatism, nearer to the grey-headed eastern birds in appearance. It is usual to treat all the above groups (within two of which taxonomists have named various slightly differing geographical races) as conspecific. On their taxonomic characters this appears a correct decision as the isolated Angola form is in-

termediate, having the sexual dichromatism of the southern form but approximating fairly closely to the eastern form in the rest of its coloration. There is, however, reason to suspect that these three main populations may have reached specific level. Pajain found that his captive birds of these three forms, although kept together, behaved as if separate species, showing no sexual interest in each other, even although he had three unpaired cocks of one of the black-faced forms and an unpaired hen of the other black-faced form among them. The numbers involved were limited and so further information is needed but Pajain's observations suggest the possibility of different species rather than races being involved. It is no proof of conspecifity if two related species, when kept captive in the same enclosure, react to each other with little or no discrimination as, for example, do the Black-rumped and Rosy-rumped Waxbills and the Golden and Amherst Pheasants, but when, in spite of enforced mutual proximity, two forms do *not* do so, it is reasonable to assume that they would probably 'keep themselves to themselves' if they ever came together under natural conditions.

Therefore, although I have here treated all forms of *E. melanotis* as conspecific, I have done so with some hesitation and it should be borne in mind that further studies may show that two, or three, of the forms involved ought to be given specific rank.

REFERENCES

Hall, B. P. & Moreau, R. E. 1970. *An atlas of speciation in African passerine birds.* British Museum (Natural History), London.
Harrison, C. J. O. 1962. An ethological comparison of some waxbills (Estrildini) and its relevance to their taxonomy. *Proc. zool. Soc. London* **139**: 261–282.
Immelmann, K., Nicolai, J., Steinbacher, J. & Wolters, H. E. 1964. *Vögel in Käfig und Voliere: Prachtfinken:* 279–290.
Kunkel, P. 1967. Displays facilitating sociability in waxbills of the genera *Estrilda* and *Lagonosticta. Behaviour* **29**: 237–261.
Pajain, H. A. 1975. Beobachtungen an Schwarzbäckchen. *Gefiederte Welt* **1975**: 41–42.
Traylor, M. A. 1968. *'Peters'' check-list of birds of the world.* Cambridge, Mass., USA.

Common Waxbill   *Estrilda astrild*

Loxia astrild Linnaeus, 1758, *Syst. Nat.* ed. 10, **1**, p. 173.

DESCRIPTION Between Avadavat and Violet-eared Waxbill in size; nearer to the latter in shape but tail less graduated and not so long in proportion. Upper parts light to medium, slightly reddish, brown to greyish brown with fine but distinct darker cross-barring on all feathers except those on forehead and (to some extent) crown of head. Sometimes a tinge of pink on the rump and upper tail coverts. Primaries and outer secondaries dull dark brown with paler fringes to the outer webs. Under wing coverts buffish. Tail dark brown, the outer webs of the outer tail feathers, and the two central feathers on both webs, are barred light and dark but usually less distinctly than the rest of the upper plumage. A bright scarlet red eyestripe, the red going both above and narrowly under the eye. Cheeks and upper throat off-white or pale greyish, usually tinged with pink. Centre of belly scarlet or rose red. Ventral patch, under tail coverts, and inner webs of all but central tail feathers black. Rest of underparts pale pinkish grey, pinkish fawn or silvery pink, each feather delicately cross-barred with brownish grey, and with a stronger pink suffusion often extending from the scarlet belly patch up the median line of the breast. Bill bright red. Irides brown. Legs and feet dark brown to black.

The female is usually less tinged with pink on the underparts, her red belly patch is often less bright and extensive and the ventral patch and under tail coverts are blackish brown rather than black. There is, however, some variation in both sexes apart from that due to plumage wear. The juvenile is more buffish brown in hue with less distinct cross-barring of the feathers. The red belly and black ventral areas are only faintly indicated. The lower part of the loral region is dull black so that instead of a red stripe from bill to and enclosing the eye, the part of the stripe between bill and orbit is red (paler than adult's) on its upper and blackish on its lower half. The bill is at first blackish but soon starts to change colour.

The nestling has 5 black spots on its flesh-coloured palate, a black crescentic mark in the under mandible, two black marks on the tongue that nearly meet across it, two bluish white, black-centred, swellings on each side of base of the upper mandible, and 2 bluish white tubercles, surrounded by black, one at each side of the base of the lower mandible (Immelmann *et al.*).

The above description is of nominate *E.a. astrild*, from much of South Africa. I do not propose here to describe each of the many, often intergrading geographical races of this species that have been named or to discuss their (in some cases questionable) validity. The following, which include the more divergent forms, are described in order to give a general picture of the extent of variation within this wide-ranging species.

E.a. damarensis, from South West Africa, has a somewhat longer tail and is considerably paler than *E.a. astrild*. Presumably because of its paleness (the red not being masked by melanin to the same extent as in darker forms) it has a delicate and pervasive pink tinge on the upperparts as well as elsewhere. Its female usually has little or no red on the belly and is dull dark brownish and/or has brownish, barred plumage on the ventral patch and under tail coverts. *E.a. cavendeshi*, from central and south-eastern Tanzania, Zambia, Zimbabwe, Malawi, Mozambique, eastern Transvaal and north-eastern Zululand, is very like *E.a. astrild* but a little smaller and shorter-tailed, a little darker brown and more coarsely barred on the upperparts and with the upper throat and front of the lower face nearly pure white. *E.a. peasei*, from the highlands of Abyssinia, is longer tailed than *E.a. cavendeshi*, rather darker above and on the flanks and sides of the breast, with the red belly patch less bright and the centre of the upper part of the breast pinkish with little or no barring. The females of these last and most other races,

show comparable differences from the males to those of *E.a. astrild*.

E.a. minor, from the lowlands of Jubaland through eastern Kenya inland to Voi, to north-eastern Tanzania south to Kilossa and the Ulugurus, Mafia Island and Zanzibar, is smaller than other races, very grey in general tone, with clear barring, little or no pink suffusion, a small rose-red belly patch and silky white cheeks and throat. *E.a. occidentalis*, from southern Ghana and southern Cameroons east to the eastern Congo, south to middle Congo, and Fernando Po, is nearly as small as *E.a. minor*, rather darker brown above than other races here described, pink-tinged below but with no well defined red belly patch and with white or nearly white face and throat. *E.a. macmillani*, from parts of the southern Sudan and Abyssinia, is very similar to *E.a. occidentalis* but paler above and with a nearly clear pinkish breast like that of *E.a. peasei*. *E.a. rubriventris*, from Gabon and Moyen Congo to the Congo mouth is another rather small race and the reddest of all. In the male all the central parts of belly and breast are predominantly bright rose-red to scarlet, the rest of the underparts are suffused with red, the cheeks and throat are pink, the rump and upper tail coverts are strongly and the rest of the upper parts to a varying extent suffused with deep rose-red. The female of this form has the red suffusion, especially on the under parts, much paler and less intense and is strikingly paler than the male on her underparts.

FIELD CHARACTERS Very small, longish-tailed, brownish bird with red bill and eyestripe and habit of switching tail from side to side. Entirely red bill and lack of red on rump or tail (in overlapping populations) distinguish it from the closely related and locally sympatric *E. rhodopyga*. Larger and browner than *E. troglodytes* and with brown, not black, rump and no white on edges of tail. Red eyestripe and barred brown plumage distinguish it from other sympatric waxbills.

DISTRIBUTION AND HABITAT Tropical and southern Africa, south of the range of *E. troglodytes* (see map). Introduced successfully into St. Helena, Mauritius, Reunion, Rodriquez, Seychelles, Amirantes, New Caledonia, Tahiti, Brazil and Portugal. Attempts to introduce it elsewhere appear (so far) to have met with only temporary success. In some of the above listed areas its distribution is limited and it may yet prove not to be firmly established.

Inhabits open country with long grass, marshes, long grass or reeds near water, cultivated areas (especially abandoned cultivation at the stage when wild grasses and weeds take over), grassy clearings and paths in forest or woodland, gardens and the vicinity of human habitations and farms, provided there are seeding grasses and cover of long grass, reeds, bushes or the like.

FEEDING AND GENERAL HABITS Known to feed very largely on grass seeds which are taken both from the growing plants and from the ground. Locally, and perhaps widely throughout its range, the seeds of the grass *Setaria*

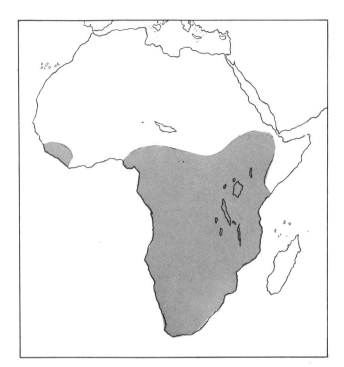

verticillata and of a grass of the genus *Paspalum* are important foods (Bates, Van Someren). Seeds of *Setaria* and *Digitaria* are important foods in the Kivu Highlands (Kunkel, *in litt.*). In Amazonia (Brazil) feeds mainly on seeds of the grasses *Panicum maximum*, *P. purpureum*, *Digitaria horizontalis*, *Sporobolus indicus* and *Echinochloa* spp. and also takes seeds of a sedge *Cyperus surinamensis* and the Amaranth, *Amaranthus spinosus* (Oren & Smith). Has been seen taking swarming termites (Immelmann *et al.*) and probably takes some other small insects.

Usually in small or large flocks. When breeding, in pairs but several pairs may nest quite near to each other in areas with a good supply of seeding *Setaria* (Van Someren). Roosts communally, often in very large numbers, in reedbeds, papyrus swamps or thick bushes. Smaller flocks may come from all directions to gather at a communal roost. Van Someren recorded many individuals roosting side by side along a single reed or papyrus stem but Immelmann (in Immelmann *et al.*), who closely observed the roosting habits of a flock of about one hundred individuals, found that the birds roosted singly, or in couples side by side, but not in rows or more than two birds together. Their roosting perches were near or in the centre of the bush, from 5 to 20 centimetres above ground, seldom higher.

In captivity this species seems usually fairly hardy. I have known individuals to live for a surprisingly long time in small cages in bird shops where they appeared to be fed on nothing but dry seed, but such treatment is not advised. Immelmann *et al.* recommend that only the smaller kinds of millet should be given (I doubt the danger of *offering* white and other larger kinds of millet provided the birds have small pannicum millet also available) and that greenfood, 'half ripe' seeds and soaked seeds, as well

as insect food should also be offered and the birds not kept at a temperature of below 15°C. Most captive breeding records seem to be of birds in aviaries where there was little certainty as to precisely what foods were being used by the Common Waxbills but Davis successfully bred this species *in a cage* in India. His birds at first fed their young mainly on the seeds of seeding grasses given them and hardboiled egg yolk but after the fifth day little egg was eaten and small maggots (from a fly that lays its eggs in dead fish), and the grass seeds, were fed to the young. As with other estrildids that perch much on abrasive reed and grass stems when wild, the claws of this species overgrow in captivity and need periodical clipping.

NESTING The nest may be sited at or near ground level in a clump of grass or other herbage or at the base of a grass entangled bush, or from about 1 to 4 metres (3 to 12 feet) above ground in a bush, shrub, tree or creeper. It is roundish to pear-shaped, built compactly of grass stems, with and without panicles attached, lined with finer grasses and occasionally also with a few feathers. There is a downward-sloping tubular entrance, usually built of grass stems with their heads outwards and from 10 to 40 centimetres (4 to 15 inches) long and about 2·5 centimetres (1 inch) in diameter inside. Often, and in some districts almost invariably, a 'cock nest', which apparently does not often get beyond the cup-shaped or half-domed stage, is built on top of the real nest (Belcher, Sclater & Moreau, Van Someren). Van Someren noted that when apparently alarmed or suspicious, one or other of the pair would fuss noisily around the 'cock nest' and carry conspicuous objects into it. Ground nests often have a cleared space in front of the entrance tube. Perhaps this is deliberately cleared and aids the sitting bird to spot and remove potentially dangerous insects such as the 'scouts' of ant troops (see *E. rhodopyga*).

Eggs 3 to 7, usually 4 to 6, most commonly 5. Both sexes incubate in turn by day. Incubation period 11 to 12 days. Young fledge at about 17 days (in Kenya, Van Someren), in captivity, and perhaps often when wild also, at about 21 days (Immelmann *et al.*). For some days after leaving the nest the young are led back into it to roost each evening by a parent, usually the father. This species is parasitised by the Pin-tailed Whydah, *Vidua macroura*.

Recorded breeding in September to January in Cape Province, November to April further north in South Africa, November to April in Southern Rhodesia, February to April in Mozambique, January to April in Malawi, November to January and March to July in Kenya, March to May in Uganda, May and June in Abyssinia, March, June and October in north-eastern Congo, November in Cameroun and September and October in Sierra Leone. In the Cape Verde Islands breeding begins in late August.

VOICE Harrison describes two contact calls, a soft 'chip' and a more abrupt 'pit', both similar to the equivalent calls of *E. troglodytes* but less nasal and higher pitched. The alarm calls, or excitement calls as Harrison terms them, are high intensity variants of the contact calls, an abrupt 'tchick' and a shrill sharp 'pit'. Members of a flock often call in flight, producing what Van Someren describes as a 'noisy twitter'.

The song is described by Harrison as 'two low harsh notes followed by a throaty bubbling note with a rising inflection: "tcher-tcher-preee".' Allowing for individual differences and the difficulties of transliteration, the descriptions given of the song by Immelmann *et al.* are essentially similar.

DISPLAY AND SOCIAL BEHAVIOUR The greeting display is similar to that of other *Estrilda* and *Lagonosticta* species (Kunkel), a quick lowering of the body, turning the head and bowing towards the other bird while uttering contact calls (see under 'Voice') and then a slower return to the normal body position. As in all excitement with most *Estrilda* species, the tail is switched or wagged from side to side so that use of the angled tail posture is indicated by the greater amplitude of the movement on the side towards the bird displayed to.

In the courtship display the bird holds a (usually long) piece of nesting material or a feather in its bill, the feathers of the belly, flank and ventral area are fluffed out and the bird often tilts itself away from the bird displayed to, so as to more fully expose the red and the black areas of plumage, the tail is angled towards the other bird and the head turned somewhat (but often only very slightly) towards it. In this position the displaying bird jerks itself stiffly up and down, bill pointing upwards, but without letting go of its perch. The male starts to sing after a few upward movements but the female, who if interested responds with the same display, is silent. This display does not usually lead to copulation which is thought to take place in the nest (Kunkel, unpublished mss and letters). Davis implies that his birds did sometimes copulate as a sequence to courtship display but is delicately ambiguous and gives no details.

Fluffed singing display shown towards known females other than the bird's mate as in *E. troglodytes* (q.v.).

OTHER NAMES St Helena Waxbill, Barred Waxbill, Brown Waxbill, Pheasant Finch.

REFERENCES

Bates, G. L. 1930. *Handbook of the birds of West Africa.* London.

Belcher, C. F. 1930. *The birds of Nyasaland.* London.

Davis, G. 1930. The breeding of St Helena Waxbills in India. *Avicult. Mag.,* 4th ser. **8**: 289–294.

Harrison, C. J. O. 1962. An ethological comparison of some waxbills (Estrildini), and its relevance to their taxonomy. *Proc. zool. Soc. London* **139**: 261–282.

Immelmann, K. Steinbacher, J. & Wolters, H.E. 1964. *Vögel in Käfig und Voliere: Prachtfinken*: 302–323.

Kunkel, P. 1967. Displays facilitating sociability in waxbills of the genera *Estrilda* and *Lagonosticta. Behaviour* **29**: 238–261.

Oren, D. C. & Smith, N. J. H. 1981. Notes on the status of the Common African Waxbill in Amazonia. *Wilson Bull.* **93**, June 1981.

Sclater, W. L. & Moreau, R. E. 1933. Taxonomic and field notes on some birds of north-eastern Tanganyika Territory. *Ibis* **3**, 13th ser., 399–440.

Van Someren, V. G. L. 1956. Days with birds. Feldiana: Zool. **38**: 491–495.

Black-lored Waxbill   *Estrilda nigriloris*

Estrilda nigriloris Chapin, 1928, *Amer. Mus. Nat. Hist. Novit.*, no. 308, p. 1.

This form may prove to be conspecific with the Common Waxbill, *E. astrild.*

DESCRIPTION Very similar to the nominate form of *E. astrild* (q.v.) but with a strong pink tinge on the barred brown upperparts, small and indefinite red belly patch, throat and upper breast tinged with an even mauvish pink, and the eye-stripe shorter (thus looking broader) and black, not red. There is a narrow pale pinkish stripe immediately above the black. Bill rather dull scarlet and perhaps slightly thicker in proportion. This description is taken from the only specimen that I have seen, a male. From descriptions of others it appears that at least the shorter black eye-stripe and lively pink suffusion are constant characters.

FIELD CHARACTERS Cannot, on present knowledge, be distinguished from *E. astrild* (should they occur together) unless the diagnostic black eye-stripe is seen.

DISTRIBUTION AND HABITAT Congo (Zaïre): on the banks of the Lualaba River near latitude 8° 46'S, and the shore of Lake Upemba. Found in a level grassy plain with tall grasses and bushes (Chapin).

FEEDING AND GENERAL HABITS Collected specimens had eaten small grass seeds. Such little behaviour as recorded not different from that of *E. astrild* (Chapin).

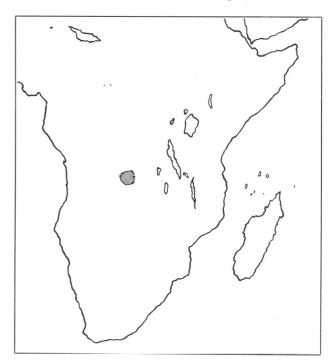

NESTING No information.

VOICE No information.

DISPLAY AND SOCIAL BEHAVIOUR No information.

REFERENCE
Chapin, J. P. 1954. The birds of the Belgian Congo. *Bull. Amer. Mus. Nat. Hist.* **75B**.

Black-rumped Waxbill   *Estrilda troglodytes*

F.[ringilla] Troglodytes Lichenstein, 1823, *Verz. Doubl. zool. Mus.* Berlin p. 26.

DESCRIPTION Slightly larger than Goldbreast in size but slimmer and with proportionately longer wings and tail. Tail between rounded and wedge-shaped when spread. Upper parts light brownish grey with delicate cross barring (in two tones of the general colour) on all the feathers except those on forehead and the wing quills. Deep scarlet eye stripe, the red running narrowly under as well as more widely above the eye. Throat and ear coverts silky white, usually tinged with pink or grey. Underparts as upperparts but much paler. Patch on ventral area (in front of vent) rosy red, this colour often spreading up from the lower belly over the median parts of the lower breast and, less often, on to the upper breast, flanks and sides of breast. Under tail coverts white, usually tinged with pink. Under wing coverts pale buffish. Rump, upper tail coverts and tail black. The outermost pair of tail feathers have white outer webs, the next pair sometimes a little white at the tips of the outer webs. There is a great deal of individual variation in the amount of rose red on the underparts and of pink suffusion generally, some birds look predominantly pinkish, others predominantly grey in colour. Bill bright red to crimson. Irides reddish brown. Legs and feet dark brown or purplish brown to brownish black.

Female as male but seldom with any definitely rose-red tipped feathers except on the belly patch. Relatively more females than males have little or no pink suffusion on the grey parts of their plumage but this is not a certain sexual difference. I once picked the pinkest and the greyest individual out of about 30 in a dealer's cage, hoping thus to obtain a cock and hen, but found out later that both were females.

Juvenile light drab brown above and pale buffish brown below, with no cross barring on the feathers. No red eye stripe but a hint of rose-red on the ventral area. Bill dark. Nestling at first with yellowish skin and pale bluish down, with conspicuous bluish white gape tubercles, and mouth pattern like that of *E. astrild* (q.v.) (Immelmann *et al.*, Russ).

A mutation occasionally occurs in which the bill is orange and the red and pink parts of the plumage yellowish orange and yellowish. It was at first thought to be a separate species and described as *Estrilda xanthrophrys* W. L. Sclater.

As is the case with some other birds, no written description can give an adequate idea of the beauty of the Black-rumped Waxbill, especially in the case of those individuals (the majority of males) with a strong pink suffusion. The sleekness of the plumage (if the bird is fit), the delicate pastel shades and fine barring, set off by the red eye-stripe and black tail, and the vivacious yet graceful movements make this one of the most beautiful of all estrildids, despite its being less colourful than many.

See plate 1, facing p. 96.

FIELD CHARACTERS Very small brownish grey bird with black, white-edged tail that is often jerked from side to side, red bill and red eye-stripe. Red eye stripe combined with generally greyish or pinkish plumage identifies it from all widely sympatric species. Of the closely related (mainly allopatric) waxbills it can be identified from *E. astrild* and *E. rhodopyga* by its black rump and tail; from *E. rufibarba* by its entirely red bill, red belly patch and (usually) pink-tinged body plumage.

DISTRIBUTION AND HABITAT Africa, in the semi-arid zone from Senegal and The Gambia east to north-eastern Congo and north-western Uganda, Sudan north to Darfur and Sennar, Eritrea and north-western Abyssinia. An isolated population in the plains around Accra, Ghana. Inhabits grassy savannas, scrub and grassy areas near water, open country with thorn scrub, marshes and sometimes cultivated areas but seldom or never in the immediate vicinity of human habitations. Appears to be often a resident but in some areas performs local (?) migrations or wanderings, absent from some of its breeding places in the dry season.

FEEDING AND GENERAL HABITS Feeds both on the ground and from growing vegetation. Known to take grass seeds

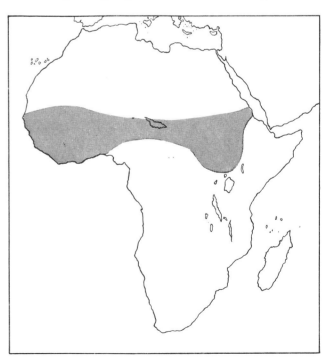

and midges. Possibly takes other seeds and almost certainly other small insects. In captivity it will eat panicum and white millet and small canary seed, the last usually only in small quantities. It is very fond of both green and ripe seeds of the Annual Meadow Grass, *Poa annua* and will also take seeds of some other grasses, Chickweed, *Stellaria media*, Knotgrass, *Polygonum aviculare*, and the growing tips of young grass. Tiny flying insects are caught on the wing and green aphids (greenfly) and the pupae of the small meadow ants of the genus *Lasius* are usually taken eagerly.

Probably the nestlings are fed at least in part on small and soft seeds in a wild state. In captivity ant pupae and larvae, greenfly, seeding grasses and soaked seed should be supplied, if obtainable, when they are breeding, but some aviculturists, including the immortal Dr Russ, have succeeded in breeding Black-rumped Waxbills on soft foods and seed alone when suitable insects could not be had. This species can usually be more easily persuaded to take egg food, milk sop and other soft foods than is the case with many waxbills (pers. obs.).

Very agile among vegetation. Holds food items, especially grass pannicles, under foot when feeding, as do other *Estrilda* species. This is one of the more hardy waxbills in captivity, although it has been less often bred than such species as the cordon-bleus or the Goldbreast. This is probably in part due to its ground nesting habits making it more vulnerable to disturbance in captivity, and in part to the disinclination of many bird keepers to devote a lot of time and space to breeding a species that could always be obtained in unlimited numbers at a trifling cost. In captivity the Black-rumped Waxbill is generally un-aggressive but competently defends the immediate vicinity of its nest, not only from larger waxbill species (pers. obs.) but even (*fide* Reichert) from such much larger and stronger birds as the Budgerigar.

NESTING Extant descriptions of wild nests seem all to derive from that of Shuel who, in northern Nigeria, found three nests built on the ground, each at the foot of a clump of long grass or a small bush. They were pear-shaped, made of dry grass heads. Each had a cock nest in the form of a 'cup-shaped extension' on one side.

In captivity the species will often nest above ground in a bush or in a basket or other receptacle but probably only when there is too much disturbance or no suitable site at ground level. The nest is ball-shaped to pear-shaped and usually has an entrance tube (downward sloping in nests above ground level) from 10 to 15 centimetres long (Kunkel, 1959, Immelmann *et al.*). Sometimes there is only the merest suggestion of a tube at the small, low entrance hole (Russ, pers. obs.). The nest is built of grass, coconut fibres or similar materials and usually more or less lined with feathers, plant wool or similar soft materials. Nests that I dissected contained numbers of feathers, some dark but most white or pale in colour, bits of tissue paper, cloth or plant wool and a few pieces of

earth and of blowfly pupa cases but always *more* of such lining materials had been carried into the cock nests. Pieces of eggshell, dry excreta, bits of white or pale paper or cloth, plant wool, bits of shiny-looking wet earth and similar materials that are whitish or dark *and* shiny are placed on top of the nest and also in and around the entrance of the cock nests. Tiny dead and rotting nestlings or dead large insects are also used for this (Karl, in Immelmann *et al.*, pers. obs.). I have seen both male and female take wet earth in their bills and make movements as if rubbing the grass at the nest entrance with the earth they held.

Cock nests are usually built beside or on top of the real nest. Boenigk found they might be completed to the point where they were identical to the real nest or to any intermediate stage. I have seen two (built together on top of a nest on the floor in my bird room) which differed from the real nest beneath them only in being smaller (about two thirds the size or a little less) and in having feathers and other conspicuous objects placed at their entrances. Boenigk found that once the eggs hatched all work on the cock nests ceased. He observed that work on cock nests took place when building behaviour at the real nest was thwarted because the other member of the pair was already building or incubating there. He concludes that cock nests are merely the functionless outcome of 're-directed' building behaviour.

I repeatedly observed with my birds, however, that when in apparent conflict (due to disturbance) between the desire to incubate and fear or suspicion, they would tend to fuss around and carry objects to the cock nests. This was most marked in a pair nesting in a basket hung on the walls of the room. They treated the next nearest basket, one about 30 centimetres away and containing an active nest of Blue-headed Cordon-bleus, as a cock nest, much to the annoyance of its owners.

Kunkel, 1959 has described in detail the building movements of this and some other estrildids. The shuddering side-to-side movement (called 'Einzittern' in German), with which many birds fix nesting material in place, has been claimed not to be used by estrildids and seems not to be in their basic nest construction but it *is* used by this species, and by *E. rhodopyga*, when fixing objects to the top of the nest. One sees it performed repeatedly at high intensity when the bird is vainly trying to make a feather or bit of tissue paper 'stay put' on the top of a basket in which it has its nest. I have sometimes, but not often, observed this species 'bundle' two or more feathers together in its bill, instead of carrying only one feather at a time, held by its end, in the usual manner of African waxbills.

Like *Estrilda rhodopyga*, and most probably other *Estrilda* species, the Black-rumped Waxbill, when collecting nest material, will reach up, grasp and pull down a grass stem, hold it under foot and then quickly and cleanly bite through the stem and sever it. Less often it will bite through the stem without first pulling and holding it down. It is thus able to obtain live stems, or dead stems still attached to a clump of grass, in a way impossible for cordon-bleus or firefinches which can only tug and jerk backwards in an often vain attempt to obtain a wanted stem.

Eggs 3 to 8, usually 4 or 5. Both sexes incubate in turn by day in the usual manner. I sometimes, when watching a pair change over at the nest, heard a soft, whispering 'tswee-tswee-tswee-tswee-tswee . . .' but at other times it was either not uttered or too quietly for my ears. Incubation period 11 days (Russ). For some days after fledging the young are led back into the nest to roost each evening and in a more apparently highly 'organised' way than by such species as the Zebra Finch. Kunkel (1959), who observed and studied this behaviour, found that one parent finds, calls and leads the young singly to the nest entrance where the other parent stands or hops about, calling and keeping them together. Only when all are gathered does one parent lead them into the nest, they follow one by one and are fed in the nest by both parents, who then leave them in the nest and roost away from it themselves. Fledged young have been observed to beg with shivering wing movements (Herkner) but, as Kunkel (1959) did not see this, probably rarely or only at high intensity. When incubating in nests on the floor of my bird room, a heavy tread in the passage outside would cause the bird to come out of the nest, look around from just in front of the entrance and then return. Presumably this behaviour functions to prevent parent as well as nest being accidentally crushed by a large mammal.

This species is believed to be parasitised by the Pin-tailed Whydah, like *E. astrild.*

VOICE Most of the calls of this species are rather loud and harsh for so small a bird though not to the same extent as those of the Crimson-rumped Waxbill. The descriptions here are from my notes on captive birds unless otherwise stated.

A repeated 'cheu-cheu' or 'chit-chit' (different versions) appear to be locomotion-intention and/or short distance contact calls. A louder, upwardly inflected 'cheeer' or 'chee-ey' is uttered in apparent alarm and perhaps in some other states of excitement. A harsher but less loud and more buzzing 'cheer' or 'cheea' is sometimes given in apparent defensive or aggressive threat. Bannerman (1953) notes the calls given by members of (wild) flocks in flight as 'tiup-tiup-tiup or something like it'.

A soft murmuring twitter: 'tswee-tswee-tswee . . .' is used as a nest call and also (sometimes) when changing over at the nest during incubation.

The song is somewhat variable and the same bird may use two (or possibly more) variants. A loud, explosive 'tche-tcheeer!', 'chee-eeer!' with the second note in each case strongly upwardly inflected, and a similarly explosive 't'chu-weee', but with the second note descending, were the commonest and most divergent variants I noted. The song of a female (females are said not to sing in display but this bird did at times) was 'pwich! cheee', the second note upwardly inflected, or merely the first explosive note

repeated: 'pwich! pwich!'. Song is given sometimes when the bird is alone but most typically by the male when giving courtship or fluffed singing displays.

DISPLAY AND SOCIAL BEHAVIOUR In the greeting display the bird approaches its partner with actual or intention movements of bill wiping, both the bowing and the subsequent head lifting movements seem a little less definite than in, for example, the cordon-bleus. The most noticeable feature of this display is the very intense, 'clockwork-like' side to side flicking or wagging of the tail, which is swung through a wide arc and tends to swing further towards than away from the partner. Soft contact notes are uttered, by females singly and by males in series (Kunkel, 1967).

In the courtship display the bird holds nesting material, usually a long grass stem or a feather, by one end in its bill. It holds its head usually at an upward angle of about 60 to 70 degrees. The plumage of the belly and the near flank is fluffed out but not so much as to present a ragged or ruffled surface. The tail is angled towards the other bird if the latter is to one side, held straight if it is immediately in front. The displaying bird then bobs stiffly up and down by bending and straightening its legs but does not let go of the branch with its feet as it does so. The male repeats his song during the display; the female tends to display less often and usually without singing. This display is not immediately followed by copulation which is believed to take place inside the nest (Kunkel, 1959). Quite often birds in breeding condition will display alone (without unilateral fluffing of the flank feathers) and I once saw a male display fully without holding anything in his bill but this is most unusual.

In the fluffed singing display (Kunkel, 1967), with plumage arranged as in courtship display but without material in his bill, the male, singing repeatedly, hops after or around the female. If she does not flee he soon tries to fly on to her back and copulate forcibly, almost always without success. This behaviour is shown to females known personally to the male but not paired to him and only rarely, perhaps never in a wild state, towards his own mate (Kunkel, 1959 and 1967 and pers. obs.).

Allo-preening is common between mates and friendly members of non-breeding groups. In captivity (and possibly also in the wild) pair bonds may loosen when the birds are out of breeding condition, leading to later re-pairing with different partners. Mandibulation and bill fencing occur in the usual situations.

OTHER NAMES Red-eared Waxbill, Grey Waxbill, Pink-cheeked Waxbill, Common Waxbill (this last sometimes used in avicultural works and leading to confusion with *E. astrild*).

REFERENCES

Bannerman, D. A. 1953. *The birds of West and tropical Africa*, vol. 2, Oliver & Boyd, London.

Boenigk, G. 1970. Verhaltensstudien zum Bau der 'Hahnennester' einiger Prachtfinken (Estrildidae). *Beitr. Vogelkunde* **15**: 402–413.

Herkner, R. 1979. Erfahrungen mit meinen Grauastrilden. *Gefiederte Welt* **1979**: 43–45.

Immelmann, K., Steinbacher, J. & Wolters, H. E. 1965. *Vögel in Käfig und Voliere: Prachtfinken*: 325–332. Aachen, Germany.

Kunkel, P. 1959. Zum Verhalten einiger Prachtfinken (Estrildinae). *Z. Tierpsychol.* **16**: 302–350.

Kunkel, P. 1967. Displays facilitating sociability in waxbills of the genera *Estrilda* and *Lagonosticta* (fam. Estrildidae). *Behaviour* **29**: 237–261.

Reicherdt, G. 1971. Meine ersten Grauastrilde. *Gefiederte Welt* **95**: 217–218.

Russ, K. 1879. *Die Fremlandischen Stubenvögel*, vol. 1. Hannover, Germany.

Shuel, R. 1938. Notes on the breeding habits of birds near Zaria, Northern Nigeria. *Ibis* **2**, 14th ser., 230–244.

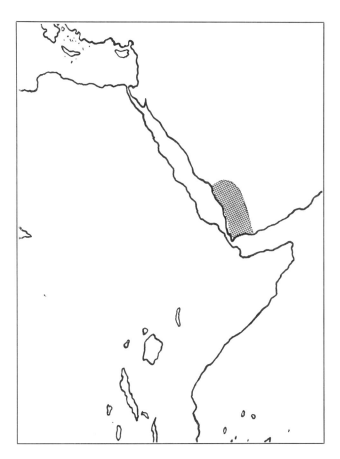

Arabian Waxbill   *Estrilda rufibarba*

H.[abropyga] rufibarba Cabanis, 1851, *Mus. Heineanum* 1, p. 169.

DESCRIPTION Slightly larger, and with proportionately rather larger bill and longer tail, than the previous species, *E. troglodytes*, from which it differs in appearance as follows: ground colour of both upper and under parts greyish brown, with no tinge of pink and much more strongly contrasted darker barring. Throat and cheeks whitish with no pink or grey tinge and contrasting with the darker sides of the neck. Whitish outer webs of outer tail feathers tinged with buff and barred and/or mottled with greyish brown. Central tail feathers and rump a less intense and more brownish black and, rarely, with some admixture of dark crimson red on the rump. Centre of lower belly, ventral patch and under tail coverts buff, palest on the under tail coverts. Eyestripe a darker red, crimson rather than rich scarlet, and in some females intermixed with black on the lores. Bill blackish, with a red mark on the sides of the upper mandible and at the bases of the sides of the lower mandible.

Female usually, perhaps always, paler buff on lower belly and ventral patch. I have not seen a juvenile of this form or a description of it.

FIELD CHARACTERS Tiny brown bird with pale edges to outer tail feathers and, at close quarters, dark red eyestripe. Not sympatric with any similar species. From *E. troglodytes* could be distinguished by its mainly dark bill, and brown and buff rather than grey and pink plumage; from *E. rhodopyga* by its blackish rump and lack of red on the wings; from *E. astrild* by its dark bill and lack of any red or pink tinge in its plumage.

DISTRIBUTION AND HABITAT South-western Arabia from Kunfuda, about latitude 19°N, south to Aden. Inhabits ravines and valleys with thick cover of bushes and/or reeds (Meinertzhagen).

FEEDING AND GENERAL HABITS Known to eat small grass seeds but genus or species apparently unrecorded. Meinertzhagen also saw it regularly taking seeds of reeds,

Juncus sp. Keeps much to cover of bushes or reeds but will come right out into the open to feed (Meinertzhagen).

NESTING Nothing known for certain. Meinertzhagen found some 'large untidy grass structures' in thick bushes that he thought were old nests of this species.

VOICE No information.

DISPLAY AND SOCIAL BEHAVIOUR No information. Probably similar or identical to its two close relatives *E. troglodytes* and *E. rhodopyga*.

REFERENCES
Meinertzhagen, R. 1954. *Birds of Arabia*. Oliver & Boyd, London.

Rosy-rumped Waxbill   *Estrilda rhodopyga*

Estrilda rhodopyga Sundevall, 1850, *Öfr. K. Sv. Vet.-Akad. Förh.*, p. 126.

DESCRIPTION Very similar to the previous species, *E. rufibarba*, from which it differs as follows: central tail feathers slightly broader; upper and under parts of a generally warmer, more buffy tone and with the fine darker cross-barring less prominent, although slightly more so than in *E. troglodytes*; white of face and throat with a creamy or buffish tinge; under tail coverts and some adjacent ventral feathers with heavy dark barring and freckling and fringed to a varying degree with carmine or dull crimson; under wing coverts pinkish buff; outer webs of greater wing coverts and inner secondaries broadly fringed with deep rose-red or carmine, forming two subdued red patches on the folded wing; rump and upper tail coverts rosy carmine to light crimson or light scarlet; central tail feathers fringed on both webs, and next two pairs on their outer webs, with the same colours; tail feathers otherwise dull dark brown, obscurely cross-barred; the two outermost pairs have their outer webs edged with off-white to pale drab, thickly freckled or barred with dull brown; bill blackish, with red or pink area at each side of upper mandible and another at each side of base of lower mandible.

Sexes alike, though possibly females average a little duller than males. Juvenile similar to adults but without cross barring on feathers and with the red parts lighter and duller. Its bill is at first black.

The above description is of nominate *E.r. rhodopyga*, from Darfur to Sennar and Khartoum, Eritrea, eastern Abyssinia and northern Somalia. *E.r. centralis*, from further south in the species' range, averages a little darker on the brown and red parts of the plumage but there is much overlap, besides individual variation. Mutants in which the normal red coloration is replaced by yellowish orange sometimes occur.

FIELD CHARACTERS Tiny brown bird with red eye-stripe, rump and wing patch, constantly flicking tail from side to side when excited or alarmed. Red on rump and tail (and wings close-up) and/or lack of any tinge of pink on back or breast would distinguish it from Common and Black-rumped Waxbills.

DISTRIBUTION AND HABITAT Eastern tropical Africa (see map), from the Sudan (Darfur to Sennar and Khartoum), Eritrea, eastern and southern Abyssinia, south through Kenya, Uganda, extreme eastern Congo (Zaïre) to northern Tanzania and northern Malawi (Nyasaland).

Inhabits dry grassland with clumps of bushes, dry acacia savanna, riparian scrub, and cultivated areas; always within easy reach of surface water. Usually a lowland bird but locally up to 1500 metres.

FEEDING AND GENERAL HABITS Little is known, or at least little recorded, of its behaviour in the wild. Takes small grass seeds both from the growing plants and from the ground and these are probably its main food. My (4) captive birds fed largely on pannicum millet but readily took green aphids (greenfly), both green and ripe seeds of the Annual Meadow Grass, *Poa annua*, and some other grasses, Knot Grass, *Polygonum aviculare*, the growing tips of young grass shoots and, though less eagerly than many waxbills, pupae of meadow ants, *Lasius* sp. Immelmann *et al.* state that this species feeds its young on relatively larger amounts of 'half ripe' seeds than does *E. troglodytes* and is consequently easier to breed in captivity.

Holds grass panicles etc. under foot and, when collecting nesting material, pulls down, holds, and bites cleanly through grass stems like *E. troglodytes* (q.v.).

In the wild it has usually been found in small parties.

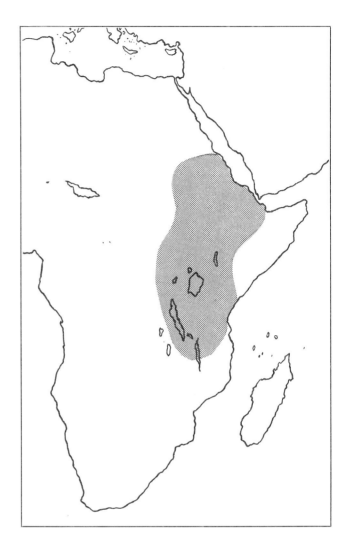

NESTING Accounts of wild nests, that I have read, seem all to derive from that of Chapin, who found a single nest, built of grass tops, with a lateral entrance, on the ground in short grass. The cock was incubating 6 eggs, 2 of which were larger than the others and presumably had been laid by the parasitic Pin-tailed Whydah, *Vidua macroura*. As Chapin makes no mention of them it seems probable that this nest did not have an entrance tube or cock nest attached.

Immelmann *et al.* state that the species has often been bred in aviaries but give no description of the nest. My own experience of the nesting of this species involved a captive male who was paired to a female *E. troglodytes*. Over a period of years many nests were built although only one egg of the numerous clutches laid ever hatched (the resultant hybrid, a female, when adult, was intermediate in tone of plumage but had an entirely red bill like her mother and red on rump and wings like her father). Most of these nests were built in a corner on the floor of the room but some in baskets on the wall. In these latter sites the birds could not build proper entrance tubes or superimpose cock nests so they will be discounted and only the floor nests described here. I dissected four of the latter, including their cock nests, and all were virtually identical. Except for very occasionally taking an odd bit of material to it, the female *troglodytes* was not seen building the real nests and although both birds 'decorated' the upper parts of the nests and carried materials to the cock nests, the consistent differences between the nests of this pair and nests subsequently built, under the same conditions in the same room, by pairs of *E. troglodytes*, made it almost certain that the male Rosy-rumped was the main if not the sole architect.

Each nest was constructed of grass stems, most of them with blades and/or seeding heads attached. Some stems of other herbage, such as chickweed and knotgrass, were also used but only in small amounts and had probably been taken only when there was a temporary shortage of suitable grass. The walls of the nest cavity were about an inch thick and surprisingly tough and compact, in great contrast to nests of *Uraeginthus* and *Lagonosticta* built in the same room. The nest lining was entirely of grass, chiefly of fine stems and of seeding or flowering panicles. None of the ground nests ever had a feather or piece of paper etc in them although sometimes such things were carried into basket nests after vain efforts to fix them on top. A few unhusked and uninjured grains of canary seed (but none of the millet that the birds mainly fed on) were sometimes found in the egg cavity and may have been deliberately carried in. The nest was roughly pear-shaped narrowing to a tubular entrance with a very small and concealed entrance hole which was surrounded by many sharp ends of grass stems so that it was impossible to insert a finger without some of them 'stabbing' it quite sharply. However, not all of the stems used for the entrance tube had been arranged in this manner although the majority had.

The outside of the nest, particularly the part immediately in front of the cock nest, was 'decorated' with (1) body feathers of Domestic Fowls, ducks, crows and pigeons; white or *glossy* black feathers being strongly preferred to brown or grey ones; (2) pieces of soft whitish tissue paper, shiny grease-proof paper, and charred, blackened paper (pieces of newspaper of similar size, which were also available, were never used); (3) small clumps of earth, both dry and damp, a very strong preference being shown for those bound by rootlets, some of which protruded from the earth mass. Some of all these objects, especially conspicuous white or glossy black feathers, were also placed in the cock nest. On two occasions when he found a tiny putrescent corpse of a nestling *Uraeginthus*, the male *rhodopyga* showed great excitement and at once carried it to and placed it in the cock nest. The shuddering side to side movement ('Einzittern' in German) is used by this species when fixing 'decoration' on to the top of the nest, all other building behaviour also as in *E. troglodytes* (q.v.).

The cock nest was (again in each case) of about the same dimensions inside as the real egg chamber below it but was otherwise smaller and with a fairly large side entrance. It had a general resemblance to the nest of a cordon-bleu, *Uraeginthus* sp., or Dark Firefinch, *Lagonosticta rubricata*, but with a larger entrance hole. In no instance was it 'completed' so as to be a facsimile, miniature or otherwise, of the real nest. The behaviour shown in connection with the cock nest was identical to that of *E. troglodytes*.

The male's behaviour made it fairly certain that in this species both sexes alternate incubation and brooding by day in the usual estrildid manner. The male, who was less timid than his mate, would take over 'out of turn' if she left the nest by day and did not soon return to it but he would not do so if the female left the nest in late evening, even if she roosted away from it. He never roosted in the cock nest. Sometimes the male *rhodopyga*, after hopping conspicuously in and out of the cock nest, after being disturbed from incubation, would remain in it for three or four minutes, as if incubating, before re-entering the real nest.

At times there were numbers of small black ants, I believe *Lasius fuscus*, in the room. These the male *rhodopyga* always killed or disabled and flung away, if he saw them near the nest entrance. On two occasions I saw him spend about five minutes squatting on the ground just outside the nest entrance and killing every ant that came within two inches of him. He ignored ants further from the nest and, like all my waxbills, never ate worker ants. I presume this to be normal innate behaviour whose function is to prevent ants from entering the nest. It is likely that even ants small and innocuous enough to be treated by the adult in this manner might still be a danger to young nestlings, should they enter the nest in numbers.

Like *E. troglodytes*, the male *rhodopyga*, when inside a nest on the floor, left the nest, momentarily, but with no sign of serious alarm, in response to any heavy tread in the passage outside the room.

VOICE Immelmann *et al.* describe a 'soft tyeek or tyeep' (my anglicisation) but all the calls that I heard from 4 males and 1 female, most of which were kept for about two years and some longer, were surprisingly harsh and loud, with a very House Sparrow-like tone. The softest I heard was the nest call 'tchŭ-tchŭ-tchŭ-tchŭ . . .', quieter than other calls of this species but of similar harsh type. The locomotion-intention and close contact call is a harsh, rather nasal 'tchă', 'tchă-tchă', 'tchek-tchek-chek' or similar with much minor variation. The distant contact call, also given in apparent mild alarm or anxiety as with other species, is a harsh, nasal, upwardly inflected 'Tchair!', 'tcherr' or 'tchaeee!' very commonly prefaced by a shorter note 'tche-tchair!', 'tche-chāā!' or similar. A male that escaped and spent most of the day in my own and other nearby gardens, maintaining almost constant vocal contact with the captives still in the house (which he re-entered, through the window he had escaped by, at dusk), uttered all calls except the relatively soft nest call very frequently but used this loud 'tchair' and 'tche-tchair' most of all.

A harsh nasal screech may be used in threat or defiance by quarrelling individuals. An abrupt di-syllabic 'tchuk-uk! tchukuk!' sometimes followed by an upwardly inflected 'tchurr' is used in apparent alarm.

The song (the word is here necessarily used without *any* musical implications) is very similar to the distance contact call and possibly not really separable from it, 'tchek-er-tcherr', 'tchĕ-chāāer!', 'tchĕ-tchāāa' and other variants, always with the last note stressed and upwardly inflected. It is used both when alone, in the courtship display, and in the fluffed singing display. A Great Tit-like chattering 'tchă-tchă-tchă-tchă-tchă-tchă-tchurr', with the churring last note upwardly inflected, appears to be an alternate form of song but, although using it also in the other song contexts my birds seemed particularly liable to utter it in the fluffed singing chases.

All the calls of this species seem to be homologous to those of *E. troglodytes* and very similar except for being louder and harsher.

DISPLAY AND SOCIAL BEHAVIOUR The greeting, courtship and fluffed singing displays of this species are identical with those of the Black-rumped Waxbill, *E. troglodytes* (q.v.) except that I have occasionally seen a male in courtship display with his head more or less horizontal (and thus at nearly right angles to his body) instead of held upward as usual. But it is quite likely that this slight difference of position is shown at times by *E. troglodytes* also. I have sometimes seen a male give the courtship display without singing at all but this is unusual. As has been said I only had one female of this species and when I saw her give the courtship display it was always in silence as is usual, but not invariable, with females of *E. troglodytes*.

I saw mandibulation and bill fencing rather more often from this species than from my *E. troglodytes* but this may have been fortuitous or due to individual differences. Allo-preening as in *E. troglodytes*.

OTHER NAMES Crimson-rumped Waxbill, Sundevall's Waxbill, Rosy-winged Waxbill.

REFERENCES

Chapin, J. P. 1954. The birds of the Belgian Congo. *Bull. Amer. Mus. Nat. Hist.* **75B**.

Goodwin, D. 1964. Some aspects of nesting behaviour in *Estrilda. Bull. Br. Orn. Club* **84**: 99–105.

Immelmann, K., Steinbacher, J. & Wolters, H. E. 1965. *Vögel in Käfig und Voliere: Prachtfinken*: 332–337.

Mackworth-Praed, C. W. & Grant, C. H. B. 1960. *African handbook of birds*, ser. 1, vol. 2.

Orange-cheeked Waxbill   *Estrilda melpoda*

Fringilla melpoda Vieillot, 1817, *Nouv. Dict. Hist. Nat.*, nouv. ed., **12**, p. 177.

DESCRIPTION About size of Avadavat but with shorter bill and longer tail which is a rather elongated wedge-shape when spread. Sides of face, including lores, area im-

mediately above and around eyes and ear coverts usually bright orange to orange-red, less often yellowish orange. In the paler-faced individuals the lores and area around the eyes are deeper in colour than the ear coverts. All top of head and sides of neck medium to darkish grey. Hind neck, mantle, back and wing coverts a uniform slightly reddish brown. Inner secondaries, and those parts of the outer secondaries that are visible when the wing is folded, a slightly darker brown; rest of wing quills darker and duller brown. Under wing coverts buff. Rump and upper tail coverts dark red to orange red, there is usually a correlation between depth of colour on the cheeks and on the rump. Tail feathers brownish black, the central ones fringed basally with red to varying degrees and the shorter outer ones tipped with pale greyish. Throat white, buffish white or greyish white, shading to a slightly less pale hue on the centre of the breast, and pale grey to buffish grey on the sides of the breast, flanks, and under tail coverts. Ventral patch buffish yellow to pale orange, rarely with some of the feathers tipped orange-red. Irides light, medium or reddish brown. Bill bright red to orange-red. Legs and feet pale brown to dark brown.

Sexes alike. Juvenile is more like adult than in most waxbills but has top of head greyish brown to dull brown, underparts and flanks paler and more buffish, and the orange of the cheeks and the red of the rump paler and less bright. The newly-hatched nestlings are quite naked (Immelmann *et al.*). Mouth markings of nestling like those of *E. astrild* (q.v.).

The above description is of nominate *E.m. melpoda*, from most of the species' range. There is much minor individual and local variation, as covered in the description. Birds from Kasai mostly have very deep orange-red cheeks and are sometimes racially separated as *E. melpoda fucata*, but so have some specimens from Liberia and elsewhere. *E. melpoda tschadensis*, from northern Adamawa, northern Cameroons and Lake Chad District, is paler, especially on the cheeks and underparts.

FIELD CHARACTERS Small brown and grey bird with orange face, red bill and red rump. The orange cheeks distinguish it from all other waxbills. If the face is not seen, its red rump would separate it from *E. astrild* and *E. troglodytes*.

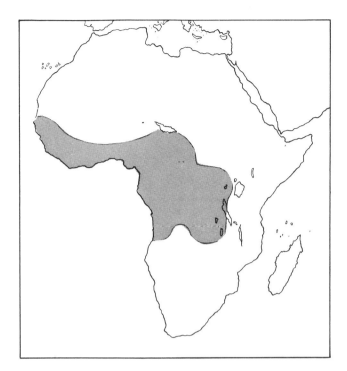

DISTRIBUTION AND HABITAT Western and central tropical Africa, from Senegal river south and east to northern Adamawa, Cameroons, Lake Chad district, the Congo except for the extreme north-east and south-west, northern Angola and the north-east shore of Lake Mweru. Introduced into Puerto Rico. Inhabits high grass savannas, grass-grown clearings and grassy areas in or near swamps, at forest edge and on the outskirts of cultivation. The presence of suitable grasses, bushy cover and water seem to be essentials of its habitat. May be in competition with the Common Waxbill as Chapin found that the two species appeared to replace each other, in similar habitats, in parts of the Congo.

FEEDING AND GENERAL HABITS Feeds both in growing grass and on the ground. Known to feed largely on seeds of grasses and there is circumstantial (and almost certainly good) evidence that it also takes aphids (Bates). Usually in flocks, single pairs sometimes seen. Movements, postures and methods of holding grass panicles under foot as in *E. astrild* and *E. troglodytes*.

In captivity requires similar food and treatment to the Black-rumped Waxbill (q.v.) but is (*fide* Immelmann *et al.*) more sensitive to cold and should never be kept at a temperature less than 18°C. It is usually very excitable, nervous and timid and it is apparently one of those birds (like the Blackbird, *Turdus merula*) whose alarm calls seem to have a particularly unnerving effect on other species. It would seem, therefore, unwise to keep it with other small estrildids, whose tameness and breeding success might be adversely affected by it. Immelmann *et al.* state that, if plenty of thick, bushy cover is provided in the aviary or bird room it will become far less nervous and panicky.

NESTING The nest is placed on or near the ground among grass or other vegetation or in a low bush. It is rounded or more or less flask-shaped, built of grass stems, blades and panicles with a usually short tubular entrance. Often there is a cock's nest on top. In captivity nests with no entrance tube but a small, well constructed entrance hole (Russ), with long entrance tubes (Kunkel, 1959), with two compartments one behind the other (Sopper), and/or with cock's nest beside as well as on top of the real nest, have been built. Kunkel's birds 'decorated' their nests in the same manner as does *E. troglodytes* but less extensively and using not bright but dull-coloured clumps of earth, bits of brown paper and small stones. A captive pair screened the entrance hole with a feather, when they had young (Alderson).

Eggs 3 to 7, usually 4 to 6. Both sexes incubate and brood in the usual way. Young fledge at 20–21 days (at least in captivity) and are independent about 12 days after fledging. A captive pair drove all other birds in the aviary, even larger species, from the vicinity of their fledged young (Reicherdt). In eastern Nigeria it is parasitised by the Pin-tailed Whydah, *Vidua macroura* (J. Nicolai, pers. comm.).

Recorded breeding in July and August in Sierra Leone, October to June, possibly also in July and August, in the Congo, in southern Congo and northern Zambia February to May (Immelmann *et al.*, Mackworth-Praed & Grant).

In captivity this species almost always nests if given reasonable facilities but its timidity prompts it to leave the eggs so often that the relative number of broods successfully reared out of all the nesting attempts is probably less than in most commonly kept species. It has, however, been bred often in bird rooms or aviaries, by Dr Russ among others, and at least once even in a cage (Alderson).

VOICE The locomotion-intention and close contact calls are soft, high-pitched repeated peeping notes (Harrison, Sopper). Harrison also records a lower, more nasal note. The distant contact call is a louder and continuous series of notes (Sopper). Most writers transliterated the alarm call in similar terms to Russ who describes it as a shrill 'tsit! tsit!' or 'tseet! tseet!' (my anglicisations) but Harrison describes an alarm call he heard given at the sight of a cat as a harsh, nasal 'cheh-cheh'. A repeated 'sree-sree-sree-sree' which is uttered when the bird is approaching something that interests it (and also seems to arouse mild alarm) and in immediate response to some *unfamiliar* sound (Russ). Sopper lists a distinctive call (not further described) which is uttered when the bird discovers something apparently pleasing to it, such as food or a suitable nest site, and which attracts its mate; and a soft, whispering nest call. The song is individually variable. Harrison describes it as 'several short notes (usually three or four) followed by two or three double notes in which the emphasis is on the first part – "de-de-de-, sweea, sweea, sweea"'; Immelmann *et al.* as a light, jingling or clinking 'tsee-ree-ree, tsee-ree-ree, tsee-ree-ree' or 'tseek-tseek-tsaylee, tseek-tseek-tsaylee' or some similar strophe. Sopper notes that his male sang a shorter version of its song in the pre-copulatory display (q.v.) than when giving the courtship display with nesting material. When performing the greeting display, the male utters repeated short trills but the female single contact calls (Kunkel, 1967).

DISPLAY AND SOCIAL BEHAVIOUR Greeting, courtship and fluffed singing displays as in the Black-rumped Waxbill (q.v.). It is thought that copulation normally occurs inside the nest but Sopper repeatedly saw his pair copulate on perches. Their copulations followed display from the male identical with that of the courtship display except that no nesting material was held in the bill and a different, rather shorter version of the song was given. From the description it would thus sound very similar to the fluffed singing display but the female, although not visibly soliciting, would apparently (sometimes) await and allow the male to mount and copulate.

Allo-preening is said (Immelmann *et al.*) to be more frequent than in other *Estrilda* species.

OTHER NAME Red-cheeked Waxbill (misleading except for the very deepest-coloured individuals).

REFERENCES

Alderson, R. 1902. Nesting of the Orange-cheeked Waxbill (*Sporaeginthus melpodus*). *Avicult. Mag.* **8**: 65–70.

Bates, G. L. 1930. *Handbook of the birds of West Africa.* John Bale & Danielsson, London.

Chapin, J. P. 1954. The birds of the Belgian Congo. *Bull. Amer. Mus. Nat. Hist.* **75B**.

Harrison, C. J. O. 1962. An ethological comparison of some waxbills (Estrildini), and its relevance to their taxonomy. *Proc. zool. Soc. London* **139**: 261–282.

Immelmann, K., Steinbacher, J. & Wolters, H. E. 1965. *Vögel in Käfig und Voliere: Prachtfinken*: 347–354.

Kunkel, P. 1959. Zum Verhalten einiger Prachtfinken (Estrildinae). *Z. Tierpsychol.* **16**: 302–350.

Kunkel, P. 1967. Displays facilitating sociability in waxbills of the genera *Estrilda* and *Lagonosticta* (fam. Estrildidae). *Behaviour* **29**: 237–261.

Mackworth-Praed, C. W. & Grant, C. H. B. 1973. *African handbook of birds*, ser. 3, vol. 2. Longman Group, London.

Reicherdt, C. 1977. Lob der Orangebäckchens. *Gefiederte Welt* **1977**: 44–47.

Russ, K. 1879. *Die fremdlandischen Stubenvögel*, vol. 1. Hanover, Germany.

Sopper, E. 1977. Anfangererfahrungen mit Orangebäckchen. *Gefiederte Welt* **1977**: 186–188.

Fawn-breasted Waxbill   *Estrilda paludicola*

Estrelda paludicola Heuglin, 1863, *J. Orn.* **11**, p. 166.

DESCRIPTION Very similar in size and shape to the previous species, *E. melpoda*, but differing as follows: grey on top of head suffused with brown and less sharply demarcated from the hind neck, mantle and back, which are of a less reddish brown and, on *close* examination, show the basic *Estrilda* pattern of fine darker and lighter cross-barring,

faintly indeed, but more clearly than does *E. melpoda*. Under wing coverts yellowish white to pale buff. Red of rump and upper tail coverts carmine to wine red. Cheeks pale grey to buffish grey. Throat yellowish white to pale buff, shading usually to a more definite pale buff on the central part of the breast and to light greyish brown at the sides of the breast and on the flanks. Centre of belly and ventral patch a brighter, light, yellowish buff with some of the feathers tipped with pinkish red. Under tail coverts whitish to pale buff. Irides red or reddish brown. Bill bright red to orange-red. Legs and feet dark brown.

The female has the buff areas on her underparts paler and the greyish brown areas at the sides encroaching more on to the buff. She has at most only a slight trace of pink on her ventral feathers, often none at all. Juvenile like adult but with black bill, paler below. Newly-hatched nestling naked. Mouth pattern of nestling very like that of *E. astrild* (illustration in Immelmann *et al.*).

The above description is of nominate *E.p. paludicola*, from eastern Oubangi-Chari and southern Sudan, south to north-eastern Congo, northern Uganda and the highlands of western Kenya south and east to Mau. *E.p. benguellensis*, from Angola to central Malanje east to northern and north-eastern Zambia, and southern Katanga to Upemba and the south end of Lake Tanganyika, has the top of its head dark grey with little or no brown suffusion and clearly demarcated from the brown of the upper parts, which is of a darker and slightly redder tone than in nominate *paludicola*. Red of rump and upper tail coverts brighter. Buff of underparts brighter and darker. Feathers of ventral patch and lower flanks broadly and extensively tipped with pinkish red. Breast feathers often tipped with pale pink. Female similar to male but averaging a little paler below and with no pink on the breast. *E. paludicola roseicrissa*, from eastern Kivu from Lake Edward to the north end of Lake Tanganyika, Rwanda, southern Uganda to the western shores of Lake Victoria, and extreme north-eastern Tanzania has its upper parts of a slightly lighter and more yellowish brown than nominate *E.p. paludicola* and the top of its head is the same shade of brown as the back. Its under wing coverts are whitish and its rump a lighter and brighter red than that of the nominate form. Its underparts are paler and greyer and it has a rose-pink ventral patch. The female is even paler beneath and has only a tinge of pink on the ventral area. *E.p. marwitzi*, from western Tanzania, is very like *E.p. roseicrissa* but is darker brown above, a more purplish and less bright red on the rump, and averages paler on the underparts. I have not seen specimens of *E.p. ruthae*, from the Middle Congo River. It is said to be very pale both above and below (Chapin).

E. paludicola ochrogaster, from Abyssinia and nearby parts of south-eastern Sudan, is a very distinct form. It has the cheeks, throat and underparts heavily suffused with a deep, rich, golden-buff, sometimes brightening to golden-orange on the lores and around the eyes. The top of its head is browner and its rump and upper tail coverts brighter red than in the nominate form. The ventral patch is no brighter buff than most of the underparts but usually has some pink-tipped feathers. Females are paler on face, breast and underparts and, in some cases, duller and suffused with grey. A very few male specimens resemble them, assuming that they have not been wrongly sexed.

FIELD CHARACTERS Tiny brown bird with bright red bill, red rump and buffish, whitish or pale greyish face and underparts.

DISTRIBUTION AND HABITAT Eastern Oubangi-Chari, southern Sudan, Abyssinia, Uganda, highlands of western Kenya, western Tanzania, Congo, Rwanda and the central plateau of Angola. Inhabits swamps, grassy savannas, along streams, grassy clearings in forest, forest edge and sometimes around villages and cultivation.

FEEDING AND GENERAL HABITS Feeds largely on seeds of grasses, which are taken from the growing plants and also from the ground. Usually in small or large flocks, often in association with other *Estrilda* species.

Probably takes some insect food in the wild, as in captivity. A pair that had previously ignored ant pupae began at once to take them when their young hatched (Schertenleib). Other pairs in captivity reared their young mainly on green (home grown) millet (Schertenleib, in Immelmann *et al.*). In captivity requires similar food and treatment to other *Estrilda* species but is less sensitive to cold than the related *E. melpoda* (Immelmann *et al.*).

Flight, gait, movements and feeding methods as in such related species as *E. melpoda* and *E. astrild*. In captivity it is lively but (unlike *E. melpoda*) not at all shy or nervous. It is fond of perching on upright reed stems and this should be borne in mind when furnishing its bird room or aviary.

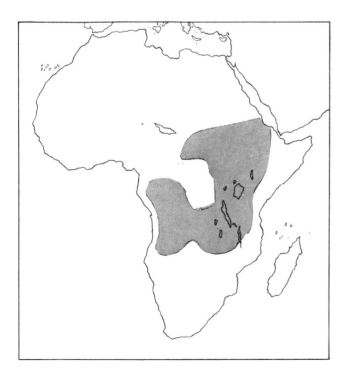

NESTING Most detailed accounts of wild nests seem to stem from two found by Weekes and one by Vincent. The former were both on the ground, well hidden at the roots of tall grass. They were built of grass heads, with a somewhat frailer but otherwise similar cock nest on top. Both real and cock nests had (surprisingly) large side entrances, apparently without entrance tubes. The nest found by Vincent was in a tuft of grass about 10 centimetres (4 inches) high. It was also roundish, built of stiff, fine, dry grass, with a downward sloping entrance tube about 2·5 centimetres (1 inch) long. On top was a 'bower', presumably an incomplete cock nest.

Eggs 4 to 6, 10 once found (Weekes), probably due to 2 hens laying in the same nest. In captivity both sexes share in incubation and brooding by day and both are in the nest at night (Schertenleib). Belcher (in Jackson) found a whydah's egg (probably *Vidua macroura*) in a nest together with 4 of the hosts' eggs. Appears to breed more readily and successfully in captivity than most *Estrilda* species (Immelmann *et al.*).

VOICE Immelmann *et al.* transcribe the contact calls of the form *E. paludicola ochrogaster* as a nasal 'tyeek', 'tyeep' or 'Tsyee', the alarm call as 'tsyee-krr' and 'kr-yee-eh'. The song is hard-sounding, similar in rhythm but different in tone to that of *E. melpoda*, 'tek tek tek teketree teketree' and variants.

DISPLAY AND SOCIAL BEHAVIOUR Probably similar or identical to that of *E. astrild*, *E. melpoda* etc but not described in detail. Has been seen to give courtship type display *without* holding a nesting symbol in its bill (Immelmann *et al.*) but probably it normally displays with nesting material in the usual way. Fluffed singing display as in related species (Lafogler, in Immelmann *et al.*).

OTHER NAMES Buff-bellied Waxbill, Marsh Waxbill.

REFERENCES
Chapin, J. P. 1954. The birds of the Belgian Congo. *Bull. Amer. Mus. Nat. Hist.* **75B**.
Immelmann, K., Steinbacher, J. & Wolters, H. E. 1965. *Vögel in Käfig und Voliere: Prachtfinken*: 337–347.
Scherterleib, K. 1961. Der Sumpastrild und seine erste gegluckte Zucht. *Gefiederte Welt* **1961**: 41.
van Someren, V. G. L. & G. R. C. 1949. The birds of Bwamba. *Uganda Journal.* **13**, special supplement.
Vincent, A. W. 1949. On the breeding habits of some African birds. *Ibis* **91**: 660–688.

Anambra Waxbill *Estrilda poliopareia*

Estrilda poliopareia Reichenow, 1902, *Ornith. Monatsb.*, **10**, p. 185. Syn. *Estrilda anambrae* Kemp, 1907.

DESCRIPTION Very similar to the previous form, *E. paludicola*, with which it may be conspecific (see p. 159), but has a proportionately slightly shorter tail and stouter, deeper bill. Most of upper parts dull yellowish brown with faint, but at close quarters clearly visible, darker cross-barring. The head tends to be slightly greyer in tone than the back, both may have a faint greenish tinge and fade to a much greyer, less yellowish hue, in worn plumage. Wings a little darker than back and mantle, inner webs of primaries and secondaries dark drab. Under wing coverts deep buff. Rump and upper tail coverts bright orange-red to bright vermilion. Tail dark drab with obscure darker cross barring, a tinge of red on the basal fringes of the central feathers and buffish tips and outer webs to the outer ones. Face and ear coverts light buffish grey to light buffish brown. Throat whitish to pale buff, shading to medium buff or greyish buff on the centre of the breast and a deeper, richer buff on the belly, ventral patch and under tail coverts. Sides of breast yellowish buff to greyish buff with faint darker cross bars, deepening to brownish buff on the flanks. A variable (often slight) amount of dull red suffusion on the flanks and sometimes also on the sides of the breast. Irides cream-coloured. Bill red. Legs and feet greyish brown.

The female is greyer and less yellowish in general tone, especially on the under parts, and has no red suffusion on the flanks. The red on her rump and upper tail coverts is less brilliant. Sexual differences can be obscured if birds in different states of plumage wear are compared. I have not seen a juvenile of this form.

FIELD CHARACTERS Very small yellowish brown to greyish brown bird with red bill and vivid orange-red rump. Bright red on rump and entirely brown (except for bill) head distinguish it at once from *E. astrild*.

DISTRIBUTION AND HABITAT South-eastern Nigeria; known only from regions of Agoulerie and Onitsha. Has been found in open deciduous forest with long grass, and on grass-grown areas of a river sandbank (Mackworth-Praed & Grant, Serle).

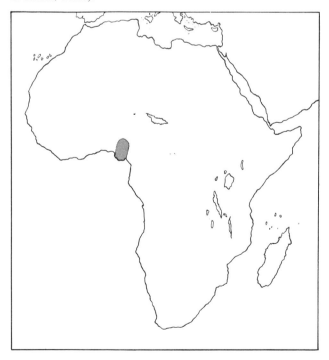

FEEDING AND GENERAL HABITS Little recorded. Serle found it in parties of up to about 20 individuals, feeding on grass seeds taken from the growing plants.

NESTING No information. A female with yolking eggs in her ovary was shot in June in Onitsha (Serle).

VOICE No information.

DISPLAY AND SOCIAL BEHAVIOUR No information. Probably very similar to that of related species such as *E. melpoda*.

REFERENCES
Mackworth-Praed, C. W. & Grant, C. H. B. 1973. *African handbook of birds*, ser. 3, vol. 2.
Serle, W. 1957. A contribution to the ornithology of the eastern region of Nigeria. *Ibis* 99: 371–418.

Black-crowned Waxbill   *Estrilda nonnula*

Astrilda nonnula Hartlaub, 1883, *J. Orn.*, **31**, p. 425.

DESCRIPTION About size of Avadavat but with longer, somewhat graduated tail, shorter bill and softer, denser plumage. Lores, forehead, crown and nape black. Hind neck immediately posterior to black of nape very pale grey with faint darker barring. Mantle, upper back and lesser wing coverts a clear or very slightly bluish grey, barred finely with dark grey. Medium and greater wing coverts similar but darker. Remaining wing quills greyish black to black, sometimes with a slight indication of cross barring. Under wing coverts silvery white. Lower back, rump and upper tail coverts rosy crimson. Tail black. Throat, cheeks, sides of head and most of under-parts silky white, usually with some pale grey suffusion on lower neck, sides of breast and flanks. Many feathers on sides of lower breast and flanks are partly or pre-dominantly rose-red to light crimson. This red tends to show as a line or edging below the wing in life, if the bird is at ease, but is sometimes concealed by the wing, as it usually is in a museum skin. Under tail coverts very pale grey with faint darker barring. Irides dark brown. Bill patterned in light red and black on both mandibles.

The female has the ground colour of her mantle and back brownish grey (barred as in the male) not clear or slightly bluish grey and can be at once identified by this feature if seen close. She also usually has the white areas more suffused with grey. The juvenile is duller and browner, its mantle and back are greyish brown and unbarred. It has no red on the flanks and the red on the rump is duller. Its bill is at first black, with conspicuous white gape flanges. The nestling has a pale yellow palate with 5 black spots, skin of gape black with two curved swollen bluish white ridges at the side, two black spots nearly meet on the tongue and there is a small black crescent beneath the tongue, or in front of it when raised, on the inside of the lower mandible (Chapin, sketch in Immelmann *et al.*).

The above description is of nominate *E.n. nonnula*, from

most of the species' range. *E.n. eisentrauti*, from Mount Cameroon, has the white parts strongly suffused with grey; its breast and underparts being predominantly a silky pale grey rather than white. *E.n. elizae*, from Fernando Po, is similar to *E.n. eisentrauti* but slightly larger. (Note: owing possibly to mistranslation from the original German description, *E.n. eisentrauti* is sometimes said to be larger than, and *E.n. elizae* smaller than the nominate form, but this is incorrect.) See plate 7, facing p. 256.

FIELD CHARACTERS Tiny grey and whitish bird with black cap and tail and red rump. Often in flocks. Black cap and rest of colour pattern distinguish it from all other waxbills except the closely related *E. atricapilla*, which is very similar in appearance but darker above and below, brighter red on rump and flanks, and has the upper mandible entirely black.

DISTRIBUTION AND HABITAT Tropical Africa south south-eastern Nigeria, Cameroons and former Spanish Guinea through northern Congo (Zaïre) to extreme south-western Sudan, Uganda, south-western Kenya, Bukoba in Lake Victoria, Rwanda, and eastern Congo south to Kivu and Fernando Po island.

Inhabits grassy forest clearings, glades and forest edge, cultivated areas or savanna with abundance of bushes and trees, locally on rather bare mountain slopes with bamboo or elephant grass. Commonly in European-type gardens where these have been made within its general habitat. Has a wide altitudinal range, in the Cameroons from near sea-level to about 2500 metres (8000 feet) (Bannerman). In the Kivu Highlands, this species is found higher than any other waxbill, in bamboo with only a few stunted trees, where the night temperatures throughout

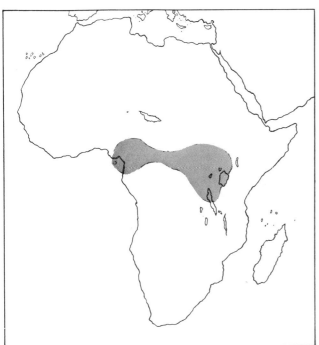

the year are only about 5°C although also common lower down and in the hot lowlands (Kunkel, 1964).

FEEDING AND GENERAL HABITS Known to feed largely on grass seeds, including cultivated millet when available. Also catches flying termites on the wing (Chapin). Probably takes other seeds and small insects although Pascha's (in Hartlaub) statement that it takes all kinds of small seeds ('allerlei kleinen Samereien') and tiny insects *including red ants* (italics mine), perhaps needs confirmation. Said also to feed on buds (Mackworth-Praed & Grant), an interesting piece of convergent behaviour (if valid), as to me this species in life irresistibly suggests a miniature Bullfinch, *Pyrrhula pyrrhula*. Kunkel (pers. comm.), who studied and kept this species in Africa, found that populations from the Kivu highlands were specialist feeders on a particular grass, *Setaria* sp., and very difficult to wean to substitute food and keep alive in captivity, whereas populations from the lowlands presented no such difficulties.

My captive birds of this species ate quantities of maw seed as well as dry and soaked millet, green and ripe seeds of many grasses but especially *Poa annua*, Knot-grass, *Polygonum aviculare*, and Chickweed, *Stellaria media*. Possibly the maw seed was too fattening for them, however, as they never bred and did not live many years (Goodwin). For some time they refused all live food except green aphids but later also took mealworms and blowfly pupae. In captivity this species has reared its young largely on ant pupae and seeding *Poa annua* in one instance (Wharton-Tiger) and on these and water fleas, *Drosophila*, in another (Kleefisch). A third successful breeder (Müller) found that his birds fed mostly millet to their young. Anyone attempting to breed this species would, however, be well advised to offer any available small insects, especially ant pupae and green aphids, and seeding grasses, besides soaked millet and grass seed.

Highly social. Commonly in small flocks. Sometimes in larger flocks and thousands may gather to feed on ripening millet crops (Mackworth-Praed & Grant). Sometimes, perhaps usually, in pairs when breeding but the pairs would appear to keep in loose contact with former flock mates (Pascha, in Hartlaub). Feeds both on the ground and in vegetation and holds objects under foot when needed in the usual *Estrilda* manner.

Kleefisch states that the male of a captive pair roosted in the rather shallow cock nest on top of the breeding nest. I think this was an idiosyncrisy of the individual bird and not a characteristic or even usual habit of the species.

NESTING Nest built in a bush, shrub, tree, creeper, hedge or grass clump, from less than 1 to about 6 metres high. Several nests may be sited in the same tree or shrub (Pascha, in Hartlaub; Chapin). The nest is built of grass stems and/or panicles and there is usually a shortish entrance tube, sloping downward. Chapin notes that the 'grass tops' 'project around this opening.' There may or may not be a cock nest on top (Bannerman, Chapin, Kleefisch, the van Somerens); probably this depends on the stage at which the nest is found and/or how much spare time the birds have had since finishing the real nest. The nest is lined with feathers, vegetable down, fine fibres and similar materials (Pascha, in Hartlaub, Mackworth-Praed & Grant, Immelmann *et al.*, Kleefisch, Müller). Four to six eggs.

Incubation period given as 11 days by Immelmann *et al.* and 13 to 15 days by Kleefisch. Probably the latter periods relate to nests at which incubation was interrupted. Young fledge at 18–20 days (Kleefisch). All the above periods from captive birds. Both sexes share incubation by day in the usual manner. In captivity young were brooded by day until about the twelfth day (Kleefisch), and roosted in the nest for some time after fledging (Wharton-Tiger).

In the Cameroons breeds at the end of the wet season and beginning of the dry season, from January to October, in north-eastern Congo from July to November, in Uganda in September and October and from January to May.

VOICE All the calls that I heard from my captive birds were very soft, though usually high-pitched, and in great contrast to the loud, harsh calls of the Rosy-rumped and Black-rumped Waxbills. I have seen no other accounts of the vocalisations of this species so this section is taken from my previous paper on it (Goodwin).

The locomotion-intention and close contact call is a thin, high-pitched 'tee-tee' or 'tsee-tsee-tsee' etc, uttered especially at the moment of taking flight. The distance contact call differs from the above only in being somewhat louder and longer: 'tseee-tseee' or 'tseee-tseee-tseee'.

The alarm call differs from the contact call in having a distinct 'r' sound in it. It could be written 'srree-sree', 'tsrreee-tsrreee-tsrree' etc. It is given in many apparent conflict situations in which some fear appeared to be involved. A rather different version, in which a single sharp high-pitched 'tchink' prefaces the trilling 'tsrreee' was heard on a few occasions when I closely approached an individual that had been put in a cage new to it. It perhaps indicates a more intense alarm or fear. The nest call is a faint soft twittering, very like that of the Goldbreast, but running up and down the scale more and very 'pure' and 'sweet' in tone. It is used by both sexes. What may be the song of the male, at least it is sometimes uttered during the courtship display, is a call much like the alarm, followed at once by one like the contact call: 'trreee-teee': that of the female a single, long-drawn 'teeee'.

DISPLAY AND SOCIAL BEHAVIOUR In the greeting display the bird with angled tail and head turned somewhat towards the other bird, hops or sidles up to it. At high intensity the body is somewhat tilted away and the flank feathers somewhat raised so that the red on the flank is contiguous with that of the upper tail coverts and both are fully visible to the partner, without the wing 'bisecting' them as it does when held normally. I observed that this behaviour was usually followed or interspersed with very deliberate bill-wiping which, being more slowly performed, was more immediately obvious than in some other species. Kunkel

(1966), although he saw incipient nodding from this species, never saw bill-wiping from it in this situation, as he did from the related *E. atricapilla*.

In the courtship display the male takes a *slender* stem of flowering or seeding grass by its firmer end, flies up to a perch and, after mandibulating the end of the stem for some moments, begins to jerk his head upwards, the body moving at each throw of the head but the feet not leaving the perch for a moment. Except in this last point, the display movements seemed more like those of *Uraeginthus angolensis* or *U. bengalus* than of *Estrilda troglodytes*. The display is usually interspersed with little jerky, side to side movements of the head. Less often I saw a more *troglodytes*-like version in which the male made deliberate upward thrusts of his head, keeping it held at an upward angle. I twice saw a female display in rather similar manner but without any material in her bill and with a more horizontal body posture. Sometimes the presumed song (see section on Voice) was uttered but more often my birds displayed in silence. In all instances when I saw these displays the mate (of either sex) was not in full breeding condition and did not respond. Possibly these were all rather low-intensity versions of courtship display. Wharton-Tiger, whose Black-crowned Waxbills bred successfully, describes the displaying male as slowly jumping up and down with a long piece of hay in his bill, 'uttering a small note', the female responding by coming to him and copulation then taking place.

Allo-preening and mandibulation occur in the usual contexts. The fluffed singing display does not occur.

OTHER NAMES Black-capped Waxbill, White-breasted Waxbill.

REFERENCES

Bannerman, D. A. 1953. *The birds of West and tropical Africa*, vol. 2. Oliver & Boyd, Edinburgh and London.

Chapin, J. P. 1954. The birds of the Belgian Congo. *Bull. Amer. Mus. Nat. Hist.* **75B**.

Goodwin, D. 1963. Some notes on Black-capped Waxbills. *Avicult. Mag.* **69**: 149–157.

Hartlaub, G. 1889. Aus den Ornithologischen Tagebüchern Dr Emin Pascha's: 3 *Estrilda nonnula* Hartl. *J. Orn.* **37**: 46–48.

Immelmann, K., Steinbacher, J. & Wolters, H. E. 1964. *Vögel in Käfig und Voliere: Prachtfinken*: 295–302. Aachen, Germany.

Kleefisch, Th. 1971. Einiger meiner Zuchterfolge 1970. *Gefiederte Welt* **95**: 50–53.

Kunkel, P. 1964. Prachtfinken im Kivuhochland. *Gefiederte Welt* **1964**: 141–142.

Kunkel, P. 1967. Displays facilitating sociability in waxbills of the genera *Estrilda* and *Lagonosticta* (Fam. Estrildidae). *Behaviour* **29**: 237–261.

Mackworth-Praed, C. W. & Grant, C. H. B. 1973. Birds of west central and western Africa. *African handbook of birds*, ser. 2, vol. 2. Longman Group Ltd, London.

Müller, J. 1976. Haltung und Zucht des Nonnenastrilds. *Gefiederte Welt* **100**: 183.

van Someren, V. G. L. & G. R. C. 1949. The birds of Bwamba. *Uganda Journal*, **13**, special supplement.

Wharton-Tiger, N. 1936. Breeding the Black-crowned Waxbill (*Estrilda nonnula*). *Avicult. Mag.* 5th ser., **1**: 323–325.

Black-headed Waxbill   *Estrilda atricapilla*

Estrelda atricapilla J. and E. Verreaux, 1851, *Rev. Mag. Zool.* (Paris), ser. 2, **3**, p. 421.

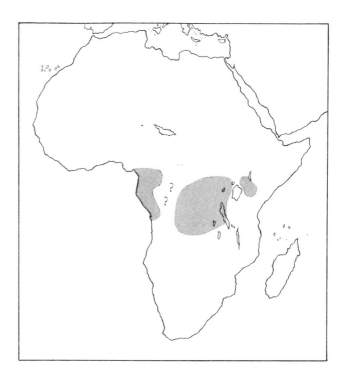

DESCRIPTION Despite its name has an identical cap-like distribution of black on the head to that of *E. nonnula* which it otherwise also resembles except as follows: the grey on the upper parts is of a slightly bluer tone, with the dark grey barring more pronounced, both the dark bars and the pale grey between them being a little wider. Throat and cheeks heavily suffused with grey except immediately contiguous to the black cap. Sides of neck, lower throat and breast smoke grey. Belly, ventral area and under tail coverts sooty black. Red on the flanks more extensive and, like the rump and upper tail coverts, of a brighter red – shining scarlet rather than rosy crimson as in *E. nonnula*. Upper mandible entirely black (lower with a pink or red triangular mark at the base, as in *E. nonnula*). The female has the mantle and back a little paler and duller grey and her grey underparts and the red on her flanks tend to be a little paler than the male's. Juvenile browner and duller with cross-barring present but inconspicuous. Juvenile males have very little red on the flanks and juvenile females none, at least this was the case with 3 juvenile males and 2 juvenile females that I examined.

The above description is of nominate *E.a. atricapilla*, from south-eastern Nigeria, southern Cameroons and through Gabon to the lower Congo. *E. atricapilla avakubi*, from the Congo lowlands from Tshuapa and Ituri districts south to Kasai and north-eastern Angola, is a paler bluish grey ground colour above, paler grey on the breast, sooty grey rather than sooty black on the belly and nearly white on throat and cheeks. *E.a. marungensis*, from the high plateaux of Marungu, is very similar but greyer on the face. I have not seen a specimen of this form. *E.a. kandti* (formerly *graueri*), from the highlands of eastern Congo, above 1500 metres (5000 feet), from north-west of Lake Edward south through Kivu to Rwanda, Mt Elgon, Aberdares and Mt Kenya, has the grey of the upper parts duller and more finely barred with dark grey than in either of the other two races. Its underparts are as pale as those of *E. atricapilla avakubi* but the grey areas often show distinct traces of cross-barring. The sexes of *E.a. kandti* differ more markedly than in the nominate form (or in *E. nonnula*), the female's mantle and back being drab brown, only slightly, if at all, tinged with grey (with the usual darker cross barring) and her underparts are pale brownish grey where the male's are grey.

Prigogine (1975a) by identifying as *E. atricapilla*, a fledgling hitherto considered to be *E. nonnula*, established the priority of the name *kandti* for the race hitherto, and in current (1978) standard works, known as *graueri*. In a longer (1975b) paper he discusses in detail the geographic variation in this species.

FIELD CHARACTERS Tiny grey or (female of the race *graueri*) drab bird with black cap and tail and brilliant red on rump and flanks. Probably not distinguishable in the field from *E. nonnula* except when entirely black upper mandible can be seen, or when the two are seen together at close quarters.

DISTRIBUTION AND HABITAT Africa from extreme south-eastern Nigeria and southern Cameroons south to extreme north-eastern Angola; Congo (Zaïre), Kivu, Rwanda, and east to Mt Elgon, the Aberdares and Mt Kenya. Inhabits grass-grown forest clearings, forest edge, paths and roadsides in forest country, mountain watercourses; similar places in bamboo-covered mountains, and gardens and cultivated areas in forest or bamboo. Not found in extensive clearings with little cover.

FEEDING AND GENERAL HABITS Known to take seeds of grasses and sedges but species apparently unrecorded (Chapin, Webb, 1934 and 1937). An immature collected by Chapin had also eaten 18 small ants. Feeds both on the ground and in vegetation. Where their ranges overlap often feeds in company with *E. nonnula*, apparently on the same foods. Webb found it difficult to wean captive birds onto millet (Webb, 1934) and the species seems seldom to have been imported into Europe and those that were not to have been kept for long. Like some other waxbills that in part of their natural range endure very cold night temperatures, it appears more delicate in captivity than many that are exclusively birds of hot habitats.

Usually in small flocks of up to about 20. Not (so far) seen in large flocks. Two were caught roosting at night in an old nest of the weaver, *Euplectes nigricollis* (Bates).

NESTING Extant descriptions all seem to derive from a nest found by a little girl at Efulen, Cameroon, another believed (on good circumstantial evidence) to be of this species also found at Efulen (Bates) and one found by Belcher on the Kinangop Plateau, Kenya on 19 November (Chapin). The first was 'water bottle shaped' and made entirely of fine grass panicles. One of the parents was caught in the nest which contained 2 eggs, presumably an incomplete clutch. The second nest was similar but empty. Below it was a smaller nest of similar shape 'pressed against the main nest like a small growing onion flattened against a larger', which contained 5 eggs. The first nest was found in a shrub at about the height of the finder's shoulders; Bates does not state the site of the second. The nest found by Belcher, on 19 November, was 2·8 metres (9 feet) high in a sapling, it was lined with feathers and contained 4 eggs; it had no cock nest attached to it.

VOICE No information. Probably very similar to that of *E. nonnula* (q.v.).

DISPLAY AND SOCIAL BEHAVIOUR Greeting display as in *E. nonnula* but with ceremonial bill-wiping at every lowering of the head (Kunkel). Other displays apparently not recorded but probably very like those of *E. nonnula*. The fluffed singing display does not occur (Kunkel).

OTHER NAMES Grey-breasted Waxbill.

REFERENCES
Bates, G. L. 1909. Field-notes on the birds of Southern Kamerun, West Africa. *Ibis*, Jan. **1909**: 1–74.
Chapin, J. P. 1954. The birds of the Belgian Congo. *Bull. Amer. Mus. Nat. Hist.* **75B**.
Kunkel, P. 1967. Displays facilitating sociability in waxbills of the genera *Estrilda* and *Lagonosticta* (Fam. Estrildidae). *Behaviour* **29**: 237–261.
Prigogine, A. 1975a. The status of *Estrilda kandti* and *Estrilda atricapilla graueri*. *Bull. Br. Orn Cl.* **95**: 15–18.
Prigogine, A. 1975b. Les populations de *Estrilda atricapilla* (Verreaux) de l'Afrique centrale et description d'une nouvelle race (Aves). *Rev. Zool. Afr.* **89**, no. 3: 600–617.
Webb, C. S. 1934. Some notes on a collecting trip in Kenya. *Avicult. Mag.* 4th ser., **7**: 1–10.
Webb, C. S. 1937. A collector in French Cameroon. *Avicult. Mag.* 5th ser., **2**, 2–10.

Black-cheeked Waxbill   *Estrilda erythrononotos*

Fringilla erythronotos Vieillot, 1817, *Nouv. Dist. Hist. Nat.*, nouv. ed., **12**, p. 182.

DESCRIPTION Very slightly smaller than Violet-eared Waxbill, with proportionately smaller bill and shorter (but still rather long) tail. Forehead medium ash grey; crown and nape a slightly darker grey, tinged with pink and with faint fine darker cross-bearing on the feathers. Mantle and back similar but with a darker pink or wine-red suffusion and the fine barring more prominent. Rump and upper tail coverts purplish red to deep scarlet. Tail black. Wing coverts and inner secondaries light pinkish grey with conspicuous blackish cross-barring. Other secondaries and primaries blackish with their outer webs a dull reddish grey, obscurely barred with dull blackish.

Underwing coverts mainly silvery grey, with faint darker barring. Face, including lores, area immediately above eyes and most of the ear coverts, black, bordered posteriorly with a lighter pinkish grey than elsewhere. Throat (except for blackish 'chin') and breast deep pinkish grey with faint darker cross-barring, the feathers tending to be tipped with wine-red or carmine towards the predominantly wine-red, carmine or, less often, deep scarlet flanks. Centre of belly, ventral area and under tail coverts black, the latter narrowly fringed with pale greyish. Irides red or, *fide* Immelmann *et al.*, brownish red. Bill blackish, usually with a bluish grey area at the base of the sides of the mandibles. Legs and feet black.

Female usually a little paler and less reddish, less extensively red on the flanks and dusky reddish grey rather than black on belly, ventral patch and under tail coverts. Immelmann *et al.* state that some have claimed that the male's iris is red and that of the female brown. Only a few of the many specimens in the British Museum (Natural History) have the iris colour noted on their labels but, with only one exception (a male whose eye colour is given as 'hazel') they corroborate this, eyes of three males being noted as 'red' or 'crimson' and of two females as 'light brown'.

Juvenile duller and less pinkish in body colour with only faint and indistinct cross-barring, except on the wings. Its red areas are a dark rusty orange-red. Mouth of nestling with five black spots on the palate, two more or less fusing spots on the tongue, interior of under mandible with (Immelmann *et al.*) or without (Steiner) a black half-moon marking on the inside of the lower mandible (probably age or individual differences are involved) Gape tubercles yellowish white, each with a large black spot on its inside.

The above description is of the southern forms of the species. Of these the western population, *E.e. soligena*, has been separated on minimal average differences of size and colour, tending to be brighter and larger. The above description is composite and covers both *E.e. soligena*, and nominate *E.e. erythronotos*.

The form from Uganda, Kenya and Tanzania, *E.e. delamerei*, is a clearly recognisable and readily differentiated race. It is slightly smaller and markedly paler. Its forehead is very pale grey, the ground colour of its upper and under parts is paler and suffused with mauvish pink or rose pink rather than dark pink or wine-red. The red on its rump and upper tail coverts is lighter and that on its flanks deep pink to rose-red. The black face patches are very clearly bordered posteriorly with very pale silvery grey or silvery beige. The black on the male's belly and ventral patch is dusky and less extensive. Base of both mandibles often more extensively bluish grey. Sexual differences as in the southern form but perhaps more marked; in particular the belly and ventral areas of the female are hardly darker than the rest of her underparts.

FIELD CHARACTERS Tiny dark reddish grey or pinkish grey bird with black cheeks, rather long black tail and red rump. For differences from *E. charmosyna* see under that species.

DISTRIBUTION AND HABITAT South Africa in northern Cape Province, Orange Free State, Griqua Land West, Transvaal and northern and central South West Africa. Botswana (Bechuanaland), Rhodesia, south-western Angola and south-western Zambia. Also East Africa in Tanzania from Lake Victoria to Iringa and Lake Manka near the Usambara Mountains; southern Kenya east to the Athi River and Doinyo Narok, and Uganda north to Lake Albert. Inhabits dry acacia thornbush country in the southern part of its range. Less information from eastern Africa where most extant accounts seem to stem from Lynes, who mentioned that trees seemed to be an essential feature of its habitat.

FEEDING AND GENERAL HABITS Feeds largely on seeds of grasses but also takes termites, small caterpillars and other small insects, some green vegetation, nectar and

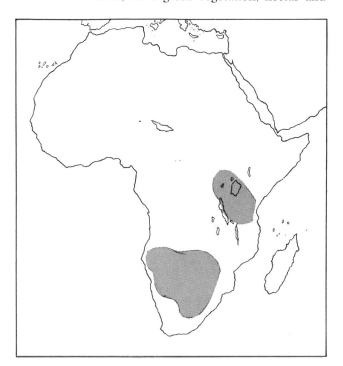

possibly fruit. Destroys the blossoms of acacias and cultivated apricots (probably of other trees too), presumably to obtain nectar or pollen. In a detailed study of this species in Central Transvaal, Skead found that seeds of the grasses *Panicum laevifolium*, *P. maximum* and *Egrarostris* spp. comprised a large part of the diet. Also taken were seeds of the grasses *Urochloa mosambiciensis*, *Tricholaena monachne*, *Cenchrus ciliaris*, *Sporobolus* spp. and *Aristida* spp., small termites (but not the large Harvester Termites) and nectar from the aloe, *Aloe davyana*. Skead thought that green grass seeds probably formed the bulk of the food fed to the young but detailed examination of droppings of nestlings showed that, in 19 out of 36 samples, the young had been fed (in part) on beetles, at least several different unidentifiable species being involved. Few or no termites had been fed to the young, in contrast to the situation with *Uraeginthus angolensis*, *U. granatina*, and *Pytilia melba* breeding in the same area (Skead).

In captivity a pair reared their young successfully largely on ant pupae (Wåhlen). Another pair fed their young almost entirely on aphids for the first 8 days and then on ant pupae and egg food (Immelmann *et al.*). Another pair fed their young on aphids, blowfly pupae (presumably the soft contents), milk sop, a soft food containing 'many nutritious ingredients', sprouting seed, grass seeds and cuttle fish bone. Usually several different items were taken by the parents prior to each feeding of the young (Osborne). The species is not usually at all easy to keep in captivity in the northern hemisphere. Immelmann *et al.* recommend abundant supplies of fresh (or deep frozen) ant pupae, aphids and newly-moulted mealworms as well as both dry and sprouted seed. Eggfood may be a partial substitute for insects when these are not obtainable. The easily bred Whiteworm is, apparently, usually refused. The Black-cheeked Waxbill, although it endures below freezing temperatures at night in winter in the southern parts of its range, is very sensitive to cold and temperature changes in captivity.

Usually in pairs or, when not breeding, small parties of from 8 to 14 birds. Very active and agile when feeding among growing grasses, will at times hang head down to feed (Skead). Pulls down grass panicles and holds them underfoot to feed from like other *Estrilda* species. Sometimes, perhaps usually, roosts in the old nests of other birds such as *Ploceus* and *Plocepasser*.

NESTING Nest usually from 3 to 9 metres (10 to 30 feet) above ground in a thorny tree (Hoesch, Roberts, Vincent); one nest found in a thickly-foliaged fig tree (Lynes). Nest large for the size of the bird, more or less retort-shaped or pear-shaped, with a downward sloping entrance tube 6 to 14 cm long. Built of grass stems and attached panicles; the thick inner walls and lining almost or entirely of flowering or soft seeding grass panicles. Feathers have apparently not been found in the real nest. Vincent noted of a nest he examined that the grass stems forming the tubular entrance were 'protruding raggedly and converging so as to conceal and practically close it'. Similar (perhaps identical) construction of the entrance seems suggested, or at least not contradicated, by other descriptions (Hoesch, Lynes, Skead).

Of the four wild nests for which I can find reasonably detailed descriptions two (Skead, Vincent) had cock nests on top and Skead found other nests with a cock nest on top and presumably none without. The cock nest is roundish, smaller than the real nest and supported at its sides by grass stems protruding from the top of the real nest. Down feathers were found outside the entrance to one cock nest. Larger feathers and/or eggshell or snailshell are placed inside it (Skead). Neither Skead nor Vincent describe the entrance to the cock nest but Immelmann *et al.* state that it is wide, presumably, therefore, more obvious than the real (tubular) entrance to the real nest.

Eggs 3 to 6. Incubation period 12 days. Young fledged at 22 days and began to feed themselves 10 days later (Wählen, observations on captive birds in Germany). Both sexes incubate, brood and feed the young but in two instances with captive birds the males were observed only to remain on the nest for short periods and the greater part of the incubation, even by day, appeared to be done by the female (Osborne, Wählen). Parasitised by the Steel-blue Whydah, *Vidua hypocherina* (J. Nicolai, pers. comm.).

VOICE Both as a contact call and as a song the male uses a thin, somewhat shivering, 'teeh-heeh' (Immelmann *et al.*, my anglicisation), what is clearly the same call is described by McLachlan and Liversidge as a melodious, slightly quavering, ascending and mournful 'fwooee'. The contact call of the female is a disyllabic 'psyee psyee' with no upward infliction (Nicolai, Immelmann *et al.*). Captive individuals can be sexed by caging them briefly apart and noting the type of contact calls they use.

DISPLAY AND SOCIAL BEHAVIOUR Kunkel describes a greeting display with pronounced nodding, that he saw when he introduced birds strange to each other and, less often, between males and females of newly mated pairs (Kunkel, 1967). Initially both birds perch side by side with their bodies somewhat turned away but their heads half turned towards each other. The body feathers are slightly fluffed and the tail angled toward to the partner. The head feathers are arranged to make the triangular head. The general posture is upright. Now the bird lowers its body till it is below the horizontal position, at the same time moving a little laterally towards the partner, the lifted tail is moved from side to side. A quick symbolic bill wipe, or its intention movements, is then performed. This may be repeated up to ten times. Usually by the time the first bird is in the low position and about to make its first bill wipe, the other begins so that at each moment subsequently when one is down the other is up. If, however, the second bird does not begin to display at the 'right' moment it does not subsequently alter its rhythm.

The courtship display is similar to that of other *Estrilda* species, the male holding a grass stem by one end in his bill, thrusting his head and body up and down and singing.

Nicolai (in Immelmann *et al.*) notes that the male often performs this display and song when alone and will deliberately withdraw from his mate apparently in order to display and sing alone.

Presumably clumping and allo-preening occur but they do not seem to have been specifically recorded (though their absence probably would have been).

OTHER NAMES Black-faced Waxbill.

REFERENCES

Hoesch, W. & Niethammer, G. 1940. Die Vogelwelt Deutsch-Sudwestafrikas namentlich des Damara- und Namalandes. *J. Orn.* **88**: Sonderheft.

Immelmann, K., Steinbacher, J. & Wolters, H. E. 1964. *Vögel in Käfig und Voliere. Prachtfinken*: 279–286. Aachen, Germany.

Kunkel, P. 1967. Displays facilitating sociability in waxbills of the genera *Estrilda* and *Lagonosticta*. *Behaviour* **29**: 237–261.

Lynes, H. 1934. Birds of the Ubena-Uhehe Highlands and Iringa Uplands. *J. Orn.* **82**: Sonderheft.

McLachlan, G. R. & Liversidge, R. 1957. *Roberts birds of South Africa*. Cape Town.

Nicolai, J. 1963. Zu den Berichten über Seltener Astrild, Schönbürzel, Wellenastrild und Blauer Honigsauger. *Gefiederte Welt* Jan. **1963**: 18.

Osborne, D. G. 1974. Breeding the Black-cheeked Waxbill, *Estrilda erythronota*. *Avicult. Mag.* **80**: 17–19.

Skead, D. M. 1975. Ecological studies of four estrildines in the Central Transvaal. *Ostrich* Supplement No. 11.

Vincent, A. W. 1949. On the breeding habits of some African birds. *Ibis* **91**: 660–688.

Wählen, W. 1973. Haltung und Zucht des Elfenastrilds (*Estrilda erythronotos*). *Gefiederte Welt* December **1973**: 227.

Pink-bellied Black-cheeked Waxbill
Estrilda charmosyna

Habropyga charmosyna Reichenow, 1881, *Ornith. Centralbl.*, **6**, p. 78.

DESCRIPTION Very similar to the previous species, *E. erythronotos*, from the paler northern race (*E.e. delamerei*) of which it differs in plumage as follows: General coloration paler and usually more evenly and intensely suffused with a paler and brighter pink. Pale posterior border to the black cheeks even more pronounced and white to pale pink in colour. Barring on wings blackish and almost clear white and even more sharply contrasted.

Red on rump and upper tail coverts usually brighter. No blackish on belly or ventral area which are almost clear pale rose-pink, salmon-pink or mauvish pink. No black on the pale pinkish throat except for a very narrow band just at the base of the lower mandible. Bill pale bluish grey tipped with sepia or blackish. Irides red, wine-red or reddish brown. Legs and feet black. Examination of skins suggests that in life this form may be a little slimmer in appearance than *E. erythronotos* and with, on average, a proportionately slightly longer tail.

Female much less strongly suffused with pink, so that she looks predominantly greyish rather than pinkish in colour. Belly and ventral area usually pink but paler than in male and sometimes greyish. Irides brown. Both sexes show much individual variation in amount and intensity of the pink suffusion but the dullest males, that I have seen skins of, are pinker than the brightest females. In very worn and bleached plumage the pink tinge may be lost. Juvenile like that of *E. erythronotos* (q.v.) but paler.

The above description is of *E.c. charmosyna* (syn. *E. nigrimentum*), from Somalia, south-eastern Abyssinia, Harar, southern Sudan, north-eastern Uganda, northern Kenya and Jubaland. *E.c. pallidior*, from the vicinity of the Guaso Nyiro river, was originally described (Jackson) as being much paler and lacking the rosy tinge on the underparts. I have seen skins of three females and one male (the type) of this race. The females are a little paler than most of the several specimens of nominate *E.c. charmosyna* species, with which I have compared them and have their bellies and ventral areas a very clear, pale pink, but they seem doubtfully separable. The male (assuming it to have been correctly sexed by the collector) is noticeably paler and less pink than males of nominate *charmosyna* but almost exactly matches the most pinkish females of that race. *E.c. kiwanukae*, from southern Kenya and northern Tanzania, is said (van Someren) to be much greyer and less pinkish in colour than other races. I have not seen specimens of it.

FIELD CHARACTERS As *E. erythronotos* but paler and brighter looking. Dr J. Nicolai (pers. comm.) found it difficult to distinguish it from *E. erythronotos delamerei* unless the pale pinkish belly was visible.

DISTRIBUTION AND HABITAT North-eastern Africa from southern Sudan (Torit), southern Abyssinia, and northern Somalia south to north-eastern Uganda, south-eastern Kenya and northern Tanzania south to Olduvai and Dodoma. Inhabits arid thorn scrub both in lowlands and hills. In South Abyssinia, Benson found it at from 900 to 1400 metres (3000 to 4600 feet).

FEEDING AND GENERAL HABITS So far as known does not differ from previous species, *E. erythronotos*.

NESTING I am indebted for this information to Dr Jürgen Nicolai who studied this species in April and May of 1980 in the Athi River District of Kenya. Nests in bushes or shrubs, usually 2 to 3 metres above ground. Usually in *Acacia brevispica*, *Commiphora schimperi* and *Capparis*

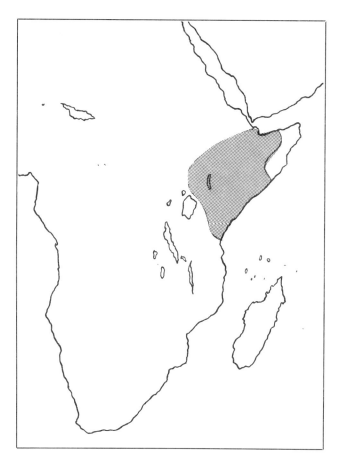

tomentosa. Nest large, pear-shaped with an entrance tube, built of grass stems and panicles. All nests found had a thinner-walled, *feather*-lined cock nest on top. All clutches found were of 4 eggs. Parasitised by the Steel-blue Whydah, *Vidua hypocherina*. Juveniles thought to be at most about two months old were collected in July in south Abyssinia (Benson).

VOICE The only calls described are 'a loud sweet whistle of two cadences' and 'a pretty warbling song' (Mackworth-Praed & Grant). Possibly this represents the male's song and contact call and the inconsequential warbling of immature birds respectively.

DISPLAY AND SOCIAL BEHAVIOUR No information. Probably very similar or identical to that of *E. erythronotos* (q.v.).

OTHER NAMES Pink-bellied Black-faced Waxbill.

REFERENCES

Benson, C. W. 1947 Notes on birds of Southern Abyssinia. *Ibis* **89**: 29–50.

Immelmann, K., Nicolai, J., Steinbacher, J. & Wolters, H. E. 1964. *Vögel in Käfig und Voliere: Prachtfinken*: 286–290. Aachen, Germany.

Jackson, F. J. 1910. Description of six new species of birds from East Africa. *Bull. Br. Orn. Cl.* **27**: 6–8.

Mackworth-Praed, C. W. & Grant, C. H. B. 1960. *African handbook of birds* ser. 1, vol. 2. London.

van Someren, V. G. L. 1919. Exhibition and description of new birds from Africa. *Bull. Br. Orn. Cl.* **40**: 52–58.

Lavender Waxbill   *Estrilda caerulescens*

Fringilla caerulescens Vieillot, 1817, *Nouv. Dict. Hist. Nat.*, nouv. ed., **12**, p. 176.

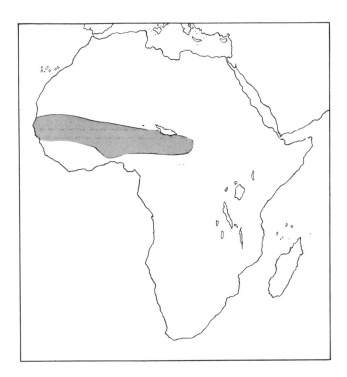

DESCRIPTION About size of Avadavat or very slightly larger with proportionately rather longer, more sharply pointed bill and wings and broader tail. Narrow black stripe from gape to and beyond the eye. Lower back, rump and the long, dense upper tail coverts, which reach about half way down the tail, a deep, rich crimson. Under tail coverts and central tail feathers a slightly duller crimson. Outer tail feathers dark grey, all except the outermost pair more or less fringed with dull crimson or carmine red on their outer webs. Inner webs and tips of primaries dark grey. Rest of plumage a delicate, slightly bluish grey shading to whitish grey on cheeks, throat and upper breast and to sooty grey to nearly black on centre of belly and the lower flanks. Lower flanks spotted with white, each small white spot near, but not quite at, the end of a feather and heightened by a black anterior border. Irides dark brown. Bill blackish at tip and usually also on culmen and lower part of lower mandible, base of bill, especially at centre, bluish grey and/or dark reddish. Legs and feet blackish brown, black or very dark olive.

Female not usually, if ever, so blackish on belly as male (Abrahams, in Butler, pers. examination of sexed skins) but voice differences (q.v.) are probably the best way of sexing live individuals. Juvenile slightly paler, with no white spots on flanks and the red parts duller and paler. Nestling has bluish white gape tubercles (Immelmann *et al.*). Its mouth pattern (*fide* Steiner) is like that of the Red-billed Firefinch, *Lagonosticta senegala*.

FIELD CHARACTERS Very small bluish grey bird with deep red lower back, rump and tail. Quite unlike any sympatric species. Its close, allopatric, relatives *E. perreini* and *E. thomensis* have black tails.

DISTRIBUTION AND HABITAT Tropical western Africa, in Senegal and former Portuguese Guinea east through Mali, northern Ghana and northern Nigeria to northern Cameroons and south-western Chad. Inhabits semi-arid country with bushes and/or trees and some open areas; rocky places with mimosa and other shrubs; areas of short grass with scattered or adjacent bushes or trees and sometimes gardens and cultivated areas that provide comparable conditions (Bannerman, Bates, Immelmann *et al.*, Mackworth-Praed & Grant).

FEEDING AND GENERAL HABITS Seeks food both on the ground and in trees and bushes. Very little information on its habits in the wild but it is known to take seeds, including, (*fide* Bates) the seeds of small fruits, and small insects. Holds grass stems etc. under foot when feeding, like other *Estrilda* species. A captive individual has been seen to hang by one foot whilst investigating a leaf held in the other (Harrison). Usually in pairs or straggling parties (Bates). Flies very fast. Locomotion-intention movements of the tail slight, in strong contrast to most *Estrilda* species

and it does not wag or switch its tail from side to side as they do (Kunkel, 1959). In captivity it is, unless ill, an extremely active, alert and inquisitive bird.

In captivity, at least in Britain and western Europe, it is usually rather delicate and sensitive to temperature changes, especially newly imported birds that have been partially plucked (as they usually have) by their companions, need warmth and careful feeding with, if at all possible, fresh ant pupae, greenfly and other small insects as well as seed, green food and soft food. The Lavender Waxbill will usually drink artificial nectar readily. It has been claimed that once 'acclimatised', it does not need artificial heat or light in winter in Britain (Boosey) but when Lavender Waxbills have survived a British winter without extra light and warmth it is probable either that exceptionally tough individuals or an exceptionally mild winter, or more likely both, were involved.

Roosts by preference in old nests of its own or other species. If forced to roost in the branches, sometimes does so hanging head downwards like a hanging-parrot, *Loriculus* (Karl, in Immelmann *et al.*).

NESTING I can find no information on wild birds. The following information is based on observations on captive birds in Europe. Builds a rounded nest with downward sloping entrance tube about 15 centimetres long. Will sometimes make use of old nests of weavers, Ploceidae, that build nests with tubular entrances. Rather large items, such as long, coarse grass stems up to 30 centimetres long and stems of Shepherd's Purse, are preferred for the outside of the nest, which is lined with finer grasses and fibres. As with other *Estrilda* species, it uses its feet to hold down material when building. Usually nests fairly high up, Kunkel found his birds always built among twigs or branches directly beneath the ceiling of the room. Munz found that his birds regularly placed feathers, bits of wood, large bird droppings and above all dead nestlings on top of their nests.

Both sexes incubate and brood in the usual way. Young fledge at 16 to 18 days and are fed by the parents for about another 14 days (Immelmann *et al.*, Kunkel, 1959).

VOICE Close contact call a short, shrill, high-pitched 'squee' or 'tsee'; in alarm this is lengthened and intensified 'tseeay' (Immelmann *et al.*) or 'a shrill, explosive "squeep"' (Harrison). The distance or high intensity contact call of the female is a two or three syllabled 'tseeeht-tseeet' or 'tseeeht-tseeht-tseeet', which the male answers with his song phrase. This latter is a two-syllabled 'seeyou' (Harrison), the first note high-pitched and short, the second longer, lower-pitched and more melodious. The nest call is a soft 'tseeteek tseeteek teek teek' (Immelmann *et al.*, my anglicisation). Güttinger & Nicolai give sonagrams of the contact and alarm calls.

DISPLAY AND SOCIAL BEHAVIOUR In the greeting display the birds perch close to and partly turned towards each other with triangular heads, angled tails and the rump and flank feathers erected but presenting a smooth surface. One raises itself high, with its head at an angle of about 60 degrees, 'freezes' a moment in this position, then bows or nods to or below the horizontal. It does not make a bill-wiping movement at the lowest point (as so many species do) but again 'freezes' for a moment. The other displays in the same manner. Commonly they display in synchrony so that when one's head is down the other's is up but quite often not. The head is usually inclined a little more towards the partner on its downward movement and a little further away from it on the upward one. Males utter their song phrase and females their contact calls during this display and thus reveal their sex to the human watcher as well as to each other.

This greeting display, or nodding display as some writers term it, is shown at high intensity if two unpaired and healthy Lavender Waxbills, who are strangers to each other, are put together. In such case it is usually interspersed with aggression and fleeing even if the birds are of opposite sex and, if they are two males or two females, is likely to be superseded by violent fighting in which the loser may be seriously hurt if it is not removed in good time. Pairing and newly paired mates perform this display together very frequently but, once the pair bond has been well established, they seldom or never do so. If, however, a strange individual is introduced to the aviary of such a pair they at once start giving this display to it *and* to each other. It thus seems certain that a good deal of latent or momentarily sublimated aggressive feeling is involved in this display in this species.

In courtship display the male, with a piece of nesting material held by one end in his bill, triangular head and angled tail, bobs up and down like other *Estrilda* species. The female at first responds by giving the greeting display but then goes over to an apparently symbolic soliciting display with quivering tail which does not (ever?) induce the displaying male to copulate. The female may also take the initiative and perform the display with the nesting symbol herself.

Copulation (on the few occasions that it has been seen) was preceded only by the male pecking a few times at the female's nape and by her crouching and quivering her tail.

All the information here on displays is derived from Kunkel (1959, 1967 and *pers. comm.*).

OTHER NAMES Lavender Finch, Red-tailed Waxbill, Red-tailed Lavender Waxbill.

REFERENCES

Bannerman, D. A. 1949. *The birds of tropical West Africa*, vol. 7. Crown Agents, London.

Bates, G. L. 1930. *Handbook of the birds of West Africa*. London.

Butler, A. G. 1894. *Foreign finches in captivity*. L. Reeve & Co., London.

Güttinger, H. R. & Nicolai, J. 1973. Struktur und Funktion der Rufe bei Prachtfinken (Estrildidae). *Z. Tierpsychol.* **33**: 319–334.

Harrison, C. J. O. 1962. An ethological comparison of some waxbills (Estrildini) and its relevence to their taxonomy. *Proc. zool. Soc. London*, **139**: 261–282.

Immelmann, K., Nicolai, J., Steinbacher, J. & Wolters, H. E. 1964. *Vögel in Käfig und Voliere: Prachtfinken*: 267–272.

Kunkel, P. 1959. Zum Verhalten einiger Prachtfinken (Estrildinae). *Z. Tierpsycol.* **16**: 302–350.

Kunkel, P. 1967. Displays facilitating sociability in waxbills of the genera *Estrilda* and *Lagonosticta* (Fam. Estrildidae). *Behaviour* **29**: 237–261.

Mackworth-Praed, C. W. & Grant, C. H. B. 1973. *African handbook of birds* ser. 3, vol. 2. Longman Group Ltd, London.

Munz, K. 1979. Die Zucht des Schönbürzels. *Gefiederte Welt* **1979**: 102–103.

Black-tailed Lavender Waxbill *Estrilda perreini*

Fringilla Perreini Vieillot 1817. *Nouv. Dict. Hist. Nat.*, nouv. ed. **12**, p. 179.

DESCRIPTION Like the previous species, *E. caerulescens*, except as follows: Tail longer and more strongly graduated. General coloration a darker grey but shaded much as in *E. caerulescens*. Thus the cheeks and throat are medium to light grey, not whitish grey, and so on. As well as a black eye-stripe there is a very small black patch at the base of the lower mandible. Rump and upper tail coverts a slightly darker red with differently textured (more glossy and less 'velvety') feathers. no white spots on the flanks. Under tail coverts dark grey to blackish, females usually dark grey and males more blackish. Tail feathers black. Bill shiny greyish blue with tip and cutting edges of mandibles black. Legs and feet greenish black.

Newly-hatched nestlings are flesh coloured with a little down on head and back. Their skin turns grey within 3 to 4 days (Pöhland, 1969). The juvenile is said (Immelmann *et al.*) to lack the black eye-stripe and be duller on the red areas.

The above description is of nominate *E.p. perreini*, from the western parts of the species' range in Gabon south to northern and western Angola and east through Katanga and northern Zambia to south-western Tanzania and the west slope of Lake Tanganyika. *E. perreini poliogastra*, from southern Tanzania south through Malawi, extreme eastern Rhodesia and Mozambique to northern Zululand is paler on the grey parts (some individuals almost if not quite as pale as *E. caerulescens*) and has the red of the rump and upper tail coverts lighter, brighter and glossier. *E. p. incana*, from southern Zululand and Natal, is very similar to *poliogastra* but averages a little darker in colour though not so dark as typical specimens of nominate *E.p. perreini*. Some authorities, sensibly in my opinion, treat *E. perreini poliogastra* as a synonym of *E.p. incana*.

Adults of the South African populations occasionally have white spots or 'white spots on red feathers' on the flanks (McLachlan & Liversidge) but I have not myself had opportunity of seeing such specimens.

FIELD CHARACTERS Very small bluish grey bird with red rump and black tail. Might easily be confused in the field with *E. thomensis*, if red flanks of the latter not seen. The allopatric *E. caerulescens* has a shorter and *red* tail.

DISTRIBUTION AND HABITAT Western, central and south-eastern Africa in Gabon south to northern and western Angola, east to Tanzania and south in eastern Africa to Zululand and Natal. Inhabits riparian woodland and thickets, evergreen forest, open woodland and sometimes rubber plantations. Usual and perhaps essential features of the habitat are some fairly thick cover and grasses growing among or near trees or bushes (Chapin, Clancey, Immelmann *et al.*, McLachlan & Liversidge, Vincent).

FEEDING AND GENERAL HABITS Usually seen in pairs or singly (mate on nest?) sometimes in small parties, these

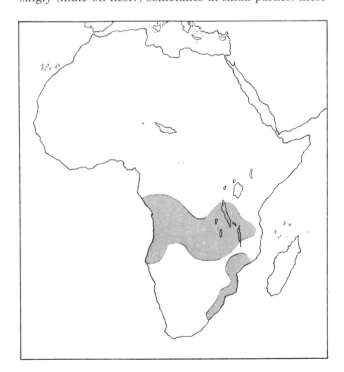

probably usually a family. Seeks food both on the ground and in bushes and trees (Immelmann *et al.*, 1964). Grass seeds (species unidentified) seem to be the only proven foods of wild birds (Chapin, Vincent) but it almost certainly takes insects when wild as it does in captivity.

In captivity Pöhland found this species took ant pupae and cut-up mealworms, readily ate a commercial insectile mixture and was extremely fond of seeding Rye Grass. His birds reared their young largely on ant pupae. Wax Moth larvae and various other small insects are also eaten (Immelmann *et al.* 1976). Of commercial seeds this species, like many other waxbills, takes mostly the smaller millets.

Holds grass panicles under foot in the usual *Estrilda* manner. Apparently less aggressive and quarrelsome, at least in captivity, than is *E. caerulescens*. Pöhland (1967 and 1969) found that his birds throve and bred successfully at a temperature of 26 to 28°C but showed immediate signs of illness if the temperature fell below 23 to 24°C.

NESTING Accounts of this species' nesting in standard works all seem to derive from Vincent's account of finding 3 nests in southern Congo. One of these, found on 1 April 1931, was about 2·5 metres (8 feet) high in a leafy shrub, not much concealed, the others found in late April, respectively, well concealed in a thick shrub and in full view in a small tree, both about 4·3 metres (14 feet) from the ground. The nests were thickly built of long, fine grass stems and grass panicles, about 12 centimetres (5 inches) in length and depth by about 10 centimetres (4 inches) across, roundish in shape with a short, downward sloping entrance tube about 5 centimetres (2 inches) or less in length. The first contained 4 well incubated eggs, the others each held 3 fresh eggs, presumably not full clutches. Further observations in the wild are needed before it can be safely assumed that the above nests had been built entirely by the Black-tailed Lavender Finches, as in captivity, this species has (so far) always taken over the completed nest of some other species, *Amandava formosa* and *Uraeginthus cyanocephala* in the case of Pöhland's birds, merely making slight additions and adding a short entrance tube.

In captivity Pöhland's birds laid clutches of 7 or 8 if they had a plentiful supply of ant pupae but of only 5 if their insect allowance was rationed or withheld during the laying period (Pöhland, 1969). Both sexes incubate and brood in the usual manner. The young are not brooded after they are 7 days old and not much after the fifth day. Young fledge at about 21 days and return to roost in the nest at night for about a week. When begging they do not (ever?) adopt the characteristic estrildid posture but stretch their heads straight up like young Cut-throats, and non-estrildid species (Immelmann *et al.*).

VOICE Contact calls; a short 'psee' and 'pseee' (Pöhland, 1967, my anglicisation). The male gives a sad, long-drawn, whistling note, sometimes followed by up to five shorter notes, in many situations, most of which seem (to me) to suggest that some degree of alarm may be the constant factor (Pöhland 1967). A (different) long, whistled note, followed by a shorter one is sometimes given during the side-to-side movements that precede the courtship display (Pöhland, 1969). Güttinger & Nicolai give a sonagram of the shorter contact call and emphasise that all the vocalisations of this species are distinct from those of *E. caerulescens* and *E. thomensis*.

DISPLAY AND SOCIAL BEHAVIOUR Courtship display as in other *Estrilda* species. Pöhland (1969) notes that long grass stems, up to 40 cm long, are preferred. Prior to displaying the male will fly conspicuously about the aviary carrying the symbol and then perch and, in a horizontal position, swing from side to side, sometimes uttering the whistling notes (see voice) until the female comes to him.

Copulation does not occur as a follow-up to the courtship display but is (*fide* Immelmann *et al.*, 1969) initiated by the female, during an allo-preening session, suddenly beginning to crouch and quiver her tail.

In the greeting display the pair, with angled tails, triangular head and slightly fluffed-out flanks bow towards one another and perform ceremonial bill wiping in synchrony on the perch between them (Pöhland, 1967). Pöhland found that his paired birds always displayed to each other at first sight when the light in their room came on in the morning as he (and I) also observed in cordon-bleus, *Uraeginthus* spp.

In agonistic situations a threatening bird may momentarily 'freeze' in a horizontal posture with spread tail. The bird at which the display is directed also 'freezes' but without spreading its tail and, after a few moments, they 'unfreeze' and there is no further immediate interaction (Pöhland, 1967). Allo-preening as in other *Estrilda* species.

OTHER NAMES Black-tailed Lavender Finch, Grey Waxbill.

REFERENCES

Chapin, J. P. 1954. The birds of the Belgian Congo, pt. 4. *Bull. Amer. Mus. Nat. Hist.* **75B**.

Clancey, P. A. 1964. The birds of Natal and Zululand. Oliver & Boyd, London.

Guttinger, H. R. & Nicolai, J. 1973. Struktur und Funktion der Rufe bei Prachtfinken (Estrildidae). *Z. Tierpsychol.* **33**: 319–334.

Immelmann, K., Steinbacher, J., Nicolai, J & Wolters, H. E. 1964 and 1976. *Vögel in Käfig und Voliere: Prachtfinken*: 273–276 and 553–557.

McLachlan, G. R. & Liversidge, R. 1957. *Roberts birds of South Africa*. Central News Agency, Cape Town.

Pöhland, E. 1967. Schwarzschwanzschönburzel (*Estrilda perreini*). *Gefiederte Welt* **1967**: 172–173.

Pöhland, E. 1969. Weitere Zuchterfolge mit Schwarzschwanz-Schönbürzeln (*Estrilda perreini*). *Gefiederte Welt* **1969**: 55–56.

Vincent, A. W. 1949. On the breeding habits of some African birds. *Ibis* **91**: 660–688.

Cinderella Waxbill   *Estrilda thomensis*

Estrilda thomensis Sousa, 1888, Jorn. Sci. Math. Phys. Nat. Lisboa, **12**, p. 155. (syn. *Estrilda cinderella* Naumann 1908).

DESCRIPTION Much like the previous species, *L. perreini*, but very slightly smaller and differing as follows: Grey of head and body paler and less bluish, with a delicate light pink suffusion on the pale breast and, less conspicuously, on the back and mantle. Lower back, rump and upper tail coverts crimson, less bright than in *E. perreini* and *E. caerulescens*. Dull crimson to wine-red patch on flanks. Centre of belly and ventral area blackish. Irides dark brown. Bill mauvish pink to pinkish red with tip, culmen ridge and lower part of under mandible blackish. Legs and feet brownish black.

The female is a very slightly duller grey, with less pink suffusion (perhaps none in some individuals) on the breast and back. I have not seen a juvenile specimen. Two bred in captivity by Pöhland (1970) were very like the adults but had no red on their flanks and dirty white bills. They showed the same sexual difference in belly colour as the adults.

There is a photograph of adults in the *Gefiederte Welt* for 1969 p. 209 and of an adult and a fledgling in *G.W.* 1970, p. 153.

FIELD CHARACTERS Tiny pale grey bird with red on flanks, red rump and black tail. Could easily be confused with the Black-tailed Lavender Waxbill if red on flanks not seen.

DISTRIBUTION AND HABITAT Western Angola from Benguella south to Bibala, Mocamedes and the lower Cunene River.

Inhabits more arid country than does *E. perreini*. Usually in mixed thorn and mopane below the escarpment but sometimes in riverine forest (Hall & Moreau).

FEEDING AND GENERAL HABITS Usually in pairs but a flock of 25 or more once seen (Rosa Pinto, in Immelmann *et al.* 1964). I can find no further information on it when wild and the following is derived from Pöhland's observations on his captive specimens.

He fed his birds successfully on the usual dry millets, with the addition of soaked and sprouted seed, sprays of half ripe 'wild millet', seeding rye grass when available honey water and ant pupae. Of the last the pupae of meadow ants, *Lasius* sp., were taken eagerly but those of the larger Wood Ant, *Formica rufa*, often refused.

Will thrive at a temperature of about 23 to 25°C but may need temperatures of up to 30°C for a period if in poor condition on arrival. Less aggressive and inquisitive than *E. perreni* and much less so than *E. caerulescens*. Roosts by preference in old or disused nests of its own or other species.

NESTING No information from the wild. Pöhland's birds (5 pairs) all built complete nests for themselves, unlike his pairs of *E. perreini* (q.v.). Nest large, built entirely of coconut fibres, with the sides and top 2 to 3 cm and the floor of the nest 4 to 5 cm thick, and with a narrow, downward-sloping entrance tube about 12 cm long. The male of one pair (but not the others) built a cock nest on top of the breeding nest and habitually roosted in it (Pöhland, 1970). I suspect, however, that in a wild state it

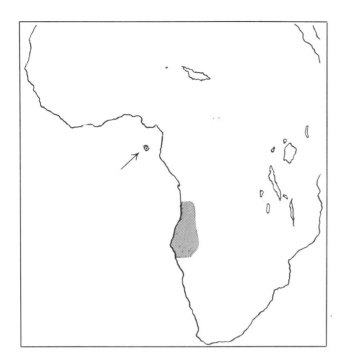

would more likely have roosted in some old nest at a little distance.

The young were seen to start feeding themselves only 2 days after fledging and were not fed by their parents after the tenth post-fledging day (Pöhland, 1970).

VOICE Contact and locomotion intention calls are soft and variable with something of an 'r' sound in them. 'tree', 'kr' etc. They are uttered almost constantly when the bird is moving about and are lengthened and intensified with apparent increase of excitement. The song (and distance contact call?) of the male is a long-drawn whistling 'see-eh, see-eh, sueee', that of the female a single 'seee'. Guttinger & Nicolai give a sonagram of a contact call.

DISPLAY AND SOCIAL BEHAVIOUR No detailed information. Probably very similar to that of *E. perreini*.

OTHER NAMES São Thomé Waxbill, Red-flanked Lavender Finch.

REFERENCES
Güttinger, H. R. & Nicolai, J. 1973. Struktur und Funktion der Rufe bei Prachtfinken (Estrildidae). *Z. Tierpsychol.* **33**: 319–334.
Hall, B. P. & Moreau, R. E. 1970. *An atlas of speciation of African passerine birds.* British Museum (Natural History), London.
Immelmann, K., Nicolai, J., Steinbacher, J. & Wolters, H. E. 1964. *Vögel in Käfig und Voliere: Prachtfinken*: 277–278.
Immelmann, K., Nicolai, J., Steinbacher, J. & Wolters, H. E. 1970. *Vögel in Käfig und Voliere: Prachtfinken*: 557–558.
Mackworth-Praed, C. W. & Grant, C. H. B. 1973. *African handbook of birds.* ser. 3, vol. 2. Longman Group Ltd, London.
Pöhland, E. 1969. Eingewohnung der seltenen Cinderella-Schönburzels (*Estrilda thomensis* Sousa). *Gefiederte Welt* **1969**: 208–209.
Pöhland, E. 1970. Zuchterfolg mit Cinderella-Schönburzeln (*Estrilda thomensis* Sousa). *Gefiederte Welt* **1970**: 152–153.

Swee waxbill   *Estrilda melanotis*

Fringilla melanotis Temminck, 1823, *Pl. Col. livr.* **37**, pl. 221, fig. 1.

DESCRIPTION About size of Goldbreast but with softer, denser plumage and less rounded tail. Forehead, crown, nape and hind neck dull slate grey. Mantle, upper back, lesser and median wing coverts a deep but slightly yellowish olive-green, with faint darker cross-barring visible at close examination. Greater coverts, inner secondaries and outer fringes of outer secondaries and primaries, olive-green, usually with some slight wash of dull red on the greater coverts and inner secondaries. Rest of wing quills blackish brown. Under wing coverts buff. Lower back, rump and upper tail coverts a very lovely shade of orange-red, sometimes inclining to light vermilion, or fading to a paler orange in worn plumage. It is a difficult colour to describe, it is always bright but glowing rather than shining. Central tail feathers black, outer ones dull drab. Throat and face (sometimes including lores, sometimes not) and ear coverts black, set off by an adjacent white border on lower throat and sides of neck. Breast pale grey to buffish grey, darkening to greyish olive on the flanks. Centre of belly, ventral area and under tail coverts buffish fawn. Irides bright red. Bill with upper mandible black, lower mandible red with pinkish area at base. Legs and feet black or brownish black.

The female lacks the black mask, her face being grey, a little paler than top of head, and her throat whitish. The fawnish buff of her belly is paler than that of the male. She seldom or never shows any red wash on the wings. Juvenile like female but green of upper parts duller and without cross barring, rump and upper tail coverts a pale, rusty orange and bill blackish. Nestling (Immelmann *et al.*, Steiner) has an unmarked palate, a black, white-bordered swelling at the base of either side of the upper mandible, two white tubercles on a black ground at the base of each lower mandible and a dark band across the tongue.

The above description is of nominate *E.m. melanotis*, from southern and eastern South Africa north to the eastern transvaal and adjacent Sul do Save, Mozambique. *E. melanotis bocagei*, from the central plateau of western Angola, has no reddish wash on the wings, the olive green upper parts are less yellowish in tone and with more pronounced fine, dark cross-barring, and similar cross-barring is also visible, though less pronounced, on the head and breast. Its breast is of a more bluish grey and its belly not buffish fawn but deep yellow or greenish yellow, shading to a little paler yellow on the ventral area and yellowish buff on the under tail coverts. Its under wing coverts are pale yellowish buff and the red on its rump and upper tail coverts a little darker (although fading to orange in worn plumage). Irides red, dark red, reddish brown or (one specimen) brown. Female differs from male as in previous race, having a grey face and being a little paler below.

E.m. quartinia, from the highlands of Eritrea, Abyssinia

and south-eastern Sudan, differs strikingly from the two races described above in the male having no black mask but a grey head like the female. Otherwise both sexes are very like *E.m. bocagei*, except for having the fine cross-barring on the back and elsewhere much less prominent. *E.m. kilimensis*, from eastern Congo, Uganda, and Kenya south through Tanzania to eastern Zambia, Malawi, the Tete district of Mozambique, eastern Zimbabwe and adjacent areas of Mozambique is very similar to *E.m. quartinia* but has the belly deep yellowish buff, often washed with orange, shading to buff on the under tail coverts. The female is like the male but averages paler below and never has orange on the belly. Juvenile like female but without cross-barring, with rusty orange rump and blackish bill.

See plate 6, facing p. 225.

FIELD CHARACTERS Tiny bird with grey head, greenish back, red or orange rump and black tail. Black mask of males of southern and eastern forms distinctive.

DISTRIBUTION AND HABITAT South Africa from Cape Town area east to Natal and eastern Transvaal, Mozambique, eastern Zimbabwe, Malawi, eastern Zambia, Tanzania, Kenya, Uganda, highlands of eastern Congo, highlands of Eritrea, Abyssinia, south-eastern Sudan and the central plateau of western Angola. Inhabits areas with plenty of fairly thick, low cover and grass; along watercourses, at forest edge, on sunny mountain slopes, and paths and clearings in forest. Often in gardens or cultivated areas if suitable cover available. Usually in hilly or mountainous country, up to 1800 metres in South Africa and higher elsewhere; usually over 1200 metres in southern Congo and up to 2500 metres in Eritrea.

FEEDING AND GENERAL HABITS Feeds largely on seeds of grasses, including *Panicum maximum*, probably also seeds

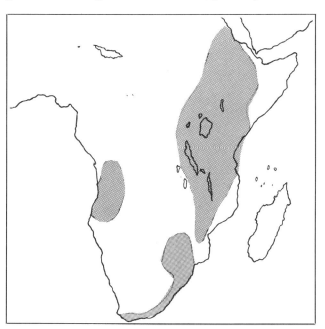

of some other plants. Also takes small insects, some of which are captured in flight. Feeds largely among and from growing vegetation, showing a tit-like agility but (*fide* Immelmann *et al.*) also seeks food on the ground. Keeps much to cover but is not at all shy of man when wild and in captivity is remarkably tame and calm (although extremely active) and not in the least inclined to panic either by night or day.

Usually in pairs or small parties. Appears not to associate with other species except sometimes fortuitously at common sources of food.

In captivity should have the smaller kinds of millet, both dry and soaked. It is very fond of fresh millet sprays with the seeds still green and will also take seeding Sow Thistle and Dandelion, Chickweed, the fresh green shoots of young grass and other seedlings, lettuce and, sometimes, chicory leaves. Small insects such as green aphids (greenfly), ant grubs and pupae and whiteworms should be given when possible and in quantity when the birds have young. Will often eat eggfood readily. Pajain recommends additional vitamin supplements even for birds that are being supplied wtih abundant greenfood and insects. Apparently less sensitive to cold than many waxbills (Robinson) but Immelmann *et al.* recommend a temperature of 17 to 18°C.

VOICE The contact call is a gentle-sounding, weak 'see-see' or 'swee-swee', at higher intensities changing to an explosive 'tswee!'. Some (McLachlan & Liversidge, Sclater & Moreau) describe the contact call of the grey-headed form *E.m. kilimensis* as 'sree'. Others, however, seem to have noted no differences in calls between the different races and Immelmann *et al.* give 'sree' and a repeated 'tseek-tseek-tseek' (my anglicisations) as high intensity variants of the 'swee' call. The alarm call of both grey-headed and black-headed forms is a sharp 'teerrrr!' (Zottmann, 1964). The song of the grey-headed form *E.m. quartinia* is soft and ventriloquial, rather suggesting the sub-song of some fringilline finch. It seems subject to some individual variation and has been variously described as 'tee-tee-tee-tee-tuuueeeh', 'teekutehleekehleekee' etc. The song of the black-faced form, *E.m. melanotis*, differs in being a single, soft but penetrating 'teeeeeeit!' or 'tuuuuueeet!' (Zottmann, 1964, my anglicisations). Begging call of fledglings is described (Sclater & Moreau) as a 'wheezy and not unmusical . . . "ss-ss-see"', loud for the size of the bird.

DISPLAY AND SOCIAL BEHAVIOUR Courtship display apparently similar to that of other *Estrilda* species but I can find no detailed description. Copulation believed to take place in the nest (Immelmann *et al.*). Allo-preening common between members of a pair.

In captivity extremely peaceful both towards its own and other species. Pajain found that several breeding pairs could be kept together without strife or stress, and that, surprisingly, his specimens of *E.m. melanotis*, *E.m. bocagei* and *E.m. quartinia* behaved as if specifically distinct, showing sexual interest only in others of the same form.

OTHER NAMES Yellow-bellied Waxbill, Dufresne's Waxbill (the black-masked forms), Green Waxbill.

REFERENCES

Belcher, C. F. 1930. *The birds of Nyasaland.* Crosby Lockwood & Son, London.

Chapin, J. P. 1954. The birds of the Belgian Congo. *Bull. Amer. Mus. Nat. Hist.* **75B**.

Immelmann, K., Steinbacher, J. & Wolters, H. E. 1965 and 1976. *Vögel in Käfig und Voliere: Prachtfinken*: 355–368 and 563–564.

McLachlan, G. R. & Liversidge, R. 1957. *Roberts birds of South Africa*. Cape Times Ltd, Cape Town.

Pajain, H. A. 1975. Beobachtungen an Schwarzbäckchen. *Gefiederte Welt* 1975: 41–42.

Robinson, E. 1934. The successful breeding of Dufresne's Waxbill. *Avicult. Mag.* 4th ser. **12**: 249–251.

Sclater, W. L. & Moreau, R. E. 1933. Taxonomic and field notes on some birds of North-Eastern Tanganyika Territory. *Ibis* 13th ser. **3**: 399–440.

Steiner, H. 1960. Klassifikation der Prachtfinken, Spermestidae, auf Grund der Rachenzeichnungen ihrer Nestlinge. *J. Orn.* **101**: 92–112.

Vincent, A. W. 1949. On the breeding habits of some African birds. *Ibis* **91**: 660–688.

Vincent, J. 1936. Birds of Northern Portuguese East Africa. *Ibis* **78**: 48–125.

Zottmann, T. M. 1960. Meine Zücht des Schwarzbäckchens (*Estrilda melanotis*). *Gefiederte Welt* **1960**: 101–103.

Zottmann, T. M. 1964. Zur Unterscheidung der Rassen von *Estrilda melanotis*. *Gefiederte Welt* **1964**: 98.

The avadavats and the Goldbreast

The three species in the genus *Amandava* are similar in shape (although not, as waxbills go, in size), they have some similarities in plumage colours and patterns, their young raise one or both wings when begging and their nestlings have similar mouth patterns (Steiner). They are all birds of areas of grass and rank vegetation, usually near water, and spend much of their time on or near the ground. The three species show more pronounced differences from each other than those between most other waxbill species now treated as congeneric and are sometimes (e.g. by Wolters, 1966) placed in three monotypic genera – *Amandava*, *Stictospiza* and *Sporaeginthus* but I concur with those who think they are best all united in *Amandava*.

The best known species is the Avadavat or Red Avadavat, *Amandava amandava*, which has long been a popular cage and aviary bird, imported into Europe in large numbers as well as being often kept in its native lands. It is unique among estrildids in the male having two distinct plumages in the course of the year: a predominantly red breeding dress and a duller non-breeding plumage in which he much resembles the female. The Avadavat is found widely in the Indian sub-continent and elsewhere in south-eastern Asia, overlapping the range of its nearest relative the Green Avadavat, *Amandava*

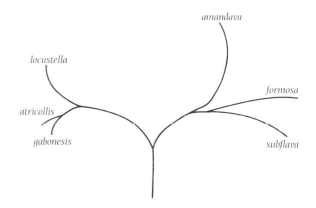

Presumed affinities within the genera *Amandava* (right branch) and *Ortygospiza* (left branch). See text for discussion.

formosa. It is possible, as Dr Harrison has argued, that these two species might be phylogenetically closer to the munias, *Lonchura*, than they are to the African waxbills. It seems, however, more probable that, as Kunkel (unpublished mss) suggests, they are representative of an early offshoot of the same stock as produced the African waxbills.

The Green Avadavat or Green Munia, *Amandava formosa*, is appreciably larger than the Red Avadavat and in its green and yellow plumage with whitish and dark barring on its flanks it is very different in colour. It is found only in relatively limited areas of India and Pakistan and, although locally common, may be a declining species.

The Goldbreast, Orange-breasted Waxbill or Zebra Waxbill, *Amandava subflava*, is a tiny bird even by waxbill standards. It shows many resemblances of plumage, voice and behaviour to the avadavats and it seems unlikely that these could all be due to convergence. Unlike the other *Amandava* species it is found, like the typical waxbills of the genus *Estrilda*, only in Africa south of the Sahara and south-western Arabia. In Africa it is widespread and abundant in suitable habitats. Kunkel points out that the comparatively slight geographical variation within this species throughout its range suggests that its ancestors may have invaded, or rather re-invaded, Africa from Asia at a comparatively recent date. The other African estrildids most likely to be related to it are represented in southern Africa and the north-western or north-eastern tropics by forms that show greater differences and in many cases are specifically distinct.

As with many other birds which perch much on the abrasive stems of rushes and large grasses, the claws of all *Amandava* species tend to overgrow in captivity. They usually need cutting back to normal length every few months. Some bird keepers are reluctant to do this but the overgrown claws cause the birds obvious discomfort, besides often leading to injury or death through their getting entangled in wire netting or nesting material, or to the breaking of eggs. The brief disturbance and fear caused by catching the bird and clipping its claws is much the lesser of the two evils. I have done it even with birds that were beginning to nest, without its having any adverse effect.

REFERENCES

Harrison, C. J. O. 1962. The affinities of the Red Avadavat. *Amandava amandava* (Linn.). *Bull. Brit. Orn. Cl.* **82**: 126–132.
Kunkel, P. 1969. Die Stammsgeschichte der Prachtfinken im Lichte des Brutparasitismus der Witwen. *Ardea* **57**: 172–181.
Wolters, H. E. 1966. On the relationships and generic limits of African Estrildinae. *Ostrich* Supplement no. 6: 75–81.

Avadavat　　　　　　　*Amandava amandava*

Fringilla amandava Linnaeus, 1758, *Syst. nat.* ed. 10, **1**, p. 80.

DESCRIPTION Between Zebra Finch and Goldbreast in size. Male in breeding plumage has forehead, face, throat, sides of neck, breast, flanks, rump and upper tail coverts red; usually a deep scarlet red but varying from coppery red to crimson. Black stripe from gape to eye; narrow short white stripe under eye. Sides of lower neck and breast, flanks, rump and upper tail coverts spotted with white, each feather having a single white spot near the tip. Top of head and nape usually a slightly less bright red and with the dark brown basal parts of the feathers showing. Mantle and back dull brown with bronzy red or dull scarlet feather fringes, the general appearance of the upper parts may vary from mainly brown to mainly red. Wings and tail blackish brown with white terminal spots on coverts, inner secondaries and outer tail feathers. Lower belly and under tail coverts brownish black, some feathers tipped reddish. Underwing coverts buff. When very new the red feathers have a distinct chestnut or coppery tone but later the same feathers become pure red. Irides reddish orange to red. Bill red with part or all of ridge of culmen dusky or blackish. Legs and feet fleshy brown.

Female and male in 'eclipse' plumage dull earth brown to dark greyish brown on upperparts except for wings, rump, upper tail coverts and tail which are as in the breeding male, but with the red parts usually a little less bright. Facial markings as breeding male but white stripe under eye creamy and less prominent. Sides of face, neck and upper breast light brownish grey. Throat and most of underparts whitish or pale buff, the latter colour suffusing the grey of the breast and shading to yellowish buff or even buffish orange on the belly.

The moult into breeding plumage is complete, involving wing and tail quills. In captivity (Goodwin, 1960, Immelmann *et al.* 1965), and possibly also in a wild state (Goodwin, 1960), many adult males begin moulting back into the red plumage before the non-breeding plumage is complete.

Juvenile dull greyish brown, shading to buffish white below, with two conspicuous pale wing bars formed by buffish tips to the median and greater wing coverts. Irides and bill at first dull. Young males moult from the juvenile into the non-breeding plumage, often with some dusky

and buffish barring on the flanks. This first moult is complete (for more detailed discussion on moults and plumages of this species see Goodwin, 1960, Harrison, 1962, Sparks, 1963 and Ticehurst, 1922). Nestling dark skinned, with brownish down, and multiple mouth markings.

The above description is of nominate *Amandava a. amandava* from India. *A.a. punicea*, from Indochina, Java and Bali (introduced elsewhere) is a little smaller and males in breeding dress are usually a brighter red, have the white spots proportionately as well as actually smaller and lack the black mark from gape to eye or have it only slightly indicated. *Amandava a. flavidiventris*, from Yunnan, Burma, Lombok, Flores, Sumba and Timor, is similar in size to *A.a. punicea*. Breeding plumage males have the red on the breast slightly less bright and shading through pinkish orange to golden or yellowish buff, more or less suffused with orange, on the belly. The white spotting extends across the front of the breast and lower neck, some feathers in these areas have whitish shaft streaks. The female has the breast more yellowish drab than grey and the belly a deeper buff and usually strongly tinged with orange.

When kept under poor conditions Avadavats are particularly prone to induced melanism. Also most captive birds, at least in Britain and western Europe, even when apparently fit and successfully breeding, replace the normal bright red with yellowish brown, dull orange or at best fiery orange (Goodwin, 1960), even individuals at full liberty in Germany failed to regain the full red colour (Nicolai, in Immelmann, *et al.*, 1965). Sufficient warmth seems the main factor necessary to enable Avadavats to retain their normal colouring. Czechowsky (1967) found that a captive male repeatedly moulted into shining red plumage when kept at a temperature of about 40°C but at one moult, when the bird was kept at only 30°C, his new plumage was yellowish. Davis (1939) found that in India caged Avadavats, fed only on dry seed, retained (or regained) their natural colour after moulting if (and only if) they were exposed to heat, sunshine and moisture.
See plate 6, facing p. 225.

FIELD CHARACTERS Conspicuous white spots on dark wings, or on red body, distinguish it from all other sympatric small finch-like birds. Juvenile not distinctive but normally with adults. Calls distinctive if known. Further information on field characters (if any) valid at a distance are needed.

DISTRIBUTION AND HABITAT West Pakistan, India and southern Nepal, Burma, Yunnan, Lombok, Flores, Sumba, Timor, Indochina, Java and Bali. Introduced into Sumatra, Singapore, Luzon in the Philippines, Hainan, Hong Kong, Fiji and Hawaii. Thought to have died out around 1930 in Egypt, after an initially successful introduction about 1900, but has recently been seen in the Suez Canal area (Immulmann *et al.*, 1976). A favourite, hardy and easily-kept cage and aviary bird it is

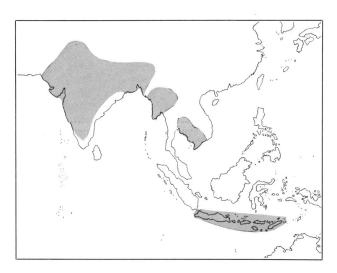

liable to be introduced or to escape almost anywhere. Has bred at liberty in Britain (pers. obs.) and Germany (Ammersbach, 1960) but cannot usually, if ever, survive an English winter in a feral state.

Inhabits especially riparian or marshy areas with tall grass, reedbeds, bushes or other rank growth; also sugarcane fields, grass-grown clearings in jungle, open woodland or cultivated areas and similar places; sometimes in gardens.

FEEDING AND GENERAL HABITS Apparently feeds mainly on seeds of grasses in a wild state but I know of no detailed study of its feeding habits under natural conditions. A pair breeding in a feral state in Germany fed their young and themselves mainly on half-ripe seeds of the grasses *Panicum crus-galli* and *Phleum arenarium*. My captive Avadavats were fond of both green and ripe seeding Annual Meadow Grass, *Poa annua*, and Common Knotgrass, *Polygonum aviculare* and of the *young* growing shoots of grasses. They also took seeds of many other grasses, and sprouting millet, but always fed largely on small yellow millet, even when other food was available. They took insects eagerly when they were feeding young, laying or moulting, not often at other times. Of the insects I was able (sometimes) to supply in quantity they took ant larvae and pupae (*Lasius fuscus* and *L. niger*), the winged male and female ants (but not worker ants of the same species), small caterpillars, very small centipedes, greenfly, small gentles and blowfly pupae, in about that order of preference.

I saw anting, with *Lasius niger* and *L. flavus*, from captive birds. One or both wings were brought forward in the usual way. Like Jays (*Garrulus glandarius*), they did not actually pick up ants but made movements as if to do so and then stroked the bill down the inner side of the primaries. On a few occasions I saw an Avadavat crawl over ants with spread, depressed tail and 'humped' back.

Takes seeds from growing grasses (Ali & Ripley, 1974) and from the ground. Behaviour of captive birds and of birds in a feral state in Britain strongly suggests that the species is primarily a ground feeder, probably feeding largely on seeds or other items picked up from the ground or plucked from low growing or prostrate plants. Does not hold seeding heads of grass or other food plants under foot. Hops on the ground but occasionally makes a few 'polka steps'. Fast and agile in flight, when flushed often rises fast at a steep angle and flies rather high (Nicolai, in Immelmann *et al*, 1965, pers. obs.). As with other estrildids that perch much on the rough stems of reeds and grasses, its claws usually overgrow and need fairly frequent clipping in captivity.

NESTING Nest roundish, strongly built of grass blades and stems, flowering or seeding grass heads, and sometimes other plant material, lined with vegetable down, fine grass, flower heads of grasses and/or feathers. Captive birds prefer white or pale body feathers of ducks, gulls, chickens and pigeons to most other lining materials offered them. Nest with a side entrance hole and often a short tubular entrance. Usually a flattish platform of grass stems and/or blades is built first and the nest erected on it (see especially Kunkel, 1959). Both sexes build but in captivity, and possibly also in the wild, only the male brings the outer materials although both bring feathers for the lining. Nest placed usually near the ground, in or at the base of a bush or in a thick grass clump, sometimes actually on the ground itself. In aviaries where there is much disturbance at floor level, often chooses to nest as high up as possible.

When given the opportunity captive Avadavats take pieces of burnt and charred wood into the nest. This habit does not appear to have been recorded in the wild but a free living pair in Germany did so (Ammersbach, Goodwin). Small bits of burnt wood are pushed into and just under the surface of the nest lining. In two nests which I dissected they were found everywhere except in the roof of the nest, but about 75 per cent of them were concentrated within a couple of centimetres or so of the nest entrance. Both sexes of my captive birds eagerly took small pieces of burnt wood, especially when their eggs were near hatching or their young were still small, but to some extent at all times from egg-laying to the fledging of the young. Nest material is carried in the typical estrildine manner, a single stem or feather by its 'hard' end, when feasible but when not the Avadavat 'bundles' it without hesitation in the more usual passerine manner.

Four to six eggs. Up to 14 recorded but this probably due to two hens laying in the same nest. Both sexes incubate in turns by day but only the female at night. In captivity males sometimes roost in the nest or its entrance but probably only in default of suitable roosting sites elsewhere. Incubation period 11–12 days. Young (in captivity in Europe) fledge at 20–21 days (Steinbacher & Wolters, 1965). Both sexes feed the young after fledging. A captive pair that adopted a newly fledged brood of Goldbreasts, *Amandava subflava*, that fledged a few days before their own young, fed their large mixed brood indiscriminately although the parent Goldbreasts discriminated and fed only their own young (Goodwin, 1960).

Breeding appears usually to take place in the second half of the rainy season and in the following dry season, in Flores entirely in the dry season. Active nests found mostly from June to August in Assam, from July to October in northern India, in southern India from October to March, in Burma from August to January, and in Flores from April to June (Immelmann *et al.*, 1965, Baker, 1934, Ali & Ripley, 1974). Fledged young crouch and raise one or both wings, when begging for food. At low intensity they may beg with only slight or even no wing movements and without crouching (Goodwin, 1960).

VOICE Wild male Avadavats (and wild-caught captives) utter a very sweet-sounding and varied though shortish song, on a descending scale. There is some geographical and possibly also individual variation. The female also sings but less often and her song is shorter. A peculiar and as yet unexplained fact is that captive-bred Avadavats not only indulge in vocal mimicry and develop abnormal songs if they fail to hear their parents singing often (Goodwin, 1960) but (*fide* Nicolai, in Immelmann *et al.*, 1965) do so even if they frequently hear their parents or other wild-caught Avadavats singing normally. A young male that I kept in a small room with his own parents and Blue-breasted Waxbills, *Uraeginthus angolensis*, however, after his initial 'rambling' warbling, sang both the (presumed) natural song (like his father's), a perfect imitation of the Bluebreast's song (quite unlike an Avadavat's) and various intermediate songs. His sister sang only an imitation of the short song of the female Bluebreast (Goodwin, 1960).

High-pitched, rather shrill but sweet-sounding calls are given in several situations. These calls are usually monosyllabic but several may be repeated at very short intervals. A rather loud, long drawn version of this 'usual' call is given when attacking or when threatening a rival but not when repulsing a lower-ranked individual. A still louder version is given by parents when their fledged young appear (to them) to be in danger. A rapidly repeated 'run-together' series of notes, with a very excited tone and on a descending scale is often given. When I have seen the bird uttering it, it has always been in typical singing posture, rather upright, with belly feathers somewhat erected and crown feathers sometimes erected and sometimes appressed. This series of shrill notes seems to function as an alternative song. The nest call is a series of soft, rapidly repeated notes that could perhaps be written 'tee-tee-tee' or 'teh-teh-teh-teh . . .'.

DISPLAY AND SOCIAL BEHAVIOUR Greeting display very similar to that of many other estrildids, with 'triangular head' and angled tail. The bird bows into a horizontal position sideways on to the partner, showing the bright rump and spotted flanks. This position is only momentarily held. In the courtship display the bird holds a piece of grass or a feather by the firmest end of its stem or shaft and, with body plumage fluffed out, bows slowly, sings, and bows again, the bows are usually first to one side of its body then to the other. The displaying bird may be beside, in front of or at an angle to its partner, it may hop around it, between bows. This display does not normally, if ever, terminate in coition and is performed by both sexes. Both Kunkel (*in litt.*) and I failed to see this display from our adult *males* of the race *A.a punicea*. Copulation is initiated by the male pecking the female's nape and/or by her soliciting with quivering tail (Kunkel, 1959), sometimes, at least in well-established pairs, it may take place without any such preliminaries (Goodwin, 1960).

The male also has a display very like the begging of the fledged young. He crouches, raises and flutters one or both wings. Sometimes his tail is pressed to the substrate and sometimes it may be twisted towards the female. He may utter a soft twittering similar or identical to the nest call or he may sing during or (more often) immediately after or in intervals between crouching and wing raising. This display may be given towards females to whom he is not paired, by a paired male, and followed by a brief attack on them or on some other bird but Sparks (1963) observed it in large numbers of captive Avadavats and was convinced that it is a 'specific pair formation display'.

Clumping and allo-preening regular between members of a pair and, at least in captivity, between males in the non-breeding plumage and between females if a red male is not present. Males in red plumage do not usually clump together and females usually show aggression towards other females, and sometimes also towards brown males, if a red male is present (Kunkel, 1959, Goodwin, 1960, Sparks, 1965).

OTHER NAMES Red Avadavat, Amaduvade, Tiger Finch, Strawberry Finch, Red Munia. (Note: bird dealers often use the name 'Strawberry Finch' for the race *A.a. punicea* only.)

REFERENCES

Ali, S. & Ripley, S. D. 1974. *Handbook of the birds of India and Pakistan*: 10. Bombay, London, New York.

Ammersbach, R. 1960. Tigerfinken (*Amandava a. amandava*) brüten in freier Wildbahn. *Die Gefiederte Welt*, Mai **1960**: 81–85.

Czechowsky, I. 1967. Über die Rotfarbung und andere Beobachtungen bei Tigerfinken. *Die Gefiederte Welt*, Mai **1967**: 94–96.

Davis, G. 1928. The breeding of Avadavats. *Avicult. Mag.* 4th ser. **6**: 241–247.

Delacour, J. 1935. Les Bengalis rouges. *L'Oiseau* **3–4**: 376–388.

Goodwin, D. 1960. Observations on Avadavats and Golden-breasted Waxbills. *Avicult. Mag.* **66**: 174–199.

Goodwin, D. 1962. Notes on the plumages of the Avadavat *Amandava amandava. Ibis* **104**: 564–566.

Harrison, C. J. O. 1962. The affinities of the Red Avadavat, *Amandava amandava* (Linn.). *Bull. Brit. Orn. Club* **82**: 126–132.

Immelmann, K., Stinebacher, J. & Wlters, H. E. 1965. *Vögel in Käfig und Voliere: Prachtfinken*: 394–408.

Immelmann, K., Steinbacher, J. & Wolters, H. E. 1976. *Vögel in Käfig und Voliere: Prachtfinken*: 11 Band: 567.

Kunkel, P. 1959. Zum Verhalten einiger Prachtfinken (Estrildinae). *Z. Tierpsychol.* **16**: 3: 302–350.

Sparks, J. 1963. The plumage of the Red Avadavat *Amandava amandava* and its effect upon contact behaviour. *Ibis* **105**: 558–561.

Sparks, J. 1965. On the role of allopreening invitation behaviour in reducing aggression among Red Avadavats, with comments on its evolution in the Spermestidae. *Proc. Zool. Soc. London* **145**: 387–403.
Ticehurst, C. B. 1922. The birds of Sind. *Ibis* (11) **4**: 646–647.

Green Avadavat   *Amandava formosa*

Fringilla formosa Latham, 1790, *Index Ornith.* 1, p. 441.

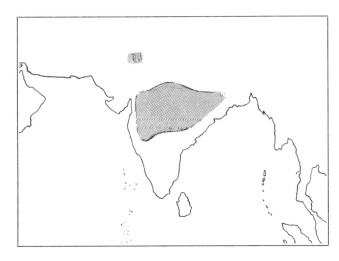

DESCRIPTION About size of Zebra Finch but slimmer in build and with a more slender bill. Head, face and neck greyish olive shading to olive green on back and wings and to greenish gold on the lower rump and upper tail coverts. Tail black. Those parts of the primaries and secondaries not visible when wing is folded brownish black. Throat pale yellow or yellowish white, shading to yellow suffused more or less with grey on the breast. Centre of lower breast and belly clear light yellow to bright yellow. Under tail coverts bright golden yellow. Sides of lower breast and flanks with relatively large, almost square-ended feathers that are boldly barred with white and greenish black. Bill dark crimson or carmine red. Irides brown or reddish. Legs and feet greyish brown to brownish flesh.

Female has all the green areas duller, the breast more suffused with grey, the belly paler yellow and the dark bars on the flanks lighter and less contrasting. Juvenile dull greyish brown above, tinged with greenish yellow on the outer webs of the wing quills and upper tail coverts. Underparts greyish buff to buff, shading to drab or deep buff on the unbarred flanks and buffish white or buffish yellow on the belly and under tail coverts. Bill at first black. The variation indicated in the above description of the juvenile plumage may be sexual. Certainly some (and possibly all) young males are brighter and more yellowish in this plumage than some (possibly all) young females.

FIELD CHARACTERS Very small greenish bird with red bill and barred flanks. Information on recognition at a distance needed.

DISTRIBUTION AND HABITAT Central India from northern Gujarat and southern Rajasthan east to Bihar, Orissa and West Bengal. Has also been recorded from near Lucknow and Lahore. Locally fairly common but in general rather scarce (Ali & Ripley, 1974). Inhabits areas with tall grass and/or low bushes, rocky scrub jungle, sugar-cane fields and other cultivated crops that provide good cover. Commonly near water.

FEEDING AND GENERAL HABITS Feeds on the ground, presumably taking grass seeds and small invertebrates but little or nothing recorded on its food in a wild state. Gregarious to some extent even when breeding and at other times in flocks of up to about 50 individuals.

NESTING Most descriptions of wild nests seem to derive from Blewitt (in Baker, 1934) who found 3 nests, each with 5 eggs, and 4 unfinished nests in a one-hectare sugar-cane field. Each nest was about 1·5 metres (5 feet) high in the upper part of the sugar-cane, supported at the back by the stem and with three of the four leaves built into the sides of the nest. Finished nests were large, roundish structures of coarse grass and strips of sugar-cane leaf, with a thick inner lining of very fine grasses. (In captivity, and possibly also in the wild when available, feathers are often used in the nest lining.) The side entrance, in each case opposite to the supporting stem, was prolonged into a short tube and well concealed by projecting grasses.

Captive birds (Kunkel, 1959) build in the same manner as *A. amandava*, first constructing a base for the nest, carrying each piece of material by one end not, apparently, 'bundling' soft materials as does the Red Avadavat. All three wild clutches found by Blewitt were of 5 white eggs. Clutches of from 4 to 7 recorded in captivity. Incubation period 11–12 days, young fledge at about 21 days (both captivity records). Both sexes incubate in turn. Kunkel found the male and female were often in the nest together but this probably happens less often in a wild state where the birds have to find their own food. Young beg with raised wings like other *Amandava* species. Recorded breeding in May and January (Ali & Ripley). In captivity needs an abundance of insect food to rear young successfully, usually refusing not only eggfood but even whiteworms (Immelmann *et al.*, 1965).

VOICE Utters a loud 'seee' or 'swee' and a similar but much softer note. The song has variously been described as twittering and less loud than that of the Red Avadavat (Immelmann *et al.*, 1965) and as starting with very soft notes but ending with 'a prolonged trill which is often quite loud' (Teschemaker, 1905). Possibly there is individual or local variation in the song.

DISPLAY AND SOCIAL BEHAVIOUR Greeting display like that of Red Avadavat but tends to fluff out plumage more and to display more intensely, repeatedly bowing forward, sometimes with ritualised bill-wiping and holding the horizontal position for a moment or two before repeating the performance.

In the courtship display does not hold material in bill. The male fully erects his body plumage, approaches the female and makes repeated short, quick bows to the side nearest her or, if he is facing her, first to one side then to the other, or frontally if display is at lower intensity. At very high intensity at the lowest part of the bow the bird's head and bill are over or even nestling in the plumage of the side of its breast and it makes a short side to side movement of bill and head (presumably derived from nest building movements). Sometimes sings softly during this bowing display. This display, which may be given by the female also, does not lead to copulation, which (always?) is prefaced by nape-pecking by the male and soliciting with quivering tail by the female (Immelmann *et al.*, 1965).

Allo-preening very freely indulged in and, at least in captivity, often by birds not paired to each other. Kunkel found virtually no intra-specific aggression between his captive birds even when breeding although (or because?) they frequently attacked some of the rather similarly-coloured but smaller Dufresne's Waxbills, *Estrilda melanotis*, that were kept with them.

Usual tail and wing-flicking flight intention movements are more pronounced and frequent than in the Red Avadavat (Kunkel, 1962).

OTHER NAMES Green Munia, Green Waxbill, Green Amaduvade.

REFERENCES

Ali, S. & Ripley, S. D. 1974. *Handbook of birds of India and Pakistan.* 10. Bombay, London and New York.

Baker, E. C. S. 1934. *The nidification of birds of the Indian Empire*, vol. 3. London.

Butler, A. G. 1894. *Foreign finches in captivity.* London.

Immelmann, K., Steinbacher, J. & Wolters, H. E. 1965. *Vögel in Käfig und Voliere: Prachtfinken*: 419–426.

Kunkel, P. 1962. Zum Verhalten des Olivgrünen Astrilds (*Amandava formosa* Lath.). *J. Orn.* 103: 358–368.

Teschemaker, W. E. 1905. The breeding of the Green Avadavat. *Avicult. Mag.* 4 (new ser.): 70–72.

Goldbreast   *Amandava subflava*

Fringilla subflava Vieillot, 1819, *Nouv. Dict. Hist. Nat.* nouv. ed. 30, p. 575.

DESCRIPTION The smallest seed-eating estrildid. Top of head and neck a rather dark olive brown, shading to a slightly darker and less olivaceous tone on back, upper rump and wings. Lower rump, upper tail coverts and superciliary stripe deep scarlet red. Short narrow buff stripe under eye and blackish loral stripe. Sides of head light olive drab, suffused with buff. Sides of breast and flanks olive drab barred with yellowish white or pale buff. Front of breast and underparts deep bright orange-red or with the centre of the breast orange-red and the lower breast and belly orange or rich yellow. Under tail coverts bright orange to orange-red. Tail brownish black with narrow white tips to the outer feathers. Bill red with the culmen ridge, a small triangular patch adjacent to the black loral stripe and the underside of the lower mandible blackish. Irides red or orange-red. Legs and feet pale brown or brownish pink.

The female lacks the red eye-stripe. Her underparts are pale buffish to pale yellowish orange, except for orange or pale orange-red under tail coverts. The barring on her flanks is less pronounced and the scarlet or orange-red of her rump and upper tail coverts less bright. The juvenile is a general dull brown above, with paler tips often showing as two buffish bars across the wing coverts, and dull buffish below, with an orange tinge on the rump. The nestling has pale buffish or whitish down and mouth markings very similar to those of the nestling Advadavat.

The above description is of nominate *A.s. subflava*, which is found in the more northern parts of the species' range, from Senegal to Abyssinia. *A. subflava clarkei*, from Gabon east to eastern Tanzania and southern Kenya, and further south, is very slightly larger and less brightly coloured below, the male having the breast and belly either entirely light golden yellow or with a variably-sized orange or orange-red patch in the centre of the upper breast.

Very prone to induced melanism under adverse captive conditions. Under better conditions and when apparently in good health it often shows a slight colour change in which the red of rump and eye-stripe are replaced by orange-red, the orange-red of the breast by bright orange, and the brown parts show a more definite green tinge. One of the few instances where such a colour change results in a bird quite as beautiful as the original.
See plate 7, facing p. 256.

FIELD CHARACTERS Tiny, shortish-tailed bird with red upper tail coverts, barred flanks and red, orange, yellow or (female) pale yellowish underparts.

DISTRIBUTION AND HABITAT Africa from Senegal to Sierra Leone east to the southern Sudan and northern and western Abyssinia. South in the west to western Angola and in the east to eastern Cape Province. Absent from extremely arid regions and equatorial rain forest. Also on Pemba, Zanzibar and Mafia Islands. In late 1962 small numbers were seen near Tais, in the Yemen, south-western Arabia (Montfort).

Inhabits marshes, reedbeds, grasslands and grassy

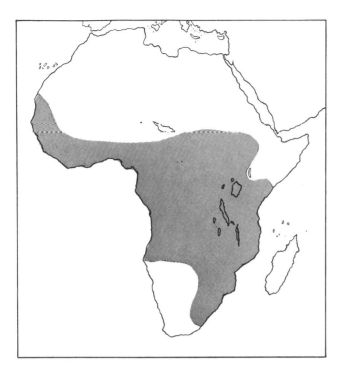

savanna. Often feeds in dryer and more open areas, including cultivation.

FEEDING AND GENERAL HABITS Feeds chiefly on the ground. Known to take seeds of grasses and almost certainly takes small invertebrates; also takes tips of growing grass (Immelmann & Immelmann) as it does in captivity (Goodwin). Perches freely on grass heads, reeds and low bushes but seldom at any height in a tree or tall bush. When not breeding usually in small parties of up to about 12 individuals but sometimes in larger flocks. When disturbed a party of birds tends to fly off in straggling rather than close formation. Roosts in reedbeds (Immelmann & Immelmann). In captivity, and probably also in a wild state, spends much time on the ground even when not seeking food. Gait, movements and behaviour very like that of Avadavat (q.v.).

Feeding habits in captivity very like those of Avadavat (q.v.). When rearing young it will eagerly pick tiny objects, presumably eggs or very young worms, from whiteworm culture although often refusing the grown whiteworms. I have had them rear young mainly on this, eggfood, soaked millet and grass seed when ant pupae and most other small wild insects were unobtainable. Can drink in the 'sucking' manner of a Zebra Finch or pigeon but seems only to do so when drinking from a thin film of liquid. Will sometimes thus drink albumen from a cracked or broken egg.

NESTING Nest from 1 to 2 metres high, sometimes lower or even on the ground, among grass or reeds or in a low bush. It is rounded, rather loosely put together, of grass, lined with grass panicles and/or feathers and usually with a tubular side entrance about 6 to 10 centimetres long. Very often, and usually in the southern parts of its range, it takes over an old or abandoned nest of some other species that builds a domed nest and, according to its size, either builds its own nest inside it or merely lines or refurbishes it. The male brings most of the material although the female may bring some for the lining. All material is carried by one end and not 'bundled' but the male will sometimes pick up and carry two feathers, managing with great difficulty, to hold both by the bases of their shafts. Eggs 3 to 9, usually 4 to 6. Incubation period 11–12 days. Young fledge at 18 to 21 days and sometimes return to the nest to roost for a few nights after fledging. Both sexes incubate in turn by day and the female only at night. The young beg with one or both wings raised, in the same manner as young Avadavats (q.v.). Sometimes a slight fluttering wing movement is used when begging. In captivity, the parents of recently fledged young repeatedly fly to them, call loudly and fly to a high perch or into cover, till the young either follow them up to a perch or hide themselves.

VOICE The contact calls and the nest call are, to my ears, very like those of the Avadavat (q.v.) but a little less loud and higher pitched. The male, when in breeding condition, utters long series of remarkably loud and strident chirps. Often 3 or 4 high-pitched chirps are followed by one on a lower key and harsher in tone. The bird utters these series of chirps in a typical rather upright singing posture, turning his head from side to side. The chirping does not appear to be homologous to the purely sexually-motivated songs of most estrildids, as it is often interspersed with or immediately followed by attacks on or fights with potential rivals (Goodwin, Russ). However, in captivity, males that are tolerant or friendly towards each other may both chirp, either at the same time or in turn, without any overt hostility breaking out and homosexually paired males may perch side by side chirping. This chirping is uttered mainly in the early morning, starting before dawn and ending a little after, and at dusk, although sometimes also during the day. The begging call of the young is a loud 'chee-chee-chee . . .', with a 'kissing' tone.

DISPLAY AND SOCIAL BEHAVIOUR In the courtship display no nesting material is held. The male hops up to the female with triangular head and angled tail and may or may not hop around her before, from beside her, performing deep bows to the side away from her. Copulation follows if the female is willing but, of course, the most intense and prolonged displays are seen when she is not. The male may spread the tail instead of angling it towards the female during the bowing display, opening and partly closing it with each bow. Except that it is not performed at a potential nest site this latter version of the bowing display is identical to the postures used when nest-calling. The nest-call, or a series of soft notes that my ears cannot separate from it, may indeed be uttered in either version of the display. Kunkel (1959) observed a display of the female in which, sometimes with a wisp of nesting material in her bill, she hops around the male and in an erect posture erects and then depresses her plumage. I have seen similar posturing (without nesting material in the bill) from the male, in which it appeared to be intention movements of mounting the female and often ended in the make making unsuccessful attempts to copulate.

Allo-preening between members of the pair is frequent and in captivity this species is very prone to solicit allo-preening from other species of estrildids.

OTHER NAMES Zebra Waxbill, Golden-breasted Waxbill, Orange-breasted Waxbill.

REFERENCES

Clancey, P. A. 1964. *The birds of Natal and Zululand.* London.

Goodwin, D. 1960. Observations on Avadavats and Golden-breasted Waxbills. *Avicult. Mag.* **66**: 74–199.

Immelmann, K. & G. 1967. Verhaltensökologische Studien an afrikanischen und australischen Estrildiden. *Zool. Jb. Syst. Bd.* **94**: 609–686.

Immelmann, K., Steinbacher, J. & Wolters, H. E. 1965. *Vögel in Käfig und Voliere: Prachtfinken*: 408–419.

Kunkel, P. 1959. Zum Verhalten einiger Prachtfinken (Estrildinae). *Z. Tierpsychol.* **16**: 302–350.

McLachlan, G. R. & Liversidge, R. 1957. *Robert's birds of South Africa*, rev. ed. Cape Town.

Montfort, N. 1965, Ornithologische Beobachtungen im Jemen. *J. Orn.* **106**: 333–339.

Russ, K. 1879. *Die fremdländischen Stubenvögel*, vol. 1. Hanover.

The quail-finches

The quail-finches, *Ortygospiza*, are confined to Africa. They live on the ground in open grassland or marshy areas. Under natural conditions they have never been known to alight above ground level, although, under certain conditions, at least one species may rise and circle high in the air. They have strong, lark-like legs and feet with nearly flat claws and long hind toes, their upperparts are cryptically coloured (with the minor exception of red upper tail coverts in one species) and their behaviour, including their displays, also shows clear adaptations to ground-living.

Their nearest relatives are almost certainly the avadavats and the Goldbreast, *Amandava* spp., to which they show resemblances in their plumage patterns and mouth markings of their nestlings (Immelmann *et al.*, 1965, Steiner). Those characters where they differ markedly from *Amandava* clearly involve their adaptation to a more completely terrestrial way of life.

The Quail-finch, *Ortygospiza atricollis* and the Black-chinned Quail-finch. *O. gabonensis* are mainly allopatric in distribution but overlap in some areas without, apparently, interbreeding. In some, but not all of the overlap areas they appear to be ecologically separated (Chapin, Traylor). Immelmann *et al.* (1976) and Wolter favour treating all forms as conspecific, pointing out that the situation is that of a (more or less) ring-shaped distribution with only some of the terminal forms overlapping (without inter-breeding however) in relatively restricted areas. The situation is thus comparable with the better known one of the Herring Gull/Lesser Black-backed gull complex. I concur with Traylor in thinking that, whilst acknowledging their close relationship, it is preferable to treat *gabonensis* and *atricollis* as species, as is usually done with the two gulls, *Larus fuscus* and *L. argentatus*.

The Locust-finch or Red Quail-finch, *O. locustella*, differs from the other two species in having white-spotted and partly red plumage, more markedly developed feet and legs and less strongly developed breast musculature. For these reasons it is sometimes placed in a separate genus, *Paludipasser*, but this does not seem justified.

Observations on *O. locustella* in the wild and on *O. atricollis* in captivity (see species' sections for details and references) suggest that male quail-finches spend much less time incubating than do the males of most other estrildids. It is difficult to see why this should be so and further observations are needed to check whether such behaviour is usual.

REFERENCES

Chapin, J. P. 1954. The birds of the Belgian Congo. *Bull. Amer. Mus. Nat. Hist.* **75B**.

Immelmann, K., Steinbacher, J. & Wolters, H. E. 1965 and 1976. *Vögel in Käfig und Voliere: Prachtfinken*: 368 and 565–566.

Steiner, H. 1960. Klassifikation der Prachtfinken, Spermestidae, auf Grund der Rachenzeichnungen ihrer Nestlinge. *J. Orn.* **101**: 92–112.

Traylor, M. 1963. Revision of the Quail Finch, *Ortygospiza atricollis. Bull. Br. Orn. Cl.* **83**: 141–146.

Wolters, H. E. 1972. Aus der ornithologischen Sammlung des Museums Alexander Koenig II. *Bonn. Zool. Beitr.* **23**: 187–194.

Quail-finch   *Ortygospiza atricollis*

Fringilla atricollis Vieillot, 1817, *Nouv. Dict. Hist. Nat.* nouv. ed. **12**, p. 182.

DESCRIPTION Between Spice Finch and Avadavat in size. Rather like the latter in shape but more heavily built with shorter tail and slightly longer legs with claws only very slightly curved and hind toe and hind claw long and lark-like.

Forehead, front of face and throat dull black except for a very small white patch at base of lower mandible ('chin'). Posterior part of face and sides of neck medium dull grey, with a slight silvery tinge on the ear coverts. Top of head, upperparts and wings very dark brownish grey with slightly paler greyish fringes to the feathers. Tail dull greyish black, the outer feathers, and occasionally to some extent also the central ones, with white apical spots or streaks. Under wing coverts mainly pale reddish buff. Front of breast very dark brownish grey, slightly tinged with chestnut and narrowly barred with white; the individual feathers have a chestnut-tinged zone, then a narrow blackish bar, then a white bar with a blackish narrow anterior edge and a paler fringe to the feather. Flanks similarly but more broadly barred and with two white bars on each feather. Median part of lower breast chestnut, shading to buffish white on the lower belly. Under tail coverts reddish buff with more or less longitudinal dark markings. Irides brownish yellow to light brown. Bill red, upper mandible often partly or entirely brownish or dusky; probably the bill is always clear red when the bird is in breeding condition but further observations are needed. Legs and feet dusky flesh, pinkish brown or flesh-coloured.

The female has no black on her face or throat, which are brownish grey. The chestnut of her breast is much paler and the white barring on her breast and flanks is less contrasting owing to the paler background. Bill with upper mandible (always?) dark brown or dusky, lower mandible pink or red. The juvenile is like the female but paler and with only very faint barring on the underparts. The nestling has six black spots on the yellowish palate, three black marks on the tongue, a black crescent on the inside of the lower mandible. There are three iridescent bluish or opalescent tubercles, with black skin between them, at the base of each upper and one at the base of each lower mandible (Chapin, Immelmann *et al.*, 1965, St Quintin).

The above description is of nominate *O.a. atricollis*, from Senegal and Gambia to northern Ghana and northern and central Nigeria. Probably the populations of northern Cameroun (Greling) will prove referable to this race. *O. atricollis ansorgei*, from former Portuguese Guinea to Liberia and the Ivory Coast, is a little darker grey in colour, with the black of the face and throat extending to the ear coverts and upper breast. *O.a. ugandae*, from southern Sudan to Uganda, extreme eastern Ituri and North Kavirondo, Kenya, is a little lighter in general coloration than nominate *O.a. atricollis*, has more white on the 'chin' and a narrow white ring round the eye. *O.a. fuscocrissa*, from the highlands of Abyssinia and Eritrea, has more white around the eye; the median part of its breast and its flanks are mainly black, so that the white barring is very conspicuous, and there is greater contrast between the dark parts of the feathers of its upperparts and their paler fringes, giving a somewhat spotted appearance. *O.a. muelleri* (syns. *O.a. digressa* and *O.a. minuscula*), from much of the species' eastern and southern range, and

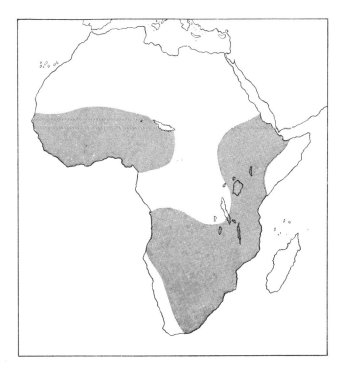

possibly also from north-western Angola, is like *O.a. fuscocrissa* but paler and greyer on the upperparts and a lighter chestnut on the breast. It is black only on the forehead, throat and the posterior edges of the breast and flank bars. *O.a. smithersi*, from north-eastern Zambia from Luapula River and Luwingu to Kasamu and Mporokomo is like *O.a. muelleri* but darker, with a blackish face and narrower white ring round the eye. *O.a. pallida*, from northern Botswana and Wankie, Zimbabwe, is similar to *O.a. muelleri* but markedly paler.

DISTRIBUTION AND HABITAT Senegal, Gambia, Mali, northern Ghana, northern Cameroun, central and northern Nigeria, Portuguese Guinea to Liberia and Ivory Coast, Highlands of Eritrea and Abyssinia, Sudan, Uganda, Kenya, Tanzania, Zambia, Zimbabwe, south-western Angola (possibly north-western Angola), Damaraland, northern Botswana south to southern Cape Province. Inhabits grasslands, usually near water. Chooses areas with tufts of grass and open sand or soil between, but often screened by the foliage of, the grass clumps. Locally on short mown grass on aerodromes etc.

FEEDING AND GENERAL HABITS Only foods recorded in the wild are small grass seeds (often) and small spiders (twice). Probably rears its young partly on insects or other invertebrates as in captivity it searches eagerly for live food as soon as its eggs have hatched (Schifter, 1964). Individuals feeding young readily take whiteworms, ant pupae, live and cooked mealworms, weevils and other live food (Ruschin, Schifter, 1963 and 1964). They are very fond of red gnat larvae and water-fleas, *Daphnia*, and will pick them out of shallow water in a dish (Schifter, 1964). A pair in an outdoor aviary eagerly searched for and pulled small earthworms from the ground after rain

(Ludwig). After the first few days both dry and soaked millet are also fed to the young. Food is sought only on the ground.

Usually in small parties or, when breeding, in pairs (Chapin, McLachlan & Liversidge, Vincent). On the ground walks, runs, uses a half walking, half hopping 'polka step' and hops when an uneven or lumpy substrate makes it convenient to do so (Kunkel, 1962 and 1966). As an initial (?) fear response crouches with head and breast flat to earth and tail erect (Kannwischer). In the wild seldom seen until flushed, when it (more often 'they') rises with fast-beating wings to a height of twenty to thirty metres and then either flies off to a distance or circles round and then drops to earth nearby (Chapin, Vincent).

Not known to perch above ground in a wild state and probably never does so, though it no doubt sings from stones or other small eminences, as it will in captivity. In captivity sometimes perches on bare boughs or ledges but this is almost certainly an artifact of the unnatural environment.

FIELD CHARACTERS Not usually seen till flushed. Small dull bird with some white on tail, that rises from ground and returns to it, after flying some way or circling high. Lack of any red or orange on rump at once identifies it from Goldbreast (q.v.) Probably easily confused with Locust-finch unless red head of male of latter seen. Probably not distinguishable from *O. gabonensis* in field, certainly not unless head with white chin and (some races) eye-ring seen.

NESTING Nests on the ground, usually between or alongside tufts of grass. The nest varies in shape according to the site but is usually dome-shaped or roundish with a side entrance that is either porched or has a short entrance tube. It is built of grass stems and blades, sometimes also rootlets, lined with finer grasses and grass panicles and sometimes (probably always if the bird can find them) with feathers (Chapin, Van Someren, Vincent). In captivity nests are always lined with pale or white feathers, if these are made available. The male finds and fetches the materials but the female does part, perhaps most, of the actual building (Ludwig). Material is held cross-wise in the bill, not by one end, and often several pieces are bundled and carried at once (Kunkel, 1966). A captive male deliberately bit through the stems of growing grass, cutting them neatly off, when collecting material. He did not touch any of the same grasses that were growing by his nest but went across a path to the further side of the aviary for them (Phillips).

Eggs 4 to 6. Both sexes incubate and brood the young in turn by day and roost together in the nest at night. Ludwig and Phillips both observed that the males of their captive pairs only sat for very short spells, while their mates were off feeding. In view of an apparently confirmatory observation in the wild on the Locust-finch (q.v.) this may, perhaps, be normal for the genus. Young first audible inside the nest 14 days after the beginning of incubation (Schifter, 1963). They fledge at about 19 to 21 days, and

can feed themselves at 30 days old (Kannwischer, Schifter, 1963). Young beg in usual postures, at high intensity with the top of the head on the ground and mouth turned upwards. The wings are lifted in a similar manner to those of young *Amandava* species. They are flapped when begging and held open and slightly fluttering or vibrating when actually being fed (Kannwischer, photograph in Immelmann *et al.*, 1965).

Recorded breeding in September to December in Nigeria; June to November in northern Uganda; April to August and in January in the Kenya Highlands; February, May, June and October in Tanzania; July in Dar-es-Salaam; December to April in South Africa and July to October in Senegal. In general it breeds at the end of the rains and the first part of the dry season (Immelmann, *et al.*, Mackworth-Praed & Grant, McLachlan & Liversidge).

VOICE Usual (contact?) calls are metallic and rather bell-like (Immelmann *et al.*), the flight call has been transcribed as a bell-like 'tirrilink (McLachlan & Liversidge).

Ludwig describes two forms of song, one consisting of call notes run together but with a particular (not described) tone and the other sounding like two stones rubbed together. Phillips gives such a vivid and amusing description of a song given by his captive male that I feel I must quote it: 'When I was a boy, . . . a certain cottager's garden had in it a cherry tree; and . . . year by year, as the season of cherries came round, in order to frighten away the birds, the old man used to fix up in the tree a clapper arrangement which was worked by a diminutive wind-mill. As the sails revolved, two loosely-hung pieces of iron were banged against an empty gunpowder canister . . . with results that were more audible than musical; and I do not know of anything that reminds me so much of this ingenious contrivance . . . as the staccato song of the Quail Finch, which goes somewhat as follows: Click clack cloik clike cluck cleck click cloik cluck click cleck clack cluck clike cloik etc etc. Now if this score be read slowly, it may appear a little tedious; it should be galloped through, as when a gust whirls round the arms of the windmill . . . so the song bursts forth at one time with startling suddenness, at another for just a little spell, at another for a prolonged period . . . no combination of words . . . can adequately describe this unrivalled composition – *but it has only to be heard to be appreciated!*'

DISPLAY AND SOCIAL BEHAVIOUR In the courtship display, the male, with angled tail and head and front of body held high, runs, lifting his feet high, three or four paces first to one side then to the other in front of the female's head and flutters his wings (Kunkel, 1966). Sometimes he may run in part circles beside or behind the female (Ruschin, Schifter, 1963). He makes upward jerks of his head which Immelmann *et al.*, interpret as homologous with the head movements of those African estrildids that display with a stem or feather in the bill but which Kunkel (1966) thinks are compensatory balancing movements to the high-stepping. This display ends in copulation if the female is co-operative (Ruschin). Said to have a display flight in which it towers up to a great height and then falls to earth 'like a stone' (Mackworth-Praed & Grant).

When trying to attract the female to the nest site the male, with nesting material in his bill and in a similar erect posture to that of the courtship display, utters a series of soft notes, shows the material to the hen and then turns, runs to the nest site and begins to build (Kunkel, 1966).

Does not usually clump or allo-preen; even members of a pair roost or rest a few centimetres apart (Kunkel). In captivity it is usually very peaceable with both its own and other species, even breeding pairs defend only a small area around their nest (Ludwig, Schifter, 1964).

OTHER NAMES Ground Finch, Partridge Finch

REFERENCES

Chapin, J. P. 1954. The birds of the Belgian Congo. *Bull. Amer. Mus. Nat. Hist.* **75B**.

Greling, C. de. 1972. New records for northern Cameroun. *Bull. Br. Orn. Cl.* **92**: 24–27.

Immelmann, K., Steinbacher, J. & Wolters, H. E. 1965. *Vögel in Käfig und Voliere: Prachtfinken*: 368–388. Aachen, Germany.

Kannwischer, H. 1974. Plege und Zucht von Wachtelastrilden im Zimmerkäfig. *Gefiederte Welt* **1974**: 174–176.

Kunkel, P. 1962. Zur Verbreitung des Hüpfens und Laufens unter Sperlingsvögeln (Passeres). *Z. Tierpsychol.* **19**: 417–439.

Kunkel, P. 1966. Bemerkungen zu einigen Verhaltensweisen des Rebhuhnastrilds, *Ortygospiza atricollis atricollis* (Vieillot). *Z. Tierpsychol.* **23**: 136–140.

Ludwig, H. 1964. Erfahrungen bei der Haltung und Zucht des Wachtelastrilds (*Ortygospiza atricollis*). *Gefiederte Welt* **1964**: 230–232.

Mackworth-Praed, C. W. & Grant, C. H. B. 1973. *African handbook of birds* ser. 3, vol. 2. Longman, Green & Co., London.

McLachlan, G. R. & Liversidge, R. 1957. *Roberts birds of South Africa*. Cape Town.

Ruschin, H. W. 1972. Etwas über Wachtelastrilde, ihre Haltung und Zucht. *Gefiederte Welt* **1972**: 141–142.

Schifter, H. 1963. Erfolgreiche Aufzucht von fünf Wachtelastrilden. *Gefiederte Welt* **1963**: 16–18.

Schifter, H. 1964. Weitere Zuchterfolge mit Wachtelastrilden. *Gefiederte Welt* **1964**: 83–85.

Phillips, R. 1909. Breeding of the Quail Finch. *Avicult. Mag.* 3rd ser. **1**: 37–47.

St Quintin, W. H. 1910. Mouth decoration of the nestling Quailfinch. *Avicult. May.* 3rd ser., **1**: 103–104.

Van Someren, V. G. L. 1956. Days with birds. *Feldiana: Zoology* **38**, published by the Chicago Natural History Museum.

Vincent, W. 1949. On the breeding habits of some African birds. *Ibis* **91**: 660–688.

Black-chinned Quail-finch   *Ortygospiza gabonensis*

Ortygospiza gabonensis Lynes, 1914, *Bull. Brit. Orn. Cl.* **33**, p. 131.

DESCRIPTION Very similar to the previous form, *O. atricollis*, with which it may be conspecific. Differs in appearance from nominate *O.a. atricollis* as follows: Head (except for the black face and throat), upperparts and wings with broader and more brownish fringes to the

feathers, contrasting with their dark brown or blackish brown centres to give a streaked and spotted appearance. Median part of lower breast a paler and more yellowish chestnut. Barring on breast and flanks similar to and as conspicuous as that of *O. atricollis fuscocrissa* (q.v.). Bill red. Sexual differences as in *O. atricollis* but perhaps less difference in intensity of the barring of breast and flanks. Bill of female dark brown or blackish, sometimes and perhaps usually with some red along the cutting edges of the mandibles. From the description given in Immelmann *et al.* (1965) it seems that some females have an entirely red or pink lower mandible, as in *O. atricollis* females. I have not seen a juvenile of this form. The mouth markings of the nestling are evidently just like those of *O. atricollis*; they were still present on two young birds that had just completed their first moult (Chapin).

The above description is of *O.g. gabonensis*, from former Spanish Guinea, Gabon and both sides of the Middle Congo River. *O.g. dorsotriata*, from the south-western shore of Lake Albert in eastern Congo (Zaïre) south to the north end of Lake Tanganyika, Rwanda, Bukoba in Lake Victoria, and southern Uganda, averages a very little larger (wing 49 to 53 as against 47–49 mm) and a little darker in colour. *O.g. fuscata* averages still larger (wing up to 55 mm) and is much darker and less brownish in colour but still with the greyish fringes of the feathers of its upperparts contrasting with their dull black centres. The white bars on its black breast are often (but not always) narrower than those of the other two races. Bill orange-red to scarlet, commonly with some sepia or blackish on the culmen and around the nostrils. Sexual differences as in the nominate form.

FIELD CHARACTERS As for *O. atricollis* (q.v.).

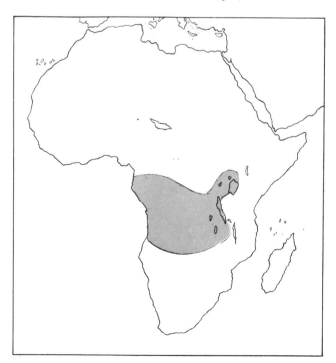

DISTRIBUTION AND HABITAT Central Africa from Gabon and north-western Angola east to southern Uganda and northern Zambia. In same types of country as previous form, *O. atricollis* (q.v.), except that in some areas of overlap it appears to prefer wetter places (Traylor). Chapin found it also in grassy fields and marshes that were surrounded by woodland.

FEEDING AND GENERAL HABITS Known to take small grass seeds and small spiders (Chapin). Feeds on the ground, sheltered by grass (Chapin). So far as known does not differ from *O. atricollis* (q.v.).

NESTING I can find no records that refer definitely (or even with probability) to this form. In all likelihood its nesting behaviour is identical to that of *O. atricollis*.

VOICE Not known to differ from that of *O. atricollis* (Benson & Irwin, Traylor).

DISPLAY AND SOCIAL BEHAVIOUR No information. Probably as *O. atricollis*.

REFERENCES
Benson, C. W. 1955. New forms of pipit, longclaw, robin-chat, grass-warbler, sunbird, quail-finch and canary from Central Africa. *Bull. Br. Orn. Cl.* **75**: 101–109.
Benson, C. W. & Irwin, M. P. S. 1965. Some birds from the north-western province, Zambia. *Arnoldia* **29**: 1–11.
Chapin, J. P. 1954. The birds of the Belgian Congo. *Bull. Amer. Mus. Nat. Hist.* **75B**.
Traylor, M. 1963. Revision of the Quail Finch *Ortygospiza atricollis*. *Bull. Br. Orn. Cl.* **83**: 141–146.

Locust-finch   *Ortygospiza locustella*

Paludipasser locustella Neave, 1909, *Bull. Br. Orn. Club* **25**: 25.

DESCRIPTION About size of Goldbreast but with shorter tail, deeper bill, larger and stouter legs and feet and long, lark-like hind claw. Face, including lores, area above and behind eyes and ear coverts, throat and breast red; usually the face is a deep scarlet and the throat and breast of a slightly paler and more orangey hue. Feathers of centre of crown brownish black with greyish fringes giving an obscurely spotted effect. Sides of crown, nape and hind neck dark greyish brown. Mantle, back, innermost greater coverts and innermost secondaries brownish black or greyish black, spotted with small white dots. The individual spotted feathers are black with dark greyish fringes and a single small white dot near the tip of each feather except for the innermost secondaries which have a narrow row of white spots along their outer edges. There is some individual, or possibly geographical, variation in the size and shape of the white dots. Wing coverts golden-orange to orange-red with paler, sometimes whitish, tips to the feathers. Innermost greater coverts partly or largely blackish brown and with clear white tips. Primaries and outer secondaries sepia with most of those parts of the outer webs that are visible when the wing is closed orange or orange-red. The outermost long primary is narrowly edged with pale buffish on its outer web. Under wing coverts pale pinkish buff and shiny in texture. Rump and upper tail coverts brownish black along the median line, otherwise bright red or orange-red. Tail brownish black, the outer feathers with white spots at their tips (one per feather). Underparts below the breast dark sooty grey, usually with terminal white dots or short bars on the lower flanks and white fringes to the under tail coverts. Irides pale primrose yellow. Bill red or orange-red with sepia or blackish culmen. Legs and feet light brown to yellowish flesh.

The female has no red on the head, the areas red in the male being dark brownish grey except for a whitish or buffish spot on the lores. Her underparts are greyish buff to off-white, the breast sometimes clouded with faint greyish barring. Sides of breast narrowly barred whitish and greyish, flanks boldly barred white and black. Plumage otherwise as male's but wings seldom quite so red as those of some males. However, the orange or red feathers of the wings of both sexes fade and bleach with wear and males in worn plumage have duller and paler wings than females in newer plumage. The juvenile is like the female but has light brown fringes to the feathers of the upper parts, giving a spotted effect. The white spots are fewer and much less distinct. Breast barred light and dark. Irides brown. Bill blackish. Some juveniles are buffier and less strongly barred on the underparts. These may be males but the few juvenile specimens I have seen were unsexed.

Irwin describes the mouth markings of a six day old nestling as follows: 'On either side of the gape are two flat red lobes protruding slightly from the corners of the mouth. The palatal pattern consists of two opposing black lines, bow-shaped and running along the roof of the mouth at the edge of the palate and all but joining anteriorly. At right angles and at the base of these two lines, are two inverted bow-shaped lines, one on either side of the mouth at a level with the gape wattles, but only about one third the length of those on the palate. Within the opposing palatal lines the roof of the mouth is bright red, the colour extending down into the throat. The tongue has three raised red lobes which overlap its edges. The posterior pair are lozenge-shaped, and placed together along the axis of the tongue and the anterior and somewhat larger one is heart-shaped.'

The above description is of nominate *O.l. locustella*, from most of the species' range. *O. locustella uelensis*, from north-eastern Congo and around Lake Leopold II, Moyen Congo, has no white spots on its upper parts and flanks. Sometimes, possibly usually, its upper mandible is more extensively dark, being red only in a narrow streak along the cutting edge.

See plate 1, facing p. 96.

FIELD CHARACTERS Tiny dark bird with red on sides of rump and *reddish or orange wings* which at once distinguish it from Quail Finch and Goldbreast, the only species likely to be confused with it. Never perches and seldom seen until flushed. Male has red face and breast.

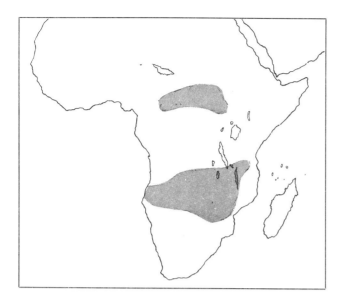

DISTRIBUTION AND HABITAT South-western and north-eastern Angola, east through southern Katanga and Zambia to Malawi and south-western Tanzania, and south to the Tete district of Mosambique and the highlands of Rhodesia. Also in north-eastern Congo and around Lake Leopold in Moyen Congo. Inhabits wet or moist grasslands, including such areas in Brachystegia woodland (Benson and Benson), where there is short or clumped grass.

FEEDING AND GENERAL HABITS Known to eat small grass seeds. Lives on the ground, never perching. Usually in parties of 3 to about 16 birds. Although a bird of damp areas, Chapin found that, in the dry season, in the Uele district of Zaïre, low marshy spots that had dried up and then been burnt over were favoured haunts. Twice the species was found on abandoned cultivation at higher levels.

Local in distribution and fluctuating in apparent numbers. May indulge in extensive migrations or wanderings but is now thought to be usually a resident with only local movements (Irwin).

When flushed may rise high in the air (Vincent) or fly off, but not very fast, the party keeps together, in steady or direct flight for 45 to 90 metres (50 to 100 yards) and then drop to earth again (Chapin). In contradistinction to Chapin, Mackworth-Praed & Grant describe the flight as rapid and dipping. Most likely, as with many other birds, the speed and form of flight is to some extent varied according to circumstances.

NESTING Nests on the ground, in either dried up or wet situations (Irwin, Vincent). Nest of dead grasses, sometimes, perhaps usually, with short stripped grass stems, apparently collected when green, in the interior of the nest, which is usually lined with a few feathers (perhaps many when the birds can find them?) and in one instance with vegetable down. One nest, examined in detail by Vincent, was well hidden among wiry grass but not

attached to it. It was ball-shaped, about three inches in diameter and with the entrance hole at one side near the top and about one inch in diameter. Irwin states the nests he found were similar in construction. Clutch 2 to 8, mostly usually 4 to 7. Irwin thought the only clutch of 2 eggs that he found was incomplete but Vincent found a nest containing 2 partly developed eggs and it is unlikely that any predator would take only part of the clutch.

Incubation, at least in larger clutches, begins up to 3 or 4 days before completion of the clutch (Irwin). Irwin's observations appeared to show that the female did most of the incubation and feeding of the young but further observations are needed. Both sexes roost together in the nest at night (Irwin). Breeds February to May in Rhodesia (Irwin, Vincent). The above information, and accounts in standard works also apparently, derive from Irwin & Vincent.

VOICE A squeaking 'chip chip' is sometimes uttered in flight.

DISPLAY AND SOCIAL BEHAVIOUR No information.

OTHER NAMES Marsh Finch, Red Quail-finch.

REFERENCES
Chapin, J. P. 1954. The birds of the Belgian Congo. *Bull. Amer. Mus. Nat. Hist.* **75B**.
Irwin, M. P. S. 1958. A description of the unrecorded gape and mouth markings of the Locust Finch, *Ortygospiza locustella*, with some breeding and other notes. *Bull. Br. Orn. Cl.* **78**: 127–129.
Vincent, A. W. 1949. On the breeding habits of some African birds. *Ibis* **91**: 483–507.

The Red-browed, Crimson, Star and Cherry finches

The Red-browed Finch or Sydney Waxbill, *Aegintha temporalis*, has occasioned much discussion among taxonomists. Although on geographical grounds its closest allies seem likely to be other Australian species, it bears a close resemblance to many of the African waxbills in the genus *Estrilda*, not only in appearance but also in behaviour. Harrison (1963), Morris & Immelmann (in Mayr) have pointed out that the plumage resemblances are not exact in detail; this is true if comparison is made to any one particular species of *Estrilda* but is a much less valid objection if the comparison is made with several species. True the post-ocular part (not all) of its eye-stripe is not identical in position with those of the Common and Black-rumped Waxbills, to match it up with the red-orange face of the Orange-cheeked Waxbill it would have to be reduced in area, and that the olive-green of its back is not precisely the same shade as that of the Swee Waxbill but, if it occurred in Africa, such differences would not be likely to be considered of more than specific significance. More cogent is Harrison's argument that other Australian estrildids also show resemblances to African forms but since theirs are fewer and/or less striking, they are usually disregarded when considering affinities.

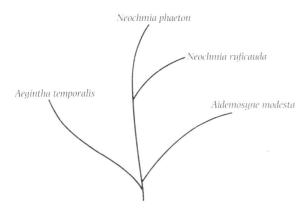

Neochmia phaeton

Neochmia ruficauda

Aegintha temporalis

Aidemosyne modesta

Dendrogram to show probable affinities of the Red-browed, Cherry, Crimson and Star Finches. See text for discussion.

Delacour unhesitatingly included *temporalis* in his enlarged conception of *Estrilda*, remarking that he considered it 'a typical waxbill in every way'. Kunkel (unpublished ms), after a very careful comparison and analysis of its displays, concluded that it was certainly close to *Estrilda* and either represented a conservative element of the stock from which such other Australian forms as the firetails had also been derived or, and more probably, that there had been several different invasions of Australia by estrildids during the climatic changes of the Pleistocene and that *temporalis* represented a relatively late and *Estrilda*-like one. Immelmann (in Mayr, 1968), however, considered its *Estrilda*-like characters as 'primitive aspects' that did not provide decisive information and was not convinced of any close relationship between *Aegintha* and *Estrilda*. Mayr decided that it 'would seem best to place *Aegintha* in the grass finches but closest to the waxbills.' Morris concluded that its affinities were with the Crimson Finch and Painted Finch and that: 'if they are not (waxbills), it is not.'

I have seen the Red-browed Finch alive both in the wild and in captivity but have not had the opportunity of observing it over a period of time in either state. Therefore my opinion, based as it is on the work of others, examination of skins and very brief impressions of the live bird, should not perhaps be given much consideration by anyone with reasons for contrary views. I think that the Red-browed Finch is probably most closely related to such Australian forms as the Star Finch, Crimson Finch and firetails and that its undoubted resemblance to the typical waxbills is a remarkable example of convergence, within related stocks. In any case this seems to be an instance where the retention of a monotypic genus is fully justified, the more especially so as it is quite possible that in assessing its relationships Delacour & Kunkel may yet be proved right and others, myself included, wrong.

The Crimson Finch, *Neochmia phaeton*, shows a close resemblance in coloration to some of the firefinches in the African genus *Lagonosticta*. This resemblance is most striking in the male although present also in the female. The firefinch-like appearance, and some similarities in behaviour to the Red-billed Firefinch, led Mitchell to consider it the Australian representative of *Lagonosticta*. As Harrison (1963) pointed out, however, in size, shape, and to some extent in the plumage pattern of the female, the Crimson Finch is nearer to the purple waxbills, *Uraeginthus granatina* and *U. ianthinogaster*, than it is to the firefinches. Immelmann's (1962, 1965) studies led him to conclude that its closest affinities were with the Star Finch, with which it agrees in many aspects of morphology and behaviour, especially if females and juveniles are compared, as the predominantly red plumage and intense aggressiveness of the male Crimson Finch are apt to distract attention from such similarities. I concur with Mayr in thinking that the Star Finch and Crimson Finch are best both included in the same genus, *Neochmia*, rather than the monotypic genus *Bathilda* being maintained for the former.

The Cherry Finch or Plum-capped Finch, *Aidemoysyne modesta*, is another species whose affinities have been in dispute. Delacour put it with the other Australian finches and actually into the same subgenus in which he included the Star, Crimson, Zebra and Bicheno's Finches. Steiner placed it in his tribe Zonaeginthae, together with the Star Finch, the Crimson Finch, the Painted Finch and the firetails. Harrison (1967) suggested that it was most closely related to the typical grassfinches and the Pictorella Finch, considering all these as representing an early invasion into Australia of mannikin-like stock, each of which was more closely related to the others than to the typical Asiatic and Australian mannikins in the genus *Lonchura*. Kunkel (unpublished mss) concluded that it was most probably an early offshoot of mannikin stock and, despite their present wide geographical separation, most closely related to the silverbills and the Bibfinch. Immelmann (1962) also allied it to *Lonchura* while Keast actually included it in that genus. Hall (unpublished mss), while recognising its apparent munia-like characters was also impressed by resemblances to the Star Finch.

The Cherry Finch has a courtship display remarkably like those of both the Silverbill and some of the more typical Asiatic Munias. It also impresses some observers as looking like a silverbill, although except for a similarly shaped and coloured tail and general rather sombre coloration those I have seen alive did not strike me as in the least like silverbills, when allowance is made for the familial resemblance. The generally brownish colour gives a somewhat mannikin-like impression but the same might, up to a point, be said of the juvenile plumages of many more colourful estrildids. The white apical spots on the wing coverts and rump seem homologous to those of the Star Finch (most specimens of the northern race) and (wings only) the Pictorella Finch, although the wing spots of the Cherry Finch are much larger than those of these two. It is of interest that another Australian species of quite a different order, the Diamond Dove, shows very similar white wing spots although in its case paired spots are involved. In the mouth markings of its nestlings, the Cherry Finch closely resembles the Star Finch. In its cherry red or 'plum' cap, the Cherry Finch evidently has visible red lipochrome pigment, another feature possessed by the Star Finch and its allies but not by the mannikins. Indeed the distribution of the red (purple) on forehead, forecrown and throat could readily come about from a slight reduction of some such pattern as that of the Star Finch.

Thus, in spite of its having some undoubtedly mannikin-like characters, I am inclined to think that the Cherry Finch's closest phylogenetic affinities may be with the Star Finch and its allies, as Steiner earlier concluded. Certainly it seems justifiable to retain it in the monotypic genus *Aidemosyne*.

REFERENCES

Delacour, J. A. 1943. A revision of the subfamily Estrildinae of the family Ploceidae. *Zoologica* **28**: 69–86.

Harrison, C. J. O. 1963. The taxonomy of the Crimson Finch and Red-browed Finch. *Emu* **63**: 48–56.

Harrison, C. J. O. 1967. Apparent zoogeographical dispersal patterns in two avian families. *Bull. Brit. Orn. Club* **87**: 63–72.

Immelmann, K. 1962. Beiträge zu einer vergleichenden Biologie australischer Prachtfinken (Spermestidae). *Zool. Jb. Syst. Bd.* 1–196.

Immelmann, K. 1965. *Australian finches in bush and aviary.* Angus & Robertson, Sydney and London.

Keast, A. 1958. Infraspecific variation in the Australian finches. *Emu* **58**: 219–246.

Mayr, E. 1968. The sequence of genera in the Estrildidae (Aves). *Vreviora* **287**: 1–14.

Mitchell, I. G. 1962. The taxonomic position of the Crimson Finch. *Emu* **62**: 115–125.

Morris, D. 1958. The comparative ethology of grassfinches (Erythrurae) and mannikins (Amadinae). *Proc. zool. Soc. London* **131**: 389–439.

Steiner, H. 1960. Die Klassifikation der Prachtfinken, Spermestidae, auf Grund der Rachenzeichnungen ihrer Nestlinge. *J. Orn.* **101**: 92–112.

Red-browed Finch   *Aegintha temporalis*

Fringilla temporalis Latham, 1801, *Index* Ornith., suppl., 48.

DESCRIPTION See plate 2, facing p. 97. About size of Zebra Finch but with smaller bill and longer (medium length), graduated, tail. In fact very similar in shape to most waxbills in the genus *Estrilda*. Lores and a broad stripe extending over and behind the eye bright red. Forehead, crown and nape medium grey. Mantle, back, wing coverts and most of outer webs of wing quills olive-green, slightly more yellowish in tone on the sides of the neck and outer fringes of the primaries than elsewhere. End third (approximately) of outer webs of primaries silvery grey. Under wing coverts buff. Rest of wing quills dark dull grey. Rump and upper tail coverts red, the ends of the feathers shining and bright but not quite so brilliant as in the firetails. Face and sides of foreneck light grey. Throat pale buff to pale grey shading to a slightly darker grey or buffish grey on breast and flanks and pale buff to greyish buff on

belly, ventral area and under tail coverts. Irides reddish brown to red. Bill red with large triangular black area on culmen and another on the underside of the lower mandible. Sexes alike but there is a good deal of minor individual variation and birds in worn plumage may be very dull and greyish on the upperparts.

Juvenile duller, with no red on the head and dark bill. Mouth markings of nestlings a 5-spot pattern on the palate, a dark bar across the tongue, dark crescent on the floor of the lower mandible and four large, black-centred tubercles in the gape, one at the base of each side of each mandible.

The above description is of nominate *A.t. temporalis*, from most of the species' range. *A.t. minor*, from northern Queensland and the Cape York Peninsula, is smaller and paler in colour. The grey of its head extends onto the upper mantle and the back is a more yellowish olive. The under tail coverts are said to 'tend towards black' (Immelmann) but in the only adult specimen I have seen, a female from Cape York, the underparts are like those of the nominate form except for being paler on throat, breast and belly and whitish on the ventral area. *A.t. loftyi*, from the Mount Lofty Ranges and Kangaroo Island, is said to be like the nominate form but browner on the head and underparts. I have not seen specimens of this race.

FIELD CHARACTERS Small greenish and greyish bird with bright red bill, face stripe and rump. Greenish back and bright red on face distinguish it from all Australian finches except Star Finch from which its unspotted breast and *bright* red rump at once separate it.

DISTRIBUTION AND HABITAT Eastern and south-eastern Australia, from Cape York Peninsula south to New South Wales and Victoria and west to coastal South Australia in the Mt Lofty Range, and Kangaroo Island. Introduced into Western Australia (Dell). Inhabits forest edge, open woodland, cover bordering watercourses, pasture land

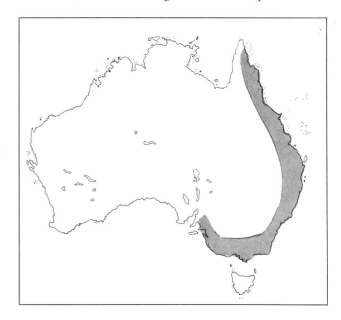

interspersed with trees and bushes, the edges of sugar cane fields, parks and gardens.

FEEDING AND GENERAL HABITS Feeds mainly on the seeds of grasses and herbaceous plants, including many introduced species such as the grasses *Poa annua* and *Digitaria sanguinalis* (Dell) and water-pepper, *Polygonum hydropiper* (Immelmann). Seeds of the grasses *Briza minor*, *B. maxima* and *Aira elegans*, of *Lepidospermum angustatum* and *Casuarina*, the seeds of many fruits and berries and small insects are also taken (Dell, Immelmann). In many places it habitually takes breadcrumbs and other human foods in gardens, parks or from windowsills and enters large mesh cages in zoos to scavenge food fed to the inmates. Mrs Barbara Triggs found that the wild Red-browed Finches she feeds prefer white millet, will eat panicum and Japanese millet but refuse linseed and husked oats. Feeds both on ground and in vegetation, can hold objects underfoot (Immelmann, 1962). Usually in pairs or small parties when breeding; when not breeding in flocks of anything up to a few hundred individuals. Roosts in nests, usually roosting nests built for this purpose and which are unlined and lack an entrance tunnel. Domestic and feral cats and the hawk, *Accipiter fasciatus* are known predators of it (Dell). Sometimes shy of man but in many places extremely tame and trusting. The locomotion intention movements involve a mainly sideways tail flicking (Immelmann, 1962).

In captivity often shy and nervous. Although some of its populations endure cold and also damp nights at some times of year, in captivity seems usually more sensitive to cold and damp than are many exclusively tropical species. Some aviculturists (e.g. Butler) have claimed that it is 'hardy' and can be safely kept even at temperatures below freezing point but this information seems based on a few exceptionally resistant birds that did not live for long after their 'winter of discontent'. Surprisingly, in view of its readiness to eat artificial foods in its free state, it will seldom do so in captivity. Besides dry and soaked seeds, it should be given a plentiful supply of greenfood, especially budding, flowering and seeding *Poa annua* grass. Green aphids (greenfly), ant pupae and other small, soft insects should be offered as available (Immelmann *et al.*). Hall (unpublished mss) noted that her captive birds 'chewed' and apparently ate grass. If, as is likely, this refers to fresh young shoots of green grass, this is a habit shared with the Avadavat and the Goldbreast. Of those species of Australian finches that were exported to and sold in Britain and Europe in *large* numbers shortly after the Second World War, this appears to be the only one of which there are no captive breeding stocks still extant.

NESTING Nests in trees, bushes or shrubs; thickly foliaged and/or spiny species being preferred. Often several pairs nest near to each other, sometimes in the same tree or bush. Immelmann found two nests with young less than a metre apart. The nest may be from 1 to 10 metres above ground. It is very like those of the firetails, a large retort-shaped or roundish structure with a downward sloping

entrance tube that may be well made and about 15 centimetres (6 inches) long or a mere suggestion of a hood over the entrance (Jasper, 1962). It is built of stalks, grass blades, grass panicles and sometimes other vegetation. Immelmann found that the outer layers of nests that he examined were made of long, fairly stiff stems of grass; the inner layer of softer grasses and grass panicles. The nest proper is lined with white feathers where these are available. In Western Australia Dell found that, before Domestic Fowls were brought into the district, nests were unlined or lined only with soft grass panicles. Immelmann, however, records thistle down and rabbits' fur being used as lining material. Jasper found that reddish brown feathers (from Rhode Island Red fowls) were ignored even though available near to the nest sites by the birds, which went about 185 metres (200 yards) to obtain white Chicken feathers. Cock nests or their equivalent are apparently sometimes, if rather rarely, built as Jasper (1962) states that 'false spouts' and 'small chambers' are occasionally added to finished nests. In captivity (and probably in freedom also) most or all of the nesting material is brought by the male but both sexes bring feathers for the lining (Russ, Jasper, 1962).

Eggs 4 to 6, usually 5 (Immelmann, 1965), up to 8 in captivity (Russ). Both sexes incubate and brood in turn by day and both roost in the nest at night (Immelmann). Incubation period 14 days; young fledge at 15 days (Dell). The young do not return to the nest but are led into suitable cover by the parents (Jasper, 1962). Immelmann state, however, that for 'long' after fledging, the parents lead the young back into the nest to roost. Possibly the presence or absence of cover and alternative roosting nests determines what takes place in this connection. Other flock members often show much interest in nests that are being built or contain young but have not been seen to participate in nest-building or parental care (Jasper, 1965). Jasper (1962) found a brood of young nestlings on the ground outside the nest, covered with ants. When he removed the ants from the nestlings and nest and replaced the former into the latter, the parents responded by immediately collecting feathers of *all* colours and packed them around the nest entrance, inside the entrance tube. Jasper implies (but does not explicitly state) that things then proceeded normally. He suggests the feathers may have been a defensive measure against the entry of ants and other insects. This may indeed be a function of the not uncommon estrildid habit of putting feathers in the nest entrance when young have been hatched, but in this case the birds seem to have done it rather late as, but for Jasper's intervention the young would certainly have died. The aggressive interference of House Sparrows, *Passer domesticus*, sometimes causes desertion and loss of nests and Brush-tailed Phascogales destroy many nests (Jasper, 1965).

In northern Australia most nesting takes place in the latter half of the rainy season, from January to April (Immelmann, 1962, 1963). Where water and food are available the nesting period may be extended. Near

Sydney nests with eggs have been found in all months except July and August (Hindwood, in Immelmann, 1965). In Western Australia Dell found it breeding from July to March.

VOICE The contact call is high-pitched and piercing, sometimes mono-syllabic but more often given as two or more syllables: 'tsee-tsee', 'seep seep' or similar. It is given both when moving about on the ground or in the branches and when in flight. When used as a distance contact call by birds that have lost sight of their companions a very loud version of up to five syllables and with a falling pitch is used (Immelmann *et al.*). The alarm call sounds like an abrupt intense variant of the contact call: 'tchip!' (Harrison). A cat-like hiss is uttered in aggressive threat (Hall, unpublished mss).

Song consists of a series of notes similar or identical to contact calls but given in a particular although individually varying sequence. Harrison describes that of one male as 'a low, almost inaudible note followed by three or four higher pitched notes . . .'. Morris transliterates the songs of two males as 'tee-te-tee teee-te-tee' and 'fee-te-teee teee-te-tee-teee-te-tee-teee' respectively. The song is given both when alone and in courtship display. The female has a shorter and lower pitched song phrase which she seldom utters except when alone. A sound spectogram of the male's song is in Hall (1962).

DISPLAY AND SOCIAL BEHAVIOUR What I take to be the greeting display has been described (Morris) as seen especially from captive males when another bird has just or recently been introduced to them. In an horizontal posture, the male, with raised tail, faces the female and performs hasty double bill-wipes. At first he is silent but then proceeds to a second stage of the display at which he sings as he rocks up and down, bill-wiping. At higher intensity the song becomes louder and clearer, the bird bows without or with only a suggestion of the bill-wiping movement and tends to align himself broadside on to instead of facing the female as at first. He also tends by degrees to lower his erect tail and angle it towards the female.

All descriptions of the courtship display show that it is very similar to that of such African genera as *Estrilda*, *Uraeginthus* and *Lagonosticta* (Immelmann, 1965, Morris, White). The male holds a long grass stem or other nesting material by one end and, with fluffed out belly and flank feathers, angled tail and upward pointing head and bill, bounces up and down, his feet letting go of the perch at each upward jump. The female responds by flying to and alighting near or beside him, throws up her head and, for a few moments, holds it pointing upwards like his. The male sings during his display. Copulation may follow. If it does the male may either drop the symbol or hold it throughout the copulation (Immelmann, Phillips). In one case the female took the grass stem from the male after copulation and flew to the nest with it (White). Immelmann (1962) states that a grass stem used to display with is held by a (partly detached) side fibre, so that it hangs

straight down. Other observers have not recorded this so it may not always be the case. A feather may be used (Phillips).

Members of a pair habitually clump and allo-preen. In captivity very ready to form allo-preening associations with other species. Highly social but the pair keep together within the flock and the pair bond is apparently strong throughout the year. When about to attack the tail is raised and fanned (Hall, unpublished mss).

OTHER NAMES Sydney Waxbill, Australian Waxbill.

REFERENCES

Dell, J. 1965. The Red-browed Finch, *Aegintha temporalis*, in Western Australia. *Western Australian Naturalist* 9: 160–169.
Hall, M. F. 1962. Evolutionary aspects of estrildid song. *Symposia Zool. Soc. London* 8: 37–55.
Harrison, C. J. O. 1962. An ethological comparison of some waxbills (Estrildini), and its relevance to their taxonomy. *Proc. zool. Soc. London* 139: 261–282.
Immelmann, K. 1962. Beiträge zu einer vergleichenden Biologie australischer Prachtfinken (Spermestidae). *Zool. Jb. Syst. Bd.* 90: 1–196.
Immelmann, K. 1965. Australian finches in bush and aviary. Angus & Robertson, Sydney and London.
Jasper 1962. Nesting notes on the Red-browed Finch. *Emu* 62: 177–180.
Jasper 1965. Further notes on the nesting of the Red-browed Finch. *Emu* 64: 145–146.
Morris, D. 1958. The comparative ethology of grassfinches (Erythrurae) and mannakins (Amadinae). *Proc. zool. Soc. London* 131: 389–439.
Phillips, R. 1902. The Australian Waxbill. *Avicult. Mag.* 8: 289–93.
Russ, K. 1879. *Die fremdlandischen Stubenvögel.* Vol. 1. Hanover, Germany.
White, S. R. 1946. Notes on the bird life of Australia's heaviest rainfall region. *Emu* 46: 81–122.

Crimson Finch   *Neochmia phaeton*

Fringilla phaeton Hombron and Jaquinot, 1841, *Ann. Sci. Nat. Paris*, ser. 2, 16, p. 314.

DESCRIPTION About size of Violet-eared Waxbill but with proportionately stouter bill and rather broader tail, which is wedge-shaped when spread and with the two long central feathers attenuated, to an individually varying degree, to blunt points. Forehead and forecrown greyish black, shading to dull brownish grey on hind crown, nape and hind neck. Mantle, back, rump, upper tail coverts and wing coverts dull blood red to crimson. Except on the rump and upper tail coverts, greyish bases and fringes to the feathers show to a varying degree. In somewhat worn plumage the red may be brighter and more shiny. The lower back is often mainly greyish. Tail carmine to crimson, the inner webs of all but the central feathers dull brownish grey. Much of outer webs of secondaries and primaries dull red but on the outer feathers (lower ones in folded wing) the red is partly or wholly replaced by olive-yellow. Rest of wings dull brownish grey. Under wing coverts mainly pale buff. Face, sides of head, breast and most of underparts crimson, dotted with small white spots on the sides of the breast and flanks. On some feathers there is a single spot on one side of the shaft, on others two 'paired' spots, one on each side. Centre of belly and ventral area dull black. Under tail coverts dull black, often or usually with dull red median areas. Irides yellowish brown, buffish or light brown; eye-rims yellowish. Bill red, whitish at base of lower or both mandibles. Legs and feet yellowish flesh to yellowish brown. In populations from north-eastern Queensland, the red parts tend to be duller, the forehead paler, often nearly concolorous with hind crown and nape, and the amount of red on the mantle and back reduced. These have sometimes been given racial status as *N. phaeton iredali* but the two forms probably intergrade (Immelmann *et al.*) and the colour of the forehead is said (*fide* Immelmann, 1965), to vary individually even within birds from a single locality.

The female has the forehead lighter than the male's, never contrasting strongly with the colour of the hind crown. Her grey areas are a little paler and more brownish and her mantle and back have less red. The red of her rump, tail and wings is lighter and duller; that of her cheeks a little and that of her throat appreciably lighter than the male's. Breast and flanks light brownish grey, sometimes suffused with light dull red, with white spots like the male's but, of course, less conspicuous. Centre of belly pale greyish cream or very pale fawn. Under tail coverts greyish fawn with some dull red suffusion.

The juvenile is a general light reddish fawn to dull drab above, paler and more buffish on belly and flanks. Some light dull red suffusion on wing coverts and secondaries. Rump dull orange-red; tail light carmine to dull orange-red. Bill black. I think that the more reddish individuals may be males but I have not seen many *sexed* specimens and other authors have not recorded a sexual difference. Mouth pattern of nestlings with five black marks on palate; gape tubercles at first bluish, later white (Immelmann *et al.*). Newly-hatched nestling very pale and almost down-less (Hall, unpublished mss).

The above description is of nominate *N.p. phaeton*, from most of the species Australian range, and of which *N.p. iredali* is, as explained above, treated as a synonym. *N.p. albiventer*, from northern Cape York Peninsula, is a little paler and has the belly and ventral area whitish. *N.p. evangelinae*, from New Guinea, is similar but has a yellowish buff or creamy belly. It is said to have a greenish yellow tinge on the head and neck but the only two specimens that I have been able to examine, a male and a female, did not. They might, however, have done so in life. Possibly some or all of the differences between *albiventer* and *evangelinae* will prove to be due to plumage state and individual differences.

See plate 2, facing p. 97.

FIELD CHARACTERS Small red and greyish bird with rather long red tail, frequently spread to a wedge (or diamond) shape.

DISTRIBUTION AND HABITAT Northern Australia from

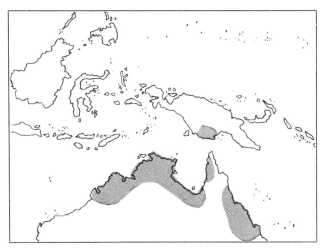

Derby and Fitzroy River in West Kimberley through northern third of Northern Territory (Storr, 1977) to north-eastern Queensland, formerly south to Rockhampton but no recent records south of Proserpine (Storr, 1973). Also in northern Cape York Peninsula. Southern New Guinea on the Fly River and the Oriomo River.

In Australia it inhabits areas near water with grass and pandanus palms, *Pandanus odoratissimus*. Now also around human habitations, in pineapple plantations and other cultivated areas so long as grass, cover and water is available (Immelmann, 1962 and 1965, Immelmann *et al.*). In New Guinea found in and especially at the edges of marshes and in savanna woodland with long grass (Rand). In parts of its former Queensland range it has, however, become extinct, probably because of destruction of waterside vegetation by cattle (Storr, 1973).

FEEDING AND GENERAL HABITS Feeds largely from growing grasses and other vegetation among which it clings and clambers adeptly. Less often feeds from the ground. Catches insects in flight. Can hold grass stems etc underfoot. Feeds largely on seeds of grasses and herbaceous plants, including those of *Echinachloa colonum*, *Iseilema* sp., *Chloris virgata*, *Cenchrus setigerus*, *Brachyachne convergens*, *Panicum zymbirformae*, *Chrysopogon latifolius*, *Sorghum plumosum* and *S. vulgare*. Also takes bits of pandanus leaf (probably also other greenstuff), winged termites and winged ants, small spiders and probably other small invertebrates (Immelmann, 1962 and 1965).

Usually in pairs but when not breeding often in small, loose flocks of up to about 20 individuals. Several pairs may breed quite close to each other and in dry periods large numbers may aggregate near the last remaining sources of water, but such groupings seem brought about as reactions to environment not through any positive sociality of the birds involved (Immelmann, 1965, Rand). Not shy of man and often very tame, or indifferent to his presence, but usually keeps among or near to cover of long grass, trees or shrubs. Does not fly over long distances and its flight appears rather weak. Tail and wing flicking locomotion movements are frequent and marked, when at all alarmed the wings are flicked up and down and the tail raised and then swung downwards and sideways (Hall, unpublished mss; Immelmann, 1962). When breeding the cock is very aggressive, not only towards conspecifics but also attacking and driving away quite unrelated and sometimes relatively large species such as, for example, the Crested Pigeon. When attacking other species the Crimson Finch often pecks at their feet but rarely does so in intraspecific hostilities (Immelmann *et al.*).

In captivity usually very sensitive to cold. Some of the earlier aviculturists (in Butler) *claim* to have kept it in good health without artificial heat throughout the English winter but I have no doubt that the advice of Immelmann *et al.* is wiser and more humane. They recommend a temperature of not less than 18 to 20°C and that, as well as the usual millets, a varied mixture of other seeds, soaked millet, greenfood, especially chickweed and half ripe seeding grasses, ant pupae and/or other small insects as available and egg food should be given. When in good health male birds are usually even more aggressive in captivity than they are when free and create havoc if kept with weaker or less aggressive species. So, as a general rule, each pair of Crimson Finches need an aviary to themselves, although some cocks, deprived of other outlets for their aggression, may then attack their mates or (and more often) prospective mates introduced to them.

NESTING Immelmann (1962 and 1965) made a detailed study of this species in Australia and the information here is derived mainly from him, with corroboration from Hall where indicated.

In the natural habitat the nest is most often placed on the bases of *Pandanus* leaves, from about 3 to 18 metres above ground; less often in a hollow stump, on projecting bark against a tree trunk, in a grass clump, bush or other site. In many settled areas the nest is usually placed in or on some nook, niche or ledge of a building. Nests readily inside occupied rooms, if permitted to do so. Immelmann observed a pair feeding their young in a nest in a forge, only a few feet above the men working there. In cultivated parts of northern Queensland nests are often sited in banana trees or pineapple plants.

The nest varies in shape according to its position but is commonly rather flattish, about 8 to 13 centimetres (3 to 5 inches) high and 10 to 18 centimetres (4 to 7 inches) long. There is no entrance tube but a mass of material often forms a rather large platform in front of the entrance. It is built of grass, strips of fibrous bark, leaves and sometimes other materials, many very long pieces of grass are often used. The nest is lined with feathers, white ones being preferred. Hall found that all the nests built by her captive birds were neatly finished with no long stalks protruding or straggling from the framework but photographs of wild nests (in Immelmann, 1962 and Immelmann *et al.*, 1965) show that this is not always the case. The male collects nesting material and does most, sometimes all of the building although sometimes the female, from inside the nest, will build with some of the material he brings. Rand (1942) watched a female (in New Guinea) collecting

nest material while her presumed mate sat nearby. This would appear, if the sexes were correctly identified, to be very unusual, perhaps due to a sudden illness and consequent inadequacy of the male.

Eggs 5 to 8. Incubation begins with the fourth or fifth egg, before then the female does not cover the eggs at night. Both sexes incubate in turn by day for periods of about 1·25 hours, the hen alone incubates at night. The cock roosts away from the nest, sometimes in long grass several hundreds of yards away. The eggs are not brooded by day when the temperature rises to about 38 to 40°C. The young are brooded by day until they are 5 to 7 days old and by night until the ninth day. They fledge at 21 days but may at times come out on to the platform in front of the nest entrance for short periods when only 17 or 18 days old. Longer fledging periods of up to 26 days have been recorded for captive young (Hall). Fledglings do not usually return to the nest after fledging but exceptionally may do so for one or two nights. They often or usually raise one or both wings when begging for food but keep the lifted wing folded when doing-so (Hall, Immelmann, 1962).

Hill found that eggs and nestlings are often destroyed by green tree ants, *Oecophylla smaragdina*.

VOICE The contact call has been transliterated 'tsee-tsee-tsee-tsee-tsee', 'tchit tchit' and similarly. When uttered as a distance contact call it is loud and polysyllabic but softer, one- or two-syllabled variants are used as close contact calls. The loud, many-syllabled form is used also as an alarm call (possibly with subtle differences not appreciable to human ears) and is very similar in sound to the alarm chatter of the Red-cheeked Cordon-bleu (Immelmann, 1962 and implicit in Hall's description of it as the 'machine gun call'). The song is a mannikin-like series of low squeezing and rasping notes, followed by three fairly loud and melodious notes (Immelmann, 1962 and 1965). Morris transliterated it as 'chu chu chu che-chee choo'. It is given as solitary song and then accompanied by tail flicking, side-to-side movements of the head and sometimes also body and wing movements and also during courtship display (Hall, unpublished mss; Immelmann, 1965). A sound spectogram of the song is given in Hall (1962). Near a prospective nest site unpaired males sometimes utter a loud, two-syllabled 'hee-heet' (my anglicisation) followed by a series of soft hissing notes (Immelmann, 1962). The usual nest call has been described as 'bubbling' (Hall, unpublished mss) and as a soft, high-pitched whimpering sound (Immelmann *et al.*, 1965); probably there are individual and/or intensity variations in this call. The begging calls of the young are at first naturally very faint but become very loud and similar to the alarmed version of the contact call (Hall, unpublished mss) when they are near fledging. Hall also mentions a 'cat-like hiss' used when attacking and similar to the corresponding note of the Red-browed Finch.

DISPLAY AND SOCIAL BEHAVIOUR In the greeting display the female (possibly sometimes the male?) flies to the mate or prospective mate, alights close to him and, with angled tail and head turned towards him, makes a deep bow. The male may respond similarly or he may respond only by turning slightly towards the female. Formalised bill wiping and mandibulation may intersperse the bows. The nest ceremony (Immelmann, 1962) is essentially a more intense, and spatially localised, variant of the greeting display. At a potential nest site, to which the male has usually attracted the female by nest calling, the pair sit side by side with angled tails, which thus cross and are usually in contact, and perform deep bows accompanied or interspersed with nest calling and mandibulation. The male (always?) bows more deeply than his mate so that his head is below hers at the lowest point of his bow. This display may be repeated at short intervals at several different potential nest sites, it is not, as in some other species, restricted to a site already chosen. Apart from copulation, this is the only time that members of a pair of Crimson Finches are normally in physical contact with each other. The nest ceremony may be performed by juveniles as well as by breeding adults (Hall, unpublished mss). The female, in butterfly-like display flight, sometimes with nesting material in her bill, will fly around a (perched) male (Immelmann, 1965).

In the courtship display the male, with a green grass stem or other nesting material in his bill, flies to and lands a short distance from the female. He then hops towards her and, when within a few centimetres, with feathers of face, back and underparts fluffed out so as to show the maximum (smooth-surfaced) areas of red and black, in a near horizontal posture with angled tail and head turned towards the female, he bobs up and down, bowing low as he does so. Shortly before copulation he assumes an erect posture, in which he continues to dance, before dropping his symbol and copulating if the hen solicits with quivering tail. In captivity at least, the courtship behaviour may start by the male bobbing up and down in an erect posture, throwing back his head at each upward movement, from which he changes to the horizontal posture when the female flies to and alights beside him (Hall, unpublished mss).

Allo-preening and clumping do not occur between adults, not even members of a pair. The (frequent) spreading of the tail is usually a sign of aggressiveness. Probably because of a tendency to increased aggression in captivity, captive birds sometimes spread their tails in courtship display.

OTHER NAMES Blood Finch, Australian Firefinch.

REFERENCES

Butler, A. G. 1899. Foreign finches in captivity. London.

Hall, M. F. 1962. Evolutionary aspects of estrildid song. *Symposia Zool. Soc. London* 8: 37–55.

Immelmann, K. 1962. Beitrage zu einer vergleichenden Biologie australischer Prachtfinken (Spermestidae). *Zool. Jb. Syst. Bd.* 90: 1–196.

Immelmann, K. 1965. Australian finches in bush and aviary. Sydney and London.

Immelmann, K., Steinbacher, J. & Wolters, H. E. 1965. *Vögel in Käfig und Voliere: Prachtfinken*: 52–66.

Rand, A. L. 1942. Results of the Archbold Expeditions. *Bull. Amer. Mus. Nat. Hist.* 79, 289–366.

Storr, G. M. 1973. *List of Queensland birds*. Western Australian Museum special publication no. 5.

Storr, G. M. 1977. *Birds of the Northern Territory*. Western Australian Museum special publication no. 7.

Star Finch   *Neochmia ruficauda*

Amadina ruficauda Gould, 1837, *Synopsis Birds Australia*, pt. 1, pl. 10, fig. 2.

DESCRIPTION About size of previous species, N. *phaeton*, but with rather smaller and less thick bill and much shorter (short-medium) and less strongly attenuated tail. Forehead, forecrown, face and upper part of throat bright red, spotted, except on lores, forehead and forecrown, with small white or pale pinkish dots, a terminal spot on each feather. Hind crown, nape and upper parts dull brownish olive. Basal half (about) of outer webs of primaries with lighter fringes; concealed parts of wing quills dull drab. Upper tail coverts pinkish carmine with large pink to pinkish white sub-terminal spots. Central tail feathers dull carmine with blackish shafts; outer tail feathers dull drab, more or less washed with carmine on the outer webs. Sides of neck, peripheral parts of cheeks, lower throat, breast and flanks dull olive brown to dull greenish, spotted with white. The white spots are small (and mostly terminal) on the outer parts of the face, elsewhere larger and subterminal, forming an oval or 'blunted triangle' mark across the feather. The white spots are edged with a darker shade of olive, which heightens their contrast. Median part of lower breast, belly and ventral area dull pale yellowish to greenish white. Under tail coverts pale dull olive with whitish cross bars. Irides orange to light red. Bill scarlet red. Legs and feet buffish yellow to pale yellowish brown.

The female has the red on the head lighter and usually confined to the lores, front of the forehead and immediately around the eyes. She is also somewhat duller, especially on the rump. The juvenile is a general yellowish olive-brown, buffish on the fringes of the wing feathers and with the rump and tail warm brownish buff, as are the under parts except for the belly and ventral area, which are paler. Tail and rump as adult but paler and with the pale rump spots buffish and inconspicuous. Bill at first blackish. The nestling has the three upper spots of the common 'domino' palate pattern, fused to form a flattish arch-shaped mark above the two lower spots, a black mark at the base of each mandible, in the gape, a nearly divided black mark on the tongue and a black crescent inside the lower mandible.

The above description is of nominate *N.r. ruficauda*, from central Queensland south to New South Wales. *N. ruficauda clarescens*, from further north and west in the species' range, is paler and brighter. Its upperparts, breast and flanks are yellowish olive-green rather than brownish olive. It often has small white apical spots on the wing coverts and its lower breast, belly and ventral area are usually clear golden yellow to pale yellow. Sexual and age differences are comparable to those of the nominate form.

There is considerable minor individual variation, especially in the amount and brightness of the red on the head (Immelmann, 1965). This is said (Caley, in Immelmann, 1965) to be due to age differences and that the individual bird becomes brighter as it gets older. Gravem found that captive-bred birds (in California) often had the red of the head replaced by yellow.

FIELD IDENTIFICATION Small finch with greenish to olive brown, white-spotted plumage and red face. Dull reddish rump and tail. Spotted breast and face at once distinguish it from Red-browed Finch and Crimson Finch female. Juvenile easily confused with the very similar juvenile Crimson Finch if no adults at hand, which there usually are.

DISTRIBUTION AND HABITAT Central and northern Queensland, along the Gulf of Carpentaria to Northern Territory,

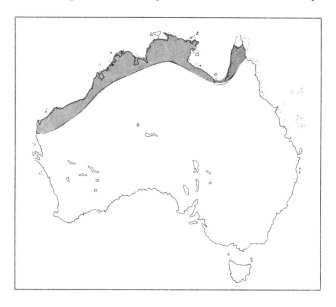

the Kimberleyes and south to the Ashburton district of West Australia. Storr (1973 and 1977) gives detailed localities for (then) recent records of distribution in Queensland and Northern Territory respectively. The type of the nominate form was taken on the Namoi River, New South Wales, but the species does not appear to have been subsequently seen in New South Wales until, in 1964, some were seen at Inverell (Baldwin). It appears to have decreased in many areas over the past century (Immelmann, 1965).

Inhabits the vicinity of swamps, creeks and rivers where there are tall grasses and rushes and damp grassland with some trees and bushes. Locally in cultivated areas, especially irrigated rice fields in northern and north-western Australia but, unlike the Crimson Finch, it does not come around human habitations (Immelmann, 1962 and 1965).

FEEDING AND GENERAL HABITS Known foods are the seeds of the grasses *Echinachloa colonum*, *Iseilema* sp., *Chloris virgata* and *Brachyachne convergens*, flying ants, *Iridomyrmex detectus*, termites, *Masotermes darwiniensis*, other small insects and small spiders (Immelmann, 1962). Like the Crimson Finch, this species prefers to feed among growing vegetation, pulling the grass panicles towards itself and holding them under foot to pick out the seeds. Only in the dry season, when it is forced to do so, does it feed largely on the ground. It drinks in a pigeon-like manner.

When not breeding usually in flocks of up to 20 individuals but sometimes, especially in periods of drought, in very much larger flocks. Several pairs often breed near to each other. Flight fast and strong, often with definite undulations but at other times, especially when in large flocks, no trace of undulations. Such large flocks often swerve, turn and alter formation in a manner suggesting flocks of Starlings, *Sturnus vulgaris* (Immelmann *et al.*, 1965–66).

In captivity sometimes hard to acclimitise but in general relatively hardy. Immelmann *et al.* recommend, however, that it should never be kept at a temperature of below 12 to 15°C. It should be given ample supplies of millet and more especially of (preferably small) canary seed, both dry and soaked, greenfood, especially unripe seeding grasses and chickweed and any small insects or spiders available. Some authorities (e.g. Immelmann) state that insects are absolutely necessary if young are to be successfully reared, that even fresh ant pupae (as the sole insect food) and eggfood will not suffice and that mealworms must not be given in quantity. Gravem, however, bred Star Finches very successfully, gave limited numbers of cut-up mealworms as the only insect food and Nicholson and Restall bred it without giving their birds any insects. In captivity, apart from defending the immediate vicinity of its nest, the Star Finch is usually very peaceable.

NESTING The nest may be in a tree or bush up to 7 metres above ground or in a grass clump, usually less than one metre above ground. Immelmann found mostly bush and tree nests in the Kimberley area and grass tussock nests in the Northern Territory. He found that they differed consistently in materials and construction. The tree and bush nests were similar to those of the Crimson Finch, made largely of grass blades already dry and partly rotten but with some green grass blades intermixed. The grass clump nests were built largely of long grass stems, mostly dry but still green, many of the ends of which stuck out untidily from the nest and especially from its apparently rather loosely put together roof (photo in Immelmann *et al.*, 1966). Both types of nest have a small side entrance with either no entrance tube or only a suggestion of one, and are thickly lined with feathers. Immelmann implies that the cock brings material and does much or all of the building and Gravem found this so in his captive birds.

Eggs 3 to 7, usually 4 to 6. Parental behaviour as in previous species (q.v.). Incubation period 12 to 13 days (Gravem, Immelmann *et al.*). Young fledge at 21 days and do not return to the nest to roost (Immelmann *et al.*). The breeding season is probably prolonged. Immelmann found that, in the Kimberleys, the Star Finch was, with the Zebra Finch, the first estrildid to begin breeding, in December, in the second half of the rainy season. In West Australia nests with eggs or young have been found in March, May and August (Serventy and Whittell).

VOICE The close contact call is a quiet 'tlit', 'tsit' or similar. It is uttered constantly by birds moving about in vegetation. The distance contact call is quite distinct, a thin, high-pitched and far-carrying 'sseet' or 'sseep'. It is given in flight and by members of large flocks as well as by any individuals that have lost contact with their mate or companions. Immelmann states that it is also used as an alarm call but Hall (unpublished mss) describes the alarm call used by her captive birds as 'a rapid, high-pitched rattle'. Possibly the 'warning' version of the contact call indicates an apparently milder or different degree of anxiety or fear as seems to be the case in the cordon-bleus, *Uraeginthus* (q.v.). The nest call is a high-pitched whispering sound, uttered by both sexes. A high 'see-see' is uttered at nest relief (Immelmann *et al.*).

The song phrase is high-pitched and only audible (to human ears) at a short distance. It is very short but the basic phrase is usually repeated many times without a break (Hall, unpublished mss). It is given both in courtship and as solitary song. In the latter context it is very freely used and Hall found that captive males sung whenever they had moved about 15 centimetres (6 inches) or more from the mate. It is given, in this context, with little feather erection except for the red face mask. Morris (1958) gives photos of both singing and normally perching males. Hall (1962) gives a sound spectrogram of the song. So far as is known only the male sings. Side to side head movements, and sometimes low intensity tail flicking, may accompany song (Hall, unpublished mss). Other individuals often 'peer' at a singing bird in a munia-like manner.

DISPLAY AND SOCIAL BEHAVIOUR Greeting display as that of previous species, the Crimson Finch (q.v.). The female has a display flight in which she flies around a (perched) male in a fluttering, butterfly-like flight while holding a long piece of grass in her bill. It is performed especially by unpaired females and may perhaps stimulate the male to courtship and pair-formation (Immelmann, 1962 and 1965).

The courtship display is very like that of the Crimson Finch. The male holds a long piece of grass, by a side fibre if it is green, in his bill and approaches the female with angled tail and the spotted feathers of his face, breast and flanks erected. He bobs up and down, turning his body from one side to another as he does so, his feet usually but not always momentarily leaving the perch with each upward movement and after it makes a deep bow. If he actually jumps he lands a little nearer the female each time, if not he sidles towards her between the upward bobs. His bill is at first held horizontally but at a later stage, just prior to copulation or attempts thereat, it is jerked to an angle of about 45 degrees with each upward movement. He usually sings frequently during this display. If the female solicits with quivering tail, the male mounts and copulates, sometimes keeping hold of his nest symbol but more often dropping it before mounting (Immelmann, 1962 and 1965). At least in captivity, minor variations of this display may occur. The upward position of the bill may accompany upward jumps from the start, the male may cease the jumps or bobs and, as a final pre-copulatory phase, sing at the female, leaning towards her in an erect posture (Hall, unpublished mss, Morris, 1958). Females and immature birds of both sexes may perform courtship display and males sometimes do so when alone. Surprisingly, and contrary to what occurs in some other species, males performing the display alone angle their tails (always?) as if there was a female on one side of them (Immelmann, 1962).

Mandibulation and bill-fencing occur in typical contexts. Allo-preening occurs between members of a pair but they do not usually clump when so-doing (Immelmann, 1962).

The pair bond appears stronger than in the related Crimson Finch and pairs keep together within the flock (Immelmann, 1962).

OTHER NAMES Ruficauda, Rufous-tailed Grassfinch, Red-faced Grassfinch.

REFERENCES
Baldwin, M. 1975. Birds of Inverell District, NSW. *Emu* 75: 113–120.
Gravem, N. 1957. Breeding the Star Finch or Rudicauda (*Bathilda ruficauda*). *Avicult. Mag.* 63: 134–136.
Hall, M. F. 1962. Evolutionary aspects of estrildid song. *Zool. Soc. London Symposia* 8: 37–70.
Immelmann, K. 1962. Beiträge zu einer vergleichenden Biologie australischer Prachtfinken (Spermestidae). *Zool. Jb. Syst. Bd.* 90: 1–96.
Immelmann, K. 1965. Australian finches in bush and aviary. Angus & Robertson, Sydney and London.
Immelmann, K., Steinbacher, J. & Wolters, H. E. 1965 and 1966. *Vögel in Käfig und Voliere: Prachtfinken*: 66–77.

Morris, D. 1958. The comparative ethology of grassfinches (Erythrurae) and manakins (Amadinae). *Proc. zool. Soc. London* **131**: 389–439.

Nicholson, A. E. 1901. Breeding of the Rufous-tailed Grassfinch. *Avicult. Mag.* **7**: 219–223.

Restall, R. 1975. *Finches and other seed-eating birds.* Faber & Faber, London.

Serventy, D. L. & Whittell, H. M. 1967. *Birds of Western Australia.* Lamb Publications Pty Ltd, Perth.

Cherry Finch   *Aidemosyne modesta*

Amadina modesta Gould, 1837, *Synopsis Birds Australia,* pt. 1, pl. 10, fig. 3.

DESCRIPTION About size of Spice Finch but with rather longer and broader (although similarly wedge-shaped) tail, smaller bill, rather longer wing (averaging about 58 to 64 mm), and softer plumage. Lores and bib dark blackish purple. Forehead and forecrown dark purplish red; in worn plumage the black feather bases show and red on the feather tips becomes a less dark shade, claret red with a hint of bronziness in it. Hind crown, nape and upperparts a rather dull coffee brown, slightly darker on the wings. White apical spots on the wing coverts and inner secondaries form an attractive barred and spotted pattern on the folded wing. Rump reddish brown, each feather broadly tipped with white. The rather long upper tail coverts are banded brown and white, the end of each feather being white. Under wing coverts barred light brown and white. Tail greyish black, the outermost pair of tail feathers are extensively white at their ends, the next three pairs have successively less white at the tip and the two central pairs usually none. Face below and behind eye silvery white lightly barred with brownish on the peripheral areas. Underparts white, conspicuously barred with coffee brown except on the belly, ventral area and under tail coverts. Irides very dark brown to nearly black; eye rims blackish. Bill blackish, usually with some bluish grey at the base of the lower mandible. Legs and feet brownish flesh to pinkish grey.

The female lacks the dark bib or has only a trace of it, her throat being whitish. She has a pale stripe extending from her bill, immediately below the nostrils, which divides the blackish triangular mark connecting her eye and gape from her purplish red forehead and extends over and behind her eye. This stripe is usually pink between bill and eye and white above and behind the eye. The red on her forehead does not extend so far on to her (mainly coffee brown) crown as does the male's. The juvenile is lighter brown above without white markings except for dull buffish white spots on the wings. Underparts pale buffish brown with only an obscure pattern, which is more spotted than barred. No red on the head. The mouth pattern of the nestling is almost identical to that of the Star Finch (q.v.) but the actual dark spots are a little larger (Immelmann, 1965, Immelmann *et al.*, 1966).

FIELD CHARACTERS Small brown finch with white-spotted wings and white and brown barred underparts. Dark forehead and (male only) bib both look blackish in most lights at a little distance.

DISTRIBUTION AND HABITAT Eastern Australia; in savanna country from south and central-western New South Wales to Nogou River and Port Denison, Queensland. Mostly a bird of the interior but in the fairly recent past has occurred near Sydney and near Richmond, New South Wales (Lane). Storr (1973) gives very full details of recorded localities in Queensland.

Inhabits riparian areas with rank grass and reeds; also open flats with bushes and trees. Locally in cultivated grain fields and gardens. The vicinity of surface water is an essential feature of the habitat for it. Has a patchy distribution within its general range. Is often nomadic and possibly only a summer visitor to the more southern parts of its range. May wander far from its usual haunts in very dry years (Immelmann, 1962 and 1965, Storr).

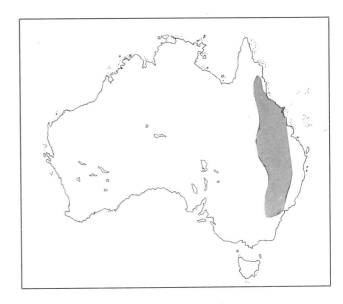

FEEDING AND GENERAL HABITS Feeds both on the ground and among growing vegetation. Often holds grass panicles under foot. Takes seeds of grasses and probably of some other plants and small insects also. In inhabited areas learns to take breadcrumbs and other human foods (Caley, in Immelmann, 1965, Immelmann *et al.*). Drinks very frequently, at least every hour, *fide* Immelmann. Usually in pairs or small flocks, at times in large flocks. Sometimes associates with flocks of other estrildids, especially Bicheno Finches. Members of a pair maintain contact within the flock. Flight strong, with slight undulations. Usually shows little fear of man. Does not roost in nests.

In captivity needs the usual seeds, both dry and soaked, and greenfood. Reicherdt found it especially fond of seeding chickweed *Stellaria media* and knotgrass, *Polygonum aviculare*. Best offered eggfood and ant pupae and other insect food when breeding (Immelmann *et al.*, Reicherdt) although some pairs refuse such things and rear their young satisfactorily without. In captivity some (but not all) pairs are sensitive to interference and may desert their nests if disturbed when at or in them. Personal incompatibility often prevents pair formation between captive individuals (Immelmann *et al.*, Restall). Some aviculturists have found this species quite hardy but they may have had exceptionally resistant individuals. Immelmann *et al.* state that the Cherry Finch is sensitive to cold and should never be kept at a temperature below 18°C.

NESTING The nest is sited in a bush, shrub, grass clump or other vegetation, usually less than a metre above ground. In northern New South Wales, Immelmann found that introduced brambles and raspberries were favoured for nesting. The nest is laterally compressed, usually 10 to 15 centimetres (4 to 6 inches) in length and height but only about 7 centimetres (3 inches) in width. It is built of green grass and growing grass in its immediate vicinity is bent over and incorporated into the walls of the nest, anchoring it more securely. Some nests are lined with feathers, others not (Immelmann). There is a side entrance and no entrance tube.

Eggs 3 to 7. Both sexes incubate in turn by day, for periods of about 45 minutes (Immelmann *et al.*). Incubation period 12 days (Russ): young fledge at 22 days (Reicherdt), both these records are of captives in Europe. Fledged young sometimes or usually return to the nest to roost for the first few nights after leaving it (Immelmann *et al.*). They are independent within 2 weeks of fledging.

Butler observed a captive female which, when flushed from her nest, performed an apparent distraction display: 'the hen was very nervous and left the nest at the least alarm, tumbling about on the earth as if wounded and gradually retreating ... until about two yards away, when she hopped up into a bush and sat quite still'.

Breeding season prolonged – commonly September to January but also at other times if conditions suitable.

VOICE Although some ornithologists have described this species as rather silent, Immelmann (1962, 1965) found it among the noisiest of Australian finches, with a great variety of calls and much variation even of the calls that can be clearly separated.

The close contact call might be written 'tlip', 'tleep', 'tlip-tlip' or similar. It is given with closed bill but noticeable throat movements. The distance contact call, used particularly by birds that have lost contact but also in flight, is quite different: 'tyeet', 'tueet' or similar. The alarm call is very variable and may be one- or multi-syllabled: 'tyait' (Immelmann *et al.*, my anglicisations). Reicherdt heard a very soft nest call from a male trying to entice his mate to the nest site.

The song is low and rather like that of the typical munias. It begins with a series of high-pitched, hardly audible sounds, then follows chirping and gargling trills and finally more flute-like notes at the end (Immelmann, 1965). It is uttered not only in courtship and when perched (more or less) alone but also in many other situations, such as when seeking food or nest building. A sound spectrogram of the song is given by Hall (1962). Captive-bred specimens may produce atypical songs (Harrison, Mitchell *in litt*). Possibly there is some variation in the wild also.

DISPLAY AND SOCIAL BEHAVIOUR The courtship display, in its complete form, is in part like that of the silverbills and in part like that of the typical munias. The male, holding a piece of grass by one end in his bill, usually in such a way that it hangs down, alights near and hops or sidles towards the female. The feathers of his bib, cheeks and belly are partly erected, his tail only slightly angled toward the hen and his bill held at or a little below the horizontal. He bobs rather slowly up and down, without his feet leaving the perch. Song is uttered without the bill being opened. After several such upward bobs, he drops his nesting symbol, ceases to bob up and down, erects his belly feathers fully so that they are separated from each other, and sings with widely-opened and downward directed bill, interspersing this with symbolic bill-wiping movements. If the female solicits, copulation follows. There is much individual variation, the same male may use different forms of courtship display at different times, some males apparently never hold nesting material and others never sing with widely-opened bill (Immelmann, 1965). Harrison had a captive male that always began to display with its bill pointing steeply upwards, at a little distance from the female. If she then came near, the male turned towards her, lowered his bill until it was level with hers and continued to display in this position. Mr Ian Mitchell (*in litt*) has also often seen this type of display but has never seen it followed by singing with *downward*-directed bill.

Peering at singing individuals is frequent. Clumping and allo-preening habitual but, at least in the wild, confined to the mate, dependent young or, in the case of young birds, siblings. Mandibulation occurs.

OTHER NAMES Plum-capped Finch, Plum-headed Finch, Modest Grassfinch.

REFERENCES

Butler, A. G. 1899. *Foreign finches in captivity*. London.

Hall, F. M. 1962. Evolutionary aspects of estrildid song. *Symposia Zool. Soc. London* **8**: 37–70.

Harrison, C. J. O. 1974. Song and display of the Plum-headed Finch. *Emu* **74**: 254–255.

Immelmann, K. 1962. Beiträge zu einer vergleichendene Biologie australischer Prachtfinken (Spermestidae). *Zool. Jb. Syst. Bd.* **90**: 1–96.

Immelmann, K. 1965. *Australian finches in bush and aviary*. Sydney and London.

Immelmann, K., Steinbacher, J. & Wolters, H. E. 1966. *Vögel in Käfig und Voliere: Prachtfinken*: 78–86.

Lane, S. G. 1966. Plum-headed Finches near Richmond, New South Wales. *Emu* **66**: 111–112.

Reicherdt, C. 1976. Zur Pflege und Zucht des Zeresastrilds. *Gefiederte Welt* **1976**: 45–47.

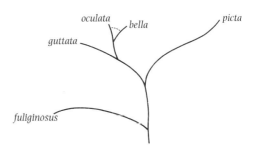

Presumed affinities of the firetails, *Emblema*, and the Red-sided Mountain Finch, *Oreostruthus*. See text for details. Dotted lines connect member of a superspecies.

The Firetails, Painted Finch and Red-sided Mountain Finch

The firetails or fire-tailed finches and the Painted Finch are fairly close to each other in size, all have boldly-spotted flanks and/or a considerable amount of finely cross-barred plumage, considerable similarities of behaviour and nestling mouth patterns and shining red rump and upper tail coverts.

The Diamond Firetail or Diamond Sparrow, *Emblema guttata* (formerly *Zonaegintus guttatus*), and the Beautiful Firetail, *E. bella*, both occur in south-eastern Australia but in different habitats. The latter is the only estrildid that occurs naturally in Tasmania. The two show differences in bill shape and wing/tail proportions as well as in coloration. Although they do not now normally occur in the same areas it is possible that some of their differences in colour pattern may have originally evolved as isolating mechanisms in reference to each other. The Red-eared Firetail *E. ocularis*, of extreme south-western Australia, shows a colour pattern which, although rather more complex than either, combines some features of both *E. guttata* and *E. bella*. It is, however, closest to *E. bella*, in behaviour and habitat as well as in coloration and seems best treated as forming a superspecies with it. All three firetails build bulky nests with an entrance tube.

The Painted Finch, *Emblema picta*, is a very distinct species and there is disagreement among authorities as to whether it is best 'lumped' with the firetails, as it was by Delacour, Hall and more recently Mayr, or whether it should be retained in a different genus from the firetails, whose generic name would then be *Zonaeginthus*, as by Immelmann. The Painted Finch is a very distinct species that has adapted to life in the arid, stony spinifex country of interior and north-western Australia. Its long, pointed bill is clearly an adaptation for efficient picking of small seeds from sand and among stones. Its usual courtship display differs from those of the firetails and its nest is smaller and without an entrance tube. These differences are also probably adaptations to, or result from adaptations to its habitat as Immelmann has pointed out. That they may, in an evolutionary sense, be rather recent is suggested by the fact that although the usual courtship is different, a male has been seen giving a courtship display similar to that of the Diamond Firetail (Webber) and that when a captive pair were given unlimited supplies of nesting material, they built a more than usually substantial nest *and attempted to build an entrance tube* (Ziegler). I therefore deem it best to follow those who give *Emblema* and *Zonaeginthus* only sub-generic rank within the genus *Emblema*.

The Red-sided Mountain Finch is found only in the mountains of New Guinea. It resembles the firetails in the brilliant shining red of its rump and upper tail coverts but its unbarred olive-brown and red plumage presents a more simplified colour pattern. Its bill is a little blunter, with a more curved culmen, and its legs and feet longer and larger. In spite of these differences, comparison of skins (I have not seen a living bird of this species) strongly suggest that it is a geographical representative of the firetails and fairly closely related. It is of course possible that this impression might be misleading. Nothing appears to be known of its nesting habits, displays or the mouth markings of its young. For these reasons, and also because it is in use in current faunal works and in *Peters' check-list*, I retain the monotypic genus *Oreostruthus* for this species. I suspect, however, that when further information on the species comes to hand, it will most likely justify reducing *Oreostruthus* to subgeneric rank within *Emblema*.

REFERENCES

Delacour, J. 1943. A revision of the subfamily Estrildinae of the family Ploceidae. *Zoologica, New York Zool. Soc.*, **28**: 69–86.

Hall, M. F. 1962. Evolutionary aspects of estrildid song. *Zool. Soc. London. Symposia* **8**: 37–55.

Immelmann, K. 1965. Australian finches in bush and aviary. Angus & Robertson, Sydney and London.

Mayr, E. 1968. The sequence of genera in the Estrildidae (Aves). *Breviora* **287**: 1–14.

Webber, L. C. 1964. Ten years with the Painted Finch and some historical notes. *Avicult. Mag.* **52**: 149–158.

Ziegler, G. 1964. Nestbau und Nest des Gemalten Astrild (*Emblema picta*). *Gefiederte Welt* **1964**: 188–190.

Diamond Firetail   *Emblema guttata*

Loxia guttata Shaw, 1796, *Mus. Lever.*, **6**, p. 47.

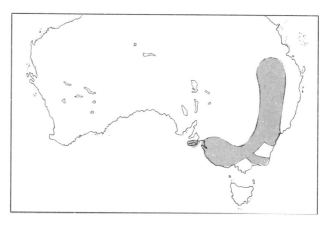

DESCRIPTION About size of Peters' Twinspot but with much longer, more pointed wing (about 65 to 70 mm), short nearly square-ended tail, and short conical bill. Crown, nape and hind neck medium grey, shading to a paler grey on the ear coverts. Broad loral stripe from mouth to eye black, narrowly edged whitish above (this not often visible in a skin but usually so in life). Back and wing coverts dull greyish brown; primaries and secondaries darker greyish brown with narrow pale brownish fringes to their outer webs. All the brown parts of the plumage may bleach to a very pale hue with wear. Under wing coverts mainly whitish. Rump and upper tail coverts shining scarlet red. Tail black. Throat and underparts silky white except for a broad black band across the breast and the sides of the breast and flanks, which are black boldly spotted with white. These white spots are single near oval or near rectangular white spots near the tip of each feather. Irides red, sometimes (*fide* Immelmann *et al.*) brown. Orbital skin pink to pinkish red. Bill deep red to reddish pink, pinkish at the base. Legs and feet dark grey to dark bluish grey.

Sexes alike except that the female tends to have a narrower (but still broad) black breast band and narrower and paler orbital skin. Loral stripe of female said to be sometimes brownish black or brown (Immelmann, Immelmann *et al.*) but this is certainly not always the case. The juvenile is paler brown above. Its head is brownish grey, its breast band dusky brown, sometimes with blackish bases and central marks on the feathers, and sometimes also concealed tiny white subterminal spots. The sides of its breast and flanks have a barred rather than spotted pattern (more pronounced on the flanks as a rule) in dull white and blackish brown. The white on its throat and underparts is duller and less silky than the adult's. The nestling has two more or less right-angled dark lines on either side of the central dark spot on the palate; the former are thought to represent a fusion of (on either side) the two spots present in many species (Immelmann *et al.*). There are two opposed dark marks on the tongue and a bluish white tubercle in the gape, at the base of each mandible.

There is an excellent coloured photograph of the adult in Hindwood and a fine colour plate, showing courtship display, in Butler.

FIELD CHARACTERS Smallish, thickset 'finch' with vivid red rump, brown back and black tail, red bill, broad black breast band across its white underparts and black, white-spotted, sides. Lack of any red plumage on head, white throat and black breastband all (together or singly) distinguish it from the Beautiful Firetail, Painted Finch, Star Finch and Red-browed Finch; the red rump from all other species.

DISTRIBUTION AND HABITAT Eastern and south-eastern Australia, from about Dawson River, Queenland, through New South Wales and Victoria to the Eyre Peninsula and Kangaroo Island, South Australia. Inhabits savanna woodland and mallee, also in pastoral country, orchards and cultivated areas provided trees and seeding grasses are at hand.

FEEDING AND GENERAL HABITS Seeks food on the ground. Feeds largely on grass seeds but also takes small insects and probably seeds of some other plants as well. Most authorities (e.g. Immelmann *et al.*, Butler) stress that besides dry and soaked millets and canary seed, greenfood and, when available, seeding grasses, chickweed, sow thistle and dandelion, animal food such as ant pupae, greenfly, cut-up mealworms and any available suitable small insects and spiders must be given to captives if young are to be successfully reared. Some, however (e.g. Massey), claim to have successfully bred the species without giving any animal food. Drinks in a pigeon-like manner, unlike its congeners.

Usually in parties of up to about 20 to 30 individuals. Even during the breeding season several birds often feed together. Very agile on the ground, often travelling surprisingly quickly in series of long hops (Immelmann, Nicolai). Does not, and apparently cannot, cling or clamber adroitly among growing vegetation (Nicolai). Flight strong and often somewhat undulating (Immelmann).

Roosts in nests built for the purpose. These are similar to breeding nests but usually lack both lining and entrance tube (Immelmann).

NESTING Builds in a tree, shrub or bush, sometimes in creepers on house walls, often in a large clump of mistletoe in a tree. The nest may vary in height from about 1·5 metres to about 30 metres. Sometimes sited among or adjacent to the sticks forming the base of some large raptor's nest. Orchard trees are often used. Several pairs commonly nest close together, sometimes in the same tree. The nest is a large, globular or retort-shaped structure, usually with a longish entrance tube. It is about 22 to 32 cm in length, of which the entrance tube is about 5 to 16 cm, and the diameter about 12 to 18 cm. There is often a second, tube-less, entrance opposite the main one. This is not usually made until after the young have hatched. It may function as an escape route should a predator enter the main entrance. The nest is usually made mostly of green grass stems but dry grass, grass blades, wiry stems of other plants and fibres are also used. It is lined with feathers and vegetable down. Charcoal does not appear to be normally placed in the nest but there is an odd, apparently authentic, record of a bird carrying a lighted cigarette end to its nest and thus starting a fire (Hindwood).

Eggs 4 to 9, usually 5 or 6. Male and female incubate and brood in turn by day. When about to relieve its mate, the bird outside calls and waits for an answer from within before entering. Both roost in the nest at night. The young are usually brooded until about 10 days old. They fledge at 24 to 25 days, at least in captivity (Nicolai). Two or more broods are usually reared in succession. The main breeding period is from August to April (Hindwood) but there are breeding records for all months except June and July (Immelmann).

In captivity breeding pairs fiercely defend the immediate vicinity of their nests and may be extremely aggressive both to their own and other species even away from the nest.

VOICE The contact call is a long-drawn mournful two-syllabled whistling sound. It is probably subject to some variation as it has been variously described as having the first syllable rising and the second descending in scale (Immelmann), a rising inflection throughout (Hindwood) or with a falling inflection in the middle only (Immelmann *et al.*, 1965). The contact calls of males are higher-pitched and longer than those of females (Immelmann). A loud buzzing 'zeep' is used in threat, by the female as a nest call, and sometimes by the male when giving the courtship display (Mitchell). Immelmann says that the call used at nest relief is similar to that of the Red-eared Firetail, which he describes as a two-syllabled 'twit-twit' which the bird inside answers with a long note followed by three short ones: 'tweet-tititit'. The alarm call is a loud 'tay tay tay' (Immelmann *et al.*, 1965, my anglicisation). The young have a loud begging call which, *fide* Mitchell, is very like the buzzing threat call. The song, which is given both in courtship display and alone, but always in the courtship display posture (Nicolai), is a series of low-pitched buzzing or rasping sounds.

DISPLAY AND SOCIAL BEHAVIOUR The spectacular courtship display was described by Butler and illustrated in colour in his book; subsequently it was described in detail by other observers, notably Immelmann & Nicolai. Before beginning to display the male, with shaking movements, arranges his plumage so that the spotted flank feathers are outside the folded wings and fully displayed. A long piece of green grass or other nesting material, sometimes held looped and often up to about a metre or more in length is carried in the bill. In the wild courtship display usually takes place on a high, dead branch (Immelmann). The male alights near the female (though at least in captivity he may fly to his favourite display perch and she goes to him there) with his neck stretched upwards but head turned down so that his bill is almost touching and nearly parallel to his neck. His neck feathers are sleeked down but most of the body feathers, especially on the belly, erected, giving him a somewhat flask-shaped appearance. In this position he bounces up and down, stretching and flexing his legs but not letting go of the perch which, if not substantial, may oscillate considerably. He sings or (*fide* Mitchell) sometimes utters the buzzing threat call. When the female comes close he at first intensifies his display then bows low towards and in front of the female, opens his bill and turns his head up towards her, thus simulating the begging posture of a fledgling.

Copulation takes place in the nest (Immelmann, Mitchell). It is sometimes or usually prefaced by the female calling from the nest entrance. The male flies to her with nesting material in his bill, she retires before him, mandibulating, and giving a shorter version of her buzzing call. She may then solicit with spread and fluttering wings and the usual tail movements. The male enters the nest, turns so that he is parallel to her, offers her the end of the grass stem he carries and copulation sometimes follows (Mitchell).

Clumping and allo-preening occur but apparently less often than with most estrildids that practise it (Hall, unpublished mss).

OTHER NAMES Diamond Sparrow, Spotted-sided Finch.

REFERENCES

Butler, A. G. 1896. *Foreign finches in captivity.* L. Reeve & Co., London.

Hindwood, K. 1966. *Australian birds in colour.* A. H. & A. W. Reed, Wellington.

Immelmann, K. 1965. *Australian finches in bush and aviary.* Angus & Robertson Ltd., Sydney.

Immelmann, K., Steinbacher, J. & Wolters, H. E. 1965. *Vögel in Käfig und Voliere: Prachtfinken:* 25–37.

Massey, J. 1975. The Diamond Firetail. *Foreign Birds* 41: 28–29.

Mitchell, I. G. (no date). *A background to estrildine courtship patterns.* Privately distributed from 21 Second Avenue, Murrumbeena S.E. 9, Victoria, Australia.

Nicolai, J. 1962. Uber die Balz des Diamantfinken. *Gefiederte Welt* 1962: 146–147.

Red-eared Firetail *Emblema oculata*

Fringilla oculata Quoy and Gaimard, 1830. *Voy. Astrolabe, Zool.*, **1**, p. 211.

DESCRIPTION Similar in size to the previous species, *E. guttata*, but with shorter, less pointed wing (averaging 55 to 58 mm), longer, round-ended tail, more sharply triangular bill and softer, looser body plumage. Top of head, mantle, back and wing coverts olive-brown to brownish grey (worn plumage) with narrow blackish brown cross-barring, finest and least conspicuous on the head and broadest on the wing coverts. Inner secondaries and outer webs of outer secondaries and primaries as back but barring less fine even than on the wing coverts. Inner webs and tips of primaries dark brownish grey. Under wing coverts pale buff with darker barring. Rump and upper tail coverts scarlet. Tail greyish brown to grey with blackish cross-barring and some dull red on the basal parts of the outer webs of the central feathers. Narrow line across forehead at base of bill, lores and a roundish patch enclosing the eye, black. A smallish patch of bright red immediately below and behind eye (involving some of the upper ear-coverts). Rest of face light olive-buff with faint, fine darker barring. Throat buffish with fine barring. Breast light brownish buff conspicuously barred with blackish brown. Underparts blackish, boldly spotted and barred with white. At the sides of the breast and on the flanks each feather has a large white subterminal spot and a large spot or bar further back; elsewhere, especially on the under tail coverts, the white markings are more definite bars. Irides red or orange, brown and grey irides sometimes recorded, possibly this may represent fading after death. Orbital skin pale greenish blue, pale blue or lilac. Bill red, sometimes pinkish or mauvish at base. A dark overlay develops on the male's bill when he is in breeding condition (*fide* Pepper). Legs and feet pinkish slate, pale hornish brown, dark brown or some intermediate shade.

Sexes alike but female's bill said not to change colour and red face patch to be, at least in breeding females, lighter than in males (Immelmann). Juvenile a little paler and duller brown with little or no barring on head. No red on cheeks and red of rump less bright than adult's. Under parts pale buff and dull white, with darker barring and crescentic markings. Bill at first dark but begins to turn red 14 days after fledging (Pepper, in Immelmann). Mouth markings of nestlings similar to those of previous species but the palate markings are of the more widespread 5 spot type. There are very conspicuous luminous gape spots (Immelmann).

FIELD CHARACTERS Small brownish finch with red bill, rump and cheek patch and boldly spotted flanks. Blackish 'goggles' around pale-rimmed eyes conspicuous close up. No similar sympatric species.

DISTRIBUTION AND HABITAT South-western Australia. Confined to the south-western corner, in the coastal belt and the Darling Range, south-east to the Hamersley estuary. After an apparent gap in distribution it then re-appears at Lucky Bay and also occurs at Mississippi Bay and Duke of Orleans Bay. In early colonial days it was more widespread and occurred near Perth (Serventy & Whittell). Inhabits forest with undergrowth, especially the forested floors of steep, stream-watered valleys. Also coastal paperbark swamps and thickets.

FEEDING AND GENERAL HABITS Takes seeds of *Lepidosperma angustatum*, *L. gladiatum* and other grasses, also small insects. Seeds of other plants and of some trees and shrubs are also taken. When feeding tends to keep above ground in low cover, perching on low or fallen branches, pulling seed heads towards itself and holding them clamped under one foot while it extracts the seeds and picking insects from foliage (Immelmann). In captivity, Pepper's birds took white, Japanese and panicum millets, Canary seed, the green unripe seed heads of these plants, various wild seeding grasses and thistles and, when breeding, aphids and other small insects. Rather surprisingly they refused termites.

Usually in pairs or singly. Immelmann found that each pair lived in an area about 90–180 metres (100 to 200 yards) in diameter. These areas were only weakly defended except in the immediate vicinity of the nest. No nest was within about 90 metres (100 yards) of that of any other pair (Immelmann). Very agile among vegetation, moves along horizontal branches with pivoting hops. Does not flick its tail. Flight not fast but twists neatly among trees; usually flies low (Immelmann). Roosts in nests as previous species.

In captivity peaceable with its own and other species but not sociable. This species does not thrive in captivity. Pepper, who seems to have been the most successful breeder of it, emphasises that large, planted aviaries are essential. In 1971 20 of this species were exported to Europe. Here they did not breed until 1974 and in the autumn of that year all died from a hepatitis infection which did not affect any of the other species in the same aviary (Immelmann *et al.*, 1976).

NESTING The nest is usually placed well up in a tree, sometimes in a prickly *Hakea* or other bush. Immelmann found that forks in the dense outermost branches of *Eucalyptus calophylla* were common sites. The nest is bulky and retort shaped, about 42–44 centimetres (15 to 16 inches) in length, of which about 17 centimetres (7 inches) is the entrance tube. The main part of the nest is about 15 centimetres (6 inches) and the entrance tube about 7·5 centimetres (3 inches) in diameter. It is made of green plant material and the egg chamber lined with feathers and vegetable down. Four nests examined in detail by Immelmann had their outer walls and entrance tubes made of strips of the liana-like twining fringe-lily *Thysanotus patersoni*, some of considerable length (up to 85 centimetres (35 inches)). The cup-shaped interior was made of grasses, mostly *Stipa elegantissima*, and lined with feathers and vegetable down. As with most estrildids the main part of the nest is built first, then the entrance tube and lining continues after incubation has begun. Usually the bottom of the nest and entrance of the nest lie above a branch (Immelmann). The nest is very strongly attached, an adaptation of the frequent violent shaking of the peripheral branches it is often built among. One nest, examined by Immelmann, contained nearly 2000 pieces of material. The male brings most or all of the nesting material, which is carried by one end, in a waxbill-like manner (Pepper).

Eggs 4 to 6. Both sexes incubate and brood in turn for periods of 1 to 1·5 hours. Nest relief accompanied by special calls as in the previous species. Wild birds usually sit very close and are not easily flushed from the nest (Immelmann) although in captivity they are sometimes nervous and readily desert (Pepper). The breeding season is from September to January (Immelmann).

Unlined nests without an entrance tube are built for roosting. They may later be converted into breeding nests. Birds still in juvenile plumage may build them (Pepper).

VOICE This species has a great many calls or perhaps, rather, a great number of variants of its major calls. Pepper has dealt very full with this (and other) aspects of the species. The following is derived mainly from Immelmann & Pepper.

The contact call (identity call) is a mournful, plaintive 'oowee' or 'wee-ee' that seems to have no beginning or ending and is difficult to locate. The female's version has a slight quaver and can be distinguished from that of the male (Pepper). This call may be uttered singly or in series. In the latter case the mate, which may be some hundreds of yards away, usually answers. Contact calling is most frequent in the breeding season and the incubating bird may call from inside the nest. A very quiet 'quirk' or 'quark' is used between members of a pair when close to each other. It has been termed 'communication call' by Immelmann. The nest relief call is a two-syllabled 'twit, twit', it is sharply defined and easy to locate. The bird inside the nest answers it with one long and three short notes: 'twee-tit-tit-tit'.

When searching for a nest site or as a preface to courtship display a call of six syllables is uttered. The first note is a variant of the contact call (identity call), the rest a series of rapidly repeated syllables similar in character to the German umlaut ü (Immelmann). It could perhaps be anglicised 'ooweeee-eu-eu-eu-eu-eu'. This call may be followed or answered by a faint, curious huffy-sounding 'huh-huh-huh'. From Pepper's observations it is clear that, at least in captivity, this call is also used in other situations. Perhaps it expresses a state of need or a searching mood that in the wild is most often felt when the bird is seeking a nest site or prior to courtship? When their young appear to be in danger the parents utter a harsh note which Pepper likens to that made by a broody Domestic Fowl when removed from her nest.

The song (Burkard, in Immelmann *et al.*, 1976) consists of single notes repeated in a definite sequence. First is a whistling or fluting note, then a long-drawn note that rises and falls in loudness four times, finally a repeated puffing or gasping sound. The song is given when the bird is alone and also during the courtship display.

Pepper heard a loud warbling from a young bird 15 days after fledging.

DISPLAY AND SOCIAL BEHAVIOUR It appears that the courtship display is subject to some variation. It may begin by the male bowing and adopting the begging-like posture as described for the previous species, *E. guttata*, hopping in this posture towards the female (who may adopt the same posture), then in an erect posture bouncing up and down (Burkard, in Immelmann *et al.*, 1976); the male may, after giving the nest site call with nesting material, usually a long grass stem held by a side fibre, in his bill, bounce up and down (Immelmann, 1962) or he may jump up and down in the bent over, head lowered position (Pepper). In the first situation the female may respond by soliciting with quivering tail and copulation take place (Immelmann, 1965). Pepper did not see copulation. Usually two or three birds would be attracted to the displaying male then all would fly into cover and out of sight.

Pepper recorded the visiting of nesting pairs (in captivity) by others but generally the species would appear to be relatively unsociable (although not aggressive). Even members of a pair do not clump or allopreen (Immelmann *et al.*, 1976).

OTHER NAME Red-eared Finch.

REFERENCES

Immelmann, K. 1962. Beiträge zu einer vergleichenden Biologie australischer Prachtfinken. *Zool. Jb. Syst. Bd.* **90**: 1–196.

Immelmann, K. 1965. *Australian finches in bush and aviary.* Angus & Robertson, Sydney.

Immelmann, K., Steinbacher, J. & Wolters, H. E. 1965 and 1976. *Vögel in Käfig und Voliere: Prachtfinken*: 17–25 and 569–572. Aachen, Germany.

Pepper. A. 1964. Notes on the Red-eared Firetail in captivity. *W. Aust. Nat.* **9**: 49–57.

Serventy, D. L. & Whittell, H. M. 1967. *Birds of Western Australia.* Lamb Publications Pty. Ltd., Perth.

Beautiful Firetail   *Emblema bella*

Loxia bella Latham, 1801, *Index Ornith.*, suppl., p. 44.

DESCRIPTION Very similar to the previous species, *E. oculata*, but differs as follows: Bill more markedly attenuated from about middle to tip so that culmen ridge may appear slightly convex and outline of bill from above slightly indented. Black eyepatch slightly larger and with the contiguous black stripe over the front of the forehead wider. No red on sides of head. Upper parts similar but the barring perhaps a little more pronounced. Rump and upper tail coverts a more vivid red and the end half (approximately) of the central tail feathers black. Most of underparts finely barred with blackish on dull white, suffused with yellowish brown on cheeks, neck and front of breast: the barring is boldest on the flanks, finest on the throat, cheeks and under wing coverts. Centre of belly, ventral area and under tail coverts black. Irides dark brown; orbital skin pale opalescent blue.

The female tends to have the yellowish brown suffusion on the breast stronger and more extensive, the barring on her lower breast and flanks extends over the centre of the belly and usually also to some extent on her otherwise duller blackish ventral area and under tail coverts. The black patch around her eyes may be smaller. The juvenile is a duller version of the adult female, with smaller eyepatch and at first a dark bill.

There is an excellent coloured photograph of an adult male in Hindwood (1966).

See plate 2, facing p. 97.

FIELD CHARACTERS Small brownish finch (barring noticeable at close view) with vivid red rump and (part of) tail and red bill. Black 'goggles' and lack of red on head distinguish it from smaller and greenish Red-browed Finch.

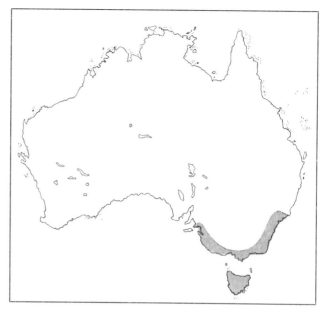

DISTRIBUTION AND HABITAT South-eastern Australia, in the coastal districts of New South Wales as far north as the Newcastle area, Victoria and south-eastern South Australia. Also Tasmania, Flinders Island and Kangaroo Island. Inhabits thick creek-side vegetation, dense heathlands, marshes, open forest and sometimes other country where there is plenty of bush or scrub cover (Immelmann, Hindwood, Sharland). In Tasmania locally in gardens (Immelmann *et al.*).

FEEDING AND GENERAL HABITS Known to feed on grass seeds, including those of *Holcus lunatus* and *Stipa* sp., the seeds of casuarinas and other trees and shrubs, small snails (Hindwood, Immelmann). Seeks food both on the ground and in vegetation. General behaviour as for previous species, so far as known, and also roosts in nests built for the purpose, but is apparently more sociable. When not breeding often or usually in small flocks of up to about a dozen birds. Sometimes feeds in company with Red-browed Finches. Often tends to become rare with increasing human settlement of an area, possibly due to predation by domestic cats (Immelmann, Sharland).

In the last century Dr Butler claimed that English and French aviculturists, unlike Dr Russ in Germany, found this species easy to keep in captivity. Later aviculturists have not found it so although it has been bred in captivity in Australia and Tasmania and is perhaps less delicate in captivity than the Red-eared Firetail. It requires similar treatment to the latter, except that it will eagerly eat termites and will sometimes eat fruit. In Europe it is apparently very sensitive to damp or cold, much more so than many tropical estrildids, in spite of inhabiting moist temperate areas when wild (Immelmann, Immelmann *et al.*).

NESTING The nest is usually in a bush, shrub or low in a tree, about 1·5 to 7 metres high. It is similar to that of the Red-eared Firetail but is usually built mainly of green grass stems, not liana-like material (Immelmann, Sharland). Eggs 4 to 8. Incubation period 11 to 13 days (Immelmann *et al.*). Parental behaviour as in *E. oculata* (Immelmann). In captivity males drive other birds from the vicinity of the nest.

VOICE The contact call (identity call) is very like that of the previous species, *E. oculata*, but monosyllabic (Immelmann). Other calls appear not to have been described in detail but are probably very similar to those of the Red-eared Firetail.

DISPLAY AND SOCIAL BEHAVIOUR No detailed information, probably similar to that of the Red-eared Firetail.

OTHER NAMES Fire-tailed Finch, Tasmanian Waxbill.

REFERENCES
Butler, G. L. 1899. *Foreign finches in captivity.* London.
Hindwood, K. 1966. Australian birds in colour. A. H. & A. W. Reed, Sydney.
Immelmann, K. 1965. *Australian finches in bush and aviary.* Angus & Robertson, Sydney and London.
Immelmann, K., Steinbacher, J. & Wolters, H. E. 1965. *Vögel in Käfig und Voliere: Prachtfinken:* 10–17.
Russ, K. 1879. *Die Fremlandischen Stubenvögel,* vol. 1. Hanover, Germany.
Sharland, M. 1945. *Tasmanian birds.* Oldham, Beddame & Meredith, Hobart.

Painted finch   *Emblema picta*

Emblema picta Gould, 1842, *Birds Australia* pt. 7 (also *Proc. Zool. Soc. London.* **10**, p. 17).

DESCRIPTION About size of previous species but with proportionately longer wing (about 55 to 59 mm), shorter tail and longer and more slender bill (see plate 2). Shorter, less soft body feathering usually gives it a slimmer appearance. Top of head, sides of neck, mantle, back and wing coverts a medium slightly reddish brown, some individuals have a considerable amount of red suffusion, mainly on the fringes of the feathers. Primaries and secondaries a slightly darker brown. Under wing coverts barred light drab and dull white. Rump and upper tail coverts a bright shining scarlet or vermilion red. Tail blackish brown with some light red on the outer webs of the central feathers. Front of forehead, face, throat, median part of upper breast and a median stripe on the lower breast and upper belly shining scarlet or vermilion. The amount of red varies somewhat individually and part of the black bases of the red (tipped) feathers may show, giving a spotted effect. Exceptionally there may be a continuous broad red stripe from throat to belly. Rest of underparts black, spotted with white except on the median part of the upper breast between the red areas. The white spots are large on the flanks, where each feather has a white subterminal spot and a band, or 'twin' spots, of white lower down, smaller at the sides of the breast and usually minute at the sides of the upper neck. Irides creamy white, white or pale buff. Bill with upper

mandible dark horn to black, usually pinkish or reddish at the tip and sometimes also on the culmen ridge; lower mandible pink, red or pinkish orange, paler towards its base and with a bluish or greyish patch at the base on either side. Legs and feet flesh-coloured to fleshy grey.

The female has the red on the head confined to the lores and around the eyes, with a tiny patch at the base of the lower mandible. Her throat and breast are black, spotted with white. She also has much less red on the lower breast and belly than the male, usually only a few red-tipped feathers. The juvenile is like the female but with reddish buff fringes to the feathers of the brown upperparts and wings, duller black and less clearly spotted below, some of the flank feathers being barred rather than spotted. Juvenile males may have more unspotted, blackish, rufous-edged feathers on the centre of lower breast and belly but this is based on only a few specimens and further information is needed. The newly-hatched young are flesh-coloured and without down (Ziegler, 1963). The mouth markings of the nestlings have the common 'domino' pattern modified so as to approach the 'horseshoe' type seen in the munias. (See sketch on p. 32.) There is a photo of begging nestlings, showing their mouth markings, in Immelmann *et al.*

See plate 2, facing p. 97.

FIELD CHARACTERS Small brown-backed bird with red on face, spotted flanks and brilliant red rump. Often very difficult to see when feeding among reddish sand or stones but red rump very conspicuous in flight.

Colour morphs in which the red is replaced by yellowish orange, and one in which the underparts were barred, have occurred in captivity (Webber).

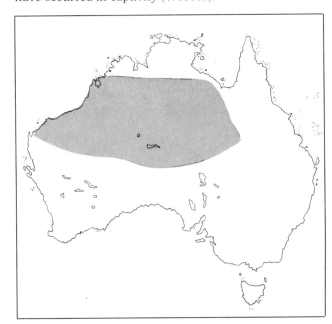

DISTRIBUTION AND HABITAT Arid parts of interior Australia from Central Australia to extreme western Queensland, the southern Kimberleys and mid-western coast south to

Boolathanna station (north of Carnarvon) and the Barlee Range. Occurrences widely outside the usual known range, as at Campbelltown, near Sydney, in 1896 (Immelmann) but probably such birds were escaped captives.

Inhabits spinifex country, preferring rocky hills and gorges but also sometimes found on open spinifex plains and locally around homesteads and in gardens. The presence of permanent water appears essential and perhaps accounts for its rather patchy distribution within its general range. Immelmann found that most Painted Finches appeared to stay near a particular water hole.

FEEDING AND GENERAL HABITS Known to feed very largely on the seeds of different species of spinifex grass, *Triodia spp.* Probably takes other seeds, insects and greenfood at times but does not seem to have been recorded doing so in the wild. Feeds on the ground, picking seeds from bare sandy places between tussocks of spinifex or among stones. Can hold grass etc. under foot. Drinks in the usual passerine manner not (ever?) with the pigeon-like method (Immelmann, Webber). Flight strong with an undulating flight path; usually flies near the ground and is very agile on the wing (Immelmann). Sometimes, when disturbed, may rise and fly round quite high before dropping to earth again (P. Colston, pers. comm.). Unlike firetails, and rather surprisingly in view of the cold nights at times in its habitat, it does not roost in nests but near or actually on the ground (Immelmann).

In captivity will eat various millets, canary seed, seeding grasses, especially *Poa annua*, chickweed and other greenfood. The small yellow or panicum millet is usually taken in greatest quantity. Immelmann and other German aviculturists recommend that insect food such as ant pupae, greenfly, termites, mealmoth larvae, mealworms and whiteworms should be given when the birds have young. Murray (in Webber) found that his birds began to take quantities of insect food as soon as their young hatched. On the other hand Webber (in Australia) successfully bred this species in numbers on seed and greenstuff alone. Ziegler (1965) found that his birds, which had not previously taken insects, eagerly took larvae of the meal moth, *Ephestia kuhniella*, and fed their nestlings largely on them. He, like other European breeders of the species, had found that young often died shortly after fledging. His studies showed that such young, although calling loudly, would not adopt the crouched, neck-twisted begging posture when the parent came to them and, presumably for this reason, were not fed. Further investigation showed that this only happened when the supplies of fresh greenfood and soaked seed had not been given first thing in the morning and in the late afternoon and the situation was remedied when half ripe seeding Annual Meadow grass was given first thing in the morning and for the last feed of the day. Ziegler presumed that the odd behaviour of the hungry young and their consequent neglect was due to lack of sufficient supply of some vitamins, trace elements or the like present in the

greenfood and half ripe grass seeds. Artificial vitamins added to other foods had no effect. In this connection Ziegler notes that Painted Finches in captivity will not eat greenfood or soaked seed unless it is very fresh (the same is true of the blue waxbills).

NESTING The nest is usually in a clump of spinifex but occasionally in some other vegetation or on the ground. Before starting to construct the nest itself a foundation platform for it is made of small stones, bits of earth, charcoal, wood or bark, short twigs or any similar materials. The function of this platform is probably, as Immelmann suggests, to lessen the likelihood of spinifex spines penetrating the nest and injuring eggs or young. The nest proper is roundish with an entrance hole at the side and usually rather small, about 10 to 12 cm (4 or 5 inches) in diameter. It is made of stems, rootlets, bark etc., usually with the softest materials on the inside, and lined with such vegetable down, hairy seeds, feathers, fern fronds etc. as may be available.

In captivity various nest sites – in baskets, boxes, bushes or on the ground may be chosen and sometimes very slight or imperfect nests are built (Webber). When, however, a pair were experimentally supplied with a superfluity of many (all possible) different materials (Ziegler, 1964), a nest with very thick base and sides was built. The birds also tried, but without much success, to construct an entrance tube. The male brings material for the base and outer walls of the nest and does most of the building but both sexes bring nest lining materials. Both cock and hen of Ziegler's pair also carried pieces of charcoal into the nest. Hargreaves (in Webber) put 12 pairs together in a smallish aviary. Under these crowded conditions 7 pairs built nests that were all piled together in contact in a banksia tree and actually reared a total of 15 young successfully.

Eggs 3 to 5, usually 4. Both sexes incubate in turn by day for periods of 0.5 to 1 hour; the female only at night (Ziegler, 1965). Incubation period from 15 days in summer to 19 days in winter in both Germany and Australia (Webber, Ziegler, 1965). The nestlings' eyes are fully open on the tenth day, at which time they usually face the entrance of the nest and the parents cease to brood them (Ziegler, 1965). Young fledge at 19 to 25 days, the longer periods in cooler weather (Webber, Ziegler 1965).

VOICE The contact calls might be transliterated as 'teek', 'trut', 'trai(r)ht' etc. When used as distance contact calls or when uttered in flight they are loud, harsh and usually given in two or more syllables. As close contact calls much softer and usually single syllabled versions are uttered. Ziegler (1964) transcribed the contact call of a captive male as 'tyok tyok' (my anglicisations) and the nest call as 'to-to-to-to' and 'o-o-o-o-o', intergrading with the contact call. The female utters a rattling alarm call: 'terrai(h)t' in response to danger near the nest; the male in this situation, however, utters only loud and penetrating versions of the contact calls (Immelmann). Song is uttered both in courtship display and when alone. It is given with the plumage of the underparts erected and head turning from side to side. Webber describes it as four quick monotone notes followed by a peculiar throaty noise. Morris transliterates it as 'che che che-che-che-che-che werreeee-ooeeeee' and an alternative version in which the two final notes sound like 'cheeurr cheeurr'. A sound spectrogram of the song is given by Hall.

DISPLAY AND SOCIAL BEHAVIOUR Ziegler (1964) describes a greeting display in which the male with angled tail and sometimes with nesting material in his bill, bows deeply towards the female slowly, makes bill-wiping movements at the lowest point of the bow, then slowly resumes an upright position in which he holds his back feathers depressed but those of his underparts erected so as to display the red and spotted areas. The female may respond with similar movements. Ziegler thinks the movements at the lowest part of the bow originates in nest-building rather than bill cleaning movements. What is probably the homologue of the courtship display of allied species appears to be seldom seen in the Painted Finch. Webber, who saw it once, describes it thus: '. . . he held a grass stalk in his bill, crouched over the perch, bobbed up and down and more or less performed the Diamond Sparrow display'. Hall (unpublished mss) also twice saw a male display in similar manner, holding a piece of grass in his bill and bouncing up and down, both feet leaving the perch at each jump. Usually courtship in this species, is prefaced either by the greeting display (Ziegler, 1964) or by the pair picking up and dropping again twigs, small stones or other such objects. The male, with the feathers of the head and belly erected in a peculiar manner so as to fully display the scarlet face and belly patch, then sings, pivoting his head. He usually begins to sing at a little distance from the female and, while still singing, nears her with jerky hops. If ready to mate the female angles her tail towards the male and then solicits with quivering tail in the usual manner. Copulation then takes place. Usually the pair court on the ground, often on a stone or some other slight eminence. Displacement bill wiping often occurs during courtship (Immelmann). Adult Painted finches neither clump nor allo-preen. Immelmann had the impression that the bond between the members of a pair is less strong in this bird than in most estrildids.

OTHER NAMES Painted Firetail, Mountain Finch.

REFERENCES

Hall, M. F. 1962. Evolutionary aspects of estrildid song. *Symposia Zool. Soc. London* 8: 37–55.

Immelmann, K. 1965. *Australian finches in bush and aviary.* Angus & Robertson, Sydney and London.

Immelmann, K., Steinbacher, J. & Wolters, H. E. 1965. *Vögel in Käfig und Voliere: Prachtfinken*: 37–49.

Webber, L. C. 1946. Ten years with the Painted Finch and some historical notes. *Avicult. Mag.* 52: 149–158.

Ziegler, G. 1964. Nestbau und Nest des Gemalten Astrild (*Emblema picta*). *Gefiederte Welt* 1964: 188–190.

Ziegler, G. 1965. Brut and Zucht des Gemalten Astrild (*Emblema picta*). *Gefiederte Welt* 1965: 112–115.

Red-sided Mountain Finch   *Oreostruthus fuliginosus*

Oreospiza fuliginosa De Vis, 1897, *Ibis*, p. 389.

DESCRIPTION About size of Peters' Twinspot or slightly larger but with larger wing (about 65 to 71 mm), much shorter tail and shorter bill. The plumage is soft and thick, probably giving a plump appearance in life, the legs are long and feet rather large. General coloration dark olive brown, slightly lighter on the cheeks and slightly darker on the wings. Under wing coverts dark reddish buff. Lower part of rump, upper tail coverts, flanks and tips of breast feathers bright red, scarlet or deep vermilion rather than crimson. Tail brownish black. Irides orange-red or dull red. Bill coral red to bright red. Legs and feet light horn colour to hornish brown, claws darker.

Female a lighter and more reddish brown on the underparts and with the red on the breast and flanks lighter and less extensive (Mayr and Rand, Rand and Gilliard). Juvenile like those from Mount Giluwe (see below) but more strongly tinged with orange-red (*fide* description of Mayr and Rand) on those areas that are red on breast and flanks in the adult; juvenile female with less orange-red tinge than male.

The above description is of nominate *O.f. fuliginosus*, from the mountains of south-eastern New Guinea. *O.f. hagenensis*, from Mount Hagen in the central highlands, is described (Mayr and Gilliard) as being generally a lighter more rufous brown and with the brown of the back 'thinly suffused with blood red'. In the British Museum (Natural History) collection there are four adult males and three juveniles from Mount Giluwe, a locality also in the central highlands. Shown on plate 7, facing p. 256. The adult males are olive brown with no red suffusion on their upper parts (and thus resemble nominate *O.f. fuliginosus*) but are a lighter and more reddish brown on the brown areas of their underparts and have some trace of red on the tips of many of the belly feathers. Their bills, eyes and legs are as in the nominate form. The two younger juveniles are a slightly more reddish brown above and have no red on their underparts. The red on their rumps and upper tail coverts is as brilliant as that of the adults but slightly more orange in tone. Their irides were dark brown. Their bills were black with the corners of the gape (which from the appearance of the dried skins were almost certainly swollen or with definite tubercles in life) bright yellow. The third juvenile is older and has begun to moult into adult plumage. It had pale brown irides and a red lower and blackish upper mandible.

I have not seen a specimen of *O.f. pallidus*, from the Oranje and Hindenberg mountains, from descriptions (e.g. Rand) it would appear to be very similar to the nominate form but with the brown parts somewhat paler. It has a yellow orbital skin as, probably, have other forms (Gilliard and Lecroy).

FIELD CHARACTERS Small, short-tailed, dark brown 'finch' with bright red rump and red bill; also some red on breast

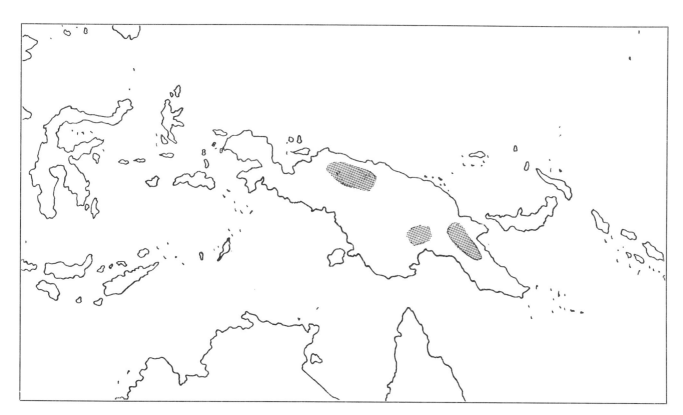

and flanks. Juvenile all brown, with dark bill but *bright red rump.*

DISTRIBUTION AND HABITAT   High mountains of New Guinea: Known (so far) from the Wharton Range, Mount Scatchley, Mount Knutsford and Winterheight in south-eastern New Guinea; Mount Hagen and Mount Giluwe in central New Guinea; and the northern slopes of the Oranje Mountains and the Hindenberg Mountains in north-western New Guinea. Inhabits transition areas between forest and alpine grassland, forest edge, in or near openings, glades, pathways or clearings in forest and in the lower growth of open forest. Grass and bushy cover appear to be essentials for its habitat.

FEEDING AND GENERAL HABITS   Known to eat grass seeds and these are probably the main food but out of four collected in the central highlands (Diamond) one had eaten insects and another fruit. Usually seen singly or in pairs, feeding in grassy places and fleeing to cover when alarmed.

NESTING   No information.

VOICE   One call has been described as exactly like that of the domestic Canary (De Vis). Which of the Canary's many different calls this comparison applies to is uncertain but quite possibly the 'Tsooeet' or 'Sweet' of alarm or anxiety is meant.

DISPLAY AND SOCIAL BEHAVIOUR   No information.

OTHER NAMES   Crimson-sided Mountain Finch, Crimson-sided Weaver-finch.

REFERENCES
De Vis, C. W. 1897. Diagnosis of thirty-six new or little-known birds of British New Guinea. *Ibis* **1897**: 371–392.
Diamond, J. M. 1972. *Avifauna of the Eastern Highlands of New Guinea.* Publications Nuttall Orn. Club no. 12.
Gilliard, E. T. 1967. *Handbook of New Guinea Birds.* Weidenfeld & Nicholson, London.
Gilliard, E. T. & Lecroy, M. 1961. Birds of the Victor Emmanuel and Hindenburg Mountains, New Guinea. *Bull. Amer. Mus. Nat. Hist.* **123**: 7–86.
Mayr, E. & Gilliard, E. T. 1954. Birds of Central New Guinea. *Bull. Amer. Mus. Nat. Hist.* **103**: 317–374.
Mayr, E. & Rand, A. L. 1937. Results of the Archbold Expeditions. No. 14. Birds of the 1933–1934 Papuan Expedition. *Bull. Amer. Mus. Nat. Hist.* **LXXIII**: 1–248.
Rand, A. L. 1940. Results of the Archbold Expeditions. No. 25. New birds from the 1938–1939 Expedition. *Amer. Mus. Novit.* **1072**.

The grassfinches, Zebra Finch and Bicheno Finch

The typical grassfinches form a close species group. The Long-tailed Grassfinch, *Poephila acuticauda*, and the Parson Finch, *P. cincta* are allopatric and very similar in habits and appearance. They seem indeed to differ more in tail length and temperament than in other characters and can certainly be treated as members of a superspecies. The Masked Grassfinch, *P. personata*, overlaps in range with both of them and is quite distinct from them in appearance. All are birds of grassy savanna and similar country. *P. personata* tends to frequent rather more open

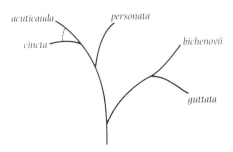

Presumed affinities of the grassfinches, Zebra Finch and Bicheno Finch, genus *Poephila*. Dotted line connects members of a superspecies.

arid areas and *P. cincta* less arid habitats but there is considerable overlap.

The very distinct Zebra Finch, *P. guttata*, is the most successful and widespread of all the Australian estrildids. It is pre-eminently a bird of the arid interior of Australia where it probably evolved but early spread to the Lesser Sunda Islands, where a distinct race occurs. As in the case of two other sympatric though quite unrelated seed-eating birds, the Budgerigar, *Melopsittacus undulatus*, and the Diamond Dove, *Geopelia cuneata*, its original adaptations to its harsh environment pre-adapted it to thrive in captivity and it has been domesticated and is kept and bred widely outside its homeland.

The Bicheno Finch is generally agreed to be most nearly related to the Zebra Finch although a very distinct species. These two are often placed in the monotypic genera *Taeniopygia* and *Stizoptera*, as by Immelmann (1962 and 1973). I concur with Mayr (1968) in thinking that they have sufficient in common with the typical grassfinches to be included with them in *Poephila*. I treat *Taeniopygia* and *Stizoptera* as subgenera.

The nearest relationships of *Poephila* are uncertain but I think that Immelmann (1962) is probably right in thinking that it represents an early offshoot from a stock ancestral both to it and to *Lonchura*, *Chloebia* and *Erythrura*.

REFERENCES

Immelmann, K. 1962. Beitrage zu einer vergleichenden Biologie australischer Prachtfinken (Spermestidae). *Zool. Jb. Syst. Bd.* **90**: 1–196.

Immelmann, K. 1973. *Der Zebrafink.* in the 'Neue Brehm-Bucherei' series, A. Ziemsen Verlag, Wittenberg, Germany.

Mayr, E. 1968. The sequence of genera in the Estrildidae (aves). *Breviora Mus. Comp. Zool.*, Cambridge Mass. **287**.

Long-tailed Grassfinch   *Poephila acuticauda*

Amadinia acuticauda Gould, 1840, *Proc. Zool. Soc. London* **1839**, p. 143.

DESCRIPTION About size of Spice Finch but bill not so large, wing longer about 58–62 cm., and with long narrow pointed tail. The two central tail feathers are greatly attenuated, ending in long wire-thin wisps. There is considerable individual variation in tail length; the longest-tailed specimen in the British Museum (Natural History) collection measures 126 mm from base of tail to the tips of the longest tail feathers. For some unknown reason, birds of this species that have been bred in captivity never grow such long central tail feathers as do wild individuals (Boosey, Immelmann, 1965) Forehead, crown and nape light, slightly bluish grey; ear coverts a paler more slivery grey. Lores black. Hind neck pinkish brown, shading to a slightly darker tone on mantle and back. Wings a darker and less pinkish brown, with the outer webs of most of the outer primaries (but not the outermost) narrowly edged with silvery white for about two thirds of their length. Under wing coverts pinkish fawn A black band (which continues downwards around the body to border the lower flanks) divides the brown of the back from the white rump and upper tail coverts. Tail black. A velvety black, pear-shaped patch includes the throat and most of the upper breast. Sides of breast and underparts light pinkish fawn with a slight mauvish tinge. A black band (continuation of the band on the lower back) divides the fawn areas from the white belly, ventral area and under tail coverts. Bill bright yellow or orange-yellow (but see under). Irides reddish brown to chestnut red. Legs and feet bright red to orange-red.

Sexes alike but the female tends to have a slightly smaller breast patch. The plumage of both sexes fades rather quickly in the wild and in old plumage the body colour is usually a very pale pinkish fawn, looking almost cream-coloured at a little distance.

Juvenile duller, with a rusty buff rather than a mauve-pink tinge; a smaller, brownish black throat patch, shorter tail and (at first) brown irides, greyish black bill and flesh-coloured legs and feet. Half grown nestlings had grey down and grey irides (Macgillivray). Newly-hatched nestlings are flesh-coloured with sparse white down. Bill at first pale horn coloured, not beginning to darken until after the eighth day but entirely black by twelfth day (Immelmann, 1965). Mouth markings of nestling with the three black palate spots joined into one curving mark and the two lower palate spots small and joined by a narrow curving line. Gape swellings bluish white, edged on the insides with black longitudinal marks; a black crescent on the lower mandible and two black marks on the tongue (Immelmann *et al.*).

The above description is of *P.a. acuticauda*, from north-western Australia. *P.a. hecki*, from Northern Territory and western North Queensland differs in having the bill orange-red. Some authorities, probably wisely, recognise no races as there is every intergradation of colour between yellow-billed birds in the westernmost and red-billed birds in the easternmost part of the species' range. However, Zann (1975, 1976b) found small differences of voice and behaviour between yellow-billed *P.a. acuticauda* from Wyndham and representatives of a population of *P.a. hecki*. When apparently pure yellow-billed and apparently pure red-billed individuals are paired together in captivity, all the first generation offspring have red bills (Boosey, Restall).

See plate 2, facing p. 97.

FIELD CHARACTERS Pale fawn finch with conspicuous large black breast patch, pale grey head, white rump, yellow, red or orange bill and long pointed black tail. The grey head and very large black bib distinguish it at once from the sympatric Masked Finch. The closely related Parson Finch is similar in colour and pattern but has a black bill and short tail. It is not sympatric with the Long-tailed Grassfinch but might conceivably occur in same area with it as a straggler or an escape from captivity.

DISTRIBUTION AND HABITAT Northern Australia from the Kimberleys (Roebuck Bay area) to western North Queensland on the Leichhardt River. Inhabits dry savanna and *Pandanus* plains in coastal areas. Locally (*fide* Immelmann *et al.*, 1966) in parts of the interior also in arid grassland with only a few small trees and bushes. Presence of surface water apparently essential but will use artificial sources.

FEEDING AND GENERAL HABITS Feeds on the ground, mainly on grass seeds. Immelmann (1962) found that seeds of *Iseilema* sp., *Eragrostis* sp. and *Eriachne obtusa* were staple foods. Also catches flying insects, especially winged ants and termites, on the wing. Drinks in a pigeon-like manner and has this drinking method developed to a greater degree than any other species except the Parson Finch and the Masked Finch (Immelmann, 1962).

Usually in small or large flocks, within which the mated pairs keep closely together. Even when breeding, flock members gather in some area near the breeding place, several times daily to feed, bathe or preen together, although feeding trips by single pairs also occur (Immelmann, 1962 and 1965). Roosts in nests; those built for the purpose being usually smaller than breeding nests and without an entrance tube (Immelmann *et al.* 1966).

Head bobbing similar but at lower intensity to that used in display (q.v.) appear to be shown as locomotion-

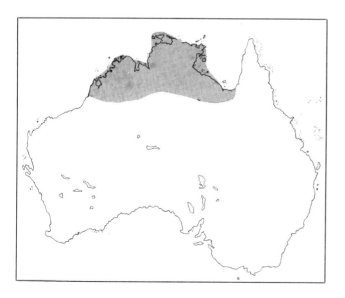

intention movements. The more usual tail movements in this context are not shown by this species or the Parson Finch.

This species appears now (1978) to be fairly well established in captivity in Europe and to a lesser extent in Britain. It is comparatively hardy and breeds freely if a compatible pair is obtained but individuals frequently refuse to pair with others to whom they are not personally attracted (Immelmann *et al.*, 1966, Restall, Zann, 1977). Can be fed on mixed millets and canary seed with the addition of soaked seed, greenfood and the usual minerals. Most successful breeders of this species recommend that the birds should be given some animal food when rearing young and Immelmann *et al.* (1966) say this is desirable at all times. Pairs may, however, refuse not only eggfood but even ant pupae. Some aviculturists have succeeded by merely giving the birds cooked or live mealworms in addition to their ordinary food (Boosey; Kirsche, in Immelmann *et al.*) but Boosey had a pair that reared fine young on only seeds and greenfood.

Immelmann *et al.* recommend that it should not be kept at a temperature below 15°C by day and, at most, a few degrees lower at night provided that warmly lined roosting nests are available. Birds that are thoroughly used to going from one to the other may, however, be allowed to fly in an open part of an aviary by day, provided they have a heated shelter at hand.

NESTING Usually breeds in loose colonies, generally with only one nest in any one tree. The nest is usually sited in a tree, bush or creeper, less often in a spinifex clump or other low vegetation. Common sites are in the dense peripheral branches of gum trees, from 5 to 18 metres high, or in the tops of pandanus palms. The nest is bulky and roundish, usually about 10 to 16 cm in diameter and with a pronounced entrance tube about 5 to 10 cm long. It is built of grasses and sometimes also wiry creepers, stems of herbaceous plants or other material and lined with feathers, plant wool or finer grasses. Small pieces of charcoal are sometimes placed inside the nest. Most, and sometimes all the nesting material is brought by the male but both sexes build.

Eggs 3 to 8, usually 5 or 6. Parental care as Zebra Finch but usually the sitting bird does not leave the nest until its mate is at or inside the nest entrance. Incubation period about 13 days. Young fledge at 21 days or a little after.

Breeds in the second half of the rainy season or shortly after, usually from January to May but sometimes later. Probably can and will nest whenever recent rains have produced abundant food supplies.

The above information is derived and condensed from Hill, Immelmann (1962 and 1965), Immelmann *et al.* (1966) and Macgillivray.

VOICE The calls of this species and its near allies have been described in detail by Zann (1975) who gives sound spectrograms of all the calls as well as discussing their ontogeny and geographical and individual variation. The relatively condensed information given here is derived from Zann's 1975 paper except (and then often only partially) where otherwise indicated.

The close contact or locomotion intention call is a short quiet 'tet'. It is given mostly when the bird is about to fly, or actually taking wing, when in flight or when out of sight of but near the mate. The distance contact call is very loud and plaintive, at high intensity it can be heard for several hundred metres. It may be one- or two-syllabled and is subject to some variation. It has been transcribed as 'weet' or (Immelmann, 1965) and 'We-WOOOOOh We-WOOOOOH' (Morris). It is given in the usual situations: by lost or temporarily visually isolated individuals, in response to such calls from other birds, when slightly alarmed and so on. If a bird hearing this call is alone, it flies towards the caller, uttering contact calls as it does so but if it is with a flock it usually only calls in reply.

Although at full intensity the distance and close contact calls are distinct (Immelmann, 1962 and 1965), intermediate forms, which Zann terms 'Beep' calls are also given, in similar situations to those that elicit distance contact calls and also by parents when approaching young to feed them.

A short, abrupt call which Zann (1975) terms the 'twit' call and shows consists of a 'tet' and a 'beep' call, so close together that they cannot be distinguished by the human ear, is given by males when apparently wishing to take wing but, for some reason, hesitant to do so. A long harsh-sounding 'squark' has been heard only from females of *P.a. hecki*. It seems to function as a contact call over a relatively short distance and was: (1) heard if a female was separated from but near her mate; (2) when young were visually separated from their parents (in which situation the mother gave this call but their father the usual distance contact call); (3) when leading young back to the nest and (4) when a female performed the courtship display to her mate.

Zann distinguishes two alarm calls: 'cha', which is given in apparently intense alarm, when danger seems imminent, and 'thuk', which is usually given when the birds are perched after the initial alarm. The 'cha' note is given in a rapid series, the 'thuk' singly. The former call causes birds that hear it to flee into cover, usually up into a tree, the 'thuk' call merely alerts them.

The short, hissing aggressive call is similar to that of the Zebra Finch. A bird that is chased by a conspecific utters a burst of calls similar to the 'cha' alarm call but louder but this calling does not deter the pursuer, whether his intent is aggressive or sexual. A high-pitched scream or screech is sometimes uttered by a bird that gets hurt in a fight. It is (I think) homologous with the squealing cry given by fledglings when seized in the hand or attacked by a conspecific. As with other birds, these cries of fear, when uttered in intra-specific contexts, have no inhibiting effect on the attacker. More surprisingly, Zann found that the parents of a squealing fledgling showed 'no detectable response'. This is in great contrast to the behaviour of *Uraeginthus* and *Amandava* (and all the many non-estrildid species I have kept) whose parents show an intense

emotional response when they hear their young cry out in terror, even although they (*Uraeginthus* and *Amandava*) do not usually, if ever, defend them actively.

What Zann terms the 'intimate call' has probably not been thought separable from contact calls by other observers. It is like the intermediate contact call but has a lower frequency and more harmonics. Intimate calls are variable and are given in many social situations, especially between members of a pair engaged in nest site selection or nest building.

A soft, grating sound, audible for only one or two metres, which Zann terms the 'kackle call', usually accompanies the head-bobbing display (q.v.). It is uttered in many social situations. The partner often responds with the same call and movements. Zann describes the 'ark call' as a longer and more rasping variant of the kackle call. It is given especially when alighting at a prospective nest site or at the entrance of a nest, apparently to entice the mate to join the calling bird.

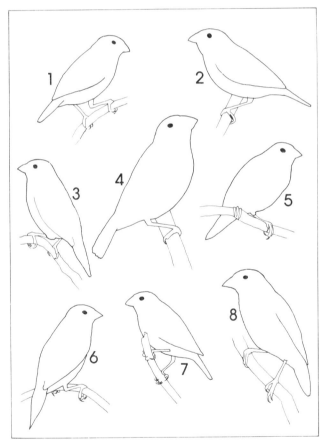

Plate 5 Some asiatic and Australasian *Lonchura* species, to show variation within the genus. (1) New Britain Munia, *Lonchura spectabilis mayri*; (2) Chestnut-and-white Munia, *L. quinticolor*; (3) White-backed Munia, *L. striata swinhoei*; (4) Java Sparrow, *L. oryzivora*; (5) Chestnut-breasted Finch, *L. castaneothorax sharpii*; (6) Indian Silverbill, *L. malabarica*; (7) Streak-headed Munia, *L. tristissima*; (8) Timor Sparrow, *L. fuscata*.

MWWoodcock

M.W.Woodcock

The nest call is a series of high-pitched whimpering or whining notes that may intergrade or develop into 'ark' notes. Longer variants of these two calls, termed copulation calls by Zann, are uttered by both sexes when copulating. Zann found that females of *P.a. hecki* uttered these calls when soliciting but his females of nominate *P.a. acuticauda* did not.

Newly-hatched nestlings (like newly hatched young of many other birds) utter soft, probably involuntary clicks. The begging call of nestlings a few days old is faint, high-pitched, pure cheeping sound but by the ninth day it has changed to a harsh, grating note. Pure cheeps may still be uttered up to the thirteenth day but only towards the end of a feeding session, presumably by partly satiated birds.

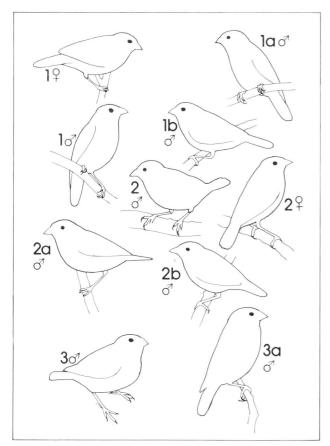

Plate 6 Some examples of geographic variation within species. Top: (1) Swee Waxbills from Natal, South Africa, (female above, male below); (1a) Male (of the sexually monochromatic form) from Malawi; (1b) Male from central Angola. Centre: (2) Avadavats from India (male left, female right); (2a) Male from Burma; (2b) Male from Vietnam. Bottom: (3) Male Zebra Finch from Australia; (3a) Male Zebra Finch from Moa island, Moluccas.
(1) Swee Waxbills, *Estrilda m.melanotis*; (1a) Swee Waxbill, *E. melanotis kilimensis*; (1b) Swee Waxbill, *E. melanotis bocagei*; (2) Avadavats, *Amandava a. amandava*; (2a) Avadavat, *A. amandava flavidiventris*; (2b) Avadavat, *A. amandava punicea*; (3) Zebra Finch, *Peophila guttata castanotis*; (3a) Zebra Finch, *P.g. guttata*.

Fledglings give recognisably distinct versions of some of the adult calls. These and their development into the adult form are fully discussed and illustrated in sound spectrograms in Zann's (1975) paper.

The song, which is given both in courtship and as undirected song, varies both individually and geographically. Zann (1976a) who investigated the song of this and allied species in great detail, says: 'each phrase consists of a soft almost inaudible introductory section of short elements followed by a main section of louder pure notes arranged in order of ascending frequency. Immelmann (1965) describes it as a series of soft notes, some flute-like and some 'squeezing' in tone, ending in a long mournful note like the distance contact call. Morris, who transcribed a song as 'tu-tu-tu-tu-tu WOO-WAH-WEEEE', remarked that the last note in the song phrase was both individually variable and also much resembled the final note in the songs of Asiatic mannikins, *Lonchura*. Zann (1975) and Hall give sound spectrograms of songs.

DISPLAY AND SOCIAL BEHAVIOUR In the head bobbing or head jerking display, the black bib is prominently displayed as the neck is stretched up and then retracted. It is used habitually as an appeasing greeting between mates and flock members and also, at usually lower intensity, as an apparent balancing movement (see 'Feeding and general habits') on alighting. Members of a pair, or a bird trying to form a pair, usually combine it with turning the head and angled tail towards the partner. It is also used by subordinate birds in agonistic encounters, often as a prelude to inviting allo-preening.

In the courtship display the male, with head up and usually holding a piece of grass in his bill, bobs up and down, bending and straightening his legs. Sometimes one or both feet temporarily leave the perch and sometimes a pivoting movement may be added (Zann, 1976b). Hall (unpublished ms) has seen this display performed without flexing the legs, the bird jumping with the legs held bent. According to Zann (1976b) this is a common invitation or prelude to precopulatory display in *P.a. hecki* but less often in nominate *P.a. acuticauda*. Zann (1975) saw a female of *P.a. hecki* give this display. A display flight in front of the mate, with grass held in the bill, may also lead to the precopulatory display in which the two birds hop to and from or around one another with formal head bobs and bill wipes. The body feathers, especially of the male, are slightly fluffed, those of the grey parts of the head rather more so, the feathers of the black bib are differentially raised so that its lower part is brought forward and the whole made more conspicuous (Immelmann, 1965). The male may sing but (*fide* Zann, 1976) if he does so he first stops jumping and stands in an upright posture to sing. The female solicits with tail quivering in the usual manner. Zann (1976) found that his captive females of *P.a. hecki* uttered the long harsh copulation calls while soliciting whereas his females of the nominate form did not.

After copulation the male lands beside the female with

head and angled tail turned towards her, makes a deep curtsey, and turns his head to one side, presenting his black throat and bill to her from below, in much the posture of a begging fledgling. Zann (1976) noted that the male gives several (symbolic?) pecks at the female's bib and ear coverts, she may peck back, and mandibulation and head bobbing follow. Neither Immelmann (1965) nor Nicolai (in Immelmann *et al.*) noted this agonistic behaviour as part of the post-copulation display so probably this is variable. There is a certain amount of minor individual and possibly also geographical variation in the sexual displays of this species and of *P. cincta*. Zann (1976) has analysed and quantified this, as observed in his captive specimens, in great detail and at considerable length.

The pair bond is very strong. In the wild the members of a pair keep continually within a metre or two of each other and seek food, preen, rest and indulge in other activities at the same time. Zann (1977) describes for both this species and the Parson Finch that: '. . . if a conspecific male landed near or gave weak sexual greeting to a mated female her mate would gently poke her on the shoulders or flanks with the top of his beak as if to push her towards the new arrival. After such a nudge she usually supplanted the new male or, if she did not, her mate would supplant the rival himself. Both sexes could nudge the partner into an aggressive response.' If this behaviour is usual it is the only case I know in which a male bird incites his mate to attack a possible rival *of his own sex* instead of (as is usual in many species, including some estrildids) either attacking the rival himself or driving her away from him.

Allo-preening and clumping are habitual and very frequent between the members of a pair and occur also between individuals not paired to each other. The allo-preening invitation, in which the head is turned back and the fluffed feathers of the bib presented, is also used as an appeasing display in agonistic situations, often with success.

OTHER NAMES Long-tailed Finch, Black-heart Finch.

REFERENCES

Boosey, E. J. 1962. *Foreign bird keeping.* Iliffe Books, London.

Hall, M. F. 1962. Evolutionary aspects of estrildid song. *Proc. Zool. Soc. London*, Symposium **8**: 37–55.

Hill, G. F. 1911. Field notes on the birds of Kimberley, North-West Australia. *Emu* **10**: 258–290.

Immelmann, K. 1962. Beiträge zu einer vergleichenden Biologie australischer Prachtfinken (Spermestidae). *Zool. Jb. Syst. Bd.* **90**: 1–196.

Immelmann, K. 1965. *Australian finches in bush and aviary.* Angus & Robertson, Sydney.

Immelmann, K., Steinbacher, J. & Wolters, H. E. 1966. *Vögel in Käfig und Voliere: Prachtfinken*: 127–143.

Macgillivray, W. 1924. Notes on some North Queensland birds. *Emu* **13**: 132–186.

Morris, D. 1958. The comparative ethology of grassfinches (Erythrurae) and mannikins (Amadinae). *Proc. zool. Soc. London* **131**: 389–439.

Restall, R. L. 1975. *Finches and other seed-eating birds.* Faber & Faber, London.

Zann, R. 1975. Inter- and intra-specific variation in the calls of three species of grassfinches of the subgenus *Poephila* (Gould) (Estrildidae). *Z. Tierpsychol.* **39**: 85–125.

Zann, R. 1976a. Variation in the songs of three species of Estrildine grassfinches. *Emu* **76**: 97–108.

Zann, R. 1976b. Inter- and intraspecific variation in courtship of three species of grassfinches of the subgenus *Poephila* (Gould) (Estrildidae). *Z. Tierpsychol.* **41**: 409–433.

Zann, R. 1977. Pair-bond and bonding behaviour in three species of grassfinches of the genus *Poephila* (Gould). *Emu* **77**: 97–106.

Parson Finch   *Poephila cincta*

Amadina cincta Gould, 1837, *Proc. Zool. Soc. London* **1836**, p. 105.

DESCRIPTION As previous species, *P. acuticauda*, but a little stockier in build, with slightly smaller bill and short tail with the tips of the two central feathers sharply pointed but only a little longer than the rest of the tail. Plumage pattern as in *P. acuticauda* and coloration very similar. Grey of head slightly bluer in tone; body plumage darker and redder, a light, rich cinnamon brown, darker and more greyish on lower back and wings. Irides brown, dark brown or brownish red. Bill black. Legs and feet red, orange-red, pinkish red or orange.

Females tend to have slightly smaller black breast bibs and slightly duller grey heads but there appears to be some overlap. Juvenile like that of previous species and showing similar differences from adult. Mouth markings of nestlings similar, sometimes (*fide* diagrams in Immelmann, 1965 and Immelmann *et al.*, 1966) with the single upper palate marking shorter and those at the sides also shorter though to a lesser extent, but at others like those of *P. acuticauda*. There is some minor individual variation in the mouth pattern (Zann, 1976).

The above description is of nominate *P.c. cincta*, from the greater part of the species' range. *P. cincta atropygialis*, from most of the Cape York Peninsula, has an entirely black rump. It is also much paler, its head being a pale silvery grey, slightly darker on hind crown and nape, and its underparts (where not white or black), mantle and upper back a delicate light, mauve-tinged, pinkish fawn, shading to a slightly darker and greyer tone on the wings.

Its irides are most often from brown to dark red, as in the nominate race but sometimes, according to the data on labels of specimens, yellowish brown or creamy brown. A hybrid zone between the white-rumped and black-rumped races has been found between Normanton and Cairns (Keast). This hybrid zone appears to have moved about 50 kilometres south since Keast discovered it, suggesting that *atropygialis* is pushing south and replacing *cincta* (Zann, 1976a).

DISTRIBUTION AND HABITAT Eastern Australia from northern Cape York Peninsula south to northern New South Wales. Inhabits similar types of country to the previous species, *P. acuticauda*, with perhaps a tendency to prefer areas with denser tree cover. Zann (1976) found it in habitats ranging from dry open woodland with a few tall trees to dense patches of two-layered woodland. The presence of seeding grasses, or their shed seeds on the ground, and surface water is essential.

FEEDING AND GENERAL HABITS In the main as previous species. In northern Queensland Zann (1976a) found that seeds of the grasses *Setaria surgens*, *Digitaria ciliaris*, *Stylosanthes humilis* and *Dactyloctenium radulans* were taken. Most seeds were picked up from the ground but some were taken from the plant, the bird leaping up, seizing the stem below the ear and then clamping the stem under one foot to pick out the seeds. Immelmann's (1962) observations led him to conclude that, when food was held underfoot by this species and its relatives, this was purely fortuitous so there may be some individual or geographical variation in this matter and further observations are desirable. Also takes seeds of *Iseilema* sp., termites and other insects (Immelmann, 1962 and 1965).

Flocks observed by Zann (1976a) fed in a dispersed group of family units, so that 15 to 20 birds were spread over an area of 10 to 15 square metres. In dry periods it usually drinks in the early morning, flying in loose flocks from the home area to the drinking place, but when water is close at hand and plentiful may drink at any time of day.

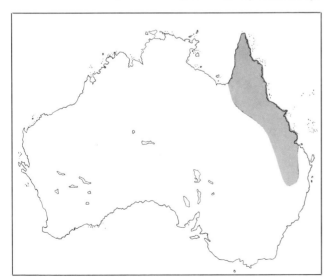

Its needs in captivity are as for the Long-tailed Grassfinch (q.v.). However, although it is just as social in a wild state, in captivity the Parson Finch is usually much more aggressive. Individuals vary and a few (even when fit) are quite peaceful. Many, however, aggressively defend a wide area around both breeding and roosting nests, habitually destroy or take over the nests of other species and often persistently attack and harass birds weaker or less aggressive than themselves. It should not therefore, except for the odd peaceful individuals perhaps, be kept with weaker species and especially not with waxbills, avadavats and other estrildids smaller than itself.

NESTING Very similar to the previous species, *P. acuticauda*, but sometimes nests in holes in trees and in termites' mounds. Quite often nests against or among the sticks forming the outer structure of some large bird-of-prey's nest (Immelmann, 1965, Immelmann *et al.*, 1966). Usually colonial but with the nests tending to be less widely dispersed than those of *P. acuticauda*, with up to 4 or 5 nests in one tree (Zann, 1976a). Of 71 nests examined by Zann, most were in the upper parts of trees, in clumps of twigs among the outermost branches and either rested on horizontal limbs or were wedged between vertical twigs. The majority of them were in *Melaleuca nervosa* or *M. stenostacha*.

Nest like that of the Long-tailed Grassfinch but tending to be bulkier and to have a slightly longer entrance tube. Zann (1976a) found that typical nests consisted of four main parts: a platform of heavy horizontal stems, a spiny outer layer of long stiff dead stems, an inner layer of finely matted soft flexible stems, an entrance tube of long stiff stems and a lining of soft grass panicles and feathers. Pieces of charcoal are sometimes placed in the nest (Iles, Immelmann, 1965).

Eggs 3 to 9, usually 4 to 6. Parental care as in *P. acuticauda*. Zann (1976a) found that true incubation only began after the fourth egg had been laid. Incubation period 14–15 days. Young fledge at 21–22 days.

VOICE Calls and song homologous with and very similar to those of *P. acuticauda* (q.v.). Some calls, especially the distance contact call, and the song are lower in pitch and hoarser and less piercing in sound. Has not apparently been heard to give the 'twit' or 'squark' calls of *P. acuticauda* or equivalents of them. Zann describes in detail and gives sound spectrograms of the calls (Zann, 1975) and songs (1976b) of this species and its two allies, *P. acuticauda* and *P. personata*.

DISPLAY AND SOCIAL BEHAVIOUR In general as previous species, *P. acuticauda*. The basic inverted curtsey type of courtship display with a nest symbol held in the bill is shown very seldom by adult males but quite often by young males (Immelmann, 1962, Zann, 1976c). Zann (1976a) found that in the black-rumped race, *P.c. atropygialis*, when a bird arrived at the social meeting place and gave the head-bobbing display, 'it was greeted by each nearby bird . . . the bird bowed down, pivoted its head and pointed the bill directly up at the head of the alighting bird (and mandibulated). This form of greeting is obviously similar if not virtually identical to the post-copulatory display which Zann (1976c) described for this species and *P. acuticauda*.

OTHER NAMES Black-throated Finch, Black-rumped Parson Finch, Diggles' Finch, Black-tailed Finch (the last three names refer only to the black-rumped form).

REFERENCES

Iles, G. W. (no publication date) *Breeding Australian finches*. Isles d'Avon Ltd, Bristol.

Immelmann, K. 1962. Beiträge einer vergleichenden Biologie australischer Prachtfinken (Spermestidae). *Zool. Jb. Syst. Bd.* **90**: 1–196.

Immelmann, K. 1965. *Australian finches in bush and aviary*. Angus & Robertson, Sydney.

Immelmann, K., Steinbacher, J. & Wolters, H. E. 1966. *Vögel in Käfig und Voliere: Prachtfinken*: 144–153.

Zann, R. 1975. Inter- and intraspecific variation in the calls of three species of grassfinches of the subgenus *Poephila* (Gould) (Estrildidae). *Z. Tierpsychol.* **39**: 85–125.

Zann, R. 1976a. Distribution, status and breeding of Black-throated Finches *Poephila cincta* in northern Queensland. *Emu* **76**: 201–206.

Zann, R. 1976b. Variation in the songs of three species of Estrildine grassfinches. *Emu* **76**: 97–108.

Zann, R. 1976c. Inter- and intraspecific variation in courtship of three species of grassfinches of the subgenus *Poephila* (Gould) (Estrildidae). *Z. Tierpsychol.* **41**: 409–433.

Zann, R. 1977. Pair-bond and bonding behaviour in three species of grassfinches of the genus *Poephila* (Gould). *Emu* **77**: 97–106.

Masked Grassfinch   *Poephila personata*

Poephila personata Gould, 1842, *Birds Australia*, pt. 6, pl. 91.

DESCRIPTION Very similar in size and shape to the Long-tailed Grassfinch but bill a little larger and deeper and the long central tail feathers shorter and tapering only to blunt points, not fine wisps. The feathers of the 'chin', loral region and at base of the upper mandible form a triangular-shaped black patch whose apex is the bird's eye. Front of forehead dark reddish brown. Rest of head, mantle, back and wing coverts a medium warm slightly reddish coffee brown; underparts (except where otherwise stated) a similar but paler brown. Primaries and secondaries a duller brown, with pale buffish fringes to the outer webs of the outermost four or five primaries. Under wing coverts pinkish brown. Undersides of primaries chestnut except at the ends, which are dark drab. Faint fine cross-barring is usually visible on the brown underparts but only at close inspection. Rump and median part of upper tail coverts white; sides of upper tail coverts black; the actual feathers are white on their inner webs and partly or largely black on their outer webs. A black band on the lower flanks similar to but broader than those of *P. acuticauda* and *P. cincta*. Narrow area anterior to the flank patch, centre of belly, ventral area and under tail coverts white. Irides blood red to dark brown. Bill bright wax yellow to amber yellow. Legs and feet pinkish red or red.

Sexes alike but females are on average a little smaller and often have the black face mask and flank patches less pronounced than those of most males. The juvenile is duller brown with brownish black and less extensive face mask and flank patches. The nestling's mouth pattern differs from that of its two close relatives and more resembles that of the Zebra Finch and Redbrowed Finch in having the five spot pattern on the palate, but it differs in having *two* crescentic black marks on the inside of the lower mandible.

The above description is of nominate *P.p. personata*, from East Kimberley east to the southwestern side of the Gulf of Carpentaria. *P.p. leucotis*, often known by the descriptive name of White-cheeked Grassfinch, from Cape York and the eastern side of the Gulf of Carpentaria, is slightly smaller. The dark reddish brown of its forehead extends over the crown. The brown of its upperparts is more strongly reddish in tone. Its cheeks, and a narrow edging to its black chin, are silvery white and there is a more extensive white area anterior to each black flank patch. Its bill is said usually to be a paler waxy yellow.

FIELD CHARACTERS Brown finch with bright yellow bill set off by black face mask. White rump and belly, black tail and flank patches. Warm brown, not silvery grey, head and lack of a *large* black patch on lower throat and breast (black only on 'chin' and front of face) distinguish the nominate race from the sympatric Long-tailed Grassfinch. The white-cheeked form is distinguished from the Parson Finch, with which it is sympatric, by its yellow, not black bill (young juveniles excepted); reddish brown top of head and lack of the black breast bib.

DISTRIBUTION AND HABITAT Northern Australia from East Kimberley and Northern Territory and north-western Queensland, south to Newcastle Waters, Thornton and Augustus Downs, and (White-eared race) Cape York Peninsula, north to the Watson and the Chester; east to Port Stewart, the upper Kennedy, Chillagoe and Fossilbrook; and south to Normanton and Georgetown (Storr).

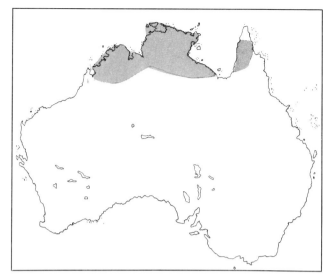

Inhabits dry open woodland savanna with scattered large trees, bushy steppe, and open grassland. Often near homesteads and sometimes in gardens. The presence of surface water is essential but cattle troughs and other artificial sources of water are widely used.

FEEDING AND GENERAL HABITS Feeds largely on seeds picked up from the ground or plucked from grass panicles by an upward jump to seize each individual seed. Seeds of the grasses *Enneapogon pallidus*, *Iseilema* sp., *Sorghum plumosum*, *Eregrostris* sp., *Eriachne obtusa* and *Sehima nervosum* are known foods. Also takes small insects, especially flying termites but also flying ants, small caterpillars and small spiders. Commonly catches (and often fails to catch) flying insects in a fluttering pursuit flight in the air. Drinks in a pigeon-like manner; usually coming to water only twice a day, in the morning and before sunset (Immelmann, 1962 and 1965). Spends much of its time on the ground although resting in the shadiest available trees during the hottest hours of the day (Immelmann, 1965).

Usually in small flocks of up to 30 birds but huge numbers may gather near the last water supplies in exceptionally dry seasons. Even when breeding flock members meet several times daily to feed, drink, bathe or socialise, although individual pairs also seek food by themselves (Immelmann, 1962, 1965). Roosts in nests, special roosting nests smaller than the breeding nest are built for this purpose.

In captivity requires similar treatment to the Long-tailed Grassfinch (q.v.) but would seem usually to be less easy to breed and slightly more delicate. Immelmann *et al.* (1966) advise that the temperature at which it is kept should not fall below 20–22°C by day and never under 15°C at night. Immelmann (1965) recommends that it be kept in a very large aviary, with dense cover in various corners and nooks, so that several pairs can be kept together and yet maintain some privacy in their individual nest sites. Whilst this is undoubtedly desirable, English aviculturists are likely to encounter problems of

space and heating expenses. One at least (Cooper, in Iles) has been very successful by keeping each pair in a small aviary (when breeding) but in sight and sound of other breeding pairs.

Roosting nests must be supplied. These can take the form of half open boxes with a *little* nesting material inside. Extra nesting material should not be supplied at times of year when one does not wish the birds to try to breed (Immelmann *et al.*, 1966).

NESTING Breeds semi-colonially; several or many pairs nesting within a small area but with only one nest in any one tree or bush and with about 20 to 50 metres distance between ground nests. The nest is built in a tree or bush or among grass or other vegetation on or near the ground. Tree nests are usually supported by a horizontal branch. Ground nests are often under a clump of grass and commonly near or beside a stump, log or fence post. Nests in holes in termite mounds have been recorded. The nest is rather large roundish or flattish-topped oval (or something between) structure with a rather large (30 to 50 mm) side entrance and the egg chamber big enough for a human fist to go inside. The nest is built of grass blades and stems and with finer grass and/or fine roots inside. There is no proper entrance tube but often a large platform in front of the entrance hole. The nest is lined with feathers, vegetable down, hair or other soft materials and pieces of charcoal, usually very many, are added. The eggs and the birds' bills are often stained blackish with charcoal. Both sexes carry material to the nest and build at all stages. Immelmann (1962, 1965) found that this species was very dilatory and slow in its nest building by comparison with its congeners and the same has been noticed in captive specimens (Iles). There are photographs of nests in Immelmann (1962) and Immelmann *et al.* (1966).

Eggs 4 to 6, commonly 5. Incubation period usually about 13 days but sometimes up to 16. Young fledge at about 22 days. Both sexes incubate and brood by day, usually for about 1·5 hours at a spell. The bird in the nest does not usually leave until after its mate has entered. True incubation begins on the day the fourth egg is laid. In very hot weather incubation stops and the bird leaves the nest. The adults of the colony all gather together several times daily to feed, drink, preen or socialise. At such times even nests with eggs or small nestlings are left unattended. For the first few days after fledging the parents lead the young back to the nest and feed them in it, and the young roost in the nest at night.

Breeding begins at the end of the rainy season, in March or April and continues to June. The Masked Grassfinch thus has a shorter breeding period than most other estrildids and usually raises (if successful) only one brood.

The above information is derived from Hill, Iles, Immelmann (1962 and 1965) and Immelmann *et al.*, 1966 and 1967).

VOICE The contact calls, the nest call and the aggressive hissing call are all very similar in sound to the corresponding calls of the Zebra Finch (q.v.). A high-pitched plaintive sound is uttered, in apparent fear, when a bird is chased by a conspecific or sees a predator. A long series of chattering calls (Immelmann, 1965), described by Zann (1975) as 'a rapid series of loud, high-pitched calls' are used in greeting at social gatherings. The song, which is given both in courtship and as undirected song, is similar to that of the Zebra Finch but the phrases are louder and clearer. There is considerable individual variation in song and, to some extent, in other calls also. Zann (1975) gives sound spectrograms of the calls (1975) and songs (1976a).

DISPLAY AND SOCIAL BEHAVIOUR This species has been intensively studied in the wild by Immelmann (1962 and 1965) from whom the information here is derived unless otherwise stated.

The courtship display is like that of the Zebra Finch (q.v.) except that the displaying male makes longer jumps and, immediately after copulating, flies back to his starting perch, repeats the display and copulates again. This process is repeated at least four times, unless the pair are disturbed. The up and down bobbing or 'inverted curtsey' is not normally performed by adult Masked Finches although occasionally (fide Zann, 1977) by young males. Courtship usually takes place among dead branches at or near the top of a tree.

Highly sociable. Even when breeding the members of the flock gather together several times daily, especially in the late afternoon. Arriving birds greet and are greeted with tail quivering, mandibulation and the characteristic calls (see 'Voice'). Usually two pairs start the social meeting and their calls appear to attract other members of the colony. At first each pair sits at a little distance from the others and indulges in allo-preening, but after a few minutes individuals approach members of other pairs and allo-preen with them; and there is frequent shifting about and changing of preening partners before the birds finally disperse in their original pairs.

It is noticeable that although the tail quivering in this context appears identical to that used by soliciting females, it does not often, if ever, elicit copulation attempts when used at the social gatherings. Under captive conditions, however, males often attempt copulation in comparable circumstances.

The bond between the members of a pair is very strong and in captivity it is often difficult to get birds to form pairs. No doubt this is often due, as is usually thought, to individual incompatibility of the birds concerned. Sometimes, however, it is probably due to the owner having unwisely kept young or unpaired adult birds with conspecifics of their own sex or other species of estrildids as their only companions with the (predictable) result that they have already formed firm homosexual or interspecific pair bonds by the time their owner decides to 'pair them up'.

OTHER NAMES Masked Finch, White-eared Grassfinch, White-eared Finch (the last two names apply only to the race *P.p. leucotis*).

REFERENCES
Hill, G. F. 1911. Field notes on the birds of Kimberley, North-West Australia. *Emu* 10: 258–290.
Iles, G. W. (no date) *Breeding Australian finches.* Isles d'Avon Ltd, Bristol.
Immelmann, K. 1962. Beitrage zu einer vergleichenden Biologie australischer Prachtfinken (Spermestidae). Zool. Jb. Sys. Bd. 90: 1–196.
Immelmann, K. 1965. *Australian finches in bush and aviary.* Angus & Robertson, Sydney.
Immelmann, K., Steinbacher, J. & Wolters, H. E. 1966 and 1967. *Vögel in Kafig und Voliere: Prachtfinken*: 154–171.
Storr, G. M. 1973. *List of Queensland birds.* Western Australian Museum Special Publication no. 5.
Zann, R. 1975. Inter- and intraspecific variation in the calls of three species of grassfinches of the subgenus *Poephila* (Gould) (Estrildidae). *Z. Tierpsychol.* 39: 85–125.
Zann, R. 1976a. Variation in the songs of three species of Estrildine grassfinches. *Emu* 76: 97–108.
Zann, R. 1976b. Inter- and intraspecific variation in courtship of three species of grassfinches of the subgenus *Poephila* (Gould) (Estrildidae). *Z. Tierpsychol.* 41: 409–433.

Zebra Finch   *Poephila guttata*

Fringilla guttata Vieillot, 1817, *Nouv. Dict. Hist. Nat.*, nouv. ed. 12, p. 233.

DESCRIPTION See plate 6, facing p. 225. Forehead, crown, nape, sides of hind neck dull silvery grey, with obscure darker central streaks to the feathers of crown and forehead. Mantle and back medium brownish grey; wing coverts and wing quills a little darker in shade but with paler fringes. Under wing coverts buffish. Median part of rump white, sides of rump black. The long upper tail coverts are broadly barred black and white, each having a white terminal band. The longest central pair of these reach to within about 3 mm of the tip of the tail so that, when the tail is folded, it appears to be barred black and white although the true tail feathers are uniform brownish black. A narrow black stripe runs along and downward from the base of the mandibles, nearly parallel to another that runs from below the middle of the eye, enclosing a white patch between them. These 'tear streaks' tend to give the bird a sorrowful expression, to the human eye. Cheeks, including ear coverts, light chestnut or brownish orange. Throat, upper breast and sides of breast finely barred black and silvery white or greyish white. A short black band divides the barred median part of the breast from the white or creamy white lower breast, belly and under tail coverts. Sides of lower breast and flanks chestnut, spotted with white 'twin spots' one on either side of the vane of each feather. Irides orange to bright red, sometimes brownish orange. Bill bright red, orange-red or bright orange. Legs and feet light orange, orange-pink, orange or flesh-coloured.

The female lacks the orange cheeks, barred breast and throat and spotted chestnut flanks of the male, having these parts light silvery grey to brownish grey. Her bill is usually a little paler than the male's. The juvenile is like the female but with a more brownish general tinge, the white on the upper tail coverts suffused with buff and a black bill. The nestling is at first flesh-coloured, later greyish on the upperparts, and has pale grey down (Hall, unpublished mss). Its mouth markings consist of a three spot pattern on the palate, with a crescentic mark below the outer spot on either side; a black crescent inside the lower mandible and two dark marks on the tongue. The swollen gape edges are at first bluish, later whitish with a narrow black line at the base of each mandible.

The above description is of *P. guttata castanotis*, of continental Australia. Nominate *P.g. guttata*, also shown in plate 6, facing p. 225, from Timor and other islands north of Australia, has the throat and breast pale grey with usually only faint indications of darker barring except at the lower periphery, on either side of the central black breast band. Its upperparts are darker brownish grey with less contrast between head and back.

The above descriptions are based on wild-taken specimens in the British Museum (Natural History) collections and on descriptions of genuine wild birds by Immelmann (1973) and others. The Australian form of the Zebra Finch has been domesticated and is bred in numbers in cages and aviaries in many parts of the world. Fawn, silver-grey, pied, white, yellow-billed and other colour varieties are regularly bred. All of them owe their (often striking) differences from the wild colour-pattern to the *loss* or partial loss of one or more of the pigments and/or markings possessed by normal wild birds. An apparent exception to this are the black or largely black varieties but these, or at least all of them that have been investigated (Immelmann, 1973) are merely cases of induced melanism through inadequate care. A form with a black breast and different tail and wing markings appears, however, to be a genuine mutation (Oppenborn). Immelmann has pointed out that very many of the so-called 'wild-type' domesticated Zebra Finches show minor differences from genuine wild birds, especially in the colour of the irides which are very frequently brown in the domestic forms.

FIELD CHARACTERS Small, noisy finch with nasal 'tin trumpet' or 'Punch and Judy' sounding call notes, red bill, 'tear streak' face pattern and short black and white banded tail (actually the long upper tail coverts). Usually highly gregarious and not like any other species in appearance.

DISTRIBUTION AND HABITAT Australia and the Lesser Sunda Islands of Lombok, Sumbawa, Flores, Alor, Sumba, Savu, Samau, Timor, Wetar, Letti, Kiser, Sermatta, Luang and Moa. Introduced to Kangaroo Island, off South Australia.

In Australia the Zebra Finch is found in many different, mostly fairly open habitats that provide a combination of grass seeds, bush or tree cover, and surface water. Probably originally a bird of those parts of the arid interior where water was present; its present wide range is in part due to man's provision of water in some dry areas and forest destruction in others. His introduction of such

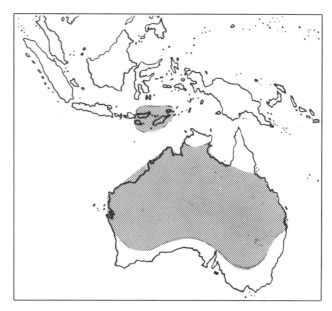

exotic food plants as Annual Meadow Grass, *Poa annua*, has also helped locally. Its present habitats include grassland with bushes and trees, savanna woodland, mulga scrub, spinifex country with some trees or bushes, saltbush flats, wood edge, cultivated and pastoral lands and around homesteads in the 'outback'. Has been recorded in forest country but probably only where man has made clearings or thinned out the trees. The above information is derived from Harrison [in Hall], Immelmann, 1962, 1965, 1973 and Serventy & Whittell.

FEEDING AND GENERAL HABITS Feeds mainly on seeds of grasses, but also takes the tips of growing grass shoots (and possibly other greenfood) and sometimes flying termites and other small insects. As usual, quantities of minerals are taken, especially by breeding birds. Immelmann (1962) observed them clinging to nearly vertical banks when thus engaged. In the Kimberleys, Immelmann (1962) found that seeds of *Iseilema* spp. were the main food in the dry season and those of *Panicum zymbirformae* in the rains. Other grasses whose seeds were eaten were *Chloris virgata*, *Arundinella nepalensis*, *Sporobolus australicus* and *Brachyachne convergens*. The seeds of *Kochia scleroptera* and some other dicotyledons were also taken. In south-western Australia, the seeds of the introduced Annual Meadow Grass are a staple food. Seeks food on the ground but will jump up to pull seeds from an ear of standing grass. Kunkel (1959) observed captive birds holding grass panicles and leaves underfoot but implied they did so less often than the typical waxbills, *Estrilda*, and the Bronze Mannikin. Immelmann (1962, p. 8) also recorded Zebra Finches, in the wild, holding grasses under foot while picking seeds from the pannicles but emphasized that only a few individual birds appeared to do this deliberately. Later, in slightly less minutely detailed works on the species (Immelmann, 1965, p. 138 and 1973, p. 10) he stated that the feet were not used to hold down grass stems. It would seem from this that at least some individuals, although probably not the majority, do at times hold objects underfoot.

Drinks in a pigeon-like manner (photo in Immelmann, 1973). Normally drinks several times a day and at all hours but can survive for a long time (up to 250 days in one instance) without water, as has been proved by unpleasant experiments (Cade *et al.*). This ability clearly increases the bird's chances of survival when, as sometimes happens under natural conditions, all the local sources of water dry up. Extremely fond of bathing, whenever it can find suitably shallow water.

Gregarious; in flocks when not breeding and even when breeding several or many pairs usually nest colonially or semi-colonially and 'off duty' birds spend much time with others. Subject to local movements, regularly to avoid enduring prolonged rainfall in the northernmost parts of its continental range and irregularly elsewhere to seek water and food in times of drought (Immelmann, 1973). Flight rapid and strong, sometimes straight or nearly so (pers. obs.) at others with slight undulations (Immelmann, 1962, 1965). Roosts in nests, either roughly-built roosting nests, old breeding nests or, less often, the old nests of other species.

In captivity, where it is now fully domesticated, it is easy to keep and breed. Immelmann (1973) states that it needs, besides the usual millet and canary seed, regular supplies of half-ripe seeding Annual Meadow Grass, Rye Grass, Shepherd's Purse, Groundsel, Dandelion and Knotgrass, when these are not available, soaked spray millet must be given daily, vitamin drops added to the water once or twice a week and cod liver oil to the food. Also that, when breeding, eggfood and/or ant pupae are essential and high mortality and low breeding success will result from a less generous regime. However, at least in Britain and Australia, Zebra Finches that have been given nothing but dry millet and canary seed and ample supplies of seeding chickweed and/or Annual Meadow Grass (and the usual minerals) with or without the addition of a little milk sop, have been bred for many successive generations (Boosey, Restall, Rogers). Miss Lexie Nicholls, who, together with her colleagues, has bred large numbers of Zebra Finches for many years in south-western Australia, informs me that their birds are fed on panicum millet, with the addition only of lettuce and seeding grasses four or five times a week, minerals, and a weekly vitamin supplement added to the water.

Immelmann (1973) recommends that Zebra Finches should not be kept at a temperature of less than 6°C when not breeding and 12°C when breeding. There are, however, many records of the species enduring lower temperatures without apparent harm. In one instance, Zebra Finches kept at full liberty in Germany, not only survived a winter during which temperatures were often well below freezing point, but actually nested and reared young, from nests built in evergreens, in December and January (Abele).

In captivity Zebra Finches, if adequately cared for even by English or Australian avicultural standards, still more

if they are cared for as in Germany, usually breed continually. It is believed alike by scientists and 'common or garden' bird-keepers that this results in a serious weakening both of the parents and the young they produce. This may be correct, though I have read of no experimental proof of it. In any case, whether the Zebra Finches suffer or not, their owner is likely to do so from the Malthusian problem that their human-like fecundity presents. Many Zebra Finch keepers solve the problem either by separating the sexes of their birds, after they have reared two or three broods, or by removing all possible nest sites and nesting materials from their enclosure. The first of these has the disadvantage that, if they are in sound of their absent mates, a good deal of mental stress is caused to the birds. The second is also stressful as the birds are forced to roost on exposed perches and, if they are in an aviary, is not easy to accomplish in any case. In my opinion the best way of solving the problem is that of Knoblauch, who lets his birds sit on sterilised eggs. Each pair will then incubate for three or four weeks before deserting and beginning to build again. This appears to be quite satisfactory so far as keeping the birds in health is concerned and they are happier under such a regime. Knoblauch evidently saved up infertile eggs but if fresh eggs were placed in warm water and gently (else they will burst) brought nearly to the boil, they would probably be suitable 'pot eggs'. I have successfully so treated eggs of cordon-bleus and Canaries for this purpose.

NESTING The nest is most often placed in a bush, shrub or small tree; thorny or prickly species being preferred. Usually only one nest is sited in any one bush or tree but sometimes two or several may be. This usually comes about, in spite of the fact that the males of breeding pairs vigorously defend the immediate area around the nest, because of shortage of alternate sites. This leads intruding pairs to persistent attempts which 'wear down' the male's aggressive response. A second pair (and later others) may establish themselves in the absence of the first pair so that, by the time the latter return, the 'trespassing' pair also feel 'in the right' and fight back when attempts are made to drive them away (Immelmann, 1962). Nests may also be sited in hollow stumps, holes in trees or banks, among the outer sticks of the nest of some large bird-of-prey, in a clump of grass or in some nook or niche of a building. Roosting nests (though not usually the one that the pair are actually using when they begin nesting), old breeding nests and, less often, nests of other species, may be renovated or a new nest built on their remains.

The nest is usually roundish, with a short entrance tube. There is much individual variation in size and shape of the nest and the entrance tube may be missing, as it is with the more roughly built roosting nests. Although the greatest variations seen between different wild nests are most likely due to their different situations and differences in available nest material, some appear to be due to differences of building behaviour. Knoblauch found, with his captive birds, that although all had similar sites and materials, there were recognisable and constant differences between the nests of different pairs, each pair always building the same individually recognisable type of nest.

Grass stems are usually the main nesting material in the wild but in default of them rootlets, small twigs and almost any possible material may be used. The nest is lined with feathers, vegetable down, softer grasses, wool or other soft material. Grass stems are carried singly by one end but softer materials are 'bundled'. Sheeps' wool is very often used but sometimes causes the loss of the brood. If it rains the wool absorbs and retains water to a very much greater extent than do natural materials, with the result that eggs or young are fatally soaked or chilled (Immelmann, 1962). Nesting material is usually sought on the ground but may also be taken from the nests of conspecifics or other species.

Usually the male finds and brings nearly all of the material and does most of the building; the female at most helping to build with what he has brought and occasionally bringing some material for the nest lining. Sometimes the female also collects material and Immelmann (1962, 1973) found this was usual in some arid areas in central Australia and enabled nests to be more quickly built, an adaptation for breeding where suitable conditions were likely to last only a short time.

Eggs 3 to 8, usually 4 to 6. Larger numbers of eggs have been found in one nest but almost certainly represent the clutches of more than one hen. Both sexes incubate in turn by day. The male roosts (with the female) in the nest at night. Immelmann (1962) found that incubating wild birds left the nest as soon as they heard the calls of their returning mate nearby, but in captivity (and probably sometimes in the wild too) the sitting bird usually waits for its mate to enter the nest before it leaves (Knoblauch). Sitting birds often leave the nest of their own volition to visit the flock for a short period. If the temperature rises above 38°C incubation ceases and the eggs are left uncovered by day (Immelmann, 1962, 1973). In captivity (and perhaps in the wild also) a bird that sees its mate away from the nest will usually go at once and take over on the eggs or nestlings 'out of turn' (Knoblauch).

Incubation period 11·25 days when artificially incubated at a constant temperature of 38·6°C but from 12·5 to 16 days, or occasionally even longer, in the wild (Immelmann, 1962). Incubation proper usually starts with the third or fourth egg (Immelmann, 1962, Knoblauch, Kunkel). Young usually fledge on the morning of the twenty-second day but for the next few days are led back into the nest to be fed, and to roost in the evening. Parents and young recognise one another. Strange young of similar age and appearance are not fed. Knoblauch experimentally arranged that 7 broods of Zebra Finches fledged at the same time in his birdroom; all the parents recognised their own young and fed them only. Knoblauch found that if newly-fledged young are adopted by other birds, their parents react by ceasing to feed them and concentrate on their next nest. I have observed identical

behaviour from Red-cheeked and Blue-headed Cordonbleus in like circumstances.

Breeding takes place whenever conditions are suitable and is strongly influenced by rainfall. In the arid parts of central Australia the species starts to breed as soon as there has been some rain and is thus able to take advantage of the temporarily increased supplies of food that result from it. In northern Australia, where rainfall is fairly regular, this results in a regular breeding season from about October to April. In south-western Australia rain is restricted to the winter months which are, however, largely too cold to permit successful breeding and there the Zebra Finch breeds twice a year, in spring when there is still some rain, and food supplies resulting from the winter rains; and in autumn when the first rains begin but while the temperature is still warm. In eastern Australia breeding periods seem similar to those in the south west. In an irrigated area in New South Wales breeding occurred in all except the coldest month, July. Even in areas where rainfall and Zebra Finch breeding times are usually regular, abnormal weather has an appropriate effect on the bird's breeding behaviour. The above paragraph is derived from Immelmann (1965).

It was formerly thought (Immelmann, 1973) that wild Zebra Finches, unlike domesticated ones, would not rear nestlings of other species. However, further experiments (Immelmann *et al.*, 1977) showed this was not so. Wild caught birds not only reared young Bengalese perfectly but also, in one instance a mixed brood of Bengalese and their own young. Experiments with (deliberately) mixed broods of both white and wild-coloured Zebra Finches have shown that both white and wild-coloured birds feed the white nestlings less eagerly, giving the coloured young priority. This is presumed to be because the white nestlings lack the normal mouth markings (Immelmann *et al.*, 1977). Doubtless this is the main reason for the parents' discrimination but, unless it is certain that equally hungry white and coloured nestlings beg with equal vigour, it might not be the only one.

VOICE The contact call is a loud, nasal-sounding 't'ya' (the 'a' as in 'have'), 'teea', 'tcheea!' or similar, subject to much minor variation. It strongly suggests the sound of a child's toy trumpet or the 'Punch and Judy' voice tone and becomes, after a little while, irritating to many human ears. Its tone is astonishingly like that of a larger and quite unrelated sympatric species, the White-browed Babbler, *Pomatostomus superciliosus*. At times when I was in the 'bush' of South Australia and Western Australia, I mistook the sound of nearby Zebra Finches for more distant White-browed Babblers or *vice versa*. It is given at varying intensities, often in a series of calls and more loudly by the male than by the female. A very high-pitched sad-sounding variant is used as an alarm call when near the nest.

The close contact call is shorter and softer but otherwise rather similar. Immelmann transcribes it as 'tet' or 'det'. The nest call has been described as 'a curious cosy little murmuring noise ... quite impossible to describe' (Boosey), and as suggestive of the distant, high-pitched whimpering of a small child (Immelmann, 1973). During copulation both sexes utter a series of notes with a 'squeezing' ('gequetschte') tone (Immelmann, 1973). A rasping note, like the rapid tearing of a piece of cotton cloth, is often uttered just before attacking another bird (Immelmann, 1973, Morris).

The song is a short repeated strophe of calls like the contact call, interspersed with softer trills or ventriloquial notes. It is individually variable. Immelmann (1969b) found that the songs of ten wild males caught in the Northern Territory all varied and showed as much difference from each other as they did from the songs of three males caught in Western Australia. Song is given both in courtship and as undirected song. It is very frequently uttered and even given by moulting birds. Immelmann (1973) noted that the output of song, as of contact calls, increased with the increasing size of the flock. Immelmann, whose paper (which contains many sound spectrograms of songs) should be read by any serious student of song in this species, found that the basic outline of the song, as a sequence of syllables with a certain approximate duration is innate. This template is completed or, if the bird has been reared by another species, covered over by a song template which is learned during the early part of the bird's juvenile life. The young Zebra Finch has a strong tendency to imitate only the songs of individuals with whom he has a strong personal bond; under natural conditions this means, of course, that he tends to mimic his father's song.

DISPLAY AND SOCIAL BEHAVIOUR The courtship display has been described in detail by Immelmann (1962 and 1973), Kunkel (1959 and unpublished mss) and Morris (1954). Usually courtship is prefaced by the cock and hen hopping to and fro with angled tails and frequent actual or symbolic bill wiping. Then the female shows her willingness to proceed further by remaining still and the male hops towards her with triangular head, angled tail and the feathers of neck, cheeks, breast and flanks fluffed out somewhat and those of the belly fully erected. He holds his bill more or less horizontal and repeats his song strophe. If on a straight perch he approaches the female by a series of pivoting jumps through 180 degrees but if he is in a bush or on the ground he hops in a circle or half circle around her, coming nearer and nearer, making frequent bowing movements and ritual bill-wipes, with head and angled tail turned towards the female. He tends to hop during the softer notes of his song and to pause while uttering the louder ones. If the female is ready to mate she solicits with the usual crouching and tail quivering and the male mounts and copulates. Immediately after copulation the male often or usually adopts the female soliciting posture with trembling tail; usually his mate does not show any positive reaction to this (Immelmann, 1962). Morris (1954) observed this display given (frequently) by males when apparently sexually thwarted and hen birds

respond to it by mounting the male and performing male-type copulatory movements.

Zebra Finches appear to prefer the bare branches of dead bushes or fallen trees as display sites and the same site may be used by many different pairs who (at different times) deliberately visit it to indulge in courtship display (Immelmann, 1962, 1973). Courtship may, however, take place on the ground or elsewhere. Sometimes the male may initially hold nesting material in his bill but this is always dropped before he begins the courtship dance.

The female often greets the male by flying to him and alighting beside him in a crouching posture with angled tail. The male responds with courtship display, nest calling or allo-preening.

When seeking a nest site the male (and sometimes also the female) hops about, pivots or turns round in the selected site, in a horizontal posture, with tail spread, mandibulating and uttering the nest call. At very high intensities the wings may be somewhat drooped but held still within the flank feathers so the latter are pushed out from the body, and a more rasping call may be uttered. Morris (1958) found that, with numbers of Zebra Finches kept together in an aviary, this display might be directed towards the mate without any apparent immediate reference to a potential nest site. He also saw it used often by a female towards her mate, when he was beginning to lose interest in her and/or show interest in another female. In this situation it was interspersed with attacks on the other female. Immelmann, in a comment on Hall's unpublished manuscript, stressed that he had only seen this display used in connection with nest-calling and by paired birds. I have, however, myself seen what are in their usual context nest demonstration displays used by some species – including the Goldbreast, *Amandava, subflava* – by a bird that was being treated coldly by one that it was courting or considered itself paired to. I do not, however, concur with Morris' idea that this display may derive from the sun-bathing pattern.

Young beg for food with the usual crouched, neck twisted posture. Morris (1954) observed adults perform it as an apparent submissive display or, perhaps, 'thwarted hostility' display might better express the motivation. It was given by a female in response to attack from a male, and (repeatedly) by a male towards a rival male when the latter showed interest in its (the displaying bird's) mate. It is, I think, significant that the male that displayed in this manner appeared to be in poor condition and that its mate shortly deserted it and paired with the rival.

Clumping and allo-preening are habitual but usually restricted to the mate, dependent young or, by young birds, to siblings. The pair bond is very strong and individual pairs keep together even within large non-breeding flocks. Mandibulation occurs in many agonistic and sexual situations of the usual kind. Ritualised or 'displacement' bill wiping is common.

Differences of behaviour between wild and domesticated Zebra Finches have been recorded, mainly involving some degree of hyper-sexuality and loss of selectivity in the latter. However, some of the recorded differences have, and others may have, been wholly or in part due to environmental conditions. Knoblauch found that, when kept in spacious quarters, the behaviour of domesticated Zebra Finches was in most respects identical to that of wild ones and such differences as were shown might be, and probably were, due to their confinement. Morris (1958) also found no differences between the behaviour of wild-caught and domesticated Zebra Finches kept under the same conditions.

A great deal of work on imprinting in this species has been done by Immelmann and his colleagues (see esp. Immelmann, 1969a and 1973, and Immelmann *et al.*, 1978). Only the more salient facts can be summarised briefly here: Male Zebra Finches imprint firmly on their parents or foster parents, when the latter are Zebra Finches of a different colour or Bengalese Finches. Nest mates have no effect on imprinting. Males of a whole brood reared together by Bengalese, in an aviary full of Zebra Finches, imprint firmly on the Bengalese. If, however, such fostered young are removed from their foster parents well before they are 50 days old and then kept for at least a week together with numbers of adult Zebra Finches and out of sight and sound of Bengalese Finches, the imprinting is reversed and they behave normally in adult life. If they are left with their foster parents 50 days or more the imprinting is irreversible.

When the foster parent is a human, Zebra Finches *will* imprint on their siblings not on the fosterer. Only young that are reared *singly* by hand become imprinted on humans.

Female Zebra Finches also imprint under comparable conditions but apparently not so completely as do males (Sonnemann and Sjölander). Experiments with Zebra Finches reared by (foster) parents, one of which was a white Zebra Finch and the other a normally (wild) coloured individual, showed that males prefer to pair with a female of their mother's colour and females with a male of their father's colour. This is irrespective of which sex is normally coloured and of the colour of the young themselves (K. Immelmann, pers. comm., Dec. 1979).

OTHER NAMES Chestnut-eared Finch; sometimes locally called 'Waxbill' in Australia.

REFERENCES
Abele, J. 1978. Zebrafinken im Freiflug. *Gefiederte Welt* **1978**: 6.
Boosey, E. 1952. The Zebra Finch and its colour varieties. *Avicult. Mag.* **58**: 29–31.
Cade, T., Tobin, C. A. & Gold, A. 1965. Water economy and metabolism of two estrildid finches. *Physiol. Zool.* **38**: 9–33.
Hall, B. P. 1974. *Birds of the Harold Hall Australian Expeditions.* British Museum (Natural History), London.
Immelmann, K. 1962. Beiträge zu einer vergleichenden Biologie australischer Prachtfinken (Spermestidae). *Zool. Jb. Syst. Bd.* **90**: 1–96.
Immelmann, K. 1965. *Australian finches in bush and aviary.* Sydney and London.
Immelmann, K. 1969a. Uber den Einfluss frühkindlicher
Erfahrungen auf die geschlechtlicher Objektfixierung bei Estrildiden. *Z. Tierpsychol.* **26**: 677–691.
Immelmann, K. 1969b. Song development in the Zebra Finch and other estrildid finches. In *Bird vocalisations*, edited by R. A. Hinde and published by Cambridge University Press, England.
Immelmann, K. 1970. Lernen durch Prägung. *Naturwissenschaft und Medizin 7*, **31**: 15–29.
Immelmann, K. 1973. *Der Zebrafink.* A. Ziemsen Verlag, Wittenberg.
Immelmann, K., Piltz, A. & Sossinka, R. 1977. Experimentale Untersuchungen zur Bedeutung der Rachenzeichnung junger Zebrafinken. *Z. Tierpsychol.* **45**: 210–218.
Immelmann, K., Kalberlah, H., Rausch, P. & Stahnke, A. 1978. Sexuelle Prägung als möglicher Faktor innerartlicher Isolation beim Zebrafinken. *J. Orn.* **119**: 197–212.
Knoblauch, D. 1978. Verhaltensweisen von Zebrafinken als Stubevögel im Vergleich zu wildlebenden Zebrafinken. *Gefiederte Welt* **1978**: 227–231.
Kunkel, P. 1959. Zum Verhalten einiger Prachtfinken. *Z. Tierpsychol.* **16**: 302–350.
Morris, D. 1954. The reproductive behaviour of the Zebra Finch (*Poephila guttata*) with special reference to pseudofemale behaviour and displacement activities. *Behaviour* **6**: 273–322.
Morris, D. 1958. The comparative ethology of grassfinches (Erythrurae) and mannikins (Amadinae). *Proc. Zool. Soc. London* **131**: 389–439.
Oppenborn, E. 1971. Neumutation Schwarzbrust-Zebrafinken. *Gefiederte Welt* **1971**: 227–230.
Restall, R. L. 1975. *Finches and other seed-eating birds.* Faber & Faber, London.
Rogers, C. H. 1964. *Zebra Finches.* Iliffe Books, London.
Serventy, D. L. & Whittell, H. M. 1967. *Birds of Western Australia.* Perth.
Sonnemann, P. & Sjölander, S. 1977. Effects of cross-fostering on the sexual imprinting of the female Zebra Finch *Taeniopgygia guttata. Z. Tierpsychol.* **45**: 337–348.

Bicheno Finch   *Poephila bichenovii*

Fringilla bichenovii Vigors and Horsfield, 1827, *Trans. Linn. Soc. London* **15**, p. 253.

DESCRIPTION About size of Zebra Finch but with longer and somewhat graduated tail, shorter upper tail coverts and rather small bill. Although it possesses no bright colours this bird's shapeliness and its unusually delicate and pleasing patterns give it a beauty surpassing that of most Australian estrildids and comparable with the choicer African forms. Forehead black. Crown dull brown to reddish brown, with faint fine darker cross-barring, shading to light greyish brown to silvery grey, with more pronounced fine darker cross barring, on hind neck, mantle, back and lesser wing coverts. Most of wing black, delicately spotted with white on all parts of feathers that show when the wing is folded, except the ends of the outer primaries. Under wing coverts creamy buff. A black band across the lower back. Rump white, long feathers from the centre of the rump come down over the black upper tail coverts, so the latter appear white. Tail brownish black. Face, including area above eyes and ear coverts, silvery white, encircled by a narrow black band running from the forehead, around the cheeks and across to divide throat and breast. Breast creamy white, pale cream or greyish white, sharply divided by another narrow black band across the lower breast from the similarly coloured underparts. Under tail coverts black. Bill greyish blue, steel blue or bluish grey, darkest on top of the culmen. Irides dark brown. Legs and feet greyish blue to dark grey. There is an excellent colour photograph in Hindwood.

The female perhaps averages a little smaller, usually has slightly narrower breast bands and (*fide* Steiner, in Immelmann *et al.*, 1966) is a less pure white around the eyes. The juvenile is browner above, with less pronounced markings; those of the wings being buffish or dull white and more bars than spots. Breast bands although less emphatic are present from fledging time (Williams). Mouth markings of nestling very like those of Zebra Finch but with the upper three palate spots elongated and the lower joined by an arching black line. Suggestive of the palate pattern of the African mannikins.

The above description is of nominate *P.b. bichenovii*, from the greater part of the species' range. *P.b. annulosa*, from Northern Territory and Groote Eylandt, has the rump entirely black. Young of a captive brood of this race (unlike young of the typical race bred by the same aviculturist) lacked the breast bands at fledging time, having only an indication of the upper band, at the sides (Williams).

There is a (racial) hybrid population in eastern Northern Territory, south-west of the Gulf of Carpentaria. When pure *P.b. bichenovii* and *P.b. annulosa* are crossed in captivity, the first generation young all have white rumps, regardless of the sex of their white-rumped parent (Boosey, Immelmann *et al.*, 1976).

See plate 2, facing p. 97).

FIELD CHARACTERS Small finch with pale greyish brown upperparts except for white (or black in Northern Territory) rump and black tail. *Entirely white, black encircled face and whitish underparts, crossed by two narrow black bands above and below breast, diagnostic.* Only bird with similar marking is the Banded Whiteface, which has a single black breast band and reddish sandy upperparts.

DISTRIBUTION AND HABITAT Northern and eastern Australia. North-western Australia west to Roebuck Bay; the northern third (approximately) of Northern Territory; Groote Eylandt and the islands of the Sir Edward Pellew Group; Cape York Peninsula and coastal Queensland south to northern New South Wales. See Storr (1973 and 1977) for details of distribution in Queensland and Northern Territory. In Queensland (Storr, 1973) it is common and widespread in the semi-arid and sub-humid zones but patchily distributed and only locally common in the humid zone.

Inhabits areas with Pandanus and long grass near water, dry plains with bushes or small trees, open woodland and forest edge. Often abundant in inhabited areas, around homesteads, at the edges of sugarcane fields and in parks and gardens. It has, however, in recent years disappeared from some inhabited parts of northern

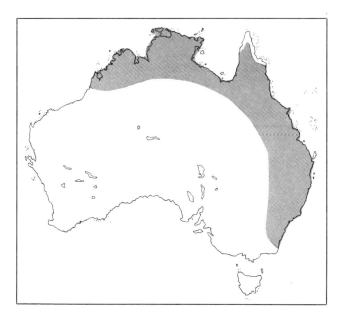

Queensland where it was formerly plentiful, probably as a result of competition from the introduced Spice Finch (Immelmann, 1965).

FEEDING AND GENERAL HABITS Feeds mainly on the ground, picking up fallen seeds and also often jumping up to pull seeds from growing plants. Takes seeds of both grasses and other plants; Immelmann (1962) listed the following food plants for it: *Chloris virgata*, *Cenchrus setigerus*, *Sehima nervosum*, *Digitaria* sp., *Setaria cornei*, *Brachiara reptans*, *Panicum zymbirformae* and *Euphorbia alsinaeflorae*. Probably also takes small insects in the wild as it does in captivity. Drinks in pigeon-like manner.

Highly social; usually in parties of up to about 20 birds but in dry seasons sometimes in large flocks. Spends much time on or near the ground. Flight appears rather weak and the bird usually flies from bush to bush and avoids long flights in the open. Roosts either in small, unlined roosting nests built for the purpose, or in old breeding nests of its own or other species. Sometimes several individuals roost in one nest (Immelmann, 1962, 1965).

In captivity usually tame, peaceable towards both its own and other species and often breeds fairly freely. It is, however, sensitive to cold, especially damp cold and although it has been safely kept in outside aviaries in summer in southern England (Boosey) this was in a sheltered, south-facing valley (at Keston in Kent) and in a period of rather warm summers. Immelmann *et al.* (1966) state firmly that it should not be allowed outside except temporarily on exceptionally warm days and should never be kept at a temperature of less than 20 to 22°C. For newly imported birds they recommend 28 to 30°C as a minimum temperature. In captivity some have successfully kept it on panicum and white millet, small canary seed and greenstuff, especially seeding chickweed with the addition of insect food such as greenfly and ant pupae when the birds have young. Immelmann *et al.* recommend, however, that in addition to the above, soaked seed and insect food should be provided at all times.

NESTING Nests most often in bushes or trees, especially in the peripheral branches. Shows a preference for dense, thorny or prickly species. Also in creepers, the old nests of babblers and other species and holes or niches in trees, posts or buildings. Several pairs often breed peaceably close to each other. Hindwood instances a case of 20 nests, at least 7 of which contained eggs in process of incubation, in a creeper growing over a dead stump; and another of 9 occupied nests in one citrus tree. The nest is roundish or oval, small and rather frail, with a side entrance which may or may not have a short entrance tube about 5 cm long. It is made of the stems of grasses and/or other plants, with finer grass and grass panicles.

Immelmann and others (in Immelmann, 1962) have found a most interesting geographical and/or racial difference: eastern populations habitually line their nests with feathers, those in northern and north-western Australia do not. At 22 unlined northern nests Immelmann experimented by placing many suitable feathers conspicuously near the nests. None of the feathers were used by the birds although if feathers were actually placed *in* the nest entrance they were then carried into the egg chamber. This was in very strong contrast to the behaviour of nesting birds of the nominate form in eastern Australia which searched widely for feathers and brought them back from a distance.

Eggs 3 to 6, usually 4 or 5. Both sexes incubate and brood in turn by day, both roost together in the nest at night. This species incubates for longer spells at a time than most estrildids, the average period per bird on the nest being nearly two hours. Young fledge at 22 days. When begging, fledglings raise one or both wings like young Avadavats (q.v.). While in the nest the young beg intensely and they adopt the characteristic estrildid begging posture when only a day old instead of only when several days like most species (Immelmann, 1962). Immelmann's observations led him to the conclusion that the parental feeding urge is relatively weak in this species and that this is compensated for by the intense begging of the young.

In northern Australia breeds mostly during the second half of the wet season but sometimes later. In eastern Australia breeds mainly in spring and autumn but nests have been found almost throughout the year (Immelmann, 1962, Hindwood).

VOICE Calls of this species are very like those of the Zebra Finch and the grass finches but higher-pitched and more plaintive in sound. The close contact call is transcribed by Immelmann (1965) as 'tat, tat' ('a' as in 'have') and the distance contact call as 'tiaat tiaat'; the latter call Morris writes as 'a plaintive twoooo-twoooo'. The nest call is very like that of the Zebra Finch (Immelmann, 1962). The song is similar to those of the Zebra Finch and Masked Finch. A sound spectrogram of the song, and that of a Zebra Finch, are given in Hall.

DISPLAY AND SOCIAL BEHAVIOUR The courtship display has been described by Morris, whose description was confirmed by Immelmann (1962) by observations on wild birds. If at a little distance the male approaches the female by a series of hops in which he tends to turn his body through an arc of about 180 degrees at each jump. He fluffs out all his body plumage so that he appears rounded in shape but with no differential degree of erection of feathers of different parts as in most other species. In a crouched posture, parallel to the hen and with his head twisted towards her, he sings and performs frequent beak-wipes. Displacement or ritualised bill wiping is also seen in other social contexts.

Highly social and usually peaceable. Allo-preening and clumping occur habitually between flock members as well as between male and female of a pair. The pair bond is very strong, the two birds keeping and roosting together throughout the year.

OTHER NAMES Double-bar Finch, Owl-finch, Banded Finch, Ringed Finch.

REFERENCES
Boosey, E. J. 1962. *Foreign bird keeping.* Iliffe Books, London.
Hall, M. F. 1962. Evolutionary aspects of estrildid song. *Symposia Zool. Soc. London* **8**: 37–55.
Hindwood, K. 1966. *Australian birds in colour.* A. H. & A. W. Reed, Sydney.
Immelmann, K. 1962. Beiträge zu einer vergleichender Biologie australischer Prachtfinken (Spermestidae). *Zool. Jb. Syst. Bd.* **90**: 1–96.
Immelmann, K. 1965. *Australian finches in bush and aviary.* Sydney.
Immelmann, K., Steinbacher, J. & Wolters, H. E. 1966 and 1976. *Vögel in Käfig und Voliere: Prachtfinken*: 86–97 and 574.
Morris, D. 1958. The comparative ethology of grassfinches (Erythrurae) and mannikins (Amadinae). *Proc. Zool. Soc. London* **131**: 389–439.
Storr, G. M. 1973. *List of Queensland birds.* Western Australian Museum special publication no. 5.
Storr, G. M. 1977. *Birds of the Northern Territory.* Western Australian Museum special publication no. 7.
Williams, H. 1902. Breeding of the Ringed Finch. *Avicult. Mag.* **8**: 264–266.

The parrot-finches

The parrot-finches, genus *Erythrura*, are a group of estrildids characterised by their predominantly green or green and blue plumage and the luminous blue gape tubercles of their nestlings. They are found from the Indo-Malayan region south and east to the Philippines, New Guinea, the Samoan and Fijian Islands, New Caledonia and north-eastern Australia. All but one species have the rump and central tail feathers red and many have red on their heads also. Some are thickset and short-tailed, others more shapely and in one, *E. prasina*, the male has a long pointed tail. Sexual dichromatism is very marked in a few forms, slight or virtually absent in others. They have recently been the subject of a detailed monograph (Ziswiler *et al.*, 1972). This work should be read in full by all who are particularly interested in this group or concerned with their anatomy.

All are, or originally were, birds of forested areas or their immediate vicinity but some have thrived as a result of man's activities and use cultivated and pasture land created by him. They seem to have had to cope in some places with competition from the numerous and successful sympatric mannikins, *Lonchura*, and elsewhere with what was originally grassless woodland. As a result some of them have departed wholly or in part from the typical estrildid grass seed staple diet and feed largely or mainly on the seeds of dicotyledenous plants, seeds taken from the insides of wild figs, and bamboo seed.

They are probably the most distinct group of estrildids and their affinities are uncertain. They share some characters with the Gouldian Finch (q.v.) and, as the Gouldian Finch also shares others with some *Lonchura* species, it seems likely that, as Ziswiler *et al.* suggest, all three groups derived from a common ancestor subsequent to its separation from other estrildids. Ziswiler *et al.* divide the genus into five subgenera: *Erythrura* (*E. prasina*, *E. viridifacies* and *E. tricolour*) *Reichenowia* (*E. hyperythra*), *Trichroa* (*E. trichroa*, *E. papuana* and *E. coloria*), *Alacanthe* (*E. psittacea*, *E. pealii* and *E. cyanovirens*) and *Ramphostruthus* (*E. kleinschmidti*). Mayr (in *Peters' Check List*) recognises the above subgenera except for *Trichroa*, which he includes in *Erythrura*. With the possible exception of *Alacanthe* and *Ramphostruthus*, as above defined, and an enlarged *Erythrura* for the rest, I prefer not to recognise subgenera within *Erythrura*. I am not competent to assess the anatomical criteria discussed by Ziswiler *et al.* but all other characters would seem to warrant treating the related forms as members of species-groups.

The Green-tailed Parrot-finch, *E. hyperythra*, has a rather scattered range in Borneo, the Philippines, Celebes, Malay Peninsula, Java and the Lesser Sunda Islands. It is mainly a bird of mountain forest where, so far as is known, it specialises in feeding on bamboo seeds. It overlaps geographically with the Pin-tailed Parrot-finch, *E. prasina* and the Green-faced Parrot-finch, *E. viridifacies* but appears to be ecologically and altitudinally separated from them. On its taxonomic and behavioural characters it seems, although a rather distinct species as parrot-finches go, likely to be most closely related to *E. prasina* and *E. viridifacies*.

The Pin-tailed Parrot-finch and the smaller, more simply-patterned Green-faced Parrot-finch are allopatric and may well be members of a superspecies as Ziswiler *et al.* suggest. In appearance, however, *E. viridifacies* is at least as close to *E. hyperythra* as to *E. prasina* and may well be as closely related to it. Both occur in Luzon but apparently are ecologically and altitudinally separated, at least they have not (yet) been found in the same places.

The Three-coloured or Blue-breasted Parrot-finch, *E. tricolor*, is the only species of *Erythrura* found in Timor and the Tenimber Islands. Ziswiler *et al.* are undecided (see

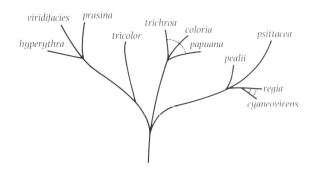

Probable relationships of the parrot-finches, *Erythrura*. The affinities of *E. tricolor* are questionable. See text for details.

pp. 110–112 of their monograph) whether it should be linked most closely with *E. prasina* and *E. viridifacies* or as a modern representative of some ancestral form. Mayr suggests that it probably forms a superspecies together with *E. coloria* and *E. trichroa*. Nothing is known of its behaviour or ecology. Its colour pattern is marginally nearest to that of the Blue-faced Parrot-finch, *E. trichroa* but could easily be a simplified derivation of such a pattern as that of *E. prasina*. I am inclined to think that it may prove closest to *E. prasina* and *E. viridifacies* but on present evidence, or rather lack of it, feel that it is best not formally linked with any other species.

The widely-distributed Blue-faced Parrot-finch, *E. trichroa*, and the Mindanao Parrot-finch, *E. coloria*, are best treated as members of a superspecies. I concur with Ziswiler *et al.* in including the Papuan Parrot-finch, *E. papuana*, in the same superspecies. *E. papuana* is extremely similar to and obviously fairly recently derived from *E. trichroa* or some recent common ancestral stock. Both it and *E. trichroa*, occur in New Guinea but they appear to be mainly allopatric there (Diamond). In at least one of the two areas where both have been found they are altitudinally separated and there is no evidence of their breeding in the same localities.

The next group consists of the forms commonly placed in the subgenus *Alacanthe*. They have bills whose construction enables them to de-husk dicotyledenous seeds with a cutting action like that of the true finches (Ziswiler *et al.*) and all of them have their heads largely or entirely red in colour.

The Red-headed Parrot-finch, *E. psittacea*, of New Caledonia is considered by Ziswiler *et al.* (pp. 114 and 115 of their monograph) to be nearest to the ancestral stock of the group. If so, it has now probably diverged appreciably from the prototype as it is a very distinct species and the only parrot-finch, except the relatively distantly-related *E. viridifacies*, that normally has no blue anywhere in its plumage.

Peale's Parrot-finch, *E. pealii*, from Fiji, has usually been treated as conspecific with the Royal Parrot-finch, *E. cyaneovirens*. I concur, however, with Ziswiler *et al.* in thinking it is better treated as a species. In habits and ecology it seems to be somewhat intermediate between *E. cyaneovirens* and *E. psittacea* but on the whole nearer to the former. In appearance it is also somewhat intermediate although closer to *E. cyaneovirens*.

The Royal Parrot-finch, *E. cyaneovirens*, embraces two geographically separated populations; the *regia* group in the New Hebrides and the *cyaneovirens* group from Samoa. The former are more markedly divergent from *E. pealii* and have become more highly specialised fig seed eaters, possibly because they co-exist with *E. trichroa* which may have competed with them for other food resources.

Immelmann *et al.* give both *regia* and *cyaneovirens* specific rank on distributional grounds, because geographically they are widely separated and *pealii* comes between them. I do not see the force of this argument. It is quite possible, as Ziswiler *et al.* suggest (p. 118 and diagram on p. 114 of their monograph) that the New Hebrides may have been colonised *from* the Samoan islands subsequent to Samoa being colonised from the Fiji Islands. In any case, although all three are clearly geographical representatives, the populations of the Samoan and Fijian islands resemble each other more closely than either resembles *E. pealii* and it seems to me best to reflect this in their nomenclatorial status.

The Pink-billed Parrot-finch, *E. kleinschmidti*, is a very distinct form, known only from Viti Levu, in the Fiji Islands. It is very similar in coloration and plumage pattern to *E. trichroa* and that its large pink bill makes it appear unusual is perhaps a reflection less on its divergence than on the considerable homogeneity within the genus. It may, as Ziswiler *et al.* suggest, represent an earlier group of *Erythrura* forms which have elsewhere succumbed in the face of competition from more recent *Erythrura* species and/or fruit doves. On the other hand it might, I think, equally well be representative of *tichroa* or proto-*trichroa* stock which has diverged in isolation.

Some of the islands colonised by *Erythrura* had no other estrildids living on them prior to their recent invasion by Europeans and Asiatics. Now, however, a variety of the more easily-kept exotic estrildids have been introduced to many of them by man. It is to be feared that competition with introduced species and the destruction of native vegetation by forestry interests may prove a serious long-term threat to some of the parrot-finches.

REFERENCES
Diamond, J. M. 1972. *Avifauna of the Eastern Highlands of New Guinea*. Publ. Nuttall Orn. Club, no. 12.
Immelmann, K., Nicolai, J., Steinbacher, J. & Wolters, H. E. 1977. *Vögel in Käfig und Voliere: Prachtfinken*: 578–581.
Mayr, E. 1968. In *'Peters' check-list of birds of the world*. Cambridge, Mass.
Ziswiler, V., Güttinger, H. R. & Bregulla, H. 1972. *Monographie der Gattung* Erythrura *Swainson, 1873 (Aves, Passeres, Estrildidae)*. Bonner Zoologische Monographien, No. 2.

Green-tailed Parrot-finch   *Erythrura hyperythra*

Chlorura hyperythra Reichenbach, 1862–1863, *Singvögel*, p. 33.

DESCRIPTION Very slightly smaller than Peters' Twinspot but tail much shorter, bill shorter and wing less rounded. Extreme front of forehead black. Rest of forehead and forecrown turquoise blue. Rest of upperparts, including upper tail coverts and central tail feathers, a deep grass green to brightish moss green. Outer secondaries, primaries and outer tail feathers blackish with moss green edges to their outer webs. Sides of breast turquoise blue, sometimes intermixed with green and shading into light moss green on the sides of the lower breast and flanks. Face, throat, breast and median areas of underparts and under tail coverts dark reddish buff. Irides dark brown. Bill black. Legs and feet flesh-coloured.

The female has the extreme front of her forehead brown; the blue on her forehead is duller and less extensive. Her green parts are a little less bright and she has no blue at the sides of the breast. I have not seen young of this species. Ziswiler *et al.* describe the juvenile as less deep in its colours, with no blue on the forehead, and with a black-tipped yellow bill. The nestling has two luminous turquoise blue tubercles at each side of the gape, one at the base of each mandible. It has a palate pattern of 3 small spots, one spot on each side of the tongue, and a spot in the centre of the inside of the lower mandible.

The above description is of *E. hyperythra brunneiventris*, from the mountains of Mindoro and northern Luzon. *E.h. borneensis*, from the mountains of Borneo, is sometimes (in one of the two specimens I was able to examine) a slightly more yellowish green. Its buff parts, except on the breast, are paler, and more intermixed with greenish on the median parts of the lower breast and belly. The green of its flanks is paler and the blue on its head reaches further back, beyond the level of the eyes. Sexual differences are comparable to those of *brunneiventris*.

E.h. microrhyncha, from the Latimodjon and Matinan Mountains of Celebes, is similar to *E.h. brunneiventris* but has a much less extensive blue area on the forehead. Its buff parts are duller, paler except on cheeks and breast, and more washed with greenish on the underparts. *E.h. ernstmayri* is similar but of a more yellowish green, especially on the rump.

E.h. malayana is known only from the type specimen, a female from Cameron's Highlands, Malay Peninsula. It is very similar to the female of *E.h. brunneiventris* but of a slightly more yellowish green above and of a more yellowish tinge on the dark buff parts. *E.h. intermedia*, from Lombok, is very like *E.h. brunneiventris* but has yellowish green upper tail coverts and central tail feathers. The only male specimen I have seen has duller blue on the forehead and less blue on the sides of the breast. Sexual differences as in *E.h. brunneiventris*.

Nominate *E.h. hyperythra*, from the mountains of western Java, is similar to *E.h. brunneiventris* but has deep golden-buff rump and upper tail coverts and yellowish olive central tail feathers. I have not seen a specimen of *E.h. obscura*, from Flores and Sumbawa. It is said to be a paler blue on the forehead, a more yellowish green, and to have the rump washed with yellowish green.

This species seems to be represented by rather few specimens in the British Museum (Natural History), and perhaps elsewhere also. It seems possible that some apparent racial differences, especially as regards the precise shade of green of the upper parts, may eventually prove to be due, at least in part, to degree of plumage wear and/or individual variation.

See plate 4, facing p. 129.

FIELD CHARACTERS Small, short-tailed 'finch', green above and buff or buffish brown on face and underparts. Blue on forehead probably only visible at close quarters head on. Buff or brown cheeks and/or green or greenish yellow rump and tail distinguish it from other parrot-finches.

DISTRIBUTION AND HABITAT Philippines, Borneo, Celebes, Malay Peninsula, Java, and Lesser Sunda Islands (see under 'Description' for details).

Inhabits open woodland, forest edge, bamboo jungle and, at least locally, the vicinity of rice fields. Usually in mountains between 1000 and 3000 metres but on Lombok, at least, sometimes as low as about 300 metres.

FEEDING AND GENERAL HABITS Apparently a specialist feeder on the seeds of bamboos but also takes some insects. Has been seen feeding in rice fields (presumably but apparently not provedly on rice) but not often. Ziswiler *et al.* found that in captivity it preferred seeds similar in shape to those of bamboos, even though they were not related to them. Lettuce seed and thistle seed were taken in preference to other dicotyledonous seeds and canary seed and the seeds of the grasses *Poa pratensis* and *Puleum pratense* in preference to various kinds of millet.

Has been encountered in pairs or singly (mate on nest?) but more often in flocks. Ziswiler *et al.* found it difficult to keep in health in captivity for any length of time.

NESTING Probably very similar to the Pin-tailed Parrot-finch but little appears to be recorded. Ziswiler *et al.* (p. 20) state that the incubation period is 13 days and that a

clutch laid in captivity consisted of 4 eggs. They did not, however, (p. 121) succeed in breeding it.

VOICE The same contact call, a very high-pitched 'tseet-tseet' (my anglicisation) is used both as a close contact and distance contact call. It is very similar to that of other parrot-finches.

The song begins with a long series of crackling notes, rhythmically uttered in different tempos. In the middle of the strophe there is a series of pure, bell-like notes. When singing the head is held with the bill horizontal, and turned jerkily from side to side through an angle of about 30°. Ziswiler *et al.* give sound spectrograms of both song and contact call. Burkard heard songs in which the first part was inaudible to his ears and only discernible from the throat movements of the singer, it was followed by four soft musical notes, each repeated twice.

DISPLAY AND SOCIAL BEHAVIOUR In courtship display the male selects pieces of nesting material and holds them 'bundled' in his bill. He then flies and perches near the female and begins to sing with the side-to-side head movements. Then he crouches, lowers his head till his bill is almost or quite touching the perch, then hops sideways towards the hen, stretching up his legs and throwing back his head at each jump. When he is nearly touching the female she responds by side to side movements of her head. Copulation was not seen to occur and is thought to take place in the nest (Ziswiler *et al.*). Burkard observed a display in which the male nodded his head vigorously up and down with hardly any movement of his body or legs.

Clumping and allo-preening do not occur.

OTHER NAMES Bamboo Parrot-finch, Bamboo Munia.

REFERENCES
Burkard, R. 1966. Die Papageiamadinen und Heinrich Bregulla. *Gefiederte Welt* **1966**: 141–143.
Ziswiler, V., Güttinger, H. R. & Bregulla, H. 1972. *Monographie der Gattung Erythrura Swainson, 1837 (Aves, Passeres, Estrildidae)*. Bonner Zoologische Monographien, No. 2.

Pin-tailed Parrot-finch   *Erythrura prasina*

Loxia prasina Sparrmann, 1788, *Mus.* Carlsonianum, fasc. 3. pls. 72–73.

DESCRIPTION About size of Peter's Twinspot but very different in shape, more slender, with more pointed wing and long graduated tail, of which the two narrow and attenuated central feathers are nearly twice as long as the next pair. The bill is rather large with sharply angled gonys and curved cutting edge of the upper mandible that give it an uptilted appearance though in fact the ridge of the culmen is straight or nearly so. Lores blackish. Forehead, face and throat a rather dull cobalt blue, paler on the throat than elsewhere. Hind crown, nape and upperparts (except where otherwise stated) a rather dark grass green. Outer webs of outer primaries, except at their tips, yellowish green. Rest of primaries and inner webs of secondaries blackish. Underwing coverts rich buff. Rump, the long upper tail coverts and the outer fringes of the

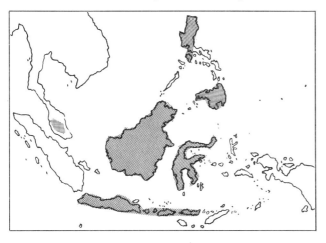

central pair of tail feathers scarlet red. Median part of central tail feathers dull red. Other tail feathers blackish, pale drab at tips and with some reddish tinge on the outer webs of some of them. Upper breast dark buff, more or less washed with dull blue, especially at the sides. A bright pinkish red patch on the median parts of the lower breast and belly. Rest of underparts dark buff. Irides brown. Bill black. Legs and feet brownish horn colour. Adult plumage attained by third month. Adults moult twice a year.

The female's tail is only about half the length of the male's, her central tail feathers being much shorter than his. Her forehead and rump are green and, like the rest of her green areas, a little darker shade of green than the male's. The red of her upper tail coverts and tail is less bright than the male's. Her cheeks vary from pale dull cobalt blue to green slightly washed with blue. Her throat, breast and flanks are dull buff, tinged with greyish blue; the median area of her underparts is pale buff. A colour phase in which the red parts are replaced by golden yellow occurs in both sexes, about 8 to 10 per cent seem to be of this phase.

I have not seen a juvenile of this species. From descriptions (Immelmann *et al.*, Ziswiler *et al.*) it appears to be similar to the female but a little greyer and duller, young males having longer tails and brighter red on the rump than females. Nestling at first naked. Mouth markings of the nestling include 3 large outer and 2 smaller inner spots on the palate, 2 dark markings on tongue, crescent inside lower mandible and two shining turquoise blue tubercles at each corner of the gape (Ziswiler *et al.*).

The above description is of nominate *E.p. prasina*, from most of the species' range. *E.p. coelica*, from Borneo, has the blue of the throat extending over the upper breast, the red patch on the underparts brighter and more extensive and the red of rump and tail brighter. Its female has blue cheeks and a predominantly pale cobalt blue throat and breast. There are no specimens of this race with yellow replacing the red in the rather small series in the British Museum (Natural History) collection.

See plate 4, facing p. 129.

FIELD CHARACTERS Small finch-like bird with darkish green upperparts contrasting with bright red rump and red, sharply pointed, tail (shortish in female, long in male). Blue face and red belly patch of male probably not good field characters except close to. Red on rump and tail at once distinguishes it from the allied *E. hyperythra*.

DISTRIBUTION AND HABITAT Western Laos, Thailand, southern Tenasserim, Malay Peninsula, Sumatra and Java. Inhabits forest (Medway and Wells), Forest edge and bamboo thickets (Immelmann *et al.*) but feeds much in open areas, especially ricefields. At least locally nomadic or migratory but relatively little is known about its habitat choice or movements in the wild.

FEEDING AND GENERAL HABITATS Known to eat cultivated rice when available. In parts of Borneo it is a major pest of

upland rice cultivation. Of hundreds of specimens dissected none contained any other food but rice (Smythies). In the Malay Peninsula it has been seen feeding on seed heads of bamboos (Medway & Wells). Usually in small or large flocks but has been little observed except when flocking to rice fields.

In captivity it seldom or never thrives unless kept in a large room or spacious aviary, at a temperature of at least 16 to 20°C. It is usually imported on a diet of paddy rice but this favourite food is evidently inadequate in captivity and experts (Immelmann *et al.*, Karl, Nicolai) are unanimous that the birds must be weaned quickly onto other foods. Karl, who seems to have been unusually successful at keeping *and* breeding this species, fed his birds on canary seed, de-husked oats, white millet and spray millet. These seeds were given both dry and soaked, the latter at various stages of germination. Ample supplies of greenfood such as lettuce, spinach, chickweed, chicory and, when available, green and ripe seeding grasses, especially *Poa annua* and *Setaria viridis* were also given. Like Nicolai, Karl found his birds entirely vegetarian even when rearing young but Immelmann *et al.* state that it will usually take ant pupae and cooked mealworms when feeding young.

Roosts on perches, never in old nests.

NESTING Usually breeds at or near the forest edge or in bamboo thickets. The nest is built among creepers and/or in a bush or tree at varying heights up to about 20 metres. It is roundish with a large side entrance, built of bamboo or rotan blades, fibres, rootlets and similar materials. It is *not* lined with softer materials. Four to six eggs. In Java breeds in February and November, in the rainy season

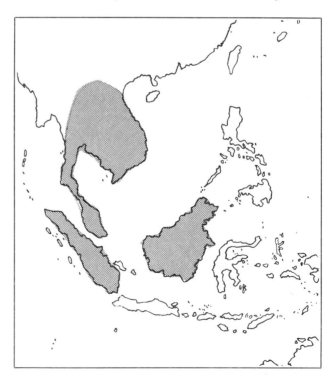

(Hoogerwerf, from whom other extant accounts of its breeding in the wild appear also to be derived).

A captive pair (Karl) used a nest box. The male enticed the female to it by sitting in front of and inside it, mandibulating. The female mandibulated when she came up and hopped in and out of the box with her mate. The nest, with a porch over the side opening, was built of sisal and coconut fibres, bast and moss by both sexes but only the male fetched material. Clutch size in captivity 2 to 5. Incubation period 12 to 14 days. Young fledge at about 21 days. Both sexes incubate and brood in turn by day, only the hen at night. Karl's birds did not brood the young by day after the eighth day or by night after the tenth. He advises that at this period the night temperature should be kept at not less than 25°C.

Fledglings of this species do not beg in the usual estrildid manner but facing their parent and fluttering their wings, just like a young Canary or other cardueline finch (Karl).

VOICE The contact call is a high-pitched 'tseet-tseet' or 'tsit-tsit'. There is apparently no difference between close and distance contact calls. The aggressive call, given when attacking or about to attack, is a sharp 'teger-teter-terge' (my anglicisation). A soft whispering call accompanies copulation (Immelmann *et al.*).

The song is variously described as a series of crackling sounds similar to the introductory phase of the song of *E. hyperythra* (Ziswiler *et al.*) and of clinking or chirping sounds (Immelmann *et al.*). Two captive-bred males perfectly mimicked parts of the song of a Green Twinspot and also produced their own species' song in typical form (Karl). Ziswiler *et al.* give a sound spectrogram of the song strophe.

DISPLAY AND SOCIAL BEHAVIOUR Immelmann *et al.* and Karl describe the courtship display as very similar to that of waxbills of the genus *Estrilda*. The male, holding a grass stem, twig or other nesting symbol in his bill bobs up and down, alternately stretching and bending his legs but without his feet leaving the perch or ground. If the female approaches he lets the symbol fall and sings with his head over hers and tail angled towards her. Karl saw copulation occur once as a finale to this display but thinks that copulation usually occurs in the nest.

Ziswiler *et al.* describe a somewhat different version in which the male, with nesting material held 'bundled' in his bill, hops towards the female, bobbing up and down. He then raises his tail and begins to switch it from side to side, at the same time lifting his head high and making similar pendulum-like side to side movements with his head. Occasionally this display may be performed without the nesting symbol in the bill. The female, if responsive, performs similar movements. The male then drops his material and the two birds perform bowing movements in synchrony. When doing so their heads cross over each others in a manner similar to that of many (perhaps all) estrildids when performing nesting ceremonies in the nest or on the nest site. Whether these different versions are due to the intensity at which courtship is performed or are

individual seems uncertain.

In captivity highly social with no sign of a rank hierarchy. Strange birds are peaceably accepted into a flock. Individual distance is maintained. Allo-preening and clumping do not normally occur.

OTHER NAMES Pin-tailed Nonpareil, Long-tailed Munia.

REFERENCES
Hoogerwerf, A. 1949. *De Avifauna van de Plantentuin te Buitenzorg (Java)*. Buitenzorg, Java.
Karl, F. 1964. Lauchgrune Papageiamadinen (*Erythrura prasina*). *Die Gefiederte Welt* **1964**: 2–4.
Immelmann, K., Steinbacher, J. & Wolters, H. E. 1967. *Vögel in Käfig und Voliere: Prachtfinken*: 179–190.
Medway, Lord, & Wells, D. R. 1976. *The birds of the Malay Peninsula*, vol. 5. H. F. & G. Witherby Ltd, London, in association with Pererbit Universiti, Kuala Lumpur, Malaya.
Nicolai, J. 1965. *Käfig- und Volierenvögel*. Kosmos, Franckh'sche Verlag. W. Keller & Co., Stuttgart, Germany.
Smythies, B. E. 1960. *The birds of Borneo*. Oliver & Boyd, London.
Ziswiler, V., Guttinger, H. R. & Bregulla, H. 1972. *Monographie der Gattung* Erythrura *Swainson 1837 (Aves, Passeres, Estrildidae)*. Bonner Zoologische Monographien, No. 2.

Green-faced Parrot-finch   *Erythrura viridifacies*

Erythrura virdifacies Hachisuka and Delacour 1937, *Bull. Brit. Ornith. Club* **57**, p. 66.

DESCRIPTION Differs from the previous species, *E. prasina*, in having a smaller bill and shorter although similarly shaped tail. Entire upper-parts green (very similar to the green of *E. prasina* but perhaps a shade brighter) except for the rump, upper tail coverts and tail which are similarly coloured to those of *E. prasina* except for being a slightly darker red. Underwing coverts buff. Throat, breast and underparts a light green. Tibial feathers and under tail coverts buff. Irides dark brown. Bill black. Legs and feet pinkish brown to flesh-coloured.

The female is a paler and more greyish green than the male. Her throat and breast are pale buffish green or greyish green shading to brownish buff on the belly, flanks and under tail coverts. The juvenile is similar to the female but pale buff or yellowish grey on the underparts.

See plate 4, facing p. 129.

DISTRIBUTION AND HABITAT Known so far only from the neighbourhood of Manila, Luzon Island, Philippines. Has been found in savanna, forest edge and bamboo thickets, from the lowlands up to about 100 metres.

FEEDING AND GENERAL HABITS Known to take seeds of grasses and of *Casuarina*; probably also takes bamboo seed. Apparently not widespread but sometimes turns up in large flocks where grasses or bamboos are seeding.

Müller found that captive birds, offered a large selection of foods, took mostly soaked, sprouting and cooked millets. He gave them vitamin supplements in their drinking water. Mealworms and soft food were not eaten.

NESTING Ziswiler *et al.* state that it breeds in March and

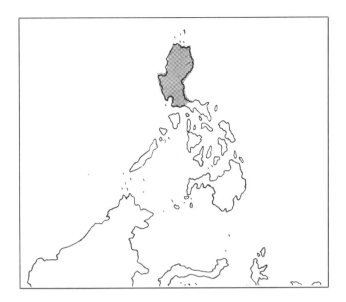

April, that the incubation period is 14 days and that a 3-egg clutch was laid in captivity. I can find no other information. Probably very similar in nesting habits to the related *E. prasina*.

VOICE Calls like those of *E. hyperythra* but Ziswiler *et al.* describe the song as much sharper and harder in sound. It begins with a rhythmical interchange of two elements and ends with a rapid repitition of a single element. Ziswiler *et al.* gives a sound spectrogram of part of the song.

Müller, however, describes the song as quiet and flowing: a high-pitched 'deedeedeedee', followed by a chattering 'day day day day – day day' and then a higher and rather grating 'graygraygrayraydaylaygray'. When singing the bird stretches its neck, lowers its tail and appresses its plumage.

DISPLAY AND SOCIAL BEHAVIOUR Courtship display like that described for the Pin-tailed Parrot-Finch (Ziswiler *et al.*); but Müller saw a courtship display in which the male takes a grass stem or strip of reed blade and holds it by *both* ends. He then holds it over the female's head and tries to force her down. She flees and is chased (Müller).

In captivity highly social with no sign of any rank hierarchy within the flock. Strange birds introduced to an established captive flock are accepted with no sign of hostility. Individual distance is maintained and clumping and allo-preening do not normally occur.

OTHER NAMES Manila Parrot-finch, Green Parrot-finch.

REFERENCES

Hachisuka, Marquis, & Delacour, J. 1937. *Erythrura viridifacies,* sp. nov. *Bull. Brit. Orn. Club* **57**: 66–67.

Immelmann, K., Steinbacher, J. & Wolters, H. E. 1967. *Vögel in Käfig und Voliere: Prachtfinken*: 176–179.

Müller, R. 1973. Beobachtungen an der Manila-Papagal-amidine. *Gefiederte Welt* **97**: 90–92.

Ziswiler, V., Güttinger, H. R. & Bregulla, H. 1972. *Monographie der Gattung* Erythrura *Swainson, 1837 (Aves, Passeres, Estrildidae).* Bonner Zoologische Monographien, No. 2.

Three-coloured Parrot-finch   *Erythrura tricolor*

Fringilla tricolor Vieilloot, 1817, *Nouv. Dist. Hist. Nat.,* nouv. ed., **12**, p. 233.

DESCRIPTION Similar to previous species, *E. viridifacies*, in shape and size. Upperparts, from nape downwards, of a similar but perhaps slightly brighter green than that of *E. viridifacies* and a similar but slightly lighter red on rump, upper tail coverts and tail. However, Ziswiler *et al.* describe the upper tail coverts as shining red so evidently there is some individual variation and some specimens are brighter than those few I have examined. Forehead, face, throat and breast dark cobalt blue, edged with a lighter blue on the crown, peripheral parts of the cheeks and sides of neck. Similar lighter blue on lower breast and belly with some intermixture of green on flanks and under tail coverts. Irides dark brown. Bill black. Legs and feet pale brown to flesh-coloured.

I have not seen an adult female of this species. It is described as being turquoise blue, washed with green, where the male is deep blue, the belly pale grey with some bluish and greenish feathers and orange-red upper tail coverts. A female juvenile is slightly paler and duller green above; buffish grey, with some green on the fringes of many feathers, shading to buffish on the lower breast, belly and under tail coverts and a darker, greenish buff on the flanks. This specimen's bill is noted as 'black' on the label but does not look as if it was the same black as an adult's in life. Ziswiler *et al.* describe (presumably younger) juveniles as having the lower mandible yellow.

See plate 4, facing p. 129.

FIELD CHARACTERS Small, short-tailed green and blue bird with red rump and tail. Not sympatric with any other parrot-finches but should it ever be seen alongside them, the combination of a blue breast and lack of any red on the head would distinguish it from any of them.

DISTRIBUTION AND HABITAT Timor, Tenimber Islands, Wetar, Babar Damar and Roma. Collected specimens were

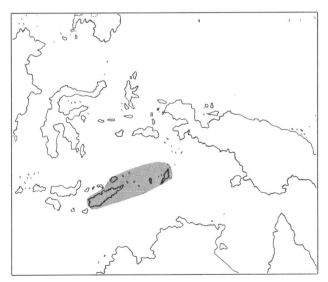

in trees but nothing of importance on habitat appears to be recorded.

FEEDING AND GENERAL HABITS No information.

NESTING No information.

VOICE No information.

DISPLAY AND SOCIAL BEHAVIOUR No information.

OTHER NAME Blue-breasted Parrot-finch.

REFERENCES
Ziswiler, V., Güttinger, H. R. & Bregulla, H. 1972. *Monographie der Gattung* Erythrura *Swainson, 1837 (Aves, Passeres, Estrildidae)*. Bonner Zoologische Monographien, No. 2.

Blue-faced Parrot-finch   *Erythrura trichroa*

Fringilla trichroa Kittlitz, 1835, *Mem. Acad. Imp. Sci. St. Pétersbourg*, **2**, p. 8, tab. 10.

DESCRIPTION About same size as the Pin-tailed Parrot-finch but less slender, with shorter tail than the male Pin-tailed (rather over half the length) with the two central feathers about 6 to 7 mm longer than the next pair and somewhat but not markedly attenuated. Bill similar to that of *E. prasina* but with less pronounced curvature of the lower edges of the upper mandible and much less sharply angled gonys. Wing measurement about 60 to 65 mm. Lores, and small feathers right at the base of the nostrils, blackish. Rest of forehead and sides of face a rather dark and slightly mauvish blue. Upperparts (except where otherwise stated) a rich, rather dark, green with a golden tinge on the sides of the neck. In some individuals an area immediately behind the ear coverts may have a reddish gold tinge suggestive of the red patch of *E. coloria*. Inner webs of outer secondaries and inner webs and tips of the primaries blackish. The green on the outer webs of the primaries is of a yellowish olive hue. Underwing coverts reddish buff. Rump and upper tail coverts dull crimson to carmine red. Central tail feathers carmine, duller along the median line; outer tail feathers brownish black with some carmine and/or yellowish olive on their outer webs. Throat and underparts a lighter and brighter green than the upperparts, sometimes with a very slight bluish or silvery tinge. Tibial feathers reddish buff. Irides dark brown. Bill black. Legs and feet brownish horn.

The female has the blue on the face paler, duller and slightly less extensive. She has less golden tinge on the sides of the neck. Her green parts are slightly less bright and on the underparts may be somewhat suffused or intermixed with buff, even in adult birds. The red on her rump and tail is of a duller and more rusty tinge. As with many other green birds, both sexes may show a strong bluish tinge on the green parts when in worn plumage. The juvenile is much like the female but duller, with predominantly greenish buff underparts and little or (more often) no blue on the head. When it first fledges the bill is deep yellow with a dark tip to the upper mandible. The mouth pattern of the nestling is like that of the Red-headed Parrot-finch (q.v.) but with a smaller central spot on the palate and a dark crescent under the tongue and there are two luminous deep cobalt blue tubercles at each side of the gape (Ziswiler *et al.*).

The above description is of *E. trichroa sigillifera*, from the tropical north-east of Australia, New Guinea, Goodenough, Sudest, Dampier and Vulcan Islands, New Britain and New Ireland. *E.t. modesta*, from the northern Moluccan islands of Ternate, Halmaheira and Batjan, is very similar to *E.t. sigillifera* but has a slightly larger bill and is of a slightly more mauvish blue on the face. *E.t. clara*, from Truk (formerly Ruk) Island in the Carolines, has the blue on the head a little brighter and more extensive and its green parts are a little brighter also. It is said (Ziswiler *et al.*) to have a very pronounced golden sheen on its back and shoulders but this feature may be variable as it was not noticeable in the few specimens that I examined. It is a little smaller (wing 55 to 60 mm). Nominate *E.t. trichroa*, from Kusaie Island in the Carolines is said to be dull green on the underparts and with a marked golden sheen on the back and shoulders. I have not seen specimens of this form. *E.t. cyanofrons*, from Banks Islands (Gaua), the New Hebridean islands of Aoba, Ambrym, Lopevi, Efate, Erromanga, Tanna and Aneitum, and the Loyalty Islands of Lifu and Maré, is like *E.t. clara* but averages a little smaller, has a shorter and blunter bill, the blue on its head is more mauvish in tint and a little more extensive and its green and red areas are a little lighter and brighter. *E.t. woodfordi*, from Guadalcanal, in the Solomons, is very like *E.t. modesta* but has a slightly larger bill and the mauvish blue area on its forehead does not reach so far back. *E.t. pinaiae*, from the southern Moluccan Islands of Ceram and Buru, is described (Ziswiler *et al.*) as bluish green above and below and with bluish grey, not green, fringes to the webs of its outer secondaries. The only specimen I have seen, however, a female from Buru, is, however, as green as and similar to females of *E.t. modesta*.

I have not seen specimens of the following three subspecies, whose descriptions are taken from those given by Ziswiler *et al.*: *E.t. sanfordi*, from the Latimodjon Mountains of south-central Celebes has its bill very broad and deep at the base and a violet-blue shade on the head. *E.t. eichhorni*, from St Matthias Island in the Bismarck Archipelago, has extensive blue on the head and a reddish orange rump. *E.t. pelewensis*, from the Pelew (or Palau) Islands, has a thick bill, pale bluish green underparts and bright red rump and upper tail coverts.

In captive-bred stocks of this species one apparently finds some overlap in the coloration of the sexes and birds cannot always be accurately sexed on this character alone. Possibly this has been due to inter-racial hybridisation in captivity or possibly (as in some other birds) there is a tendency for captive-bred males to be less intensely coloured than wild ones.

FIELD CHARACTERS Small, thickset, green bird with red rump and tail and dull blue face.

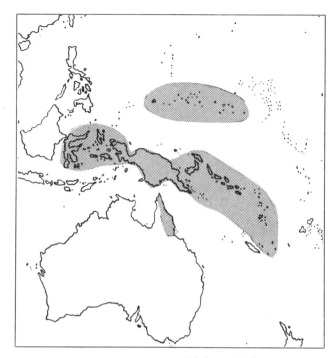

DISTRIBUTION AND HABITAT Celebes, Moluccas, New Guinea, New Britain, New Ireland, the Bismarch Archipelago, Micronesia, Solomon Islands, New Hebrides, Loyalty Islands and the tropical north-eastern seaboard of Australia. See under 'Description' for subspecific distributions. Hindwood and Marshall have discussed in detail its status and distribution in Australia. Found at varying elevations, in different parts of its range, from tropical lowlands to the chilly mist forest zone (Marshall). It and *E. papuana* in New Guinea appear to be mainly allopatric and in one of the two areas where both are known to occur, *E. trichroa* is found at higher elevations (Diamond).

Inhabits forest (probably only where there are some openings), forest edge, secondary growth, grassland, cultivated areas, plantations and, at least for feeding purposes often also playing fields, pastures and airfields. Thus in many areas it appears to benefit from man's alteration of the habitat although in Australia it is (*fide* Marshall) confined to the vicinity of relict patches of rain forest.

FEEDING AND GENERAL HABITS Feeds both on the ground and in growing vegetation. Known to take seeds of grasses, including introduced species, seeds of *Casuarina*, termites and probably other seeds and insects. In New Guinea feeds largely on bamboo seeds and also takes the seeds of figs. Usually in small flocks of up to 20 or 30 birds, sometimes in larger flocks in good feeding areas, as on parts of Efate, where man-made pastures offer it abundant grass seed. Drinks and bathes frequently, visiting the water at all times of day. When flying some distance, the flight is slightly undulating but direct and level over short distances. Can fly through young trees or other vegetation, turning and swerving nimbly to avoid boughs or stems.

In captivity needs similar care and feeding to *E. psittacea* (q.v.) but tends to be the most easily bred of all the parrot-finches and although at first wild, and often remaining so if kept in close confinement, usually becomes tame in a large aviary. Immelmann *et al.* are very emphatic that it must be kept at an even temperature of 16 to 20°C at all times but Rübner, who has bred the species successfully for 30 years, states that his home-bred birds are hardy, show no evidence of discomfort at temperatures of 1 to 2°C, and are kept from April to November in an almost shelterless outside aviary. He finds that his birds thrive on a much simpler diet than is usually recommended, they get only dry seeds (canary, oats, millet and lettuce seed), fresh ant pupae when available and mealworms. Although necessarily inbred, his stock is vigorous and broods of young are consistently reared. Others (e.g. Abrahams, Webb) have also had considerable success with this species in South Africa and England respectively.

NESTING The nest is placed in a recess of a cliff, among the adventitious roots of a banyan, among thick cover of various kinds or in the fork of a tree or shrub. It is large for the size of the bird, pear-shaped to roundish with an entrance tube about 30 to 35 mm long leading downwards at an angle from the nest chamber, built of stems, moss, the horsehair-like rhyzomes of the fungus *Marasmius equicrinus*, grass and/or similar materials.

Eggs 3 to 5, exceptionally 2 to 8. Incubation period 12 to 14 days, young fledge at about 21 days, sometimes later. From studies of wild birds on Efate, Ziswiler *et al.* conclude that most incubation, brooding and care of the young is undertaken by the female. Abrahams found that in his captive birds the female did most or all of the incubation and brooding but the male was very active in feeding the nestlings. Immelmann *et al.* state that sometimes one or both parents regularly remove the droppings of the young. Abrahams found that a nest was 'perfectly clean' after young had fledged but did not, apparently, see any nest hygiene on the part of the parent. On the other hand Ziswiler *et al.*, who both studied the species in the wild and bred it in captivity, saw no such behaviour although they observed that in this, and other parrot-finches, well-grown nestlings thrust their hindquarters through the opening and defaecate outside the nest chamber. Fledged young quiver their wings when begging (Nicolai, in Immelmann *et al.*, 1963).

In the South Pacific nests mostly in the spring and summer, from October to March but also at other times. Has been found breeding in March in Australia and in November in New Guinea (Immelmann *et al.*, Marshall, Ziswiler *et al.*).

VOICE Contact call 'tseet-tseet' or 'tsit-tsit', high-pitched and like that of other parrot-finches, as is the aggressive call. A metallic trilling 'tccrrrrr' (my anglicisation), given as a series of notes on a falling scale, is used by both sexes in pursuit flights and in some other apparently sexually-motivated situations. The nest call is a long series of notes, similar in sound to and homologous with the begging calls of the young. Recently-fledged young have a long-drawn location call 'tseeeeee' (my anglicisation). The alarm call is a series of high-pitched notes. The song is quite loud and very shrill. It is prefaced by the trilling call and is composed of six elements, three different elements being repeated at regular intervals. Ziswiler *et al.* give sound spectrograms of the calls and song.

DISPLAY AND SOCIAL BEHAVIOUR The information here is derived from Ziswiler *et al.* unless otherwise indicated. In the courtship display the male holds nesting material 'bundled' in his bill and flies to the female, uttering the trilling call and angling his tail towards her when he has alighted. She responds by angling her tail towards him and both bob up and down together but they do not bow as do the Malayan parrot-finches. The female then crouches in a horizontal posture and then flies off uttering trilling calls. The male pursues her either giving trilling calls or singing. After a short, markedly undulating flight the female perches, trilling loudly and watching the male's approach. Some when so doing adopt the crouched, neck-twisted posture of a begging fledgling. When the male reaches her the female flies off again. In most cases these pursuit flights are broken off but if the female is ready to copulate she finally solicits with quivering tail and uttering soft notes. The male bites hold of her head or nape feathers with his bill and copulates. Under captive conditions (and possibly at times in the wild) other males may join in the pursuit but if they do they are attacked and driven off by the female. If her own mate does not respond to her attempts to initiate his pursuit, the female may fly at, attack and chase him.

Display as above described is characteristic of young adults. As a pair mature they tend to decrease the preliminaries, so that finally only pursuit flights and the (sometimes) ensuing copulation are performed.

Highly social and usually very peaceable even when breeding and in captivity. Aggressive behaviour by the male towards independent young has, however, occurred in captivity (Mamlok, in Immelmann). Adults do not normally clump or allo-preen and juveniles only rarely do so if they have been reared by conspecifics. Young that have been reared by Bengalese Finches, however, habitually respond with typical allo-preening invitation postures when their foster-parents start to preen them and they also, during the period while they are still dependent on the foster parents, allo-preen each other.

OTHER NAMES Tri-coloured Parrot-finch, Three-coloured Parrot finch, Blue-headed Parrot-finch. (All these names are also used for other species so seem best not used for *E. trichroa*).

REFERENCES
Abrahams, C. N. 1939. Breeding the Tri-coloured Parrot Finch in South Africa. *Avicult. Mag.* 5th ser. **4**: 229–233.
Diamond, J. M. 1972. *Avifauna of the Eastern Highlands of New Guinea.* Publ. Nuttall Orn. Club no. 12.
Hindwood, K. A. 1948. The Blue-faced Finch in Australia. *Emu* **48**: 53–56.
Immelmann, K. 1965. *Australian finches in bush and aviary.* Angus & Robertson, Sydney and London.
Immelmann, K., Steinbacher, J. & Wolters, H. E. 1963. *Vögel in Käfig und Volière: Prachtfinken:* **15**.
Immelmann, K., Steinbacher, J. & Wolters, H. E. 1967. *Vögel in Käfig und Voliere: Prachtfinken:* 196–208.
Marshall, A. J. 1948. The breeding and distribution of *Erythrura trichroa* in Australia. *Emu* **47**: 305–310.
Rübner, I. H. 1961. Dreifarbige Papageiamadinen. *Gefiederte Welt* **1961**: 75–76.
Webb, P. B. 1932. Common or Red-headed and Tri-coloured or Blue-headed Parrot Finches. *Avicult. Mag.* 4th ser., **10**: 299–310.
Ziswiler, V., Güttinger, H. R. & Bregulla, H. 1972. *Monographie der Gattung* Erythrura *Swainson, 1837 (Aves, Passeres, Estrildidae).* Bonner Zoologische Monographiens, No. 2.

Papuan Parrot-finch   *Erythrura papuana*

Erythrura trichroa papuana Hartert, 1900, *Novit. Zool.* **7**: p. 7.

DESCRIPTION Very similar to the Australian and New Guinea race of the previous species, *E. trichroa sigillifera*, but a little larger (wing 65 to 69 mm), with proportionately longer tail and much stouter and larger bill; these points are well-shown in a photograph illustrating Neff's paper. Coloration and colour pattern like that of *E.t.sigillifera* but the hyacinthine blue on the head extends further behind the eyes both on crown and face and the upper part of the throat is also blue or strongly washed with blue. Sexual differences as in *E. trichroa*. The only female specimen I have been able to examine has the blue on its face a little paler and one or two blue-tinged feathers on the otherwise pale green upper throat. I have not seen a juvenile or nestling or descriptions of them, they are probably like those of *E. trichroa*.

DISTRIBUTION AND HABITAT New Guinea: known from the mountains of south-eastern New Guinea; the central ranges (Wissel Lakes), and the mountains of the Vogelkop. Inhabits forest edge and forest from 900–2000 metres

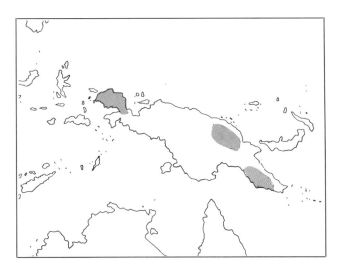

(3000 to 7000 feet). It and the Blue-faced Parrot-finch usually replace each other but in one at least of the two areas where both are known to occur, the present form is found at lower altitudes. In New Guinea both are found in similar habitats (Diamond).

FIELD CHARACTERS As previous species, *E. trichroa*, except for rather longer tail and much larger bill. Possibly the latter character would enable identification from *E. trichroa* (the only species with which it could be confused) if (and only if) seen in profile.

FEEDING AND GENERAL HABITS Virtually no information from the wild. Ziswiler *et al.* said that its food choices in captivity suggested that it was a specialist on fig seeds. However, a pair kept by Neff, eagerly took half ripe wheat and various half ripe millets in the ear and also ate the seeds of various grasses, dry canary seed and white millet and greenfood, especially chickweed. It was several months before they finally ate mealworms and ant pupae. From this it would seem likely that some seeds, other than those of wild figs, are taken in a wild state.

In captivity Neff found them peaceable and comparatively hardy, showing no discomfort in temperatures of 10° to 15°C.

NESTING No information.

VOICE The contact call is like that of the previous species, *E. trichroa*. The loud trilling call is apparently used both in (sexual?) excitement and also as a distance contact call (Neff). The song consists of a series of contact calls ending with two long trills, the first upwardly and the second downwardly inflected: 'tsee-tsee-tsee . . . srrrr . . . srrrr'. There is some variation and contact call notes may sometimes follow the trills. A more intense version of the song, in which the preliminary notes sound like 'tseea-tseea' and the trills are louder and longer, is given immediately before copulation attempts.

Neff describes the alarm call as the same as the contact call but the sound spectrograms of these calls given in Ziswiler *et al.* (who do not describe the alarm call of *E. papuana*) show the alarm call as a long connected series of contact call type notes and the contact call as a single such note. They also give a sound spectrogram of the trilling call of *E. papuana*.

DISPLAY AND SOCIAL BEHAVIOUR Sexual pursuits, followed sometimes by copulation, as in *E. trichroa*. Neff found that his pair, unlike healthy parrot-finches of other species, regularly clumped together when resting by day and when roosting at night although they did not allo-preen.

REFERENCES
Diamond, J. M. 1972. *Avifauna of the Eastern Highlands of New Guinea.* Publ. Nuttall Orn. Club, No. 12.
Neff, R. 1970. Die Papua-Papageiamadine (*Erythrura papuana*). *Gefiederte Welt* **1970**: 21–22.
Ziswiler, V., Güttinger, H. R. & Bregulla, H. 1972. *Monographie der Gattung* Erythrura *Swainson, 1837 (Aves, Passeres, Estrildidae).* Bonner Zoologische Monographien, No. 2.

Mindanao Parrot-finch   *Erythrura coloria*

Erythrura coloria Ripley and Rabor 1961, Postilla, Yale University no. 50, p. 18.

DESCRIPTION Very similar to the Blue-faced Parrot-finch but slightly smaller (wing 51 to 56 mm) and perhaps slightly shorter-tailed than most forms of *E. trichroa*. Forehead and face deep cobalt blue, the blue on the face backed and partly encircled by a more or less crescentic, large orange-red patch at each side of the neck. Rest of plumage as *E. trichroa sigillifera* (q.v.) but the green perhaps a shade darker (although quite as bright) and the under wing coverts and tibial feathers of a dark, dusky buff rather than reddish buff.

I have only seen alleged male specimens of this species, one of which I believe, however, to be a wrongly-sexed female. The blue on its head is paler and less extensive, the orange red less bright and its underparts a duller green. Ziswiler *et al.* describe this as the plumage of females under one year old but say that after this age the sexes are alike. The juvenile is described as very like that of *E. trichroa*, with no blue or red on the head. The nestling has a five-spot pattern on the palate, an un-interrupted dark band across the tongue but no dark crescent under it and luminous deep blue tubercles set in swollen yellow skin at the corners of the mouth, very like its congeners (Ziswiler *et al.*)

See plate 4, facing p. 129.

FIELD CHARACTERS Small, thickset, finch-like bird, dark green with red rump and tail and dark blue face framed on either side by red.

DISTRIBUTION AND HABITAT Philippines: known only from Mount Katanglad in central Mindanao, at elevations of

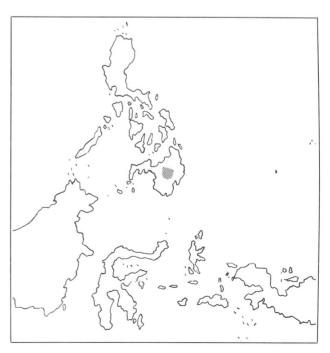

1400 to 1600 metres. Found at the forest edge and in clearings where grasses and herbaceous plants grow.

FEEDING AND GENERAL HABITS Seeks food both on the ground and in vegetation. By day frequents open mountain valleys but towards evening it ascends in family parties to forested hillsides at higher elevations. Known to take seeds of grasses, bamboos and other plants and also insects.

Captive birds (Burkard, Immelmann *et al.*) took mostly canary seed and spray millet, also mealworms and ant pupae. When rearing young they also took sprouted canary seed, seeding grass, dry grass seed and large quantities of eggfood and ant pupae.

In captivity it is active but not at all shy or nervous. It is less sensitive to cold than many of its congeners but Immelmann *et al.* recommend that it should not be kept at a temperature of less than 15°C, higher when breeding and especially when young are about to fledge or have recently done so.

NESTING No information except from captive birds. Nest similar to that of other parrot-finches, built of coconut fibres and grass stems and unlined. Readily nests in half-fronted boxes. Either sex may seek for a site, nest call there and, when the mate joins it, both perform upward-thrusting head movements and mandibulate. The male brings material and the female builds.

Eggs 1 to 3, most commonly 1 or 2 (Immelmann *et al.*, Ziswiler *et al.*). Incubation period 12 to 13 days. Young fledge at 21 days and are fed for a further 14 days or more by the parents. Both sexes incubate and brood in turn by day but only one, presumably the female, at night. The parents sit very tight and do not panic, desert or show other signs of great stress when the nest is inspected by their owner. Young birds will breed when about 5 months old but, as usual, Immelmann *et al.* say they ought not to be allowed to do so until a year old or more.

VOICE Like that of the Red-headed and Blue-faced Parrot-finches (q.v.). Ziswiler *et al.* give sound spectrograms of its calls and song.

DISPLAY AND SOCIAL BEHAVIOUR As Blue-faced Parrot-finch (q.v.), data for captive birds only, from Burkard and Ziswiler *et al.*

OTHER NAME Red-collared Parrot-finch.

REFERENCES
Burkard, R. 1966. Die Papageiamadinen und Heinrich Bregulla. *Gefiederte Welt* **1966**: 141–143.
Immelmann, K., Steinbacher, J. & Wolters, H. E. 1967. *Vögel in Käfig und Voliere: Prachtfinken*: 191–196.
Ziswiler, V., Güttinger, H. R. & Bregulla, H. 1972. *Monographie der Gattung* Erythrura *Swainson, 1837 (Aves, Passeres, Estrildidae)*. Bonner Zoologische Monographien, No. 2.

Red-headed Parrot-finch   *Erythrura psittacea*

Fringilla psittacea Gmelin, 1789, *Syst. Nat.*, **1** (2), p. 903.

DESCRIPTION Although not so colourful as some of its congeners, this species is, in my opinion, the most beautiful of all the parrot-finches as it combines a particularly unusual and attractive albeit simple colour scheme with pleasing shape and a lively demeanour.

It is about the size of the Pin-tailed Parrot-finch but plumper in shape (wing about 54 to 62 mm), the tail is medium-long, strongly graduated but not sharply attenuated, the bill proportionately shorter than that of *E. prasina* and with a curved culmen. Forehead, forecrown, face, throat and upper breast a bright yet delicate red, difficult to describe, it could perhaps be called scarlet with just a hint of pinkish vermilion. It is a colour that many would describe as cherry-red although no cherry that I have seen, fresh or bottled, could equal it. The lower rump and upper tail coverts are a similar red, as are the outer fringes to the central tail feathers, whose median parts are dull carmine. Outer tail feathers olive brown with varying amounts of dull red on the outer webs. Inner secondaries bright moss green; outer secondaries blackish brown with moss green on their outer webs. Primaries similar but the green on their outer webs, which is absent from near the ends of the feathers, is of a lighter and more yellowish hue. Under wing coverts orange-buff; some (but not all) males have a few tiny red feathers along the inner edge of the wing. Rest of plumage a rather dark but bright green, sometimes (perhaps as a result of wear) with a *very* faint silvery blue tinge on the underparts. Irides dark brown. Bill black. Legs and feet brownish horn.

The female is often, and perhaps usually, a little smaller than the male and has her red parts slightly less bright, and less extensive on the breast but there would appear, both from examination of skins and the experiences of some breeders (Boosey, Savage) to be overlap in these characters. Savage found that his hens had markedly paler legs and feet but others do not appear to have noticed this, so it may not be usual.

The juvenile is duller green above and dull yellowish olive below. The red on its rump, upper tail coverts and tail is of an orange-carmine tone. Bill at first amber yellow or orange-yellow with a dark tip or subterminal cross stripe and a dark base to the upper mandible. Captive-bred juveniles sometimes have a little red on their heads. This is almost certainly due to delayed feather growth (Immelmann *et al.*, Ziswiler *et al.*). The nestling has two luminous gape tubercles set in swollen bright yellow skin. The upper one is deep blue and adjacent to the corner of the mouth, the lower one is somewhat paler and sited immediately in front of the corner of the mouth. A five-spot pattern on the yellow palate, and two dark spots on the tongue.

See plate 4, facing p. 129.

FIELD CHARACTERS Small finch-like bird with unmarked green plumage except for bright red head (nape excepted), rump and tail.

DISTRIBUTION AND HABITAT New Caledonia. Has occurred in the New Hebrides and elsewhere but probably as a result of introduction by man. Inhabits plantations, fields or other open areas with some bush or tree growth,

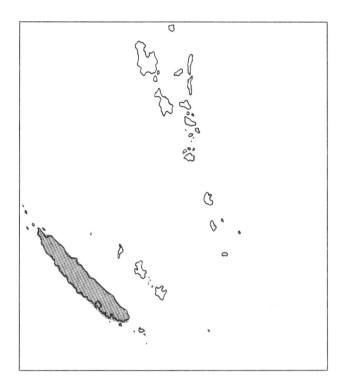

gardens, forest edge and open areas in forest. Seldom in the Niauli savanna, where *Melaleuca leucadendron* is the dominant tree, or in mangroves. Widespread and common at all altitudes where suitable habitat exists.

FEEDING AND GENERAL HABITS Feeds very largely on dicotyledonous seeds, including those of *Ageratum conyzoides*, *Pterocaulon redolens*, *Siegesbeckia orientalis*, *Ageratum mexicanum*, *Casuarina glauca*, *C. chamaecyparis*, *Helychrysum neocaledonicum* and *Erythrma glauca*. Also takes seeds of *Pennisetum purpure*, *Paspalum orbiculare*, *Eragrostis atrovirens*, *Greslana multiflora*, *Andropogon spp.* and possibly other grasses. Insects, especially flying termites, small green grasshoppers and crickets are also eaten. Uses its feet to hold down large insects (and presumably also seed heads).

In captivity it will eat a variety of seeds and other foods and in former days appears often to have been successfully kept and bred without much trouble. Savage, for example, fed his birds on canary seed, white and spray millets, flowering, seeding grasses (especially *Poa annua* when available), and chickweed.

They refused insects and soft foods until the day their young hatched, when they began at once to take ant pupae, mealworms (rationed by their owner to 6 per day) and milk sop. Webb, another successful breeder of the species, fed his birds similarly but also gave them soaked seed and seed mixed with cod liver oil. Pensold had good breeding results giving eggfood as the main source of animal protein. A wild nestling's crop contained about 60 per cent seeds of an unidentified dicotyledonous plant, 10 per cent *Casuarina* seeds (of two species) and 20 per cent insects (Ziswiler *et al.*).

Immelmann *et al.* emphasize that, in their opinion, sprouted seed, insect food, fruits and greenfood (especially when available half ripe seeding grasses and oats) should be supplied to the birds at *all* times. They warn that live mealworms may cause severe digestive troubles and recommend that mealworms should always be cooked before feeding them to the birds. They also advise against ripe oats and oily seeds such as hemp, niger, maw and rape, which are readily eaten but, they say, cause the birds to put on too much fat.

Wild-caught Red-headed Parrot-finches breed very freely in captivity but, for some as yet unknown reason, after a few or many generations, their descendants usually show greatly reduced fertility. An apparent exception to this was Nicholson, who bred the species for 18 generations with no loss of fertility or vigour. However, in spite of the fact that in the past some aviculturists bred it for many years and it was one of the few estrildids of which stocks were maintained in Germany and Britain through the difficult war years (Nicolai, Nicholson), it has never become widespread in captivity, let alone fully domesticated. In captivity it is lively, inquisitive, tame and usually peaceful towards both its own and other species. It is, however, inadvisable to keep it with other species as its lack of aggressiveness is likely to lead to its attempts to breed failing owing to other birds destroying or taking over its nests (Webb). Immelmann *et al.* recommend a minimum temperature of 15° to 18°C and at least 20°C for newly imported birds.

NESTING Usually nests in some sort of cavity or recess; in a coral cliff, among the adventitious roots of a fig tree, under an overhanging clump of grass, in or on a building etc. Probably also occasionally in thick bushes or trees as captive birds sometimes nest in such sites, although usually preferring nest boxes. The nest is roundish, built mainly of long leaves, stems and bark fibres with the usual side entrance. The egg chamber is either lined with feathers (Ziswiler *et al.*) or has merely a few feathers placed in its walls (Immelmann *et al.*). As in other parrot-finches nest material is carried 'bundled'. It is brought by the cock but the hen does much or most of the actual fixing of it into position.

Eggs 2 to 6, most often 4. Incubation period 13 days. Young fledge at 21 days, sometimes later in captivity. Both sexes incubate and brood in turn by day but the male only for brief periods (Immelmann *et al.*). At least in captivity both parents are in the nest together at night (Immelmann *et al.*). Possibly this is not invariable and may even not occur in the wild so further observations are needed. The young are brooded until 9 days old (Wagner, Ziswiler *et al.*). The male of one captive pair regularly removed the faeces of the young, after they were 9 days old (Wagner). Young 14 days old and over deposit their faeces outside the nest entrance (Ziswiler *et al.*). The young do not normally return to the nest after once leaving although young that have been reared by Bengalese Finches will return to roost in the nest together with their foster parents when the latter call them and lead them there. Ziswiler *et al.* cite an instance where, in the same aviary, two broods fledged at the same time, one of which had been reared by Bengalese and the other by their own parents. Surprisingly, the naturally reared brood followed the fostered brood when they returned to their nest at night and roosted there with them and their foster-parents, although they had not been, and were not, fed by the latter.

VOICE Ziswiler *et al.* describe the calls as virtually identical in sound to those of the Blue-faced Parrot Finch (q.v.) and other melanesian parrot-finches and give sound spectrograms of the location call, contact call, trilling call and song. Immelmann *et al.* note a sexual distinction in (presumably) the trilling calls of the two sexes, saying that the male utters a short trill and the female a short 'tsee' or 'treetree' (my anglicisations). The song consists of a very simple strophe composed of many repetitions of a single element. Boosey likens it (or the trilling call of the male?) to the sound of a policeman's whistle. A low purring sound accompanies copulation (Nicholson).

DISPLAY AND SOCIAL BEHAVIOUR Ziswiler *et al.* imply that its displays and behaviour are like those of the Blue-faced (q.v.) and other melanesian parrot-finches. Other observers of captive birds appear only to have noticed the sexual chases which, according to Immelmann *et al.*, tend not to be so wild and violent as those of *E. trichroa*. Copulation usually occurs in the nest or nest site but sometimes elsewhere (Wagner).

Adult birds do not normally clump or allo-preen although recently fledged young may roost clumped together. Young that have been reared by Bengalese Finches will, however, respond to their foster parents' allo-preening of them with typical allo-preening invitation postures.

OTHER NAMES Parrot-finch, Red-throated Parrot-Finch.

REFERENCES

Boosey, E. J. 1956. *Foreign bird keeping.* Iliffe Books Ltd, London.

Immelmann, K. Steinbacher, J. & Wolters, H. E. 1968. *Vögel in Käfig und Voliere: Prachtfinken*: 222–232. Verlag Hans Limberg, Aachen, Germany.

Nicolai, J. 1965. *Käfig und Volierenvögel.* Stuttgart, Germany.

Nicholson, N. 1950. Breeding of Red-headed Parrot Finches. *Avicult. Mag.* **56**: 249–252.

Pensold, R. 1970. Zum Beitrag 'Einiges über die Rotk. Papagei-amadine' *Gefiederte Welt* **1970**: 166–167.

Savage, E. 1897. Parrot Finches. *Avicult. Mag.* **3**: 166–167.

Wagner, J. 1961. Erfolgreiche Zucht Rotköpfiger Papagei-amiden. *Gefiederte Welt* **1961**: 74–75.

Webb, P. B. 1932. Common or Red-headed, and Tri-coloured or Blue-headed Parrot Finches (*Erythrura psittacea* and *E. trichroa*) *Avicult. Mag.*, 4th ser. **10**: 299–310.

Peale's Parrot-finch   *Erythrura pealii*

Erythrura pealii Hartlaub. 1852, *Archiv. f. Naturg.*, p. 104.

DESCRIPTION About size of the previous species, *E.*

psittacea, but with much shorter (very short) tail, of which the tips of the two central feathers project only a millimetre or two beyond the rest and the bill a very little deeper and stouter with usually a slightly more curved culmen ridge. Forehead, crown and face, including the ear coverts, bright scarlet red. Nape, and all upperparts except where otherwise stated, a rather dark but rich and bright green. Rump and upper tail coverts bright scarlet red. Central tail feathers dull red, brighter on the extreme fringes; rest of tail feathers dull brown with some buffish or dull reddish on the fringes of the outer webs. Inner webs of outer secondaries and inner webs and tips of primaries brownish black. The green on the outer webs of the primaries is a little more yellowish than elsewhere. Under wing coverts greyish buff. Throat bluish black or purplish black, shading through a narrow purplish blue zone to light turquoise blue on the central area of the upper breast. Intensely black in a narrow zone along the lower edge of the red cheeks. Rest of underparts a slightly lighter green than the upperparts. Tibial feathers greenish and drab. Irides dark blue (Ziswiler *et al.*); specimens in the British Museum (Natural History) collection are labelled by the collectors as having the irides black (2 males), reddish brown (1 male) and brown (2 females). It seems uncertain whether this reflects genuine variation or post-mortem change in the museum specimens. Bill black. Legs and feet brownish horn to pinkish grey.

Some but (*fide* Ziswiler *et al.*) not all females have the red parts less bright and the blue on the breast less bright and extensive. Juvenile paler and duller with no red on the head but throat and cheeks mainly or wholly pale dingy blue. Ziswiler *et al.* describe juveniles as also having blue on the top of the head so evidently there is individual or sexual variation, I have only examined a few juvenile specimens. Bill of recently-fledged juvenile deep yellow with subterminal dark band. Mouth markings of nestling like those of *E. psittacea* but with both upper and lower gape tubercles turquoise blue (Ziswiler *et al.*).

A mutation, which apparently occurs only in females, has the entire head blue and can easily be mistaken for *E. trichroa*.

See plate 4, facing p. 129.

FIELD CHARACTERS Small, thickset, short-tailed, green, bird, with red head, rump and tail. Not sympatric with other red-headed parrot-finches but should it be seen alongside *E. psittacea* its blackish throat, bluish breast and short tail would distinguish it. Blue-faced morph probably not readily separable in the field from *E. trichroa*.

DISTRIBUTION AND HABITAT The Fijian islands of Viti Levu, Vanua Levu, Kandavu, Ono, Yanuya, Naviti, Tavewa, Yasawa, Taviuni and Ovalau. Inhabits the periphery of both rain forest and montane forest, ricefields, grassland, forest clearings and gardens. Now most abundant in and near pastureland and ricefields provided there are dense bushes or trees at hand. Found from sea-level to about 1100 metres; only absent from the still higher mist forest zone.

FEEDING AND GENERAL HABITS Known to feed on seeds of the figs, *Ficus vitiensis, F. tinctoria* and *F. obliqua*; Casuarinas, *Casuarina nodiflora* and *C. equisetifolia*; herbaceous plants including *Hydrocotyle asiatica* and *Tephrosia purpurea* and grasses including *Sorghum vulgare, Miscanthus japonicus, Pennisetum polystachion, Isachne vitiensis, Cyrtococccum oxyphyllum* and cultivated rice. Also takes insects and spiders. The relative proportions of grass and dicotyledenous seeds apparently vary in relation to availability and the bird appears to be relatively adaptable and opportunistic in its feeding habits. Seeks food both in vegetation and on the ground.

Usually in pairs or small parties of 4 to 8. Even where abundant, as in ripening ricefields, it is seldom that parties of more than about 30 are seen together. Rather timid and wary; if in the open it flies to the cover of a bush or tree at the least alarm. It has adapted well to man's alteration of the Fijian habitat and is abundant, probably more so than it ever was in former times.

In captivity it prefers half-ripe and/or soaked and sprouted seed and only eats dry seed if forced to do so. Immelmann *et al.* stress that soaked canary seed and greenfood, especially half ripe seeding grasses, must always be available together with various kinds of millet, de-husked oats, fruit such as sweet apple, pear, orange, banana and soaked or fresh figs, and half-ripe oats and wheat in the ear when procurable. Insect food such as ant pupae and mealworms should also be given.

This species originally fed mainly on seeds other than those of grasses and has only secondarily taken to feeding also on the seeds of grasses, where they have been introduced through man's activities or (rice) are now cultivated by him. There may now or in the future be competition for grass seeds and rice from the Avadavat and Java Sparrow, also introduced by man and now locally abundant.

NESTING Usually nests from 3 to 6 metres high in the tops of densely foliaged trees and shrubs. The nest is roundish with a narrow, downward directed side entrance, built of fibres and grass stems.

Eggs 3 to 4. Incubation period 13 to 14 days. Young fledge at 21 days and are independent about 2 weeks later. Mercer (in Ziswiler *et al.*) noted that the parents always wait for 20 to 30 minutes after having filled their own crops, before they feed their young.

Breeding has been recorded in July, August and February but probably occurs at other times also.

VOICE Calls as those of *c. regia* and other melanesian parrot-finches. Ziswiler *et al.* do not specifically describe the song but imply that it is like those of other melanesian species.

DISPLAY AND SOCIAL BEHAVIOUR As in the Blue-faced Parrot-finch (Ziswiler *et al.*).

OTHER NAME Red-headed Parrot-finch (the accepted name for *E. psittacea* but unfortunately used for this species in at least one recent avifaunal work).

REFERENCE
Ziswiler, V., Güttinger, H. R. & Bregulla, H. 1972. *Monographie der Gattung* Erythrura *Swainson, 1837 (Aves, Passeres, Estril-didae).* Bonner Zoologische Monographien, No. 2.

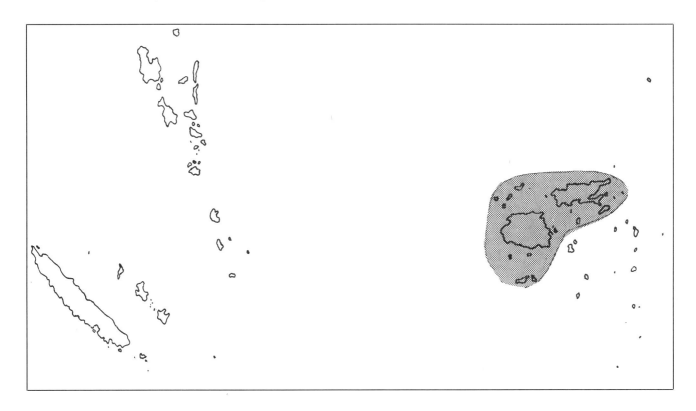

Royal Parrot-finch (*regia* group)   *Erythrura cyaneovirens*

Erythrospiza regia P. L. Sclater, 1881, *ibis* p. 544, pl. 45.

DESCRIPTION Similar to previous form, *E. pealii*, in shape but slightly larger and with a proportionately much larger bill. Head, except for the blackish lores and mauvish blue throat, deep bright scarlet red. Rump and upper tail coverts vivid bright scarlet to vermilion red. Central tail feathers dull red; outer ones dull brown with reddish olive outer webs. Neck, upper mantle and breast a deep rich blue shading into and mixed with rich green on the lower back, wings, belly and flanks. Inner webs of outer secondaries and inner webs and ends of primaries brownish black. Tibial feathers dull brown with bluish tips. Irides dark brown. Bill black. Legs and feet dark horn to brownish black.

Five female specimens in the British Museum (Natural History) differ from the six male specimens in having the blue on the hind neck and breast paler and less bright, the mantle, back and wing coverts predominantly green and more green on the lower breast, flanks and belly. Macklin described such a sexual difference in his breeding pair. Ziswiler *et al.* state, however, that females over 20 months old are indistinguishable from males.

The juvenile is rich moss green above and paler and duller green below with the red on its rump and tail coverts less bright than the adult's. Its head is a dull cobalt blue or greyish blue, shading into green on the hind crown. Bill, when newly fledged, a deep bright yellow, legs and feet pale grey (Macklin). The nestling has opalescent blue gape tubercles set on much swollen whitish gape flanges (Immelmann *et al.*, Ziswiler *et al.*). Mouth markings very like those of other nestling parrot-finches but with an un-interrupted dark band across the tongue (Ziswiler *et al.*). The dull blue feathers of the head are replaced by about the twelfth week by red feathers less bright than those of the adults. Fully adult plumage is not attained until about 20 months old, numerous intermediate stages ('zahlreiche Zwischenstadium') are passed through (Ziswiler *et al.*). Goodfellow also found that the many young that he took from wild nests and hand-reared also passed through intermediate phases between the first juvenile plumage and that of the adults.

The above description is of *E. cyaneovirens regia*, from the northern New Hebrides. I have not seen specimens of *E. cyaneovirens efatensis*, from Efate Island. It was described as having a green back and the red parts less bright. Ziswiler *et al.* believe the description is based on sub-adults and that this form is inseparable from *E.c. regia*. *E.c. serena*, from Aneiteum Island, southern New Hebrides, has the blue of the upperparts restricted to a narrow band around the hind neck and the fringes of some of the wing coverts, its belly and flanks are mainly green and all its green parts a little lighter than those of *E.c. regia*. The only female I have seen is like the male but slightly less bright. Ziswiler *et al.* think this race is also invalid and that the few extant specimens are sub-adults. I am not completely convinced

that they are right but, having seen only a very few specimens, I do not like to give a dogmatic opinion. Unfortunately it appears that the species is now no longer found on Aneiteum (Ziswiler *et al.*), probably owing to habitat destruction by man.

See plate 4, facing p. 129.

FIELD CHARACTERS Small, thickset, short-tailed, thick-billed blue and green bird with bright red head and rump.

DISTRIBUTION AND HABITAT New Hebrides. Probably now extinct on Aneiteum. Inhabits forest, forest clearings and areas of cultivation with scattered wild fig trees. On the larger islands up to 300 metres but as low as 100 metres on some of the smaller islands. Not rare but nowhere abundant.

FEEDING AND GENERAL HABITS Feeds mainly on the seeds of ripe wild figs but also takes some insects, especially larvae found in figs. Seeds of the figs *Ficus dicaisnea*, *F. acrorhyncha*, *F. obliqua*, *F. verrucosa* and *F. kajewskii* are known foods. In captivity it will eat the seeds of ripe cultivated figs. When feeding the fig may be left on its stem or plucked and carried to a branch. It is held with the feet and torn open with the curved upper mandible. The bird then inserts its lower mandible and, with to-and-fro movements, opens up the fruit and picks out the seeds. Small seeds of up to 1·5 mm in diameter are slightly crushed and swallowed husk and all, larger seeds are de-husked (Ziswiler *et al.*) Goodfellow, whose observations of its feeding habits agree with the above, found that it habitually carried figs to the same branch to eat them and this fact enabled him to catch the birds by putting bird lime where he knew they would settle.

Usually seen singly or in pairs, only when the young are still dependent, in family parties. Several birds may,

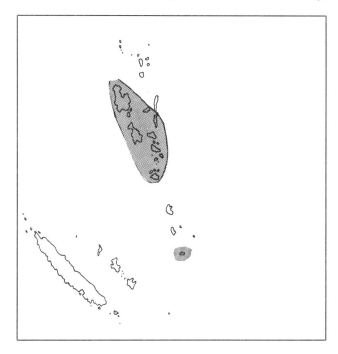

however, feed in the same tree. Keeps mainly to the upper parts of large trees. Goodfellow stresses how inconspicuous it is unless searched for, he found that many people living on the island where he caught his birds were unaware of its existence. It will go to the ground for water but prefers to drink drops from the leaves and habitually bathes by rubbing against wet leaves. When arriving to feed in a tree it alights in the very top and only gradually moves downwards as it searches for ripe fruits. When moving from place to place it flies high over the canopy.

Lories and fruit doves compete with it for food and the doves often drive it from fruiting trees. Its absence from some low altitude areas where its food trees occur plentifully may be due to the presence there of the introduced mosquito *Culex pipiens*, which carries the introduced bird malaria.

Goodfellow found nestlings of this species easy to handrear on a mixture of fig seeds (crushed at first, later whole) and eggfood made with egg and biscuit. The young so reared took canary seed readily when they began to feed themselves. All authorities (Goodfellow, Immelmann *et al.*, Neff) agree that it is difficult to get wild caught birds to take seed and that soft food, soaked seeds and insect foods must be given. On minor details and as to whether fruit should be given ad lib. there are differences of opinion and as no one seems to have been outstandingly successful with this species I hesitate to recommend one expert rather another to the would-be keeper of this evidently difficult species. Macklin, who obtained a pair of immature birds from Goodfellow, found that they readily ate a proprietary brand of softfood, spray millet, mealworms, seeding grasses, chickweed and lettuce but took very little dry seed. Subsequently they bred and reared one young one on this diet.

NESTING Nest usually in the lower part of the upper canopy of a forest tree but sometimes as low as about 2 metres above ground. The nest is built in a fork or among small branches and often incorporates the latter within its walls. It is large, elliptical or roundish, about 250 to 300 m in diameter, built of long coarse fibres, leaves, coconut fibre dried grass, vine tendrils and similar materials. The egg chamber is about 120 mm long and 100 mm high.

Clutch probably 2 to 4. Most nests found by Ziswiler contained 3 young but a few broods of 1, 2 and 4 were also found. Incubation period 14 days. Young fledge at 21 days and stay for one or two more weeks with the parents. Breeds from May till late December but some active nests may be found in January and, rarely, from February to April (Ziswiler *et al.*). There are photographs of nests and of a fledgling in Ziswiler *et al.*

VOICE The contact, trilling and aggressive calls are similar to those of the Blue-faced Parrot-finch (q.v.). The song consists of the repetition, for several seconds, of a single element and is similar or nearly identical to the songs of *E. trichroa* and *E. psittacea*, sound spectrograms of which are given by Ziswiler *et al.*

DISPLAY AND SOCIAL BEHAVIOUR Ziswiler *et al.* imply that displays and social behaviour are virtually identical in all the Melanesian parrot-finches but do not specifically describe it for this species. Probably similar to that of *E. trichroa* and *E. psittacea* except for the bird being less social.

OTHER NAMES Red-headed Parrot-finch (formerly used only for *E. psittacea* and best restricted to it), New Hebrides Parrot-finch.

REFERENCES
Goodfellow, W. 1934. The Royal Parrot Finch. *Avicult. Mag.* 4th series, **12**: 13–182.
Immelmann, K., Steinbacher, J. & Wolters, H. E. 1967. *Vögel in Käfig und Voliere: Prachtfinken*: 211–221.
Macklin, C. H. 1935. Breeding of the Royal Parrot Finch. *Avicult. Mag.* 4th series, **13**: 245–248.
Neff, R. 1971. Bemerkungen über die Papageiamadine (*Erythrura regia*). *Gefiederte Welt* **1971**: 201–203.
Ziswiler, V., Güttinger, H. R. & Bregulla, H. 1972. *Monographie der Gattung* Erythrura *Swainson 1837 (Aves, Passeres, Estrildidae)*. Bonner Zoologische Monographien, No. 2.

Royal Parrot-finch (*cyaneovirens* group)   *Erythrura cyaneovirens*

Geospiza cyaneovirens Peale, 1848, *U.S. Exploring Exped.*, ed. 1, *Birds*, p. 117.

DESCRIPTION As previous form, *E. cyaneovirens regia* (q.v.) but red on head darker and less brilliant and that on rump and tail a dull carmine. The blue areas are lighter and, except where adjacent to the red parts of nape and neck, of a more greenish blue. Females possibly average a little less bright than males but there is no constant difference.

The juvenile is described (Ziswiler *et al.*) as being dull green with a dull cobalt blue head and duller carmine rump and tail. Its bill is at first yellow or yellow-orange with a dark tip. A juvenile in the British Museum (Natural History) collection, that appears to be in its first plumage, agrees with the above description except that it has most of the blue feathers of its forehead and crown tipped with dull red. Another is similar but the red tips are larger above the eyes and on the forehead, making these areas appear mainly dull red. Two others, apparently at a later plumage stage although still with parti-coloured bills, have all the tops of their heads of the same red as that of the adults but the face blue except for a few red-tipped blue feathers. It takes about 20 months before the fully adult plumage has been acquired. The mouth markings of nestlings are like those of *E.c. regia* (Ziswiler *et al.*).

The above description is of nominate *E.c. cyaneovirens*, from Upolu. *E. cyaneovirens gaughrani*, from Savaii, is said (duPont) to differ by having the back and underparts green, the blue on the nape paler and less extensive and the throat green 'with a less extensive and paler blue wash'. It was described from one adult male and several immatures of each sex which were said to 'mirror the character of the (adult) male by being green with very little blue'. An unsexed adult, with no precise locality, in

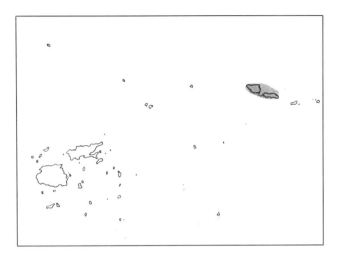

the British Museum (Natural History) collection, no 1881.5.1.4482, agrees with the above description except that its head is of a slightly paler and brighter red than those of specimens from Upolu.

FIELD CHARACTERS Small, thickset, finchlike bird, green and blue, or green, with red (adult) or (imm.) bluish or bluish and red head and dull red rump and tail.

DISTRIBUTION AND HABITAT The western Samoan islands of Upolu and Savaii. Inhabits forest openings, pasture land with some forest or secondary growth and plantations. Inhabits all elevations where suitable habitat occurs but appears to avoid very densely populated coastal areas.

FEEDING AND GENERAL HABITS Feeds on the seed of wild figs and herbaceous plants and also small insects. The crop of a nestling contained about 40 per cent fig seeds, and about 30 per cent each of weed seeds and small caterpillars. Figs are dealt with in the same way as by the previous form (q.v.). It does not appear to take the seeds of the introduced grasses. Prefers to feed in vegetation, where it can climb, cling and hang with agility, and relatively seldom feeds on the ground.

Usually in pairs or flocks of up to 40 birds. Nervous and cautious. When feeding in the open, it flies at once to the cover of tree or bush at the least alarm.

The above is derived from Ziswiler *et al.* I am, however, a little at a loss as to how to reconcile their statement (on p. 59) that the species has been able to compensate for loss of its original habitat by turning to weed and grass seeds ('durch Umstellung auf Kraut- und Grassamenernährung zu kompensieren') with two statements on p. 58 (paragraphs 2 and 5) which seem to indicate that grass seed is *not* eaten.

NESTING Nests in trees, very often in the epiphytic or parasitic growth on or around them. The nest is built of stems, fibres etc and is roundish with a narrow, downward-directed side entrance. Two nests found by Ziswiler were at heights of 6 and 8 metres.

Eggs 3 to 4. Incubation period 14 days. Young fledge at 18 days (*fide* Stunzer, in Ziswiler *et al.*). The young are

independent about two weeks after fledging. Breeds from January to April, usually (if successful) rearing two consecutive broods.

VOICE I can find no certain description. Probably similar to *E.c. regia* and *E.c. pealii.*

DISPLAY AND SOCIAL BEHAVIOUR No information, probably very similar or identical to allied species.

OTHER NAMES Samoa Parrot-finch, Red-headed Parrot-finch (usually and best restricted to *E. psittacea* but has been used for the *cyaneovirens* group in recent faunal works).

REFERENCES
duPont, J. E. 1972. Notes from western Samoa, including the description of a new parrot-finch (*Erythrura*). *Wilson Bulletin* **84**: 375–376 (includes a colour plate of all forms of this group).
Ziswiler, V., Güttinger, H. R. & Bregulla, H. 1972. *Monographie der Gattung* Erythrura *Swainson, 1837 (Aves, Passeres, Estrildidae).* Bonner Zoologische Monographien, No. 2.

Pink-billed Parrot-finch *Erythrura kleinschmidti*

Amblynura kleinschmidti Finsch 1878, *Proc.* Zool. Soc. London, p. 440.

DESCRIPTION A little larger than other parrot-finches (wing 63 to 69 mm), with short tail and rather large, broad bill with only slightly curving culmen ridge. Face, forehead and forecrown black. Hind crown and nape dark blue, shading into the dark green of the upperparts. The black of the face is divided from the lighter and more yellowish green of the posterior parts of the head by a narrow blue edging. Outer secondaries and primaries blackish brown with green on the outer webs. Rump and upper tail coverts shining red. Throat black, washed with green. Rest of underparts a lighter green than above and with a gold sheen on the green parts of the sides of the head and breast. Irides brown or dark brown. Bill pinkish flesh colour. Legs and feet flesh-coloured.

The sexes are alike or nearly so. Juvenile is described as duller and more brownish on the green parts. Clunie (1973) observed birds with the anterior half of the bill dark but which did not appear to be in juvenile plumage.

FIELD CHARACTERS Thickset green finch-like bird with red rump. *Dark face and large pale bill* are conspicuous in the field and at once identify it from the red-faced, dark-billed Peale's Parrot-finch.

DISTRIBUTION AND HABITAT Fiji Islands: Known only from Viti Levu. Inhabits rain forest at both high and low elevations. Sometimes in the forest-like cocoa plantations or at forest edge but not in native gardens and other cultivated or open areas.

FEEDING AND GENERAL HABITS The field observations of Clunie (1972 and 1973) and those of Ziswiler (Ziswiler *et al.*) give very different pictures of the feeding ecology of this species. This may be due to local differences in feeding

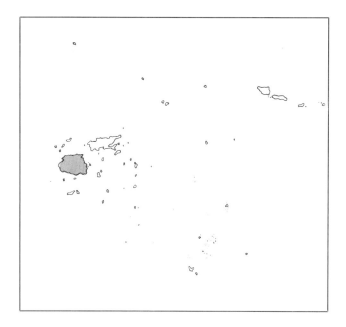

habits or, and I think much more likely, to differences dependent on the condition of the birds (perhaps whether breeding or not breeding) and/or the availability of foods. Ziswiler came to the conclusion that this bird was a specialist feeder on wild figs. It was seen feeding on the fruits of *Ficus vitiensis*, *F. tinctoria* and *Garcinia myrtifolia*. Fruits of *F. vitiensis* and *Garcinia*, were held underfood, the skin torn open and both seeds and pulp eaten, the discarded skin being left everted. The smaller, pea-sized fruits of *F. tinctoria* were plucked, crushed with up and down movements of the under mandible and swallowed whole. Feeding birds were usually seen in pairs or singly but sometimes up to 7 in the same tree. They were often driven from their food tree by the Golden Dove, *Ptilinopus luteovirens*, and the Many-coloured Fruit Dove, *P. perousii*. It fed mainly in the branches but would go to the ground for fallen fruits when driven from a tree.

Clunie observed it feeding mainly on insects, usually in pairs or singly, accompanying mixed parties of insectivorous birds. It persistently investigated bunches of dead leaves, probed in vegetation, prised off bits of loose bark and broke open dead twigs and stems in search of hidden invertebrates. One was seen to open up an ants' nest in a small dead branch and feed eagerly on either the ants or their pupae. Although it sought insects largely in the forest under-storey it also did so on the ground. One was seen to dig out and swallow a largish grub from a rotten stump. Holyoak saw it take insects from twigs and also small seeds from pea-like pods on a tree.

Apparently official forestry interests, in Fiji as elsewhere, are busy replacing the native trees by exotic conifers, and thus pose a serious threat to this and other forest species (Ziswiler *et al.*).

NESTING Clunie watched a pair building in August 1972. The nest was roundish and untidy looking, built of dead leaves, small twigs, lichens and bamboo leaves with a small, downward-facing entrance hole low down at one side. One bird (presumably the cock) brought the materials while, to judge from the movements of the nest walls, the one inside did the building. Mercer (in Ziswiler *et al.*) thinks it breeds mainly from October to January but birds in juvenile plumage have also been seen in March. Eggs said to be light red with dark red spots (Martin, in Clunie) but this seems most unlikely and some error of identification was probably involved.

VOICE Contact call a high-pitched 'tsee-tsee' (Ziswiler *et al.*) or 'chee-chee-chee' (Clunie). Also utters a single note that can be much louder and sharper than the usual contact call, and a clicking sound (Clunie, 1973).

DISPLAY AND SOCIAL BEHAVIOUR No information.

OTHER NAMES Black-faced Parrot-finch.

REFERENCES
Clunie, F. & Perks, L. 1972. Notes on the Pink-billed Parrot-finch of Fiji. *Notornis* **19**: 335–336.
Clunie, F. 1973. Pink-billed Parrot Finches near Nailagosakelo Creek, southern Viti Levu. *Notornis* **20**: 202–209.
Holyoak, D. T. 1979. Notes on the birds of Viti, Levu and Taveuni, Fiji. *Emu* **79**: 7–18.
Ziswiler, V., Güttinger, H. R. & Bregulla, H. 1972. *Monographie der Gattung* Erythrura *Swainson, 1837 (Aves, Passeres, Estrildidae)*. Bonner Zoologische Monographien, No. 2.

The Gouldian Finch

The Gouldian Finch is the most colourful and, in some people's estimation, the most beautiful of all estrildids. It is a very distinct species whose relationships have been much disputed. In bill and wing shape and in its finely attenuated central tail feathers it resembles the Long-tailed Grassfinch and was included in the same genus, *Poephila*, by Delacour & Morris. It agrees with the parrot-finches, *Erythrura*, in having green, blue and (one colour morph) red plumage, in the luminous gape tubercles of its nestlings and in a few vocal and behavioural characters (Ziswiler *et al.*). Of these resemblances to the parrot-finches the most cogent is the luminous gape tubercles. The colour pattern of the head and breast of Peale's Parrot-finch, *E. pealii*, is suggestive of a more generalised or degenerate version of that of the red-headed form of the Gouldian Finch. On the other hand *E. pealii*, like most other parrot-finches, has a red rump and upper tail coverts. No parrot-finch has either a blue rump or any bluish purple colour in its plumage, indeed the only estrildids which share these two features with the Gouldian Finch (although the shades of blue and purple are not quite the same) are two African species, the Violet-eared Waxbill and the Purple Grenadier, *Uraeginthus granatina* and *U. ianthinogaster*. Neither of these appears to be, as estrildids go, at all closely related to the Gouldian Finch.

As Hall (1962 and unpublished mss) has pointed out,

the Gouldian Finch shares many characters with some of the Asiatic mannikins and the Java Sparrow. Its plumage pattern is very similar to that of the Chestnut-breasted Finch, *Lonchura castaneothorax*, and bears some resemblance also to those of the Timor and Java Sparrows. The pale pinkish purple of the female Gouldian's breast is very similar in colour to the belly and flanks of the Java Sparrow. It is not an exact match but then neither are the greens, blues and reds of the Gouldian with those of the parrot-finches. In voice and behaviour the Gouldian Finch also shows many close, and apparently homologous, resemblances to some *Lonchura* species (Hall, Ziswiler *et al.*).

Thus the Gouldian Finch shows a mosaic of characters. Of these the *Poephila*-like wing and bill seem likely to be due to convergence but those which suggest relationship to the mannikins and the parrot-finches seem to be true indications of affinity. Probably, as Ziswiler *et al.* suggest, the Gouldian Finch derived from some stock ancestral to both *Lonchura* and *Eythrura*. Another possibility is that, especially if the characters for brightly coloured plumage and those for luminous bluish gape tubercles in the nestling are correlated, then these characters might have developed in the ancestor of the Gouldian Finch subsequent to its diverging from proto-*Erythrura* stock. At all events it seems justifiable to maintain the monotypic genus *Chloebia* for this species.

REFERENCES
Delacour, J. 1943. A revision of the subfamily Estrildinae of the family Ploceidae. *Zoologica, New York Soc.* **28**: 69–86.
Hall, F. M. 1962. Evolutionary aspects of estrildid song. *Symposia Zool. Soc. London* **8**: 37–70.
Morris, D. 1958. The comparative ethology of grassfinches (Erythrurae) and Mannikins (Amadinae). *Proc. Zool. Soc. London* **131**: 389–439.
Ziswiler, V., Güttinger, H. R. & Bregulla, H. 1972. *Monographie der Gattung* Erythrura *Swainson, 1837 (Aves, Passeres, Estrildidae)*. Bonner Zoologische Monographien, No. 2.

Gouldian Finch   *Chloebia gouldiae*

Amadina Gouldiae Gould, 1844, *Birds Australia* pt. 15, pl. 88 (also *Proc. Zool. Soc. London* **12**, p. 5).

DESCRIPTION About size of Spice Finch but general proportions similar to Long-tailed Grassfinch (q.v.) although the tail is shorter. Forehead, crown and face, including ear coverts, deep bright scarlet red. A narrow border of black behind the red area connects with the black throat. Immediately behind the black border there is a border of bright azure blue which is broadest on the hind crown and narrowest where it borders the throat. Hind neck bright green with a golden tinge, shading to a darkish grass green on the mantle, back and wing coverts and to a slightly more olivaceous green on the inner secondaries and outer fringes (except near their ends) of the otherwise dull blackish drab wing quills. Under wing coverts pale yellowish. Rump light blue; upper tail coverts a darker blue with the ends of the feathers paler and their

extreme fringes buffish. Outer tail feathers brownish black with dull white apical spots. Central tail feathers black, graduated and drawn out into fine thin wisps at the ends. Breast a rich bright purplish blue (which appears a purer purple after death), slightly darker along the sharp line of demarcation from the lower breast, flanks and belly which are bright buttercup yellow, deepening to an orange hue along the narrow line of demarcation from the purple area. Ventral area and under tail coverts yellowish white. Irides dark brown; eye-rims light blue. Bill pearl white, pinkish white or whitish horn, with a small red or pink area at the tip of the upper mandible and a more extensive red or pink area at the end of the lower mandible. Legs and feet yellowish flesh-coloured to yellowish buff.

In the wild (but seldom to the same extent in captivity) wear and bleaching of the plumage causes noticeable colour changes. At a certain degree of wear the fringes of the mantle and back feathers become a paler and brighter green, contrasting with their dark bases. With greater

Plate 7 Examples of differences between adult and juvenile plumages. All birds shown are males, the adult above in each case.
(1) Black-crowned Waxbills, *Estrilda nonnula*; (2) Chestnut Munias (white-bellied form), *Lonchura m. malacca*; (3) Red-sided Mountain Finches, *Oreostruthus fuliginosus*; (4) Goldbreasts, *Amandava subflava*; (5) Cut-throats, *Amadina fasciata*.

MWWoodcock

M.W.Woodcock

weathering these green feather tips turn light blue, except immediately behind the blue hind crown, the yellow areas of the underparts become much paler and the red of the head an orange-red colour. This extreme degree of wear is well shown by a male in the British Museum (Natural History) collection, no 1964. 870. Naturally every degree of intergradation between the above-described stages occurs.

The female has shorter central tail feathers, the red on her head is less brilliant and more or less intermixed with black. Sometimes she has only a few red feathers on her head. The green of her upperparts is duller than the male's, her breast a plae pinkish purple and the yellow of her underparts paler. When in breeding condition her bill becomes largely dark grey or blackish. Effects of plumage wear are comparable in both sexes.

Descriptions usually imply that both sexes of the juveniles are alike. They may sometimes or usually be so but in the few sexed specimens I have seen there was some difference. The juvenile male has the entire head grey

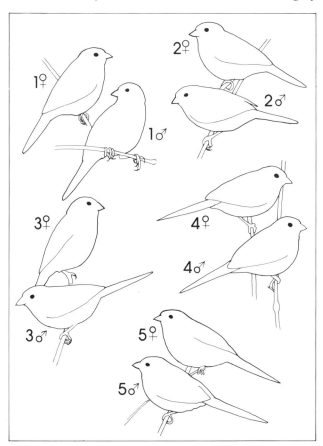

Plate 8 Differences in kind and degrees of sexual dichromatism within forms of three closely related species. A male and female of each shown, with the female above.
(1) Cordon-bleus, *Uraeginthus angolensis niassensis*; (2) Cordon-bleus, *Uraeginthus a.angolensis*; (3) Red-cheeked Cordon-bleus, *U. bengalus brunneigularis*; (4) Red-cheeked Cordon-bleus, *U. b.bengalus*; (5) Blue-headed Cordon-bleus, *Uraeginthus cyanocephala*.

except for a pale buffish grey throat. The green upperparts are of a paler and more olivaceous hue than the adult's. Rump pale greenish grey with a buffish tinge. Upper tail coverts dull bluish green with paler fringes. Central tail feathers mainly dull bluish green with dull central shafts; they are only a little longer than the outer tail feathers and only slightly attenuated. Outer tail feathers dark drab with greenish fringes to their outer webs, the outermost pair light drab with pale buffish fringes. Breast pale buffish flesh to a slightly pinkish buffish grey. Underparts, where yellow in the adult, pale buffish yellow to pale yellowish drab. Bill at first dark grey or blackish often or usually with some red suffusion on the lower mandible. The juvenile female has the green of her upperparts slightly greyer. She has no pinkish tinge on her greyish or pale drab breast and her underparts, where yellow in the adult, are off-white to pale buff. The nestling is at first naked. It has the common mouth pattern of 5 black spots on the pale palate, a crescentic mark inside the lower mandible and two dark marks on the tongue. There are two pale blue, light-reflecting tubercles at each corner of the mouth, with a less well-developed whitish tubercle between them. The nestling mouth markings and the anatomical features of the luminous tubercles were described and illustrated by Butler in 1898.

The above description is of the red-headed form. In a wild state it is always found together with the black-headed form which outnumbers it, usually, by about 3 to 1. The two are identical in appearance except that those parts of the head that are red (or black) in the red-headed form are entirely black in the black-headed.

The hereditary factor for red-headedness is sex-linked and dominant to that for black-headedness. Black-headed Gouldian Finches are thus always pure black-heads and red-headed females, even those that show only a few red feathers on their otherwise black heads, are always genetically pure red-heads. Red-headed males may be either pure (homozygous) or carrying both the black-headed and red-headed factors (heterozygous). Unless their ancestry is known, only breeding a number of young from them will prove which they are (Immelmann, 1965, Southern, 1946, Ziegler, 1963).

The yellow-headed form is similar to the red-headed but has the head yellow to tawny-orange in colour. The end of its bill is also yellowish, not red or pink. It is much rarer than the other two in the wild state and generally believed to be more delicate, or perhaps one should say even more delicate, in captivity (Immelmann *et al.*, 1968). Its coloration is due to a genetic inability to transform the yellow carotenoid pigments in its food to red carotenoids. This gene defect can occur in what would otherwise be either red-headed or black-headed birds. In the latter the black head plumage masks its presence so far as plumage is concerned but it is revealed by the yellow, not red, tip to the bill. The yellow-headed form is recessive to normal black-headed or red-headed forms.

A variety which is entirely yellow with a red head; one with a blue back and one with a white instead of a purple breast have occurred in captive-bred stocks but only the last seems to have been established. There is a good colour photograph of a pair of this white-breasted form in Iles' book.

See plate 2, facing p. 97.

FIELD CHARACTERS The black or red head, in contrast with the grccn back and/or the purple breast and yellow underparts are diagnostic. Juvenile is a light dull greenish and greyish finch with (until it starts to moult) no bright or contrasting markings.

DISTRIBUTION AND HABITAT Tropical northern Australia, from Derby to the eastern shore of the Gulf of Carpentaria and south-east to about Charters Towers (lat. 20°S), Queensland. Details of range is given by Storr for Northern Territory (1977) and Queensland (1973). Inhabits open grassy plains with groups of tall trees, savanna woodland and the edges of forest and mangrove thickets. Always near to surface water. Appears to be locally nomadic and not to breed in some of the more northerly parts of its range.

FEEDING AND GENERAL HABITS Takes both unripe and ripe seeds of *Sorghum plumosum*, *Eriachne obtusa*, *Eragrostris* sp. and probably also other grasses. Also insects, especially flying termites, and small spiders. Largely insectivorous when breeding, at least in the case of those populations observed by Immelmann. Usually feeds while perched on or clinging to grass stems or other vegetation. Will sidle down trailing branches that touch tall grasses in order to feed from the latter while still clinging to the former. Holds grass panicles and stems underfoot when feeding (Immelmann, 1962 and 1965). Drinks in pigeon-like manner. Immelmann found it rather shy of man, flying up to the tops of high trees when disturbed. Tends to perch and hold itself rather erect, more like mannikins *Lonchura*, than grassfinches *Poephila*.

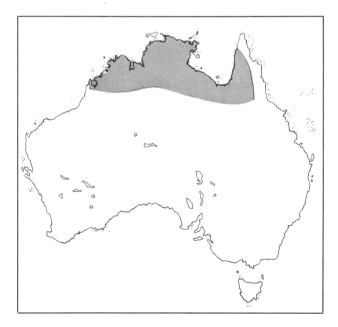

Highly social. When not breeding usually in flocks of up to several hundred birds. When breeding several pairs usually nest near to each other. Immelmann (1960) found that the Gouldian Finch, in strong contrast to other sympatric estrildids, appeared positively to enjoy the very hottest weather. It showed greatest activity when the temperature was between 30° and 40°C. In captivity usually chooses to roost on, and very often near the ends of thin twigs. Probably in the wild this serves to protect it from snakes or other nocturnal predators (Hall, unpublished mss., Mitchell). Captive birds sometimes roost in nests or under cover but only to avoid artificial light (Verborgen).

The Gouldian Finch is widely kept and bred in captivity but with very varying degrees of success. In Australia (R. H. Stranger, pers. comm.) and California (L. F. Baptista, pers comm.) it appears to be bred in numbers, without much difficulty or anything exceptionally elaborate in the way of diet or accommodation, even in areas where the temperature and humidity are not very close to those of its native haunts. In Japan it has for many years been bred in large numbers (see Ziegler, 1963 and 1975 for detailed description of methods) by treating the Gouldians as mere producers of eggs, which are collected and entrusted to Bengalese Finches for hatching and rearing.

In the past some English bird-keepers seem to have been remarkably successful at keeping and rearing Gouldian Finches under what would now seem to be inadequate conditions. Boosey bred numbers, including one brood of 9, in outdoor aviaries, feeding them only on dry seed and flowering rye grass. Teague (1932, 1933, 1936, 1946) bred them for many generations with little or no artificial heat although he took great care to supply a very varied diet, with vitamin and mineral supplements. Some aviculturists of former days (e.g. Grant-Ives) even claimed that their Gouldian Finches *enjoyed* being kept at subfreezing temperatures where their drinking water froze several inches thick each day!

These early successes may have been due to the fact that in those days of slower travel, the deplorable mortality among wild-caught Gouldian Finches was such that perhaps the few that survived to be sold in Britain (or elsewhere), and were not already fatally ill (as many evidently were, from contemporary laments about thc deaths of recently-purchased Gouldians), were a small minority of exceptionally tough and cold-resistant individuals. It is possible that some such relatively very hardy Gouldian Finches are among the present captive stocks but, if so, they would appear to be in a minority.

Ziegler has for years bred, studied, and amassed a great deal of information from other aviculturists about this species. His conclusions, which I find convincing, are that Gouldian Finches need to be kept at a minium temperature of 20 to 21°C, preferably 24°C. In addition, a very varied diet, including many kinds of dry seeds, sprouted seed, greenfood, animal food of some (and preferably more than one) kind must be given *daily*, together with extra vitamin supplements, and, of course, the usual minerals.

Humidity also has to be controlled. At a temperature of about 20°C it must be 55 to 60 per cent but at a temperature of 24°C 65 to 70 per cent. Gouldians, even those bred in captivity, are apparently much more sensitive to the stress of being caught and transported than are most other birds and this also represents a hazard to them, and to their new owner who may find even previously healthy birds fall ill through this cause. Ziegler's (1963) monographic paper on this bird should be studied in the original by all who are seriously interested in the Gouldian Finch and who can read German. What appears to be a somewhat edited and shorter version (with some apparent mistranslations) is available in English (Ziegler, 1975).

The Gouldian Finch is not a species that I have kept and its proper care would appear to be so demanding that I have not attempted here, as with many other species, to give a full summary of its dietary needs in captivity. I would advise any would-be Gouldian Finch keeper in Britain or any other cool climate to ask himself or herself three questions: Am I rich? Do I have lots of spare time *every* day? Do I think the Gouldian Finch really is the *most* attractive of all the readily available birds? If the answer to any of these questions is 'No', then he or she would be wise not to aspire to the Gouldian Finch but to be content with one of the many more easily kept birds. If, however, the answer is 'yes' in each case, then I recommend the thorough perusal of Ziegler's 1963 monograph and the contacting of the nearest *successful* Gouldian Finch keeper. In one respect the Gouldian Finch is less demanding than many otherwise more easily kept estrildids, it will usually nest even in a cage. It is also usually quite tame and will behave normally when under its owner's eye. However, its temperature and humidity requirements make it hardly suitable for the unfortunate person whose circumstances dictate that his or her birds must be kept in a cage in a living room, while, if a separate room is needed for the Gouldian Finches' cage, then there is seldom likely to be any good reason why they should be shut in the cage and not allowed to fly free in the room. The growing of orchids or other tropical plants that also need heat and humidity can be readily combined with the successful keeping and breeding of Gouldian Finches.

NESTING Sometimes builds in bushes, small trees or rank grass. The nest is then usually loosely constructed of dead grass or other materials, rather variable in shape and often with the roof slight or incomplete. More often nests in holes in trees or in holes, originally made by parakeets or kingfishers, in termite mounds. Hole nests are often similar to those in bushes but sometimes little or no nesting material is used. Nest material is collected by the male who carries it 'bundled' to the site, where the female builds. Cases of more than one pair apparently nesting in a single hollow have been recorded (in Immelmann, 1965 and Mitchell, 1958) but the eggs were all collected and such behaviour would seem to be most unusual. In captivity individuals show a preference for nesting materials similar to those of the nest in which they themselves were reared (Ziegler, 1963). Usually several pairs nest near together, sometimes in different holes in the same tree.

When seeking a nest site the male takes the lead. Both sexes, but more especially the female, show considerable caution and delay before first entering the hole. Much time may be spent together just outside it and even after the male has cautiously entered and begun nest-calling, it may be some little time before his repeated entries and calling from within induce his mate to follow. Finally both sit together inside the hole for some time. This hesitant behaviour clearly serves to lessen the risk of their entering a hole containing a snake or other predator, or one that has already been claimed by some stronger bird which, if it returned when they were inside, might attack and injure them.

Eggs 4 to 8, usually only 4 or 5 in captivity but a clutch of 9 once recorded, and all 9 young reared, from one captive pair (Boosey). Both sexes incubate in turn by day, only the female at night. When coming to take over on the eggs, the male often brings nesting material which the female builds into the nest before leaving. Incubation period 14–15 days. Young fledge at 21–22 days, often later in captivity. In the wild they do not usually, if ever, return to the nest (Immelmann, 1965) but some captive-bred cock Gouldians habitually lead their young back to the nest to roost for the first few evenings after fledging (Ziegler, 1963). In captivity (and doubtless in the wild also) parents lead fledged young up to a fairly high perch to feed them. Only when repeated attempts to make it follow to a 'safe' perch have failed will a parent reluctantly feed it on the ground (Ziegler, 1963).

Wild Gouldian Finches are said sometimes to breed while still in juvenile plumage (Immelmann, 1965). As, however, captive juveniles may feed their siblings of the next brood (Ziegler, 1963), it is possible that such behaviour in wild birds may have been mis-interpreted. Breeds in the second half of the wet season, from about January to April, rearing 2 or 3 broods in succession (Immelmann, 1965).

VOICE The voice of the Gouldian Finch has been studied in detail by Hall (1962 and unpublished mss), Immelmann (1962 and 1965), Ziegler (1963 and 1975) and Ziswiler *et al.* The information hereunder is derived from Ziegler (1963) unless otherwise indicated.

The close contact call: 'sit' or 'ssit' may be given either as a single note or in a series. The distance contact call is similar but louder, easier for human ears to localise, and usually given twice in quick succession: 'ssit-ssit', seldom singly or in series. It is used to maintain or establish contact at a greater distance but, apparently, not when the bird is feeling really anxious. In the latter situation, when a bird has become visually isolated from mate or companions, it gives what Ziegler terms the lost call (Verlassenheitsruf), a long-drawn, plaintive 'ssreeh' or 'ssreeht' (my anglicisation). This is given in a descending call series of up to seven syllables. Immelmann (1962) notes that it seems to 'hang in the air' with no definite ending. This call is also given (Immelmann, 1962) as a social call by birds gathering for a social meeting. Ziswiler *et al.* give sound spectrograms of the two contact calls.

The alarm call is very similar to the contact call, a sharp 'set-set' given as a double note or in a short series. The parents of fledged but still dependent young have a special alarm call 'dyit' (my anglicisation) which is suggestive in sound of a drop of water falling and which causes the young to 'freeze' motionless.

A pleasant sounding 'ssreeit' (my anglicisation) is uttered as a nest call by the male when he is near an actual or potential nest site and serves to attract his mate's attention to it. This call is also used as an immediate preface to the song when, and only when, the latter accompanies sexual display. A high-pitched 'weeweeweeweeweewee . . .', identical in sound to the food begging of the nestlings, is uttered by both sexes. It is given only when the caller is either inside the nest or when entering it to change over and probably serves to co-ordinate behaviour at nest relief.

The song is very like those of the Asiatic and Australian mannikins. It is high-pitched, only audible to human ears for a few metres and consists of continuous whispering, hissing and low-pitched clicking notes and also a long-drawn out whining sound. It is as Hall (unpublished mss) says and as her sound spectrograms (Hall, 1962) show, remarkably complex. It is given, prefaced by the nest call, in courtship display and as undirected song. In the latter case it is never (*fide* Ziegler, 1963) prefaced by the nest call. Although the song is often or usually given in a less extreme version of the posture in which the bird sings when displaying, Ziegler is convinced that it is not sexually motivated when given as undirected song. It may, however, then help social cohesion or amity between flock members as 'peering' (in reality almost certainly listening as the German term 'Zuhören' implies) at a singing bird by others is usual. When not performing reproductive or maintenance activities male Gouldians, young and old, spend a great deal of their time singing. A young bird that had been reared by Bengalese, and after it was independent kept with Gouldian Finches and Avadavats, copied the Avadavat's song (Baptista). Gouldians *not* reared by them have been known to mimic Bengalese (Verborgen).

DISPLAY AND SOCIAL BEHAVIOUR   The generally very *Lonchura*-like courtship display of the Gouldian Finch has been described in greater or lesser detail by many observers, especially Hall (unpublished mss), Immelmann (1962), Mitchell and Ziegler (1963) from whose accounts, especially those of Hall and Ziegler, the following information derives.

Courtship display is commonly prefaced by both birds flying about and uttering contact calls or by the male approaching a perched female. Then, either in a horizontal posture with tail somewhat raised, or in a more upright posture, the male turns towards the female and performs a series of ritualised double bill-wipes on the perch just beyond his foot. If this is done from an upright position, the head is sharply arched downwards. The bill-wiping becomes more and more rapid until it is no longer possible to see the individual movements of the bird's head. Suddenly he goes into an upright posture with the whole body drawn rigidly back so that the tarsal joints may actually be below the level of his perch. The feathers of his face are partly, those further back on the head more fully fluffed out, as are those on the rump and underparts below, and especially at the periphery of, the purple breast band. The tail is angled towards the female and somewhat depressed. In this position the male faces the female and begins to sing and to bob up and down rapidly, alternately stretching and flexing his legs, with or without his feet leaving the perch momentarily.

There is considerable apparently individual variation; some of the actions described above may be emphasised, minimised or omitted from the display. Although Hall (unpublished mss) apparently found that bobbing up and down was a normal part of the display, Ziegler (1963) found it was common in young males but very seldom performed by older (mehrjährige) ones.

The female may respond to, or initiate the male's courtship display by shaking the body plumage and turning toward the male with angled tail and (sometimes) bill-wiping and other head movements like those of the male. She may follow this by crouching and tail quivering. Copulation, however, occurs inside the nest, or nest hole, to which the male, followed by the female, often flies immediately after displaying. Tail quivering by males sometimes occurs in situations of apparent frustration (Verborgen).

When the male is uttering the nestling-like call inside the nest cavity he may (and perhaps usually or always does) adopt the postures of a begging fledgling (Nicolai, 1962).

Gouldian Finches do not allo-preen and, unless ill, do not clump. Peering at (listening to) singing conspecifics is usual. Usually very peaceable both towards its own and other species only (sometimes) defending the immediate vicinity of the nest. In captivity (and probably when wild) pairs for life but the bond between the partners seems less intense than with many estrildids.

A hand-reared male (which lived for 13 years) reacted socially and sexually to humans and also, but less intensely, to a female of its own species (Teague, 1947).

OTHER NAMES   Rainbow Finch, Painted Finch (causing confusion with the species, *Emblema picta*, usually so-called), Lady Gould (in some American bird-keeping circles).

REFERENCES
Baptista, L. F. 1973. Song mimesis by a captive Gouldian Finch. *Auk* **90**: 891–894.
Boosey, E. J. 1956. *Foreign bird keeping.* Iliffe Books Ltd, London.

Butler, A. G. 1898. On the ornamentation of the mouth in the young Gouldian Finch.

Grant-Ives, D. M. 1936. Gouldian Finch. *Avicult. Mag.* 5th ser. 1 : 125.

Hall, F. M. 1962. Evolutionary aspects of estrildid song. *Symposia Zool. Soc. London* 8 : 37–70.

Iles, G. W. (no date) *Breeding Australian Finches.* Isles d'Avon Ltd, Bristol.

Immelmann, K. 1960. *Im unbekannten Australien.* Pfungstadt/Darmstadt, Germany.

Immelmann, K. 1962. Beiträge zu einer vergleichenden Biologie australischer Prachtfinken (Spermestidae). *Zool. Jb. Syst. Bd.* 90 : 1–196.

Immelmann, K. 1965. *Australian finches in bush and aviary.* Angus & Robertson, Sydney.

Immelmann, K., Steinbacher, J., Nicolai, J. & Wolters, H. E. 1968. *Vögel in Käfig und Voliere: Prachtfinken*: 232–258.

Mitchell, I. G. 1958. The taxonomic position of the Gouldian Finch. *Emu* 58 : 395–411.

Southern, H. N. 1946. The inheritance of head colour in the Gouldian Finch. *Avicult. Mag.* 52 : 126–132.

Storr, G. M. 1973. *List of Queensland Birds.* Western Aust. Mus., special publication no. 5.

Storr, G. M. 1977. *Birds of the Northern Territory.* Western Aust. Mus., special publication no. 7.

Teague, P. W. 1932. Gouldian Finches. *Avicult. Mag.* 4th ser. 10 : 90–99.

Teague, P. W. 1933. Gouldians. *Avicult. Mag.* 4th ser. 11 : 142–146.

Teague, P. W. 1936. Experiences in removal and feeding methods. *Avicult. Mag.* 5th ser. 1 : 180–183.

Teague, P. W. 1946. Further notes on the breeding of Gouldian Finches. *Avicult. Mag.* 52 : 132–135.

Teague, P. W. 1947. Phillip – A Gouldian Finch. *Avicult. Mag.* 53 : 12–13.

Verborgen, L. & S. 1979. Bemerkungen zur Ethologie von Gouldamadinen. *Gefiederte Welt* 1979 : 45–48.

Ziegler, G. 1963. *Die Gouldamadine.* Sonderheft of *Die Gefiederte Welt.* (Note: This most important paper is not cited in the Zoological Record. I am uncertain as to what year's issue of *Die Gefiederte Welt* it accompanied as it is variously cited by German authors as for 1962, 1963 and 1964. However, my copy of the Sonderheft is clearly dated 1963 so I have thus cited it.)

Ziegler, G. 1975. *The Gouldian Finch.* Angus & Robertson, London and Sydney.

Ziswiler, V., Güttinger, H. R. & Bregulla, H. 1972. *Monographie der Gattung* Erythrura *Swainson, 1837 (Aves, Passeres, Estrildidae).* Bonner Zoologische Monographien, no. 2.

The Bibfinch, silverbills and African mannikins

These birds are discussed together, and separately from the Asiatic and Australasian mannikins, because there is much difference of opinion as to whether they should be considered generically distinct from Asiatic and Australasian forms, as advocated by, for example, Wolters, Steiner (1960) and Güttinger (1970 and 1976) or given only subgeneric rank within the genus *Lonchura* as by Delacour, Mayr, and Traylor in *'Peters'' check-list of birds of the world.*

The Bibfinch is the only estrildid native to Madagascar

and is a very distinct species. It is very small and has a proportionately rather smaller bill than most mannikins, in this latter feature and in its black bib it suggests the Australian Cherry Finch, *Aidemosyne modesta*, but the resemblance between them is probably convergent. Of possibly more significance are the decomposed shiny yellow fringes to its upper tail coverts, a character possessed by many of the Asiatic and Australian mannikins. Its rather short tail is nearly rounded and thus resembles those of the African mannikins, though it is only a little less wedge-shaped than the tails of such mannikins as *Lonchura tristissima.*

On its taxonomic characters I would ally the Bibfinch with the Asiatic mannikins (a comparable case might be the blue pigeons, *Alectroenas*, which are related to Asiatic and Australasian, not to African forms) but for the awkward fact that its courtship display resembles that of the African waxbills rather than those of Asiatic *Lonchura* species. It may represent an ancestral proto-*Lonchura* form that had developed the specialised tail coverts before losing (and never lost) the presumably primitive form of courtship display. On the other hand its *Lonchura*-like characters, including its somewhat generalised resemblance to the silverbills, might be due to convergence and it is so distinct that I concur with Güttinger in thinking that it is best placed in the monotypic genus *Lepidopygia.*

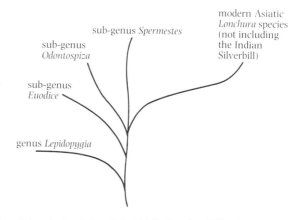

Possible relationships of the Bibfinch, silverbills, Asiatic and African mannikins. Some investigators, however, think that the resemblances of the others to the Asiatic mannikins are due to convergence (see text).

The African and Indian silverbills, *Lonchura cantans* and *L. malabarica*, differ from the other African and Asian *Lonchura* species in having longer and more pointed tails, slimmer build and from most of them in the pale sandy brown of their upper parts. These may all be merely specific characters, probably adaptations to their arid habitat. Such species as *Lonchura striata* do in fact much resemble them in appearance except for their darker coloration and somewhat less long and pointed tails. The African Silverbill has barring on its secondaries very similar to that on many typical waxbills; a feature that is absent or vestigial in the Indian Silverbill. More important perhaps are certain characters which might seem to link them with the African waxbills and their allies. These are their courtship displays, high-pitched calls and the apparent presence of masked red pigments in their rump and tail feathers which is suggested by the black feathers of these parts often showing a bronzy purple tinge and the fact that hybrids between the two species of silverbills have pink on the rump (Steiner, 1966). Also an aberrant specimen of *L. cantans* from Oman (British Museum collection no. 1977.21.47) has broad pink tips to its rump feathers. These two silverbills may, as has often been suggested, represent a very primitive group but except in their courtship display most of their differences from other mannikins appear to be adaptive. Harrison has pointed out that the differences between their displays and those of other *Lonchura* species are less definite than is sometimes thought and that the voice of the Indian Silverbill is less unlike those of some other *Lonchura* species than is that of *L. cantans.* As Kunkel (pers. comm.) says, the fact that the silverbills, unlike most dry country African estrildids, are not represented in southern Africa, suggests that the African Silverbill may represent a relatively recent invasion of Africa from the Oriental region. Dr Kunkel and Dr Baptista, who have both had extensive experience with them in life, agree in thinking them most closely allied to the Asiatic mannikins. I concur with this opinion and think that they are best put as a subgenus, *Euodice*, within *Lonchura.*

The Grey-headed Silverbill, *Lonchura griseicapilla*, bears a considerable although possibly superficial resemblance to the Indian Silverbill, but its brown parts are darker and more reddish and its colour pattern more complex. It also has a rounded, not pointed, tail. In this feature, as in its nestling mouth pattern and the nestling down (Baptista, pers. comm.) it is close to the African mannikins (q.v.). In its behaviour it seems to stand between these and the two true silverbills. Baptista, who has kept and bred it, is of the opinion that it is nearer to the former and should be put with them in the subgenus *Spermestes*. I think it is perhaps preferable to put it in a separate subgenus, *Odontospiza*, within *Lonchura*, as previously done by Steiner (1960).

The Blue-billed Mannikin, *Lonchura bicolor*, the Bronze Mannikin, *L. cucullata* and the Magpie Mannikin, *L. fringilloides* are all closely related and have similar colour patterns. The larger size and longer bill of *L. fringilloides* do not warrant subgeneric separation from its smaller relatives. They are probably adaptations to feeding on bamboo seed (Jackson).

Although in colour patterns, type of difference between adult and juvenile plumage, and structure (except for the long bill of *L. fringilloides*) the African mannikins are similar to some of the Asiatic mannikins they show consistent differences in voice and in some aspects of behaviour. Güttinger (1970 and 1976) whose papers on the subject should be read in full by anyone seriously involved with the relationships of these birds, came to the conclusion that these differences were rather basic and

that, in spite of the somewhat intermediate behaviour of the silverbills, all these forms, and the Indian Silverbill, are more closely related to firefinches and other African forms than they are to the Asiatic mannikins, their resemblances to the latter being purely convergent. Others, including Baptista and Kunkel (pers. comm.), think that these resemblances do reflect fairly close phylogenetic affinities and that the African mannikins and the silverbills are more closely related to Asiatic mannikins than they are to other African estrildids. Kunkel (1969) also suggests that the fact that none of the African mannikins or silverbills are parasitised by a whydah is another reason for thinking that they or their recent forbears evolved outside Africa. I think, although realising that I may be in error to do so, that this is so and accordingly have followed *Peters' check-list* in giving *Spermestes* only subgeneric rank within *Lonchura*.

REFERENCES

Baptista, L. F. 1973. On courtship displays and the taxonomic position of the Grey-headed Silverbill. *Avicult. Mag.* **79**: 149–154.

Delacour, J. 1943. A revision of the subfamily Estrildinae of the family Ploceidae. *Zoologica* (New York) **28**: 69–86.

Güttinger, H. R. 1970. Zur Evolution von Verhaltensweisen und Lautäusserungen bei Prachtfinken (Estrildidae). *Z. Tierpsychol.* **27**: 1011–1075.

Güttinger, H. R. 1976. Zur systematischen Stellung der Gattungen *Amadina, Lepidopygia* und *Lonchura* (Aves, Estrildidae). *Bonn. Zool. Beitr.* **27**: 218–244.

Harrison, C. J. O. 1964. The taxonomic status of the African Silverbill *Lonchura cantans* and Indian Silverbill *L. malabarica. Ibis* **106**: 462–468.

Jackson, H. D. 1972. The status of the Pied Mannikin, *Lonchura fringilloides*, in Rhodesia and its association with the bamboo *Oxytenanthera abyssinica* (A. Richard) Munro. *Rhodesia Sci. News* **6**: 342–348.

Kunkel, P. 1969. Die Stammesgeschichte der Prachtfinken im Lichte des Brutparasitismus der Witwen. *Ardea* **57**: 172–181.

Mayr, E. 1968. The sequence of genera in the Estrildidae (Aves). *Breviora* **287**: 1–4.

Steiner, H. 1960. Klassifikation der Prachtfinken, Spermestidae, auf Grund der Rachenzeichnungen der Nestlinge. *J. Orn.* **101**: 92–112.

Steiner, H. 1966. Atavismen bei Artbastarden und ihre Bedeutung zur Feststellung von Verwanschaftsbeziehungen. Kreuzungsergebnisse innerhalb der Singvogelfamilie der Spermestidae. *Rev. Suisse Zool.* **73**: 321–337.

Wolters, H. E. 1957. Die Klassifikation der Webefinken (Estrildidae). *Bonn. Zool Beitr.* **2**: 90–129.

Bibfinch   *Lepidopygia nana*

Pyrrhula nana Pucheran, 1845, *Rev. Zool.* (Paris) **8**, p. 52.

DESCRIPTION Between Goldbreast and Avadavat in size but with heavier build and proportionately larger and stouter bill. Tail bluntly wedge-shaped, the two central feathers longer than the rest but not pointed. Forehead a slightly silvery medium grey, shading through duller grey on the crown to brownish grey on the nape, darker feather centres giving a faintly spotted appearance

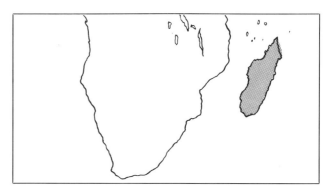

at close quarters. Lores and bib-like throat patch black. Mantle, back and most of wings a dull, slightly greyish, brown. Primaries, outer secondaries and tail brownish black. Rump and upper tail coverts pale straw yellow, glossy but not very bright. Ear coverts pale grey. Malar regions pale cream to whitish grey, contrasting with the black bib which, at certain angles, shows a slight purplish lustre. Underparts a pale, slightly pinkish, fawn to pinkish grey, with faint darker centres to the breast feathers and faint darker barring on those of the belly. Flanks slightly darker and more reddish. Under tail coverts drab or reddish drab with slightly darker subterminal bars and broad buff tips. Under wing coverts pinkish buff. Irides brown. Bill with upper mandible blackish and lower mandible reddish horn to pale pink. Legs and feet pinkish flesh. Sexes alike but some individual variation in depth of colour, apart from differences caused by wear of plumage.

Juvenile a general drab brown above, warmer and less greyish in tone than the adult and tinged with reddish buff on the rump. Underparts brownish buff, a little darker on the breast and flanks. Darker feather centres on head and breast but these are even less conspicuous than in the adult. Wing quills as adult's; tail browner. According to Immelmann *et al.* the first moult, although starting early as with other estrildids, is prolonged and fully adult dress is obtained only when the bird is about a year old. Nestling naked (Güttinger, 1976). There are good photographs of adults in Langfeldt and of both adults and mouth patterns of nestlings in Güttinger (1976).

FIELD CHARACTERS Tiny brownish finch-like bird with conspicuous black bib.

DISTRIBUTION AND HABITAT Madagascar. Inhabits grassland with some bushes or other cover, palm-plains, forest clearings, forest edge, cultivated areas and villages (Rand).

FEEDING AND GENERAL HABITS Takes seeds of grasses and other weeds, probably also some insects, but its food in the wild does not appear to have been studied at all. Rand observed it gathering about rice-pounding blocks to feed on grass or weed seeds winnowed out of the rice. Feeds both on the ground and perched among vegetation. Active and agile, reminiscent of waxbills of the genus *Estrilda*.

Probably takes some insect food, as in captivity it will take gnat larvae, ant pupae and sometimes also mealworms and gentles when rearing young (Kührer, Immelmann *et al.*).

Usually in small parties, sometimes larger flocks. When members of a flock rest, commonly up to six individuals will be side by side in line on a perch.

NESTING A complete nest may be built in a tree, bush or palm, usually at from 1 to 5 metres high, or the old nest of a fody, *Foudia* spp., may be taken over and re-lined. When built entirely by the Bibfinch the nest is oval or flask-shaped, with the entrance hole near the top and shielded by a porch-like projection above it. A nest carefully examined by Rand was composed largely of dry grass heads very firmly put together, with a few grass blades on the outside. It was lined with body feathers of Domestic Fowl 'so arranged that the free ends curled up and nearly roofed the cavity'. It measured on the outside 110 mm wide by 140 mm deep; the entrance hole was 35 mm across, the walls 20 mm thick at the sides and thicker at the bottom. Two other nests were lined, respectively, with plant down and palm fibres.

Three to eight eggs. Both sexes incubate in turn and both roost together in the nest at night. Incubation period (in captivity in Europe) 11 days. Young fledge at 25 days (Kührer), though fledging periods of as long as 31–33 days have been recorded (Landfeldt). For at least the first few evenings after fledging the young are carefully led back into the nest to roost by their parents.

VOICE A soft 'pit' and a metallic and somewhat louder 'pitsri' seem the only calls to have been described. The song has been described (Guttinger, in Immelmann *et al.*) as soft and with a purring or rattling tone ('einen leisen schnurrenden Gesäng), lasting only about 2·5 to 3 seconds, often repeated several times without pause.

DISPLAY AND SOCIAL BEHAVIOUR In courtship display the male holds a piece of nesting material in his bill, thrusts himself up and down by alternately bending and stretching his legs and sings. The female, if responsive, utters a call similar to her alarm call (not described!) and then crouches and solicits with quivering tail. Vigorous mutual bill pecking ('Schnabelkämpfe'), which gradually changes to allo-preening, follows successful copulation (Immelmann *et al.*).

Highly social. Members of flocks habitually clump and allo-preen. In captivity has been bred successfully when two or several pairs are kept in one aviary or bird room (Kührer, Langfeldt). Each breeding pair defended only the immediate surroundings of its nest but Güttinger (1976) found it aggressive even towards other species when nesting and that it was impossible to keep more than one breeding pair in an aviary.

OTHER NAMES Madagascar Mannikin, Dwarf Mannikin.

REFERENCES

Güttinger, H. R. 1976. Zur systematischen Stellung der gattungen *Amadina, Lepidopygia*, und *Lonchura. Bonn. Zool. Beitr.* **27**: 218–244.

Hartlaub, G. 1877. *Die Vögel Madagascars und der benachbarten Inselgruppen*. H. W. Schmidt, Halle, Germany.

Immelmann, K., Steinbacher, J. & Wolters, H. E. 1973. *Vögel in Käfig und Voliere: Prachtfinken*: 475–480.

Immelmann, K., Steinbacher, J. & Wolters, H. E. 1977. *Vögel in Käfig und Voliere: Prachtfinken*: 586–589.

Kührer, K. 1974. Gelungene Zucht des Zwergelsterchen. *Gefiederte Welt* **98**: 196–197.

Langfeldt, W. 1974. Überraschende Bruten mit Zwergelsterchen (*Lepidopygia nana*). *Gefiederte Welt* **98**: 161.

Rand, A. L. 1936. The distribution and habits of Madagascar birds. *Bull. Amer. Mus. Nat. Hist.* LXXII, Art. V, pp. 143–499.

African Silverbill   *Lonchura cantans*

Loxia cantans Gmelin, 1789. *Syst. Nat.* **1** (2), p. 859.

DESCRIPTION Very slightly smaller than Spice Finch and more slender in shape with blunter looking bill with more curved culmen and proportionately rather longer tail with the two central feathers markedly pointed and elongated. Forehead and crown feathers light drab brown with darker shaft markings and pale sandy buff fringes, giving a speckled and scaly effect. The dark shaft marks, and to a lesser extent the pale fringes, become progressively less pronounced through nape and hind neck and there is a progressive tendency to darker cross barring on the pale sandy brown feathers (very like the cross barring seen in many waxbills of the genus *Estrilda*) which is most pronounced on the innermost wing coverts, inner secondaries and lower back. The innermost secondaries have buffish or whitish tips made more conspicuous by dark subterminal bars – the pattern seen so often in juvenile waders, doves and larks. Outer wing coverts similarly barred but in much darker shades of brown. Outer secondaries (those near middle of wing) blackish. Primary coverts, outer greater coverts and primaries black, latter brownish black on inner webs. Under wing coverts buff. Rump, upper tail coverts and tail black, often or usually with some intermixture of a very dark brownish red hue. Face and throat light sandy brown with yellowish buff feather fringes, shading to buffish on the breast and buff, faintly barred with light sandy brown, on the sides of the breast and flanks, and to buffish white on the belly and under tail coverts. The general effect is that of a pale sandy brown bird, speckled on head, finely barred elsewhere,

with pale underparts and black rump and tail. In worn plumage the bird is usually much paler and less buffish, the upper parts then being often a very pale greyish drab with the darker barring showing more prominently and the underparts almost white. Irides brown to brownish black; eye rims bluish grey. Bill pale silvery bluish grey, sometimes darker on culmen and upper parts of the upper mandible, or with entire upper mandible darker grey. Legs and feet mauvish grey to mauvish flesh-coloured.

Sexes alike but female perhaps more apt to have tail feathers tinged with dark reddish brown. In life (as with most birds) at least some females are identifiable by their slightly smaller bills and less bold-looking heads (see Abrahams, in Butler).

The above description is of nominate *L.c. cantans*, from Senegal to western and southern Sudan. *L.c. orientalis*, from further east in Africa, and Arabia, is a little darker brown and more prominently barred on the upper parts and less buffish on face, breast and flanks. The two races intergrade in parts of eastern Africa.

I think it likely that this species has red pigment, which is masked by the black, in its rump and tail.

See plate 1, facing p. 96.

FIELD CHARACTERS Small light drab or sandy drab bird with conspicuous black rump and tail and silvery bluish bill.

DISTRIBUTION AND HABITAT Africa from Senegal east to Sudan, Somalia, eastern and southern Ethiopia, dryer parts of Kenya and northern Tanzania south to Dodoma. Also in south-western Arabia from Mecca to Aden and the western Hadramaut. Inhabits dry savannas, thornscrub, grassy areas with acacias, the neighbourhood of water in semi-desert country and cultivated and inhabited areas.

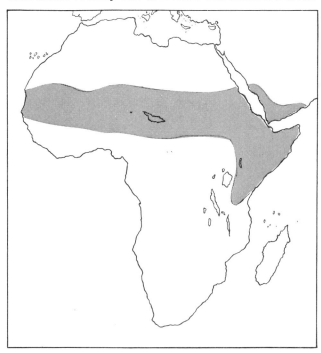

Introduced into Hawaii and breeding in an arid region there (Berger).

FEEDING AND GENERAL HABITS Feeds largely on grass seeds, mostly picked up from the ground, also plucks seeds from the growing plant with little upward hops. It does not seem to have been observed feeding while perched in vegetation but probably does so at times. May take other seeds, and Meinertzhagen records seeing it eating aphids from water mint. In captivity often refuses insect food of any kind and Bolle (in Russ), who was the first to breed it in captivity, recorded that his birds also refused greenfood and reared their young on seeds alone. Immelmann *et al.*, however, say it will usually take eggfood when rearing young.

Sometimes seen in pairs when breeding but usually in small or large flocks. As Bannerman comments ornithologists in Africa have made rather few observations on this drab and common species.

NESTING A more or less roundish grass nest with side entrance is sometimes built in a bush, tree or some niche of a building but more often the old nest of some other species, usually a weaver (Ploceidae) is taken over, lined, renovated or built on. Serle describes a substantial nest with fairly large, porched opening, built of grass and plant stems and lined inside with seeding grass heads. Probably this nest was built by the Silverbills. Kunkel found that his captive Silverbills usually chose to nest in boxes and, when so doing, made the nest entrance facing the back wall of the box, not its entrance hole. The only pair that built in the open made their nest's opening facing the wall of the room so the birds had to creep between the wall and their nest to enter it. Bolle (in Russ) observed that when nesting in some small hole or niche, his captive birds merely lined it with a little soft stuff and that only the male collected nesting material. Meinertzhagen, who observed a wild pair building, also noted that the male gathered all the materials. This nest consisted of grass, vegetable fibres and wool.

Eggs 3 to 6, up to 12 eggs have been found in one nest but almost certainly the product of 2 hens. The Van Somerens found clutches in weavers' nests together with the eggs of the weavers, thus suggesting that the Silverbills had evicted the weaver or caused her to desert. Both sexes incubate in turns by day and both roost in the nest. Incubation period 11 days. Young fledge at about 21 days and start to feed themselves at 25 days (data on captive birds, Bolle in Russ). Newly hatched young naked, and dark with waxy yellow gape swellings. The parents call and lead their fledglings one by one back into the nest in the evening and roost there with them (Güttinger, Kunkel) for at least some days after fledging (Güttinger, Kunkel). At least in captivity they learn to know their young as individuals *before* they leave the nest (Güttinger). Behaviour of captive birds strongly suggests that the species is adapted to nesting more or less colonially, as do Archer and Godman's observations on wild birds in Somalia.

VOICE The calls are high-pitched and monosyllabic. Güttinger differentiates between the contact call (Stimmfuhlungslaut) used between individuals close to one another and the version used to maintain or regain contact with others at a distance (Distanzruf) but does not describe them in detail. The begging call of the young is very similar to the latter form of contact call. The nest-call is similar to the 'close up' contact calls but softer (Güttinger).

The song is also shrill and has been variously described as 'clear and pure' (Morris), a shrill trilling and so on. Butler noted marked differences between the songs of two captive males, one uttered a 'long-drawn trill' followed by another trill in a slightly different note, the other 'a little rippling whistled song'. Harrison, who found slight but consistent differences between songs of this species and of the closely related *L. malabarica*, says the song phrase, which is always introduced by a series of rapidly repeated contact calls, consists of three parts. First 'a series of rapidly repeated notes which may show a drop in pitch or a steady descent towards the end of the phrase . . . followed by . . . a series of slurred double notes sliding from a higher to a lower pitch and becoming more rapid; and finally there is a small interrogative-sounding phrase of about four notes.' Song is given in 'undirected' situations, with closed bill and side to side head and body movements (Güttinger) and in the courtship display. Sonagrams of parts of songs are given by both Harrison and Güttinger; the latter also gives a sonagram of the begging call.

DISPLAY AND SOCIAL BEHAVIOUR The courtship display is very like that of the typical waxbills, *Estrilda*. The male holds a grass stem or other nest material by one end in his bill. He flies to the female's vicinity and then either starts his display at once or begins to sing with a side to side movement of head and body (as when singing alone) and in normal song posture and then goes over into the courtship display proper. In this he angles his tail and turns his head towards the female (if on one side of her), sometimes fluffs out his belly and flank feathers a little, sings and thrusts his head and body up and down by alternately stretching and bending his legs. Güttinger states that the upward movement is faster than the downward one (as in *Estrilda*) but Kunkel (unpublished ms on estrildine display) says this is not so. Probably there is individual variation on this point. The male continues to sing during this display. The female may respond with the same display but without song or nest symbol and usually less intensely (Kunkel) or she may crouch and solicit with quivering tail (Güttinger). The male always finishes his song strophe and drops his nesting symbol before mounting. Kunkel (unpublished mss) states that the above display does not always lead to copulation (or attempts at it) and when it does is usually a preliminary stage, after which the male drops his symbol, inclines more forward on his perch, fully erects his throat and belly feathers, sings and swings to and fro, now towards and now away from the female, and at this stage she (if willing) solicits and copulation follows. Mutual bill pecking, going over into allo-preening, follows successful copulation (Güttinger, Kunkel).

The to and fro movements and song, without the nest symbol or up and down movements, are used towards females by whom the male is (apparently) sexually attracted but not paired to or desirous of pairing (as distinct from copulating) with (Kunkel, unpublished mss).

When nest-calling the male spreads his tail. The pair also perch together on the proposed nest performing the upward thrusting movement of fixing material in the nest roof, without material in their bills. They also squat on the future site, bow their heads together and mandibulate. Güttinger, who has observed this latter display in many estrildids, believes it to have evolved from the movements used in feeding nestlings.

Highly social. Flock members know each other personally and indulge in mutual allo-preening and 'peering' at singing individuals. Strange individuals introduced into captive flocks are only mildly persecuted and are fully accepted after a few days (Güttinger). The nesting and laying of flock members is largely synchronised.

OTHER NAMES Warbling Silverbill, Black-rumped Silverbill.

REFERENCES
Archer, G. & Godman, E. M. 1961. *The birds of British Somaliland and the Gulf of Aden*, vol. 4. London.
Bannerman, D. A. 1944. *The birds of tropical West Africa*, vol. 7. London.
Berger, A. J. 1975. The Warbling Silverbill, a new nesting bird in Hawaii. *Elepaio* **36**: 27–28.
Butler, A. G. 1899. *Foreign finches in captivity*. London.
Güttinger, H. R. 1970. Zur Evolution von Verhaltensweisen und Lautäusserungen bei Prachtfinken (Estrildidae). *Z. Tierpsychol.* **27**: 1011–1075.
Harrison, C. J. O. 1964. The taxonomic status of the African Silverbill *Lonchura cantans* and the Indian Silverbill *L. malabarica*. *Ibis* **106**: 462–468.
Lynes, H. 1924. On the birds of North and Central Darfur. *Ibis* 11 series, **6**: 648–719.
Meinertzhagen, R. 1954. *Birds of Arabia*. Edinburgh and London.
Mackworth-Praed, C. W. & Grant, C. H. B. 1960. *The African handbook of birds*, ser. 1, vol. 2. London.
Russ, K. 1879. *Die Fremdländischen Stubenvögel*, vol. 1. Hannover, Germany.
Serle, W. 1933. Notes on East African birds. *Ibis* **85**: 55–82.
van Someren, V. G. L. & G. R. C. 1945. Evacuated weaver colonies and notes on the breeding ecology of *Euodice cantans* Gmelin and *Amadina fasciata* Gmelin. *Ibis* **87**: 33–34.

Indian Silverbill   *Lonchura malabarica*

Loxia malabarica Linnaeus, 1758, *Syst. Nat.* ed. 10, **1**, p. 175.

DESCRIPTION Very similar to the previous species, *L. cantans*, from which it differs as follows: bill averaging a very little smaller and less blunt-looking, with slightly less

decurved culmen. A narrow stripe above eye creamy white to pale buff. Face, throat, breast and underparts creamy white to silvery white, contrasting with the barred reddish fawn and pale buffish of the sides of the breast and flanks. Brown of upper parts slightly darker and duller, with no trace of barring. Rump and central parts of upper tail coverts white; the long upper tail coverts have their outer webs mainly black so that the live bird shows a black stripe, contiguous with the black tail, dividing the white of upper and under tail coverts. On the upper part of the rump are some feathers with white tips and narrow black or dark brown subterminal bars and/or some with two narrow wavy black or brown bars across the white part. The effect is of a very narrow area of delicately barred plumage between the brown of the back and the white of the lower rump.

Sexes usually said to be alike but Mr Alan Hayes, who has kept and bred this species for many years, tells me that in life males have clearer white lores and above the eyes and usually slightly more prominently barred flanks, and the, relatively few, sexed skins in the British Museum (Natural History) collection seem to confirm this. Juvenile has brownish face and buffish breast and dusky brown rather than black wing and tail quills.

See plate 5, facing p. 224.

FIELD CHARACTERS Small dusty brown bird with pointed black tail, white rump and bluish grey bill. Entirely whitish throat and breast distinguish from White-backed Munia, white rump from all other munias.

DISTRIBUTION AND HABITAT Extreme south-eastern Arabia, parts of Iran (and possibly of Afghanistan), Pakistan, India and Sri Lanka. A dry country species inhabiting grassland, semi-desert, scrub, secondary jungle, open woodland, cultivated areas and villages. In Sri Lanka confined to the dry-zone coastal tracts of the Mannar, Jaffna and Hambantota districts (Henry).

FEEDING AND GENERAL HABITS Feeds mainly on the seeds of grasses, including *Sorghum*, *Pennisetum*, *Saccharum*, and

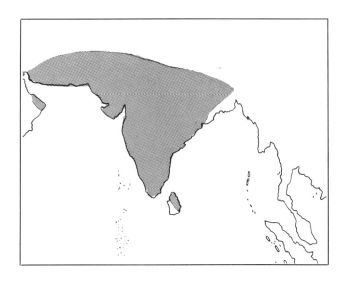

sedges. Takes cultivated millet and (*fide* Henry) rice when available. Eleven specimens examined by Mason had all eaten grass and weed seeds (not identified) but three also, respectively, one insect, one batch of insect eggs and one grain of rice. Ali & Ripley say it takes 'ants, beetles and other small insects'. Feeds mostly on the ground but also from growing vegetation. Often seeks food on or beside paths or tracks. In captivity will take millets (especially pannicum and white) and will live and rear young on dry and soaked seed and greenfood plus, of course, the necessary minerals. A pair have been known to rear two broods (of 5 and 3 young) on nothing but dry seed and greenstuff (Restall). Alan Hayes (*in litt.*) advises the use of vitamin supplements such as Abidec and vionate and the treating of the seed with halibut or cod liver oil about once a week in winter. Immelmann *et al.* state that it will usually take egg food when rearing young. Like the previous species, *L. cantans*, and unlike most estrildids, it will not infrequently breed even in a (large) cage.

Highly social, usually in large or small flocks. Roosts (always?) in small groups in old nests. Very agile and active among branches or twigs. Frequently makes side-to-side tail movements when active or excited.

NESTING In India most often nests low down in thorny bushes, from about 0·5 to 3 metres above ground; in Sri Lanka often in the crown of a Screw Pine. Many other sites are also used, including holes and niches in buildings, among projecting sticks on the outside of the nest of some large bird-of-prey, and in the deserted or appropriated nests of other species, especially those of the Baya Weaver, *Ploceus philippinus*. When built by the Silverbills themselves the nest is roundish, made of grass and sometimes also small twigs, fibres and other materials, with the side entrance hole usually in the form a short tube. Finer grasses, feathers, vegetable down and other soft materials are used as lining. Imperfect and even open-topped nests have been found (Baker) but perhaps as a result of robbing of material or other injury to the nest by other birds rather than to lack of ability by the builders. Nests are said to vary greatly in size but to be usually about 18 cm (7 inches) in diameter (Baker). However, in view of the species' habit of using the nests of other species, caution is needed in attributing unusual nests to the Siverbills themselves unless they have actually been seen building them.

Three to seven eggs. Larger numbers have often been found but probably usually as a result of more than one female laying in the same nest. Incubation and parental care as in previous species *L. cantans* (q.v.).

VOICE As *L. cantans* except that there are apparently slight but constant differences in the song (Güttinger, Harrison). Harrison describes these as follows: 'The song of *malabarica* seems at first . . . to be a confused and pattern-less series of notes but the sections of recorded song for which spectrographs were made reveal a repetition of a series of short song-phrases, each only a third of the length of a *cantans* song phrase . . . It is possible to recognise repeated notes, slurred notes and a terminal phrase, although fewer notes are involved in each section.'

DISPLAY As in *L. cantans* (q.v.). A female that is unpaired and very eager to form a pair bond will fly to a male with the nesting symbol in her bill, give a few of the upward and downward movements of the courtship display and then solicit with quivering tail (Güttinger, in Immelmann *et al.*). Probably *L. cantans* also does this.

OTHER NAMES White-throated Munia, White-rumped Silverbill.

REFERENCES
Ali, S. & Ripley, S. D. 1974. *Handbook of the birds of India and Pakistan*, vol. 10. New York, Bombay, London.
Baker, E. C. S. 1934. *The nidification of birds of the Indian Empire* vol. 3. London.
Güttinger, H. R. 1970. Zur Evolution von Verhaltensweisen und Lautäusserungen bei Prachtfinken (Estrildidae). *Z. Tierpsychol.* **27**: 1011–1075.
Harrison, C. J. O. 1964. The taxonomic status of the African Silverbill *Lonchura cantans* and the Indian Silverbill, *L. malabarica*. *Ibis* **106**: 462–468.
Henry, G. M. 1955. *A guide to the birds of Ceylon*. London, New York.
Immelmann, K., Steinbacher, J. & Wolters, H. E. 1972. *Vögel in Käfig und Voliere: Prachtfinken*: 412–421. Aachen, Germany.
Kunkel, P. 1959. Zum Verhalten einiger Prachtfinken (Estrildinae). *Z. Tierpsychol.* **16**: 302–350.
Mason, C. W. 1912. *The food of birds in India*. Mem. Dept. of Agriculture in India, Entom. Ser., vol. 3. Thacker, Spink & Co., Calcutta.
Restall, R. L. 1975. *Finches and other seed-eating birds*. London.
Ticehurst, C. B. 1922. The birds of Sind. *Ibis*, Oct. 1922. 605–662.

Grey-headed Silverbill   *Lonchura griseicapilla*

Pytila caniceps Reichenow, 1879, (*Odontospiza caniceps*) *Ornith. Centralbl.*, **4**. p. 139.
Lonchura griseicapilla Delacour 1943, *Zoologica* (New York) **28**, p. 82. New name for *Pytelia caniceps* Reichenow, 1879, preoccupied by *Munia caniceps* Salvadori, 1876.

DESCRIPTION About size of Spice Finch but wings and tail proportionately a little longer, central tail feathers rounded at ends and bill a little shorter and thicker. Outermost primary somewhat attenuated on inner web. Top of head, nape, hind neck and sides of neck a slightly silvery grey. In most individuals the feathers on the front of the forehead and those in a narrow line above the eye have silvery tips and blackish basal or subterminal areas, giving a speckled effect. Lores blackish. Face, ear coverts and upper part of throat brightly speckled with white, the individual feathers being grey with black subterminal bands and white tips. Feathers of lower throat silver grey, lightly barred with dark grey or blackish. Mantle and upper back dark dull pinkish chestnut (which fades to pinkish straw colour) shading to a more greyish hue on lower back. Wing coverts and inner secondaries dark coffee brown with a pinkish tinge. Primaries and outer secondaries blackish brown, quite black on the outer webs of most primaries except near their tips. Under wing coverts pinkish chestnut. Rump and upper tail coverts cream coloured to white. Tail black, usually with a little white on the tips of the two outermost feathers. Irides brown to blackish. Bill with upper mandible dark bluish grey, lower mandible lighter bluish grey. Legs and feet dark horn grey to blackish, soles whitish. Sexes alike.

Juvenile paler, buffish grey on head, buffish brown on mantle and buffish on underparts with no white spots on face, though sometimes some suggestion of the 'ghost' of a spotted pattern in certain lights. Palate markings of nestlings a 'double horseshoe' like those of the African mannikins (Güttinger).

FIELD CHARACTERS Small reddish brown bird with grey head, black tail and white rump. White speckled face diagnostic at close range.

DISTRIBUTION AND HABITAT Southern Abyssinia, south-eastern Sudan and adjacent areas of Uganda, through Kenya to Iringa in Tanzania. Inhabits arid grassland and thorn country; always near surface water.

FEEDING AND GENERAL HABITS Known to take seeds of grasses and (*fide* Mackworth-Praed & Grant) other seeds (unspecified). In captivity will take the usual millets and canary seed and greenfood, especially chickweed. It appears to need much insect food when rearing young. Grubbe found his birds took large quantitites of mealworms when rearing young and these had no harmful results.

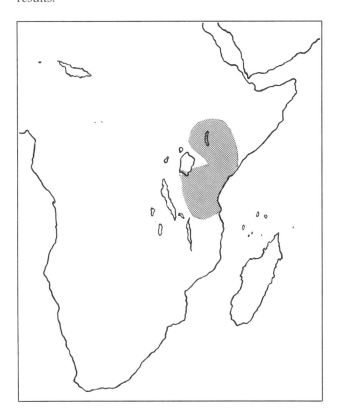

Usually in small flocks. In captivity, and probably also when wild, roosts in small groups in old nests. On at least one occasion captive birds built a roosting nest which was similar to the breeding nest (q.v.) but unlined (Pilz).

NESTING Nests have been found in the peripheral branches of trees and among the upgrowing new shoots of pollarded trees. They are large, untidy structures, with the usual side entrance and lined with feathers (Mackworth-Praed & Grant). In captivity a rounded or retort-shaped nest is built either among twigs or branches or in a half open fronted box. The outer part of the nest is built of relatively coarse materials – grass stems and blades, coconut fibre, millet stems or other materials and the inside lined with feathers, hair, wool or other soft materials.

Eggs 3 to 6, usually 4 or 5 in wild nests. Both sexes incubate in turn by day and the male roosts in the nest at night although, presumably, the female alone incubates then. When taking over on the eggs the male usually brings a piece of material for the lining. Both sexes, at nest relief, perch near the nest and utter a soft, two-syllabled note, entering the nest only when the mate inside answers (Kujawa, in Immelmann *et al.*). The newly-hatched young are dark flesh coloured with a little whitish down and pale whitish blue gape flanges. When begging they turn the head sideways but do not move it from side to side as most young estrildids do (Immelmann *et al.*). Young fledge at 24 to 28 days (captive records). They are independent 14 days after fledging (Grubbe, Immelmann *et al.*). Unlike most estrildids, fledged young make a quivering (or fluttering?) movement of the wings when begging for food, or, at lower intensity only a slight outward flicking of the wing furthest from the parent. (Immelmann *et al.*, Baptista).

VOICE Fledged young have a two-syllabled begging call that has been variously described as 'drrrr zirp' (Langberg), 'peed yee-eh' (Grubbe, my anglicisation) etc. Güttinger states, and illustrates with sonagrams, that the short note of the begging call is identical in sound with the adult's alarm call and the longer note very similar to its distance contact call. This species has (*fide* Güttinger) a special close contact call (Stimmfuhlungslaut) which is used both in flight and when feeding. A quick series of these calls are given when a large supply of food is discovered and other conspecifics are attracted to the spot.

The song is variable. It starts very soft and whispering and becomes louder towards its end. It is given both as undirected song, with bill rhythmically opening and shutting, head pointed more or less upward and turning from side to side, and in the courtship display (q.v.). Güttinger gives sonagrams of parts of the song.

DISPLAY In what appears to be the most usual form of the courtship display the male holds a grass stem by one end, flies to and perches in front of or near the female and bobs up and down, singing. The female then begins to display in the same way but without the nesting symbol in the bill. After a little the male drops the symbol, turns his bill and tail towards the female and sings a long song phrase. Ceremonial bill-wiping may introduce or intersperse this part of the display. This display is not usually followed by copulation. Baptista observed some variant forms of courtship display. One (wild caught) male habitually used only the second part of the display (as described above). Sometimes the female would respond by tail quivering and, whether she did or not, the male would finally attempt to mount her and copulate, although only once was he seen to do so successfully.

A second male performed a display, rather like the submissive courtship display of *Uraeginthus angolensis*, in which he crouched beside the female and sang at her with bill wide open and tongue protruding and moving back and forth and sometimes with a slight extension of the wing further from the female. This male used to go over to the up and down bobbing display from this submissive courtship display. The latter was also seen from another individual, sometimes with the far wing quivered like that of a begging juvenile. Three young males fathered by the male that never performed with a nest symbol, gave the usual version of the courtship display, with (at first) a stem held in the bill.

Baptista observed successful copulations after the female in response to intense (but symbol-less) display from her mate, solicited in the usual crouched posture with quivering tail and open bill.

OTHER NAMES Pearl-headed Mannikin, Pearl-headed Silverbill.

REFERENCES

Baptista, L. F. 1973. On courtship displays and the taxonomic position of the Grey-headed Silverbill. *Avicult. Mag.* **79**: 149–154.

Güttinger, R. 1970. Zur Evolution von Verhaltensweisen und Lautäusserungen bei Prachtfinken (Estrildidae). *Z. Tierpsychol.* **27**: 1011–1075.

Grubbe, O. 1967. Noch einmal die Perhalsamadine und ihre erfolgreiche Brut. *Gefiederte Welt* **91**: 168–172.

Immelmann, K., Steinbacher, J. & Wolters, H. E. 1972. *Vögel in Käfig und Voliere: Prachtfinken*: 431–440. Aachen, Germany.

Langberg, W. 1963. Breeding of the Grey-headed Silverbill. *Avicult. Mag.* **69**: 97–101.

Mackworth-Praed, C. W. & Grant, C. H. B. 1960. *The African handbook of birds*, ser. 1, vol. 2, 2nd ed. London.

Pilz, H. 1962. Weitere Beobachtungen über des Verhalten der Grauköpfigen Silberschnäbelchen (*Odontospiza caniceps*). *Gefiederte Welt* **86**: 184–185.

Bronze Mannikin   *Lonchura cucullata*

Spermestes cucullata Swainson, 1837, *Birds W. Africa*, **1**, p. 201.

DESCRIPTION About size of Avadavat but more heavily built and with larger and thicker bill. Tail rounded but with the two central feathers projecting a little beyond the rest though not pointed at their tips. Head, face and upper breast brownish black with a not very bright bottle green and/or purplish sheen; in most individuals the gloss is

mainly greenish on the forehead and crown and purplish on cheeks and breast. A variable patch or patches of glossy bottle green on the 'shoulder' of the wing due to some or most of the lesser wing coverts being partly or entirely so-coloured. Sides of lower neck, mantle, back and wings dull brownish grey, with paler feather fringes. Rump and upper tail coverts barred blackish and white or whitish grey. Tail black. Underparts below the breast white except for a bottle green patch on the sides of the lower breast, and the flanks, tibial feathers and under tail coverts which are barred blackish and white. Irides brown (orange recorded for one specimen). Bill with upper mandible black, lower pale greyish blue. Legs and feet dark grey to greyish black. Sexes alike.

Juvenile has head and face dark greyish brown, shading to light greyish brown on throat and breast, buff on the belly, brownish buff on flanks and earth brown upper parts except for buffish fringes to the inner secondaries and blackish brown primaries and tail. Bill at first entirely blackish.

The above description is of nominate *L.c. cucullata*, from Senegal south to extreme north-western Angola and east to the southern Sudan, Uganda and western Kenya. *L.c. scutata*, from more eastern and southern parts of the species' range usually lacks the glossy green patch at the side of the breast, having this area barred black and white, and its rump is usually less clearly barred. The two races intergrade in many areas and there is also much minor individual variation apart from that due to wear of plumage.

FIELD CHARACTERS Very small greyish brown bird with blackish head and pale rump (barred at close view) and white belly. Gregarious and continual nest builder. Dull greyish (not black or chestnut) upperparts distinguish from other small mannikins, much smaller size and shorter bill from Magpie Mannikin (q.v.).

DISTRIBUTION AND HABITAT Africa from Senegal and Sudan south to Angola on the west and in the east to Natal and eastern Cape Privince. Also on the islands of Fernando Po, Principe, Sao Tomé, Pemba, Zanzibar, Mafia and the Comoros. Introduced on Puerto Rico.

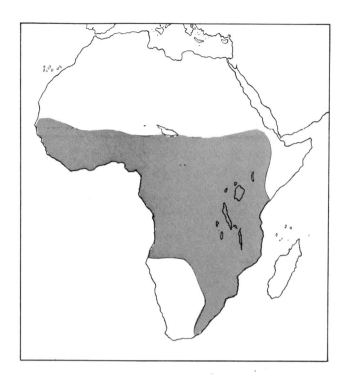

Inhabits many types of open or fairly open country, including scrub, open woodland and forest edge. Common in cultivated areas, about villages, in gardens and in some towns.

FEEDING AND GENERAL HABITS Feeds largely on the seeds of grasses, including cultivated millet when available. Kunkel (1965) found that in the parts of the Congo where he studied it (and doubtless elsewhere), it took mainly the small seeds of grasses of the genera *Digitaria* and *Setaria* and nestlings were fed on 'half ripe' seeds of these grasses. It ignored the hard-seeded grasses of the genera *Sporobilus*, *Cynodon* and *Eleusine*. Takes seeds both from the ground and from growing vegetation, where it is able to bite seed out of the panicles without having to tug to remove them. Also takes termites and possibly other insects. In captivity will thrive on seed, dry and soaked, and greenfood. When rearing young egg food and, where possible, insect food such as ant pupae should, however, be offered. It breeds freely in captivity and will sometimes do so even in cages. Often aggressive towards other species when in captivity.

Highly gregarious, usually in large or small flocks or family parties. Usually roosts in nests, often building roosting nests for this purpose, which are similar to breeding nests (q.v.) but less well put together and are built by most or all members of the party involved. These roosting nests appear to be deliberately dismantled after use and new ones built each afternoon (Holman in Bannerman, Morris).

Conspicuous side to side movements of tail, most commonly combined with a slight vertical movement, are shown at even low degrees of excitement or activity. They are basically locomotion intention movements but may function to alert conspecifics. At high intensity the wings are also flicked up and down.

This species, like its congeners and the waxbills of the genus *Estrilda* can and does hold stems or panicles under foot when building or feeding. Morris noted that a common escaping pattern was to dive into a dark corner and 'freeze' motionless. Presumably behaviour that is, under natural conditions, used in response to danger from flying birds of prey.

NESTING The nest is roundish with a small entrance hole at the side, sometimes with a short entrance tube or suggestion of one. It is built of grass stems and blades, and sometimes fibres and other materials; lined with softer grass, grass panicles, vegetable down, hair or feathers. Often sited in a small tree about 1 to 3 metres high; sometimes in larger trees, bushes, shrubs, niches or holes of buildings, among bunches of bananas or palm leaves or in the old or deserted nests of other species. Sometimes several nests may be close together, even in the same small tree. The male does most or all collecting of nest material and the female part or most of the actual building with it (Morris). When gathering material, slender grass stems are bitten through a little above ground level and carried off by the bitten end; pieces of elephant grass blades are bitten and then tugged until they split and can be torn away. Although preferring to carry material by one end, this species will hold it elsewhere when necessary. A thick layer of stems etc. is first made as a foundation and then the rest of the nest built over it (Kunkel). In some areas nests are frequently sited near active wasps' nests. In the equatorial regions has been found breeding at all times of the year, further south in the warmer months.

Eggs 3 to 8, usually 4 to 6. Both sexes incubate in turn by day and both roost together in the nest at night. Incubation period, in Europe, 12 days (Russ); young fledge at 18–21 days. Russ gives 16 to 18 days but the former probably represents abnormally early fledging induced by disturbance or some other adverse factor. The adults lead the young one by one back to the nest to roost in the evening, and roost in it with them (Kunkel, 1959). By day they call and lead them away from places or objects that arouse their alarm or suspicion (Güttinger, Immelmann *et al.*). In captivity young of the previous brood attempt to enter the nest and feed the subsequent brood. They are attacked and driven off by the parents if the latter see them but once the young fledge are allowed to feed and care for them. It appears not to be known whether this occurs in a wild state.

When begging fledged young raise the wing further from the parent (and, presumably, both if directly in front of it) like the young of *Amandava*.

VOICE Fledged young have a two-syllabled begging call similar to but less stereotyped than that of the Grey-headed Silverbill (q.v.). The alarm call has been variously transliterated, as 'tsek' (my anglicisation) by Güttinger and 'cheep cheep' by Morris. It is repeated more rapidly in correlation with the caller's degree of alarm or excitement. The distance contact call is similar to the longer note of the begging call, the song consists merely of a series of contact calls run together (Immelmann *et al.*, Güttinger). The nest call is described by Morris as 'squeaky and rasping'.

DISPLAY AND SOCIAL BEHAVIOUR In the greeting display, which is shown both towards the mate and, by the male, toward other females he is on friendly terms with, the bird, with triangular head and angled tail, and plumage somewhat erected, hops towards and around the other bird. At lower intensity there may be only a momentary angling of the tail towards the object of the display.

The courtship display has been described in great detail by Morris and also by Kunkel (1959 and 1965) and Güttinger. All these authors give good photographs of it, and Morris also of many other behaviour patterns.

No nesting symbol is held during, or immediately prior to the courtship display, which is shown only by the male. With body feathers erected except for those on the upper breast, forehead and forecrown, the male presents himself laterally to the female, with a rather upright posture, downward pointing head first mandibulates and then sings at her with widely open bill. In intervals between singing he lifts and protrudes his tongue, so that it is clearly visible, and vibrates it from side to side. These behaviour patterns may be interspersed with short periods of mandibulation. He bobs up and down, alternately flexing and stretching his legs, often combining this with jumps towards and then away from the female. In addition he performs side-to-side pivoting movements in which his body may move through an arc of 140 degrees. At high intensity he may jump round in a complete circle. With each change of position the tail is quickly re-oriented towards the female. The female may respond to this display by crouching and quivering her tail (Morris, Kunkel, 1959) but copulation does not usually follow although Morris saw, and photographed, instances when it did. Usually copulation occurs in the nest (Güttinger, Immelmann *et al.*). In captivity males often interfere with any copulation that they see (Morris). There are photographs of the courtship display in Kunkel (1959) and Güttinger, and of this and other behaviour patterns in Morris. Under captive conditions courtship display seems often to occur when impulses to escape from the too close presence of the observer are thwarted (Kunkel).

Both male and female perform a display in which the bird picks up a stem or other piece of nesting material, flies and perches beside its mate and 'freezes' motionless for a moment. This may be repeated several times and sometimes both birds may fly or hop round each other. The stems are finally dropped or carried to the nest site (Kunkel, 1959).

When fighting or threatening, and especially in defensive threat, the further wing is raised as by the juvenile when begging. At high intensity (or when the bird is directly facing its adversary?) both wings may be raised but the near one not usually so high. Fledglings beg with raised wings when attacked but neither the begging postures nor the juvenile plumage inhibit the aggressive adult's attack.

Allo-preening is common between members of a pair, family or integrated flock. In captivity strange individuals are subject to aggressive attack and/or raping attempts (Güttinger, Morris). 'Peering' at singing individuals, so prevalent in the Asiatic mannikins, does not occur (Kunkel, 1965).

OTHER NAMES Bronze-winged Mannikin, Bronze-shouldered Mannikin.

REFERENCES
Bannermann, D. A. 1949. *The birds of tropical West Africa.* Vol. 7. Crown Agents, London.
Güttinger, H. R. 1970. Zur Evolution von Verhaltensweisen und Lautäusserungen bei Prachtfinken (Estrildidae). *Z. Tierpsychol.* **27**: 1011–1075.
Immelmann, K., Steinbacher, J. & Wolters, H. E. 1973. *Vögel in Käfig und Voliere: Prachtfinken*: 460–475. Aachen, Germany.
Kunkel, P. 1959. Zum Verhalten einiger Prachtfinken (Estrildinae). *Z. Tierpsychol.* **16**: 302–350.
Kunkel, P. 1965. Verhaltensstudien an den kontinentalafrikanischen Elsterchen (*Spermestes* Swainson). *Vogelwelt* **86**: 161–178.
Morris, D. 1957. The reproductive behaviour of the Bronze Mannikin, *Lonchura cucullata*. *Behaviour* **11**: 156–201.
Russ, K. 1879. *Die fremdlandische Stubenvögel.* Vol. 1. Hannover, Germany.
Vincent, A. W. 1949. On the breeding habits of some African birds. *Ibis* **91**: 660–688.

Blue-billed Mannikin (*bicolor* group)   *Lonchura bicolor*

Amadina bicolor Fraser, 1843, *Proc. Zool. Soc. London*, **1842**, p. 145.

DESCRIPTION Similar in size and shape to previous species, *L. cucullata* (q.v.) but averaging a very little larger and with proportionately slightly larger bill. Head, breast and all upper parts intense black, slightly glossed with green except on wings and tail. Usually one or two small white spots on the outer webs of one or more of the inner secondaries. Under wing coverts mainly white. A row of feathers along sides of breast and flanks have the inner (upper) web black with a broad white subterminal band and narrow black tip and the outer (lower) web white. Rest of under parts snow white. Irides brown to dark brown. Bill greyish blue, bluish horn or bluish grey. Legs and feet dark olive, dark greyish olive or blackish. Sexes alike.

Juvenile a dull sooty brown above with obscure dull reddish brown fringes to the inner secondaries; under wing coverts dull buff. Primaries and tail brownish black. Ear coverts and sides of neck sooty grey shading to dull grey or buffish grey on the throat and upper breast and dull buff or greyish buff on rest of under parts.

The above description is of nominate *L.b. bicolor*, from western Africa east to eastern Nigeria and Mt Cameroon. *L.bicolor poensis*, from the Cameroons (where many birds are intergrades) east to the southern Sudan, eastern Congo and Rwanda, and south to northern Angola, Kasai, and Kivu, and Fernado Po island, differs as follows: it has narrow white spots and bars on the outer webs (except for about their apical third) of the primaries and most of the secondaries, forming a large, delicately white-barred patch on the closed wing. The rump and upper tail coverts are likewise delicately barred and/or speckled with white. Besides the line of parti-coloured feathers on sides of lower breast and flanks, as described above for nominate *bicolor*, the feathers immediately above these, (which are black in *L.b. bicolor*) have white edges, giving a boldly scaled or barred effect. *L.b. stigmatothorax*, from the shores of Lake Victoria, north through Uganda and Kavirondo to southern Abyssinia, is of a less intense and glossy black and what gloss there is tends to be purplish or bronzy rather than green; its mantle and back are often brownish black.

FIELD CHARACTERS Small black and white bird with bluish bill. Black upperparts and/or white barring on wings and rump distinguish it from the Bronze Mannikin (q.v.).

DISTRIBUTION Tropical Africa in Portuguese Guinea east to eastern Nigeria; Cameroons east to southern Sudan, eastern Congo (Zaïre) and Rwanda; and south to northern Angola, Kasai and Kivu; northern shores of Lake Victoria north to southwestern Abyssinia (see map).

Inhabits areas with tall grass and bushes near waterways and at the edge of marshes; forest edge, clearings and cultivated areas in or near forest and secondary growth. Often occurs together with the Bronze Mannikin in fallow lands and cultivation but typically a bird of less open areas. In the rain forest of the Congo Basin Kunkel found it one of the commonest species in native gardens and other clearings.

FEEDING AND GENERAL HABITS Feeding methods as in previous species, *L. cucullata* (q.v.). Kunkel (1965), who studied this species in the Kivu highlands, found that there its food consisted mainly of the seeds of grasses of the genera *Setaria*, *Panicum deustum* and another taller unidentified species of *Panicum*. Rice, when available, was a favourite food, the birds flocking in very large numbers to the rice fields just before it was fully ripe. Half-ripe sorghum was occasionally taken. Sometimes takes insects (Bannerman, Immelmann *et al.*).

Sometimes in pairs, more often in family parties or large or small flocks. General behaviour, including the habit of building roosting nests, like that of *L. cucullata* (q.v.) but the locomotion intention movements are much less intense. Instead of conspicuous and mainly side to side tail movements at the least excitement, this species shows only slight up and down tail movements and only when there is fairly intense readiness to fly (Kunkel, 1965). Güttinger found, however, that *his* captives of the same

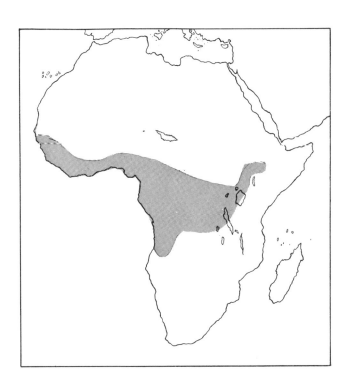

race, *poensis*, showed intense wing-flicking at the least excitement.

NESTING The nest is sited in a tree, bush, creeper, bamboo clump or similar situation, about 2 to 8 metres high. It is similar to that of the previous species, *L. cucullata* (q.v.), except in so far as its usually different habitat may result in different materials, especially beard lichen, *Usnea*, being used (Bates). Collecting and building behaviour as in *L. cucullata* (Kunkel, 1965). Eggs 3 to 6, larger numbers sometimes recorded but probably due to two females laying in the same nest.

VOICE Contact calls soft, short and whistling or piping in tone. Alarm call short and hard-sounding. Song a short, soft strophe (Immelmann *et al.*). Bannerman stresses the sweetness of the song. The head lowering movements given in courtship display (q.v.) may be used when the bird is singing alone.

DISPLAY AND SOCIAL BEHAVIOUR As in previous species, *L. cucullata* (q.v.), but there are minor differences in the courtship display. The side to side pivoting movements are more frequent and intense than the up and down movements, instead of the reverse being the case as in *L. cucullata*. Also, when displaying, the male often but at irregular intervals, bends his head down to his breast or down and sideways to shoulder or flank and sometimes then makes brief preening movements (Kunkel, 1965). On rare occasions he may make a complete head and body bow instead (Güttinger).

OTHER NAMES Black-and-white Mannikin, Black-breasted Mannakin, Fernando Po Mannikin.

REFERENCES

Bates, G. L. 1930. *Handbook of the birds of West Africa.* London.

Bannerman, D. A. 1949. *The birds of tropical West Africa*, vol. 7. London.

Güttinger, H. R. 1970. Zur Evolution von Verhaltensweisen und Lautäusserungen bei Prachtfinken (Estrildidae). *Z. Tierpsychol.* **27**: 1011–1075.

Kunkel, P. 1965. Verhaltensstudien an den Kontinentalafrikanischen Elsterchen. *Vogelwelt* **86**: 161–178.

Blue-billed Mannikin   *Lonchura bicolor*
(*nigriceps* group)

Spermestes nigriceps Cassin, 1852, *Proc. Acad. Nat. Sci. Philadelphia* **6**: p. 185.

DESCRIPTION As *L. bicolor stigmatothorax* (see above under *bicolor* group) except as follows: mantle, back, wing coverts and parts of secondaries a rather dark chestnut brown, but those parts of the secondaries that are black, barred with white in *poensis* and *stigmatothorax* are so in this form too. Some or all of the median wing coverts have pale rufous to whitish buff shaft streaks. The white-tipped black flank feathers also have white spots along their lateral fringes.

Juvenile like that of *L.b. bicolor* (q.v.) but lighter and browner, a dark reddish brown rather than sooty brown, above and paler and less greyish on the underparts. One specimen that I have seen had an indication of the adult's wing patch but in buff and blackish, not white and black.

The above description is of *L. bicolor nigriceps*, from eastern Africa in Kenya, south to eastern Transvaal, Natal and Pondoland, and west to eastern Katanga, northern and eastern Zambia, Eastern Rhodesia and Pamba, Zanzibar and Mafia Islands. *L.b. woltersi*, from southwestern Katanga and northwestern Zambia, is said to have a darker brown back. *L.b. minor*, from southern Somalia, is slightly smaller.

FIELD CHARACTERS As for *bicolor* group (q.v.) but with chestnut back which equally distinguishes it from *L. cucullata*.

DISTRIBUTION AND HABITAT Southern Somalia, Kenya south to the eastern Transvaal, Natal and Pondoland and west to eastern Katanga, northern and eastern Zambia and eastern Rhodesia; Zanzibar, Pemba and Mafia Islands.

Inhabits similar types of country to previous form (q.v.); also palm groves and (*fide* Mackworth-Praed & Grant) 'thick forest'. Probably the latter only when it is adjacent to clearings, paths, forest edge or other grassy areas.

FEEDING AND GENERAL HABITS As previous form (q.v.) so far as known but Güttinger found that captive specimens did not show the wing-flicking locomotion intention movements of *L. bicolor poensis*. In captivity a pair began to take eggfood and whiteworms as well as seed when the female started to lay (Budde).

NESTING As previous form but also very often in the old nests of weavers (Mackworth-Praed & Grant). In captivity has reared young on seed, greenfood, eggfood and whiteworms (Budde) and on these with the probable addition of ant pupae (Grannersberger).

VOICE As previous form. Güttinger gives sonagrams of parts of the song.

DISPLAY AND SOCIAL BEHAVIOUR As previous form (q.v.).

OTHER NAMES Rufous-backed Mannikin, Red-backed Mannikin.

REFERENCES

Budde, H. 1967. Die Aufzucht von Braunrückenelsterchen. *Gefiederte Welt* **91**: 32–33.

Grannersberger, K. 1967. Meine Erfahrungen mit Braunrückenelsterchen. *Gefiederte Welt* **91**: 93.

Güttinger, H. R. 1970. Zur Evolution von Verhaltensweisen und Lautäusserungen bei Prachtfinken (Estrildae). *Z. Tierpsychol.* **27**: 1011–1075.

Mackworth-Praed, C. W. & Grant, C. H. B. 1960. *The African handbook of birds*, series 1, vol. 2.

McLachlan, G. R. & Liversidge, R. 1957. *Roberts birds of South Africa*, revised edition. Cape Town.

Magpie Mannikin   *Lonchura fringilloides*

Plocus (*sic*) *fringilloides* Lafresnaye, 1835, *Mag. Zool.* (Paris) **5**, cl. 2, pl. 48.

DESCRIPTION About size of Peter's Twinspot but with proportionately much shorter tail and much larger and longer bill. The size and shape of the bill gives the bird an outline very like that of some weavers of the genus *Ploceus*. It was originally classed with these but when live birds were kept in captivity their breeding behaviour at once showed they were estrildids (Russ).

Head and neck black, glossed slightly with greenish

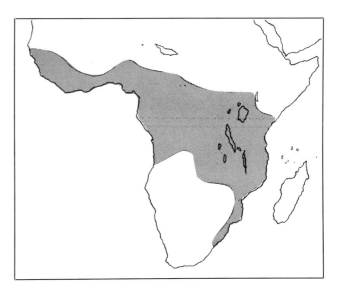

blue. Mantle and back a slightly reddish earth-brown with buffish streaks and obscure darker spots and buffish bars. This effect is produced by the individual feathers, or at least most of them, having a darker brown median area, then a conspicuous pale buffish shaft streak and buffish terminal fringe. The concealed bases of the feathers also have pale shafts. Rump and upper tail coverts black, slightly glossed with bluish or purplish. Tail black. Wings sepia brown with conspicuous creamy white shafts to the median coverts. Under wing coverts and parts of the inner webs of the wing quills, bright yellowish buff. A black patch at either side of the breast is more or less contiguous with a black and reddish buff area on the flanks. Individual feathers of this area show varying amounts of white, black and reddish buff. Rest of under parts white or creamy white shading to deep cream on the under tail coverts. In worn plumage the reddish tinge goes from the brown of the back and the creamy tinge from the underparts.

Irides brown or reddish brown. Bill with upper mandible black or very dark grey, lower mandible bluish grey to pale silvery grey, with blackish tip. Legs and feet dark grey to blackish. Sexes alike but females usually have slightly less massive bills. Juvenile a general dull brown above with wing quills and rump darker brown and tail brownish black. The wing coverts have buffish fringes which form two inconspicuous bars across the closed wing in life. The underparts, including the throat, are pale buff with a buffish brown patch at the side of the breast. When first fledged the young have much shorter and smaller bills than the adults.

FIELD CHARACTERS Small black and brown bird with white underparts and large black and bluish bill. Much longer bill, and, when in company with them, its larger size, distinguish it from *L. bicolor* and *L. cucullata*.

DISTRIBUTION AND HABITAT Africa from Senegal to Ghana, east to southern Sudan and western Uganda and south to Gabon, and northern Angola; Zambia, Malawi, Tanzania, extreme southern Kenya, north-eastern Rhodesia, Mozambique, Natal and Zanzibar. Apparently no recent records from Senegal and The Gambia (Immelmann *et al.*). Rather sparse and fluctuating in distribution within its recorded range but locally common.

Inhabits forest clearings, riparian vegetation, cultivated areas (especially where dry-soil rice is grown in tropical forest areas), bamboo thickets and (for nesting) plantations of exotic conifers.

FEEDING AND GENERAL HABITS Known to feed on seeds of grasses, including cultivated rice when available, and those of the Bindura Bamboo, *Oxytenanthera abyssinica*. One bird, shot many miles from the nearest rice-growing area, had grains of *polished* rice in its crop, that it must have found spilled by man (Sclater & Moreau). Feeding methods and behaviour as in *L. cucullata* (q.v.). In the Kivu highlands, Kunkel found that seeds of grasses of the genus *Panicum* and cultivated rice were main foods. Small grass seeds, such as those of *Digitaria*, were ignored. Jackson has shown that in Zimbabwe its presence and movements are correlated with the sporadic seeding of the Bindura Bamboo. He suggests, probably correctly, that bamboo seed is the species' primary natural food.

In captivity will thrive on a diet of seed, greenstuff and the usual minerals. Some pairs will eagerly take eggfood and insects when they have young (Immelmann *et al.*) but one pair, that bred very successfully, refused not only animal foods but even soaked seed and reared their young on white bread soaked in artificial nectar and dry seed (van Baelen).

General behaviour, including locomotor intention movements, as in *L. bicolor* (q.v.).

NESTING The nest is roundish with a side entrance, built of grass, plant stems, dead leaves and similar materials and lined with finer grass or the like. It is usually sited 4 to 6 metres above ground but sometimes much higher, in a tree, bamboo clump or shrub. Moreau found that near Amani, in Tanzania, it usually built in exotic conifers (Sclater and Moreau). Eggs 4 to 6, rarely 7 or 8. Parental behaviour, at least in captivity, as in *L. cucullata* (q.v.). Incubation period about 14 days, young fledge at 21 days (F. Hall, unpublished mss., data from captive birds).

VOICE Contact calls described as a whistling 'peeoo peeoo' and 'd'yer d'yer' (Immelmann *et al.*, my anglicisation). The alarm call is described by Moreau (in Sclater & Moreau) as a 'thin cheep' and as 'tsek' by Immelmann *et al*. The young have a more or less two-syllabled begging call which Moreau (*op. cit.*) transcribes as 't-t-t-tey-tey'. The song is a short, stereotyped strophe given both as undirected song and in display. When singing in *either* context the bird opens its bill widely, mandibulates and elevates and vibrates its tongue as its two relatives do only in the excitement of sexual display. Güttinger gives sonagrams of the song and contact calls.

DISPLAY AND SOCIAL BEHAVIOUR As in *L. cucullata* and *L. bicolor* except as follows: In the courtship display the bird assumes a horizontal or nearly horizontal body posture and erects its plumage to a much less intense degree. The up and down movements are pronounced but the side to side movements are absent or very greatly reduced (Kunkel, Güttinger). The display of nesting material to the mate is less stereotyped, it consists merely of perching near the mate, holding the material, for a moment, before flying to the nest site.

OTHER NAMES Giant Mannikin, Pied Mannikin.

REFERENCES
Güttinger, H. R. 1970. Zur Evolution von Verhaltensweisen und Lautäusserungen bei Prachtfinken (Estrildidae). *Z. Tierpsychol.* **27**: 1011–1075.

Immelmann, K., Steinbacher, J. & Wolters, H. E. 1972. *Vögel in Käfig und Voliere: Prachtfinken*: 440–450.

Jackson, H. D. 1972. The status of the Pied Mannikin, *Lonchura fringilloides*, in Rhodesia and its association with the bamboo *Oxytenanthera abyssinica* (A. Richard) Munro. *Rhodesian Science News* **6**: 342–348.

Kunkel, P. 1965. Verhaltensstudien an den kontinental-afrikanischen Elsterchen (*Spermestes* Swainson). *Vogelwelt* **86**: 161–178.

Mackworth-Praed, C. W. & Grant, C. H. B. 1960. *African handbook of birds*, Ser. 1, vol. 2.

Russ, K. 1879. *Die fremdländische Stubenvögel*, vol. 1. Hanover, Germany.

Sclater, W. L. & Moreau, R. E. 1933. Taxonomic and field notes on some birds of north-eastern Tanganyika territory. *Ibis* **75**: 399–440.

van Baelen, E. 1974. Das Reisenelsterchen (*Spermestes fringilloides*). *Die Gefiederte Welt* **98**: 122–124.

The munias or mannikins, Java Sparrow and Pictorella Finch

The munias or mannikins of the Oriental and Australasian regions are mostly medium-sized estrildids with stout and usually rather large bills, short to medium length tails, which are more or less graduated with the two central feathers often somewhat pointed, and strong, rather large, legs and feet. Their plumage shows various combinations of brown, buff, chestnut, black, grey and white, often with decomposed shining golden, yellow or chestnut feathers on the rump, upper tail coverts and tail but with no other bright primary or secondary colours. The juvenile plumage is commonly much paler than the adult's and nearly uniform, although in some species it is merely a duller, slightly paler and less strongly differentiated version of the adult plumage.

They are highly social and apparently mostly very successful species that are adapted primarily for feeding mainly on the seeds of grasses and, to a lesser extent, those of other plants. Many of them readily include cultivated rice and millet in their diet when available and, in general, they are a group that has profited from man's forest destruction and agriculture. Although 'modern' agricultural methods may well eventually prove harmful to them as to much else. The Java Sparrow and the Timor Sparrow are merely rather aberrant members of this group. The same is probably true of the Pictorella Finch. Their affinities are usually thought to be with the silverbills and African mannikins and, less closely, with the Australian grassfinches, the Gouldian Finch and possibly also the parrot-finches. Güttinger (1976) is, however, of the opinion that the resemblances that they show to African mannikins and silverbills is due to convergence, not to close relationship.

The munias have sometimes been divided into subgenera of which Wolters (1957) recognises seven and Steiner (1960) three. I think that such differences as exist do not warrant the recognition of categories above that of species-group. Even these cannot be sharply defined, as there are some intermediate forms. The first species-group is characterised by having no decomposed shining yellowish, gold or chestnut fringes to the feathers of the rump, upper tail coverts or tail. They are predominantly brown in colour and the brown body feathers have pale shafts or some indication of them. They have a simple pattern in which a dark breast contrasts with a paler or white lower breast and belly, whose feathers often show darker crescentic or barred markings.

In this species-group are the White-backed or Sharp-tailed Munia, *Lonchura striata*, ancestor of the domesticated Bengalese Finch, which has a wide range from India to southern China and south to Sumatra; the Javan Munia, *L. leucogastroides*, and the Moluccan Munia, *L. molucca*. These three forms are allopatric and seem best considered as members of a superspecies. The Dusky Munia, *L. fuscans*, has very dark plumage which only shows faint indications of the typical pattern but, like Steiner (1960), I think that its affinities are with this group.

The species in the second group have the same characters as those given above except that they all possess some feathers on the rump, under tail coverts or tail which have decomposed glossy yellowish or golden fringes. Included are the well-known Spice Finch, *L. punctulata*, which has a wide range in the Indian subcontinent and in south-eastern Asia as far as Timor and the Celebes, and the Hill Munia, *L. kelaarti*, of Ceylon and parts of India. The White-bellied Munia, *L. leucogastra*, of

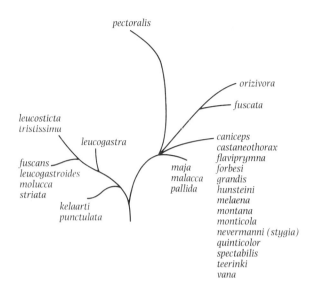

Probable affinities within the Australasian and Asiatic mannikins or munias, the Indian Silverbill excepted. Owing to the number of closely related forms, the species within each group are arranged in alphabetical order.

the Malay Peninsular, Sumatra, Borneo and the Philippines, shares the characters of this group and was placed with it by Steiner. Wolters, on the other hand, placed it in a monotypic subgenus on the grounds that, in his opinion, it also shared characters of his subgenera *Donacola* (in which he included *L. castaneothorax*, *L. monticola*, *L. montana*, *L. teerinki* and *L. melaena*) and *Munia* (in which he included *L. malacca* and several other species).

I can see no resemblances, other than those common to most munias, between *L. leucogastra* and any of the species placed by Wolters in his subgenus *Munia*. The areas of the breast and flanks that are black or marked with black in nominate *L.l. leucogastra* (less so in other races) certainly suggest a 'blacked in' version of the breast and flank pattern of *L. castaneothorax*. This might, however, be due to convergence, especially as in its juvenile plumage *L. leucogastra* is merely a dull edition of the adult, very unlike the juvenile of *L. castaneothorax*, which is of a nearly uniform pale buffish brown, strikingly unlike its parents. Modern authorities seem to have discounted the possibility of close relationship between *L. leucogastra* and *L. leucogastroides*, which were previously treated as conspecific, but I am not fully convinced they are right to do so. The two forms are allopatric, except in southern Sumatra, where *leucogastroides* may have been introduced by man and in Singapore, where it certainly was (Glenister, Immelmann *et al.*, 1970). The two are remarkably alike in colour and plumage pattern, differing mainly in *L. leucogastroides* having lighter brown upperparts with much less distinct pale feather shafts, the black on the breast not extending at either side on to the flanks and no decomposed glossy golden fringes to the central tail feathers. I think it likely that *L. leucogastra* and *L. leucogastroides* may be

closely allied. If they are it would, of course, link the two species-groups discussed above.

The Streak-headed Munia, *L. tristissima* and the White-spotted Munia *L. leucosticta*, may be conspecific. As compared to the other munias they are very distinct forms but their appearance suggests that they are more closely related to some or all of those already discussed than they are to other New Guinea species.

The next species-group contains a large number of forms all of which have well-developed decomposed glossy yellowish, golden or reddish chestnut feathers on the rump and upper tail coverts. Usually the entire head, or all of it except the throat, contrasts with the body colouring. Nine species of this group (and *L. tristissima*) are found in New Guinea where much of their present habitat has only recently, and in some cases very recently (Diamond, 1972), been produced through man's activities. Diamond concludes that there may have been rapid differentiation of species and subspecies and that their rather checker-board-type distribution pattern probably resulted from its having been largely due to chance which species got first into a new (human made) grassland area and, having established itself seemed, through competition, to have prevented later arriving congeners from doing likewise.

The Chestnut Munia, *L. malacca*, occurs in three main groups which were formerly thought to be good species. Behavioural and other evidence suggests they are now rightly treated as conspecific but for convenience, and because there is a scintilla of doubt in the matter, they are treated under separate headings in the species section. The white-bellied form, or Tri-coloured Munia, and the white-headed form from Java are geographically isolated both from each other and from the wholly chestnut and black forms that occur throughout the rest of the species' range. The Javan race differs strikingly from other forms, in having a white head contrasting with its black throat and breast instead of an entirely black head. Interestingly, the widely separated Formosan race shows a rather similar head pattern but is dark brownish grey where the Javan form is white.

The White-headed Munia, *L. maja*, is very similar in appearance to the white-headed form of *L. malacca*. It overlaps both it, and black-headed forms of *L. malacca* in Sumatra and the Malay Peninsula. Although the two species are now sympatric throughout the range of *L. maja* they appear to be closely related.

The Pale-headed Munia, *L. pallida*, is found to the east of the range of *L. maja*, of which it appears to be the geographical representative. I refrain from putting them both in the same superspecies only because *L. pallida* appears to be no closer to *L. maja* than the latter is to the white-headed form of *L. malacca*.

The Yellow-rumped Finch, *L. flaviprymna*, of Northern Australia, overlaps widely with the Chestnut-breasted Finch, *L. castaneothorax*, and the two interbreed in the areas of overlap (Immelmann, 1962). At first glance, *L. flaviprymna*, with its pale head and uniformly pale underparts (except for the black under tail coverts) differs strikingly from *L. castaneothorax* and shows considerable superficial resemblance to such other pale-headed forms as *L. maja* and *L. pallida*. Delacour treated all these forms (and some others) as conspecific. Keast (1958 and 1961), gave *L. flaviprymna* specific rank but considered it a derivative of *L. pallida*.

It has been generally held that *L. flaviprymna* must derive either from mutants of *castaneothorax* stock, which perhaps originated in inland northern Australia and later spread coastward and met again with the parent stock or relatives of it, or from some form which arrived in Australia prior to the arrival of *L. castaneothorax* or its ancestor. The latter has been the more popular theory, mainly because *L. flaviprymna* differs more markedly from its supposed nearest relatives elsewhere than does *L. castaneothorax*, races of which also occur in New Guinea. Immelmann (1962) suggests as a further possibility that it may have derived from some ancestor common both to it and *L. castaneothorax* and its resemblance to *L. pallida* be due to convergance. I believe this last to be true.

The plumage characters in which *L. flavyprymna* differs from the Australian race of *L. castaneothorax* involve only the *absence* of markings, and related melanin or phaeo-melanin pigments on head, breast and flanks. It equally lacks the well-defined (if less striking than those of *L. castaneothorax*) patterns on the breast and underparts shown by *L. pallida*, *L. maja* and *L. caniceps*. Except for the top of its head being a paler greyish it exactly agrees in the colour of its upperparts with *L. castaneothorax* and differs markedly from both *L. pallida* and *L. maja* though admittedly less so from *L. caniceps* which is, however, a much smaller bird. The differences in colour pattern between *L. flaviprymna* and *L. castaneothorax* are comparable to those between the pale-faced morph of the Red-billed Quelea, *Quelea quelea* and the more abundant black-faced morph, but for the fact that hybrids between *flaviprymna* and *castaneothorax* are intermediate in appearance and that *flaviprymna* shows (*fide* Immelmann, 1965) slight but consistent differences in courtship display, I would be tempted to consider them morphs of the same species. Indeed the possibility that slight behavioural differences may be correlated with colour differences within the species cannot be entirely excluded. Quite large behavioural differences linked with coloration have been recorded for the Ruff, *Philomachus pugnax*, and I have myself had an impression of quantitative differences in some behaviour patterns between white and blue Domestic Pigeons.

I think that *flaviprymna* derives either from a form ancestral to both it and *castaneothorax* or from mutants of *castaneothorax* stock. I do not think it derives from an early invasion of Australia by *L. pallida* stock or that it is so closely related to *L. pallida*, *L. maja* or *L. caniceps* as it is to *L. castaneothorax*.

The Chestnut-and-White Munia, *L. quinticolor*, of the Lesser Sunda Islands, is, I believe, derived from *L. castaneothorax* or proto-*castaneothorax* stock. Its rich chestnut colouring partly masks but does not fully conceal

such common features as the dark throat, contrasting with the pale-shafted ear coverts, as in nominate *L.c. castaneothorax*, and the greyish markings on the head feathers similar to those of *L.c. castaneothorax* and *L.c. ramsayi*.

A number of species occur on New Guinea and/or nearby islands. The Alpine Munia, *L. monticola*, with its relatively small bill, soft dense plumage and general colour pattern stands out from most of its congeners and superficially reminds one of an Alario Finch, *Serinus alario*. Its plumage pattern is, however, essentially like that of *L. castaneothorax* and I think there can be no doubt that it is a montane derivative of the same stock. It and the Snow Mountain Munia, *L. montana*, may be conspecific but in our present state of knowledge seem best treated as members of a superspecies.

I agree with Mees in thinking that the White-crowned Munia, *L. nevermanni*, is also closely allied to *L. castaneo-thorax*, in spite of its less complex colour pattern. Although both occur in New Guinea they are not, so far as is known, sympatric there. The Black Munia, *L. stygia*, is identical with *L. nevermanni* in everything but coloration. They are often found in mixed flocks and hybrids, or intergrades, between them have been collected (Mees). Mees has shown that previous ideas as to size differences between *nevermanni* and *stygia* were incorrect but thinks they are different species because of the differences between their juvenile plumages. To me these differences seem very slight and what might be expected, the juvenile plumage of *nevermanni* being generally more reddish in tone than that of *stygia*. I believe that *L. stygia* is a melanic morph of *L. nevermanni* but, for convenience sake and because of the possibility that I may be in error, I have dealt with them under separate headings in the species' section.

The Arfak Munia, *L. vana*, appears also to be a representative of the *castaneothorax–nevermanni* group. Except for its chestnut belly (in which point it resembles *L. nevermanni*) its plumage pattern is very like that of *L. castaneothorax* but with whitish instead of blackish throat and breast band.

The New Britain Munia, *L. spectabilis*, occurs also in parts of New Guinea. Its plumage pattern is identical to that of *L. quinticolor* and, like it, might well derive by simplification from that of *L. castaneothorax* or something similar to it. Their distribution makes it seem rather unlikely that *L. quinticolor* and *L. spectabilis* shared a common ancestor subsequent to the latter's branching off from *castaneothorax* or proto-*castaneothorax* stock.

The Grand Valley Munia, *L. teerinki*, is very similar to *L. spectabilis* in size and coloration but the greater extent of black on its underparts suggest a *castaneothorax* with 'blacked in' breast rather than, as does *L. spectabilis*, one with the black-bordered chestnut area replaced by white. I therefore doubt whether *L. teerinki* is more closely related to *L. spectabilis* than it is to others of the group.

The Grey-headed Munia, *L. caniceps*, seems of all New Guinea species the one most distinct from any of the others. Its coloration, although darker, is suggestive of that of *L. flaviprymna* of northern Australia but this slight resemblance is probably due to convergence. It seems most likely to be a very early and/or strongly divergent offshoot of the *castaneothorax* group. Hunstein's Munia, *L. hunsteini*, is rather similar in size to *L. caniceps*. They might possibly have shared a recent common ancestor but *hunsteini*'s colour pattern suggests a largely melanic form more directly derived from a *castaneothorax*-like stock.

Three large forms with very massive bills are allopatric. They are the Great-billed Munia, *L. grandis*, of New Guinea; Forbes' Munia, *L. forbesi*, of New Ireland and the Thick-billed Munia, *L. melaena*, of New Britain. *L. grandis* is very like the black-headed forms of *L. malacca* in colour pattern. However, not only is there a considerable gap in distribution between them but the details of their respective plumage patterns show some differences and the chestnut parts of the Great-billed Munia's plumage are of a much lighter and more yellowish shade than is shown by any race of *L. malacca*. Also its juvenile is said to have a spotted throat. I think, therefore, that it is more likely that the resemblances between *L. grandis* and *L. malacca* are due to convergence (within related stocks) than that they are closely related and geographical representatives. The Thick-billed Munia has a very different colour pattern from that of *L. grandis*, being largely black but with the median parts of the lower breast and belly (which are black in *grandis*) pinkish buff and a barred pattern on the flanks. Its pattern could well be derived, by increased melanisation, from one similar or identical to that of *L. castaneothorax*. *L. forbesi* is very similar to the foregoing two species in size although its bill is not quite so massive. Its coloration is similar to that of *L. grandis*, but of a less yellowish chestnut, and its plumage pattern is like that of *L. spectabilis*. It and *L. spectabilis* are completely allopatric.

These three large-billed allopatric forms may all be closely related in spite of their differing colour patterns. I think, however, that they represent separate branches (of related stocks) that have all developed large size and massive bills independently. *L. forbesi* appears to be closely related to and a geographical representative of *L. spectabilis*. *L. grandis* probably derived from some form ancestral both to it and to *L. spectabilis* and *L. forbesi*, and *L. melaena* more directly derived from *L. castaneothorax* or some form recently ancestral to both it and *L. melaena*.

The beautiful Java Sparrow, *L. oryzivora*, is widely known outside its natural range as for over a century it has been exported in large numbers to Europe, America and eastern Asia as a cage and aviary bird. It and the more sombrely coloured but similarly patterned Timor Sparrow or Brown Ricebird, *L. fuscata*, have usually been placed, as by Mayr (1968) in a separate genus, *Padda*. Even Wolters (1957), who tends to favour the 'splitting' of genera, said this decision was very questionable. Restall also questioned the advisability of keeping *Padda* distinct from *Lonchura*, and Güttinger's (1976) detailed studies of this and other species showed that it agreed in all essentials of voice and behaviour with typical *Lonchura* species.

The least trivial of the several minor characters that have been used to separate *Padda* from *Lonchura* seems to be the somewhat different formation of the vomer, a point so far investigated only in *L. oryzivora* and which will probably not prove valid for the smaller-billed *L. fuscata*. *L. oryzivora* differs appreciably in colour when adult, being largely bluish grey with a beautiful pink bill, but its juvenile plumage is very similar in its pale buffish brown colour to those of many *Lonchura* species. *L. oryzivora* is also larger than any other *Lonchura* species but in most respects the grey-billed *L. fuscata* largely bridges the gap as will be seen very clearly if one compares specimens of the two 'Padda' species and *L. castaneothorax*.

Much as I dislike departing from the nomenclature of standard works I feel bound to include these two species in *Lonchura*. To do otherwise would be illogical unless one divided *Lonchura*, as presently used by Mayr in *Peters' Check-list*, and elsewhere, into many small genera. Certainly the Pictorella Finch, the silverbills and the African mannikins all seem more deserving candidates for generic separation from *Lonchura* than do the Java and Timor Sparrows.

The Pictorella Finch, *L. pectoralis*, is distinct in appearance and differs in several points of behaviour from the typical *Lonchura* species. Immelmann (1965), though he puts it in the monotypic genus *Heteromunia*, argues, convincingly in my opinion, that its nearest affinities are with *Lonchura* and that the similarities shown to some other genera of estrildids are due to convergent adaptations to living in open country and savanna. Although its coloration and plumage pattern suggest those of some other Australian estrildids, they have, to my eye, at least as strong affinities with those of some *Lonchura*, its basic plumage *colours* being suggestive of, though not so divergent from typical *Lonchura* species as those of *L. oryzivora* and its plumage pattern easily derivable from one similar to that of *L. castaneothorax*. The coloration of its upper parts and more especially the small white spots on its wing coverts are indeed very reminiscent of another Australian species, the Diamond Dove, to which it certainly cannot be related. Its nestling palate pattern differs from that of typical *Lonchura* and approaches those of the African mannikins but as Güttinger (whose 1976 paper gives excellent photographs of the nestling mouth patterns of both) says, this is probably a chance convergence within (in my opinion) fairly closely related groups. I follow Mayr (1968) in giving *Heteromunia* only subgeneric rank within *Lonchura*.

REFERENCES

Delacour, J. 1943. A revision of the subfamily Estrildinae of the family Ploceidae. *Zoologica*, New York Zool. Soc. **28**: 69–86.

Diamond, J. M. 1972. *Avifauna of the eastern highlands of New Guinea*. Publ. Nuttall Orn. Club, no. 12. Cambridge, Mass.

Glenister, A. G. 1951. *The birds of the Malay Peninsula, Singapore and Penang*. Oxford University Press, London.

Güttinger, H. R. 1976. Zur systematischen Stellung der Gattungen *Amadina, Lepidopygia* und *Lonchura* (Aves, Estrildidae). *Bonn. zool. Beitr.* **27**: 218–244.

Immelmann, K. 1962. Besiedlungsgeschichte und Bastardierung von *Lonchura castaneothorax* und *Lonchura flaviprymna* in Nordaustralien. *J. Orn.* **103**: 344–357.

Immelmann, K. 1965. *Australian finches in bush and aviary.* Angus & Robertson, Sydney and London.

Immelmann, K., Steinbacher, J. & Wolters, H. E. 1970. *Vögel in Käfig und Voliere: Prachtfinken*: 349–353.

Keast, A. J. 1958. Intraspecific variation in the Australian finches. *Emu* **58**: 219–246.

Keast, A. J. 1961. Bird speciation on the Australian continent. *Bull. Mus. Zool. Harvard Coll.* **123**: 305–494.

Mayr, E. 1968. *Peters' check-list of birds of the world.* Cambridge, Mass.

Mees, G. F. (in press) Birds from the lowlands of southern New Guinea.

Steiner, H. 1960. Klassifikation der Prachtfinken, Spermestinae, auf Grund der Rachenzeichnung ihrer Nestlings. *J. Orn.* **101**: 92–112.

Wolters, H. E. 1957. Die Klassifikation der Webefinken (Estrildidae). *Bonn. Zool. Beitr.* **8**: 90–129.

Dusky Munia   *Lonchura fuscans*

Spermestes fuscans Cassin, 1852, *Proc. Philadelphia Acad.* **6**, p. 185.

DESCRIPTION Between Spice Finch and Avadavat in size but with proportionately larger bill than the former even. Brownish black below and brownish black to very dark dusky brown above. Lighter brown ends to the feather shafts and lighter dusky brown to pale brown tips to the median parts of the feathers on the sides of the head, crown, nape and to a lesser extent on the mantle and back give a speckled appearance and black edges to the otherwise very dark brown feathers of the lower breast, belly and flanks a slightly scaled appearance. Appreciable apparently individual differences in depth of pigment and extent of spotting or scaling, apart from those due to wear. Irides dark brown. Bill with upper mandible blackish and lower mandible pale bluish grey. Feet and legs bluish grey to slaty blue.

Juvenile like adult (except, of course, in plumage texture) but without pale tips to feathers of upperparts or black edges to those of underparts. Bill at first entirely black (Langberg, corroborated by appearance of skins of juveniles in the British Museum collection).

FIELD CHARACTERS Small, all blackish 'finch', with bluish grey on bill and feet if these visible.

DISTRIBUTION AND HABITAT Borneo and Natuna, Cagayan Sulu, and Bunguey Islands. Inhabits grassy areas, cultivation, alang-alang scrub, secondary woodland, clearings and roads in forest and sometimes towns. Harrison found it common in Kuching, the capital of Borneo, 'wherever there is grass or seed'.

FEEDING AND GENERAL HABITS Known to feed on seeds of grasses, including cultivated rice, and of reeds.

When feeding tends to keep low among the plants, approaching seeding panicles from below. Often responds to bird-scaring devices by 'freezing' where it is or by hiding in the growing rice instead of flying away

(Smythies). Feeds both in vegetation and on the ground. Sometimes seen on roads, presumably taking either mineral matter or wind-blown seeds.

In captivity has thrived and reared young when the foods given to it were millets and canary seed, both dry and sprouted and eggfood (Langberg).

NESTING Nest roundish with side entrance like that of other *Lonchura* species (Immelmann *et al.*). Usually sited in a tree or palm from 4·5 to 6 metres (15 to 20 feet) above ground. Also nests in holes or niches in trees, buildings or rocks. In the Niah Caves Harrison (in Smythies) found nests over 80 metres (250 feet) high. Clutch in upland areas of Borneo 2 to 5, usually 3. Elsewhere (*fide* Immelmann *et al.*) up to 8 eggs but usually 3 to 6.

In the Kelabit uplands of Borneo usually starts to nest in November and nests with eggs or young found in December, January and February. In Kuching nests have been found in May and October. Breeding season appears to depend largely on local food supplies (Smythies).

VOICE Smythies records a shrill 'pee pee', a 'thin chirrup' and a quick 'tek tek', the last uttered in flight.

DISPLAY AND SOCIAL BEHAVIOUR No information.

OTHER NAMES Borneo Munia, Borneo Mannikin, Dusky Mannikin.

REFERENCES

Harrison, T. 1950. Kuching bird notes. *Sarawak Mu. Journ.* **5**: 328–334.

Immelmann, K., Steinbacher, J. & Wolters, H. E. 1970. *Vögel in Käfig und Voliere: Prachtfinken*: 353–356. Aachen, Germany.

Langberg, W. 1955. The first breeding in confinement of the Borneo, or Black, Mannikin (*Uroloncha fuscans*). *Avicult. Mag.* **61**: 229–230.

Smythies, B. E. 1960. *The birds of Borneo.* London.

White-backed Munia   *Lonchura striata*
(*striata* group)

Loxia striata Linnaeus, 1776, *Syst. Nat.* ed. 12, **1**, p. 306.

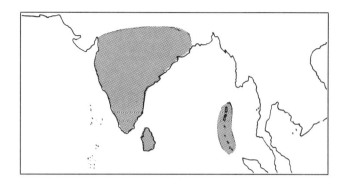

DESCRIPTION About size of Spice Finch but with bill a little larger in proportion. Tail wedge-shaped with ends of central tail feathers elongated and tapered to a blunt point (a sharp one in certain stages of wear). Forehead, face, throat, upper breast and wing quills brownish black with very faint paler shaft streaks. Crown of head slightly lighter and shading into dark dull brown, with pale buffish shaft streaks, on nape, sides of neck, mantle, back and lower rump. Under wing coverts pale buffish. A conspicuous broad white band across the lower back and upper rump. Feathers at sides of root of tail and tibial feathers dark reddish brown with whitish shaft streaks and some with whitish tips. Upper and under tail coverts blackish, lower mandible bluish grey. Legs and feet dark from lower breast to vent, creamy buff to white (according to freshness or otherwise of feathers) with inconspicuous, more or less U-shaped greyish barring on some flank feathers. Irides reddish brown. Bill with upper mandible blackish, lower mandible bluish grey. Legs and feet dark grey to bluish grey. Sexes alike. Juvenile a little paler and with the light shaftstreaks of feathers almost absent.

The above description is of nominate *L.s. striata*, from peninsular India and Ceylon. *L.s. fumigata*, from the south and central Andaman Islands, is slightly smaller. In fresh plumage it has a stronger creamy buff tinge on the underparts and is a darker brown on mantle and back. It lacks pale shaft streaks, or has them only very faintly indicated, on head, nape, mantle and rump. On the back the pale shaft streaks are evident near the tips of the feathers. The feathers of the brownish black upper breast often, especially in females, have reddish brown fringes and those near the line of demarcation with the white underparts, sometimes have white fringes. Juveniles have buff or whitish throats, buff fringes to the dark brown breast feathers and buff underparts. Captive juveniles had fully assumed adult plumage at 10–11 weeks (Siroki).

L. striata semistriata, from the central Nicobar Islands and Car Nicobar is very like *L.s. fumigata* but not quite so dark on neck, upper breast and upper parts and has more pronounced brownish fringes (in all specimens of both sexes that I have examined) on the feathers of the upper breast.

FIELD CHARACTERS Small blackish and white finch-like bird with conspicuous white band across rump.

DISTRIBUTION AND HABITAT Peninsular India and Ceylon; the Andaman and Nicobar Islands, and Car Nicobar. Widespread at low elevations but occurs up to 900 metres and locally up to 1800 metres.

Inhabits scrub, open woodland, forest clearings, waste land, cultivated areas and gardens.

FEEDING AND GENERAL HABITS Seeks food both on the ground and in growing vegetation. Feeds very largely on the seeds of wild grasses. Takes cultivated rice when available. A number have been seen eating green alga, *Spirogyra* sp., from a drying pool (Pillai). Ali & Ripley state that insects are fed to the young but give no details. The species usually refuses insect food in captivity, and the young are fed by regurgitation, so further observations are needed. In captivity it will successfully rear young if given soaked seed, egg food, chickweed and other greenstuff (Siroki).

Usually in small parties of 6 to 20, sometimes in larger flocks or in pairs. In captivity very unaggressive to its own and other species even when breeding.

NESTING Nest usually in a bush or small tree, sometimes in larger trees, reeds, or rank grass. Commonly from 1 to 4 metres above ground, sometimes lower or higher. The nest is oval or spherical and varies in size from about 15 by 15 cm (6 by 6 inches) (when round in shape) to about 20 by 20 cm (8 by 8 inches) (Baker). It is made of blades or strips of blades of grass, reed or bamboo leaves, probably also other materials at times, usually lined with finer grasses and/or grass panicles. The side entrance may have a short entrance tube and is sometimes, perhaps usually, on a level with the floor of the nest. Breeding takes place mostly during the rains but some nests may be found at almost any time of year (Ali & Ripley). Details of the nest's construction and its building probably like that described for the *acuticauda* group (q.v.).

Eggs 3 to 8, most usually 5. Incubation period 13 to 14 days (Ali & Ripley), up to 15 days recorded in captivity (Siroki). Both sexes incubate and brood in the usual manner, and both roost in the nest at night. Nest sanitation probably as in the Bengalese Finch (q.v.). Young fledge at about 21 days and are independent at 32 days (Siroki).

VOICE 'Twittering' and 'peeping' calls have been noted by various observers. The male has a purring or humming ('schnurrenden') song, uttered (when displaying?) with spread tail and head turning from side to side (Russ). Probably the calls of this form will prove similar or identical in sound and function to those of the Bengalese Finch (q.v.).

DISPLAY AND SOCIAL BEHAVIOUR Not apparently recorded in any detail. Probably essentially as in the domesticated form, the Bengalese Finch (q.v.).

OTHER NAMES Striated Finch, Striated Munia.

REFERENCES

Ali, S. & Ripley, S. D. 1974. *Handbook of the birds of India and Pakistan*, vol. 10. Oxford University Press, Bombay and London.
Baker, E. C. S. 1934. *The nidification of birds of the Indian Empire*, vol. 3. London.
Henry, G. M. 1955. *A guide to the birds of Ceylon*. London.
Pillai, N. G. 1968. The green alga, *Spirogyra* sp. in the diet of the Whitebacked Munia *Lonchura striata*. *J. Bombay Nat. Hist. Soc.* **65**: 490.
Russ, K. 1879. *Die fremländischen Stubenvögel*, vol. 1. Hanover.
Siroki, Z. 1968. Zur Brutbiologie des Spitzschwanzbronze-männchens (*Lonchura striata*). *Gefiederte Welt* **92**: 104–106.

White-backed Munia *Lonchura striata*
(*acuticauda* group)

Munia acuticauda Hodgson, 1836, *Asiatic Researches* **19**, p. 153.

DESCRIPTION As *Lonchura s. striata* (q.v.) except as follows. Central tail feathers rather more sharply pointed. Brown of ear coverts and sides of neck paler, with creamy shaft streaks and tips to the medium chocolate brown feathers. Breast feathers dark chocolate rather than blackish brown, with dull reddish brown (upper area) to whitish (lower area) fringes. Underparts, where white or creamy in *L.s. striata*, appear a light greyish buff at a little distance, due to fine, light greyish markings (mostly in elongate U shapes) on the otherwise cream or pale buff feathers. The white rump patch, at least in fresh plumage, is suffused with fawn and some of its feathers have faint brown barring. Under tail coverts dark reddish brown with paler fringes and pale shaft streaks. Upper mandible sometimes dark grey rather than blackish, or black only on the culmen. Juvenile duller above and with the underparts a pale, dull buffish with fine light drab barring on each feather. Nestling as 'chocolate' Bengalese Finch (q.v.).

The above description is of *L.s. acuticauda*, from north-central India east through the foothills of Nepal, Sikkim and Bhutan to Assam, and south and east through Bihar, West Bengal, East Pakistan, Burma and northern Thailand (Siam). *L. striata swinhoei*, shown on plate 5, facing p. 224, from southern China and Formosa, is similar but a little lighter on the brown parts and with pronounced pale cream or whitish shafts and fringes to the breast feathers. The faint greyish markings on the feathers of its underparts are, in most individuals, more elongated, and its juvenile plumage is paler and more buffish in colour. This race is probably the one from which the domesticated Bengalese Finch (q.v.) was mainly, or wholly, derived. *L. striata subsquamicollis*, from south-eastern Burma, southern Thailand, Indo China and the Malay Peninsula to Sumatra and Banka is somewhat intermediate between the two described above, but with the markings on the pale underparts rather more conspicuous than in either. All three intergrade in places and there is some micro-geographical and individual variation.

FIELD CHARACTERS Small, chocolate brown 'finch' with white rump patch and pale underparts.

DISTRIBUTION AND HABITAT Garhwal, in north-central India, east and south-east to southern China and the lowlands of Formosa, and the Malay Peninsula to Sumatra and Banka.

Occurs both in lowlands and in hills, up to 2000 metres in the Himalayas, but usually lower. Inhabits scrub, open jungle, secondary growth, cultivated and waste land, and gardens. At least at some higher elevations, it is a partial migrant, disappearing again after breeding (Immelmann *et al.*).

FEEDING AND GENERAL HABITS Feeds both from the ground and in vegetation. Takes seeds of grasses, including cultivated rice, and (*fide* Schäfer) rape seed, the latter taken, like some of the grass seeds, from the growing plant. In Bumbong Lima, Malaysia, Avery found that rice and a filamentous alga, *Spirogyra*, were the main foods. Baker states that he watched a pair bringing small caterpillars and spiders to their young but further observations on this are needed as, so far as known, no estrildid ever carries food to its young visible in its bill.

At least as social as *L.s. striata*, possibly rather more so. Schäfer noted that, even when breeding, it habitually fed in flocks. In China it was a tame and abundant species in many inhabited areas (La Touche) but I have not seen any report on its situation there since the Communist government's campaign against the Tree Sparrow and other grain-eating birds.

NESTING The nesting of this form was studied in detail in West Malaysia by Avery, from whose paper the information in this section derives except where otherwise indicated.

Nests in shrubs, bushes, trees, bamboo, creepers or large cacti; in western China Schäfer found it especially in

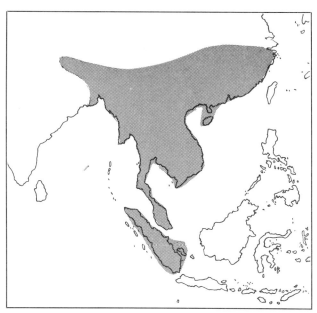

conifers. Usually about 3 to 4 metres above ground but often higher or lower. In his study area Avery found that all nests were near human habitations, usually within 5 metres of a house.

The nest is roundish, about 45 cm in circumference with a side entrance about 3 cm in diameter and the nest chamber about 6 cm in diameter. The outer layer of the nest wall is of twigs and relatively large leaves bound with pieces of thin vine and fibrous strips from the base of coconut palms, inside this is a layer of bamboo leaves, coarse grass stems or similar materials. The nest lining is of grass stems whose heads are so arranged that they hang out over the nest and nearly conceal the entrance hole and also serve to make the nest much less obvious. If they are pushed aside the shape of the nest becomes clearer and it is much more obvious. Less detailed descriptions (Baker, Schäfer) do not suggest any significant geographical differences in nest construction.

Nest material is gathered by the male but the female, who waits at the site, does most of the building. Standing grass stems were preferred to loose ones. The bird grips the stalk near its base and tugs vigorously. Baker states that to collect strips of stem or leaf the bird bites into the material then gives a quick jerk and flies off, stripping away a length. Although the species is not otherwise territorial an area of about a metre round the nest is vigorously defended from conspecifics who, if they trespass, are chased away.

Eggs usually 4 or 5, perhaps sometimes more or fewer as in other forms. Both sexes incubate in turn by day although one bird may spend more time incubating than its mate does. The nest is sometimes left for as much as 9 per cent of the total daylight hours. At the change over the bird being relieved does not usually leave the nest until after its mate has entered. Avery did not hear any calls at nest relief except from the leaving partner as it flies away. Nest predation in Western Malaysia was high, of 25 nests only two were successful. Small snakes and the Black-naped Oriole, *Oriolus chinensis*, are known predators.

In Western Malaysia recorded breeding in all months except November. In the Indian and nearby parts of its range breeds mainly from May to late August; in Szechuan from April to July, and in south-eastern China from February to November.

VOICE Schäfer says the contact call (Lockruf) resembles the call (which?) of the Serin and the alarm call is a trilling 'troi troi troi tee tee tee tee' (my anglicisation). Steiner (in Immelmann *et al.*) says the call of the male is a relatively deep 'quoi quoi', that of the female a higher pitched and rattling or churring 'terr terr'. Song, and probably in fact all other vocalisations, similar to or identical with those of the domesticated Bengalese Finch (q.v.).

DISPLAY AND SOCIAL BEHAVIOUR So far as is known identical with that of the domesticated form, the Bengalese Finch.

OTHER NAMES Sharp-tailed Finch, Sharp-tailed Munia.

REFERENCES

Ali, S. & Ripley, S. D. 1974. *Handbook of the birds of India and Pakistan*. Bombay and London.

Avery, M. L. 1978. Nesting Sharp-tailed Munias, *Lonchura striata*, in Northern Province Wellesley, West Malaysia. *Malayan Nature Journal* **32**: 85–101.

Avery, M. L. 1980. Diet and breeding seasonality among a population of Sharp-tailed Munias, *Lonchura striata*, in Malaysia. *Auk* **97**: 160–166.

Baker, E. C. S. 1934. *The nidification of birds of the Indian Empire*, vol. 3. London.

Immelmann, K., Steinbacher, J. & Wolters, H. E. 1970 and 1971. *Vögel in Käfig und Voliere*, pp. 356–365.

La Touche, J. D. D. 1925–1930. *A handbook of the birds of eastern China*. London.

Schäfer, E. 1938. Ornithologische Ergebnisse zweier Forschungsreisen nach Tibet. *J. Orn.* **86**, Sonderheft.

Bengalese Finch   *Lonchura striata*

DESCRIPTION The Bengalese or Society Finch is a domesticated form of the *acuticauda* group of the White-backed Munia, *Lonchura striata*. It occurs in three basic colours, 'chocolate', 'fawn' and white. 'Self chocolate' birds resemble the wild *L. striata swinhoei* (the race from which they were most probably derived) in colour and pattern although they show more individual variation and some are darker or lighter than wild birds. The irides of the 'chocolate' domestic birds are usually dark brown. The 'fawn' or 'cinnamon' birds are usually an attractive bright sandy fawn with the same pattern as the chocolate birds but they have red eyes. As in comparable fawn varieties of other birds, their wing and tail quills tend to be paler than the rest of the plumage. The white birds have pale flesh-coloured bills and feet but some dark pigment in their eyes. Pure albinos with pink eyes have occurred but seem to be very rare. Dilute forms of both 'chocolate' and 'fawn' also occur. In the former the colour is very similar to that of a darkish fawn but tinged with grey and the bird can be told from a fawn by its dark eye.

Self-coloured Bengalese are in the minority, most of the Bengalese Finches that are kept, and the majority of those offered for sale, are 'chocolate and white' or 'fawn and white'. Such pied specimens vary greatly in the amount of white plumage and its distribution, although forehead, crown, wings and underparts are most likely to be partly or entirely white. Eisner (1960) notes that individuals with only a very few white feathers usually have these on the forehead, upper part of the throat just below the lower mandible and among the primaries. A similar distribution of the white is usually seen on pied Domestic and Feral Pigeons that have only a little white in their plumage although in their case a few feathers around the vent and immediately behind the eye are even more likely to be white. Naturally, the bills and mouth markings of pied Bengalese also commonly show areas lacking in melanin pigment. Normally fawn behaves genetically as a simple Mendelian recessive to chocolate (Eisner, 1957). Buchan gives the expectations for the various possible matings in his useful book on the Bengalese Finch. In Germany, and possibly elsewhere, several different shades of both chocolate and fawn have been produced and given names such as 'nougat', 'cream' etc and there have been attempts to increase size and variety of colour patterns by hybridising with other *Lonchura* species.

Juveniles differ from adults in a comparable manner to those of the wild form (q.v.). They have obtained adult plumage and are capable of breeding at three months old (Eisner, 1960). When first hatched the nestlings are naked except for a little down (absent in some) on the upper parts. In self coloured chocolates the mouth markings are as in the wild form; a black horseshoe-shaped mark on the yellow palate, with two black marks below it and two on the tongue. The gape flanges are white, accentuated by adjacent black marks just inside. In fawns the mouth markings and eyeballs are fawn. Pied birds have broken or partial mouth markings (Eisner, 1960).

So-called 'crested' Bengalese Finches have some or all of their crown feathers growing at wrong angles and/or curled or otherwise distorted. The happily still rare 'frizzled' Bengalese have defective outward-curling body feathers like those of the similarly afflicted frizzled Domestic Fowls and frillback Domestic Pigeons. These gross plumage defects are pleasing to some fanciers but, in my opinion, merely add a pitiable ugliness to an otherwise attractive if hardly beautiful bird.

ORIGIN Prince Taka-Tsukasa, writing in 1922, stated that the Bengalese Finch had been imported into Japan about two hundred years before. A contemporary account said that it was obtained from China, and described the wild ancestor, quite clearly *L. striata*. About fifty years later it was kept throughout Japan but the fawn and white varieties had not then appeared. Presumably the bird was already domesticated by the Chinese before it was imported into Japan.

It evidently underwent intense selection for the ability to breed successfully in cages on a relatively monotonous diet. Hence its tameness and hardiness in captivity and its very strong parental behaviour, traits which might be lessened or lost if interbreeding with other *Lonchura* species, as now practised by some fanciers on the continent (Kirschke) becomes widespread.

NESTING Will nest in almost any type of nesting box or basket or, if in an aviary, in some near natural site in a bush or shrub. Eisner found no difficulty in getting it to breed in glass-backed nesting boxes with very little nesting material, to facilitate observation. Will use coconut fibre, grasses, plant stems, fine roots and other materials. The nest is said to be rather loosely put together (Immelmann *et al.*). Engel (in Oppenburn) found that some pairs consistently built well made nests with an entrance tube and others built inferior or grossly imperfect nests. This is surprising as the usual reason (ill health apart) for birds, whether domesticated or wild-caught, building defective nests in captivity, is lack of the right materials.

Eggs 2 to 9, usually 5 or 6. Eisner (1960) found that the incubation period (of 71 eggs) varied from 15 to 19 days with an average of 16·44 days – an astonishingly long time. However, to obtain exact timing, these eggs were removed as laid and replaced after completion of the clutch, whereas under natural conditions the eggs get some intermittent warmth, when the hen sits in the nest to lay and when both members of the pair roost in it, before regular incubation starts. Young fledge at 24 or 25 days, sometimes not till 27 days. They are fed by the parents for at least 12 days after but begin to feed themselves when a week out of the nest. For a few days prior to fledging the young move about in the nest, look out of the entrance and exercise their wings (Eisner, 1961).

The parents eat the eggshell as soon as a nestling hatches. While the young are being regularly brooded, about the first 10 days, the parents remove and eat their faeces as they are extruded. Later the young deposit their faeces high up on the sides of the nest where they soon dry and do not, even when they are dislodged, foul the interior of the nest. The parents are very careful and gentle when feeding small nestlings and may take from 10 to 15 minutes to feed the brood then. Eisner (1961) thought her birds fed the young on *crushed* seed for the first 2 to 3 days, thereafter the main diet was whole, shelled seed but, in an earlier paper (Eisner, 1960) she mentions that her birds took a commercial 'insectivorous' food also when feeding young. It would be interesting to know if this, or any other estrildid does, or can *crush* hard seeds. Bengalese will certainly often rear their young on nothing but seed and greenfood, such as chickweed, lettuce and seeding grass, and of course mineral matter, but probably they do better if the parents are given (and will take) soaked seed and milksop or eggfood in addition. It is, of course, essential that they should take such foods, and if possible insects also, if they are used to foster the young of species that rear their young on insects.

Both members of the pair often spend much time in the nest together by day, as well as roosting in it at night. Probably having little else to interest them, if caged, and no need to search for food, are as much the causes of this as their strong parental impulses.

VOICE The contact call of male and female differ and, to an experienced ear, the birds can be sexed by it. That of the female has a definite 'r' sound and has been described (Immelmann *et al.*) as 'tr-tr-tr', 'brrt brrt' and 'breet'. The male's is a more flowing 'yerk yerk' or 'quoee quoee' (my anglicisations) with no 'r' sound. The song is given only by the male. It has been described as a peculiar humming or rattling sound ('eigentümlich schnürrende Gesang') by Immelmann *et al.* Eisner (1960) notes that when, at the commencement of their first moult, juvenile males begin to sing, only a 'very quiet whispering' is uttered, which gradually becomes louder over a period of weeks, but she does not describe the adult song. Butler (1894), unmindful that fashions in childrens' toys might change, wrote that the song 'resembles nothing as closely as it does the sound made by a little woollen sheep on wheels which one sometimes sees children dragging along the pavement.' A repeated 'tscheck' is uttered when defending the territory immediately around the nest (S. & L. Verborgen).

The song is subject to much variation, apparently individual or familial. Young males partly learn their songs from other individuals, normally their father. If they have been reared by other species their songs show a definite approach to that of the fosterer (Immelmann *et al.*).

DISPLAY AND SOCIAL BEHAVIOUR In courtship display the male, with triangular head, feathers of lower breast, belly and flanks erected, tail raised a little above the horizontal, legs bent and bill held more or less horizontal, hops towards the female with a series of bowing and pivoting movements (Eisner, 1960). Usually he sings continuously and, as the display nears its end, tends to hold himself more erect and his tail at a higher angle. If responsive, the female solicits by crouching and tail quivering. Copulation is immediately followed by brief mutual aggression (Engel, in Oppenborn). From observation of a small number of pairs in aviaries Eisner (most of whose detailed observations were on caged individuals) believes that under more natural conditions, the picking up and carrying of nesting material would precede courtship display, as in the Spice Finch.

Clumping and allo-preening occur. The sociability and relative lack of aggression characteristic of the species seems to have been intensified in this domestic form. One result of this is that if several pairs are kept together, successful breeding may be hindered or prevented by several birds roosting in one nest or more than one hen laying in the same nest. Some pairs do, however, hold territory immediately around their nest, and the song appears sometimes to be given in a hostile or self assertive context (S. & L. Verborgen). As a rule, breeding is most successful when a pair have a cage or aviary to themselves.

It is sometimes said this species thrives better in a cage than when given the larger space of a room or an aviary. Except in the case of physically defective specimens, this is not so, provided other factors such as temperature, availability of food and lack of aggressive larger species, are comparable. Butler (1894) gives a vivid account of the speedy adaptation of previously caged Bengalese that he released into an aviary. Bengalese Finches would appear to be shorter-lived than most other small birds, averaging only a little over 4 years (Immelmann *et al.*).

OTHER NAMES Society Finch, Bengalee.

REFERENCES

Buchan, J. 1976. *The Bengalese Finch.* Printed by H. E. Iles, Kingswood, Bristol.

Butler, A. G. 1894. *Foreign finches in captivity.* London.

Butler, A. G. 1907. The origin of Bengalese. *Avicult. Mag.* **5**: 222–223.

Eisner, E. 1957. The Bengalese Finch. *Avicult. Mag.* **63**: 101–108.

Eisner, E. 1960. The biology of the Bengalese Finch. *Auk* **77**: 271–287.

Eisner, E. 1961. The behaviour of the Bengalese Finch in the nest. *Ardea* **49**: 51–69.

Eisner, E. 1963. A quantitative study of parental behaviour in the Bengalese Finch. *Behaviour* **20**: 134–206.

Immelmann, K., Steinbacher, J. & Wolters, H. E. 1971. *Vögel in Käfig und Voliere: Prachtfinken*: 365–384. Hans Limberg, Aachen.

Kirscke, S. 1976. Erfahrungen mit *Lonchura*-Arten. *Gefiederte Welt* **100**: 125–128.

Oppenborn, G. 1976. Fortpflanzungsverhalten des Japanischen Mövchens – wissenschaftlich gesehen. *Gefiederte Welt* **100**: 147–150.

Perreau, G. A. 1907. On the origin of Bengalese. *Avicult. Mag.* **5**: 182–186.

Taka-Tsukasa, N. 1922. Aviculture in Japan. *Avicult. Mag.*, third series **13**: 16–22.

Java Munia   *Lonchura leucogastroides*

Munia leucogastroides Horsfield & Moore, 1856, *Cat. Birds Mus. East India Co.* **2**, p. 510.

DESCRIPTION Between Spice Finch and Avadavat in size but typical *Lonchura* shape and with bill proportionately deeper than that of Spice Finch. Front of forehead, lores, front of cheeks, throat and breast, dull purplish black. Rump, upper and under tail coverts and central tail feathers blackish brown with a faint purple tinge. Primaries, outer secondaries and outer tail feathers a dull dark brown. Underwing coverts mainly buffish. Rest of upper parts a drab earth brown, slightly darker on the wing coverts and more reddish on the outer parts of the ear coverts. The feathers on the upper parts, especially on the mantle and back, have whitish or partly whitish shafts and often also a dusky subterminal bar and then a pale or whitish spot. The resultant streaked or speckled appearance is slight and not at all conspicuous. Tibial feathers reddish brown. Underparts, from lower breast to belly and flanks, white. Irides brown. Bill with blackish or

dark horn-grey upper mandible and pale greyish blue lower mandible. Legs and feet grey or bluish grey.

Juvenile a more reddish brown above, without pale shaft streaks or spots, and brownish buff below, darkest on the breast and palest on the areas that are white in the adult. Bill and eyes probably duller but not recorded.

FIELD CHARACTERS Small finch-like bird, dull brown with blackish breast and white underparts. Where they occur together (through human introduction) the entirely white flanks and blackish instead of gold-fringed tail distinguish it (at close view!) from the White-bellied Munia which otherwise has same field characters.

DISTRIBUTION AND HABITAT Southern Sumatra, Java, Bali, and Lombok. Introduced into Singapore (Glenister).

Inhabits cultivated areas, rice fields, gardens, and bushy and grassy areas. In Java mainly a bird of the lowlands but occurs up to 900 metres (3000 feet) (Kuroda).

FEEDING AND GENERAL HABITS Eats seeds of grasses and cultivated rice, both ripe and unripe (Hoogerwerf). Feeds both on the ground and in vegetation. Usually in pairs or small parties but sometimes in company with other seed-eating birds (Hoogerwerf). Perches both low down in bushes and high in trees.

NESTING Nests in bushes, the peripheral branches of trees and especially in Epiphytes. Frequently nests in the immediate vicinity of human dwellings. Nest similar to that of Spice Finch but a little smaller. Eggs usually 5 in number, sometimes 6. Breeds at all times of year in west Java (Hoogerwerf). In the dryer parts of east Java breeds only in the wet season (*fide* Immelmann *et al.*).

VOICE Hoogerwerf describes a high-pitched 'pee-ee-eet' or 'tyee-ee-ee (my anglicisation). The male has a pleasing purring or rattling song (Kaeker, in Immelmann *et al.*). The call notes of male and female differ (Immelmann *et al.*).

DISPLAY AND SOCIAL BEHAVIOUR Probably much as related species. In the earlier years of this century it was apparently imported into Europe not infrequently and

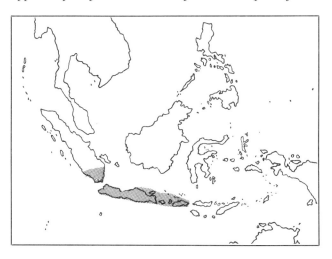

proved easy to breed in captivity. In spite, or perhaps because of this, there appears to have been little written about it, but it is known that hybrids between it and the domesticated Bengalese Finch are completely fertile (Immelmann *et al.*).

OTHER NAMES Java Mannikin, Black-rumped Munia.

REFERENCES
Glenister, A. G. 1959. *The birds of the Malay Peninsula, Singapore and Penang* (third ed.). London and New York.
Hoogerwerf, A. 1949. *De Avifauna van de Plantentuin te Buitenzorg*. Buitenzorg, Java.
Immelmann, K., Steinbacher, J. & Wolters, H. E. 1970. *Vögel in Käfig und Voliere: Prachtfinken*: 350–353.
Kuroda, N. 1933. *Birds of the Island of Java*. Tokyo.

Moluccan Munia   *Lonchura molucca*

Loxia molucca Linnaeus, 1766, *Syst. Nat.* ed. 12, **1**, p. 302.

DESCRIPTION Between Spice Finch and Avadavat in size but typical *Lonchura* shape. Head, breast, upper tail coverts and tail black. Nape, sides of neck, mantle and back medium earth brown. Wing coverts a slightly darker and more reddish brown. Secondaries, primary coverts and primaries blackish brown. Under wing coverts mainly buffish but those along wing edge barred white and black. Underparts and rump white with fine wavy and/or crescentic bars or spotted bars of black on each feather. Iris brown. Bill with upper mandible leaden grey to black, lower mandible leaden grey or bluish grey; some specimens are said on their labels to have had entirely black bills but this may be an error.

Juvenile a general rather reddish earth brown above, darker on forehead, crown and face and with the feathers of the throat and upper breast obscurely barred dull light drab and dusky grey. Wing coverts and inner secondaries with buffish tips. Rump and underparts deep buff to pale buffish, with some traces of the black and white barring of adults, this being most pronounced on the under tail coverts. Bill and legs paler and browner than adult's, to judge from their colour in specimens.

The above description is of nominate *L.m. molucca*, from the Sula Islands, Buru, Ceram, Ambon, Obi, Batjan, Ternate, Halmahera and north and central Celebes. *L.m. propinqua*, from Flores, Sumba, Kalao and Kalao-tua, is a little lighter in colour on the brown upperparts, the individual dark markings being smaller, fewer per feather, and of a less intense black; the areas of white plumage adjacent to the black breast are unmarked or almost so. The juvenile is like that of the nominate form but a very little paler. *L.m. vagans*, from the south Celebes, and Tulang Besi Islands, Timor, Timor-laut, Seramlaut, Kisui, Kur, Taam, Tajandu, Manawoka, and Kei Islands, is intermediate between the two races described above. Most specimens I have seen were rather nearer to the nominate form.

FIELD CHARACTERS Small finch-like bird with black face

and breast, whitish underparts and rump and brown back. It would probably be hard to distinguish at a little distance from *L. striata*, should the two occur in the same place through human introduction, though at close quarters the fine black barring on the white parts would distinguish it.

DISTRIBUTION AND HABITAT The Moluccan and nearby islands; the Celebes; the Lesser Sunda Islands (excluding Lombok and Bali) and the Kangean Islands. See under 'Description' for full list of islands inhabited.

Inhabits grassy and bushy areas at forest edge, clearings in forest, areas overgrown with Alang-alang, *Imperata arundinacea*, and cultivated regions (Immelmann *et al.*, Stresemann). Not wary or shy of man, whence it is called by a name meaning 'deaf Munia' in the Celebes.

FEEDING AND GENERAL HABITS No detailed information. Probably feeds largely on grass seeds. A captive pair took large amounts of soaked seed and chickweed when rearing young but did not eat live food (Deckert). In the Celebes, and probably also elsewhere, usually in family parties and small groups (Stresemann).

NESTING Nest similar to that of related species. Placed among twigs in a tree (probably also in bushes and other growth). Eggs 4 to 5, up to 7 recorded. Incubation period (in captivity) 15 days. Both sexes shared incubation in usual way. Young fledged at 21 days (Deckert). In West Flores breeds at the end of the wet season and in the early part of the dry season, that is from March to June (Verheijen).

VOICE One call has been transcribed as 'tr, tr' (Immelmann *et al.*).

DISPLAY AND SOCIAL BEHAVIOUR No information.

OTHER NAMES Moluccan Mannikin.

REFERENCES
Deckert, H. 1980. Zucht des Wellen-Bronzemännchen (*Lonchura molucca*). *Gefiederte Welt* **1980**: 184–185.
Immelmann, K., Steinbacher, J. & Wolters, H. E. 1970. *Vögel in Käfig und Voliere: Prachtfinken*: 347–350.
Stresemann, E. 1939. Die Vögel von Celebes. *J. Orn.* **88**: 1–135.
Verheijen, J. A. 1964. Breeding season on the island of Flores, Indonesia. *Ardea* **52**: 194–201.

White-bellied Munia   *Lonchura leucogastra*

Amadina leucogastra Blyth, 1846, *Journ. Asiat. Soc. Bengal* **15**, p. 286.

DESCRIPTION About size of Avadavat but typical *Lonchura* shape, with shortish tail, large head and large, thick bill. Forehead blackish brown, shading into a slightly lighter tone on crown and to dark earth brown on mantle, back and wing coverts. The individual feathers have white shafts, less fully developed on head and lower back where the feathers also have not very conspicuous whitish tips. Wing quills brownish black; under wing coverts pale buff. Lower part of rump and upper and under tail coverts, velvety brownish black with, in some lights, a purple tinge. The two elongated, bluntly pointed central tail feathers are dark brown, broadly fringed with light dull gold or straw yellow; the other tail feathers have only narrow yellowish fringes on their outer webs. Lores, cheeks, throat, upper breast and sides of lower breast brownish black. Many of the feathers at the sides of the lower breast and most of those on the flanks are marked with white (some mainly white, marked with brownish black). Rest of underparts white. Iris brown to brownish red. Bill with upper mandible dark leaden grey to blackish, lower mandible, especially at base usually paler and more bluish grey. Legs and feet leaden grey. Juvenile duller and a little paler, white on underparts suffused with buff.

The above description is of nominate *Lonchura l. leucogastra* from Peninsular Thailand (Siam), Tenasserim, the Malay Peninsula and Sumatra. The closely similar races that have been described from the Philippines and northern and eastern Borneo, *L.l. everetti*, *L.l. manueli* and *L.l. palawana*, are very like the nominate form but have

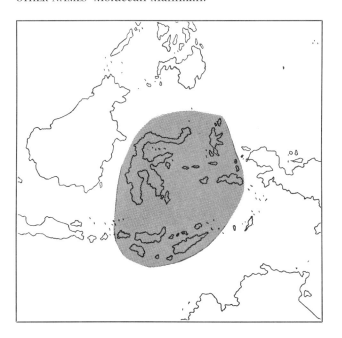

proportionately larger bills, very conspicuous white shaft streaks on the upper parts, and the white on the underparts a little less extensive. *L.l. smythiesi*, from the vicinity of Kuching, Borneo, is said to be very like them but to have less prominent pale shafts on the upperparts. The most distinct race is *L. leucogastra castononota*, from southern Borneo. It is described (Mayr, 1938) as having the upper parts rich chestnut instead of dull brown, and jet black instead of brownish black, throat, flanks and rump. I have not seen a specimen of this form or of *L.l. smythiesi*.

FIELD CHARACTERS Small, thick-billed finchlike bird, dark brown and blackish or chestnut and black, with white belly. Whitish shaft streaks on upperparts conspicuous at close quarters.

DISTRIBUTION AND HABITAT Peninsular Thailand (Siam), Tenasserim, Malay Peninsula, Sumatra, Borneo, Philippines, Palawan and the Sula Islands. Has occurred on Java, probably through escape or liberation of captives.

FEEDING AND GENERAL HABITS Presumably much as other munias but little appears to be recorded. Known to hold objects under foot (Baptista, pers. comm.). More of a forest bird than other munias (Baker, 1926, Immelmann *et al.*). Most definite records refer to forest edge, villages, gardens or similar partly open areas in or near forest, but this may, perhaps, reflect ease of observation as Davies (in Baker, 1934) found it breeding in dense forest 9·6 km (6 miles) from the nearest open space.

Usually in pairs or small parties. In Borneo rare and local (Pfeffer).

NESTING Nests in bushes or trees about 1 to 2 metres above ground. A nest examined in detail by Davison (in Baker, 1934) was globular, about 18 cm (7 inches) long by 15 cm (6 inches) wide at the broadest part and was made of grasses and bamboo leaves, lined with finer grass stems and a little fibre. Other nests have been described as

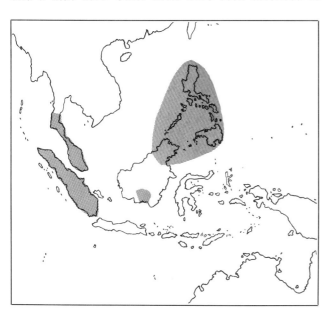

composed mainly of grass and grass panicles. Nests with eggs have been found from March to May in Tenasserim. Several broods of from 5 to 7 newly-hatched young were found in Borneo, in October (Pfeffer). Parental care unrecorded but almost certainly as in congeners.

VOICE No information.

DISPLAY AND SOCIAL BEHAVIOUR No information.

OTHER NAMES White-breasted Munia, White-breasted Mannikin, White-bellied Mannikin.

REFERENCES
Baker, E. C. S. 1926. *The fauna of British India*, Birds, vol. 3. London.
Baker, E. C. S. 1934. *The nidification of birds of the Indian Empire*, vol. 3. London.
Immelmann, K., Steinbacher, J. & Wolters, H. E. 1971. *Vögel in Käfig und Voliere: Prachtfinken*: 390–394.
Mayr, E. 1938. Notes on a collection of birds from south Borneo. *Bull. Raffles Mus.* no. 14.
Parkes, K. C. 1958. Taxonomy and nomenclature of three species of *Lonchura*. *Proc. U.S. Nat. Mus.* **108**, no. 3402.
Pfeffer, P. 1961. Etude d'une collection d'oiseaux de Borneo. *L'Oisea* **31**: 9–29.
duPont, J. E. & Rabor, D. S. 1973. South Sulu Archipelago Birds. *Nemouria*, Occ. Papers Delaware Mus. Nat. Hist. no. 9.

Spice Finch   *Lonchura punctulata*

Loxia punctulata Linnaeus, 1758, *Syst. Nat.* ed. 10, **1**, p. 173.

DESCRIPTION Between Zebra Finch and Twinspot in size but with proportionately stouter bill, closer plumage and the shortish, rounded or bluntly wedge-shaped tail with its central feathers slightly elongated and pointed at the tips. Head, neck and upper breast dark reddish chocolate brown, darkest on the throat and shading to a slightly lighter and less reddish brown on mantle, back and those parts of the wing feathers that are visible when the wings are folded. Faint darker barring and light shafts visible on most feathers of the upper parts on close scrutiny but not otherwise noticeable. Inner webs of wing quills dull dark brown, fawnish at edges. Underwing coverts mainly fawnish. Rump barred dark brown and whitish or yellowish. Upper tail coverts loose in texture, elongated and a shiny but not very bright golden colour, with traces of darker barring. Tail dull, dark brown, the pointed central feathers with a strong golden wash and yellowish edges. Lower breast and flanks with a beautiful scaled or spangled pattern in white and black, the individual feathers being white, edged and cross-marked with blackish. Centre of belly off-white or cream-coloured. Under tail coverts creamy buff with darker markings on the concealed parts of the feathers. Bill leaden grey to black, usually a paler grey at base of lower mandible. Inside of mouth blackish with pink tongue and a conspicuous white U- or horse-shoe-shaped mark on the back of the palate (Moynihan & Hall). Irides dark brown, orange brown,

reddish brown or red. Legs and feet bluish grey to pinkish grey. Sexes alike. Juvenile a nearly uniform buffish brown above, paler buffish on the underparts.

The above description is of nominate *L.p. punctulata*, from Ceylon and India. *L.p. subundulata*, from Assam and Burma in the plains and lower hills is of a less reddish brown on the head and upper parts, a duller and darker reddish chocolate on the throat, the sheen on its upper tail coverts and tail is paler and has a greenish tinge and the markings on the lower breast and flank feathers are dark brown rather than blackish. *L.p. topela*, from Siam to southern China and Formosa, is similar to *L.p. subundulata* but has the markings on the lower breast and flank feathers paler and more elongated. It thus appears a much duller and less brightly patterned bird. In *L.p. cabanisi*, from the Philippines, these last features are still more pronounced and it is a duller brown above with more pronounced pale shaft streaks and only a slight yellowish sheen on the tail coverts. *L.p. fretensis*, from Malaya, Sumatra and Nias Island, and *L.p. nisoria*, from Java and Bali are very like *L.p. subundulata* but a little redder on face and throat. *S.p. blasii*, from Flores, is like them but darker, especially on the head, and has broader and blackish marks and edges on the white feathers of its lower breast and flanks. Other races have been named, all of which are very similar to one or other of those described above. There is some minor individual variation and birds in worn plumage are often noticeably paler and duller; often they lose most or all of the golden or greenish yellow sheen on the tail and tail coverts.

FIELD CHARACTERS Small reddish brown to brown finch-like bird. Scaly pattern on underparts distinguishes it from other sympatric munias. Juveniles probably not identifiable unless with adults.

DISTRIBUTION AND HABITAT India, including foothills of Bhutan and Sikkim, Ceylon, Assam, Burma, China, Formosa, Hainan, Siam (Thailand), Indochina, the Philippine islands of Luzon, Mindoro and Panay, Malay Peninsula, Sumatra, Nias Island, Java, Bali, Bawean Island, Lombok, Sumbawa, Sumba Island, Flores, Lomblen, Savu, Timor, Kisar, Roma, Letti, Babar, Tanimbar,

south, central and Northern Celebes. Introduced into Singapore Island, Australia, Hawaiian Islands, Mauritius, Reunion, Seychelles and Palau (Philippines).

Inhabits various types of open or semi-open country with bushes, trees or scrub, secondary forest with grassy patches within it or nearby, cultivated areas, gardens and town parks. Primarily, and probably originally, a bird of fairly low elevations but occurs, following cultivation, up to 2000 metres in the Himalayas and on the Burma–China borders (Immelmann *et al.*).

FEEDING AND GENERAL HABITS Feeds largely on seeds of grasses, including cultivated rice when available; also takes seeds of other (unspecified) plants (Mason). Immelmann (1962) states that in Australia this species feeds on many species of grass seeds, but he only lists *Panicum maximum*, and *Digitalis* spp., as positively identified seeds. One of three birds dissected by Mason had eaten two small weevils in addition to seeds. Apart from this there appears to be no record of it taking insects in a wild state; possibly it does so when these are found on its food plants. In Australia it eats the crushed remains of small animals killed on the roads and locally also scraps of bread and other human foods (Immelmann). It does not appear to be known if the road casualties are eaten as a source of meat, or minerals in the form of crushed bone, or both.

In captivity readily eats various millets and canary seed and is easily kept on a diet of seeds, greenfood and minerals. Dr Alan Hayes (pers. comm.) found his captive Spice Finches eager for ant pupae when their young were small but after the first few days they reared them on soaked seed and green food, the latter mainly seeding and flowering chickweed and Annual Meadow Grass. Immelmann *et al.* advise offering live food and eggfood to breeding birds but state that many pairs will not touch it but rear their young without.

Food is taken both from the ground and from growing plants, the latter especially when feeding on ripening rice. Highly sociable, even breeding pairs are usually close to others and commonly the species is seen in flocks which may number from a few to a few hundred individuals.

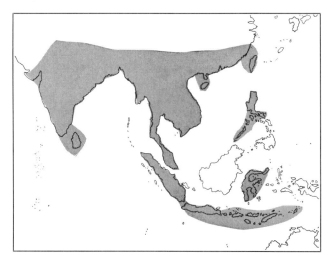

Flight may be somewhat undulating, as in many passerines, or swift and straight, the latter is seen especially and possibly only when the birds are in large flocks (Ali & Ripley, Immelmann, 1965). Conspicuous tail movements are made almost continually when hopping on the ground or among grass or branches. Moynihan & Hall describe these tail flicking movements thus: 'It takes the form of repeated and rapid, primarily lateral, swings of the tail. These lateral movements do not always follow a regular to-and-fro sequence but may, instead, comprise a quite irregular sequence, or . . . a series of abrupt movements in one direction followed by a number of jerks in the opposite direction.' The tail flicking may also at times include a vertical component. Wing flicking, in which the wings are raised quickly and, except at high intensities only slightly above the back is frequently associated and synchronised with tail flicking (condensed from Moynihan's and Hall's descriptions).

Roosts socially in thick cover, sometimes in company with other munias and weaver birds (Ali & Ripley). Often, and perhaps usually, roosts in nests, either those that have previously been used for breeding or nests built for roosting (Immelmann, 1965).

NESTING Where abundant often breeds colonially, sometimes with the nests actually touching others, but more often with at least a metre or so between any two nests. The nest is sited in a bush, tree, creeper, in the cavity at the base of a palm leaf, some nook on a building, or similar situation, often well camouflaged or among thorns. It is roundish or ovoid, very strongly built and resistant to wind and rain, owing to the materials being placed in layers in the roof and sides (Immelmann, 1962 and 1965). It is usually constructed largely of coarse green grass blades but strips of pliant bark and other vegetation are also used. Captive birds always prefer tough and green materials in preference to dry. The high side entrance usually has a short entrance funnel of up to 8 cm (3 inches) length or, at the least, a roof-like projection over the entrance. The inner cavity is lined with finer grasses, grass panicles and sometimes (but probably not often) also with feathers. Nests examined by Immelmann were 15 to 20 cm (6 to 8 inches) deep, 15 to 22 cm (6 to 9 inches) long, 13 to 15 cm (5 to 6 inches) broad and with the egg chamber 10 to 15 cm (4 to 6 inches) in diameter. Both sexes build but, in wild pairs observed in India and Ceylon (Cockburn in Baker, Henry) the male collected the material.

Eggs 3 to 7, usually 4 to 6; up to 10 have been recorded but such large 'clutches' are probably the product of two females. Incubation period given as 'about 16 days' by Ali & Ripley but this may refer to clutches where incubation was delayed or intermittent. Both sexes incubate and brood in turn, sometimes both are in the nest together for periods during the day, and the male roosts in the nest at night. Young fledge at about 18 days but the whole family continues to roost together in the nest for some time after this.

Nests with eggs or young have been found at all times of year in many parts of its range but it usually breeds during or at the end of the monsoon rains. Main breeding seasons recorded are: in parts of India from May to September, in the Ceylon (Sri Lanka) hills from January to May and again from July to December, in Burma May to October or later, in Flores March to July, and at high elevations in the Himalayas only in August and September. Breeding is restricted to the Australian summer around Sydney but is much more extended in the tropics further north (Immelmann, 1965).

VOICE The voice and displays of this species were studied in detail by Moynihan & Hall. This account is based on their work except where otherwise indicated. They used the term 'jingle' for the song of this and other estrildids to emphasise their difference in function from the songs of some other birds but I have not used that term here.

The song is very soft; its loudest elements are only audible to man up to about 6 metres (20 feet) and for this reason many observers have thought the song of the Spice Finch (and some other mannikins) quite inaudible. It is subject to much individual variation. Butler gave a good general description of it as: 'a weak metallic vibration, followed by a laboured creaking, repeated three times, and terminating in a thin long-drawn whistle, only just audible.' Moynihan & Hall go into further detail: 'The [song] . . . can be easily divided into two parts, the first of which is the longest, often lasting nearly five seconds. The majority of our males included five distinct phrases in the first part . . .; but a few birds included only three or four. Each phrase is composed of a single note repeated several times. Each note is similar, in quality, to a single "Tee" or "Tit" of the Call Note. The pitch of the first two phrases . . . is similar to the two descending notes of the soft Call Note.' If there are five complete phrases, a short pause precedes the third and fourth, which are frequently a mere repetition of the first two. The final phrase, irrespective of its number, is by several tones the lowest.

The second part . . . is a miscellany of high-pitched, flute-like whistles, mingled with harsh, low-pitched, loud Slurs (which can be transcribed as 'Myair' or 'Myaaaaan'), and a peculiar bill-rattling produced by a very rapid opening and closing of the bill (quicker than mandibulation, and without visible tongue movements). Each male seems to have his own distinctive arrangement or selection of these elements, more or less constant in different circumstances. Some birds, for example, omit the whistles completely, while others . . . reduce the rattling.

Song is given by the male both in the equivalent of the stem display and, apparently whether in breeding condition or not, without its being directed at any other bird. Under the latter conditions it usually stimulates other flock members, but *not* the mate of the singing individual, to fly or hop to the singer and 'peer' or 'listen'. Sometimes other males respond by singing themselves.

Moynihan & Hall recognise two main variants of the contact call, their 'soft call note', which they transcribe as

'Kitty' or 'Titty' with the emphasis on the first syllable, is used at close quarters between members of a pair or small group. The second main version, their 'loud call note' is transcribed as 'Kit-teeeeee' with the second syllable more emphasised and higher in pitch than the first. It functions apparently to maintain or establish contact at a distance or among members of large flocks and is the only call of the species that can be heard (by man) at a distance of 14 metres (15 yards) or so. In slight alarm a modification of this call, 'Ki-ki-ki-ki-ki-teeee', is given. In more serious alarm a sharp, creaking 'tret-tret' is uttered (Immelmann, 1965), but Moynihan & Hall only heard this creaking alarm call from females, the more usual alarm call they describe as a 'sharp "Chp"', often followed by many others in rapid succession.

A harsh rasping sound is uttered in apparent threat or protest during fights (Moynihan & Hall).

Comparative sonagrams of some of the song parts and calls of this and other *Lonchura* species are given by Guttinger (1970)

DISPLAY AND SOCIAL BEHAVIOUR   In the courtship display, the male holds nesting material by one end and hops or flies about with much tail and wing flicking. If stimulated by this the female does likewise. Soon one perches near the other and the male assumes a diagonally stretched posture, drops the symbol from his bill, bends towards the female and bill-wipes once or twice. Then, with somewhat depressed tail and feathers of head, rump, flanks and belly erected, he begins to sing. As he does so he pivots his head and body from side to side, sometimes bowing forward and sometimes also briefly bill-wiping as he pivots. The female may solicit with crouching posture and quivering tail at any point of the male's display; sometimes she may briefly adopt a diagonal stretched posture before soliciting.

The male usually finishes his song before mounting the female. Successful copulation is followed by mutual aggression, bill fencing and mandibulation, much as in the Java Sparrow (q.v.).

Clumping, allo-preening, and bill fencing occur between flock members as well as between mates. Mandibulation in which the bill is rapidly opened and shut, the pink tongue moved up and down and a cracking sound made, is used not only in hostile or conflict situations but also (*fide* Moynihan & Hall) in friendly and in such apparently a-social contexts as shortly after feeding.

In captivity males attempt to rape strange individuals of either sex that are put in their cage. Moynihan & Hall found quarrelling frequent among their caged captives (apart from the post-copulation aggression) but such little aggression as has been observed in the wild has involved defence of nest sites (e.g. Cockburn in Butler). Spice Finches kept in aviaries or bird rooms have usually impressed their owners by their peacefulness towards their own and other species.

Extreme erection of head and back feathers, termed 'ruffling' by Moyniham & Hall, is shown in agonistic situations, usually, it appears, by a bird which is becoming tired or afraid.

Experiments have shown that Spice Finches readily imprint on other species (Bengalese and Zebra Finches) if reared by them. Females however, show some apparently innate recognition of the response to the male's song. In one case a male that was not removed until 58 days old from its own species appeared to be imprinted on Bengalese Finches after 213 days with them.

OTHER NAMES   Spice Bird, Spotted Munia, Barred Munia, Nutmeg Finch.

REFERENCES
Ali, S. 1953. *The birds of Travancore and Cochin.* Oxford.
Ali, S. & Ripley, S. D. 1974. *Handbook of the birds of India and Pakistan,* vol. 10. Oxford.
Baker, E. C. S. 1934. *The nidification of birds of the Indian Empire.* London.
Butler, A. G. 1894. *Foreign finches in captivity.* London.
Güttinger, H. R. 1970. Zur Evolution von Verhaltensweisen und Lautäusserungen bei Prachtfinken. *Z. Tierpsychol.* **27**: 1011–1075.
Henry, G. M. 1955. *A guide to the birds of Ceylon.* Oxford.
Immelmann, K. 1962. Beiträge zu einer vergleichenden Biologie australischer Prachtfinken. *Zool Jb. Syst. Bd.* **90**: 1–196.
Immelmann, K. 1965. *Australian finches in bush and aviary.* London and Sydney.
Immelmann, K., Steinbacher, J. & Wolters, H. E. 1971 and 1972. *Vögel in Käfig und Voliere: Prachtfinken*: 396–412.
Mason, C. W. 1912. *The food of birds in India.* Mem. Dept. Agriculture, Jan. 1912, Entom. Section vol. 3, p. 124.
Moynihan, M, & Hall, M. F. 1954. Hostile, sexual and other social behaviour patterns of the Spice Finch (*Lonchura punctulata*) in captivity. *Behaviour* **7**: 33–76.
Whistler, H. 1928. *Popular handbook of Indian birds.* London and Edinburgh.

Hill Munia   *Lonchura kelaarti*

Munia kelaarti Jerdon (ex Blyth ms), 1863, **2**, p. 356.

DESCRIPTION   About size of Spice Finch but with rather larger bill and slightly less pointed central tail feathers. Forehead blackish brown, shading to dark coffee brown on mantle and back; the feathers of all the upper parts have pale shafts but these are not very prominent. Rump brownish black, spotted with white, there being a white, more or less cruciform spot near the end of each feather. Upper tail coverts dark brown, fringed with dull gold or dull greenish gold. Wing coverts and inner secondaries dark brown with faint paler tips; wing and tail quills blackish brown; under wing coverts buffish. Face, throat and central part of upper breast blackish or brownish black. Sides of neck and upper breast dull pinkish fawn. Belly, flanks and under tail coverts spangled blackish and white; the individual feathers having white shafts and bars or paired spots (or some similar or intermediate pattern), those of the long under tail coverts have a central white or cream streak on an otherwise mainly dark feather.

Irides brown. Bill with upper mandible dark grey, blackish or very dark horn, lower mandible similar at tip but bluish grey to silvery grey at base. Legs and feet bluish grey to greenish grey.

Juvenile has upper parts a nearly uniform warm darkish brown. Ear coverts medium brown with pale shafts. Throat dark greyish with whitish barring on feathers. Under tail coverts buffish with irregular blackish barring. Rest of underparts buffish brown with faint indications of the adult pattern, especially on the lower flanks.

The above description is of nominate *L.k. kelaarti*, from Ceylon. *L.k. jerdoni*, from India, has most of the underparts of the same pinkish fawn colour as the sides of the breast, with inconspicuous pale shaft streaks and traces of dull greyish fringes and barrings present in many feathers but not noticeable except on close scrutiny. The under tail coverts, ventral regions and rump are patterned similarly to those of *L.k. kelaarti* but in pinkish fawn and dusky drab. Juvenile very like that of nominate race but a little paler and with markings on the nearly uniform appearing buffish underparts much less evident.

FIELD CHARACTERS Small dark brown finch-like bird with spangled black and white (Ceylon) or pinkish fawn (India) underparts. Blackish breast, broadly bordered at sides with pinkish fawn, distinguish it from the Spice Finch and other munias.

DISTRIBUTION AND HABITAT India, in the Eastern Ghats (Vishakhapatnam district), and south-western India from Mysore to southern Kerala. Also the highlands of Ceylon. Found from about 600 m to about 2100 m., locally higher and lower.

Inhabits forest edge, clearings, lantana scrub, grassy areas on hillsides, gardens, tea and coffee plantations. Wait says it is also found 'deep in hill forest' but this may, perhaps, imply the vicinity of roads, gardens or other clearings in such forest. Prefers higher and wetter areas than those most favoured by *L. striata* and does not occur in the dry scrub zone. Locally migratory; a summer visitor only to areas above 2100m in the Nilghiris (Ali & Ripley).

FEEDING AND GENERAL HABITS Feeds both on the ground and in vegetation. Takes seeds of grasses, including cultivated rice where available, also, *fide* Ali and Ripley, seeds of weeds, but no detailed information on its food. In captivity will eat various millets (Immelmann *et al.*). Henry saw one 'searching among the leaves of a creeper growing on a tall stump'. He gives no further details but it suggests the species may take some invertebrate life.

Usually in pairs or small parties which are sometimes and perhaps usually family groups. Often associates with Spice Finches and Whitebacked Munias. Sometimes, and perhaps usually, builds and uses nests for roosting. Often flies high in strong, undulating flight.

NESTING Nest placed in bushes, creepers, shrubs or trees; sometimes in a large hole in a tree or some recess in a building. Usually from 1 to 6 metres above ground,

sometimes higher. It is similar to that of other Asiatic *Lonchura* species, roundish or oval, made of grass and sometimes other material such as maidenhair fern, fibrous rootlets, mosses etc. and lined with fine grasses and/or grass panicles. The male collects most or all of the nesting material; both sexes build and share in incubation, brooding and parental care.

Clutch size apparently varies geographically, from 3 to 6, usually 5 eggs in Ceylon but from 6 to 8 in India (Ali & Ripley). Larger clutches have been recorded but are probably due to 2 females laying in the same nest. Incubation period 16 days; young fledge at 15 to 17 days (Phillips, in Ali & Ripley, data for Ceylon only).

Breeds chiefly from April to August in India and from April to September in Ceylon, but breeding may occur at almost any time (*fide* Baker and Henry).

VOICE Henry records 'the usual munia type of reedy chirp' and 'a funny little song of five notes' from the Ceylon form. The contact call of the Indian form is a monosyllabic 'tay' (my anglicisation 1), nasal in tone and suggestive of calls of the Zebra Finch (Immelmann *et al.*).

DISPLAY AND SOCIAL BEHAVIOUR The courtship display is probably similar to that of other Asiatic munias as Henry says it 'jerks up and down in a quaint manner' but I can find no detailed description. Regularly clumps and allopreens with other flock members (Immelmann *et al.*). Very active in captivity.

OTHER NAMES Rufous-bellied Munia, Ceylon Munia.

REFERENCES

Ali, S. & Ripley, S. D. 1974. *Handbook of the birds of India and Pakistan*, vol. 10. Bombay and London.

Baker, E. C. S. 1934. *The nidification of birds of the Indian Empire*. vol. 3. London.

Henry, G. M. 1955. *A guide to the birds of Ceylon*. London.

Immelmann, K., Steinbacher, J. & Wolters, H. E. 1971. *Vögel in Käfig und Voliere: Prachtfinken*: 394–396.

Wait, W. E. 1925. *Manual of the birds of Ceylon.* Colombo and London.

Streak-headed Munia *Lonchura tristissima*

Munia tristissima Wallace, 1865, *Proc. Zool. Soc. London*, p. 479.

DESCRIPTION About size of Avadavat but with proportionately larger bill and rather more thick-set. Tail the usual blunt wedge-shape but with the two central feathers only slightly, if at all more pointed than the rest. Forehead, crown, nape and ear coverts dark earth brown with whitish shaft streaks. Mantle and back dark earth brown, with paler, sometimes greyish, subterminal bands on most feathers giving a slightly mottled effect, darkening to nearly black in a band just above the yellow rump. Rump and the *shorter* upper tail coverts shiny pale yellowish gold. Larger upper tail coverts and tail black with no yellow or golden fringes to the feathers. Wing coverts similar to back but with the brown parts of the feathers of a more reddish brown hue and with pale tips to some of the coverts which tend to form wing bars in life (Rand, 1938). Inner secondaries edged with dark reddish brown and the innermost ones with pale tips. Rest of wing quills brownish black. Under wing coverts yellowish buff. The sides of the breast appear spotted or barred, the dark brown feathers have large dull white subterminal spots with part of the feather shaft within the pale spot shining white. Rest of underparts brownish black, inclining to dark reddish brown on the breast and flanks in some specimens. Irides dark brown to blackish. Bill bluish grey. Legs and feet bluish grey. Immelmann *et al.* state that this species shows much individual variation.

Juvenile a more uniform and duller dark brown.

See plate 5, facing p. 224.

FIELD CHARACTERS Tiny dark brown to blackish 'finch' with streaked head and yellow rump *contrasting with black tail.*

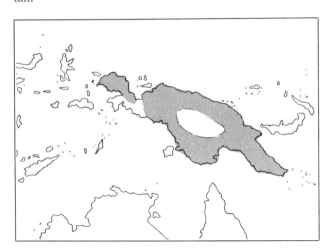

DISTRIBUTION AND HABITAT New Guinea in the Vogelkop, Weyland Mountains, on the slopes of the Oranje and Nassau Mountains east to Noord River, northern New Guinea between Mamberano and Hydrographer Mountains, and Karkar Island. In 1967 also recorded in the Port Moresby area (Mackay).

Inhabits grassy areas fringing mountain streams and at the edge of forest, native gardens and floating mats of grass in rivers. Always near to forest and not found in extensive grasslands.

FEEDING AND GENERAL HABITS Probably feeds largely on grass seeds. Usually in small flocks and, at least in some places, shy of man.

NESTING Immelmann *et al.* describe the nest as roundish with a side entrance, in (peripheral?) twigs of trees. The only other description I can find is that of Ripley, who describes a remarkable 1 metre (3 foot) long pendant nest but, as Immelmann *et al.* suggest, this was almost certainly built by some other species and later used by the munias.

VOICE No information.

DISPLAY AND SOCIAL BEHAVIOUR No information.

OTHER NAMES Streak-headed Mannikin.

REFERENCES
Immelmann, K., Steinbacher, J. & Wolters, H. E. 1970. *Vögel in Käfig und Voliere: Prachtfinken*: 343–347.
Mackay, R. D. 1969. *The birds of Port Moresby and District.* London, Sydney.
Rand, A. L. 1938. Results of the Archbold Expeditions no. 20. *Amer. Mus. Novit.* No. 991.
Rand, A. L. & Gilliard, E. T. 1967. *Handbook of New Guinea birds.* London.
Ripley, S. D. 1964. *A systematic and ecological study of birds of New Guinea.* Peabody Museum of Natural History, Yale University Bull. 19.

White-spotted Munia *Lonchura leucosticta*

Munia leucosticta d'Albertis and Salvadori, *Ann. Mus. Civ. Genova* **14**, p. 88.

DESCRIPTION Except where otherwise stated closely similar to the previous species, *L. tristissima*, with which it is known to have interbred in a wild state (Mees) and may be conspecific. In general appearance it is paler, and conspicuously spotted. The shaft streaks on the head are a purer white and tend to be wider so that the face appears predominantly whitish. There are conspicuous white terminal spots to the feathers of the upper parts, the median and greater wing coverts, and the sides of the breast. The chin, throat and under wing coverts are whitish, the underparts, except for the black under tail coverts, are predominantly rusty brown. The female is slightly duller and has the breast slightly more spotted than the male (Rand).

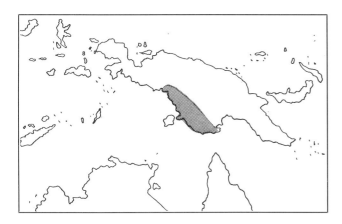

FIELD CHARACTERS Small, conspicuously white-spotted brown 'finch' with yellowish rump and blackish tail.

DISTRIBUTION AND HABITAT Southern New Guinea from Fly River to Noord River. Found in areas with grass or bamboo along forest edge, forest ridges and between forest and marsh.

FEEDING AND GENERAL HABITS Known to take seeds of grasses and of a bamboo. Has been observed feeding on half submerged grass mats on the edges of the Fly River lagoons, in grass on savanna near the forest edge and in bamboos on a forested ridge.

Has so far been encountered in small flocks of 6–8 individuals (Rand).

NESTING No information.

VOICE No information.

DISPLAY AND SOCIAL BEHAVIOUR No information.

OTHER NAMES White-spotted Mannikin.

REFERENCES
Mees, G. F. 1958. Een bastaard tussen *Lonchura tristissima* (Wallace) en *L. leucosticta* (d'Albertis and Salvadori). *Nova Guinea*, new ser., **9**: 15–19. Leiden.
Rand, A. L. 1938. Results of the Archbold Expeditions. No. 20. *Amer. Mus. Novit.* No. 991.

Chestnut Munia (*malacca* group)   *Lonchura malacca*

Loxia malacca Linnaeus, *Syst. Nat.* ed. 12, **1**, p. 302.

This is the nominate form of the species, widely known under the name Tri-coloured Munia or one of the similarly descriptive names given here under 'Other names'.

DESCRIPTION About size of Spice Finch but more heavily built with proportionately larger bill. Head, throat, breast, centre of belly, tibial feathers and under tail coverts black. rest of under parts white, usually snow white but with a creamy tinge when in fresh, new plumage. Mantle, back and most of wings a rich even rather light chestnut. Inner webs of wing quills and tips of outer primaries brownish sepia. Under wing coverts white to pale reddish buff,

sometimes with darker tips to feathers. Rump and upper tail coverts glossy dark chestnut red, the tips of the longest upper tail coverts often reddish gold rather than chestnut. The two pointed central tail feathers have narrow dull chestnut centres and broad glossy reddish chestnut to reddish gold outer fringes. Other tail feathers dull brownish chestnut with very narrow reddish or reddish gold fringes to their outer webs. Irides dark brown. Bill pale greyish blue, sometimes dusky on culmen, Legs and feet leaden blue or slate colour. Sexes alike but females seem to average paler on fringes of tail and tail coverts and in life (*fide* Butler), usually have less massive bills than males.

Juvenile a medium-light reddish brown on the upperparts, darker and greyer on crown, nape and face. Underparts a nearly uniform light buff. Bill and legs at first duller.

See plate 7, facing p. 256.

FIELD CHARACTERS Small, short-tailed, 'finch' with black head, chestnut upperparts and boldly patterned white and black underparts.

DISTRIBUTION AND HABITAT Peninsular India and Ceylon, in lowlands and hills up to 2100 metres.

Inhabits marshes, reedbeds, wet grassy areas, sugarcane and rice fields. Sometimes in rice cultivation even in forest clearings.

FEEDING AND GENERAL HABITS Known to feed on seeds various grasses, including cultivated rice when available. Takes food both from the ground and from growing vegetation. In captivity eats millets and canary seed, both dry and soaked, and greenfood, especially seeding and flowering grasses and chickweed but usually refuses insects and soft foods.

Usually in small or large flocks, sometimes and perhaps usually when breeding, in pairs or small parties.

NESTING Nest built in sugarcane, reeds, rushes, coarse grass, or bushes in marshy places; usually within 2 metres of the water or ground below. The nest is roundish, 15 or

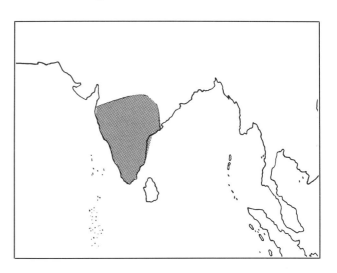

18 cm (6 or 7 inches) in diameter, made of grass, reed or rush blades and lined with finer grasses etc. There is the usual side entrance, which sometimes, and perhaps in this form usually, has a short trumpet-like entrance tube of projecting flowering grass heads (Ali and Ripley). Eggs 4 to 7, usually 5 or 6. Both sexes build and both share in incubation and parental care. Newly-hatched young naked. Incubation period 12–13 days. Young fledge at 22 to 28 days and roost in the nest for 1 to 3 weeks after fledging. These data on young and incubation from captive birds not all certainly of this form.

VOICE The contact call has been described as 'peekt' and 'pee-eet' (Immelmann *et al.*, my anglicisation). Ali & Ripley say that 'the flight call' is a triple chirp.

The song has been described in detail by Hall (especially in her unpublished ms on estrildine behaviour), Immelmann *et al.*, and Morris. It is only audible to human ears at a short distance. Each song phrase consists of three parts, a slow clapping or snapping of the bill is followed by a phase in which the bird is seen to sing but human ears (and, *fide* Immelmann *et al.*, even high sensitivity microphones) can detect no sound; the final phase consists of one or more long drawn faint and high-pitched whistling notes.

Song is uttered both in courtship and as undirected song, always with the body feathers erected and head pointed downwards.

Sonagrams of the contact call and some elements of the song are given by Güttinger and of the complete song by Hall (1962).

DISPLAY AND SOCIAL BEHAVIOUR Courtship display is usually preceded by both sexes flying excitedly about carrying nesting material, the male usually uttering a staccato call as he does so (Güttinger). Then the male alights beside the female, stands more or less erect but at an oblique angle, with his body feathers conspicuously erected, head pointing downward but slightly twisted towards the female, drops the symbol and begins to sing. At the same time he performs upward jumps, at the rate of about 3 per second, in which his feet leave the perch. If responsive, the female crouches and quivers her tail and, just before mounting, the male moves his head from side to side (Güttinger). Mutual bill pecking, with rasping calls uttered by one or both birds, then mutual allo-preening, follow copulation. The above description is taken largely from Hall's unpublished manuscript except where otherwise indicated.

Allo-preening and peering habitual. Highly social. Immelmann *et al.*, consider that the frequent failure of this and allied species to breed in captivity is often due to putting a single chance picked 'pair' of birds into an aviary instead of a number so that individuals, or at least those that first come into breeding condition, can pair with mates of their own (albeit limited) choice.

Usually said to be entirely peaceful in captivity towards birds of other species but Butler found it sometimes aggressive towards the smaller waxbills. In general,

unless an aviary is large and its inmates few, the tiny waxbills cannot be expected to breed successfully if kept with larger estrildids (and still less if kept with weavers or cardueline finches).

OTHER NAMES Tri-coloured Munia, Tri-coloured Mannikin, Tri-coloured Nun, Three-coloured Munia, Mannikin or Nun, Southern Black-head Munia.

REFERENCES

Ali, S. & Ripley, S. D. 1974. *Handbook of the birds of India and Pakistan.* Bombay and London.

Butler, A. G. 1894. *Foreign finches in captivity.* London.

Hall, M. F. 1962. Evolutionary aspects of estrildid song. *Symp. Zool. Soc. London* 8: 37–55.

Hall, M. F. Unpublished mss on estrildid behaviour.

Henry, G. M. 1955. *A guide to the birds of Ceylon.* Oxford University Press, London.

Immelmann, K. Steinbacher, J. & Wolters, H. E. 1969. *Vögel in Käfig und Voliere: Prachtfinken*: 315–328. Aachen, Germany.

Knowles, A. E. H. 1931. Three-coloured Mannikin. *Avicult. Mag.* 9, 4th ser.; 86–87.

Morris, D. 1958. The comparative ethology of grassfinches (Erythrurae) and Mannikins (Amadinae). *Proc. zool. Soc. London* 131: 389–489.

Chestnut Munia   *Lonchura malacca*
(*atricapilla* group)

Loxia atricapilla Vieillot, 1807, *Ois. Chat.*, p. 84, pl. 53.

The members of this group are widely known as Black-headed Munia (Mannikin, or Nun) in avicultural circles.

DESCRIPTION As previous form, *L.m. malacca*, except as follows: white areas of underparts replaced by chestnut. Black belly patch usually a little smaller and less sharply defined and often tinged or intermixed with dusky chestnut, as are the tibial feathers and upper tail coverts. Tips of the longer upper tail coverts and fringes of the tail feathers usually golden orange to pale yellowish gold, contrasting with the reddish chestnut rump. Juvenile as that of *L.m. malacca* but averaging a little darker and duller both above and below.

The above description is of *L.m. atricapilla*, from southeastern Nepal and north-eastern India through Assam and east Pakistan to Burma and north-western Yunnan. *L.m. rubroniger*, from Nepal and adjacent areas of northern India is very similar. When in fresh plumage it has the upper tail coverts and tail fringes darker, shining dark reddish chestnut to reddish gold, but, as in other forms of the species, these fade in worn plumage and tend to be paler in females. Three specimens from Dibrughar, northern Assam, in the British Museum (Natural History) collection illustrate this very clearly. A male in fresh plumage, no. 1887.7.1.1974 has the tail fringes reddish chestnut with a gold tinge; a male in slightly less new plumage, no. 1887.7.1.1972, has them reddish gold; a female in worn plumage, no. 1887.7.1.1973, has them pale yellowish gold.

L.m. sinensis, from peninsular Thailand (Siam), Malaya

and the lowlands of Sumatra, differs from *L.m. atricapilla* in averaging slightly smaller and having the belly patch and under tail coverts dusky chestnut with little or no suffusion or intermixture of black. *L.m. deignani*, from northern Thailand and Annam is said to differ from *L.m. sinensis* in having the upper tail coverts and tail fringes usually a deep orange red (Parkes). The above forms all intergrade and populations in some areas are intermediate.

L.m. bakatana, from the mountains of northern Sumatra, is a paler chestnut than *L.m. sinensis* but has a black belly patch and under tail coverts.

L.m. formosana, from Formosa and extreme northern Luzon (Philippines) has the forehead and face brownish black shading to dark brownish grey on crown, nape and sides of neck. The throat and breast are black and there is a large black belly patch and black under tail coverts. Its tail fringes are reddish gold to dark yellowish gold. Females mostly have the brown of the head and the gold of the tail appreciably paler than males in comparable plumage states. *L.m. jagori*, from most of the Philippines, Halmahera, Sulu Islands, Palawan, Natuna, Borneo and most of Celebes shows much local and (in some areas) individual variation (see Parkes, 1958 for discussion of this). In general it is similar to *L.m. formosana* but a brighter chestnut and with the crown and nape either a darker greyish brown or entirely deep black. Birds of the latter type, which have intensely black belly patch and under tail coverts, predominate in the southern part of its range. In the Makassar district of southern Celebes, however, the population has greyish brown heads and has been separated as *L.m. brunneiceps*. I have only seen the type of *brunneiceps*. It is a specimen in very worn and faded plumage and I much doubt if, were it in reasonably fresh plumage, it would be separable from the brown-headed specimens of *L.m. jagori*.

FIELD CHARACTERS Small, short-tailed chestnut 'finch' with black head. Bluish bill and reddish or goldish on rump and tail conspicuous close up but not diagnostic characters.

DISTRIBUTION AND HABITAT Nepal, northern India and east Pakistan, east to Assam, western Yunnan, Thailand (Siam), Indochina and Formosa, and south east through Burma, peninsular Thailand, Malaya, the Philippines and Celebes (see map).

Inhabits marshes, reedbeds, grassy areas, sugarcane and rice fields; locally in other cultivation, about villages and in scrub jungle (Baker). In the Celebes present wherever rice is cultivated, both in hills and lowland; where little or no grass is grown inhabits the Alang-alang scrub (Stresemann). In the Sulu Archipelago often colonises relatively new clearings (duPont & Rabor).

FEEDING AND GENERAL HABITS As previous form (q.v.). In Borneo, and perhaps elsewhere, does not associate with other munias in mixed species flocks (Smythies).

Up to 10 individuals have been observed roosting in one

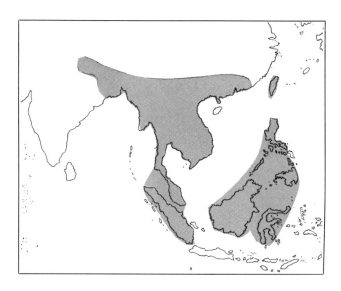

nest but it is not clear whether this represents recently fledged young or whether adults use nests for roosting. In the Sulu Archipelago many hundreds roosted, presumably not in nests, in tall grass and reeds, the birds arriving and departing in smaller flocks (du Pont & Rabor).

NESTING As previous form but (*fide* Baker) sometimes quite high above ground in a tree. It is clear, however, that low sites, such as those chosen by *L.m. malacca*, are usual. In Malaya, and probably elsewhere, sometimes nests in small colonies or at least several nests near to each other but single nests are more usual (Medway).

As with many estrildids breeding times vary locally, presumably according to food supplies. Recorded breeding from May to November in the Indian parts of its range; June to September in Burma, and December to October in Malaya.

VOICE As previous form (q.v.)

DISPLAY AND SOCIAL BEHAVIOUR As previous form (q.v.)

OTHER NAMES Black-headed Munia, Black-headed Mannikin, Black-headed Nun, Chestnut Mannikin, Ricebird.

REFERENCES

Ali, S. & Ripley, S. D. 1974. *Handbook of the birds of India and Pakistan.* Bombay, London.

Baker, E. C. S. 1934. The nidification of birds of the Indian Empire. London.

duPont, J. E. & Rabor, D. S. 1973. *South Sulu Archipelago birds.* Occ. Papers Delaware Mus. Nat. Hist. no. 9.

Immelmann, K., Steinbacher, J., & Wolters, H. E. 1969. *Vögel in Käfig und Voliere: Prachtfinken:* 315–328.

Medway, Lord, & Wells, D. R. 1976. *The birds of the Malay Peninsula.* vol 5. H.F. & G. Witherby Ltd., London.

Oates, E. W. 1883. *A handbook to the birds of British Burma,* vol. 1. London.

Smythies, B. E. 1960. *The birds of Borneo.* London.

Stresemann, E. 1940. Die Vögel von Celebes. *J. Orn.* **88**: 1–135.

Chestnut Munia   *Lonchura malacca*
(*ferruginosa* form)

Loxia ferruginosa Sparrman, 1789, *Mus, Carlsonianum*, pls. 90, 91.

DESCRIPTION As previous form, *L. malacca atricapilla* (q.v.) except as follows. Forehead and face buffish white, shading to very pale greyish brown on hind crown, nape, sides of neck and periphery of ear coverts; contrasting with the black throat and upper breast. Black belly patch large and distinct. Fringes of upper tail coverts and central tail feathers reddish chestnut to reddish gold. In worn and bleached plumage the head becomes purer and more extensively white.

FIELD CHARACTERS Small, shortish-tailed, chestnut 'finch' with whitish head. Probably easily confused with the slightly duller *L. maja* from which (when visible) its black throat and upper breast distinguish it.

DISTRIBUTION AND HABITAT Java. In areas of rice cultivation. Probably also in other typical habitats of the species, if they exist on Java.

FEEDING AND GENERAL HABITS As other forms of *L. malacca* but little specifically on this form recorded.

NESTING As for previous forms of the species (q.v.) so far as known. Has been found breeding from January to April, in June and in December (Hoogerwerf).

VOICE As described by Immelmann *et al.*, the contact call differs from that of other forms, being a whistling 'veet veet' (my anglicisation). The song is said, however, to be identical.

OTHER NAMES Javan Munia, Javan Mannikin, Black-throated Munia, Black-throated Mannikin.

REFERENCES
Hoogerwerf, J. 1949. *De Avifauna van de Plantentuin te Buitenzorg.* Buitenzorg, Java.
Immelmann, K., Steinbacher, J. & Wolters, H. E. 1969. *Vögel in Käfig und Voliere: Prachtfinken*: 315–328.

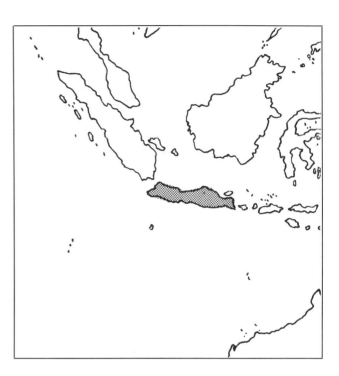

White-headed Munia   *Lonchura maja*

Loxia maja Linnaeus 1766, *Syst. Nat.* ed. 12, **1**, p. 301.

DESCRIPTION About size of Spice Finch but with proportionately thicker bill and shorter tail. Head dull white or cream-coloured, more or less washed with coffee brown on nape and throat. Mantle, back and wings dark, dull chestnut brown; inner webs of wing quills dull dark brown. Under wing coverts deep buff with brownish tips. Breast pale greyish brown, shading into a slightly mauvish dull chestnut on the sides of the breast and flanks and black on the centre of the lower breast, belly and under tail coverts. Rump and upper tail feathers glossy dark chestnut. Two central tail feathers with narrow dull brown median area, otherwise glossy chestnut red to deep reddish gold. Irides dark brown. Bill pale greyish blue, usually whitish at tip and along commissure. Legs and feet dark grey to bluish grey. The female is a little paler and duller than the male, a little more suffused with brown on the white parts of the head; the glossy parts of her central tail feathers are often lighter and sometimes golden rather than chestnut or reddish gold. These slight average sexual differences are only of use if birds in a similar state of plumage wear are compared.

Juvenile a nearly uniform-appearing light coffee brown ('café au lait') above, slightly greyer on the head and redder on the rump and tail; and buff below, palest on the throat. Bill and legs duller and probably browner than adults.

FIELD CHARACTERS Small, dark reddish brown bird with white head and pale bluish bill. Has been said to give the impression of a partly-smoked cigar.

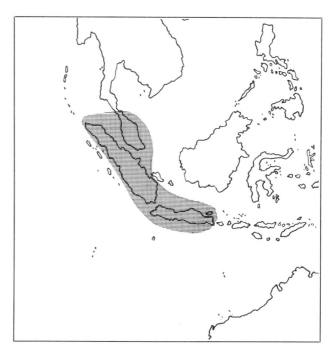

DISTRIBUTION AND HABITAT Southern peninsular Thailand (Siam), Malay Peninsula, Penang, Singapore, Sumatra, Simalur, Nias, Java, and Bali.

Inhabits grassy places, waste land, cultivated areas and gardens. Recent decrease in Singapore suspected to be due to competition from the introduced Spice Finch (Ward).

FEEDING AND GENERAL HABITS Takes seeds of grasses and said to take rice but this needs further investigation as Bernstein found that it was unable to cope with fully ripe rice and thought that it flocked to the rice stubbles to feed on seeds of wild grasses or weeds there. Perhaps, however, rice is taken when soft and not yet fully ripe. Feeds both on the ground and in vegetation. Probably takes some invertebrates as Gocht found that a captive pair eagerly took greenfly when they were rearing young. It is not clear what, of the many foods Gocht provided for his mixed collection, were actually fed to their young by this species.

Commonly in pairs when breeding and at other times in small or large flocks, often in company with other munias. Probably breeding birds also feed in flocks at times. In Java Bernstein found it tame and easily observed.

NESTING The nest is placed in a bush, low tree or grass clump, usually not much more than a metre above ground but sometimes high in the crown of a Betel Palm (Madoc). It is roundish, usually built largely of grasses but stems of other plants, bamboo leaves, fine roots and similar materials are also used. Bernstein, whose description of the nest is the most detailed, describes it as having a side entrance opening downward at an angle, appearing loosely put together on the outside but more closely and carefully built on the inside. Both sexes of a captive pair took equal parts in gathering nest material and building (Gocht). There is a good photograph of the bird at its nest entrance, by C. W. Molesworth, in Madoc's book.

Eggs 3 to 7. Both parents incubate and brood alternately by day for periods of about $1\frac{1}{2}$ hours; the female only at night. The young are brooded by day for 12 days after hatching. Incubation period 12–13 days. Young fledge at about 21 days or a little longer. Recorded breeding in February, at the end of the rainy season, in Java, and in 'the first half of the year' in the Malay Peninsula (Robinson).

VOICE The presumed contact call is a soft piping note that Bernstein transcribes as 'peekt' and 'pee-eet' (my anglicisation). The song has two strophes, of which the first is almost inaudible to human ears (quite so to some) and the second is a quickly repeated, tinkling 'heeheeheeheeheeheeheeeheeeheee' (Immelmann *et al.*).

DISPLAY AND SOCIAL BEHAVIOUR In courtship display the pair perch side by side and the male sings with upraised head, spread tail and his head moving slowly and regularly to and fro (Russ, Immelmann *et al.*).

Allo-preening occurs between members of a pair (Gocht). In captivity very unaggressive both towards its own species and others.

OTHER NAMES White-headed Nun, White-headed Mannikin, Cigar Bird.

REFERENCES

Bernstein, H. A. 1861. Ueber Nester und Eier javascher Vögel. *J. Orn.* 9: 177–191.

Gocht, H. 1966. Die Weisskopfnonne und ihre Zucht. *Gefiederte Welt* 90: 143–144.

Immelmann, K.. Steinbacher, J. & Wolters, H. E. 1969. *Vögel in Käfige und Voliere: Prachtfinken*: 310–315.

Madoc, G. C. 1956. *An introduction to Malayan birds.* Kuala Lumpur.

Russ, K. 1879. *Die Fremländischen Stubenvögel*, vol. 1. Hannover, Aachen, Germany.

Robinson, H. C. 1927. *The birds of the Malay Peninsula.*, vol. 1. London.

Ward, P. 1968. Origin of the avifauna of urban and suburban Singapore. *Ibis* 110: 239–254.

Pale-headed Munia   *Lonchura pallida*

Munia pallida Wallace, 1863, *Proc. Zool. Soc. London*, p. 495.

DESCRIPTION About size of Spice Finch but with shorter tail and larger bill. Forehead, face and throat white or creamy white, sometimes slightly tinged with brownish pink, shading to a very pale pinkish grey on the breast and light greyish brown on crown and nape. Mantle, back and wings chocolate brown with a faint mauvish tinge in very new plumage. Lower rump and upper tail coverts dark reddish chestnut. The two pointed central tail feathers are broadly fringed with shining reddish chestnut or reddish gold. Other tail feathers chocolate brown with faint and narrow reddish or goldish fringes on their outer edges. Under tail coverts dark chestnut. Rest of underparts, below the pale greyish breast, light pinkish chestnut to buffish chestnut. Irides blackish brown. Bill bright bluish grey to whitish blue. Legs and feet dark grey. Possibly females may average paler and duller but I have not been able to examine sufficient sexed specimens in comparable plumage to be sure. Birds in worn and faded plumage are considerably duller and paler than the description here given. One very worn female from Lombok has the back light earth brown, upper tail coverts golden, and the underparts pale buff. She is beginning to moult and her new feathers are normal in colour.

Juvenile a slightly lighter and different shade of brown – more warm earth brown – above, with rusty fringes to the secondaries and rusty tips (no doubt forming wing bars in life) to the median and greater wing coverts, rusty brown rump and central tail feathers, greyish brown face and nearly uniform reddish buff underparts.

The above description is of nominate *L.p. pallida*, from most of the species' range. *L.p. subcastanea*, known only from the Gulf of Palau, Celebes, is said to be darker chestnut on the underparts (Hartert).

FIELD CHARACTERS Small thickset brown 'finch' with whitish head and very pale breast. The latter would distinguish it from the brown-breasted, black-bellied *L. maja*, should they ever occur together.

DISTRIBUTION AND HABITAT South-western and central Celebes, Lombok, Sumbawa, Flores, Alor, Savu, Kisar, Sermattu, Babar, Kalaota and Madu. Presumably in the usual types of habitat (grassland) but I can find no definite statements though Heinrich (in Stresemann, 1940) implies that he found it in areas of rice cultivation.

FEEDING AND GENERAL HABITS Probably very similar or identical to those of *L. maja*. Heinrich (in Stresemann) often found it associating in mixed flocks with *L. malacca*. Peters gave his breeding birds germinated seeds, eggfood and chickweed.

NESTING In Flores nests were found in April and May (Verheyen).

Captive birds built roundish nests of broad-bladed

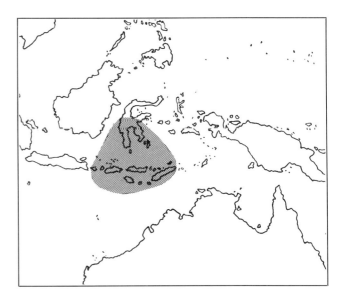

grasses, lined with sisal and coconut fibres. Eggs 4 or 5. Incubation period about 13 days (Peters).

VOICE AND DISPLAY No information.

OTHER NAMES Pale-headed Mannikin, Pale-headed Nun.

REFERENCES
Hartert, E. 1897. Mr William Docherty's bird-collection from the Celebes. *Novit. Zool.* **4**: 153–166.
Peters, J. 1979. Haltung und Erstzucht der Blasskopfnonne (*Lonchura pallida*). *Gefiederte Welt* **1979**: 27–28.
Stresemann, E. 1940. Die Vögel von Celebes. *J. Orn.* **88**: 1–135.

Chestnut-breasted Finch
Lonchura castaneothorax

Amadina castaneothorax Gould, 1837, *Synops. Birds Australia*, pt. 2, pl. 21, fig 2.

DESCRIPTION About size of Spice Finch but a little heavier in build. Tail bluntly wedge-shaped (when spread) with the central feathers pointed and somewhat elongated. Face, including lores and stripe over eye, blackish brown with pale brownish shafts to the feathers. Throat brownish black with paler feather shafts only noticeable on close inspection. Forehead, crown and nape a silvery brownish grey with darker feather centres giving a spotted effect. Mantle, back, wing coverts and fringes of the otherwise drab wing quills, warm reddish brown with indistinct greyish subterminal bands on back and mantle feathers. Lower rump and the long upper tail coverts pale golden. Tail feathers drab brown, fringed pale golden. Breast pale chestnut or deep café au lait colour, bordered at lower edge and sides with black. Lower breast and belly white. Flanks barred black and white but more or less suffused with pale chestnut. Lower flanks, tibial feathers and under tail coverts black. Irides brown. Bill pale to medium bluish grey. Legs and feet bluish grey, purplish grey, leaden grey or blackish.

Female usually a little duller than male, with a paler chestnut breast and less pronounced black band dividing the chestnut and white areas of the underparts. There is, however, a good deal of individual variation and differences due to degree of wear and bleaching, in worn plumage the greys on head and back look very pale. Juvenile predominantly light buffish drab, slightly darker and greyer on head, throat and wings than elsewhere, with pale shafts to feathers of head and face, obscure dark bars on throat feathers.

The above description is of nominate *L.c. castaneothorax*, from coastal eastern Australia, which has been introduced to New Caledonia and the Society Islands. *L.c. assimilis*, from the northern territory of Australia, the Kimberleys, Groote Eylandt and Melville Island averages a little darker in colour but is a very poorly differentiated race. *L.c. ramsayi** (formerly *L.c. nigriceps*), from South-eastern New Guinea and Goodenough Island, has the face and throat solid black, upper part of head brownish black with a grey subterminal mark on each feather giving a spotted effect, darker and more reddish brown upper parts, a darker rich golden on the rump and more boldly barred black and (pure) white flank feathers. *L.c. boschmai*, from the Wissel Lake District of New Guinea, is said to be darker on the head and breast, have chestnut flanks and paler upper tail coverts; I have not seen a specimen. *L.c. sharpii*, shown on plate 5, facing p. 224, from northern New Guinea from Astrolabe Bay to Humboldt Bay, and Vulcan (Manam) Island, is like *L.c. ramsayi* but has the forehead white or nearly white, shading to pale grey (light grey feathers with whitish fringes) on crown and nape, in strong contrast to the jet black face. its rump and upper tail coverts are glossy reddish chestnut and the fringes of its tail feathers reddish golden. Sexual and age differences of this form and *L.c. ramsayi* are comparable to those described for the nominate form. *L.c. uropygialis*, from the head of Geelvink Bay, New Guinea, of which I have not seen a specimen, is said to be similar to *L.c. uropygialis* but with paler, more yellowish, upper tail coverts and darker on crown and nape.

In parts of Australia this species regularly hybridises with the Yellow-rumped Finch, *Lonchura flaviprymna*.

FIELD CHARACTERS Small bird with thick grey bill and short golden or yellowish tail contrasting with brown back; usually in flocks. In Australia the pattern of the underparts, black throat, and pale chestnut breast divided by a black band from the white belly distinguish it from the allied Yellow-rumped Finch, but hybrids occur.

DISTRIBUTION AND HABITAT Coastal eastern Australia, from Sydney to Cape York, northern Australia, including the Kimberleys, Groote Eylandt, Melville Island, New Guinea, Goodenough Island and Vulcan (Manam) Island. Introduced on New Caledonia.

Inhabits marshes, reedbeds and tall grass bordering water, mangroves and some cultivated areas. In dry seasons sometimes in arid or semi-desert country but

*Note: if *Spermestes* is recognised the name *nigriceps* comes back.

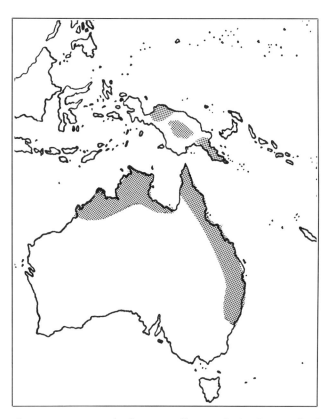

always near water (unless actually wandering in search of it). The spread of artificial irrigation in north-eastern Australia has been much to its advantage. It is now a characteristic bird of the sugar cane fields, where it breeds, and rice fields, where it feeds and does some damage. Partly nomadic or migratory in Australia, in correlation with rainfall. In the Port Moresby district of New Guinea it occurs both in open savanna and in small grassy 'pockets' in rain forest (Mackay). Usually in low-lying country but found at over 1700 metres in the Wissel Lake district of New Guinea (Junge).

FEEDING AND GENERAL HABITS Feeds mainly on seeds but sometimes takes flying termites, *Mastotermes darwiniensis*, and possibly other insects. The seeds of Wild Rice, *Oryza sativa*, are an important natural food and among other grasses whose seeds are taken Immelmann (1962) lists *Echinachloa colonum*, *Chloris virgata*, *Sehima nervosa*, *Panicum maximum* and *P. zymbirformae*. Now feeds largely on cultivated rice, barley, sorghum (dari), and millet, when they are available.

Feeds by preference perched among its food plants, much less often from the ground. Typically clings to the stem just below the seed head and, having stripped it, pulls in another seed head and holds it or its stem under either foot while feeding. It may repeat this until it is holding together 4 or 5 stems, which spring back into place when it takes flight (Immelmann, 1965).

Highly social. Outside the breeding season pairs are not obvious within the flock, suggesting that the pair bond may be less strong than in many estrildids. Single birds or small parties commonly fly with slight or marked undulations; large flocks usually direct and fast, often with Starling-like turns and twists.

In parts of Queensland, Australia, appears to be in competition with the introduced Spice Finch, which has largely replaced it in the more densely inhabited (by man) areas (Immelmann *et al.*, 1969).

In captivity will live, and sometimes rear young, on seed, soaked seed, greenstuff (especially half ripe seeding chickweed and grasses) and minerals. Immelmann *et al.* advise giving mealworms, ant pupae and egg food in addition but these are often refused.

NESTING Usually breeds colonially. Nest usually sited in reeds, long grasses or sugar cane, sometimes in bushes, shrubs, maize or bamboos, from 30 to 120 cm (1 to 4 feet) above ground. Commonly the nest is among vertical stalks that are pulled over and incorporated in the walls of the nest. The nest is small and somewhat laterally compressed so that it is usually only about 10 cm (4 inches) broad but up to 15 cm (6 inches) in depth and length. All nests examined by Immelmann (1962) were made of green grass (which quickly turns yellow on the outside of the nest), with the length of the grass used continuously decreasing towards the inside of the nest which is lined with finer and softer grasses and plant wool but not with feathers. It has a small entrance hole which may have a slight porch over it but no entrance tunnel.

Eggs 4 to 6, exceptionally 3, 7, or 8. Incubation period 12 to 13 days. Young fledge at about 21 days. Both sexes incubate and brood in the usual estrildine manner. Young, in captivity, return to the nest to roost for some nights after fledging (Immelmann *et al.*).

VOICE The only call that has been heard by observers is a monosyllabic or (less often) di-syllabic 'tit' or 'tlit' that seems to function mainly as a contact call. It may be almost inaudible (to humans) when given by members of a small group feeding near to each other, or long-drawn out and with a bell-like quality when given by birds in flight or at a distance from each other.

The high-pitched song, which lasts for up to 12 seconds, is preceded by silent mandibulation. Morris transcribes it as: 'weeeeee eeeeeee / tuee tuee tuee tuee tuee tuee tuee tuee tuee / cheeouk cheeouk cheeouk / ching-ching-ching-ching-ching'. The first note being the long whistle with which some allied species end their songs. Song is used both when displaying and when perched alone or with other members of the flock. It commonly elicits 'peering', as in the Spice Finch (q.v.).

DISPLAY AND SOCIAL BEHAVIOUR The courtship display has been described fully by Immelmann (1965), from which this description is derived. No nesting material is held. The male starts his song phrase with bill wide open and head bent down. The feathers of the head, breast, belly and rump are erected. In this position he hops up and down for a few moments. After this he bobs up and down by alternately stretching and bending his legs, frequently interrupting this with bill-wiping and body-shaking. During this the male approaches the female until the two are in contact. Then both birds, still in bodily contact, make simultaneous deep bows till their bodies are horizontal, followed by upward movements till their bodies are vertical. The birds' tails are turned towards each other and their belly feathers even more erected than in the first part of the display. During this second part of the display sequence the male is usually silent. Copulation may follow immediately.

There is much individual variation in the courtship display. Some males turn their heads from side to side while singing, others do not. Morris (1958) observed courtship displays which were initiated by both birds shaking and involved much mutual mandibulation and bill-wiping. Allo-preening occurs between paired birds but not, so far as has been observed, between other individuals (Morris, 1958, Immelmann, 1965).

OTHER NAMES Chestnut-breasted Mannikin, Chestnut-breasted Munia, Barley-bird.

REFERENCES
Immelmann, K. 1962. Beiträge zu einer vergleichenden Biologie australischer Prachtfinken. *Zool Jb. Syst.* **90**: 1–196.
Immelmann, K. 1965. *Australian finches in bush and aviary.* London and Sydney.
Immelmann, K., Steinbacher, J. & Wolters, H. E. 1969. *Vögel in Käfig und Voliere: Prachtfinken:* 286–298.
Junge, G. C. A. 1952. New subspecies of birds from New Guinea. *Zool. Mededelingen* **31**: 247–249.
Mackay, R. D. 1970. *The birds of Port Moresby and district.* Sydney, London.
Morris, D. 1958. The comparative ethology of grassfinches (Erythrurae) and Mannikins (Amadinae). *Proc. Zool. Soc. London* **131**: 389–439.

Yellow-rumped Finch   *Lonchura flaviprymna*

Donacola flaviprymna Gould, 1845, *Proc. Zool. Soc. London*, p. 80.

As has been said in the introduction to the group I believe this species to be most closely related to and possibly conspecific with the Chestnut-breasted Finch, *L. castaneothorax*.

DESCRIPTION In size and shape as previous form, *L. castaneothorax* but differing as follows in colour pattern: Top of head a paler grey. Face and throat a pale whitish grey or buffish grey. Breast and underparts a very pale buffish straw colour. Rest of plumage as in *L. castaneothorax* with which, where their ranges overlap, it interbreeds freely, producing fertile intermediates (Immelmann, 1962 and 1965). Female possibly averages a little duller than male but Immelmann (1962) found no definite sexual differences. Juvenile resembles that of *L. castaneothorax*.

FIELD CHARACTERS Thickset, shortish-tailed 'finch' with

pale head and underparts, bluish grey bill and yellowish or golden rump and tail.

DISTRIBUTION AND HABITAT Tropical northern Australia from the East Kimberleys (about Derby) to north-eastern Queensland. Exact extent of its inland range apparently not known. Habitat as *L. castaneothorax* and only less often associated with cultivated areas because of relative lack of opportunity.

FEEDING AND GENERAL HABITS As *L. castaneothorax* so far as known. Immelmann (1965) observed it feeding on seeds of the grasses *Echinachloa colonum, Chloris virgata, Sehima nervosum, Panicum zymbirformae* and wild rice *Oryza sativa*. Also takes cultivated rice when available. Probably takes some insects when feeding young as Teschemaker found his captive specimens, when rearing young, took gentles in large numbers and were constantly searching the aviary for insects.

NESTING In general as *L. castaneothorax* (q.v.) Immelmann (1965) states that clutch size averages somewhat smaller, usually 4 or 5 eggs. Breeds during the second half of the wet season. Does not construct roosting nests. During incubation and brooding the male does not roost in the nest.

Teschemaker describes vividly how a captive pair, as soon as dusk began to fall, made repeated and apparently purposive efforts to lead the young (which had fledged earlier that day) back into the nest to roost, calling and leading them and even, on a few occasions actually pushing the young from their perches when they were disinclined to make further efforts.

VOICE As *L. castaneothorax* (q.v.) except that the contact calls are said to be 'rather more piercing' (Immelmann, 1965).

DISPLAY AND SOCIAL BEHAVIOUR As in *L. castaneothorax* except that Immelmann observed consistent qualitative differences in the courtship display. The first part of this display is either omitted or combined with the second part, the male performing his bobbing movements in an almost

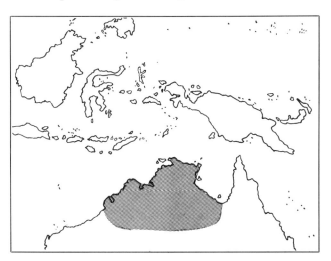

horizontal position. Bill wiping during the display is more frequent and more intense and feather erection even more pronounced. In general the courtship display of the Yellow-breasted Finch appears more intense and exaggerated and Immelmann believes that, as a result, it supplies a supernormal stimulus for females of the Chestnut-breasted Finch in spite of the less ornamental plumage of the performer.

OTHER NAMES Yellow-tailed Finch, Yellow-rumped Munia.

REFERENCES
Immelmann, K. 1962. Besiedlungsgeschichte und Bastardierung von *Lonchura castaneothorax* und *Lonchura flaviprymna* in Nordaustralien. *J. Orn.* **103**: 344–357.
Immelmann, K. 1965. *Australian finches in bush and aviary.* London and Sydney.
Teschemaker, W. E. 1907. The nesting of the Yellow-rumped Finch and the Chestnut-breasted Finch. *Avicult. Mag.*, New Ser., **5**: 113–124.

Chestnut-and-white Munia
Lonchura quinticolor

Loxia quinticolor Vieillot, 1867, *Ois. Chant.*, pl. 5, p. 85.

DESCRIPTION Shown on plate 5, facing p. 224. About size and shape of Spice Finch but head perhaps a little larger and bill a little thicker in proportion. Forehead and face dark chestnut with pale feather shafts, most noticeable on the ear coverts. Crown and nape a darker, less bright chestnut with obscure greyish sub-terminal bands or tips to the feathers. Throat very dark chestnut brown. Mantle, back, wing coverts and outer webs of primaries and secondaries a less dark chestnut brown. Inner webs of wing quills dull drab, under wing coverts buff. Rump, upper tail coverts and the wide fringes of the pointed central tail feathers, deep reddish golden to bright, light golden. Median line of central tail feathers and outer webs of others chestnut brown, rest of tail dull drab. Tibial feathers and under tail coverts black; rest of under parts below the throat, white. Irides dark brown. Legs and feet grey. Bill bluish grey. Sexes alike.

Juvenile generally light reddish drab above and buff to reddish buff below, with paler throat and pale shafts to the greyish brown feathers of the ear coverts. So far as one can judge from dried skins, their bills and feet are paler and browner than the adults'. In very worn plumage the rump may be predominantly dark chestnut and the rest of the plumage very dull.

FIELD CHARACTERS Chestnut head and upper parts and snow-white belly, in combination, distinguish from other sympatric mannikins.

DISTRIBUTION The Lesser Sunda and Timor group of Islands, on Lombok, Sumbawa, Flores, Alor, Sumba, Timor, Sermatta and Babar. Found up to 1100 metres (*fide* Immelmann *et al.*).

No information on habitat preferences.

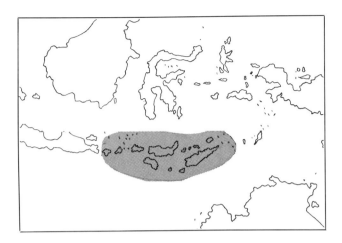

FEEDING AND GENERAL HABITS Captive birds preferred soaked spray millet but also ate dry millets, canary seed and greenstuff (Burkard).

NESTING Nests with eggs have been found, on Flores, from February to June (most in April and May), and October and November (1 in December) on Flores (Verheijen).

VOICE Burkard describes a call 'geev-geev-geev' from a captive male. The song consists of six 'geev' calls followed by scarcely audible, high-pitched, whispering trills, whistles and clucks. Close contact call 'veeveevee'.

DISPLAY AND SOCIAL BEHAVIOUR No information.

OTHER NAMES Five-coloured Mannikin, Five-coloured Munia, Chestnut-and-white Mannikin.

REFERENCES
Burkard, R. 1980. Notizen über das Verhalten meiner Funffar-bennonnen. *Gefiederte Welt* 1980: 39.
Immelmann, K., Steinbacher, J. & Wolters, H. E. 1970. *Vögel in Käfig und Voliere: Prachtfinken*: 342–343.
Verheijen, J. A. J. 1964. Breeding season on the island of Flores. *Ardea* 52: 194–201.

Alpine Munia   *Lonchura monticola*

Munia monticola De Vis 1897, *Ibis*, p. 387.

DESCRIPTION About size of Peter's Twinspot but tail shorter and bill shorter and a little thicker. The bill is, however, relatively smaller and the plumage thicker and softer than in most Asiatic forms of *Lonchura*. Forehead, face and throat black. Crown brownish black (the individual feathers largely blackish with brown central streaks), browner on nape, a dusky chestnut brown on mantle and back and a rather brighter chestnut brown on the wing coverts and outer fringes of the otherwise sepia brown wing quills. Under wing coverts reddish buff with dusky tips to the feathers but whitish under wing coverts also recorded (De Vis). Lower rump, upper tail coverts and fringes of the otherwise blackish tail feathers, shiny light golden yellow. Underparts buffish white with dark shaft streaks that do not reach quite to the tips of most feathers.

A black band across the lower breast extends on either side along the flanks and is said (De Vis) to form a barred pattern (in life?), though this was not obvious in the specimen I examined. Tibial and ventral feathers and under tail coverts black. Bill blue or greyish blue. Legs and feet bluish grey (De Vis) or brownish grey (Rand & Gilliard). Iris brown.

Juvenile brown above, brighter on the upper tail coverts, which are rufous fawn. Head slightly mottled with dusky centres to feathers. Throat blackish with white feather tips. Breast dull greyish brown, rest of underparts buffish white except for reddish buff flanks and under tail coverts (De Vis). I have only examined one specimen of this species, an unsexed adult. Where not otherwise indicated the above description is of this bird.

FIELD CHARACTERS Boldly patterned white and black underside. Head blackish, back brown, rump golden yellow. Not known to be sympatric with any similar species at the high altitudes it inhabits.

DISTRIBUTION AND HABITAT High mountains of south-eastern New Guinea at from 2800 metres to 3900 metres.
Inhabits alpine grassland and rocky areas with some grass. Has been seen both among rocks near the tops of the highest peaks and out on flat grassland (Rand & Gilliard).

FEEDING AND GENERAL HABITS Known to take seeds of a grass with very small seeds (Rand & Gilliard). Feeds both perched in vegetation and on the ground. Perches freely on grass stems, trees and rocks.
In June and July was found in compact flocks of 20 to 50. Birds in juvenile plumage were in separate and smaller flocks and were much less shy of man than the adults. (Rand & Gilliard.)

NESTING No information.

VOICE No information.

DISPLAY AND SOCIAL BEHAVIOUR No information.

OTHER NAME Alpine Mannikin.

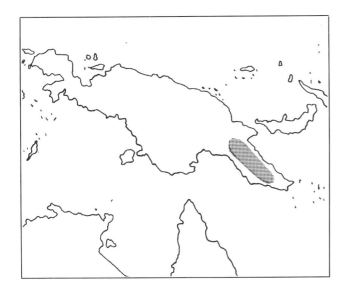

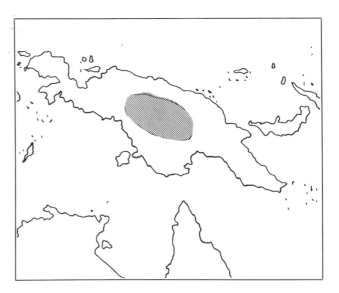

REFERENCES
De Vis, C. W. 1897. Diagnosis of thirty-six new or little-known birds from British New Guinea. *Ibis* **3**, 7th ser., 371–392.
Rand, A. L. & Gilliard, E. T. 1967. *Handbook of New Guinea birds.* London.

Snow Mountain Munia   *Lonchura montana*

Lonchura montana Junge, 1939, *Nova Guinea*, new ser., **3**, p. 67.

DESCRIPTION Very similar to the previous species, *L. monticola*, with which it may prove to be conspecific. It differs chiefly in having a buffish brown breast, the band across the lower breast is usually a band of narrow brownish black bars which continue down the flanks and the black on the head is more restricted. There is, however, some individual as well as possibly geographical variation (see especially Ripley) and some specimens have more extensively black heads and coarser barring on the flanks. The mantle and back are earth brown rather than chestnut.

FIELD CHARACTERS Brown, yellow-rumped munia with buffish breast and lower breast and flanks conspicuously barred black and whitish.

DISTRIBUTION AND HABITAT The Snow Mountains (Oranje Mountains) of interior western New Guinea, at from 2000 to 4000 metres (7000 to 12800 feet).

Inhabits alpine grassland, the edges of shrub-grown areas and, at least in the Ilaga Valley, cultivated fields (Ripley).

FEEDING AND GENERAL HABITS Little known. Ripley observed it feeding on 'weeds and grass seeds', flying from field to field in closely-packed flocks and perching freely in lalang grass and trees. In August and September Rand found it in parties of 6 to 20 and not in breeding condition.

NESTING No information.

VOICE No information.

DISPLAY AND SOCIAL BEHAVIOUR No information.

OTHER NAME Snow Mountain Mannikin.

REFERENCES
Rand, A. L. 1942. Results of the Archbold Expeditions. No. 43. *Bull. Amer. Mus. Nat. Hist.*, **LXXIX**, Art. 7, pp. 425–516.
Rand, A. L. & Gilliard, E. T. 1967. *Handbook of New Guinea birds.* London.
Ripley, S. D. 1964. *A systematic and ecological study of birds of New Guinea.* Peabody Museum of Natural History, Yale University Bull. 19.

White-crowned Munia   *Lonchura nevermanni*

Lonchura nevermanni Stresemann, 1934, *Orn. Monatsber.* **42**: p. 101.

DESCRIPTION Similar in size and shape to *L. castaneothorax* (q.v.). Forehead, crown and front of face greyish white to buffish white. Lower and posterior ear coverts dark dull brown with pale shafts. Feathers of nape, hind neck and sides of neck dark dull brown with buffish white to greyish white fringes. Upper parts dark earth brown with faint dull silvery grey subterminal bands on the feathers of mantle and upper back and rusty brown fringes to most of the wing feathers. Rump dark rusty orange shading to glossy but not very bright golden yellow on the upper tail coverts. Central tail feathers brownish with broad yellowish gold fringes. Outer tail feathers brown, narrowly fringed yellowish gold to pale greenish yellow. Throat, ventral area, tibial feathers and under tail coverts black. Rest of underparts light, rather dull, chestnut or warm reddish brown. Under wing coverts light reddish buff. Irides dark brown. Bill light bluish grey. Legs and feet dark bluish grey.

The female has the greyish white on the top of her head restricted to the forehead, her crown feathers being usually dull brown with narrow whitish fringes. She is also slightly duller generally than the male. The juvenile is earth brown above and rusty buff below. Stresemann states that young adults, already through their first moult, do not have the black throat, the feathers that first replace the juvenile plumage here being dark brown with buffish tips. Neff, who bred this species very successfully, does not specify this difference but says that young males do not attain predominantly white heads until their second moult. In their first adult plumage they are very like females. The nestling is at first quite pale flesh-coloured, naked except for a very few short greyish white down feathers on the back (Neff) and has 2 black 'horseshoe' markings on its yellow palate (Meyer). Neff's paper is illustrated with excellent photographs of nestlings at 13 and 19 days old.

FIELD CHARACTERS Small reddish brown 'finch' with largely whitish head and black throat.

DISTRIBUTION AND HABITAT Southern New Guinea between Frederick-Hendrick Island and middle Fly River. Found in savanna grassland, reedbeds, floating mats of rice grass in lagoons and flooded places and rice fields.

FEEDING AND GENERAL HABITS Feeds largely on grass seeds. Rand (1938) found that it fed both in tall densely grassed savanna and, to a lesser extent, in marshes. Usually in pairs or small parties, often in company with the probably conspecific *L. stygia*. In captivity peaceable with its own and allied species but often interferes with the nesting of other pairs so that breeding is most successful when only a single pair is kept (alone or with harmless birds of other species) in an enclosure (Neff).

In captivity will eat dry and soaked millets and canary seed, the seeds of Annual Meadow Grass, Chickweed, sweet apple and the usual minerals. A pair owned by Meyer reared young on the above foods, chiefly on soaked seed, with the addition of mealworms, but Neff found that the addition of ant pupae and other insect food, half ripe wheat and millet as well as soaked seed and chickweed were necessary for successful rearing of the young.

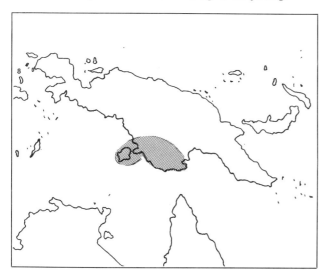

NESTING No information from the wild, the following is from studies by Neff and Meyer on captive birds. The nest may be in a box, on a ledge or in reeds or other cover. It is roundish, with a side entrance but no entrance tube, built of coarse grasses, reeds or similar materials and lined only with rather finer grasses, coconut fibre etc. The male brings the material but the female does most of the actual building (Neff).

Eggs 3 to 6, usually 4 or 5. Incubation begins with the third egg and takes 12 to 13 days (Neff), sometimes 14 (Meyer). Both sexes share parental care in the usual way, and both roost in the nest at night. Neff found that both birds were often on the nest together by day but this is probably an artifact of captivity. The nestlings beg for food in the usual estrildid manner, and wave to and fro their heads and their lifted tongues while so-doing. Their eyes open at 7 to 9 days, from which time the parents cease to brood them constantly (Neff). One captive pair ceased to brood the young at night at 12 days (Meyer) but Neff found that with broods of 4 to 5 at least one parent always roosted in the nest till their fifteenth day and in small broods both parents did so until the young had fledged (and after).

Young fledge at 20 to 22 days. For the first 2 or 3 days the parents usually lead them back to the nest to feed them there (Neff). The young begin to feed themselves about 5 days after fledging but are fed by their parents until about 14 days after fledging (Meyer, Neff).

VOICE Calls very similar to those of other Australasian *Lonchura* species. Close contact or locomotion intention call a soft short 'eeb' or 'deet'. Distance contact call a louder, more long drawn and melodious version 'dee-t, dee-et', 'drooeet, drooeet', 'dooreet' etc. (my anglicisations of Meyer & Neff), suggesting the contact call of the Bullfinch, *Pyrrhula pyrrhula*. The song is almost or (sometimes) quite inaudible to human ears. It is given with erected breast and belly plumage and head turning from side to side (Meyer, Neff).

DISPLAY AND SOCIAL BEHAVIOUR Courtship display is prefaced by flying or hopping to and fro from perch to perch. Then the male perches beside the female with his head and tail angled towards her and breast and belly feathers fully erected, and sings with wide open bill. He jerks himself upwards several times, then bows deeply, turning his bill sideways towards the female. If responsive the female solicits with quivering tail. After copulation brief mutual bill to bill fighting is usually followed by allo-preening (Neff).

Meyer's 4 captive birds were less sociable than most munias, they seldom clumped or allo-preened. Neff, however, found this species highly sociable. Allo-preening was common not only between members of a pair but also between unpaired individuals. This and clumping occurred not only intra-specifically but also with specimens of *L. spectabilis*. Peering (Zuhoren) at singing individuals occurred regularly.

REFERENCES

Immelmann, K., Steinbacher, J. & Wolters, H. E. 1969. *Vögel in Käfig und Voliere: Prachtfinken*: 333–334.

Meyer, E. 1978. Zucht der Nevermann- oder Weissscheitel-nonne (*Lonchura nevermanni*). *Gefiederte Welt* **1978**: 161–162.

Neff, R. 1979. Erfahrungen mit der Weissscheitelnonne (*Lonchura nevermanni*). *Gefiederte Welt* **1979**: 61–63.

Rand, A. L. 1938. Results of the Archbold Expeditions No. 20. *Amer. Mus. Novit.* No. 991.

Rand, A. L. & Gilliard, E. T. 1967. Handbook of New Guinea birds. London.

Stresemann, E. 1934. Zwei neue Webervögel aus Sud-Neuguinea. *Orn. Monatsber.* **XLII**: 101–103.

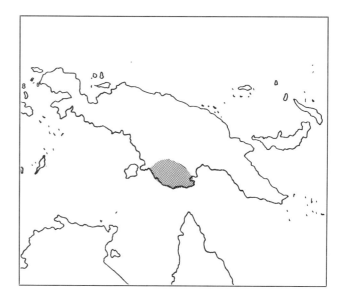

Black Munia   *Lonchura stygia*

Lonchura stygia Stresemann, 1934, *Ornith. Monatsber.* **42**: p. 102.

I think this form will prove to be a dark morph of *L. nevermanni*.

DESCRIPTION As previous form, *L. nevermanni*, with which it is probably conspecific. General plumage glossy brownish black; the feathers on crown, nape and hind neck very dark brown edged laterally with black. Wing quills a very dark dull brown, fringed with black. Owing to the make-up of the skins it was not possible to see the under wing coverts of the specimens I examined, they are described variously as pale reddish buff (Stresemann) and pale creamy buff, fading to white (Mees). Rump and upper tail coverts a light but not very bright yellowish gold. The two pointed central tail feathers have a narrow blackish median line on either side of the shaft and are otherwise brownish yellow shading into clear pale yellowish on the outer fringes; other tail feathers brownish black with only narrow yellowish fringes on their outer webs. Irides dark brown. Bill bluish grey, sometimes, *fide* Stresemann, dark grey. Legs and feet dark bluish grey.

The female is a very little duller and a little paler yellowish on rump and tail. The juvenile is dark greyish brown above, the feathers on the crown with black subterminal marks giving a spotted effect. Central tail feathers more rounded than the adults' and narrowly edged with pale yellowish. Underparts buffish grey with obscure dark spotting on the breast. Ear coverts blackish brown with white shaft streaks. The above description of the juvenile is based on that of Rand (1938), who notes that it becomes much paler with wear. This is evident in the only juvenile specimen I have seen, a male half through its first moult. Its remaining juvenile plumage is mainly light greyish brown above and very pale on the belly but I have no doubt it was as Rand describes, or very close to it, when fresh.

FIELD CHARACTERS Small black finch-like bird with yellowish rump and tail.

DISTRIBUTION AND HABITAT Southern New Guinea between Merauke District and the middle Fly River. Inhabits marshy areas with reed beds or floating mats of rice grass; also grass savannas.

FEEDING AND GENERAL HABITS Known to feed on seeds of grasses. Usually in small flocks of up to 20 individuals. Often in company with the probably conspecific White-crowned Munia. Breeding birds join feeding flocks when away from the nest.

NESTING Three nests described by Rand (1938) were all found 60 to 150 cm (2 to 5 feet) high in grass on little floating islands of grass on the edges of lagoons, where the latter changed into marsh. Two were rather solid structures made largely of flat grass blades and lined throughout, including the neck, with dry grass seed heads, from which the seeds had been removed. They were all 'lop-sided flask-shaped', the top of the nest being level but the lower edge curving up to the somewhat constricted neck of the entrance tube. One measured 20 cm long by 18 cm deep by 11 cm wide, and its entrance tube about 8 cm across and the entrance 4 cm across. The walls were 2 to 3 cm thick. The second nest was similar but the third was more globular in shape, 180 cm from entrance to back and 20 cm from top to bottom. Two clutches of 4 and one of 5 eggs were found, all in September (Rand, 1938).

VOICE No information.

DISPLAY AND SOCIAL BEHAVIOUR No information.

OTHER NAME Black Mannikin.

REFERENCES

Mees. G. (In press Zoologische Verhandelingen). Birds from the lowlands of southern New Guinea (Merauke and Koembe).

Rand, A. L. 1938. Results of the Archbold Expeditions No. 20. *Amer. Mus. Novit.*, No. 991.

Rand, A. L. & Gilliard, E. T. 1967. *Handbook of New Guinea birds.* London.

Stresemann, E. 1934. Zwei neue Webervögel aus Sud-Neuguinea. *Orn. Monatsber.* **42**: 101–103.

Arfak Munia   *Lonchura vana*

Munia vana Hartert, 1930, *Novit. Zool.* **36**, p. 42.

DESCRIPTION Similar in size and shape to *L. nevermanni*. Forehead, areas immediately above and around eyes and upper throat whitish. Rest of head pale brownish grey shading into dark earth brown on mantle, back and wings. Upper tail coverts straw yellow to pale gold. Central tail feathers blackish with wide straw yellow fringes. Outer tail feathers blackish brown with very narrow yellowish fringes on the outer webs. Upper breast dark brownish grey divided by a pale greyish white band from the chestnut brown belly. Flanks, tibial feathers and under tail coverts, chestnut, sometimes intermixed with black. Irides dark. Bill bluish grey. Legs and feet dark grey.

I have not seen a juvenile or a complete description of one. Immelmann *et al.* say that it has a greyish brown crown and nape.

FIELD CHARACTERS As for *L. caniceps*, but paler yellowish on rump and tail.

DISTRIBUTION AND HABITAT Known only from around the Anngi Lakes, in the Arfak Mountains of Vogelkop, north-western New Guinea. Inhabits grasslands at around 2100 metres (6400 feet).

FEEDING AND GENERAL HABITS No information.

NESTING No information.

VOICE No information.

DISPLAY AND SOCIAL BEHAVIOUR No information.

OTHER NAME Arfak Mannikin.

REFERENCES
Hartert, E. 1930. On a collection of birds made by Dr Ernst Mayr in northern Dutch New Guinea. *Novit. Zool.* **36**: 18–128.
Immelmann, K., Steinbacher, J. & Wolters, H. E. 1969. *Vögel in Käfig und Voliere: Prachtfinken*: 334–335. Aachen, Germany.
Rand, A. L. & Gilliard, E. T. 1967. *Handbook of New Guinea birds.* London.

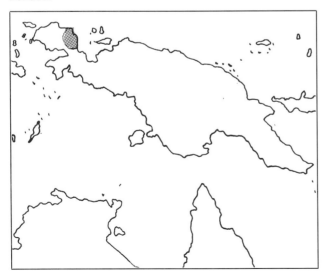

New Britain Munia   *Lonchura spectabilis*

Donacicola spectabilis P. L. Sclater, 1879, *Proc. Zool. Soc. London*, p. 449, pl. 37, fig 2.

DESCRIPTION About length of Avadavat but typical *Lonchura* shape, with proportionately much larger and thicker bill and shorter tail than Avadavat. Head and nape black, shading into very dark reddish chocolate brown, or black feathers with reddish chocolate tips, on mantle, to a slightly lighter reddish brown on back and wings. Inner webs of wing quills sepia brown. Under wing coverts buff. Rump and upper tail coverts dark reddish gold. The two somewhat elongated and pointed central tail feathers are reddish brown with broad reddish gold fringes; other tail feathers dull reddish brown narrowly tinged reddish gold at edges. Breast white to creamy buff, shading to cream or pale buff on belly. The feathers at the sides of the breast may have traces of dark greyish barring; less often both breast and flanks may be conspicuously barred. Tibial feathers, rear parts of flanks and under tail coverts black. Bill dark bluish grey to black. Irides dark brown. Legs and feet bluish grey, dark grey or blackish. Some, possibly most, females have dull brownish barring on the breast and flanks. Sexes otherwise alike, probably females averaging a little duller.

Juvenile a medium warm brown above, darker on the crown and blackish on the face. Throat greyish black with buff feather tips. Underparts buff, sometimes tinged with dusky greyish on breast and under tail coverts. Legs and bill paler and browner than adult's. Nestling at first naked and pale flesh-coloured with conspicuous bluish white gape tubercles. Mouth of nestling yellow inside, with black horseshoe mark in upper mandible, black ring round tongue and two dark spots on palate. There may be a tendency for the horseshoe marking to separate into three parts (Neff).

The above description (except for that of the nestling which may be from one of the New Guinea forms) is of nominate *L.s. spectabilis*, from New Britain. *L.s. spectabilis mayri*, shown on plate 5, facing p. 224, from northern New Guinea, has a much smaller bill. Its upperparts are a lighter reddish brown and sharply demarcated from the black of the head and nape. The gold of its rump is a paler, yellowish gold hue. Its bill, feet and legs are bluish grey. There is a photograph, probably of this form, in *Die Gefiederte Welt* **95** (1971), p. 208. *L.s. wahgiensis*, from the Bismarck, Saruwaged and Herzog Mountains of eastern New Guinea, is very like *L.s. mayri* but a duller brown above and a paler gold, almost straw-coloured, in rump and tail. Its bill is greyish white to bluish grey. *L.s. gajduseki*, from the Karimui Basin, central New Guinea, has the underparts deep buff, like that of the juvenile, and is darker on the upperparts than the two known New Guinea races (Diamond, 1967). This form lives in an area where suitable habitat appears only relatively recently to have been made available to it by man and Diamond (1972) considers that it may have developed its distinctive racial characters in as little as about 15 years.

FIELD CHARACTERS Tiny, thickset 'finch' with black head, brown back, cream or white underparts, and reddish gold to straw gold rump and tail. The unmarked underparts would distinguish it from the larger *L. monticola* should they ever occur together.

DISTRIBUTION AND HABITAT New Britain; the Bismarck, Saruwaged and Herzog Mountains of eastern New Guinea; the Karimui Basin, Central New Guinea and Hollandia area, northern New Guinea. Inhabits grassland.

FEEDING AND GENERAL HABITS Many specimens in the British Museum (Natural History) collection contained grass seeds when dissected. Immelmann *et al.* state, however, that grass *pollen* is the most important food although grass seeds are also taken. Neff (1971), who has been very successful in keeping and breeding this species in captivity, found that it readily takes millet and canary seed, both dry and soaked, half ripe wheat and millet (kept in a deep freeze to be available also in winter) and greenfood. His wild-caught birds took little or no insect food at any time but reared their young at first on half ripe seeds and chickweed, later giving them also soaked millet and canary seed. Captive bred birds, however, freely took mealworms, ant pupae and eggfood (Neff, 1972).

Associates in flocks of up to 30 or 40 individuals (Gilliard, Meyer, 1930). In central New Guinea Diamond (1967) found the species so unwary of man that it could be stalked and caught by hand. Neff found that captive birds preferred to feed clinging to hanging stems and bunches of food plants so it is probable that, when wild, they feed largely perched in or clinging to vegetation.

Builds nests for roosting. These differ from breeding nests only in having a larger entrance hole (Neff).

NESTING Meyer (1933) says the nest is shaped like that of *L. melaena*, which he describes as large, ball-shaped and made of grass; elsewhere (Meyer, 1930) he implies that it has a tubular entrance. Nests in or at the edge of grassland, in reeds, grass clumps or bushes. Neff found that nests built in captivity varied according to the site and might be either bottle shaped or oval. The outside was of coarse materials such as dried grasses and reed leaves, the lining of finer materials, mainly coconut fibres. An interesting feature (which may perhaps occur in some other estrildid nests but appears not to have been recorded) is that some nests, immediately opposite the entrance hole, had an extremely thin area in the nest wall, consisting only of a few fibres. When Neff blocked the entrance with his hand, the sitting bird invariably escaped through this weak part of the opposite wall.

Eggs 3 to 5, most usually 4 in captive birds in Germany (Neff). Incubation period 14 to 15 days (Neff). Young fledge at 21 days. Meyer (1930) recorded 14 day fledging periods for wild young but this was probably an error. Both sexes incubate by turn in the daytime the hen only at night when the cock roosts in the roosting nest, not with the sitting hen (Neff). The young become independent at 14 to 18 days after fledging (Neff).

In New Britain breeds mainly between the dry and rainy seasons, from March to May and again from September to November (Meyer, 1933). In northern New Guinea breeding birds were found in September and October (Hartert), and in central New Guinea a nest with well-feathered young was found in early May (Mayr & Gilliard).

VOICE Contact call 'geeb' or 'eeb' (my anglicisation). The song, as with other munias, is partly inaudible to human ears, the audible parts consist of clicking notes and long-drawn whistles which are repeated 2 to 4 times in a mixture of rising and falling pitches. Song is given with open bill, the head moving to and fro and head and belly feathers erect. It is given both in courtship and in 'undirected' situations, as with other *Lonchura* species. The begging calls of fledged young resemble those of Bengalese Finches. The above information is all from Neff's papers.

DISPLAY AND SOCIAL BEHAVIOUR Courtship display always takes place above ground. It may be prefaced by the male carrying nesting material but this is dropped before he begins to display. The pair perch side by side and the male makes the usual *Lonchura* up and down movements, with head pointing downwards and singing with wide open bill. The female, if responsive, solicits by crouching and tail quivering and, if not, flies off.

Allo-preening occurs both between mates and flock members. If too closely confined captive birds often pluck each other.

OTHER NAMES New Britain Mannikin, Mayr's Mannikin.

REFERENCES

Diamond, J. M. 1967. New subspecies and records of birds from the Karimui Basin, New Guinea. *Amer. Mus. Novit.*, no. 2284.

Diamond, J. N. 1972. *Avifauna of the eastern highlands of New Guinea.* Publ. Nuttall Orn. Club, no. 12. Cambridge, Mass.

Hartert, E. 1930. On a collection of birds made by Dr Ernst Mayr in northern Dutch New Guinea. *Novit. Zool.* **34**: 8–128.

Immelmann, K., Steinbacher, J. & Wolters, H. E. 1970. *Vögel in Käfig und Voliere: Prachtfinken:* 340–342.

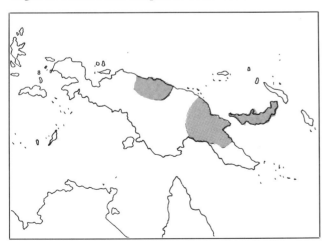

Mayr, E. & Gilliard, E. T. 1954. Birds of Central New Guinea. *Bull. Amer. Mus. Nat. Hist.* vol. 103, art. 4.

Meyer, O. 1930. Uebersicht über die Brutzeiten der Vögel auf der Insel Vuatom (New Britain). *J. Orn.* **78**: 19–38.

Meyer, O. 1933. Vogeleier und Nester aus Neubritannien, Sudsee. *Beitr. Fortpflanzungsbiologie der Vögel* **9**: 122–136.

Neff, R. 1971. Die Prachtnonne (*Lonchura spectabilis*). *Die Gefiederte Welt* **95**: 234–236.

Neff, R. 1972. Weitere Beobachtungen an der Prachtnonne (*Lonchura spectabilis*). *Die Gefiederte Welt* **1972**: 68.

Grand Valley Munia   *Lonchura teerinki*

Lonchura teerinki Rand, 1940, *Amer. Muse. Novit.*, no. 1072, p. 14.

DESCRIPTION Similar in size and shape to previous species, *L. spectabilis*. Forehead blackish, shading to dark brown on crown, nape and hind neck. Back, wing coverts and outer edges of the blackish brown wing quills, dark reddish brown, with greyish fringes to feathers in fresh plumage. Under wing coverts buffish. Lower rump, upper tail coverts and broad outer fringes of central tail feathers pale gold or straw-yellow; other tail feathers blackish brown, narrowly fringed with straw-yellow. Face, throat, upper breast, tibial feathers and under tail coverts black. Rest of underparts white with black or black and light reddish brown blotches or flecks on the sides of the lower breast and flanks. Bill leaden grey (*fide* Immelmann *et al.*). Irides and legs apparently unrecorded. Female a little duller than male with a tendency for the flank markings to appear as definite bars (Rand, 1940).

Juvenile dark brown above, paler on rump and edges of tail feathers. Throat pale reddish brown. Breast greyish brown. Rest of underparts pale buffish with brown spotting on the flanks.

The above description is of *L.t. teerinki*, from the Grand Valley of the Balim and Bele Rivers, on the northern slope of Mt Wilhelmina in the Orange Mountains. *L.t. mariae*, from Bokindini, 50 km north of the Balim Valley is said to be of a more intense black on the head and a richer, deeper brown on the upperparts (Ripley).

FIELD CHARACTERS Small brownish 'finch' with face and throat black and belly white.

DISTRIBUTION AND HABITAT New Guinea, north of the Snow (Oranje) Mountains from 1300 to 2300 metres (4200 to 7300 feet) (see also under 'description'). Inhabits grassland, especially the extensive secondary grassland resulting from native clearing of the forest, and abandoned native gardens.

FEEDING AND GENERAL HABITS Little recorded. Almost certainly feeds largely on grass seeds. Has been seen in flocks (Ripley).

NESTING No information.

VOICE Ripley heard 'typical low one-note *Lonchura* calls'.

DISPLAY AND SOCIAL BEHAVIOUR No information.

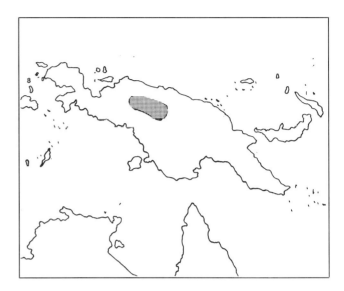

OTHER NAME Grand Valley Mannikin.

REFERENCES

Immelmann, K., Steinbacher, J. & Wolters, H. E. 1969. *Vögel in Käfig und Voliere: Prachtfinken*: 283–284. Aachen, Germany.

Rand, A. L. 1940. Results of the Archbold Expeditions. No. 25. *Amer. Mus. Novit.* No. 1072.

Rand, A. L. & Gilliard, E. T. 1967. *Handbook of New Guinea birds.* London.

Ripley, S. D. 1964. *A systematic and ecological study of birds of New Guinea.* Peabody Museum of Natural History, Yale University Bull. no. 19.

Grey-headed Munia   *Lonchura caniceps*

Munia caniceps Salvadori, 1876, *Ann. Mus. Genova*, 9: p. 38.

DESCRIPTION About length of Avadavat but heavier build and with thicker bill, though the bill is not quite so large in proportion as in many *Lonchura* species. Head, including nape and throat, light, slightly brownish grey, a very little paler on face and crown than on nape. Mantle, back and wings a dark dull chocolate brown, sharply demarcated from the grey nape. Under wing coverts bright buff. Rump, upper tail coverts and the broad fringes of the two central tail feathers reddish gold to glossy tawny orange. Median line of central tail feathers dark brown. Outer tail feathers dark chocolate brown with narrow gold or reddish tawny fringes. Underparts, below the grey throat, dull greyish brown shading into the black of the belly, lower flanks, tibial feathers and under tail coverts. Irides black (*fide* D'Albertis, in Sharpe). Bill dark greyish blue, probably with the basal part of lower mandible paler in life, to judge from appearance of museum specimens. Legs and feet dark grey to blackish. Female said to be duller than male (Rand & Gilliard, Immelmann *et al.*), the 2 specimens I have examined were unsexed and probably both males.

I have not seen a juvenile of this species or description of one. From a specimen moulting from juvenile to adult dress, it is clear that the juvenile plumage is largely light brown above and buffish on the underparts.

The above description of nominate *L.c. caniceps*, from the lowlands of south-eastern New Guinea. *L.c. kumusii*, from the lowlands of the north coast of south-eastern New Guinea, of which I have not seen a specimen, was separated as being much paler on the upper parts and with the belly slaty brown not black. *L.c. scratchleyana*, from the mid-mountain grasslands of south-eastern New Guinea, differs from *L.c. caniceps* in being lighter and more reddish brown above, having the rump and tail fringes yellowish gold, the underparts paler and more reddish with the black of the belly more restricted and the head of a more buffish grey.

FIELD CHARACTERS Very small dark brown to reddish brown 'finch' *with pale greyish head* and gold on rump and tail.

DISTRIBUTION AND HABITAT South-eastern New Guinea, west to Hall Sound and Huon Gulf. Found in lowlands and from 1000 to 2000 metres up in mid-mountain grassland. Inhabits grassland, areas of mixed grass and scrub, marshes, pockets of savanna in rain forest areas, plots of

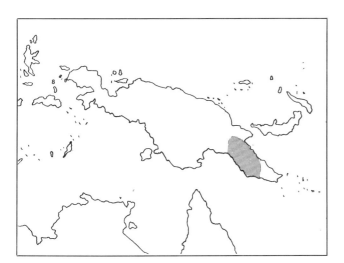

swamp rice, lawns, airstrips and similar manmade habitats.

FEEDING AND GENERAL HABITS Known to feed on grass seeds. In some areas habitually feeds on lawns (Bell). Has been observed both in small parties of 3 or 4 to 20 individuals and larger flocks of up to 100 or more both in mid-mountain regions (Bell) near Port Moresby when grass on which it feeds was seeding (Mackay).

NESTING No information.

VOICE No information.

DISPLAY AND SOCIAL BEHAVIOUR No information.

OTHER NAME Grey-headed Mannikin.

REFERENCES
Bell, H. L. 1971. Field-notes on birds of Mt Edward, Papua. *Emu* **71**: 13–19.
Immelmann, K., Steinbacher, J. & Wolters, H. E. 1969. *Vögel in Käfig und Voliere: Prachtfinken:* 331–333.
Mackay, R. D. 1969. The birds of Port Moresby and district. London, Sydney and Johannesburg.
Rand, A. L. & Gilliard, E. T. 1967. *Handbook of New Guinea birds.* London.
Sharpe, R. B. 1890. *Catalogue of the birds in the British Museum,* vol. 13. British Museum (Natural History) London.

Hunstein's Munia   *Lonchura hunsteini*

Donacicola hunsteini Finsch, 1886, *Ibis*, p. 1, pl. 1.

DESCRIPTION Between Spice Finch and Avadavat in size but thick-set and short-tailed in shape, perhaps even more so than the Chestnut-breasted Finch (q.v.) which it much resembles in proportions. Forehead, crown and nape silvery grey, with black centres and bases to the feathers giving a spotted effect. Ear coverts similar but darker. Lores, mantle, back and wing coverts and underparts coal black. Rump, upper tail coverts and broad fringes to central tail feathers reddish gold. Rest of tail and wing quills brownish black. Under wing coverts buff. Irides dark brown. Bill blackish (probably with a steely grey sheen in life). Legs and feet blackish. Female as male but with feathers of belly and flanks buffish white at base and some visible speckling and barring with buffish white elsewhere. This description is, however, based on only 2 specimens, and the differences may be individual not sexual.

A female juvenile (the only juvenile I have been able to examine) has the head, neck and upper breast blackish brown, with dull grey tips to the feathers of forehead, crown and nape and pale shaft streaks to the ear coverts. Rest of upper parts dark earth brown, tinged with yellow on the upper tail coverts and fringes of the central tail feathers. Underparts buffish.

The above description is of nominate *L.h. hunsteini*, from northern New Ireland. *L.h. minor*, from Ponape Island is (surprisingly) said to differ only in being slightly smaller. *L.h. nigerrima*, from New Hanover, differs in lacking the grey tips on the head feathers and having the bases of the feathers of the underparts conspicuously tipped with brownish white. I have not seen specimens of *minor* or *nigerrima*.

FIELD CHARACTERS Small, thickset 'finch', mainly (female) or entirely (male) black in plumage except for silvery grey, dark-speckled top of head and reddish gold rump and central tail feathers.

DISTRIBUTION AND HABITAT The Kavieng District of northern New Ireland; New Hanover Island and Ponape Island.

On New Hanover found in high jungle grass (Finsch).

FEEDING AND GENERAL HABITS Four collected in New Hanover had eaten seeds of grasses and of other (unidentified) plants (Heinroth).

NESTING No information.

VOICE No information.

DISPLAY AND SOCIAL BEHAVIOUR No information.

OTHER NAME Hunstein's Mannikin.

REFERENCES
Finsch, O. 1886. On two new species of Birds from New Ireland. *Ibis* **13**, 5th ser., 1–2.

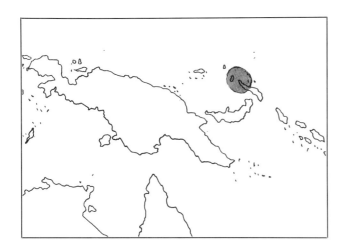

Heinroth, O. 1903. Ornithologische Ergebnisse der '1 Deutschen Südsee-Expedition von Br. Mencke'. *J. Orn.* **51**: 65–125.
Immelmann, K., Steinbacher, J. & Wolters, H. E. 1970. *Vögel in Käfig und Voliere: Prachtfinken:* 336–338.

Great-billed Munia   *Lonchura grandis*

Munia grandis Sharpe, 1882, *Journ. Linn. Soc. London, Zool.* **16**, p. 319.

DESCRIPTION About size of Spice Finch but with shorter tail, larger head and much larger and thicker bill. Head, nape, breast, median part of lower breast and belly, tibial feathers, lower flanks and under tail coverts black. Sides of lower breast most of flanks, mantle, back and lesser and median wing coverts, a clear light yellowish chestnut. Greater wing coverts and most of those parts of the primaries and secondaries visible when wing is folded, slightly darker, more reddish brown. Inner webs of wing quills sepia. Under wing coverts buff. Rump and upper tail coverts light reddish gold to deep yellowish gold. Tail the usual blunt wedge shape, the two pointed central feathers having broad yellowish gold to greenish gold fringes and a narrow dark median line. Outer tail feathers drab with narrow yellowish outer fringes. Irides brown or dark brown. Bill greyish blue or whitish blue. Legs and feet greyish blue.

I can find no description of the juvenile. Immelmann *et al.* imply that it is like that of *L. malacca* except for having a spotted throat.

The above description is of nominate *L.g. grandis*, from south-eastern New Guinea, westward on the southern coast to Hall Sound and on the northern coast to the upper Watut River. *L.g. ernesti*, from northern New Guinea, from Astrobabe Bay to the Ramu and Sepik Rivers, was separated as having straw yellow fringes to the central tail feathers (Stresemann, 1921). The only specimen that I have been able to examine, an unsexed adult from Arwar, also has a much smaller and less deep bill than 3 specimens of *L.g. grandis* that were available for comparison. *L.g. destructa*, from the Hollandia district of northern New Guinea, is said to have a browner back than *L.g. grandis* and yellower upper tail coverts. *L.g. heurni*, from the Idenburg and Memberano Valleys of northern New Guinea, is like *L.g. grandis* but a darker chestnut on the upperparts. I have not seen specimens of either *heurni* or *grandis*.

FIELD CHARACTERS Huge-billed 'finch' with black head and breast, yellowish chestnut to brownish chestnut back, and reddish gold to straw yellow rump and tail.

DISTRIBUTION AND HABITAT New Guinea (see map for approximate known distribution). Inhabits grassland and cane brakes, both at low altitudes and the mid-montane grasslands (Diamond). Also, and perhaps preferentially where available, floating mats of marsh grass in lagoons and flooded areas (Rand, Rand & Gilliard).

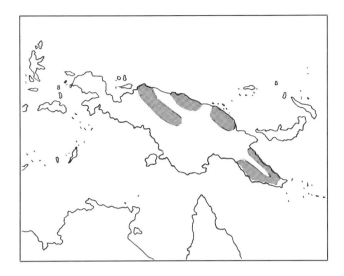

FEEDING AND GENERAL HABITS Known to eat seeds of marsh grass (Rand). Associates and moves about in small, compact flocks, even when breeding.

NESTING Has been found nesting on floating mats of marsh grass, in flooded areas of the Idenburg River region, in March, April and May. The nests were placed, sometimes singly, sometimes several close together, in shrubs and on floating logs or stumps with projecting branches. One stump, that projected only a metre or so above the water, held 10 active nests. Nests shaped like 'lop-sided flasks, lying on their sides'. Built of broad dead grass blades and lined inside with fluffy flowerheads of grasses and seed panicles from which the seeds had been removed or had fallen. Some nests had lots of grass rootlets used in them also. A nest which was measured was 20 cm long, 13 cm wide by 16 cm deep. The inside chamber was 9 cm by 8 cm and the entrance 6 cm long. All the above information is from Rand (1942). The race *L.g. ernesti* has been found nesting in January (Immelmann *et al.*). Eggs 5 or 6.

VOICE No information.

DISPLAY AND SOCIAL BEHAVIOUR No information.

OTHER NAME Great-billed Mannikin.

REFERENCES
Diamond, J. M. 1972. *Avifauna of the eastern highlands of New Guinea.* Publ. Nuttall Orn. Club, no. 12. Cambridge, Mass., USA.
Immelmann, K., Steinbacher, J. & Wolters, H. E. 1969. *Vögel in Käfig und Voliere: Prachtfinken:* 328–331.
Rand, A. L. 1942. Results of the Archbold Expeditions. No. 43. *Bull. Amer. Mus. Nat. Hist.* LXXIX, Art. 7: 425–516.
Rand, A. L. & Gilliard, E. T. 1967. *Handbook of New Guinea birds.* London.
Ripley, S. D. 1964. *A systematic and ecological study of birds of New Guinea.* Peabody Museum of Natural History, Yale University Bull. 19.
Stresemann, E. 1921. Communication in *Anz. Orn. Ges. Bayern* 5: 33–42.

Forbes' Munia   *Lonchura forbesi*

Munia forbesi P. L. Sclater, 1879, *Proc. Zool. Soc. London*, p. 449, pl. 37, fig 3.

DESCRIPTION About size of Spice Finch but thicker set, with larger head, shorter tail and large, deep bill. Head, nape, tibial feathers and under tail coverts black. Mantle, back, wing coverts and outer fringes of the otherwise dull sepia wing quills, deep chestnut brown, shading to light yellowish chestnut in worn plumage. Often with a faint grey tinge on the feather fringes. Lower rump, upper tail coverts and all but the brownish median area of the pointed and slightly elongated central tail feathers, brownish gold to dull yellowish gold. Outer tail feathers reddish brown with dull brownish gold fringes. Under parts light chestnut to reddish buff with faint silvery fringes to the breast feathers giving a slightly barred effect at very close inspection. Some individuals have blackish markings at the tips of some of the median belly feathers and blackish under tail coverts. Under wing coverts reddish buff. Irides dark brown. Bill described as 'black' and 'slate and black' in 2 adult males in the British Museum (Natural History) collection, and as 'slaty black' by Hartert, who examined several other specimens. Probably the base of the lower mandible is a little paler than rest of bill, as in many munias. Legs and feet slate blue or dark slate (above specimens and Hartert).

I have not seen a juvenile. Hartert describes one as paler above and below than the adult and with its crown striped dark brown and blackish.

FIELD CHARACTERS Small, short-tailed large-billed 'finch': reddish brown with black head and dull gold on rump and tail.

DISTRIBUTION AND HABITAT New Ireland. Presumably in similar habitats to those of other munias.

FEEDING AND GENERAL HABITS The crops and stomachs of 3 collected specimens contained grass seeds, other small seeds and fragments of mussel shell (Heinroth).

NESTING No information. Three (out of 4) specimens collected by Heinroth in March had fully developed gonads.

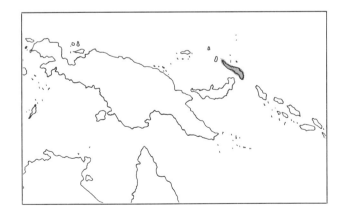

VOICE No information.

DISPLAY AND SOCIAL BEHAVIOUR No information.

OTHER NAME Forbes' Mannikin.

REFERENCES
Hartert, E. 1925. A collection of birds from New Ireland (Neu Mecklenburg). *Novit. Zool.* **32**: 115–136.
Heinroth, O. 1903. Ornithologische Ergebnisse der '1 Deutschen Südsee-Expedition von B. Mencke'. *J. Orn.* **51**: 65–125.

Thick-billed Munia   *Lonchura melaena*

Munia melaena P. L. Sclater, 1880, *Proc. Zool. Soc. London*, p. 66, pl. 7, fig 2.

DESCRIPTION About size of Spice Finch but much more thickset, with longer wing, shorter tail, larger head and very large and deep bill. Greater part of plumage coal black. Primaries and secondaries brownish black with a rusty brown tinge on the fringes of the outer webs. Lower rump and upper tail coverts dark reddish gold to rusty orange. The pointed and elongated central tail feathers have narrow blackish brown median areas and broad reddish gold fringes, the outer tail feathers are blackish brown with narrow rusty orange or dull reddish gold fringes. Centre of lower breast and belly, and under wing coverts, pinkish buff; some of the flank feathers marked pinkish buff and black. Irides dark. Bill blackish or dark

grey, whitish on base of lower mandible. Legs and feet dark grey.

I have not seen a juvenile of this species. Immelmann *et al.* describe it as dark brown above and light brown below, with reddish brown upper tail coverts.

Judging from descriptions and colour slides kindly sent to me by Mr D. W. Hadden, the form found on Buka, Solomon Islands, differs in having the back, mantle and wings dark chestnut and the reddish buff on the underparts more extensive. See sketch.

FIELD CHARACTERS Small, mainly black 'finch' with huge, thick bill and reddish gold or rusty rump and tail.

DISTRIBUTION AND HABITAT New Britain; also on Buka, Solomon Islands (Hadden, *pers. comm.*). Inhabits grassland and bushy areas with some grass (Immelmann *et al.*).

FEEDING AND GENERAL HABITS Feeds largely on grass seeds, possibly also seeds of some other plants and known to take pieces of grass blade also. Frequently seen on beaches bare of vegetation, presumably it obtains mineral matter there (Immelmann *et al.*). Found in flocks in swamp vegetation (Hadden, *pers. comm.*).

NESTING Nests colonially in tall grass. Usual roundish munia nest with narrow side entrance, made of grass blades and panicles, coarser outside and finer inside. A nest found by Don Hadden (pers. comm.) was well concealed about 2 metres high in tall vegetation. Eggs 3 to 6. Breeds at almost all times of the year (Immelmann *et al.*).

VOICE No information.

DISPLAY AND SOCIAL BEHAVIOUR No information.

OTHER NAMES New Britain Mannikin (used in one check list for both this species and *L. spectabilis*), Thick-billed Mannikin.

REFERENCES
Immelmann, K., Steinbacher, J. & Wolters, H. E. 1969. *Vögel in Käfig und Voliere: Prachtfinken*: 280–283. Aachen, Germany.

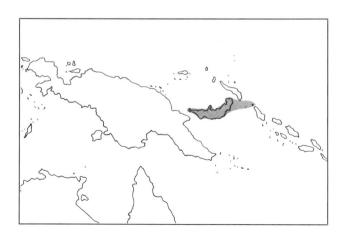

Java Sparrow   *Lonchura oryzivora*

Loxia oryzivora Linnaeus, 1758, *Syst. Nat.*, ed. 10, **1**, p. 173.

DESCRIPTION Shown on plate 5, facing p. 224. Rather shortish tailed and large-billed; would appear thickset but for the very sleek, close-fitting plumage. Top of head, lores, throat and a narrow border behind the snow white cheeks, rump, upper tail coverts and tail deep black. Primaries dark grey with a paler slightly silvery area on the inner webs. Underwing greyish with silvery tinge. Underparts below the breast a rather dull mauvish pink, shading to creamy white on ventral regions and under tail coverts. Rest of plumage a delicate clear bluish grey. Bill deep rose pink, sometimes almost crimson, at base, shading to white or very pale pink at the tip and along the cutting edges of the mandibles. Irides reddish brown to deep blood red, 'wood brown' and crimson once (each) recorded. Eye rims pink. Legs and feet flesh pink. Sexes alike in plumage but females usually have less massive bills than males. When birds in similar condition are compared the female's bill is usually paler. Only males sing.

Juvenile a general dull, greyish fawn above, a little darker and greyer than elsewhere on top of the head and with broad rusty fawn fringes to the dull grey secondaries and greater wing coverts. Throat whitish or pale fawn shading to deep fawn with faint darker streaks or spots on the breast and to pale yellowish fawn on lower breast and belly. Tail dark grey. Bill at first blackish. Legs dull flesh-coloured. Irides presumably duller than adult's. A nestling a few days old, that I examined, was pinkish with dusky down, blackish bill, creamy white gape and gape tubercles. The inside of its mouth was pinkish and unmarked but (*fide* Immelmann *et al.*) later, or perhaps in most specimens at all ages, there is a crescentic black mark on the palate. Dorn states that the nestlings have *no* down so there may be some variation here.

White and pied forms of this species have long been bred in a domesticated state in China and Japan, and more recently elsewhere. In its homozygous state the white Java Sparrow is dominant over the normal wild colour pattern (Immelmann *et al.*).

FIELD CHARACTERS Small finch-like bird with large bright pink beak. When bill not visible general blue-grey colour and black rump and tail distinguish it. Juveniles nondescript and probably not easy to identify unless with parents or bills already partly pink.

DISTRIBUTION AND HABITAT Believed to be native only in Java and Bali but has been widely introduced elsewhere, having long been a favourite and (especially in hot and warm temperate climates) easily kept cage and aviary bird. Found in a feral state in Malaya, Sumatra, Borneo (local), Lombok, South Celebes, Moluccan Islands, Fiji Islands, the Philippines, Formosa, Indo-China (South Vietnam), the central plains of Siam (Thailand), Christmas and Cocos Keeling Islands, Zanzibar and Pemba Islands and nearby coastal areas of Tanzania, and St

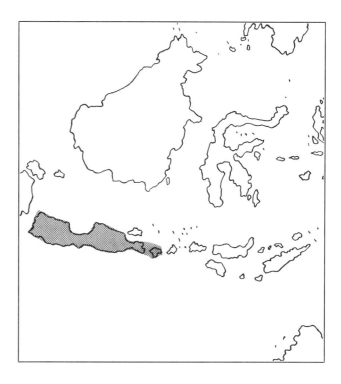

Helena. Bred in Hawaii as recently as 1968 or 1969 (Berger) but may not have a viable population there now. Often recorded in southern China and formerly established on Mauritius and the Comoro Islands. Introduced and abundant on Fiji.

The species is liable to human persecution both because of its destructiveness to rice and its own edibility. Hence the fortunes of local populations may be very unstable and the situation is usually complicated by the possibility of recent escapes and the lack of interest generally shown in this familiar bird by visiting ornithologists.

Typically in cultivated and inhabited areas but may occur far from human habitations in bush grown grassland or open woodland.

FEEDING AND GENERAL HABITS Takes food both from the ground and from growing vegetation. When available cultivated rice is the main food, at other times wild seeds and, according to Bernstein, small fruits and possibly insects, are also eaten. Apart from its rice-eating, its food in the wild seems to have been little studied. In captivity may refuse all other foods (apart from consuming quantities of mineral matter) if paddy rice is available. Otherwise readily takes canary seed, the larger millets (probably, like most birds, refusing red millet), and ripe or 'milky' wheat, oats or rye if given in the ear. Some individuals will take egg food soft foods, broken peanuts and insects (Brown, Dorn, Goodwin, Immelmann *et al.*) especially when rearing young.

Holds seed heads and nesting material under foot. One individual tested was found to be consistently right-footed (Baptista, pers. comm.).

Bernstein found it (in Java) in pairs or small parties

when the rice fields were under water but as soon the water was run off and the rice began to turn yellow large flocks gathered to feed on the rice.

NESTING Nests may be in holes of trees or buildings or in trees, bushes or parasitic growth. Bernstein found that nest varied in size according to the site. The nest is more or less rounded or, if the site dictates, a half-ball shaped structure, built of grass stems (and other tough stems?) with a large side entrance hole. A captive pair choose the longest, toughest and most wiry grasses from an assortment given and took even more eagerly tough bindweed stems. This pair (Goodwin, 1963) lined the deep cup of their nest with white and pale-coloured feathers, these were taken to the nest and put in place by both male and female but only the male carried and built with the grasses etc that formed the main part of the nest. Dorn's Java Sparrows, which successfully reared young, also lined their nest with feathers. Immelmann *et al.* say that the nest is not lined, other than with coconut fibres and fine grass and that some pairs make very poor and slight nests. Possibly there are individual differences, some domesticated Java Sparrows may have partly lost the full nest building behaviour or, and perhaps most likely, too small nest boxes or lack of suitable materials is to blame.

Three to 8 eggs, most often 4 to 6. Both sexes incubate in turn by day and only the female at night, in the usual manner. Incubation period 13 to 14 days (Rückert, Jugelt). Immelmann *et al.* give the fledging period as 3 to 4 weeks but quote periods of 33 (Kapzynski) and 35 days (Radtke) that have been recorded for young of the white form. Young bred from wild-caught parents fledged in 26 to 28 days. (Jugelt). There seem, however, to be no records of incubation or fledgling periods for in the wild, all the above being from captive Java Sparrows in Europe.

Young begin to feed very soon after fledging but may be fed by their parents for another 2 to 3 weeks. While still dependent they return to roost in the nest at night.

VOICE The song is evidently subject to much apparently individual variation. Immelmann *et al.* describe it as beginning with a few bell-like single notes that follow each other more and more rapidly and finally flow together in a continuous strophe of trilling and clucking sounds interspersed with both higher pitched and deeper notes and sometimes ending in a long-drawn whistling note. Morris found that all the individuals (number not stated) that he studied ended their songs with this long-drawn whistling 'weee'. Butler, who kept and bred both the wild and the white domesticated forms, described the song of the former as a 'metallic whistling' sounding like 'Torcumtee, turcumtong; torcumtee, torcumtong; torcumtee, torcumtong; whirri-urra-urra', the last phrase being 'a clear water-bubble trill'. He stated that the song of the white variety is very different and transcribed it as 'Tseeow, tseow, tseow; tsee, tsow, irri-irri-urra; chow, chow, chow, chow, cheea; whirri-hurra-urra; irry, irrihu' 'the long words being true water-bubble trills'. I transcribed the song of one of my two wild-caught captive

males as 'chu-chillik, chu-chillik, chillik-eeee'. The song of the other, who was more timid and less vociferous, was much softer, sweeter and more complex.

The song is given by the male when in breeding condition (and, *fide* Immelmann *et al.*, also when *not* in breeding condition), typically when he is alone or at least out of sight of his mate. I have, however, sometimes heard (and seen) it uttered when the pair were together or in sight of each other. Immelmann *et al.* state that the song is never uttered when displaying to the female and that those who think it is have mistaken the ticking or clucking contact calls (see below) for the song. I do not think, however, that I made this mistake with my captive Java Sparrows or that Butler, who described the displaying male as 'singing all the time' did so. I think that at least some male Java Sparrows do sing when displaying. Pialek's description of the display as being accompanied by a pleasing whistling or fluting ('Einem recht wohlklingenden, einfachen Geflöte') must also almost certainly refer to the song.

What I have termed the contact call (Goodwin, 1963) is a short, rather liquid-sounding 't'luk' or 'ch'luk' (short 'u' as in 'but'), which others have transcribed as 'tik' or 'tack'. It is monosyllabic but usually repeated many times. It appears to function in maintaining or re-establishing contact between individuals; also probably at times as a flight-intention call as it often seems to indicate some degree of disquiet or alarm and readiness to fly away. It is given at many different degrees of intensity. It is usually uttered very loudly and emphatically by birds which are separated from their companions or which take flight in alarm. If a pair are shut in different rooms both utter this call in response to the same call from the unseen mate. This and the trilling call (q.v.) may intergrade. Some males evidently either utter this call when displaying and also in other situations, instead of the song (Kunze, Radtke) or else in some Java Sparrows the song (or its equivalent) consists only of these, or very similar, notes.

The alarm call sounds to my ears merely a very loud, 'hard sounding', variant of the contact call, but further observations on these and the species' other calls are needed.

The trilling call is a trill of varying length, with a strong 'r' sound in it and usually with a rising inflection. It may intergrade with the contact call but is typically very distinct from it. A very hard-sounding, long-drawn, rattling version is given during successful copulation. This call seems to express any form of (presumably) pleasurable excitement connected with reproductive behaviour. It was given by the female (possibly also by the male), when greeting the mate after a brief separation. When they bowed in greeting to each other just after hopping out of the basket they had roosted together in, when the light was switched on in the morning. By the female when alighting near the nest with a feather in her bill and *more* intensely a moment later when she entered the nest with it. By one (or both) of the pair during copulation, at the precise moment that cloacal contact was, apparently, achieved. It was never given during attempts at copulation in which cloacal contact was not achieved. Sometimes by the female entering the nest (with a feather) if the male was already inside. The female often gave this call when the male was uttering other calls, or when she was very close to me. I am not sure whether or not the (less tame) male also gave the trilling call as at all times when I thought he might have done the female was very near him, and this call is uttered without any noticeable bill or throat movements.

The very distinctive version given in copulation might be considered a different call but a version intermediate between the 'normal' high-intensity form of the trilling call and the very long, hard, rattling version given during copulation could be artificially induced in the following way. If I shut the male in a different room for an hour or so and then allowed him to fly back into the room where the female was, she would give this intermediate version while he was still in the air flying towards her. It was always followed by very intense greeting display.

That the more usual (non-copulatory) version of the trilling call depends for its intensity and duration on the degree of excitement was suggested by the behaviour of the female when taking feathers to the nest. She preferred large, fluffy, white feathers and gave much louder, longer trills when she alighted and (later) slipped into the nest with such a feather than she did when she had only a small, dull-coloured feather.

A growling or rattling (Schnarren) call, which Baptista, Butler and Immelmann *et al.* say is given in hostile situations but do not describe more fully, may possibly be an aggressive variant of the above. I have not heard it.

The moaning or mewing call is difficult to describe but unmistakeable as, although it varies greatly in loudness, pitch and duration, it bears no resemblance to any other Java Sparrow call that I have heard. It is a low-pitched moaning sound, sometimes inclining to a mewing sound. At high intensity it is so loud and drawn-out that it reminds one of the mew call of the Herring Gull, *Larus argentatus*. It always has a querelous and 'complaining' tone. Hearing it, one is almost forced to assume that it *must* be a note of protest, but I am far from sure that it is. On the only occasions when I was certain that the female of my pair uttered this call (because the male was singing as she did so), she gave it in a much higher-pitched and 'sweeter' sounding form than more usual variants (which may have been uttered by the male).

This call was only given when both members of the pair were in the nest, or nest site, at the same time. Usually it was heard when one bird entered the nest basket in which the other was already present. Thus it was uttered (but I do not know by which individual) when one bird entered with nesting material while the other was in the basket or when it entered to take over brooding or incubation. It was also heard when, at roosting time, a second bird entered the basket into which its mate had already retired. In this last situation it was also heard from two birds, believed both males, that were not in breeding condition.

On a very few occasions the male introduced short, low intensity variants of this call into his song. It is likely that this call has some appeasing function. As, in my experience, it is only given when both birds are together in the nest or roost site it cannot be equated with the nest calls of other estrildids.

I sometimes heard a series of very soft, repeated notes suggestive of very tender, soft, run-together variants of the contact call. It was very suggestive of the nest-calling of some other estrildids but I only heard it when both members of the pair were together in the nest or nest site. Kunze says that the hen Java Sparrow has a very pleasant-sounding nest call that sounds like 'tuituituit'.

A rather loud snapping or clicking sound, apparently made by snapping the mandibles together, was usually given by the male of my breeding pair just before beginning to sing in the courtship display.

DISPLAY AND SOCIAL BEHAVIOUR In the courtship display the male adopts a peculiar, bent-over posture. In this posture he bounces up and down, sidling nearer to his mate as he does so. His feet usually leave the perch at each jump and make quite a loud noise as they strike it again. His lowered head is slightly above perch level and only slightly turned towards his mate most of the time but every few seconds he lowers it more deeply, until it is at or even below perch level, at the same time making a waggling movement that appears to be an exaggerated symbolic 'bill-wiping' and as he does this his head is turned slightly more towards the female. There is some suggestion of the triangular head and tail twist but these are less marked than in, for example, the waxbills.

The male of my pair used to utter very excited sounding versions of the contact call, which became more intense as he adopted the bent posture and changed to loud bill clicking which in turn gave way to song as he neared the female. Often the male began to display in silence and sometimes the clicking sounds were omitted but he always sang as he began to draw himself more erect in readiness to mount his mate, even if he had not sung before, unless, as sometimes happened, the female forestalled him by soliciting at an earlier stage of the display. Once the male had begun this display he would always respond to soliciting of the female by mounting her, even if this occurred before he had begun to utter bill clicks or song. As has been said (see under 'Voice'), some male Java Sparrows appear not to sing during this display.

The female's response to this display varies. Sometimes she adopts the same bent over posture and bounces up and down with the same head movements. As the pair come together, or shortly after they have done so, she goes into the usual estrildine soliciting posture, crouching with somewhat raised and quivering tail. I have seen this from Java Sparrows in zoos and public aviaries but I never saw the female of my pair display in this manner. If she was in the mood to copulate she would respond to the male's display by hopping or sidling towards him and then immediately solicit. Often she did this the moment the male began to display and before he had even got fully into the bent over posture. Kapzynski's description of the display of his (white) specimens suggests that the females he observed behaved similarly. If my female was unwilling to mate she would hop up to the male and put her head *above* his as soon as he got ready to mount her, or before, at other times she would hop away, stay where she was and peck at the male's bill when he neared her, or simply take no notice and slip away from under him when he tried to mount her.

Successful copulation is followed immediately by mutual aggression. In my pair this was usually (but not always) initiated by the female, who at once pecked fiercely at the male's bill and face. He would peck back and a brief but vicious-seeming pecking match would follow. As aggression dies down the pecking goes over to mandibulation, and then to a mutual greeting display. I have seen similar post-copulatory behaviour in other pairs of Java Sparrows not in my possession but some, at least of the white domesticated form, show less aggression. Kapzynski describes the female as *gently* pecking at the head of the male (who crouches) after copulation and the male of Radtke's pair always sang at this time so evidently could not have been attacked.

The greeting display is shown when the pair come together after a separation, brief or otherwise. Or when they first *see* each other after the light is put on in a room where they have roosted. The birds hop or sidle towards each other, as they come together they bow their heads towards their own or the partner's feet, then lift their heads and each in turn puts its head above its partner's, then they bow again. The trilling call (q.v.) accompanied or prefaced this display in my captive pair. If the partners had been separated for half an hour or so (by shutting them in different rooms), they performed very intense greeting display and then sat pressed very closely together side by side for some minutes.

Baptista observed threat displays in which the bird, in a horizontal posture, pointed its bill towards its opponent. This was often combined with twisting the head to one side, opening the bill and waving the head from side to side. This head waving may also be performed with the bird's neck stretched backward so that its nape nearly touches its back.

Clumping and mutual preening occurs between the members of a pair and, at least at times in captivity, between members of a non-breeding group or flock.

A peculiar and frequent habit of captive Java Sparrows is that of roosting at night and resting by day beside, underneath or even on top of doves that are kept with them. This has been seen with Turtle and Spotted Doves, *Streptopelia turtur* and *S. chinensis* (Goodwin, 1952 and 1963, Morris, 1956) and with Bleeding-heart Pigeons, *Gallicolumba luzonica* (Brown, 1963). It does not seem to be primarily, if at all, a means of obtaining warmth as it is done in tropical as well as temperate climates (Brown). It has been observed from many different individuals of both the wild and domesticated forms. Brown observed that his

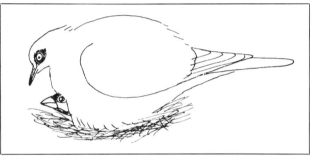

many Java Sparrows showed no such behaviour towards Emerald Doves, *Chalcophaps*, or Masked Doves, *Oena capensis*. It might be mentioned that the colour pattern of the latter is less unlike that of the Java Sparrow than is that of the species which they have been seen to exploit.

Even if this behaviour proves an aberration of captive birds, it is of interest but, as behaviour that has been so dismissed has in some cases (such as the habit of whydahs, *Vidua* spp., attempting copulation with birds of other genera), later been proved also to occur under natural conditions, anyone able to observe wild Java Sparrows should be on the alert for it.

OTHER NAMES Ricebird, Java Temple Bird (an unfortunate name concocted by American bird dealers), Java Finch.

REFERENCES
Baptista, L. F. & Atwood, A. D. 1980. Agonistic behaviour in the Java Finch. *J. Orn.* **1980**: 171–179.
Bernstein, H. A. 1861. Ueber Nester und Eier javascher Vögel. *J. Orn.* **9**: 177–192.
Brown, R. E. B. 1963. Java Sparrows. *Avicult. Mag.* **69**: 239.
Butler, A. G. 1899. Foreign finches in captivity. London.
Dorn, J. 1966. Brutbeobachtungen an Reisfinken. *Die Gefiederte Welt* **90**: 227–228.
Goodwin, D. 1952. Recollections of some small birds. *Avicult. Mag.* **58**: 24–29.
Goodwin, D. 1963. Observations on Java Sparrows. *Avicult. Mag.* **69**: 54–69.
Immelmann, K., Steinbacher, J. & Wolters, H. E. 1968 and 1969. *Vögel in Käfig und Voliere: Prachtfinken*: 258–269. Aachen, Germany.

Jugelt, S. 1968. Über die Zucht von Reisfinken. *Der Falke* **15**: 132–133.

Kapzynski, B. 1961. Freude am weissen Reisfinken. *Die Gefiederte Welt* **1961**, 228–229.

Kunze, H. D. 1962. Zum Verhalten der Reisfinken. *Die Gefiederte Welt* **1962**. 57–58.

Mackworth-Praed, C. W. & Grant, C. H. B. 1960. *African handbook of birds*, ser. 1, vol. 2 (second ed.). London.

Medway, Lord, & Wells, D. R. 1976. *The birds of the Malay Peninsula*, vol. 5. London.

Morris, D. 1956. The feather postures of birds and the problem of the origin of social signals. *Behaviour* **9**: 75–113.

Musil, A. 1960. Aufzucht von Reisfinken. *Die Gefiederte Welt* **1960**: 14–16.

Pialek, W. 1958. Einiges über Reisfinken. *Die Gefiederte Welt* **1958**: 236–238.

Radtke, G. A. 1959. Zum Balzverhalten und zur Haltung der Reisfinken. *Die Gefiederte Welt* **1959**: 23–25.

Rückert, K. 1968. Bleibt der Blaue Reisfink ein schlechter Zuchtvogel? *Der Falke* **15**: 99.

Timor Sparrow   *Lonchura fuscata*

Loxia fuscata Vieillot, 1807, *Ois. Chant.*, p. 95, pl. 62.

DESCRIPTION Shown on plate 5, facing p. 224. About size of Peters' Twinspot. Shape as Java Sparrow but bill a little smaller in proportion and with a slightly less curved culmen. Pattern of plumage almost identical to that of Java Sparrow but coloration very different.

Cheeks, under wing coverts and underparts below the breast a faintly yellowish white. Rest of plumage a darkish chocolate brown, shading to black on the forehead, sides of crown, throat and a narrow band dividing the white underparts from the brown breast. Wing and tail quills blackish chocolate. Bill steely grey, lighter at cutting edges. Irides very dark brown, eye rims bluish grey. Legs and feet brownish horn colour. I have not seen a juvenile or a description of one. It is probably a fawnish colour like that of the Java Sparrow and the related *Lonchura* species, this is suggested by Martin's description of it as similar to a young Bullfinch, *Pyrrhula pyrrhula*.

FIELD CHARACTERS White cheeks contrasting with otherwise dark head and neck distinguish it from other small finch-like birds.

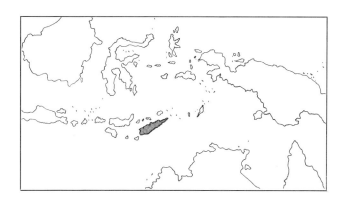

DISTRIBUTION AND HABITAT Timor and the adjacent Samau Island. No information on habitat.

FEEDING AND GENERAL HABITS No information from the wild. Probably very similar to *P. oryzivora*. In captivity highly social (Burkard).

NESTING No information for the wild. A pair that reared a brood in captivity (Martin) built a nest of hay, moss, bits of paper and feathers in a Budgerigar nest box. Four white eggs were laid and both sexes took turns in incubating, brooding and feeding the young. Live insects were left untouched by the parents but they ate, and presumably fed to the young large amounts of chickweed (or seeds thereof?) and seeding grasses. Burkard has bred this species in captivity to the fourth generation. Clutch size varied from 2 to 9 eggs. One pair reared 19 young in 3 consecutive broods. Breeds when kept in flocks, the pairs breeding in synchrony.

VOICE I can find no information apart from Silver's statement that 'The call note is very like, but quite distinguishable from' (that of the Java Sparrow).

DISPLAY AND SOCIAL BEHAVIOUR No information.

OTHER NAMES Brown Ricebird, Brown Mannikin (a most unfortunate choice as, descriptively, it could apply to most mannikins and to many much better than to the present species).

REFERENCES
Burkard, R. 1980. Von einigen seltneren Psittaciden und Prachtfinken. *Gefiederte Welt* **1980**: 1–2.

Immelmann, K., Steinbacher, J. & Wolters, H. E. 1969. *Vögel in Käfig und Voliere: Prachtfinken*: 270–271.

Martin, A. 1961. Breeding of the Brown Mannikin. *Avicult. Mag.* **67**: 89–90.

Silver, A. 1939. The Brown Padda or Ricebird. *Avicult. Mag.* **4** (5th ser.): 317–318.

Pictorella Finch   *Lonchura pectoralis*

Amadina pectoralis Gould, 1841, *Proc. Zool. Soc. London* **8** (1840), p. 127.

DESCRIPTION A little larger than Spice Finch, with proportionately rather longer bill and shorter, rounded

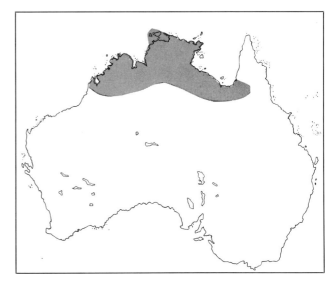

tail. Face and throat an intense black with a purple lustre; some of the black feathers, especially on the maler regions, have minute white spots. A bright buffish fawn stripe runs from the base of the upper mandible, over the eye and follows the line of the black area to become a broader stripe or patch on the side of the neck, behind the ear coverts (see sketch). Upper parts light brownish grey, a little darker on the tail and duller on the wing quills. There are tiny white terminal spots on the outer wing coverts. Underwing, and under wing, coverts mainly pinkish fawn. A broad band across the breast, of feathers with broad snow white tips and black subterminal bands. Except where feathers are missing or disarranged this area usually only appears barred with black at the upper part of either side of the band. Underparts a delicate fawnish pink with a faint mauve tinge, shading to buff on the central part of the belly. Some of the feathers on the upper parts of the flanks are greyish with white tips and black sub-terminal bands but these seem to be mostly concealed by the wings when the bird is active. Under tail coverts barred white and dark grey, with pinkish fawn tips. Irides dark brown. Bill bluish grey, culmen often darker than rest of bill. Legs and feet flesh-coloured, pinkish buff or pinkish brown.

The female is duller and paler, having the black of the face intermixed with brownish grey, especially on the upper parts of the ear coverts. The subterminal bands on her breast-band feathers are blackish grey and more extensive and, when new, the white does not extend quite to the tip of the feather, which is narrowly fringed with greyish black. Hence her breast band appears barred white and black throughout. Her underparts are paler and more buffish than those of the male.

Juvenile dull brown above, darker on face and throat, and on wing and tail quills, and with reddish buff tips and fringes to most wing feathers. Throat dusky grey, rest of underparts pale pinkish buff. This description is of newly fledged birds, the juvenile plumage soon fades and bleaches to a pale buffish brown on the upperparts. Bill brownish black. Newly hatched nestling naked and dark flesh-coloured with two luminous tubercles at gape (Langberg, in Immelmann *et al.*). Palate pattern with double horseshoe marks very similar but not identical to those of African mannikins (good photo in Güttinger, 1976).

See plate 2, facing p. 97.

FIELD CHARACTERS Small finch-like bird with uniform pale greyish upperparts, including rump and tail, black face and grey bill. Greyish rump and tail and white or white and black breast band, distinguish it from Chestnut-breasted Finch. These characters and black face from Yellow-rumped and Zebra Finches.

DISTRIBUTION AND HABITAT Tropical northern Australia, from about Derby through the Kimberleys and Northern Territory to near Charters Towers, Queensland.

Inhabits open country, usually grassland with scattered bushes near to creeks or waterholes. Sometimes found far from surface water but probably only when wandering in search of it. In the western Kimberleys has been found in true spinifex country (Immelmann, 1965).

FEEDING AND GENERAL HABITS Feeds on seeds of the grasses, *Echinachloa colonum*, *Chloris virgata*, and several species of *Iseilema*, probably also of some other grasses. Takes cultivated rice when not fully ripe but not to the same extent as do the Chestnut-breasted and Yellow-rumped Finches. Also takes insects, including flying ants and termites, beetles and spiders. Takes food both from the ground and from growing vegetation but appears to prefer to feed on the ground, unlike some other *Lonchura* species.

In captivity will take millet and canary seed but needs soaked seeds and greenfood, especially chickweed and annual meadow grass when available, in addition. When rearing young, should be given live foods, of which ant pupae, whiteworms, mealworms and wax moth larvae are readily taken (Langeberg, in Immelmann *et al.*).

Commonly in small parties or pairs but often in larger flocks and immense flocks may form in the vicinity of water during times of drought. Sometimes associates with grassfinches, *Poephila* spp., and Zebra Finches. Usually drinks in typical manner but very speedily, with repeated quick sips (Immelmann, 1965) but has been seen drinking by sucking (Harrison, in Hall, 1974).

NESTING The nest is placed in a low bush or grass clump,

usually from only a few centimetres to 60 centimetres above ground, rarely higher. It is described by Immelmann (1965) as an untidy-looking, bottle-shaped structure, without an entrance tube; made of dry grass stems, rootlets and small twigs and sometimes lined with a few feathers. Four to six eggs, sometimes fewer in captivity. Both sexes incubate by day but only the female at night, as usual. The male does not roost in the nest and no roosting nests are built.

In captivity (and probably also when wild) small pieces of charcoal are placed in the nest and the growing stems of supporting vegetation may be built into its walls. The young fledge at 3 weeks but for the first few nights thereafter return to the nest to roost. When begging, fledged young raise the far wing, like Bicheno Finches and avadavats. They begin to feed themselves 4 to 6 days after fledging and become independent about 16 days after fledging (Pilz, in Immelmann *et al.*).

VOICE The contact call used at close quarters is a soft rather sparrow-like chirp, 'chip' or 'tscheep' etc. The distance contact call, or identity call as Immelmann calls it, is a penetrating 'tlit', which is intensified to a long-drawn 'tleet' or 'teet' by lost individuals. A soft call, sounding like 'g'ee', uttered with open mouth during courtship display, and sometimes when perched alone, seems to be the equivalent of the song of other estrildids.

DISPLAY AND SOCIAL BEHAVIOUR The courtship display deviates from that of typical *Lonchura* species and shows some, possibly convergent, resemblances to that of the Painted Finch. It takes place on the ground and is prefaced by both sexes making pecking movements and sometimes also picking up and dropping small objects. The courtship display proper has two phases. In the first the male usually holds a piece of nesting material in his bill. With bill pointing upwards, body feathers fluffed out and tail fully spread he hops in a semicircle in front of the female, uttering, as a rule, his song equivalent 'g'ee' and dragging his spread tail audibly over the ground. The hopping movements get quicker and the semicircles smaller and smaller until the male is just in front of the female. The

male then drops the nest symbol and hops round behind the female in a half circle until his body is parallel to hers. Then with tail still fanned out but angled a little towards the female, the male bows deeply then again hops around behind the female until he is standing parallel to her on the other side, and bows again. This may be repeated several times until the female begins to solicit with quivering tail, and copulation takes place. Two other displays have been regularly observed by Güttinger (1976). Prior to and during the nest-building period, the pair, with angled tails, peck at the ground together, picking up small stones and letting them fall again. This ritual is not followed by further display or copulation. During the building period the male often persistently chases the female in flight and, shortly after, calls her to the nest.

Does not clump or allo-preen (Immelmann, 1965), in this respect contrasting greatly in behaviour with more typical munias. Peering (at a male Spice Finch who was singing) has been observed in captivity but not in the wild, though Immelmann suggests it might occur naturally in similar inter-specific situations when this species is in company with Chestnut-breasted and Yellow-rumped Finches.

Very unsuited to cage life but often does well in aviaries, if at least part of the floor is kept covered with clean, dry sand. In captivity usually unaggressive and even when breeding only defends the immediate surroundings of its nest.

OTHER NAMES Pectoral Finch, Pictorella Mannikin, White-breasted Finch.

REFERENCES

Güttinger, H. R. 1976. Zur systematic Stellung der Gattungen *Amadina, Lepidopyga* und *Lonchura. Bonn. Zool. Beitr.* **27**: 218–244.

Hall, B. P. 1974. *Birds of the Harold Hall Australian Expeditions 1962–1970*: 326–327. British Museum (Natural History), London.

Immelmann, K. 1965. *Australian finches in bush and aviary.* Sydney and London.

Immelmann, K., Steinbacher, J. & Wolters, H. E. 1969. *Vögel in Käfig und Voliere: Prachtfinken*: 271–280.

Index of Common Names

Index of scientific names

Figures in *italic* indicate a major entry
Figures in **bold** indicate a colour plate